ACC

Adult Corrections in Canada

Second Edition

Weinrath & Winterdyk

Library and Archives Canada Cataloguing in Publication

Weinrath, Michael and Winterdyk, John A.
   Adult Corrections in Canada, Second Edition/ Edited by Michael Weinrath and John A. Winterdyk

ISBN 978-1-897160-93-0

A catalogue record for this book will be available from Library and Archives Canada Cataloguing in Publication.

Cover image: Barbed Wire On A Post By katyphotography. Adobe Stock, File # 123144644.

Cover and book design by de Sitter Publications

de Sitter Publications
111 Bell Dr
Whitby, ON, L1N 2T1
CANADA

289-987-0656
www.desitterpublications.com
info@desitterpublications.com

Contents

CONTENS

About the Authors

Gillian Balfour is an Associate Professor of Socio-Legal Studies and Feminist Criminology. Her research examines feminist engagement with the victimization, criminalization, and incarceration continuum. She has published widely in areas of sentencing law reform impacts on Indigenous women and the implications of restorative justice in the context of gender-based violence. With her colleagues, she has examined how rape narratives and legal narratives intersect in sexual assault sentencing decisions, as well as the role of victim impact statements in sentencing practices. She is currently conducting an archival study of discipline in Canadian women's prisons and is a co-investigator on a national study looking at the lived experiences of incarceration. Her most recent project explores the place of organized labour inside prisons. She is a member of Canada's Walls to Bridges collective that provides prison-based learning for incarcerated and non-incarcerated students.

James Bonta received his Ph.D. in Clinical Psychology in 1979 and began his career as a psychologist at a maximum-security remand centre, and later as Chief Psychologist. In 1990, he joined Public Safety Canada and he is presently Director of Corrections Research. Dr. Bonta is a Fellow of the Canadian Psychological Association and recipient of the Criminal Justice Section's Career Contribution Award for 2009. Dr. Bonta's interests are in the areas of risk assessment and offender rehabilitation. He co-authored with the late D. A. Andrews *The Psychology of Criminal Conduct* (now in its fifth edition). He is also a co-author of the various *Level of Service* risk/need instruments that have been translated into five languages and used by correctional systems throughout the world.

Nicolas Carrier is Associate Professor of Criminology & Criminal Justice at Carleton University. He is notably the author of La politique de la stupéfaction: pérennité de la prohibition des drogues (Presses Universitaires de Rennes, 2008). His research interests include criminological and social theory, social control, the sociology of law and moralization processes.

Tracey Cyca has been an Instructor in the Department of Public Safety and Justice Studies at MacEwan University since September 2003. Prior to this she was an instructor in the Bachelor of Applied Justice Studies at Mount Royal University in Calgary. She has taught distance and on-line courses for both MacEwan and Mount Royal. Tracey's educational background includes a Bachelor of Arts (Honours Psychology) from the University of Manitoba and a Master of Criminology (Applied) from the University of Ottawa. Tracey's current research and teaching interests include youth, addictions, and resiliency. She has worked as a case manager and program facilitator for several youth correctional facilities; has participated in youth justice committees and other alternative measures programs; and has taught social skills and substance abuse programs to youth at risk. She has also been involved in mentoring and board work.

Myles Ferguson (J.D., MA) received his Ph.D. in Applied Social Psychology in 2016. He is a research associate with the Centre for Forensic Behavioural Sciences and Justice Studies at the University of Saskatchewan. Myles has published several reports for various federal and provincial Ministries and departments that address public health and safety, diversity and inclusion issues, justice issues and public policy development.

Paul Gendreau, O.C., Ph.D. is a native of Winnipeg, Manitoba and was raised in Ottawa, Ontario. He began working at Kingston Penitentiary, Ontario in 1961 and has had appointments at several universities including Trent University (1968-1972), Carleton University (1972-1986), University of Ottawa (1972-1986), and the University of New Brunswick, Saint John (1986-2005). Between 1972-1986 he also worked in Ontario corrections as Chief Psychologist and acted as a consultant on corrections projects in Jamaica, New Zealand, the United States, and Canada. Between 1986-2005 he was visiting scholar at Edith Cowan (2000) & Griffith (2004) Universities in Australia as well as the University of Cincinnati (1996-1997; 2007-2008). He is currently Professor Emeritus at UNB and a visiting scholar at the University of North Carolina, Charlotte (2010-2012). Dr. Gendreau is a former President of the Canadian Psychological Association and has received numerous awards from CPA, the American Psychological Association, the International Community & Corrections Association, and the Correctional Service Canada (CSC). He has published extensively on "what works" in the assessment and treatment of offenders [also see the CPAI-2010© which has been widely used to evaluate offender treatment programs], program implementation, the effects of prison life, and the use of statistics in knowledge cumulation. In 2007 Dr. Gendreau was appointed an Officer of the Order of Canada for achievement and merit of a high degree, especially service to Canada or humanity at large.

Claire Goggin, Ph.D. is an Assistant Professor in the Department of Criminology and Criminal Justice at St. Thomas University in Fredericton, New Brunswick where she teaches courses in Research Methods and Statistics, Corrections, Psychology of Criminal Behaviour, and Programme Evaluation. Current research interests include offender risk assessment and classification, correctional program evaluation, including the effects of imprisonment, empirical research methodologies and statistics, particularly meta-analysis, and knowledge cumulation and transfer. She has co-authored several articles, book chapters, and conference presentations on the above topics.

Kelly Hannah-Moffat is a Professor and Vice Dean Undergraduate at the University of Toronto Mississauga. She joined the Department of Sociology in 1999. She is cross-appointed to the Centre of Criminology and Socio-legal Studies and is a Massey College Senior Fellow. Professor Hannah-Moffat also worked as a policy advisor for Madame Justice Louise Arbour on the Commission of Inquiry into Certain Events at the Prison for Women in Kingston and was the President of the Toronto Elizabeth Fry Society. She has published numerous articles and books on risk, punishment, parole, gender and diversity, women's imprisonment, specialized courts, actuarial sentencing and criminal justice decision-making.

Amy Klassen is a Ph.D. student in the Department of Sociology at the University of Toronto. Her research work is on the various ways people with mental illness are governed inside and outside of the criminal justice system. More specifically, her current research includes theoretical understandings of prison resistance, choice, and the conflation of mental illness with disorderly conduct among female prisoners; the use of community treatment orders to manage people with severe mental health issues in community mental health; and the influence of risk-based thinking to prisoner rights.

Katharina Maier is an Assistant Professor of Criminal Justice at the University of Winnipeg. She is particularly interested in people's experiences of punishment, prisoner re-entry, front-line workers, and community penalties. Her current research examines the role of non-state actors in prisoner re-entry. Katharina's work has appeared in *Theoretical Criminology and Punishment & Society*.

Aja Jacqueline Manning is a graduate of the Applied Justice Studies Program of Mount Royal University and completed her Master of Science majoring in Criminal Justice through Indiana State University.

Aja has worked in both non-profit and Government agencies helping develop community programs, social return on investment projects and providing prevention and intervention services to vulnerable children, youths and their families in the Calgary and area region. Aja continues to expand her research in areas of counselling and mindfulness meditation with the focus of future program development for social services and the criminal justice system.

Olga Marques is an Assistant Professor (Criminology) at the University of Ontario, Institute of Technology. Her research interests include the construction, policing and regulation of gendered, sexed and raced bodies, and the inter-relationships between gendered/sexed social norms, social control, and resistance. Her current research projects focus on the impacts of spousal and/or children's incarceration on mothers; and revenge and non-consensual intimate image dissemination.

Lisa Monchalin teaches in the Department of Criminology at Kwantlen Polytechnic University. She is of Algonquin, Métis, Huron, and Scottish descent. Proud of her Indigenous heritage, and driven by personal and family experiences, she is determined to reduce the amount of crime that affects Indigenous peoples through education. Lisa is the author of *The Colonial Problem: An Indigenous Perspective on Crime and Injustice in Canada* (University of Toronto Press, 2016).

Amanda Nelund is an Assistant Professor of Sociology at MacEwan University in Edmonton AB. She has published in areas of restorative justice and criminalized women, restorative justice and gendered violence, and public criminology. Her current research focuses on alternative justice responses to sexual violence on post-secondary campuses.

Debra Parkes holds the Chair in Feminist Legal Studies in the Peter A. Allard School of Law, University of British Columbia. She teaches and researches in a variety of areas related to constitutional and human rights law with a focus on gender inequality, criminal law, and penal law and policy. She has published widely in these areas and has received funding from the Social Sciences & Humanities Research Council of Canada (SSHRC) to study life sentences, to examine mechanisms for oversight and accountability of imprisonment in Canada, and to study experiences of incarceration in Canada. She was Editor-in-Chief of the *Canadian Journal of Women and the Law* from 2009-2013 and she recently guest edited a special volume of the *Canadian Journal of Human Rights* on solitary confinement and human rights.

Justin Piché is Associate Professor in the Department of Criminology and Director of the Carceral Studies Research Collective at the University of Ottawa. He is also Co-editor of the *Journal of Prisoners on Prisons* and Co-founder of the *Criminalization and Punishment Education Project*. Professor Piché has over 50 peer-reviewed publications and more than 200 media appearances in three areas: 1) the construction of new jails and prisons; 2) alternatives to incarceration and punishment, and 3) cultural representations of confinement and penality. Justin was awarded the Aurora Prize in 2012 from the Social Sciences and Humanities Research Council of Canada "for excellence, creativity and originality in research and a deep commitment to sharing knowledge that enriches Canada's intellectual and cultural life." He was also the University of Ottawa's Faculty of Social Sciences Young Researcher of the Year in 2016 "for the importance, and exceptional characteristics of his research work." He was an organizer of the Fifteenth International Conference on Penal Abolition held on Algonquin Territory in 2014 and is currently involved in a campaign to stop the construction of a bigger jail in Ottawa so that the Government of Ontario reinvests funds currently earmarked for the project towards community supports and building capacity for transformative justice.

Rick Ruddell is the Law Foundation of Saskatchewan Chair in Police Studies at the University of Regina. His work has been published extensively in the fields of corrections, juvenile justice, and policing, and recent books include *Oil, Gas, and Crime* (Palgrave Macmillan), the third edition of *Making Sense of Criminal Justice* (Oxford University Press), the second edition of *Exploring Criminal Justice in Canada* (Oxford University Press) and the forthcoming *Corrections: A Critical Examination* (Routledge).

Rosemary (Rose) Ricciardelli, Ph.D., is a Professor of Sociology, the Coordinator for Criminology, and Co-Coordinator for Police Studies at Memorial University of Newfoundland. She is an Associate Director of the Canadian Institute for Public Safety Research and Treatment (CIPSRT) and Correctional Services Sector Lead. Beyond her position as Senior Research Fellow with Correctional Services Canada, she has new affiliations and appointments at Ontario Shores Centre for Mental Health and Toronto Rehabilitation Institute. She has published over 70 journal articles, 25 chapters and over 150 presentations and invited talks, all in a range of academic journals including the *British Journal of Criminology*, *Punishment & Society*, *Sex Roles*, and *Theoretical Criminology*. She has authored three edited collections and five monographs (2 of which are forthcoming). Her research interests include gender and experiences and issues within different facets of the criminal justice system. Her current research looks at prisons, desistance from crime, and the mental health and lived experiences of prisoners, prison officers, and police officers. Her sources of ongoing research funding include Correctional Services Canada, the Social Sciences and Humanities Research Council of Canada, the Canadian Institute of Health Research (CIHR), and the 2018 Canadian Federal Budget.

Paula Smith, Ph.D. is an Associate Professor in the School of Criminal Justice at the University of Cincinnati. Her research interests include offender classification and assessment, correctional rehabilitation, psychological effects of incarceration, program implementation and evaluation, transfer of knowledge to practitioners and policymakers, and meta-analysis. She is the co-author of *Corrections in the Community* and has also authored more than thirty journal articles and book chapters. Dr. Smith has directed numerous federal and state-funded research projects, including studies of prisons, community-based correctional programs, juvenile drug courts, probation and parole departments, and mental health services. Furthermore, she has been involved in evaluations of more than 280 correctional programs throughout the United States. In addition to her research experience, Dr. Smith has considerable experience working with various offender populations, including juvenile offenders, sex offenders, and perpetrators of domestic violence. Currently, she provides training and technical assistance to criminal justice agencies throughout the United States and Canada.

Derek Spencer is an Assistant Professor of Criminal Justice at the University of Winnipeg. He researches criminal law, with a particular focus on sentencing. His Master of Laws thesis was a groundbreaking exploration of *Protecting Canadians by Ending Sentence Discounts for Multiple Murders Act*. Articles adapted from his thesis have been published in leading criminal law journals. In 2018, Professor Spencer was awarded the University of Winnipeg Faculty of Arts Excellence in Research Award for his judicially cited comparative law study of the Multiple Murders Act.

Kevin Walby is Associate Professor of Criminal Justice and Chancellor's Research Chair at the University of Winnipeg, Canada. He has authored or co-authored articles in *British Journal of Criminology*, *Qualitative Inquiry*, *Qualitative Research*, *Punishment & Society*, *Policing & Society*, *Australian & New Zealand Journal of Criminology*, *Criminology and Criminal Justice*, *Surveillance & Society*, and more. He is the author of *Touching Encounters: Sex, Work, and Male-for-Male Internet Escorting* (2012, University of Chicago Press). He is a co-author with R. Lippert of *Municipal Corporate Security* *in International Context* (2015, Routledge). He is co-editor of *Access to Information and Social Justice* with J. Brownlee (2015, ARP Books) and The Handbook of Prison Tourism with J. Wilson, S. Hodgkinson, and J. Piche (2017, Palgrave). He is co-editor of *National Security, Surveillance, and Terror: Canada and Australia in Comparative Perspective* with R. Lippert, I. Warren and D. Palmer (2017, Palgrave). He is co-editor of the *Journal of Prisoners on Prisons* as well as book review editor for *Surveillance & Society and Security Journal.*

Michael Weinrath is Professor and Past Chair of Criminal Justice and Director of the Justice Research Institute at the University of Winnipeg. He recently published *Behind the Walls: Inmates and Correctional Officers on the State of Canadian Prisons* (2016, UBC). His research recently has focused on procedural justice in corrections, problem-solving courts, adult and youth intensive supervision probation programs and prison-based therapeutic communities. His current projects include a study of police decision making on diversion and restorative justice referrals and the relationship between the prison environment and prisoner misconduct.

Tim Williams is an Assistant Professor in the Department of Public Safety & Justice Studies at MacEwan University. He has 19 years of professional experience in community corrections and has worked as a parole officer and halfway house manager. He has also held positions as the vice president of the Alberta Criminal Justice Association and as an Outside Review Board Chair, investigating inmate grievances at federal institutions. His current research and teaching interests include risk assessment, correctional interventions, and institutional subcultures.

Andrew Woolford is a Professor of Sociology at the University of Manitoba. He is author of *'This Benevolent Experiment': Indigenous Boarding Schools, Genocide and Redress in the United States and Canada* (2015), *The Politics of Restorative Justice* (2009), and *Between Justice and Certainty: Treaty-Making in British Columbia* (2005), as well as co-author of *Informal Reckonings: Conflict Resolution in Mediation, Restorative Justice, and Reparations* (2005). He is co-editor of *Canada and Colonial Genocide* (2017), *The Idea of a Human Rights Museum* (2015), and *Colonial Genocide in Indigenous North America* (2014). He is currently working on two community-based research projects with residential school Survivors: 1) Embodying Empathy, which will design, build, and test a virtual Indian Residential School to serve as a site of knowledge mobilization and empathy formation; and 2) Remembering Assiniboia, which focuses on the commemoration of the Assiniboia Residential School.

J. Stephen Wormith is a Professor in the Psychology Department at the University of Saskatchewan (U of S) and Director of the Centre of Forensic Behavioural Science and Justice Studies, which is also at U of S. Previously, he was Psychologist-in-Chief for the Ontario Ministry of Community Safety and Correctional Services. He is a Fellow of the Canadian Psychological Association (CPA). He co-authored the Level of Service/Case Management Inventory (2004) with D. A. Andrews and J. Bonta and participates internationally in research and training on risk assessment. He is on the editorial board of *Criminal Justice and Behavior, Psychological Services* and the *Canadian Journal of Criminology and Criminal Justice.* He is also on the Board of Directors of the International Association for Correctional and Forensic Psychology (IACFP). Dr. Wormith's research activities have concentrated on the assessment and treatment of offenders. He consults with provincial and federal government departments and serves as an expert witness on matters of offender assessment and treatment.

John Winterdyk was the first Director of the Centre for Criminology and Justice Research (CCJR) at Mount Royal University (2009-2012). He is also an Adjunct Professor at St. Thomas University (Fredericton, New Brunswick), University of Regina (Regina, Saskatchewan), and the Polytechnic in

Namibia (Windhoek, Namibia). He is also a Visiting Scholar at KIIT University in Bhubaneswar, India. He has published extensively in the areas of youth justice, human trafficking, international criminal justice, and criminological theory. To date, he has authored and(co)edited some 30 textbooks and is currently working on a new young offenders book (OUP) as well as a new edition of his *Introduction to Criminology* textbook (OUP), and is co-Editor in Chief of a *Handbook on Human Trafficking* (Palgrave). Current areas of research interest include identity theft, corrections, human trafficking, teen courts, and crime prevention.

An Introduction to Adult Corrections in Canada

Michael Weinrath and John Winterdyk

This book is designed to meet the needs of most standard introductory level corrections courses in undergraduate criminology and criminal justice programs. It examines and evaluates a wide range of themes and issues that relate to adult corrections in Canada.

Unlike other areas of the criminal justice system, the selection of textbooks on corrections is somewhat limited. This book intends to help expand the options available to instructors and students. In preparing the latest edition of this book, we recognize that, like all areas of the criminal justice system, corrections is a continually evolving area that is influenced by the changing economic, political, and social events that characterize Canadian society. For example, since Canada became a nation in 1867, we have seen dramatic shifts within corrections such as moving from a nationwide federal and provincial prison system in the latter portion of the 19th century and into the mid-portion of the 20th century to a system with many community corrections alternatives such as probation, parole, conditional sentences, fine option, pre-trial supervision, and halfway houses. As is discussed in various chapters throughout the book, many of these changes are unnoticed because corrections remains a mostly "hidden element" of the system.

We live in an era bombarded continuously by "breaking news," where human and civil rights have now taken centre stage, and there is an ever-increasing awareness among the general public about crime and criminal justice issues. For example, we hear about prison escapes within hours, the released inmate who reoffends, and major abuses by staff within a correctional setting (e.g., the Ashley Smith case, which is also used in the book as a case example regarding some of the challenges adult corrections still faces). Such facts also confront us as an overburdened and under-resourced correctional system, which is presented with new challenges such as gangs, mental health, an increasing number of women and Indigenous in the system, greater ethnic and cultural diversity, as well as a growing and ageing inmate population. We are also witnessing the expansion of alternatives such as community-based corrections, electronic monitoring, and restorative justice programs. These offer the judicial system an increasing number of options to consider when sentencing an offender.

In short, adult corrections is a dynamic and exciting field of study and most worthy of having its dedicated course(s) and textbooks in order to do justice to the issue and subject matter. The correctional changes and challenges have practical, political and administrative implications which are all addressed at various levels throughout this book. In addition to merely providing an overview of the diversity of corrections, each chapter also explores, to varying degrees, some critical issues that will serve to stimulate further discussion, research, and inquiry either inside or outside of the classroom.

Even though we are now fully into the new millennium, there remain many areas of corrections which deserve to be examined to ensure that its operations reflect the values of Canadian society and our Charter of Rights and Freedoms. Also, this leads to many questions, such as: Should some offenders be restrained in a custodial setting? Moreover, for how long and under what conditions? What constitutes cruel and unusual punishment in prison? We need to delve into areas that are less understood such as the increasingly punitive nature of community corrections. Does the greater use of electronic monitoring, house arrest and urinalysis make parole and probation much more intrusive?

Also, how hard can the state push these measures on offenders who are placed into the community based on some correctional principle or ideology?

Hence, the key goals of this book are to:

1. Provide the reader with a comprehensive and time-sensitive overview of adult correction that traces the historical roots of Canadian corrections to its current expression.
2. Provide an overview of the principal elements and topics confronting the different areas of correctional practices in Canadian corrections.
3. Introduce the reader to some of the seminal and critical research studies done in corrections, as well as recent cutting-edge inquiries into Canadian adult corrections.
4. Challenge the reader to examine the pros and cons of some of the classic debates in corrections, such as the use of custody versus community alternatives.

ORGANIZATION OF THE TEXTBOOK

This book is composed of 13 chapters written by a cross-section of individuals who have the academic background and boast the practical knowledge and experience of their subject area.

The chapters are ordered in a logical sequence starting with the historical, practical, and factual trends within adult corrections. However, course curriculums may not necessarily follow the order. Therefore, some content and facts are repeated to some degree throughout the book. However, we ensure that redundancy is kept to a minimum.

In **Chapter 1**, John Winterdyk and Aja Jacqueline Manning begin with an overview of the concepts and description of the complexity of corrections. The authors trace the concept of penology to its present form. The remainder of the chapter reviews the basic operations and mandates of adult correction within the practical and philosophical framework. The first chapter lays the foundation for the remainder of the book.

In **Chapter 2,** Winterdyk provides an historical overview of adult corrections in Canada. The chapter begins with an exploration of how penitentiaries came into existence and the ways that corrections differ from today. The author then provides a summary of some of the significant inquiries and reports that helped to forge and change the face of corrections. Attention is paid to significant events, such as the 1996 Arbour Commission and the Transformation Agenda in 2006.

Derek Spencer, in **Chapter 3**, shifts attention to Canada's criminal law, and issues around the application of legislation to the exercise of sentencing. He provides the reader with knowledge of Canadian sentencing purposes and principles and how they apply to the correctional system.

In **Chapter 4**, Michael Weinrath provides an overview of probation, the most commonly utilized and, perhaps, least understood form of correctional intervention. He points out the flaws that plague probation practice but offers some examples of recent, promising forms of intervention.

In **Chapter 5,** Rosemary Ricciardelli and Weinrath draw on a broad set of literature, and their recent research into remand, and provincial and federal prisoner populations to paint a grim but realistic view of contemporary Canadian prison life. The authors track prisoners inmates from their admission into the system through to how they manage their day-to-day lives, as well as assessing new challenges such as prison gangs.

In **Chapter 6,** Gillian Balfour looks at women in corrections, particularly recent events regarding the landmark "Creating Choices Report" in the 1990s. Balfour discusses the promise of the report to fundamentally change the way women offenders are housed and treated in federal corrections, only to observe the failures of the CSC in effectively following through on several key recommendations.

Indigenous mass incarceration is explained in **Chapter 7** by Lisa Monchalin and Olga Marques. The authors link colonialism, the impact of residential schools and the imposition of white settler law on consequent Indigenous over-representation in our prisons. They also offer hope in discussing methods of "decolonizing" Canadian society and resilience in the Indigenous community.

In **Chapter 8,** Debra Parkes, Kelly Hannah-Moffat and Amy Klassen address the issue of prisoner rights, tracing its history, and reviewing some of the landmark legal decisions and government inquiries that resulted in some improvement in prison conditions. At the same time, they chart the difficulties inmates experience in receiving fair treatment, as correctional organizations struggle to meet their "duty to act fairly."

In **Chapter 9,** Claire Goggin, Paula Smith, and Paul Gendreau provide an excellent overview of the history of rehabilitation programming in corrections. Building on the latest research, including their own, the authors review the key features of effective programming, warn of misguided efforts and strategies to "treat" offenders, and point the way forward for practitioners wishing to incorporate the best techniques in helping offenders positively change their behaviour. Stephen Wormith, Myles Ferguson, and James Bonta give a fascinating overview of the development and use of evidence-based classification and case management in Western corrections. They provide the reader with the latest cutting-edge research and give insight into its most appropriate applications in institutional and community settings.

Tracey Cyca and Tim Williams discuss parole and conditional release in **Chapter 10**. In addition to providing an overview of the purpose and principles of conditional release (CR), the authors offer a thorough review of the success of CR. The chapter also provides an overview of the often misunderstood role and purpose of parole. Both CR and parole are discussed regarding their respective roles and impact on corrections.

In **Chapter 11**, Andrew Woolford and Amanda Nelund explore the emerging practice of restorative justice (RJ), a relatively new form of corrections intended to reduce the adversarial nature of the criminal justice system and provide a more collaborative means of resolving offences between the victim and offender. They work through RJ's history – the various theoretical models are considered, as well as recent research findings. They caution the reader about the many challenges posed by the successful implementation of restorative justice but conclude with examples of promising programs around the country.

In **Chapter 12,** Justin Piché, Kevin Walby, and Nicolas Carrier provide readers with an abolitionist critique of the justice system. They provide students with foundational abolitionist concepts. Abolition can be a very abstract concept, but the authors bring their chapter to life through stories from academics and activists who have worked to reduce or eliminate the use of prisons in Canada.

Rick Ruddell and Katharina Maier, in **Chapter 13,** bravely tackle what the future could look like for corrections in Canada. They explain that while the science of predicting is not a precise science, forecasting efforts are helpful for operational issues across a wide range of factors. The chapter explores the potential impact of the ever-changing inmate population, the evolving nature of technology, and even the relative effectiveness of violence reduction strategies. Perhaps one of the more concrete forecasting issues is trying to explain the potential costs and benefits to the system.

SPECIAL FEATURES OF THIS TEXTBOOK

In addition to this textbook representing a collection of original contributions from academicians and scholarly practitioners, it also includes the following pedagogical features to assist the reader and instructors:

- Textbox inserts that highlight key supplementary material to enrich the chapter content
- Useful web links for further reading and/or inquiry
- Review and critical thinking questions
- Key terms and concepts (in bold text) relevant to the topic area being discussed in the chapter

ACKNOWLEDGEMENTS

First and foremost, we want to acknowledge the invaluable contribution of the contributors to this textbook. We intentionally sought contributors who are recognized for their expertise in their subject area. All the contributors provide a level of insight on their topic that we feel further enriches the depth and quality of the content. We are delighted to have added ten new authors to the book, mostly younger scholars but a few who are older and leaders in their field. All the contributors prepared their chapters in a complementary manner that will allow the reader to feel that they are reading a textbook with a familiar tone and similar features. For example, not only are the chapters prepared in a student-friendly manner, but they also include a set of common pedagogical elements such as key terms and concepts, "boxes" that supplement learning objectives, study questions, and helpful web links.

This is the second edition of *Adult Corrections in Canada*. This time Michael Weinrath has taken the lead on this new editor as John Winterdyk is nearing retirement. This has been a fruitful partnership, and we thoroughly enjoyed the sometimes exasperating nature of organizing an edited text together! We want to acknowledge and thank the anonymous reviewers for their feedback. While their input is most beneficial, we recognize that any shortcomings of the book are ours alone. Finally, but not least of all, we would be very remiss if we did not recognize the support of our wives, who supported our taking on another book project and the evenings and weekends that went with it.

We extend a hearty "thank you" to our publisher, Shivu Ishwaran, de Sitter Publications for encouraging us to undertake this second edition. It is always great to be in demand! To our copy editor, Gayle Gonsalves, we express our indebtedness since we know that sometimes an external set of eyes can and will see things that we overlooked. While this book is the result of input from many people, as editors we assume responsibility for any oversights. We welcome your feedback should you have any suggestions to improve our book.

Adult Corrections within a Canadian Context[1]

John Winterdyk and Aja Jacqueline Manning

1

Learning Objectives

After reading this chapter, you should be able to:

- Describe the complex nature of corrections.

- Define corrections in terms of its evolving nature.

- Explain corrections as a political and social concept.

- Describe the mandate and principles of adult corrections.

- Explain the different practical and philosophical orientations of (adult) corrections.

- Describe the role of corrections within the Canadian criminal justice system.

...to cause justice to prevail in the land, to destroy the wicked and the evil, to prevent the strong from oppressing the weak, to go forth like the sun..., to enlighten the land and to further the welfare of the people.

–Hammurabi (circa 2130-2087) in the Code of the Babylonian King, commenting on the purpose of punishment.

When we were preparing the first edition of this chapter in 2010, the then Conservative government was pledging to pass Bill C-10, also known as the Omnibus Bill. It made Canadians think that crime is not only everywhere, it is an inextricable part of our social fabric. Based on the sweeping conservative measures of the Bill, it leads some people to believe that the only way to address crime was to "get tough" on it. As Karl Menninger (1968, p. 6) wrote: "crime is *everybody's* temptation. It is easy to look with proud disdain upon 'those people' who get caught…. But who does not get nervous when a police car follows closely?" Therefore, if we are all capable of transgressions, how do we justify responding to those who get caught? However, almost a decade has passed and in addition to a new government, we have some new ideas about correctional practices in Canada.

Although we have witnessed a general decline in the crime rate since the mid-1990s and well into the new millennium, crime rates are still considerably higher compared to when the current Uniform Crime Reporting practice was introduced in the early 1960s. Also notable is the decline in crime severity, with 2014 seeing the lowest level of crime severity since 1998, when the first Crime Severity Index (CSI) was introduced (see Police Reported Crime Statistics, 2014). The increase, followed by the recent decline, raises a number of questions about whether any of the measures taken by the different elements of the Canadian Criminal Justice System (CJS) might account for the change. Pertinent to this text, one of the questions is what role, if any, does the correctional system play? While arguably a cynical statement, corrections has not managed to completely shed Robert Martinson's (1974) unwelcomed mantel that "nothing works" in corrections (see Chapter 9). Even though most academicians agree that the assertion is overstated, penological theory (see below) continues to be shrouded in an air of skepticism, and public support or faith in corrections is seldom static.

Since crime is generally a normative concept, most people have a reasonable sense of what constitutes crime. The public, however, is less well-informed about the complexities underlying the causes of crime. People tend to view crime as a violation of the values and norms of society that undermine their moral sense of order. As the father of American sociology, Charles Cooley proposed at the turn of the 20th century that all humanity shares a common core of "values and rules on how to act" (cited in Christie, 1996, p. 179).[2] Yet, our compliance can be neutralized by various economic, individual, political, and social circumstances. Hence, social scientists try to define the concept of crime in more precise terms. In so doing, their frame of reference influences the various factors of criminal behaviour that a criminologist focuses on. Although there are a variety of definitions and explanations (e.g., biological, economic, psychological, & sociological – see, Winterdyk, 2016), given the context of this textbook, we will use the legalistic definition: **crime** is defined as an act, or omission, that violates the criminal law and is subject to a legal response that is sanctioned by the state. **Criminal law** is the formal means by which society attempts to protect the public and define guidelines for public order and stability based on "how close the law is the core of common human experience" (Christie, 1996, p. 181). Imposing **sanctions**[3] on convicted offenders provides four rationales to protect society: deterrence, incapacitation, rehabilitation, and retribution (see below). When these rationales for intervention are officially applied to the convicted offenders through the judicial process euphemistically, they are collectively referred to as **corrections**.[4] The forums where the rationales are applied in contemporary society are varied and diverse. They include, among other options, probation, conditional release,

4 Rationales:
1) Deterrence   3) Rehabilitation
2) Incapacitation 4) Retribution

incarceration, fines, restitution orders, and a variety of other alternatives that have evolved over the years. Most of these subject areas are covered throughout the book. However, as reflected in Box 1.1, different societies apply different informal and formal measures to prevent people from committing crimes or disrupting social order.

Although representing a diverse collection of options, Canadian adult correctional (i.e., 18 years and older) practices often comes under fire as the public tends to perceive that corrections does not properly carry out the sanctions of the courts. In addition, as reflected in the sample of the dramatic media stories below, correctional practices also seem to violate the public's sense of justice, for example:

- Suicide attempts spike amid Ontario prison system overhaul. "At a time when Ontario prison officials have vowed to take a more humane approach to inmate care, the province has recorded a significant rise in the number of suicide attempts in its correctional facilities. Over the past decade, provincial institutions have averaged 106 suicide attempts a calendar year." (White, 2017)
- Canada's jailhouse secret: Legally innocent prisoners are dying. "Nearly 270 people have died in Canadian provincial jails over the past five years. Two-thirds of them were legally innocent." (Paperny, 2017)
- Young Women Keep Killing Themselves in Canada's Jails. "Her jailer, Corrections Service Canada (CSC), knew she had attempted suicide a week earlier, and was aware of her history of similar suicide attempts and self-harm, including once setting herself on fire—but still they classified her as a low-risk for suicide, her family alleges in a recently launched lawsuit." (Beaumont, 2016)
- Canada's prisons are the 'new residential schools. "A months-long investigation reveals that at every step, Canada's justice system is set against Indigenous people." (Macdonald, 2016)
- No rehabilitation in Alberta federal prisons, correctional investigator says. "Inmates in federal custody are often poorly equipped to reintegrate into society after their sentences due to sub-par conditions at Canadian prisons, the country's prison watchdog said." (Wakefield, 2017)

As illustrated in the above media captions, current dissatisfaction focuses on the well-being of inmates, the "leniency" of the system, the investment in the system, and an apparent confusion around the objective and mandate of corrections. These issues represent serious concerns that deserve closer scrutiny. Hence, throughout this chapter, we will examine the diverse nature of correctional practices, policy, and issues in Canada. In addition, the chapter will provide information which the reader can assess whether the various forms of corrections are either too lenient or too harsh. Finally, by offering an overview of corrections, we hope you will gain a richer understanding and appreciation of the diversity and complexity of adult corrections in Canada, and thereby begin to bridge an understanding of the purpose of corrections with constructive social policy and educative options.

In one of the first Canadian textbooks exclusively devoted to corrections in Canada, Ekstedt and Griffiths (1984) argued that the need for a textbook on the subject was premised on the "expansion of criminal justice and correctional courses…and the development of staff training programs for correctional personnel" (p. vii). Almost forty years later, the general rationale still applies but the scope has evolved in its depth and mandate. For example, until recently, corrections in Canada was synonymous with incarceration (see Chapter 3), and the concept of community-based corrections (see Chapter 4) did not really emerge until the early 1990s; the treatment of women in prisons also underwent dramatic reforms after the release of the 1990 report, *Creating Choices: Report of the Task Force on Federally Sentenced Women* (see Chapter 10). In addition, the impact of the media and public perception (see

Chapter 2) on victims of crime, conditional sentencing, restorative justice, and the use of aftercare services, among other community-based options, have all become part of the correctional enterprise. For example, while the public tends to view corrections as the practice of incarceration (as reflected in the media excerpts above), actual incarcerations decreased between 1995 through till 2006, after that date they went up slightly. However, since 2012 the overall incarceration rate has been declining steadily with exception to a slight increase in 2015 and 2016 (see Chapter 5). By contrast, the use of remand has increased dramatically since the mid-1990s and continues to exceed sentenced population today. In addition, the average number of stays spent in remand has also steadily increased across the country (Adult Correctional Services in Canada, 2016/2017). The overall trend supports Christie's (1996) argument that "the growth in prison populations within major industrialized nations has only accelerated."[6]

Through the efforts of Amnesty International and with the 50th anniversary of Human Rights Declaration in 1998, and the passing of the Canadian Charter of Rights and Freedoms in 1982, there are mandates that maintain the delicate balance between individual freedom and social order at a national scene, and this heralds a higher profile more than ever before. For many, this profile constitutes

Box 1.1 – Social Order in a Complex World

While crime and social order share a universal concern, they mean different things in different cultures. Societies use diverse response mechanisms to attain and maintain social order. How different cultures achieve social order tends to reflect variations between these cultures and their social, economic, political, and historical characteristics. In summary, the meaning of crime is dependent on four factors (Morrison, 2005, pp. 12-15):

(i) Crime is a social construction;
(ii) Crime is a product of religious authority/doctrine;
(iii) Crime is a reflection of nation-state legality; and
(iv) Crime is derived from social and political Theory.

How countries respond to crime can be, in part, described by examining their incarceration rates (see Table 1.1). For example, the United States tends to have one of the highest incarceration rates in the world because it emphasizes penalization as the appropriate response to maintaining social order. On the other hand, Japan has a very low incarceration rate. Corrections in Japan relies on social conformity and prefers informal sanctioning (e.g., public shaming), while Poland, which has a comparatively high incarceration rate, is characterized "by appealing to each person's sense of civic obligation" (Reichel, 1994, p. 266). Nevertheless, since the mid-1990s, Poland has begun to use more community-based services, although limited resources hampers their effectiveness (Reichel, 2007). Meanwhile, even within countries there can be noticeable differences in their incarceration rates. In Canada there is considerable variation between the provinces and territories (see Reitano, 2017, Table 1). For example, Manitoba recorded having the highest incarceration rate while Nova Scotia recorded the lowest between 2016-2017 (Adult corrections Services in Canada, 2017).

And while most countries (and their states or provinces) share similar justification and goals for punishment, there is considerable variability in their justification. For example, even though more than 40% of all nations abolished the death penalty by the end of the 2010s, it is

continued...

still used in countries such as Iran, Iraq, China, South Africa, Japan, and the United States. Of these countries, only Japan and the United States employ protracted processes in the execution of offenders (Death Sentences and Executions, 2010, 2010).[6] Nevertheless, contrary to pleas from the United Nations' *Universal Declaration of Human Rights*, they still practice the death penalty. In fact, the United States is among the few countries that still use the death penalty as a "corrective" measure for certain types of crimes committed by young persons.

By engaging in a **comparative analysis** of different correctional systems, we observe how the concept of social control varies and how different systems achieve control. Comparative studies allow researchers to explore questions such as which model works best, under what conditions do they work best, and how and why they vary.

Should we strive for universal concepts of social control? What problems does it pose for social order when the concept of crime is not universal? What challenges (i.e., economic, social, human right, and/or political) might such efforts pose for correctional systems?

Table 1.1 International Prison Population Rate -- Highest to Lowest

Country	2018 Incarceration rates (per 100,000 population)
United States	655
Russian Federation	411
Belarus	364
Bermuda	319
South Africa	280
Guyana	259
Greenland	225
Chile	225
New Zealand	220
Tunisia	206
Singapore	201
Paraguay	199
Poland	198
Saudi Arabia	197
Kazakhstan	194
Australia	167
United Kingdom	141
Canada	114
France	102
Greece	93
Lesotho	92

continued...

Cyprus	83
Netherlands	59
Sudan	46
Japan	45
Iceland	38
India	33

Source: World Prison Brief (2018, June).

Not withstanding possible changes in legislation and recording practices, it is observed that the per capita incarceration rate has climbed in most parts of the world since 1999. In fact, since 2000, the total prison population is estimated to have increased 20 percent (World Prison Population List 11th (ed), 2016).

How can this be explained?

a negative image. Moreover, when we take into account that symbolically, corrections and the law (i.e., legal system) still represent the failure of the criminal justice process to deter potential offenders, the negative profile and general skepticism bears an additional burden for Canadian society.

We will begin by examining the current meaning of corrections. This will be followed by examining the concepts of punishment and intervention that largely define operational principles of corrections. From here, we will describe the scope of adult corrections in Canada before offering an overview of some of the practical elements of corrections in the country. Then, we will explore the various justifications for punishment before examining some of the political, social, and legal aspects of corrections. The chapter will conclude with a general overview of corrections within the criminal justice system.

Since antiquity, all societies view certain behaviours, or acts, as unacceptable, for instance, they are in conflict with defined concepts of social harmony and social order. These acts are referred to as **proscribed** behaviours. Conversely, societies encourage, or prescribe, other behaviours such as marriage, working for a living, and respecting other people and their property. Hence, all behaviours can be placed along a continuum of unacceptable to acceptable behaviours. The Canadian sociologist John Hagan (1984) used a pyramid analogy to illustrate this continuum as it relates to perceived deviance in societies. At the top of the pyramid are the *consensus* acts of crime and deviance that are

Box 1.2 – Moving Beyond Penology: Corrections

What are the ultimate consequences for society and the offender (and victim) regarding what we do in the name of corrections? For example, in Iran, your hands can be cut off for stealing, and in Thailand, a person can receive the death penalty for drug smuggling; whereas, in Canada, the death penalty is abolished and there is a distinct focus on the rehabilitation of criminals.

How are our actions towards criminals a reflection of society?

uniformly sanctioned, while at the bottom of the pyramid are the vast range of behaviours that he describes as social diversions that have no uniform agreement regarding whether these behaviours constitute any social harm and whether there should be any formal response.

Historically, the focus of corrections was on punishment and imprisonment (see Chapter 2). In fact, it was not until the mid-1900s that the term **penology** became a part of corrections. Penology is derived from the Latin word *poena*, which means punishment. Hence, penologists, as social scientists, study the relative effectiveness of different punishments which, in-turn, is translated into policy.

This chapter documents that historically, punishment is the primary mode of righting wrongs. It is only the method by which punishment is administered that has changed. Although some of these methods can still be found in some societies today, we have evolved from self-help justice and blood feuds between families to the state assuming responsibility for administering punishment. After the state assumed the role of administering punishment, prisons were introduced to simply serve as remand or detention centres until an appropriate punishment is delivered. Hence, the role prisons played in early times, when prisons and institutional experiences served as a *punitive* and *retributive* response to wrong doing, served no corrective function. Therefore, as a social science, penology represents a narrow focus, but one that is not completely neglected. People interested in the study of penal reform, as illustrated throughout this textbook, continue to explore various rationales for justifying the punishment of certain types of offenders.

Meanwhile, corrections embraces three elements: punishment, treatment, and prevention. Some critics such as Michel Foucault (1977) suggest that modern corrections do little more than engage in surveillance, control, and management. Nevertheless, the concept of corrections reflects the broader range of responses and programs, and available alternatives that deal with convicted offenders. When the term and concept of corrections replaced penology in the late 1800s, it reflected the broad range of facilities, programs, and services that deal with convicted criminals. Much of the impetus for the conceptual change originated at the first International Prison Congress in 1872, held in London, England, where the ideas of rehabilitation and humane treatment were highlighted. This transition and its implications on corrections in Canada are explored in Chapter 2.

Regardless of the name change, the historical review of (adult) corrections in Canada will reveal that our correctional system continues to emphasize punishment over other objectives. It is, in part, our long history of relying on punitive strategies that pose challenges for correctional reforms today. In addition, the process of administering corrections is also complicated by its complex relationship with the rest of the criminal justice system. For example, the police are often seen as the "gatekeepers" of the criminal justice system. Under certain circumstances, the police can make decisions whether formal actions should be taken against an offender. Meanwhile, the courts can exercise a certain degree of discretion as to whom and how many offenders enter the correctional system. Corrections then became the last vanguard that attempts to deal with people who could not be deterred from committing a crime. However, competing correctional objectives (i.e., punishment vs. treatment/rehabilitation vs. maintenance of the offender – see below) have seldom made good partners. In fact, one of the most enduring questions in corrections is: "can you punish and treat someone at the same time?" For example, a few decades ago, **hydrotherapy** was used as a treatment modality for violent offenders. It involved wrapping the offender tightly in a wool type blanket and then placing the patient in either an ice-cold bath or outside during winter. Today, many view this as a form of "cruel and unusual punishment," even though it was once thought to be therapeutic!it was once thought to be therapeutic![8]

In addition to philosophical issues, correctional services in Canada must also contend with a range of practical issues. For example, corrections is administered by various levels of government including federal, provincial, and municipal. There are also private and voluntary agencies in society that provide services such as supervision, reintegration, employment advocacy, human service delivery, and a host of other services that are privatized in some provinces. Collectively, the levels of delivery and variation in services provide numerous administrative and practical challenges in the performance of corrections.

THE EVOLVING NATURE OF CORRECTIONS

As described in Chapter 2, the meaning and nature of corrections has evolved throughout Canadian history (see Winterdyk, 2018a, 2018b). Corrections, whether in Canada or elsewhere, is an alluring yet complex subject area. However, it can generally be said that while the practice of corrections involves the use of punishment as the measure of enforcing social order, the process of applying corrections has varied. For example, a recent report observed that jails across Canada hold more adults awaiting trial than convicted offenders serving sentences (Donnelly, 2017). This is sharp contrast the Canadian frontier days when most persons imprisoned were serving a sentence. Nevertheless, today's prisoners have rights (see Chapters 8) and opportunities (see Chapter 10) that were unknown to prisoners in earlier times. During pre-Confederation, for example, we used correction practices such as branding, flogging, hanging, placing felons in the stocks or the pillory, and cutting off people's ears for certain crimes (Carrigan, 1991).

The early Canadian "prisons" were initially modelled after the British Elizabethan **Bridewells**, which were workhouses used to house everyone from the poor, the sick, the insane to petty criminals. However, as the Bridewells fell out of favour in England, Canadian prisons were then modelled after the Pennsylvania and Auburn prison systems (see Chapter 2; also see Box 1.3). And unlike today when we consider the social and political mindset, little concern was given to the well-being of the inhabitants of these correctional facilities.

Although we have offered a glimpse into the evolving nature of adult corrections, and before we begin to examine any issues surrounding corrections, it is important to define and explain adult

---

Box 1.3 – Kingston Penitentiary

According to Correctional Service Canada, the first penitentiary was introduced by the Philadelphia Quakers in 1789 as a way to move away from harsher punishments to a system, whereby offenders could be rendered "penitent" and reformed after a period of reflection during imprisonment. Before Canada was a nation, its first penitentiary, called the "Provincial Penitentiary of Upper Canada" was built in Kingston, Ontario in 1835. It represented a move from the practice of administering severe and often public punishment for crimes, to keeping criminals away from other members of society, in a place where they were punished, but where they also had the chance to think about their actions and hopefully reform their behaviours. In 1868, the institution came under Upper Canada's first Penitentiary Act, which proclaimed that "if many offenders convicted of crimes were ordered to solitary imprisonment, accompanied by well-regulated labor and religious instruction, it might be the means under Providence, not only of deterring others from the commission of like crimes, but also of reforming the individuals, and inuring them to habits of industry." The institution opened on June 1, 1835, housing nine inmates and is still in operation today, housing between 350 and 500 inmates. While several prison riots have occurred at the site, it remains open and is one of the oldest prisons in the world still in operation. Now called the "Kingston Penitentiary," the institution was designated a National Historic Site of Canada in 1990 (History, 2011).

One of the worlds oldest prisons

corrections within a contemporary context. Its meaning and scope, as suggested by Griffiths and Cunningham (2000), is influenced by such factors as the social and political elements underlying corrections, its legal relation to the criminal justice system, as well as by its relative conceptual diversity.

ADULT CORRECTIONS: A POLITICAL AND SOCIAL CONCEPT

As is the case with all concepts unique to the study of crime and criminal justice, the term corrections is both *relative* and *evolving* (see Box 1.4). Corrections is a term that is neither well understood, nor is there a universal agreement about its objective.

This general level of perplexity has its roots in the context of who is defining corrections and the time-period being defined. During Canada's frontier days, a criminal's social status was no better than an animal (Carrigan, 1991). Criminals were generally viewed as being atavistic and deserving of punishment (see, for example, Gould, 1996). Hence, the notion of corrections evolved around the practice of *retribution* and *just deserts* (see below). Corrections involved punishment that, by today's standards, is considered inhumane. Yet, given the understanding of whom and what a criminal was, these practices were seldom questioned (other than by prisoners, perhaps). Nevertheless, not knowing differently, the political and social concept of corrections prevailed until the Age of Enlightenment (c.

Box 1.4 – The History and Evolution of Corrections and Punishment

Antiquity to 1700 AD:

- Self-help justice or sometimes referred to as "vigilantism":
- Retaliation and vengeance: blood feuds (i.e., vendettas) were a common practice in early times.
- Retribution: The Sumerian Codes (1850 BC), while often associated with the legal principle *lex talinos* – "an eye for an eye and a tooth for a tooth," served to place limitations on the degree of retaliation allowed. Even so, punishments under these codes were harsh and often administered by the injured party. *Are victim impact statements today a "civilized" form of vengeance?*
- Capital punishment: Code of Hammurabi (1750 BC) is the first codified law that legislated social interactions. A sentence of death was a common disposition for many offences.
- Measured justice: Justinian Code (600 AD) during the Roman Empire attempted to match the punishment to the perceived gravity of the crime. The concept of proportionality was introduced, for example, "scales of justice."
- *Wergeld*, also known as *lex scalia,* is a form of retaliation involving payment to the victim. This practice is still evident in a number of Middle Eastern and Far Eastern countries. Payment is proportionate to the injured party's position in society.
- *Friedensgeld*: During the Middle Ages (c. 1200 AD) as the state and church gained in power, wergelds were replaced by friedensgeld. The administration of punishment became the responsibility of the state. Hence, payment was no longer made to the victim but to the state which also served as a measure for addressing collective wrongs.
- In 1865, Canada introduced the death penalty for murder, treason, and rape. In 1961, murder was classified as capital (i.e., premeditated) and non-capital offences. In 1976, capital punishment was abolished as a punishment in Canada.

1700s) when several scholars expressed concern for the rights of humanity.

A variety of intellectual scholars, during this period, began to apply a scientific and rational approach to the understanding of their society. Among some of the more notable scholars are: Charles Montesquieu, Francois Marie Arouet Voltaire, and Jean-Jacque Rousseau of France; Jeremy Bentham, John Howard, David Hume, and Adam Smith in England; and Cesare Beccaria in Italy. These and other scholars argue that regardless of class, occupation, or race, all people are equal and deserve to be treated as such. For example, Rousseau (1712-1778), in his earlier writings, argues that the growth of civilization corrupted the natural goodness and increased inequality within society. Along these lines, he also targeted private ownership of land as a causative factor of crime and corruption. In his epic, *The Social Contract*, published in 1762, Rousseau lashed out against the political status quo and called for equity, fraternity, and liberty for all. In fact, these words became the battle cry of the French Revolution in 1812. In the book, he also wrote of **natural law** and the concept of natural rights (e.g., freedom of speech, equality before the law, and freedom of persons). Collectively, these ideas helped to redefine the social and political notion of justice and corrections.[7]

Beccaria (1738-1794) is another intellectual who profoundly influenced the concept of justice, and indirectly corrections. His pinnacle work, *On Crimes and Punishment*,[8] published in 1764, complemented the ideas of Rousseau by calling for equality for all, liberty for all, humanitarian treatment of all people regardless of the type of crimes they commit, and a utilitarian approach to justice. That is, it is better to prevent a crime than to punish it. However, if someone has done harm, then punishment should be certain, severe (i.e., in measured proportion to the offence), and swift. And if someone does harm, then the state has no right to use torture prior to the determination of guilt.

The works of Rousseau, Beccaria, and scholars from the Enlightenment Period instrumentally forged penal and correctional reform at a social and political level. Bentham (1748-1833), for example, called for the reform of criminals using education and adequate provisions upon release. He also outlined a set of criteria to precisely calculate punishment. Meanwhile, John Howard (1726-1790) devoted his life to the introduction of humane conditions and handling of all prisoners. Arguably, a more recent Canadian contemporary is Frank P. Miller (see Box 1.5).

In summary, the social and political notions of corrections influenced our understanding of corrections and will continue to do so. Our thoughts and political agendas, combined with scientific findings, will impact future correctional policy and practices. In this light, it becomes ever more important to understand corrections within this context, so that the process of corrections can continue to strive towards a balance of respecting individual freedoms and the protection of society.

CORRECTIONS AS A LEGAL AND CRIMINAL JUSTICE SUBSYSTEM

Corrections and the criminal justice system, in general, have their own social structure. The structure is made up of the social values in society, the various statuses found in corrections (e.g., prisoners, offenders, correctional officers, caseworkers), and the norms specific to or of concern to corrections (see Chapters 4-7).

In terms of the latter component, the law gives corrections its specific meaning. The law defines the programs and agencies that have legal authority over the custody or supervision of persons who are convicted of a criminal offence and sentenced by the court.

In Canada, several legislative acts influenced the mandate of correctional services. The *British North America Act* of 1867 defined the distribution of power between provincial and federal governments. Specifically, s. 91(27) of the Act granted the federal government exclusive jurisdiction to make criminal law and to define procedural matters. Section 92(14), meanwhile, granted the provinces the power to administer matters pertaining to justice. Hence, the Act gave the federal government control

Federal Government = serious offences
Provincial Government = less serious offences

Box 1.5 – A Canadian Pioneer in Corrections

Frank P. Miller is one of the true pioneers of the modern corrections system in Canada. Starting as a classification officer in the Canadian penitentiary system just after World War II, over the course of his career, he helped move Canada towards a system incorporating rehabilitation, conditional release, and parole. In 1952, Frank Miller left his job as a classification officer to become an Assistant Director with the Remission Service. Along with the other Assistant Director, Benoit Godbout, and Allan McLeod, the recently appointed Chief of the Remission Service, Miller felt they had a mandate to bring Canadian parole into the 20th century. Their key ideas included individualization of treatment and gradual release, as well as supervision, aftercare support, and earlier consideration for release (after half of the sentence is served, rather than two thirds). In 1959, the three helped draft Canada's Parole Act, establishing the Parole Board of Canada as a completely independent parole decision-making authority, and Miller was appointed as one of its first members. According to him: "The purposes of parole, like the purposes of the sentence in the first instance, are the protection of society and the rehabilitation of the offender. Ideally, these two purposes are inseparable. While society can be protected temporarily by the detention of the criminal, if he is not reformed, society is no longer protected when he is released" (Vandoremalen, 2000, p. 13). Miller remained a Parole Board member until 1965, when he replaced Benoit Godbout as Executive Director of the National Parole Service. In 1972, Frank left the Parole Service and was appointed Canadian Coordinator to the Fifth United Nations Congress on the Prevention of Crime and the Treatment of Offenders. He retired from the Public Service in 1976 having made a substantial impact on the correctional system and criminal justice reform in Canada and around the world (Vandoremalen, 2000).

over serious crimes, while the provinces became responsible for administering justice over the less serious offences. Today, the responsibility for corrections continues to be shared between federal, provincial, and municipal levels of government. However, as defined in the Constitution, the federal and provincial correctional agents are the most important.

The Act underwent a number of major amendments until 1982. At that time, under the stewardship of then Prime Minister Pierre Elliot Trudeau, the Act was consolidated with the signing of the *Constitution Act*.

Further clarification of correctional jurisdiction is defined by the legal system, the *Criminal Code*. When first passed in 1892, the *Criminal Code* entrenched many of the British common law traditions into a Canadian context. However, over the years, amendments slowly eliminated the common law crimes (e.g., felonies and misdemeanors) and replaced them with *indictable* and *summary* offences. Indictable offences are defined as serious offences punishable to a sentence of two years or more; sentences are served in federal institutions. Summary offences are considered less serious crimes and generally do not exceed six-month sentences of incarceration and/or fines up to $5,000 (see section 787 of the CC). Summary conviction offences are tried by a provincial court judge, and terms of incarceration are served in provincial or territorial correctional facilities.

MANDATE AND PRINCIPLES OF ADULT CORRECTIONS

In Canada, the handling of young offenders is legislated under the *Youth Criminal Justice Act* (see Box 1.6). And since the primary focus of this text is on the adult offender, we will not discuss youth corrections (generally, see Youth Justice, 2017).[9]

As noted earlier, corrections is faced with trying to "maintain the delicate balance between individual freedom and social control" (Mandate and Principles of Corrections in Canada, 1998). And, as reported by the Canadian Criminal Justice Association, some of the guiding principles that are universally defined under the *United Nations Covenant on Civil and Political Rights*, of which Canada became a signatory member in 1978, are also among those challenges which are not fully addressed in the Act.

Box 1.6 – *Youth Criminal Justice Act*

On April 1, 2003, the *Youth Criminal Justice Act* (YCJA) replaced the *Young Offenders Act* of 1984, in an attempt to clarify Canada's youth justice philosophy, and allow for increased rehabilitative measures to facilitate the re-integration of delinquent youth back into Canadian society. The Act sets out legislative parameters for the application of correctional and criminal law to those who are between the ages of 12 and 18 at the time of committing an offence (see sec. 2 of the *YCJA*). It also indicates that youth, ages 14 to 18, may, under certain circumstances such as murder, be tried as adults. Overall, the Act places less emphasis on custody as punishment for non-violent or less serious offences, and rather reserves this punishment for violent and repeat offenders. Further, alternative sentencing is emphasized, leaving room for punishment such as referrals to community programs, meetings with police, and formal letters of warning as options in youth sentencing. Critics of the *YCJA* argued that the legislation is too lenient, and, in 2006, the Harper Conservative Government lobbied for harsher sentences to deter offenders and to reduce recidivism rates. The Supreme Court, however, ruled that "since no basis can be found in the *Youth Criminal Justice Act* for imposing a harsher sanction than would otherwise be called for to deter others from committing crimes, general deterrence is not a principle of youth sentence under the new regime" (*Youth Criminal Justice Act*:…, 2006).

More specifically, however, the principles governing corrections and the other elements of the criminal justice system can be found in the *Canadian Charter of Rights and Freedoms*, the *Criminal Code*, the *Corrections and Conditional Release Act* (1992) (also see Chapter 10), and various relevant provincial legislation.

The primary principles of corrections in Canada include the following elements:

1. Throughout the correctional process the rights and dignity of the offender must be respected;
2. While a convicted person's liberty and mobility are restricted, Correctional Services cannot impose further punishment that exceeds those defined under the court disposition;
3. In accordance with the *Corrections and Conditional Release Act*, Correctional Services must adhere to the guidelines and standards established to ensure the fair treatment and handling of all offenders;
4. Inmates must be treated with dignity. Hence, they must, within reason, be granted the opportunity to maintain positive family and other supportive relations. Corrections also has an

obligation to provide/offer a wide range of programs that will allow offenders to seek assistance and improve their odds of reform and rehabilitation;

5. Correctional agencies must be accountable and subject to regular independent and public assessment; and

6. Ultimately the reintegration and protection of society (Mandate and Principles of Corrections in Canada, 1998).

THE SCOPE OF CORRECTIONS

As is evident throughout this textbook, correctional practices involve more than the incarceration and institutionalization of offenders. Until recently, probation is the most common disposition for provincially charged offenders, and depending on the province, many others are placed into some community-based program such as conditional sentencing. As a result of this evolution in corrections, today the correctional process includes:

- Absolute and Conditional Discharges (Chapter 3);
- Fines and Fine Option Programs (Chapter 3);
- Conditional Sentencing (Chapter 4);
- Probation (Chapter 4);
- Women in custody and other 'special' populations (Chapters 6);
- Incarceration (Chapters 5, 8);
- Conditional Release/Parole/Community Residential Centres (Chapter 10), and
- Restorative Justice (Chapter 11).

These broad classifications can be further divided into municipal, provincial, and federal based programs. The range of programs is presented in greater detail in subsequent chapters. For a schematic illustration refer to Figure 1.1 (p. 24).

Although there is a degree of variability regarding how the different levels of jurisdictions operate, they share some common denominators. For example, all jurisdictional levels include public and private correctional programs.

In recent years, there is a concerted effort at all levels of corrections, and the criminal justice system in general (in particular the courts), to move towards greater use of alternative measures for both adult and young offenders. What needs greater clarity is who drives the operational realities of correctional programming? Is it social, political, economic, or some intricate combination of factors?

Today, the alternative measures options are commonly referred to as *restorative justice, circle sentencing,* or more recently, *transformative justice.*[10] These programs are embraced, in subtly different ways, at all levels of the system, both by the public and private sectors. While not a new concept, the idea was popularized by John Braithwaite's 1989 treatise, *Crime, Shame and Reintegration.* In his text, Braithwaite advocates "reintegrative shaming" as a more humane and utilitarian way of dealing with offenders. The concept of shaming as a correctional strategy will be explored in Chapter 11.

Ekstedt and Griffiths (1984), among others, note, the range of correctional programs impacts the "style of management and organization within correctional programs" (p. 7). Regardless of the type of program, they must all subscribe to the mandate and principles of corrections (see above). However, the different levels of corrections tend to subscribe to different correctional ideologies (see Box 1.7). Nevertheless, collectively they reflect the shifting philosophies and ideologies that characterize the history of corrections.

In order to understand the complexity of corrections today, its issues and concerns, as well as its future direction, it is helpful to examine the varying ideologies. An **ideology** is essentially a frame of reference that we rely upon to explain and understand some aspect of our culture – past and present. There are three broad ideologies that apply to correctional practices: **punishment, treatment,** and **prevention**. They are not mutually exclusive and may overlap, depending on the level and type of correctional program. Nevertheless, the divisions are useful in understanding the ideologies.

Box 1.7 – The Changing Face of Correctional Ideologies

Should we be allowed to execute Elric MacArthur, Travis Winsor and Bruce McArthur? How would Canadians have reacted to them prior to the abolition of capital punishment in 1976?

While Canada abolished the death penalty, many countries, including the United States, continue executing individuals who commit certain crimes.[13] This can be problematic when extradition from Canada is requested from the United States and the death penalty is a possible outcome. For example, in 1995, Atif Rafay and Glen Burns, two Canadians, were charged with the murder of Rafay's parents and sister in Washington State. They fled to Canada, and Washington subsequently requested their extradition. At the time, there was no formal requirement to seek assurances that the death penalty would not be applied if the prisoners were sent back to the United States. The case, however, went to the Supreme Court, and in 2001, the court ruled that Canada is required to "seek assurances" that the death penalty will not be applied before prisoners are extradited.

Punishment:

The oldest form of societal response to a wrong-doer is punishment. It usually falls into one of two categories: death or a wide array of **corporal punishments** (any act that when inflicted produces physical pain short of death). Although some countries still practice these methods, in earlier times corporal punishment involved such practices as mutilation, flogging, branding, and torture. In addition to the physical pain inflicted on the offender, one of the most significant aspects of corporal punishment was its public nature. Many of the punishments were administered in public to add humiliation, set an example for others, and provide an opportunity for public retaliation; hence, "adding insult to injury." Compared to the past, there is a gradual reduction in the current level of severity of punishment. Today, rationales for punishment are couched in specialized terminology and scientifically rationalized approaches that can be found in the works of several key classical scholars. For example, Karl Marx (1818-1883), Georg Hegal (1770-1831), and Jeremy Bentham (1748-1832), all wrote on the merits and purpose of punishment and spoke of the need for punishment to exist, but felt that punishment should always be based on the "proportionality principle," which means that no more punishment should be imposed than is absolutely necessary (Tonry, 2011).

There are three general rationales that are used to justify the use of punishment. They include **retribution, deterrence**, and **incapacitation**. *Retribution* dates back to very early times when an offender was considered a threat and an enemy of society who deserved to be punished, put to death, or banished. In earlier times, the administration of such justice, although often swift, did little to deter people from committing similar (or other) crimes. We refer back to the observation made by Menninger at the beginning of this chapter. Is not retribution both a crime against the individual and against us?

It is interesting to note that in 1976, the now defunct Canadian Law Reform Commission essentially embraced a non-utilitarian version of punishment. The Commission observed: "Organizing the future… is not the major function of the criminal law. Even if we cannot control the future, this does not mean we must ignore the present and the past. We still need to do something about the wrongful act" (cited in Walker 1991, p. 29). Surely, this raises some question about the purpose of punishment! If it does not deter crime, or rehabilitate offenders, is it acceptable to justify punishment simply as a measure of **just deserts** (i.e., individual responsibility where imprisonment is seen as an appropriate consequence and one that is *deserved*)? In many respects, this notion represents a return to the more basic rationale for incapacitation – punishment. Citing several concrete examples, Schmalleger (1998) makes a sound argument for the assertion that in the late 1990s, prisons in the United States moved away from any notion of rehabilitation, prevention, or treatment to simple warehousing and management of prisoners. Similar opinions are expressed by the Canadian author, David Cayley (1998), in his book, *The Expanding Prison*. To offset the growing problems of overcrowding, corrections introduced such practices as selective incapacitation and other community-based programs. Yet, as Menninger (1968) notes, the concept of just deserts is little more than an illusion that offers the offender and the victim little, if any, opportunity for reparation for the harm done.

Based on classical school principles, *deterrence* is premised on the notion that we are capable of free will and if the threat or risk of punishment is sufficient, then we are less inclined to offend. The concept also assumes that if someone is punished, they are less likely to re-offend because deterrence implies premeditation (Cayley, 1998). This is referred to as *primary deterrence*, while the deterrence of others is referred to as *secondary deterrence*. When Ben Johnson was caught using illegal drug performance enhancing products in the 1988 summer Olympics, it neither deterred him or other athletes from using similar drugs. More recently, in 1998, the Alberta and Manitoba governments proposed an amendment to the *Criminal Code* that will create a mandatory minimum two-year sentence for "repeat offenders who commit a second offence of break and enter within two years of expiry of their last sentence" (Roberts, 1999, p. 2). Yet as research shows, mandatory sentences, over-punishment, let alone expected severity of punishment are ineffective – hence, no deterrent effect (Cayley, 1998; Koerth-Baker, 2016). For example, did your first speeding ticket stop you from speeding again? Did getting caught telling a white-lie as a young person stop you from telling another one?

Walker (1991) argues that deterrence is only marginally effective provided that the offender does not have a long history of prior convictions. Critics question to what extent the rationale of deterrence is used as a cloak for vengeance? The philosopher, Immanuel Kant (1724-1804), notes that the purpose of punishment is not to deter but to make the offender suffer as part of a higher moral order. Nevertheless, some criminologists continue to explore new variations of the concept. John Braitewaite's (1989), *shaming*, is a recent example. Representing an extension of Frank Tannenbaum's idea of labelling in the 1930s, shaming is premised on the notion that people prefer not to be negatively labelled (see Heidt & Wheeldon (2015) for a general review of the Tannenbaum's labelling theory). However, what remains unclear is to what extent do such factors as the offender's social, personal, cognitive, and even spiritual circumstances play in determining whether any orientation designed to serve as a deterrent works? Based on the voluminous amount of research involving labelling theory, the findings show that while most ex-offenders are aware of the stigma they carry, it is less clear how they process it, or how or why the label has a lasting negative or positive influence (see Box 1.8). Therefore, any notion of deterrence is based on a subjectively distorted understanding of norms that cannot be predicted or quantified.

The third reason for punishing an offender is *incapacitation*. The intention is to prevent the offender from committing any further offence(s) by literally incarcerating them. While at one time

> ### Box 1.8 – Section 718.1 of the *Criminal Code*
>
> Section 718.1 of the *Criminal Code* states: "a sentence must be proportionate to the gravity of the offence and the degree of responsibility of the offender." Canada already has a number of mandatory minimum sentences, particularly for crimes related to firearms (introduced in 1995). Through Canada's pending 'tough on crime' legislation (Bill C-10), new mandatory minimum sentences were introduced for various drug, sex, and violent crimes. While many jurisdictions still leave room for judicial discretion with respect to mandatory sentences, Courts in Canada have no discretion to impose lesser sentences for those crimes involving minimum sentences. According to the Canadian Bar Association: "A fundamental sentencing principle in *Criminal Code* section 718.1 is proportionality...proportionality reflects the necessary and delicate balance that must be achieved in fashioning a just sentence. This balance is also necessary for the administration of a justice system that is explicable and responsive to its citizens. Logic and fairness requires an individualized and proportional sentence" (Bill C-215 2005).
>
> ### *In what ways can mandatory sentence be justified under such conditions?*

offenders were simply placed into prisons for the duration of their sentence, it has only been in the last two hundred years that incapacitation is used in conjunction with one or more of the other forms of punishment. Today, incarceration is seen as the standard response to achieve justice, despite a growing body of evidence that questions its plausibility. The law is not well structured to enable the courts and correctional officials to predict future risk. Furthermore, the notion of justice being served is a subjective term. As Menninger (1968) comments, depending on the context, justice offers to help some, while creating pain for others. What justice is achieved by incarcerating someone? In a more concrete sense, the esteemed Norwegian criminologist, Nils Christie (1928-2015) (1996), notes that the more serious and frightening the crimes, the poorer our ability to predict the risk of recidivism.

Treatment:

Tracing its history back to the Enlightment Period and the Positivist School of Criminology, the treatment approach reflects a more humane ideological approach to responding to criminal behaviour. The Positivists Approach subscribes to the notion that human behaviour, including criminality, is physiologically based. It may be either inherited or environmentally influenced. Hence, offenders are thought to have some ailment or "sickness" that is analogous to the medical model and assumed to be treatable. Like the medical model within the correctional environment, treatment modalities or therapies attempt to "remove" criminal behaviour by using a wide variety of approaches. They range from community-based programs or minimal security settings that provide offenders with an opportunity to "heal" their anger, frustration, or other "ills" to physical and chemical interventions (e.g., lobotomies and chemical castration for chronic sex offenders). Correctional treatment is a principle that has persisted throughout the history of corrections in Canada, but it conceptualization has evolved and morphed. We will next review the various treatment ideologies.

Historically, the treatment ideology can be divided into four sub-categories. They include:

1. *Medical Model:* Dating back to the earlier part of the 20th century and coinciding with the emergence of psychology as a discipline, corrections officials embraced the notion that the

problem of criminality was somehow associated with the constitutional make-up of the individual. The solution was to develop assessment tools to diagnose the "ailment" and then apply the appropriate treatment program. Then the "patient" is considered well if they are deemed 'cured,' rehabilitated, and they are either returned to the community, or placed on probation or parole (see Chapters 4 and 10 for the difference between probation and parole).

2 *Reformatory Model*: Introduced during the late 1800s, the reformatory approach was rooted in Quaker and Calvinistic doctrines. Offenders were thought to be culturally, educationally, and socially disadvantaged in some way. Reformatories were places that emphasized practical education, teaching basic vocational and occupational skills within a regime of strict discipline designed to reform criminal tendencies by offering offenders more socially acceptable outlets.

3 *Reintegration Model*: Although the concept of reintegration can be traced back to ancient times (see Winterdyk, 2001), it did not emerge as a formal correctional option until the late 1960s. The basic premise of reintegration entails a process where a mutually acceptable resolution between the offender and victim(s) is sought so that harmony (i.e., emotional, mental, physical, and spiritual) is restored. Unlike the other models, the causes of crime are thought to be community related. That is, crime is the by-product of a lack of legitimate opportunity (e.g., poverty, being unskilled, insufficient education, and urban decay) to attain socially prescribed goals (e.g., home, decent paying job, and safe community).

A recent variation of the reintegration model that emerged in the mid-1990s is transformative justice. Briefly, it involves a process to resolve conflict, whether between individuals or in social settings, through the justice system, in workplaces, or in other communities. We will explore this concept and other aspects of reintegrative and transformative models in Chapter 11.

Since the late 1980s, the variety of reintegrative approaches has burgeoned. Some of the more common programs include community service orders, fines, fine option programs, probation, and electronic surveillance. All the programs are designed to enable the offender to remain in the community and demonstrate their desire to be a part of the community. Correctional personnel act as brokers for services. Relying on established criteria, correctional personnel must apply the doctrines of *proportionality* (i.e., the perceived level of risk the offender poses to themselves and/or the community) and *parsimony* (i.e., how much freedom can the offender be afforded).

4. *Treatment Model*: Essential to the treatment model is the option of using indeterminate sentences, i.e., allowing the system to detain an offender until they are deemed "reformed" or rehabilitated. Based on the medical model, intervention is deemed to be in the best interest of the offender. Canadian prisons and correctional initiatives include programs such as anger management and other cognitive behavioural programs, educational or vocational programs, life skills workshops, addiction management courses, family intervention initiatives, and multimodal programs. Today, the treatment model is generally seen to be analogous to the medical model. However, it is included here to reflect its historical legacy and subsequent refinement of the treatment ideologies.[11]

Researchers do not agree on the effectiveness of the treatment modality. Yet, as Gottfredson (1979) and Lab and Whitehead (1990) observe, the skeptics tend to apply overly rigorous methodological standards that make even positive results appear questionable. For example, based on his extensive review of the literature, American criminologist, Ted Palmer (1992, p. 76), concludes that "in the past three decades with studies whose designs and analysis were at least adequate leaves little doubt that many programs work, and not just with one or two types of offenders and programs." However, he indicates that, usually, it is not a single type of program but a multiple-intervention strategy that works best. This observation is congruent with some of the emerging integrated and interdisciplinary theories of crime (Barak, 1998; Winterdyk, 2016).[12]

Aside from methodological issues, the notion of rehabilitation implies a return to a former condition or competence, which raises the question: how do you return someone to a former state when they have never experienced it?

Prevention:

The final correctional ideology that we will discuss is prevention. Since there are only a few exceptions that enable the correctional system to detain someone for the remainder of their life due to: a real risk of overcrowding, incarceration being an expensive option, and the physical (and moral) impracticality of incarcerating all offenders, then prevention offers another option. Furthermore, without an offender there is no crime; therefore, the criminal justice enterprise attempts to prevent crimes from occurring and utilize strategies to prevent convicted offenders from re-offending. Given the rather variable success rate (e.g., property offenders vs. corporate offenders) of the present correctional programs, the public and the justice system are calling for crime prevention (i.e., primary, secondary, and tertiary) initiatives as possible solutions (see Winterdyk, 2018b).

Theoretically, prevention methods are designed to divert potential offenders away from criminal or delinquent activity. Prevention initiatives operate on the premise of identifying the cues that can either trigger criminal behaviour (e.g., environmental, social, and economic) or the signs of criminal propensity (e.g., victim of abuse and neglect, and family and personal difficulties). Unfortunately, the literature is replete with examples illustrating the difficulty and complexity of the prediction process. Crime prevention programs target factors (i.e., risk factors) either in the individual's life (e.g., self-defence, safe walk, educational based programs) or they target environmental and social factors designed to reduce criminal opportunity (e.g., alarm system, door locks, street lighting, and window bars).

As a partial response to the questionable effectiveness of treatment and punishment initiatives, in recent years there is a shift back to prevention initiatives in provinces like Alberta, British Columbia, and Ontario. In earlier times, people and communities took proactive steps to protect their person and environment. Beccaria (1963, p. 93) observes: "it is better to prevent crimes than to punish them" and, among other points, he suggests "by perfecting education" (p. 98) and involvement in constructive change. Today, prevention initiatives reflect the broad spectrum of ideas put forth by Beccaria and others of his time. Prevention strategies are divided into three major categories. They include:

- *Primary prevention* involves initiatives aimed at factors within the physical or social environment that are believed to contribute to criminal behaviour. Physical changes can range from using security alarms, while social changes might involve taking steps to reduce poverty, reducing population density, and reducing social inequality between the genders. For example, in the late 1990s, Ontario corrections identified programs that could provide social services to children and their families in a community context. The programs were designed to prevent young people, living in socially-economically disadvantaged communities, from developing emotional and behavioural problems that are recognizable risk factors.
- *Secondary prevention* initiatives are premised on the assertion that the seeds of criminal and delinquent activity begin early in life. Hence, secondary prevention strategies focus on developmental factors such as providing early intervention programs for high-risk families and individuals, providing opportunity for those who are economically and socially deprived, and expanding resources for groups such as abused children and women. For example, within the

correctional facilities' secondary prevention programs for inmates already identified at-risk of committing suicide (i.e., recognised through expressed intent or individual actions), most detention facilities have designated "observation aides" to assist staff in monitoring at-risk inmates (for some recent examples, see: https://www.publicsafety.gc.ca/cnt/cntrng-crm/crm-prvntn/nvntr/index-en.aspx).

- *Tertiary prevention* approaches to crime prevention tend to be criminal justice initiatives. Since research has shown the limited effectiveness of imposing criminal sanctions (e.g., imprisonment), advocates of this orientation focus on projects such as community-based corrections, making prisons more community friendly, repealing those crimes that have no deterrent effect (e.g., certain drug offence laws and the death penalty). Other examples of tertiary prevention in corrections include programs and initiatives that focus on treatment, rehabilitation, prosecution, and isolation of the inmate from the inmate population.[13]

In this section, we have examined the three major ideologies that corrections situationally employs in handling certain offenders. The corrective orientation is influenced by a variety of factors ranging from traditional beliefs and folkways to political and economic factors. Hence, contemporary influences play a significant role in directing corrections and the contextualization of social order. As McCormick and Visano (1992) note, the study of corrections is not "independent of social life but emerges out of complex interactive processes." However, as we will see in various chapters throughout this book, the media continues to offer dramatized, unrepresentative vignettes that confound the direction of corrections.

Finally, it is worth noting the origin of punishment and pain, and how they are woven into the fabric of corrections. The word punish comes from the Latin word *punire* – "to see to it that the duty of *poena* is fulfilled." *Poena* is Latin and means "the compensation value to be paid in order to resolve a criminal conflict" (Cayley, 1998, p. 124). These concepts are imbedded into correctional rationales. For example, rather than ask "what needs to be done?" – corrections operates (under the direction of the courts) from a stance where it asks, "how much punishment does this person deserve?" Whether it is punishment, treatment, or prevention, they all share an element of compensation, either to the state and (usually indirectly) to the victim. Until recently, this was reflected in the practice where the state is compensated, while the rights and pains of the victim were largely overshadowed. Although by the late 1990s, this orientation appeared to have sifted somewhat, and we will see in other chapters in this textbook that this orientation is also fraught with various issues.

Our response to crime resembles that of a pendulum whose weight is not perfectly balanced. While correctional practices swing back and forth between retribution to treatment to management, criminological and penological theories introduce variations of the otherwise rhythmic swing. Hence the "proper" corrective response is not a question of crime control or what works, but to what extent is the correctional response based on cultural values. As a number of academicians and scholars observe, "justice must be seen to be done." But as philosopher and critical criminologist, Jeffery Reiman (2012) remarks in his classic work, *The Rich Get Richer and the Poor Get Prison,* if we wanted to design a criminal justice system (i.e., correctional system) that would fail, it would look very similar to the one we have. As the esteemed psychologist, Karl Menninger, notes in his treatise, *The Crime of Punishment* (1968), society gets the crime and criminals it deserves! However, on the up side of such gloomy observations, there may be a silver lining in the cloud. Menniger suggests that it is our increased level of awareness about the plight of the criminal justice system that will enable us to devise more effective crime prevention and crime control remedies. However, according to Nils Christie (2009), any effort of prevention should focus on public health rather than turning to the criminal justice/corrections approach.

ADULT CORRECTIONS WITHIN THE CRIMINAL JUSTICE SYSTEM

As noted earlier in this chapter, corrections is an integral element of the criminal justice system. The major elements consist of law enforcement, prosecution, courts, and corrections (see Figure 1.1). In addition, there is the hidden element known as the public. While it is beyond the scope of this book to discuss the nuances of the meaning of "system," it warrants a brief comment at this point (see Cox & Wade (1985) for a more detailed discussion). For our purpose, we will assume that based upon its operational (i.e., legislative and jurisdictional), interdependent, and interrelated links to the CJS, corrections fulfills the basic mandate of processing those persons "who have been screened through one or more of the system's other components" (Ekstedt & Griffiths, 1984, p. 9).

As part of its link to the criminal justice system, corrections is responsible for the accused and convicted. Therefore, in this final section, we will take a brief look at the characteristics of the correctional population and how fiscal resources are deployed to deal with this segment of society.

The Demographics of the Adult Correctional Population

As noted earlier, corrections in Canada is diverse in its scope and involves four major offender population categories. Throughout most of the 1990s, approximately two-thirds of all adult provincial court cases resulted in a conviction. As the *Juristat* report (1999) indicates: "on any given day in 1997-98 an average of 157,766 adult offenders were in prison or under community supervision" (p. 4). Between 1996-97, there was a dramatic shift from probation (approximately 65%) to remand custody in 1997-98 (33%), followed by provincial/territorial or federal facilities (31%), then probation (21%),

Figure 1.1 – Overview of the Canadian Criminal Justice Process

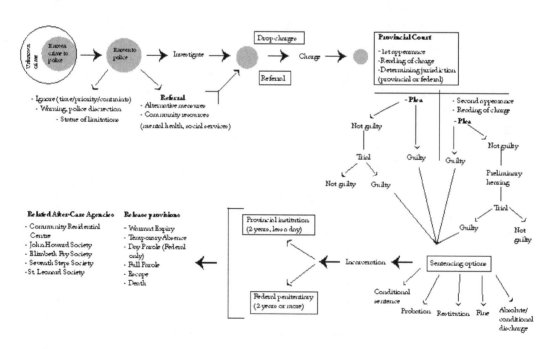

We want to acknowledge the input of Mr. Roland LaHaye in preparing this Figure.

conditional sentences (approximately 5%), conditional releases[19] (approximately 4%), and finally remand custody (approximately 4%).

Based on 2016-17 data, the trend has changed a bit as there were only 117,645 adult offenders supervised in either a custody or community program on any given day – despite a sizeable increase in the Canadian population. This translates to a rate of 4232 offenders per 100,000 adult population - a decline of 3% from 2015/16, and a 17% decline from 2012/13 (Malakeih, 2018). The decline parallels the decline in police-reported crime data. Regionally, Prince Edward Island had the largest decrease at -11%, followed by Alberta at -8% (ibid.). Meanwhile, Manitoba had the highest incarceration rate of 240 per 100,000 for 2016/17 – compared to the national average which was 136 per 100,000 adult population. Another notable change from the late 1990s has been the gap between remanded and provincial/territorial sentenced populations. Malakeih (2018, p.2) reports that for 2016/17 "remand made up the largest proportion of total initial entries." Again, there are regional variations. However, consistent with the trends in the late 1990s, males and younger adults are overrepresented in custody admission, and this also remains true for offenders who are Indigenous (see Chapter 7).[14]

Finally, for 2016-17, admissions to remand continued to account for the largest proportion of all admissions (41%), followed by probation (27%), and provincial and territorial sentenced custody (20%). Approximately 3.7% of admissions went to federal custody (Reitano, 2017; Malakieh, 2018).

Even though public opinion reflects the general notion that the correctional system is "soft" on offenders (see Roberts, 2005), the distribution of offenders has remained consistent since the early 1980s and well into the new millennium (Reitano, 2017). For example, in 1997-98, there were 9,200 offenders incarcerated in federal institutions; while in 2008-09 there were slightly fewer offenders incarcerated totaling 8,323 (Calverley, 2010). However, in 2016-17, there was a marked increase of offenders being held in federal custody on any given day. According to Malakieh (2018) there were 14,425 offenders were in federal custody on any given day. However, given the increase in the overall population, the actual rate of incarceration hasn't changed as dramatically.

In the mid-1970s, Griffiths, Klein, and Verdun-Jones (1980) reported that the federal incarceration rate of adult female offenders to adult male offenders in the mid-1970s was 1:20 (approximately 5%). In 2015-16, women accounted for only 8% of admissions to federal custody, up slightly. Provincially women in custody are higher in proportion. About 17% of admissions to provincial and territorial sentenced custody are female, and 14% of admissions to remand (Reitano, 2017). However, as with all types of dispositions, there is considerable variation between the provinces. For example, in 2016-17 Manitoba was reported in having the highest incarceration rate while Nova Scotia recorded the lowest (Malakieh, 2018) (see Chapter 3 for further discussion).

In addition to the shifting distribution of dispositions (i.e., more remands and fewer custody dispositions) over the past two decades, there was a shift in the demographic distribution of offenders and their presenting issues (e.g., mental health and graying inmate population) (see Figure 1.2).[15] These are issues that present new challenges to adult corrections and these will be addressed in other chapters in this book.

The Cost of Corrections

Increasingly we hear about the rising cost of administering the criminal justice. In 1977-78, adult correctional services accounted for 21.1% of the total justice services budget. This converts to $551 million or $23.62 per capita (Griffiths et al., 1980, p. 4). The total criminal justice budget for 1977-78 was around $2.5 billion. Griffiths et al. (1980) predicted that the budget will soar to "between $5 and $7.5 billion annually by 1986" (p. 3). By 2015/16, the federal correctional budget reached $2.4 billion and included over 18,000 employees who worked in at least one of their 43 facilities, across the

Figure 1.2 – Adult Admissions to Federal and Provincial/Territorial Custody, by Age Group, 2016-17

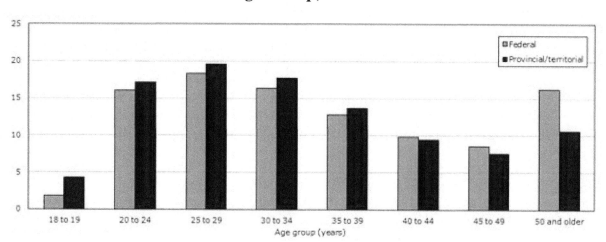

Source: Maleikieh (2018, Chart 2).

country (CSC Statistics, 2017). Overall, the operating expenditures only increased 1% from 2015/16. For the same budget period, "it cost an average of approximately $116,000 and $31,000 to maintain an offender in a CSC institution and in the community, respectively" (ibid). In terms of long-terms spending, the proposed budget is expected to increase only about $291 million between 2016-17 actuals and 2017-18 forecasted spending is $291 million and increase from $2.3 billion in 2017/18 to $2.4 billion by 2020/21 (2018-2019 Departmental Plan, 2018). As reflected in Table 1.3 the estimated spending will remain stable across the primary options of CSC.

This results in an average cost per inmate of $288 in federal institutions and $213 in provincial institutions, with the per capita inmate cost varying from province to province. For example, in Prince Edward Island the cost was $297 (highest) while it was only $144 per person in Alberta (lowest – excluding the territories) (Malakieh, 2018). Some 81% of the provincial expenditures were accounted for by custodial services even though the custodial population only accounted for 22% of the correctional services population. While perhaps this it to be expected, it raises issues about the use of alternatives to custodial sentences.

Even though it was thought that the decisions to support a "tough on crime" (i.e., *Truth in Sentencing Act* and Bill C-10 - the "Omnibus Bill") agenda by the former Conservative government would result in dramatic increases in the correctional budget, CSC data does not support this. Arguably, the anticipated increase has been waylaid by the new Liberal government and various other initiatives (see, e.g., Power, 2017) that will be discussed in other chapters in this book.

Throughout the remainder of this book we will offer a comprehensive introduction to corrections in Canada. Students will learn that despite often being maligned, corrections represents a dynamic and complex element of the criminal justice system. And although we began this chapter by commenting on the public's general level of dissatisfaction with corrections (i.e., the "lenient treatment" of convicted criminals), it must be remembered that the mandate of corrections is dictated by the overriding orientation of the criminal justice system. The type of disposition a convicted offender receives is administered by the courts. And in Canada, judges are independent agents of the CJS and are not polit-

Figure 1.2 – Adult Admissions to Federal and Provincial/Territorial Custody, by Age Group, 2016-17

Core Responsibilities and Internal Services	2015-16 Expenditures	2016-17 Expenditures	2017-18 Forecast spending	2018-19 Main Estimates	2018-19 Planned spending	2019-20 Planned spending	2020-21 Planned spending
Custody	1,519,751,744	1,510,190,155	1,648,924,804	1,539,111,387	1,539,111,387	1,537,126,925	1,536,755,801
Correctional Interventions	398,165,375	398,249,136	454,567,369	440,605,483	440,605,483	440,037,388	439,931,144
Community Supervision	141,891,344	154,796,731	163,569,477	162,635,455	162,635,455	162,425,761	162,386,544
Subtotal	2,059,808,463	2,063,236,022	2,267,061,650	2,142,352,324	2,142,352,324	2,139,590,074	2,139,073,489
Internal Services	297,976,182	299,568,379	386,710,595	301,693,278	301,693,278	301,304,288	301,231,541
Total	2,357,784,645	2,362,804,401	2,653,772,245	2,444,045,603	2,444,045,603	2,440,894,362	2,440,305,030

Source: Maleikieh (2018, Chart 2).

ically or publicly accountable. Hence, we might want to ask to what extent are correctional practices true reflections of public and/or political will? Furthermore, as mentioned earlier (and will be discussed in greater detail throughout this book), the breadth of corrections is much greater than the public realizes. In fact, much of corrections is hidden from public view. For example, in 2015, the Human Rights Committee of the United Nations "called upon Canada to reduce prison crowding, limit solitary confinement, and improve access to treatment for mental ill prisoners" (Latimer, 2015). The success of corrections only attracts public attention when problems arise (e.g., refer to the media headlines at the beginning of this chapter). Furthermore, as we will see, many of today's problems have a long history that is rooted in-part by public fear, their misconceptions, and the societal conditions when they occurred. Still, corrections has and continues to evolve, hence making it an interesting and exciting topic for study and research.

As human behaviour is inextricably linked to societal issues and trends, how we respond to wrong-doers can only be understood in a historical context. Therefore, in the next chapter, we will trace the historical roots of corrections in Canada to better appreciate how historical antecedents have forged contemporary correctional practices.

SUMMARY

We began this chapter by observing that crime is an integral part of our social fabric and that (adult) corrections plays a pivotal role in our formal response to it. Our notions and practices of how to "correct" transgressors of the law are dominated by a pejorative approach – that is, revenge and just deserts. In fact, the term penology was used, until recently, to represent the nature and study of how to address offenders. Yet, research has repeatedly shows that such measures, however contrived, seldom produce the desired results of abating and deterring offenders.

Next, we briefly examined the dynamic and evolving nature of corrections. We explored the role of politics and how various social forces impact corrections. Then we looked at the influence of the legal system on corrections. From here we provided an overview of the complexity of corrections while also reiterating how corrections continues to evolve in its practice and ideology.

In the final section we presented a summary of some of the practical issues facing corrections such as correctional populations, budgetary matters, and the process behind corrections.

Throughout the remainder of this book, we present greater descriptive and critical insight into the major elements that make-up corrections. The chapters are prepared by many leading academicians in their respective field. In so doing, we provide a rich and insightful understanding of the intricate aspects that make-up adult corrections in Canada.

Finally, each chapter includes a set of discussion questions designed to help the reader distill the essence of each chapter. Furthermore, since many students have a working knowledge of the internet and information is constantly changing, each chapter includes several web links that are intended to provide the reader with additional information on the general topics covered. Therefore, you are encouraged to review the questions and explore the links provided.

KEY TERMS AND CONCEPTS

Bridewell	Classical School	Comparative Analysis
Crime Prevention	Criminal Law	Deterrence
Frank P. Miller	Incapacitation	Just Deserts
Penology	Punishment	Sanctions
Treatment		

STUDY AND DISCUSSION QUESTIONS

1. The concept of corrections has a long history. How has it evolved throughout the ages? Do you agree with the current orientation of adult corrections?
2. The costs of delivering corrections (and criminal justice in general) have increased dramatically since the late 1970s. Which correctional philosophy might best serve to help reduce such costs?
3. Scholars like Nils Christie argue that intervention and prevention of offending should focus less on correctional practices and more on public health prevention/intervention approaches. What you do you think of this position? Support your decision.
4. Towards the end of the millennium, there has been a noticeable shift to community-based programs such as conditional release. What possible pitfalls might such a move represent for adult corrections?
5. Throughout this chapter, corrections is described as a dynamic and evolving component of the criminal justice system. How might we begin to better determine the direction programs and services should take? What role/influence might politics, public opinion, and jurisdictional boundaries play in forging such initiatives?

6. The recent proposed Omnibus Bill (C-10 - 2011) includes possible provisions for new and increased mandatory minimum sentences, the selective elimination of conditional sentences, and longer waiting times before individuals can apply for pardons. What possible implications will this have for adult corrections?

HELPFUL WEBLINKS

www.sgc-scc.gc.ca is the homepage for Corrections Service of Canada. Dsp-psd.pwgsc.gc.ca/dsp-psd/pilot/statcan/85-002-XIE/85-002-XIE.html is the homepage for *Juristat* reports released by Statistics Canada.

NOTES

[1] This chapter is based on the framework of an earlier rendition, see Winterdyk (2001).

[2] This notion of "right" and "wrong" is based on the consensus model of justice. The consensus view of justice is based on the premise that most citizens in a society share common values and norms and work toward a common good.

[3] A sanction is generally defined as a "consequence or punishment for violation of accepted norms of social conduct" (Gifis, 1975, p.186). Sanctions can be used to redress either civil injuries or criminal offences.

[4] The first mandate of Correctional Service Canada is *rehabilitation*.

[5] In 2017, the website for Amnesty International noted that in 2017 over 1032 people were executed around the world. The numbers have fluctuated from 1253 executions in 2008 to a low of 682 in 2012. Yet, the site notes that on average 1 execution takes place every 9 hours (but, this does not include China were executions are believed to be in the thousands) (see https://www.amnesty.org/en/latest/news/2018/04/death-penalty-sentences-and-executions-2017/).

[6] The same can be said of ECTs or electroshock therapy. First introduced in the late 1930s by an Italian neuropsychiatrist, the treatment became widely used in the 1950s for various forms of depression, mania and catatonia. Although claimed to be a treatment, its side effects have also arguably been described as cruel and unusual punishment.

[7] It is somewhat ironic perhaps to note that Rousseau's personal life was less than exemplary. He was abandoned at age ten and wandered the country-side of France for most of his life. He sired five children with a servant girl whom he later left to an orphanage setting (Cranston, 1968).

[8] Graeme Newman and Pietro Marongiu (1990) questioned whether Beccaria wrote this work. Drawing on his academic and professional track record, they suggest that some of his colleagues may have helped pen his treatise. Regardless, the work stands as the cornerstone to the classical school of criminological thought.

[9] See Winterdyk (2016) for an overview of issues pertaining to young offenders in Canada.

[10] You might be interested in visiting the webpage of the Australian transformative justice organization – one of the first to be established.

[11] Note these are elements shared by those who advocate the reintegrative, restorative, and transformative approaches.

[12] Cox and Wade (1985, p. 5) suggest that the best way to view the criminal justice system is as a "network of interrelated, but independent individuals who are subject to many internal and external pressures…"

13 You can view the list and range of current crime prevention initiatives across the country at: https://www.publicsafety.gc.ca/cnt/cntrng-crm/crm-prvntn/index-en.aspx

14 For example, in 2017, while Indigenous represent 2.7% of the Canadian population they represent almost 17% of admissions into correctional facilities.

15 Canada's population is aging. Between 1951 and 2015 children (ages 0-14) outnumbered seniors (65+). However, as of 2016, the trend has reversed, and the gap is expected to continue to grow significant over the next several decades (Grenier 2017).

REFERENCES

Amnesty International. (2011). *Death sentences and executions 2010*. London: Peter Benson House. Retrieved from http://www.amnesty.org.au

Barak, G. (1989). *Integrating criminologies.* Needham Heights, MA: Allyn & Bacon.

Beaumont, H. (2016, August 10). Young women keep killing themselves in Canada's Jails: Now the families of two women who died are suing the government. *Vice.* Retrieved from https://www.vice.com/en_ca/article/nnk58m/young-women-keep-killing-themselves-in-canadas-jails

Braithwaite, J. (1989). *Crime, shame and reintegration.* Cambridge, U.K.: Cambridge University Press.

Brennan, S., & Dauvergne, M. (2011). Police reported crime Stats in Canada, 2010. *Juristat, 85* (2).

The Canadian Coalition Against the Death Penalty. (2010, 23 December). *The only Canadian on death row in the U.S.: Ronald Smith – death row Montana.* Retrieved from http://www.ccadp.org

Carrigan, D.O. (1991). *Crime and punishment in Canada: A history.* Toronto: McClelland and Stewart.

Calverley, D. (2010). Adult correctional services in Canada, 2008/2009. Retrieved from http://www.statcan.gc.ca

Cayley, D. (1998). *The expanding prison.* Toronto: House of Anansi Press.

Canadian Centre for Justice Statistics. (1994). Police personnel and expenditure in Canada. *Juristat, 16*(1).

Canadian Centre for Justice Statistics. (1997). Justice spending in Canada. *Juristat,* 17(3).

Canadian Centre for Justice Statistics. (1995). Adult correctional services in Canada, 1994-95. *Juristat,* 17(4).

Canadian Centre for Justice Statistics. (1997). The justice data factfinder, 1997. *Juristat,* 17(13).

Canadian Centre for Justice Statistics. (1997). Adult correctional services in Canada, 1996-97. *Juristat,* 18(3).

Canadian Centre for Justice Statistics. (1999). Adult Correctional Services in Canada, 1997-98. *Juristat,* 19(4).

Canadian Statistics Centre. 2018-2019 Departmental Plan. Ottawa: CSC. Retrieved from http://www.csc-scc.gc.ca/publications/005007-2606-en.shtml#dp11

Christie, N. (1996). *Crime control as industry* (2nd Ed.). London, UK: Routledge.

Christie, N. (2006). Empty the prisons. *Wired Magazine.* Retrieved from http://www.wired.com

Cox, S.M., & Wade, J.E. (1985). *The criminal justice network: An introduction.* Dubuque, Iowa: W.C. Brown.

Cranston, M. (1968). *Jean Jacques Rousseau: The social contract.* (Translated). NY: Penguin.

CSC Statistics – key facts and figures. (2017). CCS, Ottawa. Retrieved from: http://www.csc-scc.gc.ca/publications/005007-3024-eng.shtml

Donnelly, A. (Jan 11, 2017). More than half of Canadian adults in jail awaiting trials rather than serving sentences in 2014 and 2015: StatsCan. *National Post.* Retrieved from http://nationalpost.com/news/canada

Dormer, D. (2011, October 9). Son says dad should stay in jail 'forever'. *The Toronto Sun.* Retrieved from http://www.torontosun.com

Ekstedt, J., & Griffiths, K.T. (1984). *Corrections in Canada: Policy and practice.* Toronto: Butterworths.

Fairchild, E. (1993). *Comparative criminal justice systems.* Belmont, CA: Wadsworth.

Foucault, M. (1977). *Discipline and punish: The birth of the prison.* London, U.K.: Penguin.

Gifis, S.H. (1975). *Law dictionary.* Woodbury, NY: Barron's Educational Series.

Gould, S.J. (1996) *The mismeasure of man.* NY: W. W. Norton.

Gottfredson, M.R. (1979). Treatment destruction techniques. *Journal of Research in Crime and Delinquency,* 16: 39-54.

Grenier, E. (May 03, 2017). Canadian seniors now outnumber children for first time, 2016 census shows. CBC. Retrieved from https://www.cbc.ca/news/politics/2016-census-age-gender-1.4095360.

Griffiths, C.T., & Cunningham, A. (2000). *Canadian corrections.* Scarborough, ON: Nelson.

Griffiths, C.T., Klein, J.F., & Verdun-Jones, S.N. (1980). *Criminal justice in Canada: An introductory text.* Toronto: Butterworths.

Hagan, J. (1984). *Disreputable pleasures: Crime and deviance in Canada* (2nd Ed.). Toronto: McGraw-Hill.

Heidt, J., & Wheeldon, J.P. (2015). *Introducing criminological thinking: Maps, theories, and understanding.* Thousand Oaks, CA: Sage.

History. (2011). Retrieved from http://www.csc-scc.gc.ca

Koerth-Baker, M. (2016). *Crime despite punishment. Undark – Truth, beauty, science.* Retrieved from https://undark.org/article/deterrence-punishments-dont-reduce-crime/

Lab, S.P. & Whitehead, J.T. (1990). From "Nothing works" to "The appropriate works": The latest stop on the search for the secular grail. *Criminology,* 28: 405-418.

Latimer, C. (Oct. 4, 2015). How we created a Canadian prison crisis. *The Star.* Retrieved from https://www.thestar.com

Macdonald, N. (2016, February 18). Canada's prisons are the 'new residential schools': A months-long investigation reveals that at every step, Canada's justice system is set against Indigenous people. *Maclean's.* Retrieved from https://www.macleans.ca/news/canada

Malakieh, J. (2018, June 19). Adult and youth correctional statistics in Canada, 2016/2017. *Statistics Canada.* Retrieved from https://www150.statcan.gc.ca/n1/pub/85-002-x/2018001/article/54972-eng.htm

Mandate and principles of adult corrections in Canada. (1998). Retrieved from http://home.istar.ca

Mandel, M. (1992). The great repression: Criminal punishment in the nineteen-eighties. In K.R.E. McCormick & L.A. Visano (Eds.), *Canadian penology.* Toronto: Canadian Scholars Press.

Martinson, R. (1974). What works? – Questions and answers about prison reform. *The Public Interest, 35,* 22-54.

McCormick, K.R.E., & Visano, L.A. (Eds.). (1992). *Canadian penology: Advanced perspectives and research.* Toronto: Canadian Scholars Press.

McKie, D. (2011, January 14). Inmate programs fall short of capital spending. *CBC News.*

Menninger, K. (1968). *The crime of punishment.* NY: The Viking Press.

Morrison, W. (2005). What is crime? Contrasting definitions and perspectives. In C. Hale, K. Hayward, & A. Wahidin. *Criminology* (pp. 3-22). Oxford: Oxford University Press.

Newman, G., & Marongiu, P. (1990). Pennological reform and the myth of Beccaria. *Criminology, 28,* 325-346.

Palmer, T. (1992). *The re-emergence of correctional intervention.* Newbury Park, CA: Sage.

Paperny, A.M. (2017, August 03). Canada's jailhouse secret: Legally innocent prisoners are dying. *Reuters.* Retrieved from https://www.reuters.com/article/us-canada-jails-deaths-insight/canadas -jailhouse-secret-legally-innocent-prisoners-are-dying-idUSKBN1AJ19V

Police reported crime statistics. (2010). *Juristat.* Retrieved from http://www.statcan.gc.ca

Power, P. (April 14, 2017). Federal prisons have become less deadly, crowded under Liberals, numbers show. *Globe and Mail.* Retrieved from https://www.theglobeandmail.com

R. *v.* B.W.P.; R. *v.* B.V.N., [2006] 1 S.C.R. 941, 2006 SCC 27. Supreme Court of Canada. (2006, June 22). Retrieved from http://csc.lexum.org

Reichel, P. (2007). *Comparative criminal justice systems: A topical approach* (5th ed.). Englewood Cliffs, NJ: Pearson Prentice Hall.

Reichel, P. (2014). Comparative criminal justice systems: A topical approach (7th ed.). Englewood Cliffs, NJ: Pearson Prentice Hall.

Reiman, J. (2010). *The rich get richer and the poor get prison* (10th ed.). NY, NY: Allyn and Bacon.

Reitano, J. (2017). Adult correctional statistics in Canada 2015/16. *Statistics Canada.* Retrieved from https://www150.statcan.gc.ca/n1/pub/85-002-x/2017001/article/14700-eng.htm

Roberts, J.V. (1999). Mandatory sentencing rides again. *Juristat Report, 14*(1), 1-3.

Roberts, J.V. (2005). Public opinion and corrections: Recent findings in Canada. *Correctional Service of Canada Report.* Ottawa: Evaluation and Review Branch, Performance Assurance Sector.

Smandych, R. (2019). From 'misguided children' to 'criminal youth': Exploring historical and contemporary trends in Canadian youth justice. In J. Winterdyk, K. Gorkoff, & D. Antonowicz (eds.), *Youth at risk and youth justice* (3rd ed.). Don Mills, ON: OUP.

Solicitor General and Public Security, Government of Alberta. (2009). *Annual Report, 2008-2009.* Edmonton: Government of Alberta.

Statistics Canada. (2005). Adult correctional services in Canada, 2003/04. *Juristat Report*, 85-211-XIE.

Stone, L. (2011, October 12). Barriers on the road to redemption: Eleven years after prison system reform, many problems persist, and new ones have surfaced. *The Vancouver Sun.* Retrieved from http://www2.canada.com

The Vancouver Sun. Retrieved from http://www2.canada.com

The Daily. (2009, December 08). Adult and youth correctional services: Key indicators. Retrieved from http://www.statcan.gc.ca

Tonry, M. (Ed.). (2011). *Why punish? How much?: A reader on punishment.* London: Oxford University Press.

Tory crime bill cracks down on drug, sex offences. (2011, Sept. 20). Retrieved from http://www.cbc.ca

Trevethan, S., & Rastin, C.J. (2004). A profile of visible minority offenders in the federal Canadian correctional system. Retrieved from http://www.csc-scc.gc.ca

Vandoremalen, J. (2000). A pioneer in Canadian corrections. *Let's Talk, 25*(2), 13.

Walker, N. (1991). *Why punish?* Oxford, UK: Oxford Press.

Wakefield, J. (2017, October 31). No rehabilitation in Alberta federal prisons, correctional investigator says. *Edmonton Journal.* Retrieved from https://edmontonjournal.com

Walmsley, R. (1999). *World Prison Population List.* London: King's College London, School of Law, International Centre for Prison Studies. Retrieved from http://www.prisonstudies.org

Walmsley, R. (2005). *World prison population list* (6th Ed.). London: King's College London, School of Law, International Centre for Prison Studies. Retrieved from http://www.prisonstudies.org

World Prison Brief (2018, June). *Highest to lowest world prison brief data.* London: Birkbeak University of London, Institute For Criminal Policy Research. Retrieved from http://www. prisonstudies.org

White, P. (2017, June 25). Suicide attempts spike amid Ontario prison system overhaul. *The Globe Mail*. Retrieved from https://www.theglobeandmail.comfacilities-record-rise-in-inmate-suicide-attempts/article35460149/

Winterdyk, J. (1998y). It's time, it's time… is it time for restorative justice? *Law Now,* April/May, 20-22.

Winterdyk, J. (2000). *Young offenders in Canada: Issues and perspectives* (2nd ed.). Toronto: Harcourt Brace.

Winterdyk, J. (2001). Corrections and the criminal justice system. *Corrections in Canada: Social reactions to crime.* Toronto: Pearson.

Winterdyk, J. (Ed.). (2004). *Adult corrections: International systems and perspectives.* Monsey, NY: Criminal Justice Press.

Winterdyk, J. (2016). *Canadian criminology* (3rd ed.). Don Mills, ON: Oxford University Press.

Winterdyk, J. (2018a). *Pioneers in Canadian criminology*. Oakville, ON: Rock Mill's Press.

Winterdyk, J. (ed.). (2018b). *Crime prevention: International perspectives, issues, and trends*. Boca Raton: FL: CRC Press.

Youth Criminal Justice Act: Changing the Law on Young Criminals. (2006, June 23). *CBC News Online*. Retrieved from http://www.cbc.ca

Youth Justice. (2017). Ottawa: Department of Justice. Retrieved from http://www.justice.gc.ca/eng/csj-sjc/just/11.html

An Historical Overview of Adult Corrections in Canada

2

John Winterdyk[1]

Learning Objectives

After reading this chapter, you should be able to:

- Recognize and describe some of the early correctional history that led to the Kingston era in Canada.

- Understand how and why penitentiaries came into existence.

- Describe some of the key concerns with using prisons for rehabilitation and punishment.

- Recognize and describe some of the key correction inquiries and prison commissions – and how they contributed to the change in correctional philosophy in Canada.

- Examine the emergence of a new "kind" of corrections – Community Corrections.

- Understand that Canadian corrections is taking a drastic "turn" in direction as a result of the Arbour Commission in 1996 and the Transformation Agenda in 2006.

INTRODUCTION

In this chapter we review the development of adult corrections in Canada from a chronological perspective. An attempt is made to highlight events, personalities, legislation, and reports that had a profound effect on present day Canadian correctional philosophy. An important emphasis is placed on government initiated Royal Commissions and other formal inquiries (such as the 1953 Fauteux Report and the 1996 Arbour Report) to illustrate the significance of their role in the changing face of corrections in Canada. Indeed, corrections in Canada is a dynamic process, ever changing in nature, and continues to "correct" itself by adapting to its environment even as this is being written (Griffiths & Murdoch, 2013).

The origin of Canadian corrections (formally referred to as penology) dates to ancient times when values and norms, and the value of life, were very much different from today (see Ruddell, 2017). As noted in Chapter 1, corrections or justice, during antiquity was severe and harsh with an emphasis on punishment. Depending on one's social status, life was considered cheap and authorities believed that punishment was a swift, fair, and a sure deterrent. Our oldest surviving criminal code, the laws of Hammurabi of Babylon (1750 BC), prescribed death sentences for almost everything and nobody questioned the state's right to take a life. The community had the right to defend and protect itself. Moreover, if the means of retaliation was out of proportion to the offence, so be it. At least it would serve as a warning to others.

Hebrews were more restrained than the early Babylonians. There were only 15 capital offences in the early Mosaic Code (see Chapter 1) including murder, bestiality, blasphemy, cursing parents, adultery, and practicing witchcraft. Under subsequent Roman law (circa 700), death sentences were carried out for such offences as treason, adultery, sodomy, murder, forgery by slaves, and corruption – pick-pockets and thieves plied their trades in the very shadows of the noose.

As presented in Chapter 1 (see Corrections as a Political and Social Concept), a variety of intellectual scholars during the Age of Enlightenment (c. 1700s) began to ask: If the death penalty does not deter, what good is it? The basis for this argument was that capital punishment for even minor offences was not just cruel – it also appeared useless. By 1810, only 10% of those condemned to death in England were, in fact, hanged. The rest were either imprisoned (a new form of corrections) or transported to other lands.

The new philosophy of liberty and equality contributed to the impetus for correctional reform, and emphasized the dignity of men and women, and the rights of the individual (see Beccaria in Chapter 1). It inspired a growing sensitivity to the harm of physical torture and cruelty, while capital and corporal punishment began to look barbaric. During the 1700s, the Quakers (formally known as the Religious Society of Friends) and evangelicals revived the idea of spiritual reform through solitude, penitence, and strict discipline (the basic correctional philosophy of the future penitentiary system); they believed that prisons should improve people.

PIONEERS OF PENAL REFORM: JOHN HOWARD, ELIZABETH FRY AND ALEXANDER MACONOCHIE

Arguably, the real watershed in modern corrections occurred in 1777 when **John Howard** (1726-1790) published his historic, *The State of the Prisons in England and Wales* (see Box 2.1). The book was an account of his exhaustive investigations of jails across England and Europe (see Chapter 1 for further details). Howard was one of the first reformers to apply scientific methods to social research. His conclusions jarred the complacency of polite English society and forced the British government to act.

Box 2.1 – John Howard's ideas on prison reform

In order to redress this hardship, I applied to the justices of the country for a salary for the gaoler in lieu of his fees. The bench was properly affected with the grievance, and willing to grant the relief desired: but they wanted a precedent for charging the country with the expense. I therefore rode into several neighbouring counties in search of a precedent; but I soon learned that the same injustice was practiced in them; and looking into the prisons, I beheld scenes of calamity, which I grew daily more and more anxious to alleviate. In order therefore to gain a more perfect knowledge of the particulars and extent of it, by various and accurate observations, I visited most of the *Country Gaols* in England. Seeing in two or three of them some poor creatures whose aspect was singularly deplorable, and asking the cause of it, I was answered, "they were lately brought from the *Bridewells.*" This started a fresh subject of inquiry. I resolved to inspect the Bridewells; and for that purpose I travelled again into the counties where I had been; and, indeed, into all the rest; examining *Houses of Correction, City and Town-Gaols.* I beheld in many of them, as well as in the *County-Gaols,* a complication of distress: but my attention was principally fixed by the *gaol-sever,* and the *small-pox*, which I saw prevailing to the destruction of multitudes, not only of *felons* in their dungeons, but of *debtors* also.

Source: *The State of the Prison in England and Wales.* John Howard, 1777.

Howard proposed a new prison system which he believed would be both fair and humane. He called for "special houses of penance – penitentiaries" (Petersila & Reitz, 2013, p. 393). This "model" prison, Howard conceived, would be quiet, clean, and orderly. The "keepers" would be paid civil servants who were accountable to the government. There would be no corporal (i.e., physical) punishment. The inmates would be isolated in their cells and protected from all corrupting influences.

The British *Penitentiary Act* of 1778 was the direct result of Howard's recommendations. It provided for several major reforms, including safe and sanitary buildings (referred to as "penitentiary houses"), regular prison inspections, abolition of the "fee system" (i.e. illegal payments to the jailers) and a reformatory program inside the prison walls. Unfortunately, many years passed before these ideals were put into practice.

In 1790, the father of prison reform died, ironically, of jail fever contracted while in Russia. Howard lived to see the abolition of most tortures as well as the building of the first penitentiary at Wymondham in Norfolk, England in 1785. However, he never knew that the regime he fought so hard for – the system of solitary confinement – would come to be feared as the cruelest punishment of all.[2]

Elizabeth Fry (1780-1845) was a wealthy Quaker matron who was active in various 19th century English philanthropies. Between 1812-1813, she visited the female prisoners at New Gate Prison in London and was horrified by what she saw: a horde of filthy, ragged, and drunken women stacked on top of each other. (It was "almost like a slave ship," she later told the English House of Commons.) The women's quarters had no heat and babies lay unclothed and "blue with cold"; the women survived by begging and prostituting daily (DoBash et al., 1986).

Fry's visit to New Gate marked the beginning of a lifelong commitment to prison reform. Like her male counterpart, John Howard, she inspected prisons all over Britain, including convict ships before they sailed to foreign lands (transportation of convicts). Fry insisted that the female inmates be kept separate from the men and supervised by other females; she wanted the jails to rehabilitate women convicts through education and job training. In 1822, she helped to open the first half-way house for female ex-convicts in London, England.

Fry's influence was very evident in the *British Prison Act* of 1823, which ordered jailers to separate men and women, and to hire female guards for female prisoners. At the time, society believed that women offenders must be innately corrupt and abnormal and could not be reformed; a criminal woman was believed to be evil and a monster.

Fry was one of the very few people who subscribed to the theory of *social determinism*: she believed that women broke the law because they were in needy and desperate circumstances. To this day, the reform movement for female offenders continues under the Elizabeth Fry Society banner carrying on her legacy of bringing an element of humanity and hope to incarcerated females and their families.

The third British citizen whose penal reform ideas had a profound influence on Canada's correctional system was the work and ideas of **Alexander Maconochie** (1787-1860). Although a geographer by training, he spent time in what is now know as Australia (then referred to as Van Diemen's Land) and was the private secretary to the Lieutenant-Governor. In 1840, while in charge of the penal colony of Norfolk Island, Maconochie explored a range of treatment-oriented ideas with his prisoners. As Carrigan (1991) notes, the "central thrust in (his) program was rehabilitation" which was achieved through "a better system of classification, more humane discipline, the indeterminate sentence, education, recreation programs, and measures to prepare prisoners to return to free society" (p. 345). As the reader might know, virtually every one of these concepts were incorporated into the Canadian penal system (see http://www.caefs.ca/ – the Canadian Assoc. for Elizabeth Fry Societies).

EMERGENCE OF THE PENITENTIARY SYSTEM IN CANADA IN THE 1800s

The prison reformers, following Howard, believed that they could change offender's minds by regulating their bodies. They even dared to hope that the penitentiary would become the model of order and morality for the rest of the community (UNODC, 2018). Now crime was viewed as a kind of moral disease; the carriers must be quarantined.

Although the idea of the penitentiary originated in Europe, it was the Americans who became its earlier enthusiasts. In fact, even in colonial times the Americans resisted the British system of corporal and capital punishment. As early as 1682, the Quaker leader, William Penn (1644-1718), established a penal code for whipping and mutilation. Capital punishment was retained for the crime of murder only.

In 1787, William Bradford, Benjamin Rush, and Caleb Lowes formed the Philadelphia Society for Alleviating the Miseries of the Public Prisons. In 1790, they persuaded the state legislature to create the first true correctional institution in North America, in a wing of the Walnut Street Jail.

In this penitentiary, most inmates were still housed together in large rooms but hardened criminals were placed in solitary confinement. The disciplinary regime of the Walnut Street Jail became known as the Pennsylvania System.

The most drastic experiment with solitary confinement took place in 1821 at the Auburn Penitentiary in New York State. A group of prisoners were locked up in their cells with absolutely no distractions – not even let out to perform manual labour jobs. Many of the subjects (more than half) committed suicide (shades of Alcatraz in the near future) and the project was stopped two years later. The French criminologists, Alexis de Tocqueville and Gustave de Beaumont, condemned this extremism: "it does not reform, it kills" (Anderson, 1960, p. 211).

The regime at Auburn was subsequently modified to permit prisoners to work in silence during the day, returning to solitary confinement only at night. This became known as the Auburn System (or silent associated system).

In Pennsylvania, prison authorities were still committed to the principle of total isolation and giving criminals their **just deserts** (see Chapter 1). The show place of the Pennsylvania System (also known as the Separate System) was the huge Eastern State Penitentiary at Cherry Hill, built in 1829.

At Cherry Hill, all prisoners were kept in solitary confinement 24 hours a day. They were not permitted visitors and worked alone in their cells. Their only human contact was their keeper who checked on them three times a day. "Solitary confinement, first conceived as a humane and redemptive discipline, became the dreaded 'Hole' – immeasurably worse than any torture of the body," wrote Charles Dickens, who later toured Cherry Hill in the 1840s (Baehre, 1977, p. 31).

In 1849, members of Canada's Brown Commission visited this infamous prison and found that: "the prisoners as a group have a shallow, worn-out appearance: the eyes are deeply sunk…and the eyeballs glare with a mad look and feverish brightness" (Baehre, 1977, p. 32). The prison authorities reluctantly admitted that at least 50 of their 300 prisoners were in fact mad. John Howard, himself, had not advocated total separation. He thought prisoners should be allowed to work and exercise together. Unbroken solitude, he warned, might lead to "insensibility or despair."

Despite its drawbacks, the Pennsylvania System was eventually adopted in most parts of Europe, whereas the Auburn System prevailed in the United States and Canada. (During the 19th century in Canada, only the Prison of Isolation at Kingston Penitentiary was based on the Pennsylvania model.)

Regardless of the system used, the 19th century mania for silence and segregation continued. By the late 1880s, overcrowding in the penitentiaries made traditional discipline irrelevant. Silence and segregation could scarcely be enforced when cells had to be shared (see, generally, Ruddell, 2017, p. 268-269). Solitary confinement ceased to be a reformatory method and soon evolved into pure punishment and revenge. The dungeon, or "hole," became the prison-within-a-prison.

The penitentiary, as conceived by Howard, had failed; yet, the system continued to thrive long after its original practices and rationale were abandoned.

Corrections in Early Canada (1830-1867)

"There is one thing which can hardly fail to strike an emigrant from the old country, on his arrival in Canada. It is this – the feelings of complete security which he enjoys…he sees no fear – he need see none. This is a country where the inhabitants are essentially honest – here you may sleep with your door unbarred for years" (Catherine Parr Traill, cited in Carrigan, 1991, p. 15). Canada was hardly this idyllic in 1857. Crimes like robbery, assault, and murder have always existed in Canada and can be traced back to the very earliest days of exploration and settlement. In fact, Canada has had more than its fair share of lawbreaking in New France, the Maritimes, Upper and Lower Canada, and of course, in the "Wild West" (Griffiths & Murdoch, 2013). Out of this developed the need for a corrections system; a system that would ideally both correct and rehabilitate (see the overview of Maconochie above).

This system effectively began with the passing of the *British North America Act* (BNA Act) on July 1, 1867. Canada's legal system is based on England's Common Law System, while our correctional system would be divided forever – Parole and Penitentiaries to Ottawa and the rest to the provinces (see Chapter 1).

Prior to the *BNA Act*, there was little interest in jailing Canadians. In the early 1800s in Canada, jails were not viewed as a common punishment for criminals and there was little interest in reform, and even less interest in rehabilitation programs. The punishments were swift, severe, and progressive with little to no uniformity in sentencing; for example, for a similar offence one offender might be hanged while another was sent to servitude on a galley ship. Punishment was designed to shame and humiliate the offender (Griffiths & Verdun-Jones, 1994).

In 1800, a Canadian could be hanged for stealing a shirt, and robbery was one of several dozen offences that carried the death penalty (see Cayley, 1998 for a detailed account). For less serious offences, the sanctions included branding, banishment, transportation, and whipping. The people of Upper and Lower Canada inherited the British **bloody code**.

Writing as an editor of the *Toronto Globe* in 1846, George Brown[4] (Beattie, 1977, cited in Ekstedt & Griffiths, 1988, p. 37) expressed early Canadian sentiments about whipping and punishment in the jail system (see Box 2.2).

Any early correctional reforms in Canada were minimal, simply along the lines of basic improved medical treatment, better food, and more sanitary accommodations. An early advanced idea was applied in 1830 at the Hamilton jail where inmates were given a limited opportunity to practice their trade. A further progressive idea was suggested where prisoners could work together outside during the day and return to jail at night, a common practice today in minimum security Canadian prisons. Unfortunately, this early idea received no support.

According to Carrigan (1991), Western Canada had no need for jails in the early 1800s as the population was sparse (less than 4 million) and crime was dealt with instantly and on-the-spot. Like Britain, hangings were frequent enough to begin to cause widespread revulsion. By 1833, the number of capital crimes in Canada was reduced to 12 from over 300, including murder, rape, robbery, burglary, and arson. By 1841, only murder and treason were punishable by death.

The first real correctional facility was opened at **Upper Fort Garry** (in what is now Winnipeg, Manitoba) in 1835. It was a simple courthouse with two jail cells, and was one of five local forts built in the area. Prisoners had to provide their own food and other amenities. For those who could not afford this, the province provided a daily ration of one pound of pemmican (at the public's expense) and water.

The first quarter of the 19th century saw a reasonably well-defined correctional philosophy in this country. While there was a strong belief in punishment, both as the wages of sin and as a deterrent,

Box 2.2 – *The Globe*, 4 November 1846, Kingston Penitentiary

Lash! - Lash!! - Lash!!!

It appears from statements which are not contradicted, that from 200 to 300 punishments are inflicted on the prisoners of the Penitentiary every month. Supposing these average to 20 lashes, it follows that 1300 lashes are given in a month, and 50,000 in a year, a far greater amount we are sure than the whole British Army and Navy undergo. A hundred and fifty lashes must be given in this den of brutality every day the sun rises. Who can calculate the amount of pain and agony that must be imposed in this pendemonium [sic]. Who can tell the amount of evil passions, of revenge, and of malice, that must be engendered by such treatment? A penitentiary is a place where the prisoner should reflect on the past, and be placed under such a system of moral training as may fit him for becoming a better member of society. Will the lash do that? Did it ever do anything but harden the person whose body was torn by its infliction?

there was also a growing belief that criminals could be reformed as law-abiding citizens. To achieve this, prisoners began to be placed in separate cells, and classified according to their crimes and past records. This included hard labour, strict discipline, and silence; the major program was religious instruction, given by the prison Chaplain. This system was known as **Moral Reformation**. Thus, the Christian Church influence in both French and English Canada was the predominant penal philosophy. Canada's correctional philosophy was one of spiritual change through penitence, which later became known as the **Reform Model**. Although this was the underlying rationale, unfortunately for early Canadian Reformers, the conditions in most early Canadian jails were not conducive to penance, discipline, or reform.

In these early years, few Canadian communities could afford to build any jails, let alone spend money on lavish jail items like food, staff, repairs – reform was not a high priority. Most jails, like the Fort Garry, were small and isolated, with a single, poorly paid keeper (see History of… n.d.).

In the first part of the 19th century, a large immigrant wave from Europe significantly increased Canada's population, which was the natural formula for a rise in crime, and thus increased jail use as a punishment and deterrent. The existing small jails could no longer accommodate this increase in inmates and an alarmed public began worrying about recidivism rates, inmate behaviour, and terrible jail conditions (Carrigan, 1991). The overcrowding led the newspapers of the day to describe Canadian jails as "schools for crime" – a concept that is still subscribed by many today.

Birth of Kingston Penitentiary

As the crimes punishable by death decreased, an alternative form of punishment was growing by leaps and bounds – hard labour and the tight regime of control in a penitentiary (Miethe & Lu, 2005). Canada's first penitentiary, in Kingston, opened on June 1, 1835 and Henry Smith (1812-1868), a lawyer and political figure, was the first official warden from 1835 till 1849 (Ruddell, 2017).

In the common Canadian jails of the 1830s, one could still find most of the abuses that John Howard condemned in the British prisons of the 1770s. They were filthy, disease-ridden, and chaotic. Until 1836, prisoners in the Toronto jail received around 700 grams of dry bread a day, they had no work and no exercise, and many were kept in chains.

In partial response to the deplorable conditions of Canadian prions, Canadian lawmakers were greatly interested in the American penal experiments. The respective strengths and weaknesses of the Auburn and Pennsylvania Systems were passionately debated in Parliament by both sides. Finally, in 1831, a select committee of the House of Assembly of Upper Canada called for the building of a penitentiary near Kingston (then known as Portsmouth). A board of commissioners settled on the Auburn, or silent associated system, as the most productive penal philosophy; moral re-education had been born in Canada.

The first Canadian *Penitentiary Act* was passed in 1834. It set out the new objectives for the Kingston jail. It provided "the means…not only of deterring others from the commission of like crimes, but also of reforming the individuals and inuring them to habits of industry" (Carrigan, 1991, p. 330). Thus, moral re-education was to replace intimidation.

Brown Commission (1848-1849)

The actual experience during the early years was quite different from what the legislators envisioned. Whereas Kingston was conceived as a humane alternative to the cruelty of the bloody code, the first warden, Henry Smith, soon instituted his own reign of terror, all in the name of reform (History of the…. n.d.).

Shoom (1966) notes that prison violations of rules were met by punishment of a "swift and often brutal nature" (p. 215). It involved flogging with the cat-o'-nine-tails and rawhide, as well as the use of irons, solitary confinement, and rations of bread and water. To illustrate this, Shoom (1966, p. 216) presents the following entries from the *Kingston Punishment Book* for 1843:

Offence	**Punishment**
Laughing and talking	6 lashes; cat-o'- nine-tails
Talking in wash-house	6 lashes; rawhide
Threatening to knock convicts' brains out	24 lashes; cat-o'- nine-tails

Smith was finally removed in 1849 after an investigation by a special government commission headed by the Honourable Adam Ferguson and chaired by its secretary, George Brown, then editor of the Toronto Globe newspaper and soon to be elected Reform member of the legislature in Upper Canada (Brown Commission of 1848, cited in Beattie, 1977).

In its first report (also commonly referred to as the "Brown Report"), issued in 1848, the Commission:

- Condemned the use of corporal punishment;
- Recommended removal of the warden;
- Criticized the way Kingston operated; and
- Did not condemn the structure or the regimen imposed on the inmates.

In its second report in 1849, the Commission recommended:

- The major objective should be reformation;
- The operation of the jail should be more efficiently run;
- Moral suasion should replace physical force;
- Chaplains should be regularly employed; and
- Government penitentiary inspectors should be employed to regularly inspect prisons.

Beattie (1977) argued that: "what was really on trial was the system itself, the silent or congregate system under which Kingston was established... Ultimately, the Commission concluded that the silent system was fine – it was the warden who had failed to get the most out of it" (pp. 28-29). At the time of the second report, three children under the age of 12, including one 8-year-old, and 12 youths under the age of 16 were serving time in the Kingston penitentiary.

The Commission comprised of Brown and his five commissioners toured the United States and concluded that the Auburn System should be retained and modified to provide for the best parts of the Pennsylvania System. Some of the modifications included:

- A maximum of six months in solitary confinement;
- A separate facilities for young offenders;
- The construction of a separate asylum for criminally insane offenders,
- The improvement of small local jails;
- The establishment of education programs; and
- The creation of private prison societies to help offenders re-adjust back into the community.

The Brown Commission concluded that the primary purpose of a penitentiary was "simply the prevention of crime and that aim demanded the reclamation of prisoners whenever possible through using the minimal amount of force, making every attempt at rehabilitation" (cited in Bellomo, 1972, p. 22).

The two reports by the Brown Commission were the first formal inquiries into Kingston's operation, but only the first in a long line of Royal Commission investigations into the running of Canada's penitentiary system. The Brown Report resulted in Warden Smiths' resignation and the dismissal of several other key prison officers at Kingston's penitentiary (Ruddell, 2017).

While there is still debate to this day about the real impact of the Brown Commission on correctional reform (see Steeves, 2018), one thing is certain, in the following years, several pieces of legislation were passed to implement many of the Commission's recommendations, such as:

- The *Penitentiary Act* of 1851 provided for the construction of new *cells, reduced* corporal punishment, appointed two jail i*nspectors, and* the removal of mentally ill offenders;
- The *Prison Inspection Act* of 1857 allowed for the transfer of insane *convicts and young* offenders to separate, and newl*y built facilities; and*
- Subsequent legislation in 1859 established a system of regular prison inspection.

By the 1860s, these government penitentiary inspectors were characterizing the Canadian System as "one of rigid repression, of uncompromising coercion, one which admits no change or improvement in the condition of the convict as a consequence of good conduct" (Ouimet, 1969, p.8). They advocated the adoption of a progressive system like the one used in Ireland (making use of a mark system for graduated, early release because of good behaviour).

British North America Act (1867)

In the Irish, or Crofton System, the convicts could gradually work their way back to freedom. They would begin their sentences in solitary confinement (Pennsylvania System) and then move on to working together by day (Auburn System). During this second phase, good behaviour could earn marks or chips which could, in turn, further privileges including a ticket of leave or early release (i.e., parole) (Carrigan, 1991).

At the time of Canadian Confederation in 1867, the prisons were deteriorating and the Federal Government, in accordance with the *BNA Act*, assumed responsibility for the provincial penitentiaries at Kingston, Halifax, and Saint John, New Brunswick. This came under the legislative authority of Parliament with the passing of the *Penitentiary Act* of 1868. Conditions did not noticeably improve in the prisons, but Canada, at last, had a federal penitentiary system. Additional penitentiaries were constructed across the country (see Box 2.3).

Some of these prisons are still in operation today, with the most notable improvement being the five, new decentralized prisons for women. In 1997, the prison for women at Kingston (P4W as it was known) was finally closed, and five cottage style, small prisons were opened for women in each of the five federal regions in Canada.

The *BNA Act*, then, laid the very foundation for our present federal correctional system in Canada. And as reflected in Box 2.3 above, after the initial construction of our federal prisons, it was not until the 1960s, 1980s and even into the 1990s and the new millennium that additional prisons were, and are, being built.

The Emergence of Canadian Penitentiaries

The new penitentiaries constructed in Canada between 1873 and 1882 helped to ease inmate overcrowding and relieve the pressure, but the alarming frequency of prison riots, in Canada and the United States, made it clear that the system itself was fundamentally flawed. The deprivation of liberty did not reform anymore; better methods had to be found.

Like the reformers of the 18th century, the 19th century Victorian prison reformers were part of a larger progressive social movement. But now, there was an increasing emphasis on professionalism. Prison reformers in Canada and the United States strived to make criminology a respectable science.

Box 2.3 – Federal Prison* Construction Prior to 2015

Before the 1940s
Kingston Penitentiary – 1832
Laval Penitentiary - 1837, closed in 1989
Dorchester Penitentiary - 1880
Saskatchewan Penitentiary - 1911
BC Penitentiary – 1878, closed in 1976
Stony Mountain Institution - 1877
Collins Bay Institution - 1930s
Prison for Women - 1930s

The 1950s
Federal Training Centre
Leclerc Institution
Joyceville Institution

The 1960s
Springhill Institution
Correctional Development Centre (Quebec)
Archambault Institution
Cowansville Institution
Millhaven Institution
Warkworth Institution
Drumheller Institution
Matsqui Institution

The 1970s
Regional Reception Centre (Quebec)
Regional Psychiatric Centre (Prairies)
Edmonton Institution
Kent Institution
Mission Institution

The 1980s
Atlantic Institution
Drummond Institution
Donnacon Institution
Port Cartier Institution
Special Handling Units
La Macaza Institution
Bowden Institution

As of August 2018, there are 5 Institutions and Centres in the Atlantic provinces, 10 federal Institutions and Centres in Quebec, 7 Institutions in Ontario, 12 Institutions, Centres and healing lodges in the Prairie region, and 8 facilities in the Pacific region. There are currently a

continued...

total of 43 federal facilities plus 15 Community Correctional centres and 200+ Community Residential facilities. Under the former federal Conservative government, between 2008 and 2011, the federal government allocated $32 million over several years to renovate and expand a number of existing federal facilities across the country which increased the bed capacity by 562.

Source: CSC (2018). Retrieved from http://www.csc-scc.gc.ca/institutions/001002-5000-eng.shtml

National and international organizations were formed, and Canadians participated in the first penal Congresses held in Boston and New York in the latter part of the 19th century. At this time, in 1874, groups like the Prisoner's Aid Association of Toronto were formed to help ex-convicts. The old religious explanations for crime were no longer accepted, but there was still no consensus about what caused crime or what could cure it. With ever spiralling recidivism rates, penal reformers began to explore other correctional philosophies (Ruddell, 2017).

Biological explanations were popular. This was the heyday of phrenology (analysis of head bumps) and the theory of the *born criminal*. Cesare Lombroso (1835-1909), who, for example, called himself a criminal anthropologist wrote *L'Uomo Delinquente* in 1889. In this book, he claims that criminals were evolutionary throwbacks, who could thus be identified by their sloping foreheads, extra-long arms and prominent ears (Winterdyk, 2016a). As late as 1930, most Canadians still believed that crime was hereditary and that habitual offenders should be sterilized. J.G. Moylan, Inspector of Penitentiaries from 1875 to 1895, remarked that:

> convicts are excellent subjects for experiment; for they are not allowed to have any will of their own...the interior of our prisons is a grand theatre for the trial of all new plans in hygiene, education, physical, and moral reform. (Baehre, 1977, p. 112)

Canada's correctional system was about to enter the medical arena. By the turn of the 20th century, the criminal became viewed as sick and in need of treatment and rehabilitation. The recommendations of royal commissions began to reflect this new theme in corrections. In 1914, for example, a royal commission was called to investigate the state and management of Kingston Penitentiary. They found that many of the guards were not qualified (Carrigan, 1991). The Commission further concluded by calling for "a careful and scientific study of the individual...prisons can no longer be run like factories, processing human material into interchangeable units" (Carrigan, 1991, p. 388).

There was a notable gap between theory and practice in the Canadian correctional system. Fluctuations in the crime rate, financial constraints, shifting political priorities, and countless administrative problems interfered with the implementation of desirable programs. Penal reformers and correctional authorities did not always see eye-to-eye. The reformers' first concern was in assisting the offender, while the wardens' priority was with keeping institutional order.

In 1924, then Superintendent of Penitentiaries, W.S. Hughes, commented in his *Report on Prison Affairs* that: "the treatment of inmates in a penitentiary continues to be a subject of debate, and many people who know little of crime and nothing of criminals still continue to offer suggestions...for the treatment of offenders. It is most fortunate for the convicted ones that the suggestions of these inexperienced ones are seldom tried" (Archambault, 1938, p. 9) (see Box 2.4).

Reforms were slow to come, but by the late 1920s, Canadian corrections began to introduce inmate classification; create special juvenile facilities; launch a system of industrial prison farms; and implement legislation for earned remission and parole (Curtis et al., 1985).

Box 2.4 – What is Prison Reform?

In 1924, a former warden of three large prisons (including Auburn and Sing Sing prisons), Thomas Matt Osborne, published the following basic tenets of prison reform:

1. Prisoners are human beings; for the most part remarkably like the rest of us.
2. They can be clubbed into submission – with occasional outbreaks; but they cannot be reformed by that process.
3. Neither can they be reformed by bribery in the shape of privilege; special favours or tolerant treatment.
4. They will not respond to sentimentality; they do not like gush.
5. They appreciate a "square deal" when they get one.
6. There are not many of them with mental defectives; on the contrary, the majority are embarrassing clever.
7. All of these facts must be taken into consideration, if we want prisons which will protect society. Unless they are taken into consideration, our correctional institutions will continue to be what they have been in the past – costly schools of crime – monuments of wasted effort, of misguided service.
8. To date, all forms of severity, all forms of kindly mental and moral pauperizing, have been tried; and all have failed and will continue to fail.

Source: (Osborne, 1924, pp. 7-8)

During the Depression there was a surge of economic crimes, especially among unemployed men. In 1929, there were 2,769 offenders in Canadian penitentiaries. In 1933, there were 4,587, an increase of 66% in just four years. As discussed in Chapter 1, this continued to escalate up to 1997, when Canada was listed as the third leading nation in the Western world in terms of incarceration rates – 256 per 100,000 population – a very dubious honour (Solicitor General Canada, 1997). By 2004-05, the rate dropped significantly to 131 per 100,000 (Facts and Statistics, 2008), but it was still well above most western European countries, yet still lower than the United States. And according to Roberts and Grossman (2016), although the rate continues to decline, Canada's incarceration rate is still not comparatively high by international standards.

The Canadian authorities were beginning to take a hard-line on crime and criminals during the Depression. Once again, reform was subordinated to repression. During General D.M. Ormond's militaristic regime as superintendent of prisons (1928-1938), there were 20 riots and disturbances. All seven penitentiaries, at the time, were beset by disturbances including strikes, fires, and fatal shootings.

A Watershed Report: The Archambault Commission (1936-38)

The violence in Canadian prisons stirred public and media attention, and certainly served as a catalyst for the Archambault Commission of 1938 which was chaired by Justice Joseph Archambault (1878-1964) (see Ruddell 2017, p. 275). As Carrigan (1991) points out, the disorder within the prison system belied the fact that few, if any, of the recommendations from the **Brown Report** were addressed. The recommendations in the Archambault report represented a major point for modern Canadian correctional reform. The report included 88 recommendations which covered almost every aspect of the system and still serves for much of today's 21st century penal philosophy in Canada.

The main thrust of the report was that punishment does not create change. Rather, the overall goals of the correctional system should be to:

1. Prevent crime;
2. Rehabilitate offenders; and
3. Deter other habitual criminals.

Under the direction of Justice Archambault, this first of many future Royal Commissions, held its first meeting in 1936. The Commission toured most Federal Penitentiaries before releasing its final report in 1939. What it found was disheartening, The Commission noted:

- An almost complete lack of rehabilitation programs;
- A prison system that completely focused on punishment and cruelty;
- Inmates were locked up in their cell for over 16 hours per day,
- Filthy living conditions;
- No granting of privileges; and
- No education programs or instructors.

Most alarmingly, they found a very high recidivism rate amongst inmates. In 1936-37, it was more than 70%. Thus, it was not surprising that the Commission's report was highly critical of the existing Canadian Federal Correctional System. Some of its major recommendations for change, included:

- Improvements in prison education, recreation and work programs;
- A better deal for female prisoners;
- Greater diversity of facilities including facilities for first time offenders;
- Reforms to the probation and parole systems;
- Better after-care services;
- Administrative reorganization;
- Improved inmate classification;
- Combine the provincial and federal systems under Ottawa;
- Retrain existing staff and hire new, more qualified staff; and
- Improved medical and psychiatric services. (Carrigan, 1991, pp. 367-368)

Post World War II and Treatment

The Second World War diminished further public interest in prison reform and the full implementation of Justice Archambault's recommendations were temporarily shelved. Only a few inmate liberties such as earned remission, easier visiting, and increased recreation were granted to offenders.

Arguably, the real start of modern penal change in Canada happened in 1946 when Ottawa created the new job of Commissioner of Penitentiaries (Jaffery, 1963; Ruddell, 2017). The Commissioner had the power to review and influence change through his recommendations on the system. By 1950, the Commissioner reported that Canada had:

- Implemented a prisoner classification system;
- Psychological testing for inmates;
- Improved educational and vocational programs; and
- Complete social histories on all prisoners.

Canada had finally entered the modern age of corrections and was using a rehabilitative approach towards correcting offender behaviour.

By 1953, Ottawa appointed a Committee of Inquiry to study remission services. Chaired by Justice Joseph Honoré Gérald Fauteux (1900-1980), this commission concluded that the main purpose of the correctional system was the rehabilitation of the offender. The goal was to re-train, not punish the offender.

Carrigan (1991) maintains that it was this committee which truly adopted the word *corrections* in Canada, a term they explained as "the total process by which society attempts to correct the antisocial attitudes or behaviours of the individual" (p. 374).

This resulted in the development of specialized after care programs for addicts, sex offenders, and psychopaths. Other areas to benefit were:

- The construction of new medium security jails;
- Liberalizing probation and parole;
- Mandatory review of parole;
- The development of specialized aftercare programs for addicts, sex offenders, and inmates suffering from various psychological disorder,
- Increased use of pre-sentence reports; and
- The creation of a new, national Federal Board.

In short, the **Fauteux Report** accomplished what many previous committees did not – a Canadian correctional system based on the inmates' rehabilitation as its guiding philosophy. Canada entered, albeit late, the Age of the **Medical Model** in corrections.

From 1946 to 1960, the Correctional System was led by Major General Ralph Gibson. During his tenure, the number of federal jails increased from 7 to 15 and Gibson implemented many of Archambault's and Fauteux's suggestions. Psychological services (1947), a full-time psychiatrist (1958), and a new staff training college in Kingston were just three of the many changes implemented under Gibson's leadership.

For almost thirty years after the Archambault report, the penitentiary system continued to come under scrutiny by royal commissions, government committees, and private sector organizations. These reports seldom questioned the original penitentiary goal of reform! They remained steadfast to the idea that most inmates could be rehabilitated while in prison. However, in time, the rehabilitation philosophy began to crack, and opponents criticized it as excessively oppressive, too lenient, and anti-humanitarian. For example, in the **Ouimet Report**, the Commissioners concluded that most "reformable convicts would probably do better outside the prison walls" (Ouimet, 1969, p. 367). This report advocated the idea that offender change "might be more profitably pursued within a community setting than inside correctional institutions" (Ouimet, 1969, p. 365). This is generally described in most texts as the start of the Reintegration Era (i.e., "community corrections") of corrections in Canada. This second correctional philosophy maintained a move: away from institutionalization and towards decentralized; community run models that deviated from the traditional "experts" and the medical model and more towards open institutions; and one environment that promoted/supported prisoner rights.

The Report of the Task Force on Community-Based Residential Centres spelled out the means to be used in this new model:

- Divert persons entirely from jail (jail is a last resort);
- Divert persons from the Criminal Justice System;
- Shorten sentences by the court;

- Shorten actual incarceration; and
- Provide temporary relief from jail. (Outerbridge, 1972, p. 133)

The 1970s saw many changes implemented in the Correctional Service Canada. During this decade, prisoners began to be called by their names, they could grow beards, and even have a say in prison conditions through their inmate committee representatives. The psychiatric period and medical model in Canadian penitentiaries was at an end. Almost every conceivable form of therapy had been tried, including various forms of psychotropic drug treatments, electro-shock, behaviour modification, sensory deprivation, weekend marathons, and even nude encounter groups!

The 1970s saw an attempt to humanize some aspects of daily life in a jail. There was even an attempt to give prisoners a limited degree of self-government, through their inmate committees. In 1971, the **Mohr Committee** suggested that inmates could better be rehabilitated in a small group setting. Living units were created where inmates and staff members could reside in a family-like setting (Griffiths & Murdoch, 2013).

In 1973, the Solicitor General's Perspectives paper recommended diversion for non-violent offenders. According to its authors, prison had to be regarded as the sanction of last resort. Also, during this period, community service orders began to replace prison sentences and there was a renewed interest in using restitution as a means of helping to rehabilitate offenders by making them accountable for their actions. In fact, in 1969, the Canadian Committee on Corrections endorsed restitution as a correctional method, and in1974, the former Canadian Law Reform Commission did the same (Waller, 2002).

In the mid-1970s, a report of the Law Reform Commission of Canada said that "prisons had failed both as deterrents and rehabilitators." It declared that offenders could "not be re-educated for life in society while separated from it" (Gosselin, 1982, p. 89).

Reparation in the 1980s

By 1980, the old British Columbia Penitentiary at New Westminster was shut down for good. The old fortress stood for more than a century, and its closing signalled the beginning of the end for Canada's Victorian prisons and the philosophy they represented.

Throughout the 1980s, Ottawa continued its interest in the concept of Community Corrections and sanctions. Bill C-19 (*Criminal Law Reform Act* of 1984) proposed that the sentencing policy in Canada focus on community alternatives to prison. According to this proposal, emphasis was given to non-custodial sanctions, with imprisonment reserved for cases where such non-custodial sanctions are appropriate. However, despite these suggestions and given the delays caused by the two World Wars and the depression; lead by Allen J. MacLeod, there was a gradual shift toward what appeared to be a *get-tough* approach with correctional policies (see Box 2.3 above). The antiquated Auburn model was gradually replaced with a multiple-model system that included, among other changes, with a broad range of institutional alternatives, including reformatories, halfway houses, juvenile detention centres and isolated work camps.

The 1980s punishment objective was based on the theory of reparation which meant an "emphasis on offender responsibility for rehabilitation" (Ekstedt & Griffiths, 1988, p. 70).

Carson Report (1984)

On July 27, 1984, the Advisory Committee to the Solicitor General of Canada on the Management of Correctional Institutions (Carson Committee) was formed. Its mandate was to review and report on the management of the Correctional Service of Canada in response to earlier concerns and studies on suicide and violence in the system. The Committee's report was submitted on November 30, 1984.

One of the major findings was that Canadian prison wardens had little autonomy and, because of the excessive centralization of control by the Correctional Service of Canada, they were often reduced to paper shuffling bureaucrats (Carson Report, 1984).

The Carson Committee also raised serious concerns about the viability of the existing seven-level security system and the practice of "cascading" inmates (i.e., moving them to progressively lower levels of security over the course of their confinement).

Concern was also expressed about the over classification of inmates in maximum security prisons. The Committee noted that:

> since the overcrowding is particularly serious in medium security institutions, there are many inmates presently in maximum security who would, under normal conditions, be in medium security. The difficulties associated with the proper classification of offenders and the fact that such a process is often subjective rather than premised on established predictive guidelines must be a major consideration in any discussion of correctional treatment. (Ekstedt & Griffiths, 1988, p. 194)

The concerns raised in the Carson Report continue to this very day. A major concern of the Federal Correctional System in 1998-99 was a process known as accelerated review or the extensive review of inmates in penitentiaries who are serving their first term of imprisonment for non-violent offences. The hope was to release them on full parole after they served one-third of their sentence. The controversy in 1999 over this federal policy was related to a leaked Federal Government memo and related rumours about a 50-50 formula for federal release; that is, a plan by the correctional system to release as many as 50% of its federal prison population back into the community after one-third of their sentence was served (McGuire, 2015). Naturally, this has spawned the backlash of many citizen and government representatives and then received major attention when in 1996 the Arbour Commission (see below) called for the improvement of inmate treatment and training programs. The report lead to the creation of CORCAN Corporation which allowed for the first-time inmates to make products that were sold outside prisons. Their motto was "in the business of employability) (Winterdyk, 2001). However, despite the increased allocation of resources and opportunities to such treatment programs, the relative impact on reoffending remained relatively unchanged. Hence, in response to the challenges of specialized programming, CSC underwent another shift in its correctional ideology.

Emergence of the "Opportunities Model" (1980s)

Punishment dressed-up as reparation witnessed in the 1970s continued in the 1980s. A new name emerged to present this corrections philosophy to the Canadian Public: "the program opportunities model" (Subcommittee on the Penitentiary System in Canada, 1977). The model is based on the idea that "the offender is ultimately responsible for his behaviour…he is convicted and sentenced on the basis of his criminal behaviour, not on the basis of some underlying personality disorder or deprived socio-economic condition" (Subcommittee on the Penitentiary System in Canada, 1977, p. 71).

In using the opportunities model, corrections shifted total responsibility for reformation onto the shoulders of the offender. The system did retain responsibility for making basic and essential programs and services available to prisoners, should they choose to participate as the inmates were responsible for choosing whether they wanted to participate or not (The Sawatsky Report, CSC, 1986). The two and three headed model management style was established (see Ekstedt & Jackson, 1997, pp. 76-80). Meanwhile, the Gallagher Report, in 1988, identified flaws in offender programming. In addition, in 1989, the CSC redefined its mission statement as follows:

The Correctional Service of Canada, as part of the criminal justice system and respecting the rule of law, contributes to the protection of society by actively encouraging and assisting offenders to become law-abiding citizens, while exercising reasonable, safe, secure and humane control. The mission provided a clearer mandate on how to manage correctional facilities and its inmates.

Hence, by the early 1990s, as Duguid (2000) observed, CSC experience yet another ideological shift in its correctional directive. The shift represented a merging of the opportunistic model with the old rehabilitation model.

Corrections in the 1990s: Victim's Rights and Restorative Justice

As the 1990s, neared, correctional philosophy was a "mixture of the program opportunities model, with a strong emphasis on control of offenders, and perhaps a dash of what remains of the rehabilitation model of the 1960s" (Griffiths & Verdun-Jones, 1994, p. 288).

The Mission Statement of the Solicitor General of Canada, Correctional Service of Canada (1991, p. 4) describes it best:

The Correctional Service of Canada, as part of the Criminal Justice System, contributes to the protection of society by actively encouraging and assisting offenders to become law-abiding citizens, while exercising reasonable, safe, secure and humane control. Obviously the goal is to balance the concepts of assistance and control: "our aim is to assist and encourage to the extent that is possible and to control to the extent that is necessary."

This age-old dilemma is still unresolved today. Its philosophy is contained within the *Corrections and Conditional Release Act* (1992) which states that the main purpose of the Federal Correctional System is twofold:

1. To carry out sentences imposed by the courts through the safe and humane custody and supervision of offenders; and
2. To assist the rehabilitation of offenders and their reintegration into law-abiding citizens through the provision of programs in penitentiaries and in the community.

Section 10 of this Act goes on to state that the service should "use the least restrictive measures consistent with the protection of the public, staff members and offenders." The Task Force on Reintegration of Offenders (1997) states:

1. That low-risk offenders will receive more of their programming in the community, and
2. Program referrals will be monitored more closely to ensure that only offenders who require specific programs are referred. These points reflect the risk/needs model of justice supported throughout much of the 1990s.

Furthermore, the Act includes provisions that allow for the victim to be present but not heard during (or at) an offenders parole hearing. In accordance with the Act, a victim is also entitled to be told about the release and whereabouts of the offenders. The Act was followed in 1996 by the establishment of a Restorative Justice and Dispute Resolution Branch, which was created to help meet emerging needs for victim-offender mediation, and to address conflicts within the correctional setting (Corrections in Canada, 2010).

Arbour Commission (1996)

In 1994, a series of events occurred in the Prison for Women (P4W) in Kingston that went on to define the new face of corrections in Canada. It is ironic that the smallest group of inmates in

Canada's Federal Correctional system (in 1996 there were 320 women in prison; 142 in Kingston) would help to redesign a system that was, at the time, "hopelessly afloat in a sea of chaos and confusion" (Arbour Report, 1996).

On April 10, 1995, a Commission, chaired by then Justice Louise Arbour (see Narayan, 2017, p. 234-235), was appointed to "investigate and report on...the incidents which occurred at the Prison for Women in Kingston...beginning on April 22, 1994 and further to make recommendations to the policies and practices of the Correctional Service of Canada" (Arbour, 1996, p. ix). The impetus for the inquiry emerged after several female inmates at P4W were strip-searched and chained by male guards wearing riot gear (see below).

Without a doubt, this was probably the most exhaustive and thorough Royal Commission Inquiry in the history of Canadian Federal correctional practices. The inquiry process took place in two phases:

Phase I: Judicial public hearings were held for 43 days and heard 21 witnesses.
Phase II: Policy discussions held over 9 days with staff from the Correctional Services of Canada, inmates and correctional experts from across Canada and abroad. In total, the Commission interviewed more than 130 people and took evidence from 21 witnesses.

In addition, Madam Justice Arbour visited correctional facilities across Canada and met with staff in Kingston, as well as staff in several other Federal penitentiaries. The Report was released on March 28, 1996. What happened to cause such a major crisis in Canadian corrections? As Justice Arbour stated in her report: "the incidents that gave rise to this inquiry could have gone largely unnoticed" (Arbour, 1996). The public viewing of a videotape and the release of a special report by the Correctional Investigator in 1995 helped to shed light on the current state of our Correctional system; otherwise Correctional Service Canada would have essentially "closed the book" on these events.

The series of events in 1994 that gave rise to this inquiry, consisted of a number of incidents. This included a "brief but violent physical confrontation" took place between six female inmates and several correctional staff. A couple of weeks later this resulted in Correctional staff demonstrating outside the Prison for Women, demanding the transfer of the inmates. Ultimately most of the women were transferred to a psychiatric treatment centre and then returned to segregation. After pleading guilty to related criminal charges on December 22, 1994, the women were finally released from segregation and returned to general population in January 1995.

Because of these incidents, Justice Arbour's report made 14 wide-sweeping major recommendations to the Correctional Service of Canada. Some of the key suggestions included:

1   Male emergency response teams not be employed in women's institutions, nor allowed to strip search and cavity search female prisoners;
2   A position of Deputy Commissioner for Women must be created with all the powers necessary to implement appropriate changes;
3   Special training programs should be implemented to allow more sensitive responses;
4   Segregation can only be used in compliance with the law;
5   Input from other criminal justice agencies and staff should be included and used in such future situations; and
6   Correctional Service improves their accessibility on all levels.

The Prison for Women was closed in 1997 and all female inmates transferred to their respective five regional prisons in Canada (see Chapter 6). However, the first call for its closure came in 1938, four years after it opened.

There is no doubt that the Arbour Inquiry and its report helped to hasten the slow process of change within Canadian corrections. As Madam Justice Arbour notes in her Report, "they were part of a prison culture which did not value individual rights" (1996).

Since then, many of these recommendations have impacted the way Correctional Services of Canada now treats all its Federal prisoners (see, generally, Griffiths & Murdoch, 2013). Male inmates have also received better, accelerated reviews of their cases with respect to their needs, rights, and ultimate review for release. This is referred to as a risk and need responsivity model (see Bonta & Wormith, 2007).

The risk and needs model was intended to provide a fair assessment for both public protection and inmate release into the community. For the model to work, it was necessary to improve and expand staff training, improve prediction models, as well as engage and support more correctional research into crime and offender behaviour.

2000 – Present: A Time of Continued Transformation

As discussed by Winterdyk (2016b), among others, the terrorist attack on the United States on September 11, 2001, marked not only a dramatic shift in public safety and security in Canada, but globally. Canada, and most of the world, began to evaluate public safety as never before in the history of Canadian corrections. The establishment of the Canadian Borders Service Agency (CBSA) and Public Safety Canada, in 2003, not only highlighted a shift in national security, but also promoted a transformation within Canadian correction by focusing on public safety as the move resulted in the merger of several border services activities and resources "to enhance public safety and minimize risk to Canadians from a wide range of threats" (Correctional Services Canada, 2014).

According to the CSC website on Corrections in Canada, there was a shift in acknowledging that there is a broader range of risk and needs among the inmate population. For example, since 1997 there was a 50% increase in the number of incarcerated, violent offenders (Corrections in Canada, 2010). The demographic profile of the inmate population has changed and continues to evolve. For example, CSC must now contend with higher rates of inmates with infectious diseases such as HIV/AIDS, an aging population, more inmates with mental health related issues (with estimates as high as 20%), and an inmate population who, relative to the general population, are less well educated, are less likely to have full time jobs, lack problem-solving skills, and a host of other challenges. Finally, in 2007, when Stockwell Day, then Minister of Public Safety, commissioned an independent review board to examine how the government could best address the crime problem a report was produced and referred to as the Transformation Agenda.

Transformation Agenda

The report included 109 recommendations grouped around five themes. They included: offender accountability, eliminating drugs from prison, offender employability to enhance reintegration, improving physical infrastructure, and moving to earned parole. Then, starting in 2008, the Government allocated some $122 million over two years to the CSC to ensure they could respond to these recommendations. In addition, for the fiscal year 2018-19, CSC identified four priorities, further reflecting its corporate priorities and transformation. The priorities include:

1. CSC will implement a National Indigenous Plan in an effort to further reduce waiting periods and expand/improve culturally-appropriate programs.
2. CSC will further implement and monitor its Refined Model of Mental Health Care to "maximize efficiency and effectiveness of mental health services" in all federal institutions.

3. CSC will continue to work to "achieve a higher percentage of offenders completing correctional programs and vocational training."
4. CSC will continue to strengthen security protocols in order to improve inmate safety and security. This includes, among other initiatives, further reducing the entry of illicit contraband, etc. (Correctional Service Canada, 2018).

Collectively, these factors place a unique burden not only on CSC but also on the management of its facilities and available resources. However, as reflected throughout the history of correctional services in Canada, CSC has been ready, if not willing, to adapt to the changes and demands placed on the services it provides. For example, in 2005, new uniforms were introduced which the CSC felt were more respectful of human rights and reflective of its mandate. In addition, in 2007, the CSC added a section to its website for victims of federal offenders. The site provides victims with easy-to-access, up-to-date information about the services offered by its National Victim Services Program. In addition to other resources on the site, it also provides victims with a wealth of information to better help victims understand the justice and correctional systems. The site, furthermore, explains the role a victim's voice can play in the Federal Government's ongoing response to the needs of victims of crime.

Being mindful of protecting the rights and well-being of inmates, in 2006, the CSC banned smoking in all its penitentiaries and community-based correctional facilities.

Currently Canada offers a wide variety of correctional services to offenders. The offender-community style of corrections emphasizes values such as inclusion, democracy, responsibility, reparation, safety, healing, and reintegration. Community corrections allows an offender to carry out their sentence through community supervision, where they can reintegrate as law-abiding citizens with continued support and access to programs (see Chapters 3 & 4).

Examples of community corrections include bail supervision programs; when an accused awaits trial in the community instead of being held in custody, the accused is supervised by a community member. Alternative measure programs/restitution allow an accused to enter into a contract answering to their crime; they perform community service, make a charitable donation, attend counselling or perform a service to the victim or pay victim back (e.g., repair a broken fence, fix damage to a stolen vehicle or vandalized property). Fine option programs have an offender works for an hourly rate (e.g., $5.00) in an approved community work environment until the monetary debt of the crime is repaid.

The most common disposition used in corrections is probation wherein an offender is supervised within the community while following a set of conditions (see Chapter 4). A community service order, when the offender works in the community, can be a part of probation. Levels of supervision are dependent on risk of recidivism and level of crime. A conditional sentence, when the prison sentence is less than two years and a day, can be served within the community.

Attendance centre programs use non-residential facilities where offenders are on a temporary absence, they report frequently for supervision and/or programs. Temporary absences are granted for inmates who are working in the community. Electronic monitoring is used in some provinces and has been recently introduced in federal corrections. An offender is given an ankle bracelet which emits either a continuous signal or alternatively the bracelet only responds when the computer calls it and notes the offenders location (passive locator). Federally, Parole officers work with the National Monitoring Centre to analyze data received from the tracking device, reporting whether the offenders are obeying their parole restrictions or not.

Parole/conditional release has an offender serve part of their sentence in the community, this is a function of the National Parole Board under the authority of the Solicitor General of Canada. The parole Board reviews applications made by inmates from federal penitentiaries. Under federal law, most offenders must be released on some form of conditional release (called statutory release) to serve the last third of their sentence in the community. Halfway Houses are utilized as an intermediate step between prison and freedom, particularly for those on day parole (see Chapter 10 in this textbook for further discussion).

The benefits of community corrections compared to custody are reduced cost, less prison over-crowding, agency collaboration and access to community-based programs (Steiner, Wada, Hemmens, & Burton, 2005).

To date, there has been some public reaction to the Transformation Agenda (see, for example, Jackson & Stewart, 2009; Winterdyk, 2010) but given its relative newness, the final verdict appears yet to be scripted. However, one thing remains certain, the history of adult corrections in Canada is evolving and dynamic on many levels, not only within Canada, but in recent years, also within the international community. Adult corrections in Canada has come a long way from following in the foot-steps of Britain to be a recognized international leader and model on a range of levels (see, for example, Chapters 9 & 13).

Finally, as much as the CSC may appear to be transforming towards a restorative and reinte-grative model, in 2009, Ottawa doubled (approximately $195 million) its federal prison construction budget, in partial response to an expanding list and diversity of criminals. Although rationalized by the government as being reflective of its concern for public safety, there is ample evidence that building more prisons does not deter criminals from offending (Curry, 2009; Hackler, 2011). Furthermore, according to their 2015-2016 "Quick Facts" data sheet, it still cost approximately $116,000 and $31,000 to maintain an offender in an institution and in the community respectively. In addition, in 2016, Canada's crime rates reached a 45-year low, yet paradoxically the incarceration rates hit an all-time high (see Chapter 1 & 5) (Chan, Chuen, & McLeod, 2017)! Therefore, time will bear the mark on whether such measures truly serve to promote public safety and deter criminals.

SUMMARY

The purpose of this chapter was to provide an historical overview of adult corrections in Canada, with a focus on prisons in the 20th and 21st century. The history of Canadian corrections is characterized as one of punishment. Until recently, this orientation had an enduring influence on our correctional practices. During pre-Confederation, Canada's correctional system was based on the Auburn (congre-gate) system of penitentiaries – a combination of punishment and penitence. It became the dominant model for early prisons across Canada, including our first penitentiary, the Kingston Provincial Peni-tentiary.

This approach lasted throughout the 1800s and for most of the 1900s century. It was not until we adopted the medical model of corrections in the 20th century that ideologies such as rehabilitation, deterrence, reintegration (1980s - 90s), and finally, restorative justice (1990s - 2000) emerged. The Transformation Agenda in 2006 marked a potential shift or transformation in adult corrections in Canada. However, its true impact remains to be seen.

The evolution of corrections in Canada, although influenced by American trends, is tied more directly to the Royal Commission Inquiries throughout the 20th century. The current *Federal Correc-tions and Conditional Release Act* (1992) still supports reintegration ideology. Hence, Canada has moved from just deserts (where the punishment is equal to the crime) to a reintegrative approach. And although these changes have not always met with public or political support, they do reflect the dynamic nature and the role that social, economic, and political interests play in the administration of criminal justice, and in this case corrections. Furthermore, Canada's correctional practices have garnered inter-national respect in many areas (see Chapter 9).

Of all the treatments described in this chapter, the relatively recent move towards restorative justice and addressing victims' rights appears to offer the most promise. There is also increasing discussion of the increased use of modern technology such as electronic monitoring, security of offenders, facility design and inmate classification, institutional security information, special interest groups (e.g., gangs and organized crime and home confinement (e.g., curfew; see Chapter 4 for further discussion), among other considerations. What the future holds for the immediate and long-term future of adult corrections remains unclear, but some ideas and issues are discussed in the final chapter of this book, as well as touched on in several chapters.

Whatever the final direction, Canadian corrections has taken some unique and positive steps forward since 1835. Unlike our American counterparts, Canada has decided to tackle the problems of prison violence and over-crowding with healing programs as opposed to constructing more jails and executing more offenders.

Canadian correctional philosophy appears to have discarded the traditional deterrent sentencing model and adopted a risks-needs model (see Chapter 9). By assessing individual offender's risks and needs, with trained staff, we are better able to determine our program and service direction. And while the treatment may be far different from what our predecessors planned for in the early part of this century, it does appear that they were correct on one count. The environment required to carry out these new treatments and programs will be the community – the *hidden element* of the criminal justice system.

Only in the community will we have a fighting chance to battle and control crime. Only in the community will we be able to have any future for long-term successes, with the reintegration of offenders, assistance to victims, and protection of the public.

As Madam Justice Louise Arbour stated in her Report: "the history of women and crime is spotted with opportunities most of which have been missed. We hope that history will not dictate our future" (1996). (Justice Arbour has gone on to chair the United Nations War Crimes Tribunal and in 1999, was appointed to the Supreme Court of Canada.)

It appears that the past and present history of the Canadian Federal Correctional system practices does not accurately reflect the views of average Canadians. Nevertheless, it is important to note that the problem is much broader than an Indigenous peoples issue, mental health issue, or a female inmate issue. If it is a social ill to jail too many people for too long, then we desperately need new alternatives in the community, alongside increased and expanded existing resources.

Judges, as a body, are now finally realizing that incarceration as a long-term solution is not the answer. As many past Royal Commissions have recognized, in Canada jail should be nothing more than a last resort. Attempting to explain why this is obvious to us, since these same judges stress that jails only temporarily remove offenders from our midst (Arbour, 1996). Arbour further notes that, imprisonment has thus far failed to satisfy a basic function of the Canadian judicial system, which is to protect society from crime in a manner commanding public support while avoiding needless injury to the offender.

KEY TERMS AND CONCEPTS

Carson Committee	Opportunities Model	Justice Louise Arbour
Fauteux Report	Ouimet Report	Brown Report
Archambault Commission	Bloody Code	Medical Model
Retaliation	John Howard	Walnut Street Jail
Pennsylvania System	Cherry Hill	Just Deserts
Upper Fort Garry	Moral Reformation	Reform model

STUDY AND DISCUSSION QUESTIONS

1. What role did John Howard and Elizabeth Fry play as early correctional reformers? What major contributions did each of them make?
2. How did Canadian jails come into existence? What role did the Kingston Penitentiary play?
3. How did the Brown Commission impact Canadian penitentiaries?
4. Contrast the Archambault Commission (1938) with the Carson Report (1984). What are the similarities and differences?
5. Why was the Arbour Commission (1996) necessary? How did it affect 1990s correctional philosophy?
6. What is the significance of the Transformative Agenda for the future of adult corrections in Canada?

HELPFUL WEBLINKS

www.csc-scc.gc.ca/ The homepage for Corrections Service Canada – in addition to offering a variety of links relating to historical information on corrections in Canada, it also offers a wide range of links to current correctional issues, research reports, and correctional data.

NOTES

[1] An initial version of this chapter was prepared by Alan Erdahl before he retired from Mount Royal University and it appeared Corrections in Canada, 2001, J. Winterdyk (Ed.). Jessica Wood, a former student at Mount Royal University, assisted with the second edition (2013).
[2] John Howard became the first civilian to honoured with a statute at St. Paul's.

REFERENCES

Anderson, F.W. (April 1960). Prisons and prison reforms in the old Canadian west. *Canadian Journal of Corrections,* 209-15.

Andrews, D., Bonta, J., & Wormith, S. (2006). The recent past and near future of risk and/or need assessment. *Crime & Delinquency, 52*(1), 7-27.

Annual report of the commissioner of penitentiaries, 1949. (1950). Ottawa: King's Printer.

Arbour, the Honourable Louise. (1996). *The prison for women in Kingston - A commission of inquiry into certain events.* Ottawa: Public Works and Government Services of Canada. Retrieved from http://www.justicebehindthewalls.net

Archambault, J. (Chairman). (1938). *Report of the royal commission to investigate the penal system of Canada.* Ottawa, ON: King's Printer.

Baehre, R. (1977). Origins of the penitentiary in Upper Canada. *Ontario History*, Vol. 59, 185–207.

Beattie, J.M. (1977) *Attitudes towards crime and punishment in Upper Canada, 1830 - 1850.* Toronto, ON: Centre of Criminology, University of Toronto.

Bellomo, J.J. (1972). Upper Canadians attitudes towards crime and punishment. *Ontario History, 54,* 11-26.

Bonta, J., & Cormier, R. (1999). Corrections research in Canada: Impressive progress and promising prospects. *Canadian Journal of Criminology, 41,* 235-247.

Bonta, J., & Wormith, S. J. (2007). Risk and need assessment. In G. McIvor & P. Raynor (Eds.), Developments in social work with offenders (pp. 131-152). Philadelphia, PA: Jessica Kingsley Publishers.

Chan, J., Chuen, L., & McLeod, M. (2017, July 20). Everything you were never taught about Canada's prison systems. Intersectional analyst. Retrieved from http://www.intersectionalanalyst.com

Correctional Service Canada. (2018). Retrieved from http://www.csc-scc.gc.ca

Correctional Service Canada. (2014). Retrieved from http://www.csc-scc.gc.ca

Carrigan, D.O. (1991). *Crime and punishment in Canada, a history.* Toronto, ON: McClelland & Stewart Inc.

Carson, J. (Chairman). (1984). *Report of the advisory committee to the Solicitor General on Management of Correctional Institutions (Carson Report).* Ottawa: Ministry of Supply and Services.

Cayley, D. (1998). *The Expanding Prison: The Crisis in Crime and Punishment and the Search for Alternatives.* Toronto: House of Anansi Press.

Coles, D. (1979). *Nova Scotia corrections – An historical perspective.* Halifax: Corrections Service Division.

Corrections and Conditional Release Act. (1992). Retrieved from http://laws-lois.justice.gc.ca

Correctional Service of Canada. (2008). Retrieved from http://www.csc-scc.gc.ca

Corrections in Canada. (2010). Retrieved from http://www.csc-scc.gc.ca

Community Corrections. (1998). Retrieved from http://www.johnhoward.ab.ca

Correction Services Canada. (2011). Correctional Service Canada: National facility directory. Retrieved from http://www.csc-scc.gc.ca

Curry, B. (2009). Ottawa will expand prisons to suit tough crime laws. Retrieved from http://www.theglobeandmail.com

Curtis, D., Graham, A., Kelly, L., & Patterson, A. (1985). *Kingston penitentiary: The first hundred and fifty years.* Ottawa: Supply and service Canada.

DoBash, R., & Gutteridge, S. (1986). *The imprisonment of women.* New York, NY: B. Blackwell Publishers.

Duguid, S. (2000). *Can Prisons Work?: The Prisoner as Object and Subject in Modern Corrections.* Toronto: University of Toronto Press.

Ekstedt, J.W., & Griffiths, C.T. (1988). *Corrections in Canada: policy and practice* (2nd ed.). Toronto, ON: Butterworths.

Ekstedt, J.W., & Jackson, M.A. (1997). *The keepers and the kept, introduction to corrections in Canada.* Toronto, ON: ITP Nelson.

Facts and Statistics. (2008). Retrieved from http://www.prisonjustice.ca

Federal Corrections and Conditional Release Act (1992). Retrieved from http://laws-lois.justice.gc.ca

Gendreau, P., Goggin, C., & Paparozzi, M. (1996) Principles of effective assessment for community corrections. *Federal Probation, 60,* 64-70.

Goff, C. (1999). *Corrections in Canada.* Cincinnati, OH: Anderson.

Gosselin, L. (1982). *Prisons in Canada.* Montreal, PQ: Black Rose Books.

Griffiths, C.T., & Murdoch, D.J. (2013). *Canadian corrections* (4th ed.). Toronto: ON: Nelson Ed. Ltd.

Griffiths, C.T., & Verdun-Jones, S.N. (1994). *Canadian criminal justice.* Toronto, ON: Harcourt Brace.

Hackler, J. (2011). Reducing crime the intelligent way. Building parenting not prisons. *Justice Report, 26*(3), 3-6.

History of Canadian correction system. (n.d.). Retrieved from: http://www.csc-scc.gc.ca

Howard, J. (2013). *The states of prisons in England and Wales.* Cambridge, UK: Cambridge University Press.

Jackson, M. & Stewart, G. (2009). A flawed compass: A human rights analysis of the roadmap to strengthen public safety. Vancouver, UBC: Allard Research Commons. Retrieved from https://commons.allard.ubc.ca

Jaffery, P. (1963). *Sentencing of adults in Canada.* Toronto, ON: University Press of Toronto.

McGuire, J. (2015). CHAPTER 16: Treatment Approaches for Offenders with Mental Disorder. Ottawa: Correctional Service Canada.

Narayan, R.D. (2017). Pioneers in the Canadian legal system. In J. Winterdyk (ed.). *Pioneers in Canadian criminology.* Oakville, ON: Rock's Mills Press.

Melossi, D., & Pararini, M. (1981). *The prison and the factory: Origins of the penitentiary system.* Totowa, NJ: Barnes and Noble.

Miethe, T.D. & Lu, H. (2005). *Punishment: A Comparative Historical Perspective.* New York, NY: Cambridge Un. Press.

Motiuk, L., Bonta, J., & Andrews, D. (1986) Classification in correctional halfway houses: The relative and incremental predictive criterion validities of the megargee-MMPI and LSI systems. *Criminal Justice Behavior, 13*(1), 33.

Osborne, M.T. (1924). *Prisons and common sense.* Philadelphia, PA: J.B. Lippincott.

Ouimet, R. (Chairman). (1969). *Report of the Canadian Committee on Corrections – towards unity: Criminal Justice and Corrections.* Ottawa, ON: Information Canada.

Outerbridge, W.R. (1972). *Report of the task force on community-based residential centres.* Ottawa, ON: Information Canada.

Petersilia, J. & Reitz, K.R. (2015). *The Oxford Handbook of sentencing and corrections.* New York, NY: Oxford University Press.

Roberts, J. & Grossman, M.G. (eds.). (2016). *Criminal Justice in Canada: A Reader,* 5th ed. Toronto: Nelson Pub.

Ruddell, R. (2017). Pioneers in Canadian corrections. In J. Winterdyk (ed.) *Pioneers in Canadian Criminology,* Oakville, ON: Rock's Mills Press.

Shoom, S. (1966). Kingston penitentiary: The early decades. *Canadian Journal of Corrections*, 8, 215-220.

Solicitor General Canada, Correctional Service of Canada. (1997). *Basic facts about Corrections in Canada.* Ottawa, ON: Public Works and Government Services Canada.

Solicitor General of Canada, Correctional Service of Canada. (1991). *Mission of the Correctional Service of Canada.* Ottawa, ON: Supply and Services of Canada.

Steeves, J. (2018). The right to remain silent? *The Signal.* Retrieved from: http://j-source.ca

Steiner, B., Wada, J., Hemmens, C., & Burton, V. (2005). The correctional orientation of community corrections: Legislative changes in the legally prescribed functions of community corrections 1992-2002. *American Journal of Criminal Justice, 29*(2), 141-159.

Subcommittee on the Penitentiary System in Canada. (1977). *Report to Parliament by the sub-committee on the penitentiary system in Canada.* Ottawa, ON: Supply and Services Canada.

The Juristat Reader: A statistical overview of the Canadian Justice System. (1999). Toronto, ON: Thompson Educational Publishing Inc.

The Sawatsky Report, CSC. (1986). Ottawa: Correctional Service Canada. Retrieved from https://www.publicsafety.gc.ca

The Task Force on Reintegration of Offenders. (1997). Retrieved from http://www.csc-scc.gc.ca

UNODC. (2018). Retrieved from: https://www.unodc.org

Waller, I. (2002). Crime Victims: Doing Justice to Their Support and Protection. University of Ottawa: Unpublished.

Winterdyk. J. (Ed.). (2001). *Corrections in Canada.* Toronto, ON: Pearson Education Canada.

Winterdyk, J. (2016a). *Canadian Criminology* (3rd ed.). Toronto: OUP.

Winterdyk, J. (2016b). The long shadow of 9/11: should we be afraid of what might be lurking in the dark? *Justice Report,* 31(4): 6-9.

Winterdyk, J. (January 2010). A call for reflection: Sampson et al. vs. Jackson and Stewart or "the CSC 'roadmap'" vs. "a flawed compass." *Justice Report.*

Sentencing and Correctional Sanctions

3

Derek Spencer

Learning Objectives

After reading this chapter, you should be able to:

- Know the different populations of offenders housed in Canadian correctional facilities.

- Understand the impact of bail and remand time on sentencing.

- Know the major purposes and principles of sentencing in Canada.

- Appreciate the key aggravating and mitigating factors in sentencing.

- Understand the *Gladue* principle and key misunderstandings about this principle.

- Understand the differences between the main types of sanctions that can be imposed.

INTRODUCTION

Sentencing plays a pivotal role in the criminal justice system. As James Fitzjames Stephen aptly surmised in 1863, "[s]entencing is the gist of the proceeding. It is to the trial what the bullet is to the powder" (as cited in *R v Gardiner*, 1982, p. 413). Sentencing links the criminal law process, which determines whether an accused charged with an offence is guilty or not guilty, with the correctional process, which enforces sanctions imposed on those found guilty of crimes. At sentencing a judge determines what sanctions will be placed on the offender and the duration of these sanctions. The offender is then turned over to corrections for the implementation of the imposed sentence.

Sentencing law operates in a rather unique dichotomy between strict formality prescribed by statute and a large amount of judicial discretion. Legislation, largely codified in the *Criminal Code* outlines elements of a sentence, sometimes with great precision. Aside from instances where specific legislation requires a certain sanction as part of a sentence, judges have a broad discretion in sentencing. Sentencing is a highly individualized process, and judges are mandated to consider the circumstances of the offence and the circumstances of the offender when passing a sentence. This chapter will provide a brief overview of the sentencing process, the purposes and principles of sentencing law in Canada, and the sentencing options available to a judge, as applicable to adult offenders. Before discussing sentencing in-depth, I will provide a brief overview of un-sentenced inmates who are on remand or held in immigration detention, as they too are part of the group corrections practitioners will interact with.

In this chapter, I have used the terms "offender" and "accused" in ways consistent with Canadian jurisprudence. At the time of sentencing, the individual on trial has been found guilty of a crime, removing the presumption of innocence. An individual being sentenced is therefore commonly referred to as the offender by the courts. Where individuals have not been found guilty, such as individuals being held in custody pending trial, they retain the presumption of innocence and are referred to as accused in this chapter. They are also referred to as pre-trial detention cases or remand prisoners (see Chapter 5).

In this chapter I also refer to the Supreme Court without qualification. When this is done, the Supreme Court being referred to is the Supreme Court of Canada, Canada's final appellate court.

NON-SENTENCED INMATES

Remand

Not all individuals in custody have been sentenced for an offence. In some provincial jails or correctional institutions, the majority of inmates may not actually have been sentenced, but rather, have been denied bail. Remanded inmates are legally innocent and are held in custody to await trial or a bail hearing. As the Canadian Civil Liberties Association (CCLA) reports, in 2012/13 there were over 25,000 individuals detained in provincial jails across Canada, and over half were held on remand. The CCLA notes that remand rates have tripled in the past three decades, despite a falling crime rate. Further, there are large regional disparities in remand rates. In Manitoba, 66% of inmates were on remand, the highest rate in Canada, followed by rates of 61% in Alberta, and 60% in the Yukon and Ontario. Conversely, in Prince Edward Island only 18% of the jail population was on remand (for further discussion see Chapter 5).

Remand, also known as **pre-trial detention** plays an important function in maintaining public safety and confidence in the justice system. As the Supreme Court explains:

[t]he repute of our criminal justice system rests on the deeply held belief of Canadians that the right to liberty and the presumption of innocence are fundamental values of our society that

require protection. However, that repute also depends on the confidence citizens have that persons charged with serious crimes will not be able to evade justice, harm others or interfere with the administration of justice while awaiting trial. (*R v St-Cloud*, 2015, para 1)

An accused may be a high risk to attempt to avoid justice by fleeing, or may commit further crimes if released, causing further harm in the community. Public confidence in the justice system would be eroded if these accused could not be held by authorities, particularly when they pose a risk to public safety and there is a strong case against the accused.

For the vast majority of criminal offences, the Crown bears the onus to show grounds why the accused should be detained in custody. For a handful of offences, listed in s. 469 of the *Criminal Code*, the onus for bail is reversed and the accused must demonstrate why he or she should be released. The most notable offence under s. 469 is murder. Section 515(6) of the *Criminal Code* also contains provisions that reverses the onus for bail, requiring the accused to show why they should be released.

The legal framework for judicial interim release, also known as bail, is set out in s. 515(1) of the *Criminal Code*. In sum, this section states that other than for s. 469 offences, a judge shall order the accused be released unless the prosecutor shows cause why the accused should be detained or why another form of bail should be used.

Section 515(10) sets out three grounds when detention of the accused may be necessary. These are:

1) ensuring the accused attends court (s. 515(10)(a));
2) ensuring protection of public, including victims or witnesses of the offence (s.515(10)(b));
3) maintenance of confidence in the administration of justice (s. 515(10)(c)).

Bail is governed by the "**ladder principle**." As the Supreme Court of Canada explains the ladder principle "requires a justice or a judge to impose the least onerous form of release on an accused unless the Crown shows why that should not be the case" (*R v Antic*, 2017, para 4). Under the ladder principle, judges should consider, in order:

1) releasing the accused without conditions;
2) releasing the accused with non- monetary conditions;
3) releasing the accused with monetary conditions.

When releasing with monetary conditions, again the judge must follow the ladder principle and impose the least onerous form of release. These options include whether to require the deposit of money or another asset or whether to require a third party like a family member or friend to agree to supervise the bail and forfeit money if the bail is breached. Such a third person is known as a surety.

The ladder principle operates in reverse for s. 469 offences, requiring the accused to show why they should be released and why each of the rungs should not be imposed, starting with release with monetary conditions and working in reverse to release without conditions.

The Supreme Court has set out 11 principles and guidelines that should be followed when applying bail provisions:

(a) **Accused persons are constitutionally presumed innocent, and the corollary to the presumption of innocence is the constitutional right to bail.**
(b) Section 11(e) [of the *Charter*] guarantees both the right not to be denied bail without just cause and the right to bail on reasonable terms.
(c) Save for exceptions, an unconditional release on an undertaking is the default position when granting release....

(d) **The ladder principle** articulates the manner in which alternative forms of release are to be imposed. According to it, "release is favoured at the earliest reasonable opportunity and, having regard to the [statutory criteria for detention], on the least onerous grounds"....This principle **must be adhered to strictly**.

(e) If the Crown proposes an alternative form of release, it must show why this form is necessary. The more restrictive the form of release, the greater the burden on the accused. Thus, a justice of the peace or a judge cannot impose a more restrictive form of release unless the Crown has shown it to be necessary having regard to the statutory criteria for detention.

(f) Each rung of the ladder must be considered individually and must be rejected before moving to a more restrictive form of release...

(g) A recognizance with sureties is one of the most onerous forms of release. A **surety should not be imposed unless all the less onerous forms of release have been considered and rejected as inappropriate.**

(h) It is not necessary to impose cash bail on accused persons if they or their sureties have reasonably recoverable assets and are able to pledge those assets to the satisfaction of the court to justify their release. A recognizance is functionally equivalent to cash bail and has the same coercive effect. Thus... **cash bail should be relied on only in exceptional circumstances** in which release on a recognizance with sureties is unavailable.

(i) When such exceptional circumstances exist and cash bail is ordered, the amount must not be set so high that it effectively amounts to a detention order, which means that the amount should not be beyond the readily available means of the accused and his or her sureties. As a corollary to this, the justice or judge is under a positive obligation, when setting the amount, to inquire into the ability of the accused to pay. **The amount of cash bail must be no higher than necessary to satisfy the concern that would otherwise warrant detention and proportionate to the means of the accused and the circumstances of the case.**

(j) Terms of release imposed under s. 515(4) may "only be imposed to the extent that they are necessary" to address concerns related to the statutory criteria for detention and to ensure that the accused can be released. **They must not be imposed to change an accused person's behaviour or to punish an accused person** (*R v Antic*, 2017, para 67. Emphasis added).

The ability for a judge to remand an accused into custody awaiting trial is an important feature of the justice system and ensures public safety and confidence in the justice system. However, the high proportion of inmates who are remanded into custody calls into question whether remand is being over used (Myers, 2017; Weinrath, 2009).

Credit for Remand Time

If an accused is remanded into custody, they receive credit for the time spent in prison towards the sentence imposed. However, remanded inmates do not receive statutory remission that sentenced prisoners receive. The lack of credit towards statutory release is part of the reason why remand time is normally credited at a rate of 1.5 to 1, or 1.5 days of credit given for every 1 day spent on remand. Prior to 2009, offenders typically received 2:1 credit, and some cases offenders were granted credit at a 3:1 rate.

In 2009, the Conservative government enacted the *Truth in Sentencing Act*, one of several legislative actions taken by the government from 2006-2015 while they emphasized a "tough on crime" agenda. The *Truth in Sentencing Act* capped credit at 1.5:1.

In *R. v. Summers*, the Supreme Court stated that "the loss of early release, taken alone, will generally be a sufficient basis to award credit at the rate of 1.5 to 1" (2014, para 71). By granting a remanded accused 1.5 to 1 credit, 12 months of custody is credited at 18 months, making their sentence quantitatively equivalent to that of any other provincial inmate.

The **go forward sentence** is calculated by subtracting credit for remand time from the sentence imposed by the trial judge. The go forward sentence is used to determine the locus of confinement. If an offender receives a sentence of 3 years, which ordinarily would be served in a federal penitentiary, but was on remand for 1 year and received 1.5 to one credit, the go forward sentence would therefore be 18 months, which the offender would serve in a provincial prison. Thus, time in pre-trial custody can have a significant impact on an offender's final disposition.

Immigration Detention

One controversial issue arising in the United States during the presidency of Donald Trump is the use of immigration detention, with a particularly contentious debate over the separation of children from their parents. While Canada also uses immigration detention, it does so at a lesser rate that the United States and focuses on the best interests of the child. Canadian immigration policy only detains children as a last resort. The majority of children held in Canadian immigration custody are held to avoid separating them from their parent or guardian. In 2016-2017, 151 minors were in custody accompanied by a parent or guardian, compared to just 11 minors detained without accompaniment. These minors were held for an average of 13.1 days. (Canada Border Services Agency, 2018)

Individuals detained for immigration reasons are held under authority set out in the *Immigration and Refugee Protection Act*. This Act allows for detention of an individual:

1) where an officer has reasonable grounds to believe is inadmissible into Canada and is a danger to the public (2001, s. 55(1), 55(2))
2) where the officer has reasonable grounds to believe is inadmissible into Canada and is unlikely to appear for examination, an admissibility hearing, removal from Canada, or at a proceeding that could lead to the making of a removal order (s. 55(1), 55(2)), or
3) the officer is not satisfied of the identity of the foreign national in the course of any procedure under the *Immigration and Refugee Protection Act*. (s. 55(2)(b)).

Individuals detained for immigration detention may be placed in one of the few centres operated by Canada Border Services Agency, while others are placed in provincial remand centres. The *Immigration and Refugee Protection Act* requires that immigration detention be reviewed by the Immigration Division within 48 hours of the foreign national being taken into detention (s. 57(2)). A second review is required after a further 7 days (s. 57(2)), and at least every 30 days "the Immigration Division must review the reasons for the continued detention" (s. 57(2)). Decisions of the Immigration Division can be judicially reviewed by the Federal Court of Canada (s. 72(1)).

In 2017, a total of 3,585 individuals in Canada were detained under the *Immigration and Refugee Protection Act*. The vast majority, 3,127 (87%) were detained for 0-90 days. In 297 cases (8%) detention was for 91-180 days, and a further 81 (2%) were held for 181-365 days. Eighty (2%) immigration detentions were in excess of one year (Canada Border Services Agency, 2018).

SENTENCED INMATES

Sentencing takes place "as soon as practicable after an offender has been found guilty" (*Criminal Code*, 1985, s. 720(1)). In many cases, an offender pleads guilty and the sentencing hearing begins and concludes in a matter of several minutes. More complex sentencing hearings may occur weeks or months after the finding of guilt, especially when the sentencing requires additional evidence such as the preparation of a pre-sentence *Gladue* report. Compared to a criminal trial, sentencing hearings are often more informal, and the rules of evidence are not applied as strictly. Although witnesses may be called to testify at sentencing hearings, most sentencing hearings do not involve witnesses.

The offender may elect to submit letters of support from family, friends and members of the community that serve the purpose to present mitigating factors to the sentencing judge, such as strong family and communities ties, employment and volunteering history and general good character apart from their offending. Such information is also gained from a pre-sentence report prepared by a probation officer (see Chapter 4).

Victim impact statements may be read to the court, either by the victim themselves or by the Crown Prosecutor. The purpose of these statements is to ensure the consequences of the offender's actions are palpably brought home to him or her, and to make the sentencing judge aware of the damage the offence has caused. Victim impact statements may include description of the physical or emotional harm, property damage or economic loss suffered by the victim as the result of the commission of the offence and the impact of the offence on the victim, but cannot make assertions of fact, criticism of the offender or recommendations of punishment.

Sentencing is an individualised process, and at times highly controversial. The Alberta Court of Appeal stated it "is notorious amongst judges... that one of the most controversial subjects, both in theory and practical application, is sentencing" (*R. v Arcand*, 2010, para 8). While judges must attune sentences to the facts of a given case, they do so drawing on various purposes and principles of sentencing outlined in **section 718** of the *Criminal Code*.

PURPOSES AND PRINCIPLES OF SENTENCING LAW

The principles and purposes of sentencing in Canada are codified in section 718 of the *Criminal Code*, but this has not always been the case. In *R. v. Arcand*, a five justice panel of the Alberta Court of Appeal wrote a lengthy judgment that canvased history and evolution of sentencing law in Canada. As the majority in *Arcand* wrote:

> The approach to sentencing in Canada is a product of this country's experience and history, and of steps taken – and not taken – through the years. It took almost 130 years from Confederation before Parliament codified, through Bill C-41, the purpose and principles of sentencing that courts must follow in imposing sanctions on offenders. As part of these sentencing reforms which came into effect in 1996 (collectively the "1996 Sentencing Reforms"), Parliament underscored how vital public confidence is to the authority of law. It accomplished this by providing in s. 718 of the *Criminal Code*[2] that the fundamental purpose of sentencing is "to contribute, along with crime prevention initiatives, to respect for the law and the maintenance of a just, peaceful and safe society". How is that purpose to be achieved? The answer is also found in s. 718 – "by imposing just sanctions" that have one or more of the objectives specified in the section...

> From the time Canada was created, the task of sentencing offenders fell, as it had in the motherland of the common law, England, to the judiciary. In 1892, Canada's first *Criminal Code* was adopted. Parliament carried forward into that *Code* the sentencing discretion in favour of trial judges. Parliament's general approach historically has been to define a crime broadly, covering a range of acts of varying degrees of seriousness, and provide for an equally broad

range of sentence left to the judge's discretion. Typically, it would prescribe no minimum sentence, only a maximum.

For many decades, Canadian trial judges were essentially on their own in sentencing offenders. Indeed, it was not until 1921 that courts of appeal were given the power to review fitness of sentence. Prior to that, the sentencing discretion exercised by trial judges was essentially unfettered. Courts of appeal could merely consider the technical legality of the sentence imposed...

Reform, when it came, was driven largely by dissatisfaction with unjustified disparities in sentencing. Inconsistent application of principles had been seen to produce inconsistent results, thereby attracting public concern about the perceived – and actual – unfairness of the criminal justice system. First to take up the challenge were the appeal courts. With a view to assuring fair and equal justice while maintaining flexibility in sentencing, some appeal courts adopted starting points or other guideline sentencing tools. (2010, paras 2, 19, 20, 22)

The majority in *Arcand* overviewed three large studies of sentencing practices in Canada, a white-paper published in 1982 (Canada, 1982), a report published in 1987 by a Royal Commission that had been appointed (Canada, 1987) and a 1988 report known as the *Daubney Report* (Canada, 1988). The Court in *Arcand* noted how these three reports led to reforms, culminating in the codification of purposes and principles of sentencing in the *Criminal Code*:

In response to these initiatives, Parliament decided to reform sentencing practices in a principled way. The 1996 Sentencing Reforms would be Parliament's first attempt to statutorily define – and confine – the scope of the courts' discretion in sentencing. But it would not be its last...

The 1996 Sentencing Reforms fundamentally reconfigured Part XXIII of the *Code* on sentencing. For the first time ever, in accordance with the recommendations of the *Sentencing Commission Report*, Parliament included in the *Code* an express statement of both the purpose and principles of sentencing. The legislative history and Parliamentary record confirm that one of Parliament's primary motivations was to provide a uniform approach to sentencing in Canada. Courts would henceforth be bound to serve the purpose, and apply the principles, of sentencing that Parliament prescribed. (1985, paras 27, 29)

The principles and purposes of sentencing were codified in section 718 of the *Criminal Code* which remains in force to this day. Since the coming into force of this section in 1996, Parliament has made various changes to section 718 and related sections, but the general structure and content remains similar to the version enacted in 1996.

The fundamental principle of sentencing, proportionality, is codified in s. 718.1 of the *Criminal Code*. A number of secondary principle are set out in section 718.2 of the *Criminal Code*. These include the principles of individualization, parity, restraint, totality and *Gladue* which are discussed below.

While the sentencing principles set forth in section 718 of the *Criminal Code* give guidance to judges, judges maintain a broad degree of discretion over sentencing. As the Supreme Court of Canada stated in *R. v. Ipeelee* "[t]he determination of a fit sentence is, subject to any specific statutory rules that have survived *Charter* scrutiny, a highly individualized process. Sentencing judges must have sufficient maneuverability to tailor sentences to the circumstances of the particular offence and the particular offender" (2012, para 38). The principles of sentencing do not operate in a hierarchy. As the Supreme Court explains in *Nasogaluak*:

No one sentencing objective trumps the others and it falls to the sentencing judge to determine which objective or objectives merit the greatest weight, given the particulars of the case. The relative importance of any mitigating or aggravating factors will then push the sentence up or down the scale of appropriate sentences for similar offences. The judge's discretion to decide on the particular blend of sentencing goals and the relevant aggravating or mitigating factors ensures that each case is decided on its facts, subject to the overarching guidelines and principles in the *Code* and in the case law. (2010, para 43)

While no objective of sentencing trumps any other, all sentences must follow the rule of proportionality. As the Supreme Court has stated, "[w]hatever weight a judge may wish to accord to the various objectives and other principles listed in the *Code*, the resulting sentence must respect the fundamental principle of proportionality" (*R v Ipeelee*, 2012, para 37).

Proportionality

The fundamental principle of sentencing is that of **proportionality**. Set out in section 718.1 of the *Criminal Code*, this principle dictates:

> A sentence must be proportionate to the gravity of the offence and the degree of responsibility of the offender.

While proportionality was codified as part of the 1996 amendments to the *Criminal Code*, it has been a central tenet of sentencing for much longer. As the Supreme Court stated:

> It is basic to any theory of punishment that the sentence imposed bear some relationship to the offence; it must be a "fit" sentence proportionate to the seriousness of the offence. Only if this is so can the public be satisfied that the offender "deserved" the punishment he received and feel a confidence in the fairness and rationality of the system. (*Re B.C. Motor Vehicle Act*, 1985, p. 533)

The Supreme Court has often described proportionality as "the *sine qua non* of a just sanction" (*R v Ipeelee*, 2012, para 37), meaning proportionality is absolutely essential and indispensable. The Court has also noted that proportionality "is intimately tied to the fundamental purpose of sentencing — the maintenance of a just, peaceful and safe society through the imposition of just sanctions" (para 37).

As the text of section 718.1 states, a sentence must be proportionate to 1) the gravity of the offence and 2) the degree of the responsibility of the offender. The gravity of the offence considers factors such as the harm caused by the offence, the potential for harm and the moral blameworthiness of the offender. The degree of the responsibility considers the role of the offender before the courts, such as whether they actually committed the offence or aided and abetted the offence.

In cases of an offender being sentenced for multiple crimes, proportionality expresses itself through the totality principle. Codified in section 718.2(*c*), totality states "where consecutive sentences are imposed, the combined sentence should not be unduly long or harsh." When an offender is being sentenced for multiple crimes, the sentence is not simply determined by passing an appropriate sentence for each individual offence and adding the totals together. As explained by Clayton Ruby in an oft-cited passage:

> A cumulative sentence may offend the totality principle if the aggregate sentence is substantially above the normal level of a sentence for the most serious of the individual offences involved, or if *its effect is to impose on the offender "a crushing sentence" not in keeping with his record and prospects* [emphasis added]. (Ruby, 1994, pp. 44-45)

The procedure for applying totality is to first determine whether the sentences should be served consecutively or not. In part this is determined by the transaction concept which asks whether there is a nexus to the offences, such as the offences being of the event or of the same nature. Ordinarily crimes that are part of the same transaction will receive concurrent sentences, but there are many exceptions to this. Where sentences are to be consecutive, the second step of applying totality is to determine the sentence for each offence. Totality is then applied to determine if the sentence is excessive, and if it is, the sentence is adjusted, sometimes significantly (*R v Draper*, 2010, para 30).

Mandatory Minimum Sentences

One of the most controversial, and high-profile issues in Canadian sentencing is the use of mandatory minimums. While mandatory minimum sentences have received heighted media attention and public scrutiny in recent years, they are far from a new sentencing tool. The first *Criminal Code*, enacted in 1892, carried six crimes with mandatory minimum sentences (Crutcher, 2001, p. 273). Over the next 100 years mandatory minimums remained relatively rare, but in the 1990s the Liberal government enacted numerous mandatory minimums for firearms offences. Mandatory minimums became a favoured legislative tool by the Conservative government during the "tough on crime era," with 51 mandatory minimum sentences added to the *Criminal Code* or amended to increase the punishment from 2005 until the Conservatives lost power (Bronskill, 2016).

Unlike many other jurisdictions, in Canada mandatory minimum sentences are truly mandatory. A judge must impose the minimum term of imprisonment unless they rule the provision is unconstitutional pursuant to the *Charter of Rights and Freedoms*. The *Charter* test sets a high threshold, requiring a court to answer in the affirmative that the mandatory minimum requires the judge to impose a sentence that is grossly disproportionate to a fit and proportionate sentence, which the Supreme Court has stated "is aimed at punishments that are more than merely excessive" (*R v Smith*, 1987, p. 1072).

Mandatory minimum sentences can place judges at odds in sentencing. As McLachlin CJC wrote in *R. v. Nur*:

> Mandatory minimum sentences, by their very nature, have the potential to depart from the principle of proportionality in sentencing. They emphasize denunciation, general deterrence and retribution at the expense of what is a fit sentence for the gravity of the offence, the blameworthiness of the offender, and the harm caused by the crime. **They function as a blunt instrument that may deprive courts of the ability to tailor proportionate sentences at the lower end of a sentencing range.** (2015, para 44. Emphasis added)

The Supreme Court has struck down four mandatory minimum sentences:

- In 1987, a 7-year mandatory minimum for importing narcotics into Canada (*R v Smith*, 1987);
- In 2015, a 3-year mandatory minimum for possession of a prohibited firearm that is loaded or has readily accessible ammunition for a first offence (*R v Nur*, 2015);
- In 2015, a 5-year mandatory minimum for possession of a prohibited firearm that is loaded or has readily accessible ammunition for a second of subsequent offence (*R v Nur*, 2015);
- In 2016, a 1-year mandatory minimum for possession of controlled substance for purposes of trafficking where the offender has been convicted of any drug offence except possession in the previous 10-years (*R v Lloyd*, 2016).

The Court has also upheld numerous mandatory minimums, including:

- In 1990, life with no parole eligibility for 25 years for first degree murder. At the time of this sentencing the offender was eligible to apply for early release after 15 years, a key factor in the courts decision. The removal of the faint hope clause may open the door to a further challenge to this minimum (*R v Luxton*, 1990);

- In 2000, four years for criminal negligence causing death with a firearm (*R v Morrisey*, 2000);
- In 2001, life with no parole eligibility for 10 years for second degree murder (*R v Latimer*, 2001);
- In 2008, four years for manslaughter when committed with a firearm (*R v Ferguson*, 2008).

Lower courts have also considered mandatory minimum sentences, with several having been struck down by various courts across Canada.

Maximum Punishments

All *Criminal Code* offences have a maximum sentence. Section 718(1) of the *Criminal Code* dictates for summary conviction offences, the maximum punishment is a $5,000 fine and/or six months in jail, unless otherwise stated. Some summary offences have longer maximum sentencing, such as impaired driving which has a max of 18 months set forward in s. 255(1)(c) of the *Criminal Code.*

Box 3.1 – Maximum Sentences for Indictable Offences

Two Years	Five Years	Ten Years	Fourteen Years	Life
Taking part in a riot (s. 65(1)).	Possession of a forged passport (s. 57(3)).	Possession of a prohibited weapon (s. 92(3)).	Forgery of a passport (s. 57(ii)).	Street racing causing death (s. 249.2).
Duelling (s. 71).	Pointing a firearm (s. 86(3)(ii)).	Prison breach (s. 144).	Bribery of a judicial officer (s. 119(1).	Murder in the first or second degree (s. 253)(1)).
Failing to comply with an appearance notice (s. 145 (5)(a)).	Sexual exploitation of a person with a disability (s. 153.1(1)).	Bestiality (s. 160(1).	Street racing causing bodily harm (s. 249(3)).	Kidnapping (s. 279)(1)).
Spreading false news (s. 181).	Impaired/Over .08 Driving (s. 255(1)(b)).	Assault with a weapon causing bodily harm (s. 267(b).	Aggravated assault (s. 268(2)).	Stopping the mail with intent to rob (s. 345).

For indictable offences, the *Criminal Code* specifies a maximum of either 2, 5, 10, 14 years or life in prison (see Box 3.1). It was previously stated that the maximum sentence should only be given to the "worst offender who committed the worst offence." The Supreme Court has laid the "worst offender, worst offence" principle to rest, instead preferring proper application of other sentencing principles to determine whether the maximum sentence should be given (*R v Solowan*, 2008, para 3). It is rare to see an offender receive the maximum punishment, expect in cases of murder where the maximum and minimum sentence are the same – life in prison.

Denunciation and Deterrence

Section 718(*a*) of the *Criminal Code* states on objective of sentencing is "to denounce unlawful conduct and the harm done to victims or to the community that is caused by unlawful conduct." The Supreme Court has stated that **denunciation** is "a symbolic, collective statement that the offender's conduct should be punished for encroaching on our society's basic code of values" (*R v M (CA)*, 1996, para 81) and the communication of society's condemnation of the offender's conduct" (*R v Proulx*, 2000, para 102). Denunciation is typically linked with the principle of deterrence as both principles typically call for harsher sanctions to be imposed on an offence.

Section 718(*b*) of the *Criminal Code* states the principle of **deterrence** states should be used "to deter the offender and other persons from committing offences." As the Supreme Court explains "[d]eterrence, as a principle of sentencing, refers to the imposition of a sanction for the purpose of discouraging the offender and others from engaging in criminal conduct" (*R v BWP*, 2006, para 2). There are two forms of deterrence, specific deterrence and general deterrence. Specific deterrence is aimed at the offender before the court, while general deterrence is aimed at deterring other members of the public from offending.

The *Criminal Code* specifies that when offences involve the abuse of a child under 18 (1985, s. 718.01), certain crimes against police officers or other justice system participants (s. 718.01), or killing or injuring police or military animals the principles of denunciation and deterrence shall receive "primary consideration."

While denunciation and deterrence are factors a judge considers when imposing a sentence, you can see in other chapters that these principles are not the focus of most corrections practice. While correctional officers enforce security procedures within a correctional centre, it is not their function to punish prisoners. They are to maintain a humane environment. Probation and parole officers enforce conditions of the courts or a parole board, but in cases of non-compliance, they do not proactively breach or suspend offenders for punitive reasons. That said, it may be that actions by corrections agents can be perceived as punishment by offenders caught up in the corrections systems (see Chapter 8).

Rehabilitation

Section 718(*d*) of the *Criminal Code* states sentencing should "assist in rehabilitating offenders." As the Supreme Court stated, "[r]ehabilitation is one of the fundamental moral values that distinguish Canadian society from the societies of many other nations in the world, and it helps the courts impose sentences that are just and appropriate" (*R v Lacasse*, 2015, para 4).

Rehabilitation gains larger attention when dealing with youthful offenders. As the Nova Scotia Court of Appeal states "[t]here is ample authority for the proposition that sentences for youthful offenders should be directed at rehabilitation and reformation, not general deterrence…. This is common sense. A youthful offender… who has an interest in a vocation and can be equipped with the tools to earn an honest living, is more likely to be diverted from a life of crime than would a career criminal"

(*R v Bratzer*, 2001, para 40). Rehabilitation is closely allied with the objective of restraint (*R v Moriarty*, 2016).

Reparations and Restraint

A series of restorative sentencing principles are codified in sections 718 (*e*) and (*f*) as well as 718.2 (*d*) and (*e*) of the *Criminal Code*.

In *R. v. Gladue*, the Supreme Court noted that while some of the s. 718 principles were a codification of existing practices, ss. 718 (*d*), (*e*) and (*f*) are new and underpinned by a restorative approach to justice. The Court states:

> as a general matter restorative justice involves some form of restitution and reintegration into the community. The need for offenders to take responsibility for their actions is central to the sentencing process.... Restorative sentencing goals do not usually correlate with the use of prison as a sanction [citations omitted]. (1999, para 43)

The principles of restraint must be read in light of other sentencing principles. In *R. v. Proulx*, the Supreme Court stated that restraint from incarceration is important, but alternatives to imprisonment must be reasonable and appropriate (2000, para 96).

Gladue

Section 718.2(*e*) is one of the most misunderstood sentencing principles of the *Criminal Code*. Section 718.2(*e*) was enacted in light of the plight of over-incarceration of First Nations in Canada. As the Court in *R. v. Gladue* wrote in 1999, "[i]n the mid-1980s, aboriginal people were about 2 percent of the population of Canada, yet they made up 10 percent of the penitentiary population. In Manitoba and Saskatchewan, aboriginal people constituted something between 6 and 7 percent of the population, yet in Manitoba they represented 46 percent of the provincial admissions and in Saskatchewan 60 percent" (para 58).

The ***Gladue*** principle, as it became known, was designed to help to address this issue, which stems from a legacy of colonialism. As the Court stated:

> The background factors which figure prominently in the causation of crime by aboriginal offenders are by now well known. Years of dislocation and economic development have translated, for many aboriginal peoples, into low incomes, high unemployment, lack of opportunities and options, lack or irrelevance of education, substance abuse, loneliness, and community fragmentation. (1999, para 67)

The Court notes that as factors such as employment and education reduce an offender's chance or length of incarceration, and systemic background issues facing First Nations make them more prone to being incarcerated. These and other factors contribute to a higher incidence of crime and incarceration.

The *Glaude* principle was revisited by the Supreme Court over a decade later in the 2012 decision of *R. v. Ipeellee*. The Court noted that cautious optimism arising from *Gladue* has not borne out in practice, noting that from 1996 to 2001, the general prison population fell 22% while Aboriginal admissions increased 3%. Furthermore, when *Glaude* was decided in 1999 First Nations made up 12% of federal inmates, a number that increased to 17% in 2005 (*R v Ipeelee*, 2012, para 62).

In *Ipeelee* the Supreme Court addressed three interrelated criticisms of the *Gladue* decision, these being "(1) sentencing is not an appropriate means of addressing overrepresentation; (2) the *Gladue*

Box 3.2 – Misconceptions of *Gladue*

To see public misconceptions of the *Gladue* principle, all one needs to do is find a news article online involving the sentencing of a First Nations offender and read the public comments. A 2018 article published in the Winnipeg Free Press discussing a First Nations offender who was sentenced to life with no parole for 15 years for a second degree murder provides an example of typical comments seen in public debates about sentencing across Canada.

Reader comments on this article, written by four separate readers, include:

Reader 1: I dont [*sic*] agree that there should be consideration for indigenous life circumstances ... a murderer is murderer and not worth the air he breaths.

Reader 2: This gladue [*sic*] consideration is biased by race . [*sic*] You do the crime you do the time. One court system for all.

Reader 3: Gladue...what a crock!

Reader 4: Toews [the sentencing judge, Mr. Justice Vic Toews, (who coincidently was a Federal MP and Justice Minister during part of the "Tough on Crime" era)] said he decided on 15 years after considering Ryle's background and life circumstances. If not for the Gladue factors courts are legally bound to take into consideration for Indigenous offenders, Toews said he would have increased the parole ineligibility. Seems clear use of race to lessen sentence [*sic*].

These comments, which are similar to what can be found in most news articles across Canada relating to a First Nations offender, misunderstandings of section 718.2(e) highlighted by the Supreme Court in *Ipeellee*.

principles provide what is essentially a race-based discount for Aboriginal offenders; and (3) providing special treatment and lesser sentences to Aboriginal offenders is inherently unfair as it creates unjustified distinctions between offenders who are similarly situated, thus violating the principle of sentence parity" (2012, para 64). The Court found these critiques a fundamental misunderstanding of *Glaude*.

Regarding the first criticism, the court noted while sentencing may not be the sole or even primary matter of addressing overrepresentation, "that does not detract from a judge's fundamental duty to fashion a sentence that is fit and proper in the circumstances of the offence, the offender, and the victim" (*R v Ipeelee*, 2012, para 69) and "judges can ensure that systemic factors do not lead inadvertently to discrimination in sentencing" (para 67).

Regarding critics of a race-based discount, the Court stated:

This critique ignores the distinct history of Aboriginal peoples in Canada. The overwhelming message emanating from the various reports and commissions on Aboriginal peoples' involvement in the criminal justice system is that current levels of criminality are intimately tied to the legacy of colonialism.... Furthermore, there is nothing in the *Gladue* decision which would indicate that background and systemic factors should not also be taken into account for other, non-Aboriginal offenders. [citations omitted]. (para 77)

Finally, addressing concerns that *Gladue* violates the principle of parity, the court stated "[n]o two offenders will come before the courts with the same background and experiences.... To the extent that *Gladue* will lead to different sanctions for Aboriginal offenders, those sanctions will be justified based on their unique circumstances – circumstances which are rationally related to the sentencing process" (para 79).

Parity

The principle of **parity** states that "a sentence should be similar to sentences imposed on similar offenders for similar offences committed in similar circumstances" (*Criminal Code*, 1985, s. 718.2(b)). This has two main components, parity among similar offenders, and parity among co-accused.

The principle of parity addresses one of the five sentencing truths discussed by the Alberta Court of Appeal in *Arcand*, where the Court stated "[t]he proposition that if judges knew the facts of a given case, they would all agree, or substantially agree on the result, is simply not so" (2010, para 8). However, given the vast array of circumstances to be considered at sentencing, parity may at times give way to a call for individualization, and sentences that appear disparate are explainable. As the Supreme Court stated in *R. v. Lacasse*:

> although ensuring parity in sentencing is in itself a desirable objective, the fact that each crime is committed in unique circumstances by an offender with a unique profile cannot be disregarded. The determination of a just and appropriate sentence is a highly individualized exercise that goes beyond a purely mathematical calculation. It involves a variety of factors that are difficult to define with precision. (2015, para 58)

Both the judiciary and legislature have taken steps to bring sentences into greater parity. Starting points and sentencing ranges are two judicial tools used for sentencing parity. Parliament has also enacted mandatory minimum sentences that are used in part to promote parity.

Starting points are set by an appellate court to give judges in the relevant province an idea of the minimum sentence a typical offender should receive for a certain offender. Sentencing ranges operate similarly, giving a defined range. Starting points and ranges are not binding, judges may still go above or below the range depending on the circumstances of the offence. The Supreme Court has stated:

> Sentencing ranges are nothing more than summaries of the minimum and maximum sentences imposed in the past, which serve in any given case as guides for the application of all the relevant principles and objectives. However, they should not be considered "averages", let alone straitjackets, but should instead be seen as historical portraits for the use of sentencing judges, who must still exercise their discretion in each case. (*R v Lacasse*, 2015, para 57)

Both starting points and ranges are typically articulated by a Court of Appeal. Rules of *stare decisis* makes this range only directly applicable in the province where it was set, although it may be influential elsewhere. The Manitoba Court of Appeal discussed sentencing ranges in the case of *R v Burnett*. The Court had previously stated "absent exceptional circumstances, someone who breaks into another's home once should generally expect a sentence in the range of two years" (*R v Burnett*, 2017, para 11). The Court expanded on this range and set a general range of 30 months for breaking into a house and stealing a restricted firearm and three years for a break and enter with a theft of a firearm (para 15). Both ranges assume "a mature offender pleading guilty with no record and prior good character" (para 15). Sentences would be higher for offenders with criminal history or who lose the mitigation of a guilty plea. Likewise, aggravating factors such as subsequent use of the firearm in a violent crime, connection with a criminal organization or use of violence in the break and enter would be aggravating but are not considered in the range; offences with these characteristics would call for a sentence at the top-end or even exceeding the range.

Aggravating and Mitigating Factors

Section 718.2(a) states that "a sentence should be increased or reduced to account for any relevant aggravating or mitigating circumstances relating to the offence or the offender, and, without limiting the generality of the foregoing."

Aggravating factors are circumstances that increase the gravity of the crime and call for harsher sanctions to be imposed. The Crown must prove aggravating facts beyond a reasonable doubt.

There are a number of statutory aggravating factors, and further aggravating factors can be found in the common law. Aggravating factors listed in section 718.2 of the *Criminal Code* include:

- evidence that the offence was motivated by bias, prejudice or hate based on race, national or ethnic origin, language, colour, religion, sex, age, mental or physical disability, sexual orientation, or gender identity or expression, or on any other similar factor;
- abuse of a spouse, common law- partner, person under 18 years of age or abuse of a position of trust;
- commission of a terrorist offence or offence for a criminal organization;
- an offence committed while subject to a conditional sentence, or while on parole, statutory release or unescorted temporary absence.

Section 10(2) of the *Controlled Drugs and Substances Act* also lists a number of aggravating factors that apply to crimes under the purview of that statute. These include:

- if the offender carried, used or threatened to use a weapon;
- if the offender used or threatened to use violence;
- trafficking near a school or public place frequented by those under 18;
- using a person under 18 to commit or be involved in the offence.

The common law has additional aggravating factors, common examples being:

- previous criminal record, especially when recent, related and demonstrates escalating criminality;
- actual or threatened use of violence or a weapon;
- substantial planning and organization of the offence.

Box 3.3 – Common Factors for Sentencing

Mitigating	Neutral	Aggravating
• Guilty plea • No prior record • Remorse and rehabilitation • Positive community engagement (social, education and employment)	• Not pleading guilty • Not cooperating with authorities • No evidence or remorse	• Motived by hate or bias • Abuse of trust or romantic partner • Use of violence or weapons • Prior record, especially when recent and related

Mitigating factors call for less severe sanctions to be imposed. The defence must prove mitigating factors on a balance of probabilities. Some common mitigating factors include:

- no previous record;
- youthful offender;
- guilty plea;
- prior good character, including employment history;
- rehabilitative efforts.

Guilty pleas are mitigating for several reasons. First, they are a way to demonstrate remorse, save judicial resources and spare victims from having to testify. The earlier a guilty plea is entered, the more mitigating its effect can be. An accused who pleads guilty on the eve of the trial where the state has clear and concrete evidence will receive limited, if any, mitigation based on this late guilty plea.

There is no consensus as to when an offender is no longer youthful, as this concept refers to not only age but also maturity (*R v Priest*, 1996, para 21). Allan Manson writes that as a general rule, those 18-25 will be youthful (2001, p. 106).

There are several factors that should be treated as neutral factors (see Box 3.2). A lack of a guilty plea is neutral, given that accused have a constitutional right to a fair trial. As a guilty plea typically indicates remorse, the lack of remorse is neutral, otherwise anyone who contested their charge would receive aggravation to sentencing. Likewise, given accused have various protections such as rights against self-incrimination, failing to cooperate with authorities is a neutral factor. This does not extend to failing to comply with lawful demands, such as interfering with the lawful execution of a search warrant or resisting a lawful arrest which may themselves lead to further criminal charges, but failing to provide a statement to the police or otherwise self-incriminate is not aggravating for the purposes of sentencing.

SENTENCING OPTIONS

The sentencing factors discussed above help guide the judge in picking the appropriate sanctions to place on the accused. Judges are also guided by legislation and precedent. When legislation prescribes a mandatory minimum sentence, judges must impose incarceration of at least that length. As noted, starting points or ranges also give a judge guidance in setting a sentence.

Alternative Measures

Alternative measures serve as a substitute to the formal sentencing process in Canada. Section 717 of the *Criminal Code* permits alternative measures when "not inconsistent with protection of society" and several conditions are met, including that the measure be part of an authorized program, the offender "fully and freely consents to participate" and accepts responsibility for the offence. Alternative measures are typically used in minor crimes such as common assaults, mischief, theft and simple possession of small amounts of narcotics. Alternative measures are aimed at first time offenders or those who have significant gaps in their criminal record. On successful completion of the alternative measure, the charge is withdrawn, resulting in no criminal record.

Alternative measures may be administered as part of the regular court process or may be part of a problem solving or therapeutic court. Common forms of problem solving courts include Domestic Violence Courts, Drug Treatment Courts, Mental Health Courts, and First Nations Courts (see Chapter 4).

Alternative measures are also permitted for drug offences pursuant to section 10(4) of the *Controlled Drugs and Substances Act*. One unique feature of the drug treatment court provision is that where an offender successfully completes a drug treatment court program, the court is not required to impose the mandatory minimum sentence.

Discharges

A discharge is the lowest form of adult sentence a court can impose, allowing an offender to not only avoid incarceration but also avoid having a criminal record. With an **absolute discharge**, the offender is found guilty but a conviction is not registered. **Conditional discharges** are similar to absolute discharges, the primary difference being that an offender is placed on probation for a period of time up to three years and is not discharged until completing probation.

Discharges are registered on the National Criminal Records Repository, more commonly known as CPIC (Canadian Police Information Centre), a central database storing information on criminal records, stolen property and individuals wanted by the police. Discharges are stored on CPIC for a period of 1-3 years depending if the discharged is absolute or conditional.

The legal requirements of a discharge are that:

1) The offence does not carry a minimum punishment;
2) The maximum sentence is less than 14 years;
3) The discharge be in the best interest of the accused;
4) The discharge is not contrary to the public interest.

In *R. v. M. (B.J.)*, the Alberta Court of Appeal discussed factors to be considered in the exercise of granting discharges, including:

- the nature of the offence;
- the prevalence of the particular offence as it may exist in the community from time to time;
- whether an accused stood to make some personal gain at the expense of others, as distinct from some activity which might be in the nature of a prank or in respect of which his motives were other than self-interest;
- where the offence is relating to property, as here, the value of the property destroyed or stolen must be relevant. The theft of a ball-point pen would not ordinarily be regarded as seriously as the theft of a colour television set;
- whether the crime was committed as a matter of impulse, and in the face of unexpected opportunity, or whether it was calculated;
- whether the circumstance that an accused has committed the offence is something which should be a matter of record so that members of the public may have the opportunity of being aware of the fact that that accused had committed the offence in question. (1976, paras 15-20)

Absolute discharges are often reserved for first-time offenders who have committed minor offences. Sometimes personal circumstances of an offender can also weigh in favour of an absolute discharge. In *R. v. Cormier-Ohalloran*, a 2013 decision of the Alberta Provincial Court, a 21-year old who suffered a significant brain injury was charged with assault of his care workers. The Crown sought a 1-year suspended sentence while the defence sought a discharge. While the offences were serious, the fact the offender was young and had reduced culpability due to his brain injury led the sentencing judge to order an absolute discharge.

A conditional discharge was imposed in the case of *R. v. Bertuzzi* (2004). In this case, Todd Bertuzzi, then a professional hockey player for the Vancouver Canucks, pled guilty to assault causing bodily harm for an on-ice attack of Steve Moore, a player for the Colorado Avalanche. Given Bertuzzi's age, 29, requirement of international travel in his career, the sentencing judge found it was in his best interests to receive a discharge. The sentencing judge considered Bertuzzi's lengthy suspension from professional hockey, financially costing him over $500,000, as well as opportunities to play international competitions, as meeting the objectives of both specific and general deterrence, and found the discharge was not contrary to the public interest. Ultimately Bertuzzi was given a conditional discharge with a one-year probation order that included 80 hours of community service.

Probation

The most commonly imposed sentence in Canada is **probation**, which was imposed in 42.9% of cases with a guilty verdict in 2015/16 (94,505 of 220, 233 cases). As noted above, probation orders are given as part of conditional discharges. Probation orders can also be given on their own, which is known as a suspended sentence. An offender may also receive a fine plus probation, or incarceration up to two years accompanied with a probation order. The "two out of three rule" dictates that an offender cannot be given prison, probation and a fine, they can only receive two of these punishments in any given sentence. This rule comes from the wording of s. 731(1)(*b*) of the *Criminal Code* that states "in addition to fining or sentencing the offender to imprisonment for a term not exceeding two years, direct that the offender comply with the conditions prescribed in a probation order."

Probation orders are a rehabilitative sentencing tool. As the Saskatchewan Court of Appeal stated, in a passage later endorsed by the Supreme Court "the innate character of a probation order is such that it seeks to influence the future behaviour of the offender" (*R v WBT*, 1997, para 30). The Court went on to state that a probation order:

> seeks to secure "the good conduct" of the offender and to deter him from committing other offences. It does not particularly seek to reflect the seriousness of the offence or the offender's degree of culpability. Nor does it particularly seek to fill the need for denunciation of the offence or the general deterrence of others to commit the same or other offences. Depending upon the specific conditions of the order there may well be a punitive aspect to a probation order but punishment is not the dominant or an inherent purpose. (para 30)

While typically attached to a provincial prison sentence, a probation order can be attached to a federal sentence if the offender is given exactly two years in custody, calculated by the go forward sentence (*R v Black*, 2014, para 23).

Suspended Sentence

A suspended sentence is similar to a conditional discharge, with the key difference being that the offender does receive a criminal record when given a suspended sentence. With a suspended sentence, an offender is placed on a probation order for up to three years.

Section 731(a) of the *Criminal Code* notes that when contemplating a suspended sentence the judge must consider "the age and character of the offender, the nature of the offence and the circumstances surrounding its commission." Suspended sentences cannot be given for an offence with a minimum sentence. As the British Columbia Court of Appeal explained:

> If an offender who is on probation is convicted of an offence, the suspension of the sentence may be revoked and the offender may be brought back before the court for sentencing. At that point, the judge may impose any sentence that could have been imposed at the time the sentence was suspended. (*R v Voong*, 2015, para 19)

The Court stated that "[b]ecause a breach of the probation order can result in a revocation and sentencing on the original offence, it has been referred to as the '*Sword of Damocles*' hanging over the offender's head" (para 39). However, in most cases when a probationer is charged with a breach, they are sentenced for the breach as a stand-alone incident, including new criminal charges that formed the basis for the breach, rather than being re-sentenced for the predicate offence.

A suspended sentence with three years of probation was given in the case of *R. v. Rushton* to an 18-year-old offender who pled guilty to possession of methamphetamines, possession of cocaine and cannabis for the purposes of trafficking and failure to comply with a youth sentence. The Crown sought a sentence of 2 years incarceration. The judge considered mental health issues and drug addiction of the accused and "a dramatic turnaround since his arrest" (2017, para 23) including volunteering in the community, positive employment and several letters of support. While the principle of parity directed a federal penitentiary sentence for a hard drug trafficker, based on a number of mitigating factors the judge elected to pass a suspended sentence. The judge noted while incarceration may serve as a deterrent in the short term, the suspended sentence gives meaningful incentive for the offence to continue his rehabilitation and if he does not he can be brought back for re-sentencing. Therefore, the suspended sentence "can provide deterrence and denunciation without interfering with all of Mr. Rushton's accomplishments toward rehabilitation" (para 100).

Fine

Section 734 of the *Criminal Code* grants judges the discretion to impose a fine on an offender. For offences that do not include a minimum term of imprisonment, judges may impose a fine "in addition to or in lieu of any other sanction a court is authorized to impose" (1985, s. 734(1)(a)). For offences with a minimum punishment of imprisonment, judges may impose a fine in addition to other sanctions, but not in lieu of the imprisonment; this power remains subject to the "two-out-of-three rule" where judges cannot impose prison, a fine and probation on the same offender as part of the same sentence. Statistically, fines are a common sentencing option, being imposed in 32% of cases where a guilty verdict was made in 2015/16 (69, 842 of 220, 233) (Statistics Canada, 2018).

Some offences carry a minimum fine. One of the most commonly imposed mandatory fines comes from section 255(1)(a)(i) of the *Criminal Code* which imposes a minimum fine of $1,000 for a first offence of impaired driving or driving while over .08. When a minimum fine is required by law, the judge must impose a fine of this amount regardless of the offender's ability to pay. Where no minimum fine is included, the judge can only impose a fine if satisfied the offender is able to pay or discharge the fine under a fine option program which is offered in several provinces.

The judge can set out the time or time by which the fine, or portions of the fine, must be paid. If an offender defaults on payment of the fine, imprisonment is imposed. The length of imprisonment is determined by a mathematical equation set forward in s. 734(5) of the *Criminal Code*. In effect, this section calculates prison as a result of an unpaid fine as: **Amount of unpaid fine/(provincial minimum wage x 8)**. For example, an offender is fined $800 and fails to pay any of this fine by the specific date, the numerator is therefore $800. Suppose the provincial minimum wage where the fine was imposed is $10/hr. The denominator is therefore 80 (10x8) The fine is therefore converted into a sentence of 10 days incarceration ($800/80). The maximum term of imprisonment that can be imposed for default of a fine is six months in the case of a summary conviction offence and 5 years in the case of an indictable offence (*Criminal Code*, 1985, s. 734(5)(b)).

CUSTODIAL SENTENCES

Conditional Sentences

Conditional sentences of imprisonment are a relatively new sentencing option, brought forward as part of the sentencing amendments enacted in 1996, with the Supreme Court stating this option was "clear message to all Canadian judges that too many people are being sent to prison" (*R v Proulx*, 2000, para 1). Since that time, Parliament has placed an increasing set of restrictions on the availability of conditional sentences.

While technically classified as a form of custodial sentence, offenders given conditional sentences can avoid incarceration in a custodial setting if they abide by the terms of their conditional sentence. In common parlance, a conditional sentence may be seen as house arrest.

While a conditional sentence may on its face appear very similar to a probation order, there are several key distinctions. While probation is generally seen as a rehabilitative sentencing tool, conditional sentences are designed to address "both punitive and rehabilitative objectives" (*R v Proulx*, 2000, para 23) of sentencing. Conditional sentences have a greater number of compulsory conditions than probation orders, and a judge can mandate treatment without the consent of the offender with a conditional sentence. While probation orders should not have conditions that were imposed as a form of punishment, the Supreme Court of Canada has made it clear that "conditional sentences should generally include punitive conditions that are restrictive of the offender's liberty" (*R v Proulx*, 2000, para 23) stating "[c]onditions such as house arrest or strict curfews should be the norm, not the exception" (para 36).

At the time conditional sentences were first enacted, judges could impose a conditional sentence when four criteria were met:

1) the offence not punishable by a mandatory minimum;
2) the court must impose a term of imprisonment of less than 2 years;
3) the safety of the community would not be endangered by having the offender serve their sentence in the community; and
4) a conditional sentence would be consistent with the fundamental purpose and principles of sentencing.

Since that time, Parliament has placed increasing restrictions on the availability of conditional sentences. Conditional sentences must now meet three additional criteria:

5) the offence cannot be an indictable offence punishable by a maximum sentence of 14 years or life;
6) the offence, when prosecuted by indictment, cannot have a maximum of 10 years or more if the offence is a terrorism or criminal organization offence, resulted in bodily harm, involved the import, export, trafficking or production of drugs or involved the use of weapon;
7) the offence is one of 11 offences listed in 742.1(f) of the *Criminal Code* when prosecuted by indictment (offences in this section include sexual assault, kidnapping, motor vehicle theft, and theft over $5,000).

The ever-increasing restrictions on the use of conditional sentences has led to a decline in their use as a sentencing option. In 2011/2012, 11,830 offenders received a conditional sentence, representing 4.7% of all sentences imposed. In 2015/16, only 8,022 conditional sentences were imposed, representing 3.6% of all cases.

Intermittent Sentences

Intermittent sentences are available pursuant to criteria set forward in s. 732 of the *Criminal Code*. Intermittent sentences are only available when a court imposes a prison sentence of ninety (90) days or less.

Intermittent sentences allow offenders to serve their sentence at times specified in the order, typically on weekends. This allows an offender to keep community ties such as employment and family relations while serving a period of incarceration.

While intermittent sentences are attractive to a judge imposing a sentence and the offender, correctional facilities have difficulties accommodating intermittent sentences. As inmates serving intermittent sentences continually move back and forth between custody and their ordinary lives, they may become a source for contraband to enter correctional facilities (Québec Ombudsman, 2018, p. 15). Further, intermittent sentences may lead to over-crowding, inter-facility transfers which in turn leads to more strip searches (Québec Ombudsman, 2018, p. 14).

Offenders receive credit towards their sentence only for days when they are in custody. When not in custody, offenders abide by terms of a probation order. Under a typical intermittent sentence, an offender may enter the custodial facility Friday evening and be released Sunday afternoon, getting credit for three days of their sentence, plus 1.5 days of statutory remission. For an offender able to serve three days over a week, a 90-day intermittent sentence would take 20 weekends, or approximately 5 months to serve. The extended period of punishment may be unpleasant for an offender who wishes to get their punishment over with. The *Criminal Code* allows an offender to apply to the court to convert their intermittent sentence into a consecutive sentence (1985, s. 732(2)).

Provincial and Federal Prison Sentences

When an offender is sentenced to imprisonment, the length of sentence determines whether they will serve their sentence in a provincial prison or federal penitentiary. Judges do not have the power to dictate what custodial facility an offender will serve their sentence in, but may make a recommendation in this regard, for example, suggesting the offender should be incarcerated in a facility offering mental health treatment. Offenders in provincial prisons are eligible for statutory remission and can be released after serving two-thirds of their sentence.

Offenders sentenced to a life sentence or a sentence of two years or more serve their sentence in a federal penitentiary (*Criminal Code*, 1985, ss. 734.1(1)(a), 734.1(1)(b)). Offenders sentenced to a sentence of under two years serve their sentence in a provincial prison. This is why a sentence of "two-years less a day" or "a deuce less" may be imposed by a judge who seeks to keep an offender out of the federal system. As noted, the go forward sentence is used to determine whether a sentence is below or above two years. A judge may sentence an offender to over two years in prison, but if credit for remand time reduces the go forward sentence under two years the locus of confinement will be a provincial prison.

Fixed Parole Eligibility

Most offenders serving a sentence in a federal penitentiary will have a fixed parole eligibility date. In most cases offenders are eligible for day parole once they have served "one half of the portion of the sentence that must be served before full parole may be granted" (*Corrections and Conditional Release Act*, 1992, s. 119(1)(d)) although this is subject to numerous exceptions (see Chapter 10).

Ordinarily, offenders are eligible for full parole at the lesser of one third of their sentence or 7 years. Therefore, an offender sentenced to 12 years in a federal penitentiary will be eligible for full parole after 4 years, an offender sentenced to 21 years of more will be eligible for full parole after 7 years. Again, there are multiple exceptions to these general rules.

Dangerous and Long-Term Offenders

Part XXIX of the *Criminal Code* outlines provisions for dangerous and long-term offenders. Long-term offender orders allow courts to impose community-based supervision on an offender for a period of up to 10 years following their release from custody. The Supreme Court has noted long-term offender orders have two objectives: "(1) protecting the public from the risk of reoffence, and (2) rehabilitating the offender and reintegrating him or her into the community" (*R v Ipeelee*, 2012, para 48). Dangerous offender orders allow for indefinite incarceration.

An application for a dangerous or long-term offence can be made when an offender is convicted of a serious personal injury offence that is a designated offence, and the offender has been convicted twice prior of designated offences and received a sentence of two years or greater for each conviction (*Criminal Code*, 1985, s. 752.01). There is a lengthy list of designated offences that include sex offences such as sexual interference and incest, and violent offences such as attempted murder and assault with a weapon. Once an application is made, the offender is remanded for assessment for up to 60 days.

Section 753.1(1) allows long-term offender orders to be imposed on offenders meeting specified conditions if the court is satisfied of three conditions:

(a) it would be appropriate to impose a sentence of imprisonment of two years or more for the offence for which the offender has been convicted;
(b) there is a substantial risk that the offender will reoffend; and
(c) there is a reasonable possibility of eventual control of the risk in the community.

Long-term offenders are incarcerated for the imposed sentence and supervised in the community for up to 10 years after. Their release may be suspended if an offender breaches a condition or a suspension is necessary to prevent a breach of a condition or protect society (*Criminal Code*, 1985, s. 135.1(1)). Offenders are placed in a federal penitentiary during the duration of their suspension.

Dangerous offender status can be ordered when a court is satisfied the offender shows a failure to restrain behaviour and likelihood to cause serious injury to another, indifference to consequences of future actions or is unlikely to be inhibited by normal standards of behavioural restraint or shows a failure to control sexual impulses and there is a likelihood of causing harm due to this. Persons declared dangerous offenders may apply for parole after 7 years of their sentence and every 2 years thereafter, but release is rare.

Life Sentence

The harshest maximum punishment available in the *Criminal Code* is life imprisonment. Offenders sentenced to life imprisonment remain eligible for parole, but if paroled will remain under the supervision of Correctional Services Canada their entire life. Where an offender is convicted of second degree murder, the judge will set parole ineligibility at between 10 and 25 years. For first degree murder, offenders are not eligible for parole for 25 years. Under the faint hope clause, convicted murderers can apply for a reduction of parole ineligibility after 15 years. The faint hope clause is not available for multiple murders, or a case of a single murder where the offence occurred on or after December 2nd, 2011.

The *Protecting Canadians by Ending Sentence Discounts for Multiple Murders Act* is a new sentencing provision and also applies to crimes committed on or after December 2nd, 2011. This law gives sentencing judges the discretionary power to make parole ineligibility consecutive in cases of multiple murder. Therefore, an offender convicted of three murders could face up to 75 years in prison before being eligible for parole. While some judges have taken the view this power should be used sparingly and offenders should be left with a hope, but not a guarantee, of eventual release, other judges have used this power to create sentences that amount to life with no possibly or release. At least eight offenders have been sentenced under this law to parole ineligibility periods of 50 (*R v Millard*, 2008; *R v Kahsai*, 2018; see also Hixt, 2018), 70 (*R v Borutski*, 2017), and 75 years (*R v Bourque*, 2014; *R v Garland*, 2017; *R v Ostamas*, 2015; *R v Saretzky*, 2017).

Corollary Orders

A sentence may also include one or more corollary orders in addition to the main punishment imposed. These corollary orders may include prohibition from possession firearms and/or other weapons, requirement to provide a DNA sample or register as a sex offender, forfeiture of crime related property and driving prohibitions.

There are times when the *Criminal Code* requires a judge to impose a certain corollary order and other times it is discretionary. For example, section 109 of the *Criminal Code* imposes a mandatory firearms prohibition order for a number of circumstances, including:

- An indictable offence where violence was used, threatened or attempted and the maximum sentence is 10 years or more;
- An indictable offence where violence was used threatened or attempted against a current or former intimate partner, a child or parent of an intimate partner or anyone in their residence;
- Certain weapons offences including using firearms in an offence, unlawful possession of certain firearms, trafficking weapons;
- Trafficking, importing or production of certain narcotics.

Section 110 of the *Criminal Code* gives a judge discretion to impose a firearms prohibition in certain cases, including for offences where violence against a person was used, threatened or attempted and section 109 does not make a prohibition mandatory.

CONCLUSION

Sentencing is one of the most important, albeit often over-looked, parts of the criminal trial process. Sentencing is the connective tissue bringing together the criminal law with corrections, as sentencing determines whether offenders will be monitored in the community or incarcerated. Judges are given a wide-degree of discretion in determining a just and appropriate sentence and determining which of the *Criminal Code* principles should be emphasized in any given case. Parliament also plays a role in sentencing and may modify sentencing legislation. Recent years have seen Parliament limit the amount of credit an offender can receive for time spent on remand, increase the number of mandatory minimum sentences and allow for longer, harsher sentences in cases of multiple murder. All these changes have an impact of both provincial and Federal corrections, who must house and manage the inmates who are sentenced.

KEY TERMS

Remand	Pre-trial detention	Ladder Principle
Go forward sentence	Section 718	Proportionality
Mandatory minimum sentences	Denunciation	Deterrence
Rehabilitation	*Gladue*	Aggravating Factors
Mitigating factors	Absolute discharge	Probation
Conditional discharge	Two-years less a day	Intermittent Sentence

HELPFUL WEBLINKS

CanLII (https://www.canlii.org/).

This website contains court judgments, as well as statues and regulations from all Canadian jurisdictions. The full text of the court decisions discussed in this chapter can be accessed via CanLII.

Criminal Code (http://laws-lois.justice.gc.ca/eng/acts/C-46/).

The *Criminal Code* of Canada can be accessed at this web address. The full text of the sections discussed in this chapter can be found here. Amendments to the *Criminal Code* are updated at this link. You are also able to see previous version of the entire *Code* or of a particular section.

Controlled Drugs and Substances Act (http://laws-lois.justice.gc.ca/eng/acts/C-38.8/).

The *Controlled Drugs and Substances Act* can be accessed here. Like the *Criminal Code*, this is updated as the *CDSA* is amended and can be used to access the legislative history.

Corrections and Conditional Release Act (http://laws-lois.justice.gc.ca/eng/acts/C-44.6/).

This legislation pertains to issues in the federal penitentiary system, including eligibility for parole. Equivalent legislation dealing with provincial prisons can be found for every province.

"Set up to Fail: Bail and the Revolving Door of Pre-Trial Detention"
(https://ccla.org/dev/v5/_doc/CCLA_set_up_to_fail.pdf).
This report outlines issues with bail in Canada.

REFERENCES

Bronskill, J. (2016, December 13). Justice tracking over 100 court challenges to mandatory minimum penalties. *CBC News*, Politics. Retrieved from http://www.cbc.ca/news/politics/mandatory-minimums-constitutional-challenges-1.3893961

Canada Border Services Agency. (2018). Annual Detention Statistics - 2012-2017. In *Arrests, Detentions and Removals*. Retrieved from https://www.cbsa-asfc.gc.ca/security-securite/detent/stat-2012-2017-eng.html

Canada. Department of Justice, *The Criminal Law in Canadian Society*. Ottawa: n.p. 1982.

Canada. The Canadian Sentencing Commission. *Sentencing Reform: A Canadian Approach. Report of The Canadian Sentencing Commission*. Ottawa: Supply and Services Canada, 1987.

Canada. Standing Committee on Justice and Solicitor General. *Taking Responsibility. Report of the Standing Committee on Justice and Solicitor General on its Review of Sentencing, Conditional release and Related Aspects of Corrections*. Ottawa: Queen's Printer for Canada, 1988.

Crutcher, N. (2001). The Legislative history of mandatory minimum penalties of imprisonment in Canada. *Osgoode Hall Law Journal*, *39*(2/3), 273-285.

Hixt, N. (2018, April 5). Calgary man sentenced to life in prison, no parole for 50 years for killing mother and woman she cared for. *Global News*, Crime. Retrieved from https://globalnews.ca/news/4124327/emanuel-kahsai-murder-sentencing-calgary/

Manson, A. (2001). *The Law of Sentencing*. Toronto, Canada: Irwin Law.

Myers, N. M. (2017). Eroding the presumption of innocence: Pre-trial detention and the use of conditional release on bail. *The British Journal of Criminology*, *57*(3), 664-683.

Québec Ombudsman. (2018, March). *The consequences of the increase in intermittent sentences in Québec correctional facilities*. Retrieved from https://protecteurducitoyen.qc.ca/sites/default/files/pdf/rapports_speciaux/consequences-increase-intermittent-sentences.pdf

Ruby, C. *Sentencing*, 4th ed. Toronto: Butterworths, 1994.

Statistics Canada. 2018. Table 35-10-0030-01. *Adult criminal courts, guilty cases by type of sentence*. Retrieved from: https://www150.statcan.gc.ca/t1/tbl1/en/tv.action?pid=3510003001

Weinrath, M. (2009). Inmate perspectives on the remand crisis in Canada. *Canadian Journal of Criminology and Criminal Justice*, *51*(3), 355-379.

LEGISLATION

Criminal Code, Revised Statutes of Canada [1985, c. C-46].
Immigration and Refugee Protection Act, Statutes of Canada [2001, c. 27].
Corrections and Conditional Release Act, Statutes of Canada [1992, c. 20].
Truth in Sentencing Act, Statues of Canada [2009, c. 29].

CASE LAW

R. v. Antic, 2017 SCC 27, [2017] 1 S.C.R. 509
R. v. Arcand, 2010 ABCA 363, [2010] A.J. No. 1383 (QL)
R. v. Bertuzzi, 2004 BCPC 472, [2004] B.C.J. No. 2692 (QL)
R. v. Black, 2014 ABCA 214, [2014] A.J. No. 659 (QL)
R. v. Borutski, 2017 ONSC 7762, [2017] O.J. No. 6876 (QL)
R. v. Bourque, 2014 NBQB 237, [2014] N.B.J. No. 295 (QL)
R. v. Bratzer, 2001 NSCA 166, [2001] N.S.J. No. 461 (QL)
R. v. Burnett, 2017 MBCA 122, [2017] M.J. No. 348 (QL)
R. v. B.W.P., 2006 SCC 27, [2006] 1 S.C.R. 941
R. v. Cormier-Ohalloran, [2013] A.J. No. 1488 (QL)
R. v. Draper, 2010 MBCA 35, [2010] M.J. No. 94 (QL)
R. v. Ferguson, 2008 SCC 6, [2008] 1 S.C.R. 96
R. v. Gardiner, [1982] 2 S.C.R., 1982 CanLII 30 (SCC)
R. v. Garland, 2017 ABQB 202, [2017] A.J. No. 1126 (QL)
R. v. Ipeelee, 2012 SCC 13, [2012] 1 S.C.R. 433
R. v. Kahsai, 2018 (Alberta Court of Queen's Bench)
R. v. Lacasse, 2015 SCC 64, [2015] 3 S.C.R. 1089
R. v. Latimer, 2001 SCC 1, [2001] 1 S.C.R. 3
R. v. Lloyd, 2016 SCC 13, [2016] 1 S.C.R. 130
R. v. Luxton, [1990] 2 S.C.R. 711, 1990 CanLII 83 (SCC)
R. v. M. (C.A.), [1996] 1 S.C.R. 500, 1996 CanLII 230 (SCC)
R. v. Millard, 2018 ONSC 1299, [2018] O.J. No. 1036 (QL)
R. v. Moriarty, 2016 ABPC 25, [2016] A.J. No. 465 (QL)
R. v. Morrisey, 2000 SCC 39, [2000] 2 S.C.R. 90
R. v. Nur, 2015 SCC 15, [2015] 1 S.C.R. 773
R. v. Ostamas, 2015 MBQB 136, [2015] M.J. No. 205 (QL)
R. v. Priest, [1996] O.J. No. 3369 (QL), 1996 CanLII 1381 (ONCA)
R. v. Proulx, 2000 SCC 5, [2000] 1 S.C.R. 61
R. v. Rushton, 2017 NSPC 2, [2017] N.S.J. No. 23 (QL)
R. v. Saretzky, 2017 ABQB 496, [2017] A.J. No. 831 (QL)
R. v. Smith, [1987] 1 S.C.R. 1045, [1987] S.C.J. No. 36 (QL)
R. v. Solowan, 2008 SCC 62, [2008] 3 S.C.R. 309
R. v. St-Cloud, 2015 SCC 27, [2015] 2 S.C.R. 328
R. v. Voong, 2015 BCCA 285, [2015] B.C.J. No. 1335 (QL)

Probation and Community Corrections

4

Michael Weinrath

Learning Objectives

After reading this chapter, you should be able to:

- Define probation and explain what type of conditions can be used and why.

- Understand the history of probation and its development alongside other correctional interventions.

- Describe trends in the use of probation as a disposition by the court, particularly over time and in comparison to other criminal justice sentencing options.

- Describe the process of the enforcement of probation, understand issues around its use and recent trends.

- Describe the major job functions of a probation officer including classification, pre-sentence investigation, report writing, case planning, case management and enforcement.

- Understand the criticisms of probation and explain some of the methods proposed to improve its practice in Canada.

- Explain what conditional sentences, electronic monitoring drug treatment courts entail, and their strengths and weaknesses as a form of community corrections in Canada.

INTRODUCTION

This chapter offers an overview of adult probation and community corrections options which are administered by the provincial and territorial governments in Canada. Probationary supervision is a critical component of the criminal justice system; it is the most frequently applied sanction by the judiciary and represents one of the more popular alternatives to confinement. More individuals are on probation in Canada on any given day than are on bail supervision, parole, conditional sentences, and provincial or federal custody, *combined* (Statistics Canada, 2018). Despite its large numbers, probation is essentially an understudied phenomenon in Canada and elsewhere. In this chapter, I draw on available Canadian studies, and consider relevant data from the United States, Britain, and other jurisdictions, as well as relevant case law. A recurring theme in this chapter is the often-overlooked onerous nature of probationary supervision for offenders, and criminal justice trends towards more stringent enforcement.

Community corrections other than probation for adult offenders have increased significantly in Canada over the past 20 years. Intensive supervision probation, conditional sentences, electronic monitoring and problem-solving courts emerged in the mid 1990s to early 2000s and provide alternatives to custody that are more structured than probation. While ostensibly helping offenders avoid incarceration, these programs have their critics who argue that these initiatives have increased, not reduced the amount of state surveillance of offenders.

WHAT IS PROBATION?

Following a determination of guilt, the courts have several options: fines, probation, conditional sentences, and custody. As can be seen in Figure 4.1, the option most often selected is probation. It is commonly perceived by the public as a rehabilitative sentencing option that involves a friendly counsellor helping offenders with their life problems. For those assigned probation, however, it might also be considered punishment. Imagine being a young person in your 20s and having to complete 240-hours of volunteer community work, making monthly restitution payments, not being able to drink recreationally with your friends, and having to see someone once or twice a month and discuss things you would rather keep private. Some might view this as punitive! The case law on probation sentencing, however, is clear in outlining that judges must use probation as an alternative to custody and emphasizes principles of rehabilitation over denunciation or deterrence (see *R. v. Deis,* 1996).

Probation is assigned by a judge and falls principally under section 731, subsections 1 and 2 of the *Criminal Code of Canada* with standard and optional conditions. Optional conditions pursuant to section 732.1(3) are intended to help the probationer avoid further trouble with the law. For almost any crimes without a minimum penalty, probation may be administered by the courts in these forms:

a. A *conditional discharge* or *suspended sentence* of up to three years, with *standard conditions* to keep the peace and maintain good behaviour, appear before the court when required to do so, notify the court or probation officer in advance of any change in name or address and notify the court or probation officer of any change in employment or occupation.

b. A conditional discharge or suspended sentence, with standard and additional *optional conditions* such as reporting to a probation officer, abstaining from alcohol and drugs, provide bodily samples (e.g., cheek swab or urinalysis), make restitution, complete up to 240 hours of community service, abide by a curfew and undertake designated treatment programs, as well as any reasonable conditions "for protecting society and for facilitating the offender's successful reintegration into the community."

c. A conditional sentence, plus probation of up to three years with *optional conditions.*

d. A *split sentence* of a fine and a period of probation of up to three years with *optional* conditions, or a jail sentence of up to two years less a day, and up to three years probation with optional conditions.

On the one hand, probation may be viewed as a rehabilitative sentence, particularly in cases where a conditional discharge is granted. Successful completion of a conditional discharge results in no record of an offence. On the other hand, probation can also incorporate punitive elements such as custody and restrictive conditions such as a curfew. An individual sentence may range from a conditional discharge of a short one-month period with no conditions or two years less a day custody sentence followed by another three years probation with many onerous conditions. While probation is often viewed by the public as a soft disposition and by others as "getting off" from a crime, for offenders, the actual experience can be quite different. Probation can involve some demanding reporting requirements, extensive treatment commitments, work service, curfews, and restricted drinking, not to mention the possibility of custody if these conditions are violated.

Case Law on Probation Conditions

R. v. Shoker (2006) emerged as a key Supreme Court decision regarding the suitability of probation conditions and it is highly cited in recent appellate decisions. Shoker was convicted and assigned conditions that he abstain from alcohol and illicit drugs, attend treatment as directed by his probation officer, and provide blood or urine samples as directed by his probation officer. Any violation of these conditions would result in a breach of probation. The Supreme Court held that the sentencing judge certainly had authority to assign an abstain condition given Shoker's history of alcohol related crime. It was observed that the courts are given broad power to craft reasonable conditions for protecting society and facilitating the accused's reintegration into the community. However, such authority is not unlimited, and it was held that the urinalysis condition was intrusive, involved self-incrimination, and an inappropriate law enforcement role for the probation officer. Thus, although the court has great latitude in creating conditions for probation, they must reasonably connect to either the protection of the public or reintegration of the offender into society. Conditions that appear purely punitive in nature or are tangentially related to the offender's situation or circumstances, may be struck down.

The British Columbia Supreme Court affirmed the importance of utilizing probation for primarily rehabilitative purposes and not punishment. In *R. v. Deis* (1996), they struck down community work service conditions that the sentencing judge added to several probation orders that already included custody. The sentencing judge made no reference to the rehabilitative purpose of the conditions and appeared to be using community work as a punishment. The conditions were, therefore, struck from the order by the appellate court.

The use of probation conditions to coerce offenders into treatment has been a controversial area. Revisions to the *Criminal Code* resulted in the creation of section 723.1(1)(g), which indicates that a treatment condition may only be used: "*if the offender agrees...[to] participate actively in a treatment program approved by the province.*" This condition, thus, puts the probationer in control of whether s/he receives treatment. The assumption here is that treatment will not assist individuals who are not genuinely interested in participating, and that treatment itself, particularly psychiatric treatment involving medication is very intrusive. The counter argument is that probationers rarely occupy the most objective vantage point to determine whether they need treatment, and that it is best that the court determine this and compel them if need be. In fact, section 3. (g).1 indicates that a probationer can be directed to attend an alcohol/drug treatment facility approved by the province, suggesting that certain types of treatment can be ordered for offenders.

As discussed earlier, *R. v. Shoker* reaffirmed the requirement that the court needs the agreement of the offender before they can assign this condition. Yet, appellate courts have provided different rulings on this issue, even in determining the "treatment." The British Columbia Provincial Court (BCPC) in *R. v. Harris* (2001) determined that "treatment" in condition (g), however meant psychiatric treatment and/or medication, a significant personal intrusion violating section 7 of the *Canadian Charter of Rights and Freedoms*, which guarantees an individual protection against intrusive actions by the government. However, while the treatment condition is allowable in cases when the offender agrees, to "psychological" treatment, this does not necessarily apply to other forms of programming. Surprisingly, the BCPC ruled that Harris was indeed required, as directed by his probation officer, to attend a sex offender treatment program. They ruled this was a "counselling" program and not "treatment" in the form that the *Charter* could consider too intrusive, thus no agreement by the offender was necessary beforehand. The BCPC ruled that the group counselling and educational aspects of sex offender treatment were different from the "mental techniques" and physical intrusiveness (medication) of psychiatric treatment. Although one can agree that medication can have significant physical side effects on an individual's body, it seems debatable that counselling offered in sex offender or domestic violence programs is dramatically different from psychiatric interventions. Indeed, many anger management and addictions programs are built around cognitive behavioural psychological models.

THE DIFFERENCE BETWEEN PROBATION AND PAROLE

When it comes to adult corrections, the most common mistake made by the public (and many students) is the difference between probation and parole. The simplest way to distinguish them is to realize that probation is administered by the courts, while parole is administered by a national or provincial parole board. A judge will assign twelve months of probation, and probation officers must go through the court to breach or revoke a probation order, a process that can take months. Charges must be proven in court and may involve a trial. Parole is part of a custody term and administered by a federal or provincial parole board. An offender serving three years may be released after 18 months on full parole by the parole board. In the event of misbehaviour, parole officers can give a brief report to the parole board and get a warrant to suspend parole, requiring an inmate to return to custody as soon as arrested. After a hearing in front of the parole board, an offender might be sent back to prison to serve the remainder of his or her custody term. The legislative authority for probation is set out in the *Criminal Code of Canada*; parole is set out in the *Corrections and Conditional Release Act*.

History of Probation

In Canada, our early forms of justice were exported from the founding nations of France and England. Corporal and capital punishment were meted out until the Kingston penitentiary was built in 1835 (Carrigan, 1991). Probation began in the United States through the work of John Augustus (1785-1859), a volunteer who spoke on behalf of the offenders brought before the courts. Augustus conducted inquiries into the background of offenders and appeared in front of judges with them, and offered to look after the offenders if they were discharged. Not only did Augustus provide the earliest version of probation supervision, his information gathering for the courts was also a precursor to the presentence investigative report.

In Canada, probation was used informally for younger, first-time offenders (*An Act Permitting the Conditional Release of First Offenders in Certain Cases*). The probation was unsupervised, however, and offenders were released on a recognizance that might have conditions. The Act was further amended over the years to allow for terms for repeat offenders (two offences within the last five years) and offences punishable by more than two years incarceration (McFarlane, Coughlan. & Sumpter, 1966).

Initially, supervised probation in Canada was only granted to young offenders with the passage of the *Juvenile Delinquents Act* in 1908. For adults, supervised probation did not occur until 1921 when the *Criminal Code* was amended to allow this; subsequently, Ontario implemented the first probation system a year later in 1922. In Ontario, at that time, there was substantial controversy and debate over the introduction of this system (see McFarlane, Coughlan, & Sumpter, 1966). Many thought probation would coddle offenders, while others resented the added cost of probation staff to the public purse. Reformers were steadfast in their belief that probation would provide a cost-effective alternative to incarceration. In the end, the reformers won the day, but it is noteworthy that there was little interest in probation outside of Ontario for many years (McFarlane, Coughlan, & Sumpter, 1966).

Carrigan (1991) believes that early developments in probation were fueled by changes in assumptions of individual responsibility. Society moved away from an emphasis on individuals being totally responsible for their actions, and towards an understanding that some needed help, particularly if they came from disadvantaged backgrounds. Probation officers were thought to take on the parental role, providing guidance to young men who lacked proper upbringing and socialization. Over the years, such an approach was critiqued for its inherent class and racial bias (Rothman, 1980). Furthermore, the labelling school of criminology also argued that the court process followed by probation contributed to offenders developing a "master status" as an offender; young men might start off as minor offenders but develop a self-identity as a "criminal" through constant reminders such as reporting to a probation officer (Becker, 1963).

The national royal commission into correctional services, *Archambault* (1938) was the first to recommend an increase in adult probation services and the creation of a national (not provincial) probation service. It was felt that a federal branch could provide more uniform services than those currently being delivered (or not) by individual provinces (Jubinville, 1967; McFarlane et al., 1966). Later, the federal *Fauteux Committee Report* (1956), likewise, supported the expansion of adult probation services, but observed that, unfortunately, with the division of federal and provincial powers, the provinces retain responsibility for the administration of justice, including probation services. To this day, there has been no progress with respect to a national service, meaning that programming may vary greatly from province to province (also, see Chapter 1).

For the first sixty years of the 20th century, adult probation growth in Canada was slow. Except for Ontario, provinces did not begin providing adult probation services until after World War II (Carrigan, 1991). Ontario, Canada's largest province and one of its wealthiest, had only 15 probation officers by 1952. The service expanded more quickly thereafter and by 1956, there were 94 probation officers. In Saskatchewan, adult probation was established in 1948, but from 1951 to 1962, there were only three probation officers for the entire province (Skinner, Driedger, & Grainger, 1981). Manitoba did not hire its first adult probation officer until 1957 (Toupin & Ouellette, 1972). Through the years, the use of adult probation was quite restrictive; recall that second offenders were only allowed probation after five years and certain serious offences were ineligible for probation. In 1969, the *Criminal Code* criteria for probation was revised to eliminate virtually all impediments; repeat offenders were now eligible, and all offences, except those with a minimum penalty, prescribed by law (Toupin & Ouellette, 1972).

The Ouimet Report (1969) is the government committee document most closely associated with the modern era of community corrections. *Ouimet* advocated not only for an expanded use of probation but a greater emphasis on community alternatives to custody. Unlike *Archambault* and *Fauteux*, whose reports did not impact probation services significantly, the Ouimet report is correlated with some remarkable and progressive changes to adult probation. Probation officers (PO) in the 1970s were generally the first to supervise fine option programs, community work service, temporary absences from provincial institutions, and place clients in halfway houses. The legal impact of the 1969 changes to the *Criminal Code* should not be understated, however. For example, in the year the amendment eliminating the repeat offence restriction took effect, Manitoba reported increasing its probation count by 60%. Legislation can make a difference.

GETTING A PICTURE OF PROBATION, ITS RECENT PAST AND CURRENT USE IN CANADA

Probation grew in the 1970s and 1980s while the crime rate increased; but this trend has now changed. Probation use has changed significantly since the 1980s. To assess and understand this trend carefully, we can draw upon our national agency, Statistics Canada, for some helpful data through their Adult Corrections, Integrated Court and Criminal Court Surveys. The data is not perfect or exhaustive, largely because not all the provinces and territories willingly (or care to) provide data.

In accessing criminal justice statistics, there are some key distinctions that help us interpret them. For instance, the number of new offenders assigned probation in any given year, or admissions, is a helpful statistic to understand whether probation use is increasing or decreasing. The number of admissions, however, might not translate exactly into the number of people who are on probation, because probation terms vary in length; some offenders' probation may be terminated early or they may reoffend and be incarcerated, and so on. Thus, the daily count of probationers tells us how many probationers are being supervised by probation officers. Unfortunately, raw numbers do not tell us whether probation use is increasing relative to Canada's overall population, nor can it compare a densely populated province like Ontario to a smaller one like Prince Edward Island. So, a *rate per 100,000* is a helpful statistic for people wanting to know more about probation (calculated by taking the number of probationers, dividing by the adult population of Canada, or a specific province/territory and multiplying by 100,000).

In sum, the data tells us that probation use has increased, the terms are longer, and that breach of probation has also increased. However, there is variation in probation use by province/territory; some make extensive use of this court disposition, others less so.

Table 4.1 provides a comparison of probation data over approximately thirty years, and also compares the most recent two year period. First, we observe that from 1978-2017, probation admissions increased from 62,925 to 77,110, a substantial increase of 22.5%. During this same period, the number of offenders supervised by probation staff also increased significantly, by 57.6%, from 53,937 to 84,978. The rate per 100,000, however, has started to decline after years of increase. Consider that in 1978 probation rate was 322, up to 470 in 1998 before starting to decline. In many respects it is surprising that this decline did not happen sooner and have more of an impact, given that Canada's crime rate has declined significantly since 1992.

A disturbing trend is the over-representation of Indigenous Canadians, who only make up 4% of the Canadian adult population. They have increased from 12% to 22.5% and are five times as likely, as non-Indigenous Canadians, to end up on probation. This is particularly disappointing, especially considering several government commissions in the 1990s recommending action to reduce the over-representation of Indigenous Canadians in the criminal justice system, and the recent Truth and Reconciliation Commission (Cawsey, 1991; Hamilton & Sinclair, 1991; TRC, 2015).

Figure 4.1 depicts the average number of probationers per 100,000 by each province/territory for 2017. There are some interesting differences between these jurisdictions, particularly if one considers the local crime rates. The Maritimes provinces have comparable rates of crime, yet Newfoundland averaged half as many probationers per 100,000 compared to Prince Edward Island (PEI). When

Table 4.1 – Probation Trends					
	1978	**1998**	**2008**	**2017**	**Change 1978-2017**
Probation Admissions	62,925	64, 500	86,222	77,110	+22.5%
Daily Count	53,937	68,475	95,795	84,978	+57.6%
Rate per 100,000	322	342	391	305	-5.3%
Median Age	21	26	NA	33*	+12
% Female	15	18	18	20	+5%
% Indigenous	12	13	19	22.5	+10.5%

Source: Statistics Canada Tables 35-10-0021-01, 35-10-0154-01, 35-10-0020-01.
*Estimate. There are limitations on the reliability and validity of data by province/territory in some years. Those interested in particular jurisdictions should consult Statistics Canada data by individual province/territory.

Figure 4.1 – Probation Rate per 100,000 by Province, 2017

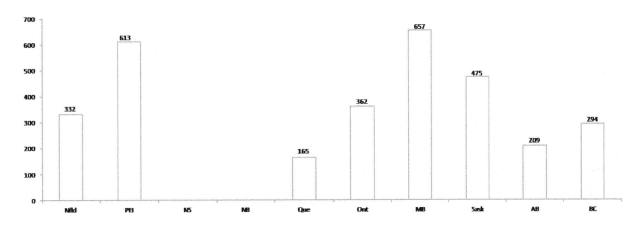

Source: Statistics Canada Table: 35-10-0154-01 Average counts of adults in provincial and territorial correctional programs. Nova Scotia and New Brunswick have not provided estimates for some years.

looking at our two most populous provinces, Ontario makes heavy use of probation, while Quebec averages only about half as many offenders per day (165 compared to 362).

The data from both custody and probation use suggests that those jurisdictions that use probation extensively also tend to use custody more often (see Chapter 5). This is partially driven by the crime rate in Canada's prairies, but not so in the case of Prince Edward Island. Beyond this, differences may arise from cultural traditions, organizational styles, and bureaucratic initiatives. For example, Quebec has a reputation for extensive use of social service alternatives, and they do not imprison as much as other provinces. This is certainly an area where more comparative research is needed.

The adult criminal court survey shows that, in 2016, adult offenders generally end up on probation for more serious offences. Crimes against the person (32.8%) and property crimes (32.0%) are the two most common categories, and this has not changed much over the years (see Figure 4.2). Administration of justice offences (19.4%) comprise a surprisingly substantial category, and often involve breach of probation offences that can result in more probation (probation violation = more probation). Drug related (3.6%), and traffic offences involving either dangerous or drunk driving (6.6%) or "other" make-up the other probation crime groups.

Figure 4.3 provides us with a general picture of where probation fits into the sentencing schemes of judges. Those found guilty receive probation as the most common disposition for convictions, assigned to 42.9% of all cases. Prison (38.3%) and fines (31.7%) are the next most popular, while conditional sentences were only accessed 3.6% of the time. These figures are a bit misleading, however, as the dispositions do not "stand alone" and they might be used in conjunction with one another. For example, some offenders who received both prison and probation would be noted in both categories. In addition, Statistics Canada places conditional discharges, community work services, and suspended sentences (no supervision) into an "other" sentencing category, thus our table likely *underestimates* probation use.

ADMINISTRATION AND ENFORCEMENT OF PROBATION

Offenders are placed on probation on trust, and if they fail to abide by the conditions of their probation, they are subject to penalty. Violation of a probation order condition can result in a charge of **breach of probation**, pursuant to section 733.1 of the *Criminal Code*. Much more rarely used to deal with violations is revocation of a probation order under section 732.2(5), which can be initiated if a probationer commits a new offence, including one under section 733.1.

Proceeding with a charge of breach of a condition typically involves a probation officer submitting a *violation report*, and forwarding it to the Crown's office, and then having the police issue a summons. The charge is subject to the court process, and probation officers must testify and present evidence in court to prove the violation. A significant change to probation enforcement occurred in the mid-1990s, when legislation amended the *Criminal Code* burden of proof from a probationer demonstrating a *"wilful failure to comply,"* to a more easily proven criteria of *"without a reasonable excuse."* Furthermore, in 1995, breach of probation changed from a summary conviction offence (i.e., maximum six months in jail or $500 fine) to a hybrid offence,[1] with the indictable offence meriting up to two years in prison. Even more significantly, the summary conviction maximum increased from six months to up 18 months imprisonment. This certainly toughened up the consequences for breach of probation. It should be noted that police officers can also lay breach of probation charges. For example, police might observe offenders violating curfews or no-contact breaches (i.e., associating with known offenders, or spending time near an off-limits victim), and then charge them.

In practice, probation officers have considerable discretion regarding whether to lay a charge. Violation of probation charges are not automatic in most jurisdictions, and probation officers follow

Figure 4.2 – Probation by Crime Type, 2016

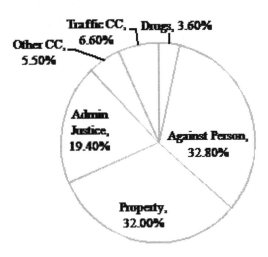

N=86,802 **Note**: Crimes Against Person can include Manslaughter, Attempted Murder, Robbery and Sexual Assault, but mostly comprises level one Assault.
Source: Statistics Canada, Table 35-10-0035-01. Adult criminal courts, guilty cases by mean and median length of probation.).

Figure 4.3 – Guilty Cases in Criminal Court by type of Sentence Canada, 2016

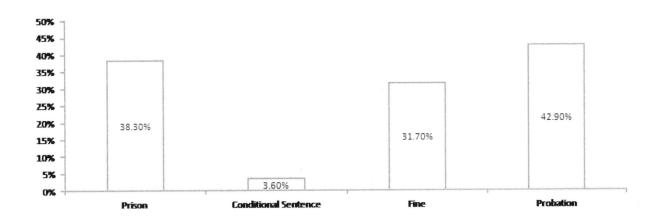

N=220,233. **Note**: These dispositions may be combined with each other; (e.g., a single case may get prison and probation, so totals do not add up to 100%).
Source: Statistics Canada, Table 35-10-0030-01 Adult criminal courts, guilty cases by type of sentence.

systems of **graduated sanctions**, increasing penalties if an offender continues to be uncooperative. This might include disciplinary interviews addressing inappropriate behaviour, warnings of possible breach action, and increasing reporting from monthly to weekly. A probation officer will consider an offender's overall behaviour when deciding on case action. For example, a client who violates an alcohol consumption condition by becoming quite drunk might agree to participate in an addictions program, and again just get a warning. To initiate a charge, the probation officer must prepare a violation report for the crown prosecutor who has ultimate authority over proceeding with a breach. While official data is difficult to obtain, informal discussions with probation officials suggests that *revocations of probation* are much more rarely processed than breach of probation charges.

Enforcement of probation orders can be complicated and require considerable time and effort on the part of probation officers, a significant difference from parole and conditional sentences. For example, a violation of parole can result in an immediate suspension and, shortly after, a complete revocation – it does not require following the same legal processes nor the evidentiary burden of probation. Likewise, the conditional sentence is easier to enforce, as it reverses onus on an offender charged with a violation to prove their innocence, and the charge need only be proven on the "*balance of probabilities*," a much lower burden than the "reasonable doubt" required in criminal court for a probation breach.

Case Law on Breach of Probation

The Manitoba Provincial Court addressed the issue of *mens rea*, or guilty intent in a probation breach in *R. v. Di Pietro* (2000). The court found a probationer guilty of a breach for not reporting for six months, despite the accused's defence that he missed messages left by his probation officer and forgot to report. The court ruled that the probation order put some responsibility on the probationer to abide by its conditions. Likewise, the Alberta Provincial Court ruled that a probationer "forgetting" to report upon release from jail was not an acceptable deffence. In *R. v Bremmer* (2006) the offender had signed the probation order prior to custody and had a letter sent (which he signed) while in custody. His argument, that he became preoccupied with "personal survival" upon his release from prison and just forgot to contact probation authorities, did not sway the court.

In the Saskatchewan Provincial Court, the well-reasoned R. v. Bolen decision, however, makes clear that the prosecution does not escape the requirement to prove *mens rea*. In this case, a probationer failed to pay restitution while residing on a reserve, where unemployment was high, and he lived on social assistance. The prosecutor argued that the probationer could have picked up bottles or found odd jobs to pay his $50 per month restitution. The judge found the crown's position unreasonable and ruled that it had not proven beyond a reasonable doubt that the probationer intentionally violated his probation order, and the charge was dismissed. Family violence cases sometimes see probation orders applied with conditions restricting contract between the offender and his victim. Are they strenuously enforced? In *R v. Wilson* (2017), the probationer insisted that the victim manipulated him into contacting her, only to later report him for violating the order. In this case the Ontario court ruled that inducements to breach were not an excuse – there was no urgency or crisis precipitating these contacts, meaning he could have explored other options, or even applied to the court for relief.

Is Probation Working? Recidivism

Does probation work? Clearly, there are many ways to define success. Did an offender comply with their conditions like completing treatment, pay restitution, or complete their community work? Did they improve their personal relationships, maintain steady employment or graduate from school or post-secondary education? While all these measures are used, in the end, researchers and the public are mostly stuck on recidivism as the measuring stick to gauge the program's success. Recidivism usually concerns re-involvement with the criminal justice system, and is appraised through new charges, new convictions, readmission to prison, and in the case of probation, breaches of probation. If a breach is the outcome, it makes the evaluation of probation difficult as these violations typically do not involve any direct harm to anyone. The term **technical violation** is used to denote a violation of a probation condition, other than a breach, for a new crime (i.e., failure to keep the peace and maintain good behaviour).

Unfortunately, most jurisdictions do not publish recidivism statistics. Therefore, this makes it more difficult to assess whether probation practice is improving, in decline, or conversely, whether probationers become a higher risk or more dangerous. From 2001-2005, Alberta reported recidivism rates of 31% - 40%, but they included outstanding charges that may or may not have resulted in convictions (ASG, 2005). The way recidivism is measured greatly affects how success looks. The Alberta study gives us some insight into breach of probation *failure rates*, or the percentage of adult offenders who do not successfully complete probation without a breach. In a study population of 14,438 adult probationers, 34% breached or failed. Proportionately, some optional conditions were less likely adhered to. About one in four restitution/compensation orders (27.4%) were not completed, and about one in five community work orders (20.7%) were also not completed. Overall, mandatory conditions were most likely to be breached; when looking more carefully at the statistics behind this, failure to report changes in address or employment/education was about one in ten (11.1%), about the same as not reporting to a probation officer (9.6%). These figures can appear in a more positive light if we consider *success rates* instead of failure rates. Ninety percent of probationers reported to their probation officers, 70%-75% paid restitution or completed compensation or community work service, and 85% abided by their curfews or attend work/school. How the numbers are presented can have a big impact on how a program is perceived!

PROBATION OFFICERS AND PROBATION PRACTICE

Probation officers work for provincial governments and each province provides additional legislative structure through individual Corrections Act(s). While there is some variation from province to province, most jurisdictions provide similar services. Probation officers (PO's) are officers of the court and provide presentence investigations to the judiciary on request. Once assigned to probation, PO's classify offenders according to risk and need, and develop a case management plan. In addition, a probation officer may supervise remanded accused on a pre-trial recognizance and conditional sentence cases. They may also manage the Fine Option Program and supervise those who must do volunteer community work to compensate for their fine. In some jurisdictions, PO's may also supervise volunteer probation officers.

Presentence Report

The **presentence report** (PSR) provides a social history of the offender and is intended primarily to assist the judiciary in sentencing. Judges may request presentence reports under section 721(1) of the *Criminal Code*, which specifies that this function is performed by probation officers. This section generally requires information on the offender's age, maturity, character, behaviour, attitude and willingness to make amends, as well as criminal history. Section 721(3)(d) allows significant discretion to each province and territory in determining content. The *Code* provisions are quite limited and most PSR's cover a substantial history of the offender, including family, education, employment, addictions, use of leisure time, and mental health. The authority for probation officers to investigate and prepare these reports is further authorized by provincial corrections legislation. The judge, crown, defence counsel and offender receive a copy of the report. The report is subject to challenge by the accused and the probation officer may be cross-examined.

Probation officers may still give oral reports to judges, but generally most information is provided in a report form. The PSR uses a social history format, starting with the subject as an offender and then chronicling his or her life and circumstances. Some PSR's include risk scales, which affects the focus of different sections of the report and the way they are weighted by the probation officer in assessing the offender.

Presentence reports can only be used after a guilty plea and have other uses besides assisting the sentencing judge. They provide information for both the crown and defence to use when speaking to sentence. PSR's are important casework documents that can assist the probation officer in classifying an offender and devising an appropriate case plan. In the case of a custody sentence, they can also assist prison staff in their classification and release planning.

Use of the Presentence Report

The most extensive survey of Canada's provinces and territories provides important data on the presentence report and its use in Canada (Bonta, Bourgon, Jesseman, & Yessine, 2005). They found a favourable consensus on the utility of PSR's amongst all groups. Judges felt the information contained in a PSR was useful in sentencing because it provided independent, objective information, particularly for violent offenders. Probation officers were more likely to express dissatisfaction with the current state of presentence reports, often feeling they were requested for minor offences too frequently. Probation officers, in some jurisdictions, expressed dissatisfaction with their training, or felt that too much repetitive information was required.

Presentence reports tend to be resource heavy. In five Canadian jurisdictions, the average time spent preparing a PSR was 14.1 hours, although it ranged from 6.1 to 17.1 hours, indicating some substantial differences by province/territory. PO's averaged three hours interviewing clients and 1.8 hours talking to collaterals, such as police, partners, parents/family members, employers, and teachers. Writing time averaged seven hours. The PSR is a significant document – the average length is 11 pages. In comparing presentence reports, Bonta and his colleagues found that PSR cases did tend to be more often charged with violent or multiple offences. In other words, judges did seem to be assigning PSR's in the case of more serious offenders.

Recommendations, Sentence Bias and Risk

An enduring issue with presentence reports is its possible negative influence on the sentencing process (Hagan, 1975; Hannah-Moffat & Maurutto, 2010; Weinrath, 1999). Probation officers can have very conservative or liberal views, which may create differences in the recommendations they make to judges. This is potentially significant, because studies find an 80%-85% concurrence rate of judges following the probation officers' recommendations.

Most researchers conclude, however, that the influence of the probation officers' recommendation on judges is overstated. The over-rating of the recommendation's influence is perhaps best supported by research that shows that it is the current offence and prior criminal history that wield the largest influence on sentencing. Current and past crime severity tends to outweigh age, race, gender, and other possible biasing factors when it comes to final sentence (Boldt et al., 1983; Hagan, 1975; Leiber, Reitzel & Mack, 2011).

Are presentence reports helpful to judges when assigning probation? One might assume that the social history information and PO's evaluation is helpful, yet studies in the United States, Britain and Canada found no difference in recidivism rates between PSR probation clients and those assigned to probation without a PSR (Davies, 1971; Rumney & Murphy, 1952; Weinrath, 1999). This has led to questions about the utility of the PSR as a risk assessment instrument, and the need to focus on providing community alternatives to the judiciary at the point of sentence. Another strategy advocated for PSR's is the addition of **actuarial risk and needs scales**. These risk instruments are based on recidivism studies that allow probation officers to rank risk more accurately by assigning a score to age, prior criminal history, employment background, educational needs and so forth, thereby creating a statistical likelihood of the success of probation. It is thought that the use of such instruments will likely make probation officers more objective and their recommendations more accurate. In their Canadian survey, Bonta and his colleagues (2005) found that only two provinces (Alberta and Quebec) were not using an instrument and still assessing risk intuitively by experience. In their study, they used a simulation design to assess if probation officers using risk instruments followed guidelines. They found that PO's did generally adhere to the risk criteria. Offenders ranked lower risk were more likely to receive a probation recommendation. Most judges supported the use of actuarial information – this is promising given the short time risk scales have been in use.

Hannah-Moffat and Maurutto (2010) criticize risk scales because they are not designed to consider the social disadvantages faced by racial minorities and women. Using the example of race, they point out that Indigenous Canadians are disadvantaged in terms of employment, schooling and other areas, which, in turn, means that they will be scored higher risk than non-Indigenous Canadians. The PSR, in other words, embeds racial discrimination within the sentencing process. They argue for more narrative reports, and offer the example of the Gladue Reports, adopted in parts of Ontario because of dissatisfaction with risk based PSR's. In *R. v. Gladue* (1999), the Supreme Court articulated that judges had to consider Aboriginal disadvantages such as marginalization, residential schools, substance abuse in local communities, and family problems in sentencing decisions. In such cases, judges will need more information to sentence an accused Indigenous person; thus, a report prior to sentence is necessary.

The contribution of presentence reports to sentencing may well be over-rated, yet it still plays an important part in the court process and is one of the more complex functions performed by probation officers. The move to actuarial risk-based instruments to help guide PSR assessment provides a more objective way of structuring probation officers decision-making, but the risk approach does move PO's away from their more traditional, individualized justice assessment. One solution creates other problems. It is likely that the "restructuring" of the presentence report in Canada is not finished yet.

Classification

Classification is a key probation officer responsibility and occurs after sentencing. While a presentence report is helpful, PO's will proceed to assess new clients, with or without a PSR. At this point, a probation officer must consider the needs of the offender - what will help him/her live a stable, law abiding lifestyle, and balance this with the relative risk that they pose to the community. Classification of probationers has been around for as long as probation; however, it has arguably only recently become more standardized and research-based.

Originally, probation officers used their experience and intuition to classify offenders, coupled with, perhaps, a review of their criminal history. Since the late 70s, probation officers in most Canadian provinces have utilized classification instruments that are based on recidivism risk factors, or better yet, local studies that identify correlates of reoffending. Using the previously mentioned actuarial approach, probation officers now complete classification interviews using instruments that list *criminogenic* (associated with recidivism) risk and need factors. PO's then use the results to fashion a case management plan. This model is also referred to as the RNR (**Risk Need Responsivity**). Systematic follow-up from the initial classification, such as program referrals or counselling approaches is referred to as "evidence-based practice," if the risk instrument is based on research. This is considered a more scientific approach and assumes that PO's should be more successful if they use risk instruments and programming approaches that are steeped in research results, as opposed to their own intuition or experience. These issues are discussed more extensively in Chapter 9.

Case Management

Case management essentially involves the probation officer's development of a plan to help the offender stay out of trouble and develop a law-abiding life style. Based on the initial classification, the PO determines the number of times a probationer will have contact each month. Depending on the case, the PO will set topics for counselling sessions, assign program referrals such as addiction or anger management, and schedule community work service or restitution payments. Additionally, probation officers may have to set up collateral contacts with parents or employers, and sometimes victims, to monitor a higher risk probationer. Case management may also involve greater supervision or surveillance responsibilities if a probationer has more restrictive conditions, such as a curfew, a requirement to reside in a certain place, or to abstain from alcohol or a no-contact order with negative peers or crime victims (see Chapter 9).

Probation Officer Roles

Like a parent, probation officers must manage the dual roles of helper and enforcer. When a PO helps and encourages their clients, they take on the role of a treatment counsellor. When they check up on their client and find that they have violated their conditions, then they end up assuming the role of law enforcer and may even play a hand in their clients going to prison. These dichotomous roles are a challenge for probation officers, particularly as most enter this field interested in helping others.

In his classic study of a downtown US probation office, Klockars (1972) identified four types of probation officers. The "law enforcer" placed a heavy emphasis on surveillance and enforcement of probation orders, while the "time server" took a similar but more bureaucratic approach to the job and just followed policy and bare compliance with the probation order. On the other hand, the "therapeutic agent" was more interested in helping the client through counselling and problem-solving, and not interested in probation conditions. Klockars found the most effective probation officer was the "synthetic officer," a hybrid of the law enforcer and therapeutic agent, who combined a genuine caring for their client with a practical attention to leading a law-abiding lifestyle (ibid.). The synthetic officer first established himself as a control agent, and then gradually moved to a counselling, problem-solving focus, deferring coercive authority to his supervisors ("Gee, if you do that, I'll have to report it to my bosses…"). In this way, the PO establishes a strong rapport and motivates the client, but maintains an emphasis on control, without being overtly controlling. This strategy has the bonus of relieving some of the role strain facing the PO who is trying to balance being a helper with the surveillance requirements. A recent review of relevant studies, including the classic Canadian research by Andrews and Kiessling (1980), provides considerable support for the synthetic officer approach (Skeem & Manchak, 2008). The research suggests that this strategy is particularly effective when it is combined with an evidence-based approach.

CRITICISMS OF PROBATION AND ITS PRACTICE

Probation has a tremendous potential to assist offenders – as noted earlier, it is easily the most common disposition in adult corrections; hence, initiatives to change offenders or simply ensure that they are treated fairly will certainly reach the greatest number. Most of the research suggests, however, that in terms of reaching its potential, probation is likely an underachiever (see Bonta et al., 2011;

Cohen, 1985). Progress has certainly been made in terms of identifying ways to improve probation practice over the past 30 years, however, seeing promising methods successfully implemented in the field is rare. Despite research support and a well-articulated framework, not everyone is enamoured with the RNR model. Finally, there are some perennial criticisms of probation that must be considered.

Technical Criticisms

Bonta and his colleagues research illustrates some of the problems with current probation practice and some of the challenges in implementing positive changes (Bonta, Rugge, Scott, Bourgon, & Yessine, 2008). They reviewed probation files to assess case focus and progress, but in a unique approach they also used actual audio tapes of sessions between probation officers and their clients to determine how well PO's used their initial classification assessment, and whether they focused on criminogenic risks and needs. The file reviews revealed that follow-up by probation officers on identified criminogenic needs was inconsistent and needed improvement. For example, 40% of clients had employment needs but only 10% had a plan. Probation officers did not discuss criminogenic needs frequently enough in sessions and tended to follow-up on program needs only when they were mandated by the courts. In general, Bonta et al. (2008) found probation officers were adequate in working with clients, but not highly skilled in relationship building.

Criticisms of Probation Agencies' Adoption of RNR

Not everyone supports the direction of probation and the suitability of the RNR model, and researchers have raised larger issues about our "risk society" and the direction of managing offenders (see Feely & Simon, 1994). Prior to the rise of risk classification, the emphasis in corrections was on the individualization of treatment and trying to address the specific concerns of each probationer. The use of research-based instruments and classification has changed that. The practice of using actuarial instruments, which categorize individuals into "risk groups" and organizes probation officers into "risk professionals," is thought to have redirected corrections away from the individual and into a more bureaucratic, rigid view of offenders and their treatment. Instead of being worried about individual probationers and engaging them in planning for their future, PO's are thought to be much more directive and forceful in telling offenders about their problems and what to do about them (Ward, 2010).

The RNR is linked with social psychologists, but other branches of psychology take a different view of the best way to manage offenders. Humanistic psychologists argue that assessment by way of criminogenic needs results in blaming the offender. They offer a **Good Lives Model** which argues that offenders should have input into developing a plan to reach their life goals (Ward, 2010). In this approach, counsellors are more like facilitators in helping offenders achieve what they want in life, which are usually universal needs such as a good job, supportive relationships, and housing. In response, Andrews, Bonta, and Wormith (2011) have been vigorous in defending the RNR and criticized the GLM as lacking in empirical support. They also note that the proper use of criminogenic needs involves a respectful relationship with the offender.

Probation is Becoming More Punitive

Earlier it was noted that historically probation was used as rehabilitation, and even appellate courts have emphasized it is not to be used as a punishment. Recently, however, probation programs have evolved by placing a high premium on enforcement. A recent change to probation enforcement is the introduction of intensive supervision programs (ISP). In these initiatives, probation officers maintain close ties with local police forces. They help them enforce zero tolerance policies for offenders, particularly in the early stages of the program. Probation staff generally do not provide as much latitude for ISP offenders who violate their conditions because they are a high risk, mostly violent group. ISP programs like Winnipeg's Criminal Organization and High-Risk Offender Unit (COHROU) run almost analogous to parole with warrants issued in some cases for missing appointments. Unlike normal breach practices, these cases receive a swift police response and offenders might be picked up the same day (Weinrath, Doerksen & Watts, 2016).

Trend data indicates that breach charges are increasing and dispositions more severe. Table 4.2 shows that probation breaches are increasing, and dispositions are getting tougher. Over a 22-year period, a significant rise has occurred in probation findings of guilty in Canada, from 20,278 to 24,552, which is a 21.1% increase (Table 4.2). Probation breaches appear to be taken seriously by the courts as well. Most recently 57.6% of all breach convictions resulted in prison sentences, while the rest were split between more probation, fines, and a small proportion of conditional sentences. These statistics do not consider the time in pre-trial custody for those offenders picked up on warrants, so the prison time is likely underestimated. For probationers, the outcome of prison has increased over 12% since 1993-94.

Despite the large number of offenders on probation and the large number of breach of probation charges laid each year in Canada, we know little beyond the broad statistics provided by Statistics Canada. The increase in probation breaches is significant – does this tie in with changes made to the *Criminal Code* in the mid-1990s? How many charges proceed by way of indictment?[2] If we include pre-trial detention, how long is the average stay in custody for breach of probation charges? Are there differences by type of violation (e.g., non-reporting versus treatment or curfew)? One may well wonder

Table 4.2 – Trends in Breach Charges: Is Probation Getting Tougher?				
	1993-94	**2005-06**	**2015-16**	**% change 1993-2016**
Breach of Probation	20,278	21,754	24,552	+21.1%
Breach of Probation Outcomes				
Prison	45.0%	51.6%	57.6%	+12.6%
Probation	22.0%	35.5%	34.1%	+12.1%
Conditional Sentence	-	3.1%	2.7%	-0.4%
Fine	32.0%	22.9%	34.1%	+2.0%*

Source: Statistics Canada: Table 35-10-0030-01 Adult criminal courts, guilty cases by type of sentence.
Note: *More than one disposition may be given per sentencing, so totals may exceed 100%.

whether this aggressive enforcement of probation affects the relationship between offenders and probation officers. Do probationers feel they get fair treatment? We might also ask if the punishment for breach of probation fits the crime? Recall that many breaches might be for not reporting or not completing community work service, technical violations that do not hurt anyone directly.

More General Criticisms of Probation as a Correctional Practice

Probation has been criticized by social theorists as sounding good in the abstract, but in practice, it is increasing, not decreasing, retribution and control by governments. Is the science of "treatment" advanced enough to say with certainty that offenders should go under specific program regimes, or are we simply creating jobs for a professional class of psychologists, probation officers, and program workers? Stanley Cohen (1985) argues that the expanded use of probation in places like Britain and the use of experts were often done to benefit a self-serving professional class whose expertise was questionable, given the failure of so many correctional programs. For Cohen (1985, p. 185), his "hell on earth" was being an offender caught up in a "case conference" of corrections professionals: He felt that probation continues to survive and grow despite no firm evidence that casework helps. This is because it serves the interest of government: probation is relatively inexpensive and gives the appearance to the public of "doing something," rather than just releasing offenders outright from the courts. Critics, like Cohen, or historian, David Rothman (1980), argue that the relatively high success rate of probation reflects that many offenders who are given counselling as part of their probation, do not need it. A cost-effective alternative for low risk offenders is the assignment of unsupervised, suspended sentences or fines, rather than supervision (see Box 4.1).

IMPROVING PROBATION PRACTICE

As noted earlier, more offenders are under probationary supervision than any other disposition. Thus, improving probation practice has the greatest potential to improve the lives of offenders and

Box 4.1 – Two Probation Experiences

Jennifer is a first time, eighteen year old offender who has broken into two residences and found guilty of two counts of Break, Enter and Theft. A *presentence report* (PSR), completed by probation services, recommends that she is suitable for probation and restitution should be made for damages caused by the break-ins. The judge, in this case, sentences the young woman to one year supervised probation with standard conditions to: keep the peace; be of good behaviour; report any change of address or occupation to the court; report to a probation officer, as directed; and pay restitution. Jennifer reports to a probation officer, who *classifies* Jennifer according to the risks and needs scale used in his province. Jennifer has reasonable family support and no serious addiction or other problems noted. She is classified as *low risk* and reports, in person, between once to twice a month. She later obtains steady employment, makes full restitution after six months, and her reporting is reduced to every six weeks. Finally, after nine months, she is granted an *early termination* of reporting responsibilities entirely. This could have been done through the courts and her probation order could have been formally amended, but her PO simply used his discretion that she did not need to report.

continued...

Box 4.1 – Two Probation Experiences

George has a long criminal history and was convicted of several property crimes and a serious assault. Because he served a number of months in pre-trial detention, he avoids a federal sentence and receives a year in provincial custody with two years probation, with conditions to report to a PO and attend programs. When released from custody, George is directed to report to a probation officer. Martha, his PO, classifies George as *high risk,* partly due to his criminal history and severe needs in areas such as addiction, personal relationships, and negative peer involvement. The client not only must report weekly but is referred to more intensive treatment such as anger management and addiction counselling. George was on probation before, and is not happy about being on probation after having served time in custody. He is a difficult case to manage. Initially, things go well and he reports regularly and goes for programming. After a while, however, he starts missing appointments and stops going to his program sessions. After several warnings and registered letters sent to his last known address, a *breach of probation* charge for not reporting as required and refusing to attend treatment is laid.

reduce re-offence. Notable recent efforts to better probation officer performance and reduce recidivism include intensive probation supervision, motivational interviewing, and strategic counselling training on criminogenic needs.

Motivational Interviewing

Motivational interviewing (MI) had its start in the field of addictions (Prochaska & DiClemente, 1983), and promotes a therapeutic relationship between counsellor and client. In the probation field, advocates argue that it will help probation officers move away from more aggressive, confrontational, unproductive supervision styles. Instead, POs will use this approach to better develop rapport, and create a stronger relationship base to positively influence and assist clients in dealing with ineffective behaviours. MI offers a strengths-based approach to dealing with probationers. The focus is on having offenders develop skills to solve their own problems and help them decide to change. They use OARS techniques: open questions, affirming positive talk and behaviour, reflecting on what is heard and said, and summarizing what was spoken, which is thought to create an effective structure to meetings. Used properly, MI should result in the PO talking less and engaging in more "productive talk" in support of change. Probation officers do not abandon their supervisory responsibilities, nor do they advise of consequences in a non-threatening manner (Clark, 2006). This approach fits well with the RNR model and is currently being used by a few Canadian probation jurisdictions. It answers, to a degree, criticisms that evidence-based practices have encouraged a deficit-based approach to managing offenders.

The empirical tests of motivational interviewing in corrections has obtained mixed results. For instance, some US studies have found that POs can be successfully trained to practice MI, however, no differences in probation reoffence outcomes were observed between treatment and control groups of probationers (Shaul, Koeter & Schippers, 2016; Walters, Vader, Nguyen, Harris, & Eells, 2010). More favourably, a New Zealand test, comparing two inmate groups, saw a reduction in recidivism rates (Anstiss, Polaschek, & Wilson, 2011). Finally, in a US study of parole officers, Lin (2017) found motivational interviewing reduced reoffence. More research is needed to assess its effectiveness (and

Canadian research would assist in assessing the viability of its use in our country), but clearly the MI model offers a positive alternative to more coercively oriented approaches to probation.

Better Technical Application of the RNR Model,
Core Correctional Practices and Therapeutic Alliance

It was outlined earlier that although PO's used classification instruments that identified criminogenic needs, in practice they were not a focus of client meetings. To test the notion that a stronger application of the RNR model would improve probation officer performance and reduce recidivism, Bonta and his colleagues (2011) organized the **Strategic Training Initiative in Community Supervision** (STICS). Involving three provinces, this project used a control and comparison group of probation officers to test whether better applications of RNR would reduce recidivism. The initiative involved a three-day training session for PO's, monthly coaching sessions, and one-year follow-up training. Analyzing audio taped probation-client meetings, the training and coaching had a clear impact on the ability of POs to focus on criminogenic needs and apply proper techniques to structure client meetings, even though most were only twenty minutes. Significantly, STICS showed a 15% reduction in recidivism for the treatment group. While the study authors correctly caution about the size of their sample and the need for replication, STICS is an important study and may well promote a more professional approach to probation practice.

Application of core correctional practices such as the STICS model has also proven of interest to American corrections agencies. Going under various names, American probation has introduced variants of STICS notably EPICS (Effective Practices in Community Supervision) (Smith, Schweitzer, Labrecque & Latessa, 2012). Despite variation in implementation, most programs include applications of motivational interviewing, and such **core correctional practices** as emphasizing empathy, non-blaming communication, and structures of positive reinforcement, problem solving and rehearsal (Dowden & Andrews, 2004). Finally, more and more programs also incorporate features emphasizing the **therapeutic alliance**, the building of a relationship between the probation officer and offender. Building such a relationship tends to reduce client resistance and increase engagement in counseling and treatment (Blasko & Taxman, 2018; Kennealy, Skeem, Manchak, & Louden, 2012).

Probation will likely continue to be the predominant form of correctional supervision because it is economical and less costly than prison. Given the cost of incarceration and the complex needs of offenders, other community alternatives have emerged or re-emerged over the past 25 years.

OTHER FORMS OF COMMUNITY CORRECTIONS

Intensive Probation Supervision

The use of reduced caseloads is tied to the notion that probation officers can be more effective if they have more time to spend with their clients. With high caseloads, probation officers see many clients only once a month or less, providing little opportunity to counsel and work with their clients. Early efforts at **intensive probation supervision** found that lower caseloads and frequent contact resulted in increased technical violations (Robison, Wilkins, Carter, & Wahl, 1969). In other words, increased surveillance simply resulted in probation officers getting better at detecting breaches. In the 1980s, Americans looked to ISP as an intermediate sanction that could help reduce their burgeoning prison population. They emphasized surveillance objectives and tactics that included home checks, drug testing and **electronic monitoring**. Electronic monitoring involves the addition of offenders wearing an electronic bracelet that can alert probation officers if they are not at a designated residence. A Canadian study (Bonta, Wallace-Capretta, & Rooney, 2000) showed that ISP, coupled with electronic monitoring, had little to no affect, something also found in a more recent study with federal parolees (Olatu, Beaupre, & Verbrugge, 2009). In a Manitoba study with mostly violent, high risk offenders, once again it was found that ISP increased technical violations but had a suppressive effect on violent crime (Weinrath, Doerksen & Watts, 2015).

While early efforts were promising (Erwin & Bennett, 1987), larger studies found that ISP did not reduce recidivism, and, indeed, once again higher technical violations were observed (Petersilia & Turner, 1989). Recent research reviews suggest that ISP is more effective when coupled with treatment interventions and evidence-based practice (WSIPP, 2018). In the most recent review the influential Washington State Institute for Public Policy concluded ISP that included treatment had a positive effect in reducing reoffence, while surveillance-based programs had no impact.

Intensive probation supervision may yet prove to have some benefit if it targets more serious offenders and involves stronger treatment regimes. The current research evidence supporting its use is not strong.

Conditional Sentences

Conditional sentences were introduced in 1996 by Canada's Liberal government, with an objective to reduce the use of custody for offenders who did not pose a risk to the public (Roberts, 2004). Conditional sentence orders, or CSO's, fall under section 742.1 of the *Criminal Code* can only be assigned for crimes that merit a sentence of two years less a day. There must be no minimum penalty for the offence, no danger presented to the public, and the disposition not be inconsistent with the fundamental principles and purposes of sentencing under the criminal code. This legislation left very few offences that were ineligible, thus serious violent crimes such as manslaughter, sex offences, causing death by impaired or dangerous driving were eligible. Ostensibly, this meant that sentencing goals of denunciation and deterrence (see Chapter 3) were de-emphasized and the courts were to focus more on incarcerating only those offenders who posed a risk to the public. Conditional sentences in Canada were consistent with other programs being introduced in the 1990s and early 2000s in the US and Europe that used a notion of house arrest or "community custody" (Roberts, 2004).

Conditional sentences were almost immediately controversial as individuals convicted of bodily injury offences and drug trafficking were placed on conditional sentences with few conditions, thus looking like offenders were "getting off." In the landmark *R v. Proulx* (2000) the Supreme Court of Canada (SCC) tried to situate CSO's more clearly between probation and prison. More onerous and restrictive conditions of house arrest, curfew, and work service were to become standard features of CSO's, making these dispositions more consistently punitive than probation.

Despite the changes introduced by the SCC conditional sentences have remained controversial. The federal Conservative government in the mid-2000s and into the 2010s has greatly restricted the number of eligible offences for CSO's. Now many serious personal injury offences such as Manslaughter are no longer eligible. What is perhaps more surprising is that non-violent crimes such as Break and Enter, Theft over $5,000 and most drug trafficking offences no longer qualify.

In many respects, supervision of conditional sentence cases is like probation. Conditions of keeping the peace, reporting to a probation officer, abstaining from alcohol/drugs and so on are consistent with what might see on a probation order. As mentioned, more exacting conditions such as curfew, home confinement and work service will be more often present on a CSO. Enforcement differs as well; violations of a CSO are reverse onus, which means it is incumbent on the offender to show why he did not breach. Furthermore, the court can determine on "the balance of probabilities" whether or not a breach occurred, as opposed to the higher burden of "beyond a reasonable doubt." Punishment differs as well, as CSO's have their sentences "stop" when charged, and if found guilty they may serve the remainder of their conditional sentence in custody. For example, offender has 12-month CSO, is charged at 6-month period but can't be located. Arrested after 2 months at large. If found guilty, the judge can then sentence the offender to the remaining 6 months in custody or put the individual back on the conditional sentence to finish it.

In many respects it is unfortunate that conditional sentences have become so limited in their application. In its early years, Roberts (2004) found that CSO's reduced the number of custodial admissions provincially. No recent research has been done but given the more limited application of the conditional sentence, it is unlikely to be able to wield the same impact. Conditional sentences represented an important step for Canada to reduce its use of custody and emphasize community placement. The conditional sentence offers many advantages over prison; maintenance of employment and contribution, keeping family and other social ties, less cost than prison, the conditional sentence offers many advantages socially and in the long term. There were still 7,249 offenders placed on conditional sentences in 2017, but this was a drop of 40% from the peak of 12,128 in 2011 (Statistics Canada, 2018).

Electronic Monitoring

Electronic monitoring (EM) began use in the 1980s but the technology, its application and efficacy have undergone significant changes since then. The equipment typically features a device strapped to an ankle, or more recently wrist devices (Gable, 2015). The device emits a signal to a corrections staff who can monitor where a person is. Originally, the EM device was limited in scope, relied on telephone lines and could only ascertain whether an individual remained in their residence or not. Today, Global Positioning Systems (GPS) allow corrections staff to monitor the whereabouts of EM cases throughout a city or rural area.

The rationale for electronic monitoring is generally associated with reducing costs due to incarceration, while allowing an offender to maintain community ties, and education initiatives, treatment and/or employment. Certainly, the idea of constantly monitoring someone and deterring crime, or swiftly apprehending him or her in the event of reoffence has an appeal. Technology, and the thought it is making the world a better place undoubtedly has its allure. Touted as a cost-effective alternative to custody, its early promise was not fulfilled (Bottos, 2008). Initial applications of electronic monitoring found it to "widen the net" of corrections, adding lower risk individual who would have normally been on probation. The technology was troublesome and often did not work. It did not reduce recidivism, and like many intensive supervision programs it increased the rate of technical violations detected (Bottos, 2008; Renzema & Mayo-Wilson 2005). Electronic monitoring still relies to a great degree on the cooperation of the offender; he or she can simply rip off their bracelet and go "on the run" if they decide they no longer want to be under supervision.

Bonta, Wallace-Capretta, and Rooney, J. (2000) conducted early studies of Canadian electronic monitoring in Saskatchewan, using the older radio frequency technology. They concluded that EM had little impact on recidivism. More recently, US research outcomes for electronic monitoring have been more positive. Perhaps because of the better tracking of the GPS technology, large scale studies of EM in Florida and California have been more favourable on the ability of EM to discourage reoffence. (Bales et al., 2010; Turner, Chamberlain, Jannetta & Hess, 2016). Bales and his colleagues found general reductions in reoffence for moderate and high-risk Florida probationers and a superiority of GPS over Radio Frequency systems. Turner et al. found high risk sex offenders were more likely to register as sex offenders, less likely to abscond and had lower reoffence rates. Despite the improved technology there are still issues with electronic monitoring. Offenders can still encounter "dead spots" where the GPS signals do not work. House arrest can also create stress within a household between the offender and family, and the offender can end up feeling isolated (Renzema & May-Wilson, 2005). The sheer volume of information generated by hundreds of offenders on EM can incur staff costs – someone must monitor all that data. There will always be a degree of cost to EM, so unless prison use is substantially reduced, it is difficult to justify its funding. Jones (2014) also points to the general problem of "penal excess," the notion that EM inevitably makes traditional probation or parole more onerous and increases the punitive aspects of community supervision. It may be that EM will not be used to reduce prison use, but rather make probation/parole less rehabilitative.

The United States has made significant use of electronic monitoring, but Canada has been much more cautious in its application (McDonald, 2015). US states have statutes that mandate EM's use, but this is not the case in Canada. Federal corrections have been actively planning in recent years to utilize electronic monitoring for higher risk parolees, although earlier efforts have not worked well (McDonald, 2015; Olatu, Beaupre, & Verbrugge, 2009). McDonald reports that electronic monitoring has seen limited use by provincial agencies. Examples of EM include lower risk prisoners on provincial parole or temporary absence release (Ontario and Saskatchewan), conditional sentences with house arrest (Ontario, Nova Scotia), and higher risk auto thieves and domestic violence probationers (Manitoba). Newfoundland used electronic monitoring for medium risk inmates on temporary absence and probationers from 1994-2013, but discontinued its use due to costs and unclear benefits.

Despite some recent positive outcomes in US research, electronic monitoring cost and benefits have not been proven to provincial agencies. Federal corrections may have the best chance to more successfully implement electronic monitoring. Research is essential that carefully monitors its offence outcomes and the social as well as fiscal costs of the program.

Problem-Solving Courts

Introduced as an alternative to custody, problem solving courts more actively involve the judiciary and court actors in the management of offenders, rather than leaving it solely to probation officers. In this section we will focus on drug treatment courts (DTC), although other examples in Canada include mental health, domestic violence, and wellness courts. The problem-solving approach to court cases is referred to as **therapeutic jurisprudence**, or TJ (Winnick & Wexler, 2002). TJ applies

> principles (that) include ongoing judicial intervention, close monitoring of and immediate response to behavior, the integration of treatment services with judicial case processing, multidisciplinary involvement, and collaboration with community-based and government organizations. (p.480)

Drug treatment courts share several common features (see Goldberg, 2011; Justice Canada, 2018). They involve the voluntary diversion of drug addicted offenders who would otherwise be imprisoned into 12-24-month addictions programs. Participants appear in front of a regular judge once a week, usually appearing less regularly as they progress in the program. The drug court team consists of the judge, a consistent crown prosecutor, a representative of legal aid and treatment counselors or probation officers. Clients participate in individual counseling and/or groups, delivered by treatment staff or through outpatient services provided by an addictions agency. Curfews are usually required at the beginning of a program, and drug use is monitored through urinalysis. Counselors provide weekly reports to the court team prior to the weekly client appearances. The programs run on a harm reduction basis; thus, failing drug tests do not result in incarceration, addicts are expected to have slips. The judge and court team will be encouraging in these situations and sometimes try alternate treatment strategies. The court makes use of sanctions and incentives; sanctions might include admonishment by the judge, more frequent court appearances and urinalysis, or more stringent curfews. Incentives might include praise, more generous curfews and less drug testing, and sometimes coupons for store goods.

Problem solving courts have been in use in Canada for over 20 years (Goldberg, 2011). The original drug treatment court began in Toronto, Ontario in 1998, now the Yukon and all provinces except Newfoundland and New Brunswick operate a version of one. Canadian courts use a pre-plea or guilty plea approach (e.g., in Toronto offenders can agree to enter the drug court without pleading guilty). In other provinces guilty pleas are required. There are other variations in the program models; some involve probation staff and outpatient services (Edmonton), some have in-house counselors and direct services (Regina). The programs were initiated with mostly federal funding, but over the years the provinces have assumed more responsibility for the cost. Programs are focused on illicit drug users, those alcohol addicted are generally not eligible.

American studies have shown that drug treatment courts result in reduced recidivism rates, lower subsequent drug use and better well-being (Mitchell, Wilson, Eggers, & MacKenzie, 2012). Cost-benefit studies indicate that drug courts are very effective; they achieve savings from less prison time, less use of the health system, less subsequent crime and benefits from regular employment. In Canada, studies in Vancouver and Winnipeg showed reductions in recidivism rates between drug court clients and matched addicted comparison groups (Somers, et al., 2012; Weinrath et al., 2018a).

Drug treatment courts have their critics. Retention rates in Canadian courts run from 11% to 38%, meaning less than half of referrals complete the program (Weinrath et al., 2018b) While alternatives to custody and harm reduction is laudable, critics point out that the drug treatment court still relies to a great degree on coercion and punitive sanctions (Fischer, 2003). Regular treatment and court attendance, curfew and intrusive urinalysis makes it much more restrictive than probation or many conditional sentences. Appearing in front of a supportive judge is one of the strong visual selling features of DTC's, but Lyons (2013) has argued that it is stigmatizing for participants to appear in open court in front of other drug court clients and share intimate details about drug use and other personal matters. Fischer has argued that using the criminal justice system in this way takes resources away from other drug treatment, still criminalizes addicts and distracts from efforts at legal reform such as decriminalization of narcotics and other drugs.

Drug treatment courts have their weaknesses but stand as an innovative way to divert offenders from prison. Getting legal players like judges, prosecutors and defence counsel involved in programming is a positive step, and a move towards getting criminal justice players to "think outside the box" when dealing with offenders. Unlike many diversion programs most DTC's are resourced well – they can deliver strong programming. The results from Vancouver and Winnipeg are promising. More outcome research, cost-benefit analysis and efforts to improve retention are recommended as priorities for Canadian drug courts.

SUMMARY

As with most areas of adult corrections, adult probation had a slow start in the 20th century, but since the 1960s, it has become the most common form of state sanction. While ostensibly thought of as a form of rehabilitation, it tends to be under-rated as a form of punishment, particularly when coupled with a period of incarceration and stern conditions such as no-drinking, curfew or non-association with certain others.

Probation has increased in use, despite a decline in Canada's crime rate, and arguably has become tougher; breaches of probation incur stiffer penalties and intensive supervision programs place offenders under closer scrutiny. Efforts to professionalize the probation officer function using more objective classification and risk assessment has been criticized by some as moving probation further away from its roots in individualized treatment and concern for offender well-being. Despite these criticisms, however, probation still offers an important alternative to custody and recent efforts offer the potential to provide better service to offenders.

Intensive probation supervision, conditional sentences, electronic monitoring and problem-solving courts have been introduced in community corrections over the past 25 years as efforts to decrease the use of custody while safeguarding the public. Of these initiatives, conditional sentences have shown the most significant impact on custody, but legislative changes have muted their potential impact on Canada's rate of imprisonment. Electronic monitoring and drug courts have some supportive research, but the costs incurred with their operation suggests that provincial authorities be cautious in their use – rather than use any of these measures, why not just use probation with treatment?

Probation and conditional sentences will likely continue to be favoured sanctions because they allow the judiciary an option other than custody. Critics of community dispositions must still contend with the unpalatable alternative – an increase in the number of Canadians in prison, which includes a discouraging number of the socially marginalized. We need more research to get a better understanding of whether probation and other community initiatives are helping, punishing, or reducing custody or if it is simply increasing social control.

KEY TERMS AND CONCEPTS

Actuarial Risk and Needs Scales

Breach of Probation

Classification

Conditional Discharge

Conditional Sentence

Criminogenic Risk and Needs

Daily Count

Electronic Monitoring

Good Lives Model

Graduated Sanctions

Intensive Probation Supervision

John Augustus

Motivational Interviewing

Presentence Report

Probation Standard and Optional Conditions

Problem-solving courts

Revocation of Probation

Risk-Needs-Responsivity Model

Split Sentence

Strategic Training Initiative in Community

Suspended Sentence

Technical Violation

Therapeutic Jurisprudence

Violation Report

Wilful Failure to Comply Without a Justifiable Excuse

STUDY AND DISCUSSION QUESTIONS

1 Define probation and explain what type of conditions can be used.
2 Describe trends in the use of probation as a disposition by the court, particularly over time, and in comparison, to other criminal justice sentencing options.
3 How do probation officers go about enforcing a probation order? What are some of the legal issues around enforcement?
4 Describe the major job functions of a probation officer including classification, presentence investigation, report writing, case planning, case management and enforcement.
5 What are some of the most serious criticisms of probation and probation practice?
6 Discuss some of the methods proposed to improve probation and its practice in Canada. Which do you favour and why?

HELPFUL WEBLINKS

This provincial websites below give you an understanding about how probation is structured, Some discuss career opportunities and job requirements.

- **Alberta Probation:**
  https://www.solgps.alberta.ca/careers/probation_officer/Pages/default.aspx

- **British Columbia Community Corrections:**
  https://www2.gov.bc.ca/gov/content/justice/criminal-justice/corrections/about-us/divisions/community-corrections

- **Nova Scotia Probation:** http://www.gov.ns.ca/just/Corrections/community_programs.asp

- **Ontario Probation Officer's Association:** http://www.poao.org

- **Yukon Probation:** http://www.justice.gov.yk.ca/prog/cor/prb/index.html

- **John Howard Society of Canada:** http://www.johnhoward.ca

  This venerable society advocates on behalf of offenders and provides programming for them. The site is informative and gives critical commentary on federal and provincial correctional initiatives, as well as offering community alternatives to custody.

- **Elizabeth Fry Society: http://www.elizabethfry.ca/**

  This group advocates on behalf of female offenders and provides programs for women. Like John Howard, they can be quite critical of federal and provincial governments and the lack of options for female offenders, particularly compared to males in the correctional system.

NOTES

[1] The Crown has the option to proceed by indictment or summary conviction in the case of a hybrid offence. Indictable offences generally have much stiffer penalties than summary convictions, and consequently are treated more seriously by the courts.

REFERENCES

Alberta Solicitor General. (2005). *Alberta Solicitor General annual report*. Edmonton: Alberta.

Andrews, D., & Bonta, J. (2010). *The psychology of criminal conduct* (5th ed.). New Providence, N.J.: LexisNexis.

Andrews, D., Bonta, J., & Wormith, S. (2011). The risk-need-responsivity (RNR) model: Does adding the good lives model contribute to effective crime prevention? *Criminal Justice and Behavior, 38*, 735-755.

Andrews, D., & Kiessling, J. (1980). Program structure and effective correctional practice: A summary of CaVIC research. In R. Ross & P. Gendreau (Eds.), *Effective correctional treatment* (p. 24). Toronto, ON: Butterworths.

Anstiss, B., Polaschek, D., & Wilson, M. (2011). A brief motivational interviewing intervention with prisoners. *Psychology, Crime & Law, 17*, 689-710.

Archambault, J. (1938). *Report of the royal commission to investigate the penal system of Canada*. Ottawa, ON: Queen's Printer.

Becker, H. (1963). *The outsiders*. New York, NY: The Free Press.

⚹Blasko, B. L., & Taxman, F. S. (2018). Are supervision practices procedurally fair? Development and predictive utility of a procedural justice measure for use in community corrections settings. *Criminal Justice and Behavior, 45*(3), 402-420.

Boldt, E., Hursh, L., Johnson, S., & Taylor, W. (1983). Presentence reports and incarceration of natives. *Canadian Journal of Criminology, 25*, 269-276.

Bonta, J., Bourgon, G., Jesseman, R., & Yessine, A. (2005). *Presentence reports in Canada*. Ottawa, ON: Public Safety Canda.

⚹Bonta, J., Bourgon, G., Rugge, T., Scott, T.-L., Yessine, A. K., Gutierrez, L., et al. (2011). An experimental demonstration of training probation officers in evidence-based community supervision. *Criminal Justice & Behavior, 38*, 1127-1148.

Bonta, J., Rugge, T., Scott, T.-L., Bourgon, G., & Yessine, A. (2008). Exploring the black box of community supervision. *Journal of Offender Rehabilitation, 47*, 248-270.

Bonta, J., Rugge, T., Sedo, B., & Coles, R. (2004). *Case management in Manitoba probation*. Ottawa, ON: Public Safety and Emergency Preparedness Canada.

Bonta, J., Wallace-Capretta, S., & Rooney, J. (2000). A quasi-experimental evaluation of an intensive rehabilitation supervision program. *Criminal Justice and Behavior, 27*, 312-329.

Bottos, S. (2008). *An overview of electronic monitoring in corrections: The issues and implications*. Ottawa, ON: Correctional Service of Canada.

Carrigan, D.O. (1991). *Crime and punishment in Canada, a history*. Toronto, ON: McClelland & Stewart Inc.

Cawsey, R.A. (1991). *Alberta task force on the criminal justice system and its impact on the Indian and Metis people of Alberta: Justice on trial*. Edmonton, ON: The Task Force 1991.

Clark, M. (2006). Motivational interviewing for probation staff: Increasing the readiness to change. *Federal Probation, 69*(2), 22-28.

Cohen, S. (1985). *Visions of social control: Crime, punishment and classification*. Glasgow, Scotland: Polity Press.

Davies, M. (1971). *Probationers in their social environment*. London, UK: Her Majesty's Stationary Office.

Dowden, C., & Andrews, D. A. (2004). The importance of staff practice in delivering effective correctional treatment: A meta-analytic review of core correctional practice. *International Journal of Offender Therapy and Comparative Criminology, 48*, 203-214.

Erwin, B., & Bennett, L. (1987). *New dimensions in probation: Georgia's experience with intensive probation supervision (IPS)*. Washington, DC: National Institute of Justice.

Fauteux, G. (1956). *Report of a committee appointed to inquire into the principles and procedures followed in the remission service of the department of justice of Canada*. Ottawa, ON: Queen's Printer.

Feely, M., & Simon, J. (1994). Actuarial justice: The emerging new criminal law. In D. Nelken (Ed.), *The futures of criminology* (p. 256). Thousand Oaks, CA: Sage Publications Ltd.

Fischer, B. (2003). Doing good with a vengeance: A critical assessment of the practices, effects and implications of drug treatment courts in North America. *Criminal Justice, 3*(3), 227-248.

Gable, R.S. (2015). The ankle bracelet is history: An informal review of the birth and death of a monitoring technology. *The Journal of Offender Monitoring, 8*, 4-8.

Goldberg, S. (2011). *Problem-solving in Canada's courtrooms: A guide to therapeutic justice*. Ottawa, ON: National Judicial Institute, Retrieved from www.nji-inm.ca.

Hagan, J. (1975). The social and legal construction of criminal justice: A study of the pre-sentencing process. *Social Problems, 22*, 620-635.

Hamilton, A.C., & Sinclair, M.C. (1991). *Report of the aboriginal justice inquiry of Manitoba.* Winnipeg, MB: Public Inquiry into the Administration of Justice and Aboriginal People.

Hannah-Moffat, K., & Maurutto, P. (2010). Re-contextualizing pre-sentence reports: Risk and race. *Punishment & Society, 12,* 262-286.

Healy, W. (1915). *The individual delinquent: A text-book of diagnosis and prognosis for all concerned in understanding offenders.* Boston, MA: Little, Brown.

Hogarth, J. (1971). *Sentencing as a human process.* Toronto, ON: University of Toronto Press.

Jones, R. (2014). The electronic monitoring of offenders: penal moderation or penal excess? *Crime, Law and Social Change, 62:*475-488.

Jubinville, R. (1967). *Proposals for development of probation in Canada.* Canadian Corrections Association.

Justice Canada. (2018). *Drug treatment court funding program evaluation.* Accessible at: http://www.justice.gc.ca/eng/rp-pr/cp-pm/eval/rep-rap/2015/dtcfp-pfttt/p3.html

Kennealy, P. J., Skeem, J. L., Manchak, S., & Louden, J. (2012). Firm, fair, and caring officer-offender relationships protect against supervision failure. *Law and Human Behavior, 36,* 496-505.

Klockars, C. (1972). A theory of probation supervision. *Journal of Criminal Law, Criminology, and Police Science, 64,* 549-557.

Leiber, M., Reitzel, J., & Mack, K. (2011). Probation officer recommendations for sentencing relative to judicial practice: The implications for african americans. *Criminal Justice Policy Review, 22,* 301-329.

Lin, J. (2017). Program evaluation in the context of supervision regime change: Motivational interviewing in Colorado. *Justice Quarterly,* 1-24. doi: 10.1080/07418825.2017.1367027.

Lyons, T. (2013). Judges as therapists and therapists as judges: The collision of judicial and therapeutic roles in drug treatment courts. *Contemporary Justice Review, 16,* 412-424.

Mcdonald, D. (2015). Electronic monitoring in Canada: Federal and Provincial/Territorial law and practice. *The Journal of Offender Monitoring, 27,* 13-27.

McFarlane, G., Coughlan, D.W.F., & Sumpter, A.H. (1966). *The development of probation services in Ontario.* Department of the Attorney General. Toronto, ON: Queen's Printer.

Olatu, M., Beaupre, M., & Verbrugge, P. (2009). *Evaluation report: Electronic monitoring program pilot.* Ottawa, ON: Correctional Service of Canada.

Ouimet, R. (1969). *Toward unity: Criminal justice and corrections. Report of the Canadian committee on corrections.* Ottawa, ON: Queen's Printer.

Petersilia, J., & Turner, S. (1989). Comparing intensive and regular supervision of high-risk probationers: early results from an experiment in California. *Crime and Delinquency, 36,* 87-111.

Prochaska, J., & DiClemente, C. (1983). Stages and processes of self-change of smoking: Toward an integrative model of change. *Journal of Consulting and Clinical Psychology, 51,* 390-395.

Renzema, M., & Mayo-Wilson, E. (2005). Can electronic monitoring reduce crime for moderate to high-risk offenders? *Journal of Experimental Criminology, 1,* 215-237.

Roberts, J. V. (2004). *The virtual prison: Community custody and the evolution of imprisonment.* Cambridge University Press.

Robison, J., Wilkins, L., Carter, R., & Wahl, A. (1969). *San Francisco project – A study of federal probation and parole – final report.* San Francisco, CA: University of Berkeley, School of Criminology.

Rothman, D.J. (1980). *Conscience and convenience: The asylum and its alternatives in progressive America.* Toronto, ON: Little, Brown and Company.

Rumney, J., & Murphy, J.P. (1952). *Probation and social adjustment.* New Brunswick, NJ: Rutgers University Press.

Rush, C., & Robertson, J. (1987). Presentence reports: The utility of information to the sentencing decisions. *Law and Human Behavior, 11*, 147-155.

Shaul, L., Koeter, M. W., & Schippers, G. M. (2016). Brief motivation enhancing intervention to prevent criminal recidivism in substance-abusing offenders under supervision: A randomized trial. *Psychology, Crime and Law, 22*(9), 903-914.

Skeem, J.L., & Manchak, S. (2008). Back to the future: From Klockars' model of effective supervision to evidence-based practice in probation. *Journal of Offender Rehabilitation, 47*, 220-247.

Skinner, S., Driedger, O., & Grainger, B. (1981). *A history of corrections*. Regina, SK: Canadian Plains Research Center, University of Regina.

Smith, P., Schweitzer, M., Labrecque, R. M., & Latessa, E. J. (2012). Improving probation officers' supervision skills: an evaluation of the EPICS model. *Journal of Crime and Justice, 35*(2), 189-199.

Somers, J. M., Currie, L., Moniruzzaman, A., Eiboff, F., & Patterson, M. (2012). Drug treatment court of Vancouver: An empirical evaluation of recidivism. *International Journal of Drug Policy, 23*(5), 393-400.

Statistics Canada. (2011). CANSIM Correctional Services. Retrieved from http://www5.statcan.gc.ca

Statistics Canada (2018). Table 35-10-0030-01   Adult criminal courts, guilty cases by type of sentence. Available at https://www150.statcan.gc.ca/t1/tbl1/en/cv.action

Stein, L.A.R., Colby, S.M., Barnett, N.P., Monti, P.M., Golembeske, C., & Lebeau-Craven, R. (2006). Effects of motivational interviewing for incarcerated adolescents on driving under the influence after release. *American Journal of Addictions, 15* (Suppl. 1), 50-57.

Toupin, R.E., & Ouellette, J.A. (1972). *The rise of the sparrow; A paper on corrections in Manitoba*. Winnipeg, MB: Department of Health and Social Development.

Truth and Reconciliation Commission of Canada. (TRC) (2015). *Honouring the truth, reconciling for the future: Summary of the final report of the Truth and Reconciliation Commission of Canada*. Available at: http://www.trc.ca/websites/trcinstitution/File/2015/Findings/Calls_to_Action_ English2.pdf

Turner, S., Chamberlain, A. W., Jannetta, J., & Hess, J. (2015). Does GPS improve recidivism among high risk sex offenders? Outcomes for California's GPS pilot for high risk sex offender parolees. *Victims & Offenders, 10*(1), 1-28.

Walters, S.T., Vader, A.M., Nguyen, N., Harris, T.R., & Eells, J. (2010). Motivational interviewing as a supervision strategy in probation: A randomized effectiveness trial. *Journal of Offender Rehabilitation, 49*, 309-323.

Ward, T. (2010). The good lives model of offender rehabilitation: Basic assumptions, aetiological commitments, and practice implications. In F. McNeil, P. Raynor & C. Trotter (Eds.), *Offender supervision: New directions in theory, research and practice* (pp. 41-64). New York, NY: Willan.

Ward, T., & Maruna, S. (2003). Criminogenic needs and human needs: A theoretical model. *Psychology, Crime & Law, 9*, 125-143.

Washington State Institute for Public Policy (WSIPP). (2018). *Inventory for evidence-based, research-based, and promising programs for adult corrections*. Olympia, WA. Accessible at http://www.wsipp.wa.gov/ReportFile/1682/Wsipp_Inventory-of-Evidence-Based-Research-Based-and-Promising-Programs-for-Adult-Corrections_Inventory.pdf

Weinrath, M. (1999). Are new directions warranted for the presentence report? An empirical test of its validity in the adult court system. *Crime and Justice, 22*, 113-129.

Weinrath, M., Doerksen, M., & Watts, J. (2015). The impact of an intensive supervision program on high-risk offenders: Manitoba's COHROU program. *Canadian Journal of Criminology and Criminal Justice, 57*, 253-288.

Weinrath, M., Gorkoff, K., Watts, J., Smee, C., Allard, Z., Bellan, M., Lumsden, S., & Cattini, M. (2018a). Accessing drug treatment courts do age, race or gender matter? *Australian & New Zealand Journal of Criminology, 0*, 1-19.

Weinrath, M., Gorkoff, K., Watts, J., Smee, C., Allard, Z., Bellan, M., Lumsden, S., & Cattini, M. (2018b). Accessing diversion from custody: Retention and classification in a drug treatment court. *Annual Review of Criminal Justice, 7*, 315-345.

Winick, B. J. & Wexler, D. B. (2002). Drug treatment court: Therapeutic jurisprudence applied. *Touro Law Review, 18*, 479-486.

CASES CITED

R. v. Berg, 2014 B.C.J. No. 2084

R. v. Bolen, 2003 SKPC 163 (CanLII)

R. v. Bremmer, 2006 ABPC 93 (CanLII)

R. v. Deis, 1996 CanLII 612 (BC SC)

R. v. Di Pietro, 2000 CanLII 11405 (MB PC)

R. v. Gladue, [1999] 1 SCR 688

R v. Harris, 2001 BCPC 97 (CanLII)

R. v. Proulx, [2000] 1 S.C.R. 61

R. v. Shoker, [2006] 2 SCR 399 2006 SCC 44

R v Wilson, 2017

Prison Life: Doing Time in Canadian Institutions

5

Rosemary Ricciardelli and Michael Weinrath

Learning Objectives

After reading this chapter, you should be able to:

- Understand recent trends in prisoner custody.

- Describe and understand the socialization process of prison admission.

- Outline the major theories of prison adjustment and their criticisms.

- Explain subcultural theories and how they shape the prisoner social system.

- Describe the overcrowding situation in Canada and its impacts.

- Understand the issue of violence in correctional institutions.

- Outline the problem of illicit drugs in prison and various methods of interdiction.

- Describe the issue of prison gangs, their formation, activities and the strengths and weakness of proposed solutions.

INTRODUCTION

In this chapter, we go "inside" Canada's federal and provincial correctional institutions to understand the inner workings of prisons and the day-to-day life of those living and working within closed custody spaces. We use both quantitative and qualitative data sources to inform the reader about prison spaces. National and provincial statistics alongside empirical research reveal external trends, such as the more frequent use of remand that adversely impacts persons charged with a criminal offense, and the changing landscape of prisons in the country. Indeed, it is the qualitative studies conducted by academic researchers, prisoner advocates, or prisoners themselves, men and women who have spent time in prison observing and systematically recording their experiences that provide nuanced insights into the day-to-day interworking of prison spaces. Prisoners, current or formerly incarcerated, and prison ethnographers or scholars have a rich history of informing and creating prison research. This includes pioneering efforts by Clemmer (1940), Sykes (1958), and Irwin (1962) as well as more recent qualitative efforts by prison sociologists Ben Crewe in England (2005a), former prisoner Victor Hassine in the United States (US) (2006), and sociologists Elizabeth Comack (2008), Michael Weinrath (2016) and Rosemary Ricciardelli (2014a) in Canada. These studies provide insight into the so-called "inmate" subculture and the difficulties faced by prisoners. In the latter portion of this chapter, after discussing the changing norms of prison living, we examine the traditional problems of violence and drugs that confronts prisoners in their institutional life, and newer challenges such as prison gangs and extremism and changing legislation around transgender prisons. Our focus in this chapter is on men's life in prison, while female prisoners will be covered in Chapter 6.

TRENDS IN CANADIAN CUSTODY

Persistent Custody Use despite Declining Crime Rates – with More on the Horizon

Crime rates have some utility when comparing criminal behaviours and the use of custody over time and across space. Statistics Canada has also added the Crime Severity Index (CSI) (Wallace et al., 2009) to assess the problem of crime by weighting different types of crime by severity. The CSI allows for a differentiation in the crime rate between more trivial and more serious offences. For instance, an increase in the number of armed robberies would be rated higher than an increase in the number of thefts.

Since 1992, the official crime rate has shown movement downwards (Keighley, 2017). Looking at a the most recent 16-year period, 2000-2016 (Table 5.1), we see the crime rate continues to decline at a substantial rate of 31.3%, and the CSI has dropped similarly by 33.5%. The violent crime rate and the Violent Crime Severity Index have also declined by 29.6% and 23%, respectively. The good news for Canadians is that not only is the crime rate shrinking, but so is serious crime.

Why consider the crime rate when this chapter is supposed to address prison life? Well, the number of people in prison, should, in principle, be linked to changes in the crime rate, or so we might think. Logically we expect that the number of adults in custody will also have declined in the past sixteen years corresponding with the decreased rates of crime. Surprisingly, this is not so, in fact, there was an *increase of 2.6%* in rates from 2000-2016. We view a likely decline in custody in recent years as stymied by the 2013 legislative change, formally known under the short title of the Safe Streets and Communities Act (e.g., the omnibus crime bill or Bill C-10).

Bill C-10 was intended and successful in seriously limiting the use of conditional sentences as an alternative to custody and established mandatory minimum custody sentences for other crimes. These measures continue to be counter-intuitive; if the crime rate is going down and custody is going up, why do we need to further increase the use of custody?

	2000	2016	% Change
Table 5.1 – Crime Rates and Custody Rate 2000-2016 (Per 100,000)			
Overall Crime Rate	7,607	5,224	-31.3%
Crime Severity Index	106.7	70.9	-33.5%
Violent Crime Rate	1,494	1,051.6	-29.6%
Violent Crime Severity Index	97.8	75.3	-23.0%
Custody Rate	126.3	133.6	+2.6%

Source: Statistics Canada (2018).
Table 35-10-0154-01 Average counts of adults in provincial and territorial correctional programs,
Table 35-10-0155-01 Average counts of offenders in federal programs, Canada and regions.

The elevated use of custody is only part of the problem for prisoners. The provincial authorities have been reluctant to grant early releases for prisoners, thus further explaining Canada's continued high use of custody. Provincial parole boards in Ontario and Quebec have reduced their rate of awarding parole. Ontario went from 60% approvals in 1986-87 to 32.4% in 2009-2010 (Ontario Parole Board, 2010). In fact, British Columbia eliminated their provincial Parole Board in 2007, requiring their provincial prisoners to apply to the federal National Parole Board (NPB). It takes nearly six months for the Correctional Services of Canada (CSC)to process a prisoner application through to the NPB, meaning that provincial prisoners serving nine months or less cannot be realistically processed in time to make it worthwhile. Provincial prisoners serving a nine-month sentence are usually out after six months, due to a third of their sentence being taken off as earned remission.

While much attention is focused on federal and provincial parole boards, less attention has been given to the serious decline in provincial temporary absence (TA) programs. Designed for quick processing for prisoners serving short terms, these programs were more effectively used in the past. For example, Alberta in the 1990s had as many as 1,000 former prisoners per day on TA (Personal Communication, Alberta Solicitor General, 2011). As shown in Figure 5.1, very few provincial prisoners are released early, and that number is going down. From 778 prisoners per day on TA in 2002-03, the latest figures indicate that there were only 457 in 2015-16, a drop of 41.3%. Considering there were 11,000 sentenced individuals in provincial custody on average in 2015-16, 457 appears to be a very low number!

More Prisoners Serving "Harder" Time on Remand

There have been serious increases in the federal day-to-day custody totals over the past 10 years, from 11,040 to 14,498 in 2015-16, a jump of 3,458, or 31% (Figure 5.2). But while more federal

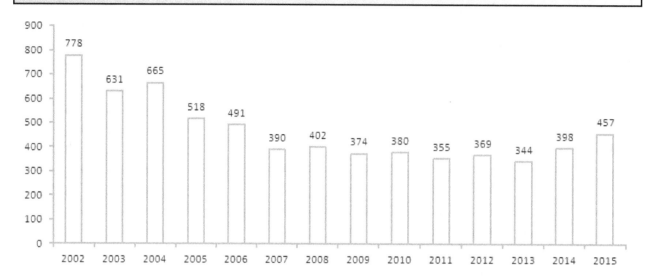

Figure 5.1 – Provincial Daily Temporary Absence Count

Source: Statistics Canada (2018) Corrections Program.

prisoners are a looming crisis for Canada's prisons, there is another significant (but largely unnoticed) problem; more prisoners who are yet to be convicted of a crime are serving time under increasingly difficult circumstances. In Canada, we have experienced a phenomenal (and lamentable) increase in the pre-trial detention population which prisoners and releases have continued to describe as the hardest time they must serve (see Ricciardelli, 2014a; Pelvin, 2017; Weinrath, 2016).

Prisoners are directly affected by their legal status. Remanded accused adults are placed in high security detention centres while awaiting trial or sentencing. Remand centres are generally designed as maximum security, thus pre-trial detention prisoners will begin their custodial experience in the most secure units in such facilities. Moreover, their legal status – they are charged, considered a flight risk or threat and thus not eligible for bail, and yet to be convicted or sentenced – leaves them incarcerated without the opportunity to work, only an hour of recreation each day, perhaps eligible for a few literacy programs, scant access to religious counselling, and no control over their conditions of confinement. In contrast, sentenced prisoners are assigned a security rating, sent to serve their sentence at a correctional facility, and work on a release plan with a staff member (e.g., a probation officer or case manager). They also have better access to programs, work, and recreation where available. The irony is, we must remember, that remand prisoners have not been convicted of anything, but must endure worse living conditions and greater uncertainty than sentenced (e.g., found guilty or who have plead guilty) prisoners (Pelvin, 2017; Weinrath, 2016).

In 1985-86, Canadian provincial remand centres and correctional institutions averaged 3,424 pre-trial detention cases and 12,690 provincial/territorial sentenced prisoners. By 2016, 14,899 of the daily prisoner count were on remand, and only 10,091 were sentenced (see Figure 5.2). This represents an increase of over 335% in remands, and a decline of 20.5% in sentenced offenders. While this almost 30-year trend is striking, the accelerated growth of remand in the last ten years is even more remarkable.

Figure 5.2 – Provincial Remand and Sentenced In-House Count

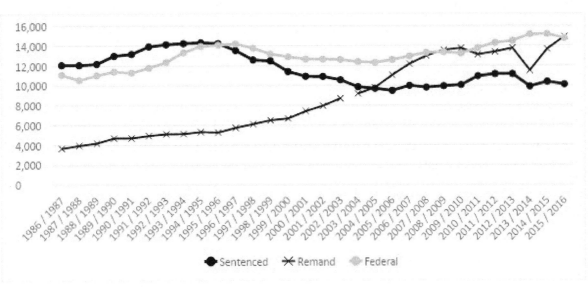

Source: Statistics Canada (2018) Table 35-10-0154-01.

For the ten-year period 1986-1995, pre-trial cases jumped by only 1,600, but for the decade 2005-06-2015-16, remands escalated by almost 4,000 prisoners! Increasing more federal sentences (2 years+) is not a viable explanation for the decline in provincial/territorial *sentenced* prisoners, especially when one considers that the daily number of federal prisoners changed marginally, from 12,581 to 14,471, between 2006 and 2016. The in-house prisoner count data illustrates a crisis across Canada. Despite regional variation by provinces and territories in their use of custody (Statistics Canada, 2018), each has faced an upsurge in persons held in remand custody. Provincial data indicates that by 2016 Nova Scotia, Alberta, Manitoba and Ontario had 65-68% of their prisoner populations on remand (Statistics Canada, 2018).

There were three common explanations offered for the increase in remanded prisoners:

1. **Two-for-one credit**: prisoners are staying in remand because they earn enhanced credit when sentenced for their time in remand custody due to the poor facilities (e.g., overcrowding and lack of movement, programs, and recreation), remission, and parole while on pre-trial detention (e.g., prisoners with one year in remand custody get two years taken off a three-year sentence).

2. **Increase in administrative offences**: such offenses include charges such as failing to appear in court, curfew breaches, and violations of non-contact orders for domestic violence cases (Taillon, 2006). These violations of court orders are more likely to result in detention until trial, and this has likely contributed to increases in the remand rate.

3. **Longer wait times for trial**: in Canada, it is now taking much longer for cases to get to trial. The average number of days to conclude a case increased from 121 to 215 during 1994-2004 (+77%). Also, during that period, the percentage of cases that took more than eight months to dispose of doubled from 13% to 27% (Taillon, 2006; Weinrath, 2009a).

Despite having no empirical evidence that prisoners were colluding regarding "two-for-one," under Harper the federal government passed Bill C-25, which effectively limits remand credit to "one-for-one," except in exceptional circumstances. Weinrath (2009a), in his survey research of Manitoba prisoners, found that only about 20% opted for the "two-for-one," most were simply frustrated by the amount of time it took to get to trial. Moreover, many of his participants felt that Crown prosecutors were, most often, the ones asking for the delay (Weinrath, 2009a). Despite hearing about his research and the submissions by other criminologists and legal scholars who opposed Bill C-25 in open Senate Hearings, the Bill was passed and proclaimed in February 2010. Among other features, the bill proposed to reduce pre-trial credit to one-to-one.

The legislation has obviously had little to nil effect on remand rates. The Supreme Court struck down the one-for-one part of new law and substituted 1.5-for-one (*R. v Summers*, 2014). As the previously noted statistics show, the provincial remand situation has not improved at all since 2010; instead it has only worsened. A 2016 Supreme Court decision, however, may finally have an impact on pre-trial detention rates. The *Jordan* SCC case has placed a "presumptive ceiling on time to trial of 18 months for less serious cases tried in provincial court and 30 months for serious crimes tried in a superior court" *(R v. Jordan)*. In consequence, a burden is placed on police and the Crown to get cases moving through the system, as they risk public criticism and embarrassment for any such cases that are thrown out.

Tougher Time Being Served on Remand, Less Programming?

The shift to higher numbers of remand prisoners has the dubious effect of lowering or stabilizing the federal custody rate and seeing the custody rates rise in provincial institutions (Figure 5.2). Due to the conversion of provincial correctional centres into remand institutions, less programming is available to prisoners (Weinrath, 2016). In federal institutions because there are fewer admissions and prisoners are there for longer periods of time, they can typically access longer, more intensive programs. In provincial sentenced institutions, work and treatment programs may be available during the day, and recreation is available for a few hours in the evening. However, this is not the case with remand; for example, Weinrath (2016) found that remanded prisoners serving time in large institutions, like Fort Saskatchewan Correctional Centre in Alberta and Headingley Correctional Centre in Manitoba, get as little as 45 minutes recreation, three days a week. Similarly, Ricciardelli (2019) in her work with correctional officers found that programming was scarce across institutions in the Atlantic region and what did exist was largely unavailable to remand prisoners. Prisoners on remand, then, simply spend a lot of unconstructive time on their unit, either in their cell or playing cards (if allowed) or watching television. This is regrettable, as previous research shows that at least 60% of remand prisoners recognize that they have problems and desire treatment (Weinrath, 2007).

In summary, in Canada there continues to be a greater use of custody despite a decline in the crime rate. More onerous living conditions for most prisoners are the result of the upward remand trend. Thus, in Canada, many prisoners are doing "harder" time.

THEORIES OF PRISONER ADJUSTMENT

As noted in Chapter 2, prisons became popular in the 18th and 19th centuries because they held the promise of changing prisoners for the better. In the 19th century, institutions promised different regimes to drive this change through the prison, penitentiary, reformatory or correctional institution. Custodial facilities however have yet to live up to this early ideal of rehabilitating or deterring prisoners (see Carrigan, 1991; Rothman, 1971).

The early prisoner theories used to explain adjustment to institutional life include **prisonization, deprivation, importation, and integrated theories**, as well as the idea of prisons as "total institutions." These models were developed during the late 1930s to early 1960s, remain popular in empirical work by punishment scholars, and still resonate with a lay person's concept of prison life. Clemmer (1940) first coined the term "prisonization," a play on the sociological concept of "socialization," to describe the way prisoners learn and become accustomed to the informal and formal prison cultures when incarcerated – including oppositional subculture. Said another way, prisonization is the process of prisoner assimilation and adaptation to prison culture and living. He saw prisoners holding values and adopting folkways that differed from individuals on the "outside," culminating in holding oppositional values to the administration. Of course, Clemmer's hypothesis was criticized by other scholars who voiced concern about his methods and description of the process (see Jacobs, 1977, Zamble & Porporino, 1988).

Building on Clemmer's work using Talcott Parsons' systems theory, Gresham Sykes (1958) outlined a deprivation theory of prisoner socialization. Deprivation theory holds that prisons are negative places with deprivations inflicted on prisoners that create destructive attitudes and behaviours, and an oppositional prisoner subculture. Traditional deprivation theorists, then, have depicted prisoner life within a framework of "schools for crime," where, over time, prisoners are socialized into a prisoner subculture with a rigid prisoner code that supports illicit activity and promotes opposition to correctional administration and staff). Driving this "prisonization" and creation of the prisoner code are the five **pains of imprisonment**, also referred to as the deprivations prisoners' experience upon admission to a closed custody facility: they lose their autonomy in decision-making, privacy, safety, access to sexual relations, and access to material goods (Sykes, 1958). Deprivations, it must be recognized, are not just the loss of freedom and agency within the restrictive nature of prison living, prisoners also live in deprived conditions, with minimal independence or access to goods and services, loved ones, and are disassociated from all their possessions, everything they have worked for or ever had, and their supports. Nonetheless, the theory of deprivation has also being met with criticism, largely tied to the lack of attention directed at social factors, such as race, and prison gangs (Jacobs, 1977).

Taking Sykes (1958) work as a point of departure, some early prison theorists tended to focus their efforts on understanding how the persuasive and rigid organizational characteristics of prisons shaped the movements and space of those housed within: the prisoners (Goffman, 1961). Goffman's enduring depiction of the "**total institution**," alerts us to the potential impact of prisons and other formal organizations such as the military and mental asylums on human behaviours and actions. He saw such formal institutions as isolating the individual from external society and essentially forcing values and routines on his or her daily existence. Basing much of his analysis on mental health facilities, commonly referred to as "asylums" at the time, Goffman saw prisoners as enduring humiliating experiences upon admission that he termed **mortification rituals**. These rituals were designed to break a person down, strip them of their prior identity and then mark the first step toward the creation and shaping of a new self. They include: first, taking worldly possessions away (e.g., to start breaking the person down); second, shaving their heads (e.g., to remove their sense of self); third, being assigned a number as your identity (e.g., stripping of prior identity); and lastly, being forced to wear a uniform (e.g., marking the "new self").

Goffman has been criticized. Some observers argue that the deleterious effects of incarceration discussed in his work are overstated, as he extrapolated from his experiences in mental health facilities (Bonta & Gendreau, 1990). While his concept of the total institution remains popular, there is much dispute over the ability of current institutions to totally isolate and re-socialize individuals (Jacobs, 1977). With the advent of television, civil liberties legislation and oversight boards, the notion of an institution effectively cutting off its members from the outside world and any influence by others is not tenable (Farrington, 1992). Moreover, authors, such as Irwin (1962) have written on the ongoing influence of outside trends on the prison.

As a prison scholar with first-hand prison experience, John Irwin particularly felt that deprivation theory grossly over-estimated the ability of the prison to socialize individuals because prisoners did not live in a "total institution" or institutional vacuum, they are impacted and shaped by their experiences on the street both before and while inside prison. His importation theory (1962), built on his own experiences and observations when incarcerated in the California prison system. He posits that individuals who enter prison, by and large, already possess "antisocial" attitudes and values. Said another way, he argued that the prisoner subculture and predatory, oppositional behaviours simply reflect pre-existing subcultures. Prison itself, then, does not make a person "worse" because they are already prone to predatory activity and hold negative attitudes towards the police, correctional staff, and law enforcement people. (Ricciardelli, Maier, & Hannah-Moffat, 2015, p. 5; see also: Irwin, 1962; Jacobs, 1977). While holding different central premises, these theories share the view that the prisoner subculture limits the ability of the prison to change those incarcerated.

More recent scholarship has shown that both importation and deprivations shape prisoner behaviour (Sorenson et al., 1998). As such prison scholars including, Crewe (2005a), Sparks and colleagues (2009) and Lacombe (2008), suggested an **integrated theory** to explain prison culture and living that includes both importation and deprivation hypotheses. Here, prisons are interpreted as informally organized by the juncture of past and present experiences, institutional organization and current restrictions.

Nonetheless, a slightly different version of the importation theory is provided in a seminal study by Canadian psychologists Zamble and Porporino (1988). The authors apply coping/stress theory to offenders, hypothesizing that prisoners with poor coping skills while in the community will struggle in prison. Using a longitudinal design that followed upwards 150 prisoners, the study found clear evidence that offenders with difficulty dealing with others, problem solving or controlling aggression also exhibited similar behaviour while in prison, and upon release. This has also been referred to as the **"deep freeze" hypothesis**, which asserts that prisons do little to help or hurt those in custody (Bonta & Gendreau, 1990). Prisoners then merely do their time with no real deterioration or improvement (for other studies on prisoner "coping," see McCorkle, 1992; Ricciardelli, 2014).

THE PRISONER SUBCULTURE AND THE CONVICT CODE

Theorists of all persuasions, such as deprivation and importation, concede that prisoners not only live but are socialized into a separate prison community with its own **subculture** (Cohen, 1955), which includes, at times, opposition to and rejection of the dominant order or formal rules imposed by prison administration and staff (Clemmer, 1940). In men's prisons, the subculture and "code" is highly gendered, influenced by "masculinities"; specifically, hyper-masculinities are found to underpin how identities are formed or maintained by adult male prisoners (Comack, 2008; Ricciardelli, 2013). **Masculinities** are comprised of traditional male attributes that are valued by "real men," such as physicality, aggressiveness, a willingness to be violent, a more stoic demeanour, and hierarchical view of group status. Male prisoners gain status if they are physically and mentally tough and stand-up for themselves. In contrast, so-called feminine behaviour such as expressing feelings and emotions are actively devalued by prisoners. Attributes of prisoners, such as their gender positioning and presentation, and the prison environment itself together inform the prisoner experiences of adjustment and the development of a prisoner social system guided by a "**convict code**" or prisoner code (Sparks et al., 1996; Crewe, 2005a; Ricciardelli, et al., 2015).

This "code,: a series of informal norms, structures prisoners' day-to-day behaviours. Historically, this set of unwritten rules was thought to help prisoners get along, but ultimately it promotes negative attitudes by actively working against the dominant order (Clemmer, 1940). More recently, the code has been thought to be less about having prisoners "get along" and more focused on maintaining order, promoting individualism and countering unpredictable behaviours by prisoners (Ricciardelli, 2014b; Ricciardelli, et al., 2015). Researchers in Canada, the US, and Britain, however, show that the code has declined in importance over the last few decades, but some form of these subcultures and organizational rules continue to exist. For example, Cooley (1992) found that rather than a strict "convict code," only a set of "informal rules" guided prisoners in day-to-day life; rules that might or might not be adhered to depending on the situation. This notion of "situational compliance" to the code is echoed by Hassine (2006) in his account of doing time in US state prisons and Crewe (2005a) in his participant observation study of residents in a British prison. Said another way, both authors found that prisoners adhere to the convict code only when it suits them.

Thus, although the "convict" code may change between institutions, there remain some consistencies in its tenants across institutions. No matter what the central objectives of the code, it always dictates what behaviour are, versus are not, acceptable, which will include provisions for *status, appropriate behaviour and mutual respect* (Mann, 1967; Ricciardelli, 2014c; Sykes, 1958).

The central tenets of the inmate code include:

- Status
  - Prisoners who stand-up for themselves (i.e., do not back down in a fight), and are smart and discreet in their dealings are respected in the prison
  - Prisoners who commit more serious violent crimes have more status (murderers, than perhaps, thieves).
  - Prisoners who are new have less status until they prove themselves to be "solid" or "stand-up."
  - Informants, "snitches," or "rats" rank in the lower rungs of prisoner hierarchy and could be beaten or killed for their transgressions.
  - Sex offenders are ranked the lowest among prisoners and are thought acceptable targets of violence and victimization. Amongst persons convicted of sex-related offenses, people whose victim was a child (or children) rank the lowest.

- Appropriate Behaviour and Respect
  - Do not talk to staff unless you have to.
  - Oppose administration.
  - Do not inform.
  - Do your own time, and do not involve yourself in the problems/concerns of others.
  - Stand up for yourself, be strong, and don't be weak.
  - Do not talk to staff unless you must (i.e., do not act friendly with staff or have extended conversation as it suggests one could be "snitching").
  - Avoid making eye contact with prisoners.
  - Do your own time, and do not involve yourself in the problems/concerns of others.
  - When threatened, stand-up for yourself and fight back, and do not appear weak or show fear.
  - Repay all debts.
  - Do not ask another prisoner about their business.
  - Do not look into another prisoner's cell or enter without an invitation.
  - Do not steal from another prisoner.
  - Do not call another prisoner a "goof" unless calling out a fight (although "goof" is now

used to suggest a prisoner's charge or conviction compromises their status as a "solid" prisoner, prisoner lore suggests that "Goof" originally served as an acronym for "Get Out or Fight" and was used to call out a fellow prisoner to fight.)

Despite its suggested utility, the code appears to have declined in its adherence. The question, however, is why?

In the US, Irwin (2005) viewed the influx of state-raised, violent, young prisoners in the 1970s as leading to a less supportive network, generally among prisoners, and an increase in violence. However, in Canada, this trend is reported by federal prisoners, yet the situation appears more complex. Citing interviews conducted in the early 1990s, Weinrath (2016) and Jackson (2002) report that the rules governing the prisoner subculture may have lessened due to efforts by correctional authorities. Although dynamic supervision by correctional staff and intelligence gathering efforts by preventative security officers may have diminished the influence of a prisoner code, more recent scholars have suggested that the code has not necessarily declined in adherence, rather, it has changed form but stays oriented toward decreasing unpredictable violent behaviour and snitching among prisoners (Ricciardelli et al., 2015).

More "Snitching" and less "Solidarity"

Weinrath (2016) found that Canadian prisoners and staff generally agree that the code has declined in influence in both federal and provincial prisons (See Box 5.1). This deficiency is viewed as a negative phenomenon by staff and prisoners, but for different reasons. Prisoners are very concerned about what they perceive to be an increase in the amount of informing on other prisoners. They express anger over how this restricts their ability to solve prisoner problems within their own group. They also decry the current lack of mutual respect and courtesy; they feel that this was an important organizing feature of prisoner life "back in the day." Ricciardelli (2014c) learned of similar concerns in her study of formerly incarcerated federal prisoners. She also found that former prisoners spoke most of "young" prisoners who did not understand consequences or show respect as being of most concern in the institution. Prisoners with longer histories of incarceration, just like many citizens in the outside world, tended to reminisce about the "old days" where elders were shown respect and prisoner solidarity had meaning. Weinrath found staff (particularly correctional officers) do not necessarily view the amount of informing as a problem, because, of course, this usually means that they have more knowledge of prisoner activities, improving their ability to manage their units and hold trouble-makers accountable. Staff feel, however, that the decline in prisoner respect for each other is a negative feature of day-to-day prison life.

The Code in Present Day: A Continuum?

In Canada, prison researchers have found that some prisoners insist the code still exists, but not all prisoners subscribe to it – or recognize that they are subscribing to a code. Weinrath found that older prisoners are more likely to subscribe to the code, having either learned it from prisoner mentors when they were first incarcerated, or having picked it up over the years using common sense and street smarts. Similarly, federal prisoners are more likely than provincial prisoners to adhere to the code in some form. No matter how it is viewed, the key objectives of the code in the current Canadian prison context remains to create an informal prison culture that reduces unpredictable prisoner behaviours (i.e., uses sanctioned violence in essence to reduce instances of unpredictable violence), encourages individualism (i.e., minding one's own rather than getting mixed in someone else's relations), and ensures that people living in overly close and overcrowded quarters have some privacy in otherwise impossibly non-private spaces (Ricciardelli, 2014b; Ricciardelli et al., 2015).

FEATURES OF DAY-TO-DAY PRISON LIFE

More recent efforts to assess prisoner adjustment have studied the initial transition for first-time prisoners into prison. In his UK study of younger, new prisoners, Harvey (2007) reports initial contact with the system put prisoners in a **liminal state**. The liminal state is a sort of limbo or transitional state for new prisoners trying to adjust and understand their new world and its routines. Prisoners are in a

Box 5.1 – Prisoner and Staff Perceptions on Changes in the Inmate Code

The unwritten rules that supposedly guide the day-to-day life of prisoners have undergone some changes in recent years. The following quotes are from prisoners who have served time at a number of provincial and federal correctional institutions in Western Canada, as well as staff. The data originates from a study by Weinrath (2009b).

"The unwritten rules of jail are basically gone. There's so much rattin' and shit on these ranges. It's fuckin' sickening. Like, when I started doing my time, you learned and you learned fast what jail was about. It was jail, it wasn't what it is today. If you didn't learn fast, you got straightened out and that was it. And then obviously you learned" (**Dean, federal experience, sentenced Headingley Correctional Centre**).

"It is all dog eat dog. There use to be a time where I would come in, lets say I just got arrested, by the time I got upstairs in the remand centre they'd have a package put together for me. Coffee, junk food for people coming off drugs and stuff, they always had a package for you. There is nothing anymore, nobody does nothing for nobody" (**Tori, female, federal experience, remand at Fort Saskatchewan Correctional Centre**).

"Yeah, there is so little of the code in here right now, I can give you example after example of people stealing from each other, from jealousy, the envy that comes out. As we speak right now, I wouldn't be surprised if there was a lockdown because of tobacco stealing. Here the code doesn't matter. Like, for instance, there are coffee jugs, someone took the glass tube out of one last week, to use for a crack pipe, I guess, and that's what gives crack heads a bad name. There is no code, there is no code in here" (**Danny, lifer, Matsqui Institution, Fort Saskatchewan Correctional Centre**).

"Is there an inmate code of ethics? No, it's changed, now it's pathetic. It used to be, pay your bills don't snitch, don't be loud, don't be a mouth piece. It's, respect to your fellow inmate, that's how it used to be. Now guys are pumping music all night long, they don't give a fuck about the next guy and that's what's changed. It used to be inmates against guards, inmates would stick together as a collective against the guards and now it's inmates against inmates. It's every man for himself. Now there is racketeering, they now have this two for one shit. Used to be ten years ago, here buddy I'll help you out just give it back to me when you can. Now it's, you take that you're gonna owe me two for one. Pay me on two you owe me four next pay day, you don't pay me four next pay I'm punching you out. Everybody's an entrepreneur (laughs)" (**Remy, ex-gang member, Stony Mountain Institution**).

W: Is it just the old school guys who adhere to the inmate code?

continued...

"My best friend in the joint, is now 21, and we're not great friends, but he's young and he's got it" **(JM, lifer Matsqui Institution)**.

"There are still a lot of guys who hold true to that. And I am one of them you know what I mean."

W: Is it true more of the older guys?

"Not necessarily, some of these younger kids are right in there too. Some of them are very much about the code, because a lot of these kids are growing up on the street, so they know the street code. So, when they come here they follow the code here too. Which is impressive, you get some more the crack kids that have no code. No code in life they have no code in jail, right? You know what you have out there is what you have in here, as far as I am concerned"

W: You think there are still stand up guys (i.e., reliable inmates who are circumspect in their communication)?

"There are stand up guy's, lots of them here and I see it everyday. Of course, you see the other kind but that is in every walk of life you know what I mean" **(Rod, remand Fort Saskatchewan Correctional Centre)**.

"The code has changed, yes and no. They steal from each other more now, there is no one on one for fighting, and they do talk to staff. But they don't tell us everything and we don't expect them to. Some of them maintain more of a code than others; some inmates try to be solid. But there are still some aspects of the code inmates stick to that might surprise you. For example, male inmates don't assault a female officer. I feel safer on a male unit than a female unit" **(Petunia, staff Fort Saskatchewan Correctional Centre)**.

"Parts of the code exist, and other parts are kind of minimized. You know a guy gets beat up, they are not going to talk to staff when we do an investigation. They didn't see it, or I fell in the shower, you know? So not cooperating with staff, not listening to staff, a lot of that still exists. So, there is an inmate code, there always will be an inmate code, it's just that some of the rules, like talking to staff, have changed because times have changed" **(Mr. A., staff HCC)**.

state of shock and spend considerable time in their cells for the first few days. After this initial period, however, Harvey found most prisoners adjust to their surroundings. In the US, Schmid and his co-investigator, prisoner Jones (1993) investigated the adjustment of first-time, short-term prisoners in a maximum-security custody, using a rare "complete" observation design. They found that shorter-term prisoners took on some of the norms of the prisoner subculture, but they generally remained low in status and never fully took on the prisoner identity. During their initial period of custody, their activities were defensive in nature, spending time in their cells, moving carefully through the institution and sizing up risky situations, all the while gathering information on appropriate behaviour.

Generalizing about a prisoner's "first time" in prison is difficult because there are many possible custodial experiences and they may all be serious, depending on the friends a prisoner might make, the time they spend in custody, and the degree of supervision by staff. The remand experience, it is argued, may not be as difficult to navigate in prison if placed with less serious offenders. New first time prisoners enter prison on a lower rung in the institutional hierarchy; they are fair game to be hazed by both prisoners and correctional officers until they learn the ways of the institution. But in situations of overcrowding or placement error, an offender may be placed next to seasoned and less patient prisoners, which can become uncomfortable or put pressure on the new prisoner to adopt the experienced prisoner's values. If not facing a prior custody remand, the individual's first actual prison experience starts after court and is likely more difficult, for example going for the very first time to a large provincial or federal correctional institution.

For prisoners, starting when they wake up in the morning, their day will be different depending on where they are serving time (Weinrath, 2016). It further varies due to the prisoners they serve time with, and the opportunities for work or programming. Another variable that also influences them is whether they are placed in remand, provincial sentenced or federal sentenced facilities. Provincial remand prisoners are usually serving time with other prisoners who may be anxious about their upcoming cases or they might be serving for very serious offences, have long criminal histories, or are first time offenders. Hopefully, a remand admission will be placed in a unit with prisoners who have similar offender backgrounds. As mentioned, remand cases do not have much recreational time (an hour a day), can access few programs, and do not earn remission. Their future is uncertain, as cases may be remanded, applications for bail denied, and their final disposition may or may not involve more custody. Sentenced provincial prisoners (i.e., those who serve sentences less than two years) are generally housed with less serious prisoners, have some access to programs, and have reasonable access to recreation in the evenings. Sentenced prisoners, in some situations, do not have access to as much programming because they are now sharing correctional institutions with remands, restricting their movements and access to services (Weinrath, 2016). Federal offenders serve, on average, the longest sentences and are more likely to be housed with the most serious and violent offenders. While more long-term programs are available, federal offenders must compete with other prisoners for spots, sometimes making access difficult (Weinrath, 2016).

What type of work is available for prisoners? Many institutions have a prisoner job manual that identifies the available jobs (Alberta Solicitor General, 2008). Almost every correctional facility needs prisoner kitchen workers and cleaners to support day-to-day operations. From this point, opportunities vary. For example, prisoners can work in local garages, or they can do gardening, snow removal or farming. Opportunities also exist for barbers, hairdressers, hobby crafts assistants, or recreation assistants. Some federal and provincial institutions offer industrial program experience, the most well-known program, the federal CORCAN program, engaging prisoners in light manufacturing of goods (Corcan, 2008). Prisoners with an educational background can tutor other prisoners who are trying to upgrade their education. Prisoners in minimum security settings can work in bush camps, clearing brush and cutting firewood.

Prisoners interested in leadership positions may become a Prisoner Secretary, or head of a Prisoner Committee (Solicitor General, 2007). Most provincial corrections and federal institutions allow for the creation of prisoner committees to promote self-governance. Prisoner committees can arrange for fund allocation from the proceeds of canteen sales. These committees might organize recreation leagues and socials involving outside groups. They also meet with institutional representatives to raise concerns and negotiate privileges. Prisoner committees can make suggestions and recommendations to institutional authorities, but they have no formal authority.

OVERCROWDING

Canada's Current Situation

Overcrowding occurs when a prison exceeds its rated capacity for housing prisoners. For example, if 400 prisoners are held in an institution with 300 beds, then it is overcrowded by 33.3% (one-third of 300). Another definition for determining overcrowding is the proportion of capacity. For instance, our example of 400 prisoners in a 300-bed institution would be running at 133% of capacity. Consequences of overcrowding are alleged to increase violence for prisoners and correctional staff, and decrease employment, recreation and program opportunities, and generally, overall, create a more stressful environment (Demers, 2014; Paquin-Marseille, Grant, & Michel, 2012). Overcrowding typically results in **double-bunking**, or the sharing of a cell by two prisoners (if not more than two prisoners). The United Nations (UN) minimum standards on the treatment of prisoners specifies that prisoners should be housed in single cells (UN Congress on Prevention of Crime, 1958).

Canada's provincial and federal correctional systems are both having trouble with overcrowding, and it is getting worse. Consider Figure 5.1 again, while remand and sentenced prisoner populations are rising, new prisons are not being built fast enough to manage them. The federal Auditor General in 2014 concluded that despite some improvements from previous years, Correctional Service Canada had not planned adequately for long term expansion of the prisoner population, and were likely to continue to need to double-bunk to manage overflow. The AG observed that adequate space for health care and programs were not considered in future expansion plans.

The most significant harms with overcrowding have occurred in the provincial correctional systems, and this is not surprising given the large increases in prisoners over the past ten years. Overcrowding, and double and even triple bunking has become a fact of life in many Canadian provincial correctional institutions. In Ontario, ongoing crowding and reports of miserable conditions such as prisoners sleeping in shower stalls resulted in a formal inquiry being called into conditions at the Ottawa-Carleton Detention Centre (OCDC Task Force, 2017). In Manitoba in 2015, there were 2,555 prisoners housed in space for 2,010, or 127% overcapacity (Kavanagh, 2016). The Brandon, Manitoba Correctional Centre had the gymnasium converted to a dorm-like setting to house prisoners. British Columbia's Auditor General reported that despite adding 800 new cells since 2007, BC Corrections was still operating at 140% of occupancy (Office of the Auditor General of BC, 2016).

Overcrowding ultimately can result in an increase in the use of incarceration and construction of more prisons. Piché (2014) found in his review of government documents through access to information requests that 6,300 additional beds had been proposed by provincial corrections by early 2010, most of them aimed at remand prisoners. He found the motivation and rationales by bureaucrats for more prison space varied from more punitive to more humanitarian. On the one hand, expanding prisons could ensure greater staff and public safety, because overcrowding was causing tension and the system was supposedly seeing more gang members and violent offenders who required more secure housing, On the other hand, more correctional facilities were also argued necessary to reduce over-crowding and associated pains for prisons such as double-bunking and to increase programming to address the specific needs of women, Indigenous offenders, and prisoners with mental health conditions. Piché challenged both views, arguing that such positions distracted policy makers from considering that the crime rate was in decline and that more alternatives to the use of incarceration should be pursued, rather than more prisons.

Effects of Overcrowding

Critics of overcrowding routinely argue that it adds to the stress of the correctional environment and increases violence. While stress and overcrowding are consistently being associated together, surprisingly, studies have failed to find any correlation between overcrowding and violence – sometimes prisoner-prisoner assaults and staff assaults *decrease* as the prisoner population *increases* (Franklin, Franklin, & Pratt, 2006; Wooldredge & Steiner, 2009). Wooldredge and Steiner (2009) argue that these conflicting findings may be attributed to the differences in measurement. So, how do we best measure overcrowding? One way is to use spatial density which is calculated by dividing the rated capacity of a prison by its current population. This method is easily understood and provides a straightforward measure. For example, if an institution is running at 130% of capacity, at least 30% of prisoners are in crowded quarters, whether that is double, or triple bunked or in a dormitory setting. Others suggest that perceptions of crowding are important because that will indicate the prisoners' level of comfort, their stress and hence, how potentially violent they might become (Wooldredge & Steiner, 2009).

While there is very little Canadian research on overcrowding, most researchers conducting studies in the US, using different measures, have generally found that prison crowding seems to have only a small effect on increasing violence, and some studies even show a negative effect (Paquin-Marseille et al., 2012; Franklin et al., 2006). Walters (1998) suggests that this lack of effect may be due to improved performance by correctional authorities. If a prison becomes crowded, staff may take steps to reduce the likelihood of violence through more careful control and monitoring of movement. Conversely, Wooldredge and Steiner (2009) argue that findings of less or minimal change in violence with overcrowding may instead result from the undercounting of assaults; correctional staff may not have the time or means to effectively monitor the prisoner population when it reaches a certain size.

While the effects of violence are variable, researchers are more supportive of other problems associated with crowding. Crowding and greater stress on prisoners are found consistently in the literature (Bonta & Gendreau, 1990; Paquin-Marseille et al., 2012). Stress is logically related to suicide ideation and completion, and not surprisingly, death by suicide among prisoners tend to increase as the prisoner population rises (Bonta & Gendreau, 1990; Huey & McNulty, 2005).

VIOLENCE IN INSTITUTIONAL SETTINGS

Social control theorists interested in prisons put efforts into unpacking the role of formal controls, those imposed by the administration, versus informal control (e.g., the prisoner code) in structuring the behaviours of prisoners, including the use of violence (Woolredge & Steiner, 2009). As in free society, there are rewards and punishments tied to actions that conform or deviate from the norms that govern behaviours in prisons. Maier and Ricciardelli (2018) found that, for federal prisoners in Canada, adhering to the formal norms or administrative controls of prison living often means deviating from the informal norms of the prisoner subculture. Said another way, what is rewarded in one context is punished in the other. Among other concerns, this opens the possibility for violence in institutions in response to what can be viewed as transgressions of the prisoner code. Looking at former prisoners' experiences with administrative controls in federal prisons, Ricciardelli and Sit (2016) found that, from the perspective of their participants, formal coercive controls in units classified as high security encouraged violence and left prisoners feeling vulnerable and unsafe. Yet, remunerative controls, as often found in prisons of a lower security classification, deterred violence and encouraged pro-social conformist behaviours because prisoners were keen to stay. Nonetheless, violence is described as "omnipresent" in prison, as there remains an undercurrent of the potentiality for violence that increases with the security classification of the prison and always shapes prison living. For this reason, among others, whether one is a prisoner or correctional officer, the prison can be a difficult place to spend time, perhaps now more than ever before.

The Trend towards More Violent Prisoner Profiles

From the 1990s to the early 21st century, objective empirical data and the qualitative impressions of CSC managers indicate that prisoners entering the federal prison system have become more difficult to manage and prepare for release (Boe et al., 2003; CSC Review Panel, 2007; Weinrath, 2016). For example, from 1997-2002, federal male admissions were more likely to be maximum security (14% to 21%). Gang affiliation rose to about 1 in 6 prisoners, with prison gang membership running as high as 36% in some institutions. Not only are prisoners more likely to have a history of prior incarceration in provincial or youth facilities, but about 25% of federal prisoners are serving sentences for homicide. While this increase was gradual, it represents the cumulative effect of the 1976 legislative change that abolished capital punishment and sentenced those convicted of first degree murder to 25-year minimum sentences and ten-year minimum sentence for second degree murder. Although the homicide rate has decreased substantially since 1992 (Keighley, 2017), the sheer number of 10-25 maximum sentences has raised the proportion of lifers.

How Much Violence is there in Correctional Institutions?

Assessing violence trends in prison is difficult. Tracking institutional violence rates over time reveals whether the situation is worsening, improving, or stable in any prison. For administrators, it allows for benchmarks to assess individual prisons and how well they are managing their institutional populations. Regrettably, few if any provincial authorities release institutional assault statistics, while annual official rates of prisoner-on-prisoner and prisoner-on-staff assaults have only recently been generated by the CSC. They also have varied the way they report assaults, using rates, moving averages and three-year summaries, making it difficult for outside parties to track trends. Given the current context about "modernizing" or changing prison practices, including, for example, eliminating or reducing the use of administrative and disciplinary segregation, it is fundamentally important to be able to empirically assess how policy change impacts the prison violence.

In addition to the organizational obstacles tied to recording violence, many prisoners do not report assaults, which results in undercounting. This is also a well-documented problem in police reported and recorded crime, but it is believed that non-reporting is likely greater among the prisoner group where there has historically been undeniable pressure not to inform on others (Cooley, 1993). Researchers investigating violence in Canadian prisons are generally confined to federal penitentiary studies. The few quantitative studies in the area are rather dated, however the findings are valuable. For example, in a self-report survey of prisoners in five medium/maximum penitentiaries in the Prairies, Cooley (1993) found 34% of prisoners were the victims of physical aggression (mostly assault) in the past year. The national federal prisoner survey reported an assault rate of 26% (Robinson & Mirabelli, 1996).

PERCEPTIONS OF VIOLENCE

Journalists Kevin Marron and Michael Harris both wrote books on Canada's federal penitentiaries. They each observed how violence diminished the quality of life for both staff and prisoners (Harris, 2003; Marron, 1996). These investigators visited penitentiaries throughout the country and interviewed staff, prisoners, and the families and friends of those incarcerated. They reported everyday violence as a fact of prison life. Marron completed his story just around the time double bunking became a persistent problem in the early 1990s. Compared to Marron, Harris tends to focus more on the threat of violence towards staff and appears to rely on staff sources for information. He expressed concern over the many rights afforded to prisoners, yet his book is marred by several factual errors as well (for a more general critique of Harris's book, see Jackson, 2004).

Canadian prisoner autobiographies outline the necessity of aggression in prison and the inevitability of violence. For example, Wayne Carlson (2001), an escape artist who was in and out of Canadian and US prisons from the 1960s to the late 1990s, describes developing a willingness to be violent as essential to establishing a reputation when he was first admitted to an adult prison. Likewise, during his journey through Canada's penitentiary system in the early 1990s, lawyer Julius Melnitzer

(1995) reports being threatened and intimidated when first admitted. Eventually, he ended up as an aggressor in a fight, causing him to lose his minimum-security status and chance at parole.

The question then becomes, is prison violence inevitable? Prisoner narratives by Carlson and Melnitzer reveal a belief that violence can be evaded by prudent caution and social skills, typically picked up through experience. Carlson views violence as something a smart prisoner can avoid. After being raised to medium security because of his fight and other issues, Melnitzer reports that it was his own personal improvements in getting along with others which enabled him to avoid further problems. He eventually earned his way back to minimum security and was paroled.

Violence, nevertheless, has been described as a sort of "rite of passage" among federal prisoners; required in some ways to confirm status (i.e., appearing tough) and show adherence to the prisoner code (Ricciardelli et al., 2015). Consider the paramount prisoner rule of "no ratting or informing," or "do your own time." Since it is impossible for a prisoner to always do their "own time," it is likely that a prisoner will be accused of engaging in problematic behaviour (e.g., making eye contact). Moreover, a prisoner's efforts to appear strong then make it difficult, if not impossible, to avoid physical confrontation without going into protective custody.

The use of **protective custody** (PC) and the designation of prisoners as **incompatibles** are traditional methods used to reduce prison violence (Weinrath, 2016). PC is thought to offer prisoner's protection. Essentially, prisoners in danger, or potential danger, are isolated from other prisoners and put in a separated protective custody unit. The need for PC is usually identified upon admission, or when a prisoner's stigmatized status becomes apparent after they tried being housed in general population (GP). Examples of typical residents of PC units are informants, sex offenders, persons who are severely in debt to other prisoners (e.g., due to gambling or drug purchases) and, in some cases, prisoners who are considered vulnerable because of age, mental or physical health, or naiveté about prison life. "Incompatibles" is a term now used in contemporary corrections to designate prisoners who cannot be housed with others on a unit because of current conflicts with other prisoners, often gang members, or due to their crimes (e.g., sex offenders) or being an informant. Basically, prisoners in PC are considered "incompatible" with other prisoners.

Staff are to refrain from identifying a prisoner as incompatible because it labels them, which also makes scheduling activities and coordinating who is on each unit (or who shares cells) awkward within a prison because one always must check to ensure antagonists are not present (Weinrath, 2016). Prisoners, however, report that careful placement is a way to keep them safe and makes them feel more secure. Dynamic security by staff (use of interaction to proactively deal with potential prisoner problems) and the use of prisoners as intelligence sources to help manage violence was grudgingly acknowledged by prisoners as having a certain measure of effectiveness. By using communication and uncovering information from prisoners, staff have reduced violence by targeting predators, managing incompatibles, and using PC when needed. Dynamic supervision practices, however, are also resented, at times, by prisoners who often prefer to manage situations either by themselves, or by senior prisoners (Weinrath, 2016).

DRUG USE

Recent CSC statistics indicates that about 50% of persons admitted to federal prisons have a substance use disorder (CSC, 2015), while researchers in an earlier study suggested that up to 80% of admitted prisoners had addiction concerns (Motiuk, Boe, & Nafekh, 2003). Addiction is an important problem to address, especially because of the persistent link between drug use and criminal activities (Pernanen, Cousineau, Brochu, & Sun, 2002). Illicit drug use is related to: robbery and theft to support a habit; crimes committed while under the influence; drug trafficking; and the violence associated with

Box 5.2 – Prisoner Suggestions to Reduce Violence

Prisoner suggestions to reduce institutional violence are quite varied. Some recognized a positive influence from dynamic security and dialogue between staff and inmates. Many prisoners are simply not that worried about violence or accept it as a fact of everyday life.

"Pretty hard to have violence in here because you're pretty well locked up most of the time in remand. A slap to them today is violence, you start yelling at somebody nowadays, you're charged for violence or assault. You don't see the violence here (provincial institution) that you do in the penitentiaries. It's just not here, you get a lot of whiny, snivelling little kids here that can't do time" (**Bernie, gang member federal experience, remand at Headingley Correctional Centre, HCC**).

"When I was in protective custody, it's calm there. If you mix certain guys that get along, it's good. But if you mix like wrong guys then it gets violent" (**Jazz, ex-gang member on remand HCC**).

"They protect people now. In the old days, there was no incompatibles and we never ratted, everybody just did their time. If you had a known rat you had them moved off the unit. You did your time right and you got the fuck out of there. Now people telling on each other and there is just such a young crowd. But now, everybody thinks, okay, I don't like that girl, so she is a rat and I will tell everybody that. We will just get rid of her. Well it doesn't work that way. They protect those people now they get to stay, and anything happens to them, we go. Which is pretty harsh. You can't just pick and choose who you want to do time with anymore, sorry. You pick and choose who you want to do time with on the street so you should stay out there if that is the way you want it. You shouldn't come here" (**Tori, female, federal experience remand Fort Saskatchewan Correctional Centre**).

"To reduce violence, have anger management. You can go to classes and take the sharing circle, it's part of anger management too, you know, you need to talk about it" (**JJ, federal experience, sentenced HCC**).

"To reduce violence, I would like to have a native (Indigenous) guard on every range. It doesn't even have to be a native guard, but a guard on the range, instead of sitting in the office all the time, communicating with the inmates, that calms everything right down. Or have a native liaison worker, or a chapel guy. Aboriginal culture is important too. Take us to a sweat" (**Jazz, ex-gang member on remand HCC**)

"Matsqui, in the pacific region, has always been the shiny star of heroin connection. We had a big change when they allowed the methadone maintenance program in. They kept it out the door for 20 years. It's been a good change. We used to have the nurses run back and forth because of overdoses, you don't see that anymore. I have not seen anyone

continued...

get hit like that in two years, they got all the heroin guys on methadone. It made Matsqui, an easier place to do time, because it is quieter. Drugs do not circulate like they used to. It is still a curse. There is less stealing in here, which contributes to less violence. So overall, it's probably better than it was. Considering we're a campus of users, we are still doing pretty good here" (**Gary, Lifer Matsqui Institution**).

smuggling and marketing drugs (see Box 5.2). The problems associated with drugs and street crime reappears inside the prison as drugs constitute a significant underground economy within institutions (Crewe, 2005b). According to MacPherson (2004), drug use, specifically, is associated with:

- Violence over control of the drug trade inside; Violence over unpaid drug debts; intimidation of prisoners on day release to smuggle drugs inside, or through their visitors, or other means;
- Maintenance of an addicted lifestyle, instead of using prison time for treatment; threatening or corruption of correctional or support staff to bring in drugs;
- Transmission of infectious disease such as Hepatitis and HIV through injection drug use; and
- Overdose and death; in a recent review of 105 overdose incidents occurring from 2012-2015, the federal correctional investigator found 11 fatalities, within which 31 cases of male deaths involved prescribed medications.

The reasons that prisoners may use drugs in prison are explained by deprivation, importation and integration perspectives. Generally, deprivation theorists view drug use to cope with the day-to-day stress of incarceration as a means of managing the pains of imprisonment. Importation theorists note that most prisoners admitted to correctional institutions in Canada have substance abuse problems. Integration theorists suggest the combination of addiction or past experiences on the street and the deprived conditions of confinement in prison together encourage prisoner's continued drug use (Crewe, 2005b).

Shewan and his colleagues (1994) surveyed Scottish prisoners and found 73% continued to use cannabis during their current incarceration, but that only 2%-6% used hard drugs – they reported lessening their drug use while incarcerated, challenging some of the precepts of deprivation theory. In Britain, Boys and colleagues (2002) found support for both importation and deprivation – 60% of heroin and cocaine users continued use while in prison, while 12% reported first using heroin or cocaine while incarcerated. In a Canadian study of male and female federal prisoners, Plourde, Brochu, Gendron and Brunelle (2012) found that 70% of respondents reported using drugs less often, and that taking drugs before being incarcerated increased the likelihood of using drugs when incarcerated. They also found prisoners in maximum/medium security used drugs more often than those placed in a minimum setting. Overall, evidence gives more credence to importation theory to explain long term drug use among prisoners and supports deprivation theory in explaining first time drug use in prison.

How Do Drugs Get Into an Institution?

Researchers have found that two primary means of getting drugs into prisons: visitors and correctional staff (Inciardi & Lockwood, 1993). Prisoners report drug smuggling methods such as hurling concealed drugs into prison yards or "throw overs." Drugs are also transported when prisoners are first admitted into the institution as they may smuggle in drugs in their body orifices (e.g., "hooping"), or in items that they keep such as footwear by hiding drugs in the linings or shoe tongues (Weinrath, 2009b). In provincial facilities that house prisoners serving intermittent sentences (e.g., serving "weekends"), these "weekend" prisoners are often pressured to bring in a steady supply of drugs as well. Visitors may also transplant drugs through kisses (orifice to orifice), or surreptitiously passing them to the prisoner while visiting, who, in turn, may secrete them in his or her anus, or swallow, and excrete later. Prisoners take great pains to secure drugs in visiting areas as they are subject to a strip search after a visit. Another method is hiding the drugs in the visiting area which are later retrieved by prisoner cleaners.

How Much Drug Use?

A consistent source that is now available to learn about the extent of drug use is official agency records of drug testing. Random drug testing through urinalysis has been conducted since the mid-1990s in Canada, UK, and the US. Urinalysis consists of an analysis of urine secreted by a prisoner. The urinalysis system is not perfect. In comparison to Canadian prisoner self-report studies, urinalysis underestimates the amount of drug use in prison (Plourde & Brochu, 2002). This may be due to prisoner motivation to avoid detection and circumvent tests.

But, does drug testing deter? In Canada, the CSC found a large impact after the first year of implementing tests in 1995; levels decreased substantially from 34% to 11% (McVie, 2001). In recent years, CSC has reported progressively lower positive rates:

- 2000-2007 range of 12%-13%
- 2008-10 average of around 8%
- 2015-17 mean of around 6%

The CSC attributes the decline in drug use to efforts at interdiction (CSC, 2011; Office of the Correctional Investigator, 2017). Equating these results with actual drug use should be done cautiously, however. The case can be made that federal officials should also consider anyone who refuses to be tested as testing positive. Refusals are complex, perhaps linked to how drug testing can be considered intrusive and refusers may be willing to be charged and happy to avoid the inconvenience and shame of drug testing. Counting "refusers" as users would certainly impact annual estimates. For example, in 2003-04, the CSC reported that 13% of prisoners were using drugs because that is the number that tested positive via random testing. Now, imagine if they added the 12.5% who refused the tests that year, then the rate is more likely to be 26%, a much more substantial number.

Drug Interdiction and Treatment

There are two primary methods of dealing with the use of drugs in prison: **interdictions**, which intends to halt or limit the supply of drugs available in prison (supply-side); and **drug treatment**, which seeks to have prisoners deal with the substance abuse issues that creates the need (demand-side). The CSC uses rather controversial ion scanners to examine the personal items of prospective visitors and reports on possible drug tainting in wallets, keys or other items prior to visitors entering the correctional facility. It also uses drug sniffing dogs for visitors and random checks throughout an institution (CSC, 2006). Correctional staff in federal and provincial institutions also use general security procedures to discourage drug use, such as cell and unit searches, prison yard searchers, vehicle patrols to discourage "throw overs," intelligence gathering, and punitive consequences for those who violate the rules (Weinrath, 2009b). Prisoners caught using or selling drugs face segregation, denial of visits or glass visits only, and can incur institutional charges that increase their sentence length inside or delay their parole eligibility.

On the treatment side, some units are designated "drug-free" and prisoners who reside there submit to regular urinalysis. Drug treatment is also used, but there remains some question regarding its accessibility; federally, the demand is too high and provincially, a high number of remands do not take treatment (Weinrath, 2007). At the federal level, methadone maintenance – a harm reduction strategy that recognizes recovery from addiction is a lifelong challenge, is an option available to persons with heroin addiction. The literature is generally supportive of methadone programs (Kinlock et al., 2007).

PRISON GANGS AND SECURITY THREAT GROUPS

As noted earlier in this chapter, **prison gangs** (PG) are a concern because they tend to be extremely predatory, promote violence, and are aggressively oppositional to staff (Griffin & Hepburn, 2006; Weinrath, 2016). They are likely to control the institutional drug trade and sub-rosa or illegal economic system (Crewe, 2005b; Trammell, 2012). In some respects, these gangs represent the most negative features of the prisoner subculture. Any identifiable clique of three or more prisoners involved in activities that threaten the security of other prisoners, staff or the institution generally are called **security threat groups** (Fong & Vogel, 1994-95).

In Canada, prison gangs have become a notable problem, both provincially and federally. Biker gangs were active in federal institutions in the 1980s but, arguably, posed manageable problems (Weinrath, 2016). In the 1990s, street gangs and other members of criminal organizations emerged in Canada's correctional institutions and their threat has escalated as they recruited more members. In their interview of police informants across Canada, Kelly and Caputo (2005) reported that prison gangs can serve as sources of recruits for street gangs. In their assessment of criminal organization members admitted from 2006-2009, the CSC estimated about 9.6% of admissions serving prisoners were associated with Outlaw Motorcycle Gangs (OMG), Street Gangs (SG), Traditional Organized Crime groups (TOC) (e.g., Mafia), Indigenous and Asian gangs (Ruddell & Gottschall, 2011). Compared to other prisoners, Indigenous, Asian and Black prisoners are over-represented in prison gangs, while whites are under-represented. Gang members tend to be younger, more violent, and involved in more assaultive behaviour and the drug trade. They also have higher needs, pose higher risks yet offer low potential for successful reintegration (Ruddell & Gottschall, 2011).

Indigenous prison gangs are a problem in federal and provincial jails in the Prairie Provinces (Ruddell & Gottschall, 2011; Weinrath, 2016). In Manitoba, for example, Headingley Correctional Centre and Stony Mountain Institution both report that about 30% to 35% of their prisoner population has a gang affiliation. Grekul and Laboucane-Benson (2008) found that Indigenous gangs appear to arise from structural inequalities in Canadian society. Discrimination and ruptured families has resulted in the Indigenous youth, in some cases, seeking out the gang to provide social support.

More recently, violent extremist gangs and their efforts to radicalize other prisoners have become a concern in Canada and other Western nations (Neumann, 2014). Estimates runs as high as 100,000 Islamic terrorists in custody world-wide (Krughlanski, Gelfand, & Gunaratna, 2010), other extremists include the Irish Republican Army, and Red Army. Skillicorn (2006) defines radicalization as a change in beliefs, feelings and actions towards one side versus another in a conflict. Such definitions are problematic of course; individuals pushing for gender or racial equality then, might be considered as radicalizing individuals to get support for pay equity for women or amendments to the **Indian Act**. Issues with radicalization in custody settings include the recruitment of prisoners into the organization who could then engage in extreme violence upon release. Still, it appears that there are relatively few violent extremists in custody: recent Canadian research suggests that less than 1% of federal admissions are radicalized (Skillicorn, Leuprecht, Stys, & Gobeil, 2015). In their study, Skillicorn and his colleagues also found it difficult to distinguish violent extremists from other prisoners but indicated extremist do experience alienation from others and employment problems but show greater involvement in programs. They indicated that even with a plethora of available data from CSC, there were simply too few violent extremists to identify prisoners at risk of being radicalized.

While, we will draw on several studies, our focus in the remainder of this chapter will be on Weinrath's work on Prairie gangs. Specifically, we review the etiology of gangs in prison; their formation, recruitment practices, impact on day-to-day prison life, and impacts on institutional management.

Etiology of Prison Gangs

Prison gangs tend to be associated with the importation model of prisoner adjustment (i.e., members of the street gang once incarcerated join their associates in prison – the prison gang). Yet, it has been found that prisons can spawn their own home-grown gangs, which is arguably a response to the pains of imprisonment and associated deprivations (see Sykes, 1958). Fong and Buentello (1991) outline the following five step process for prison gang formation:

1. Prisoner enters prison.
2. Enters into clique of other prisoners.
3. Group evolves for self-protection.
4. Group evolves to become predators.
5. Group evolves into more formal prison gang structure, ongoing entity, extends out into street gang.

Fong and Buentello (1991) note that, at any time, the process can stop; a clique may never evolve into a group, and some self-protection groups may not become predators. An example of this type of formation of a full-fledged gang is drawn from Texas, where prisoners formed the Texas Syndicate initially as a self-protection group to fend off other prison street gangs. The Syndicate eventually expanded their criminal operations onto the street. This process of prison gang evolvement is linked to the deprivation model; the lack of safety within the institution from other gangs spawned the formative self-protection group. In Western Canada, examples of both are evident. The Indian Posse street gang, one of the largest in Manitoba, began as a "jail house" gang in the late 1980s and early 1990s (Weinrath, 2016). The Aryan Brotherhood was formed in Saskatchewan Penitentiary purportedly to fend off Indigenous gangs. Examples of street gangs who continued their activities in prison include the Manitoba Warriors in Manitoba and Red Alert in Alberta.

Recruitment

One of the significant differences in prison gang structure from the 1980s to the 1990s and up to today is recruitment. At one time, biker gangs were very selective, and prisoners had to earn trust and confidence over time. However, now the focus is on strength in numbers; the more gang members, the greater the power and influence. In the Prairies, where prison gangs are plentiful, members are recruited while on remand or even on their way from court to Stony Mountain Penitentiary (Weinrath, 2016). Based on his qualitative study, Weinrath found that the motivations for some prisoners were for safety, status, power, access to drugs, and/or other illicit goods. Also, without a gang affiliation, prisoners had concerns about being targeted for assault. On the other hand, gang leaders argued that threatening people to generate recruits was overblown; gangs had more applicants than they needed.

Strategies to Manage Prison Gangs

Correctional strategies to deal with prison gangs may include intelligence gathering. This may involve using informants, monitoring prisoner telephone calls and mail and financial records, and even

Box 5.3 – Prisoners on Prison Gangs

Prison gangs are a source of problems for corrections administrators and prisoners. Views are generally negative towards gangs, and suggestions to ameliorate the problem often focus on isolation or prevention strategies.

"They should segregate them, you know if you want to be down in a gang stick them all in one fricken warehouse. This way they cannot go around recruiting anybody else. That's the biggest thing for me, their picking on these little kids and stuff like that. The little kids are scared for their lives and stuff, so they're joining and before you know it they got a taste of it" (**Donny, sentenced prisoner Fort Saskatchewan Correctional Centre, FSCC**).

"And the problems that come with gangs are just retarded. Like I said you get a few of them together and all of a sudden you can watch them change and you know that pisses me off because you get the people alone and they are not bad guys. You play sports with them, you do this with them, but I don't understand the whole gang mentality. If you get the wrong people together you're going to have violence right" (**Todd, sentenced prisoner, FSCC**).

"No, done with gangs. Done with the gang life. It was getting too serious. People are getting shot and stuff like every day" (**Jazz, former gang member, remand, Headingley Correctional Centre, HCC**).

"If you got problems with certain gangs, you don't know where you're gonna end up. They got to break that whole lifestyle before they end up in jail. I know they've been starting to touch base on it, but they need to go more in-depth and work with the kids better, growing up in bad families." (**Ed, remand HCC**).

"They need more in-depth work with the kids growing and encourage them not to get into the gang scene. For weak families, find other things to replace the social support, open more community centers, get the kids involved in stuff. Take some in-depth looks at the parents. Fight the problem when they're young, not when it's too late and they've already had how many victims" (**Jason, remand HCC**).

recording involvement in violent incidents. Intelligence officers also work with related police and community corrections intelligence workers to monitor the link between PG and street gang activity.

In Western Canada, variants of containment and dispersal strategies have been tried (Ruddell, Decker, & Egley, 2006; Weinrath, 2016). At the provincial level, for example, at the Headingley Correctional Centre, correctional services maintain larger gangs on separate 20 or 30 bed units while smaller gangs are dispersed throughout the institution. The disadvantage to this approach occurs when institutions are crowded, and beds are scarce, then a 20-bed unit may have 10 prisoners because they are the only gang members in custody. In a sense, control is ceded to the gang that is housed, and they can choose who is allowed admission to the unit, obviously undermining the authority of the institutional staff. The PG gains status from their isolation. Also, once on the unit, program and work opportunities are limited, thereby reducing opportunities for gang members to change.

How well do program intervention efforts work for PG members? There are mixed results regarding programming and treatment. A Manitoba PG program combined criminogenic needs and Indigenous spiritual practices to assist prisoners in leaving the gang. The program focused on single gangs at a time and produced positive in-program results (e.g., lower scores in criminal thinking over time, and positive ratings of facilitators); however, once released into the community, program participants fared no better in recidivism than an untreated control group (Weinrath, Murchison, & Markesteyn, 2012). Better results were observed when gang members participated with other prisoners in traditional CSC cognitive-based treatment programs for anger management (Di Placido et al., 2006). In a study focused on traditional organized crime gang members, Stys and Ruddell (2013) found no differences in success rates between TOC members and a matched non-gang group; in other words, gang membership did not impede program effectiveness.

Overall, PGs continue to pose a serious challenge to correctional staff and are a scourge in the day-to-day prison life of prisoners. Continued attention needs to be paid to this problem, and much more research is required on the various intervention strategies to see what might prove most effective.

KEY TERMS AND CONEPTS

Subculture	Deprivation Theory	Prisoner or Convict Code
Importation Theory	Integration Theory	Protective Custody
Pains of Imprisonment	Incompatibles	General Population
Deep Freeze Hypothesis	Urinalysis	Masculinities
Drug Interdiction	Liminal State	Prison Gang
Security Threat	Group Containment	Dispersal

STUDY AND DISCUSSION QUESTIONS

1. Imagine you have just been admitted to a correctional centre. What do you expect to face during your first few days? What will you do to make sure that you adapt?
2. What challenges do prisoners face when they are first admitted to custody?
3. Outline the two major theories of prisoner adjustment. Which do you favour and why?
4. What is the 'prisoner' subculture? How does it form? What are its rules? What is the current status of the subculture in Canada and other nations?
5. Why are drugs such a problem in prison? What can be done about drugs in prison?
6. Discuss prison gangs and their impact on a correctional institution: What can be done about them?

HELPFUL WEBLINKS

- **Correctional Service of Canada** http://www.csc-scc.gc.ca/text/index-eng.shtml
    This is a useful website in many ways. It includes reports and research studies performed by their staff. While one should be always cautious of government based research, many of the studies are competent and well done and cover a number of areas.

- **Justice Behind the Walls**: http://justicebehindthewalls.net/index.html
    A resource established by prisoner advocate and legal scholar, Michael Jackson. In addition to helpful information on prisons, and inmate personal stories, it includes a copy of his book, Justice Behind the Walls, which can be read on-line for free.

- **Don't do it Video**: http://www.csc-scc.gc.ca/security/001003-6001-eng.shtml
  A short video identifying the consequences of trying to smuggle drugs in prison.

REFERENCES

Alberta Solicitor General. (2008). *Inmate job manual*. Edmonton, Alberta.

Alberta Solicitor General. (2011). Personal communication, ASG staff November 3, 2011. Edmonton, Alberta.

Auditor General of Canada (2014) Spring Report, Chapter 4 – *Expanding the capacity of penitentiaries – Correctional Service Canada*, retrieved at: http://www.oag-bvg.gc.ca/internet/English/parl_oag_201405_04_e_39335.html#hd3c

Boe, R., Nafekh, M., Vuong, B., Sinclair, R., & Cousineau, C. (2003). *The changing profile of the federal inmate population: 1997 and 2002*. Ottawa, ON: Correctional Service of Canada.

Bonta, J., & Gendreau, P. (1990). Reexamining the cruel and unusual punishment of prison life. *Law and Human Behavior, 14*, 347.

Boys, A., Farrell, M., Bebbington, P., Brugha, T., Coid, J. et al. (2002). Drug use and initiation in prison: Results from a national prison survey in England and Wales. *Addiction, 97*(12), 1551-1560.

Carlson, W. (2001). *Breakfast with the devil: The story of a professional jail breaker*. Toronto, ON: Insomniac Press.

Carrigan, D.O. (1991). *Crime and punishment in Canada, a history*. Toronto, ON: McClelland & Stewart Inc.

Clemmer, D. (1940). *The prison community*. Boston, MA: Christopher Publishing.

Cohen, A. (1955). *Delinquent boys: The culture of the gang*. New York, NY: The Free Press.

Comack, E. (2008). *Out there/in here: Masculinity, violence and prisoning*. Black Point, NS: Fernwood Publishing.

Cooley, D. (1992). Prison vicimization and the informal rules of social control. *Forum on Corrections Research, 4*. Retrieved from http://www.csc-scc.gc.ca/text/pblct/forum/e043/e043ind-eng.shtml.

Cooley, D. (1993). Criminal victimization in male federal prisons. *Canadian Journal of Criminology, 35*, 479-495.

Correctional Service of Canada (CSC). (2015). Mental Health Branch Performance Measurement Report Year End Results 2014-15. Ottawa, ON.

Correctional Service of Canada Review Panel. (2007). *Report of the Correctional Service of Canada Review Panel*. Ottawa, ON: Correctional Services of Canada.

CSC. (2011). Departmental performance reports 2003-2010. Retrieved from http://www.cscscc.gc.ca/text/pblcttl-eng.shtml.

CSC. (2006). Drugs in correctional facilities: A dangerous situation. Ottawa, ON: Correctional Service of Canada.

Corcan. (2008). *Annual Report*. Ottawa, ON: Correctional Service of Canada.

Crewe, B. (2005a). Codes and conventions: The terms and conditions of contemporary inmate values. In A. Liebling & S. Maruna, (Eds.), *The effects of imprisonment* (pp. 177-2008). Portland, OR: Willian Publishing.

Crewe, B. (2005b). Prisoner society in the era of hard drugs. *Punishment & Society*, 7(4), 457-481.

Demers, J. (2014). *Warehousing prisoners in Saskatchewan: A public health approach*. Canadian Centre for Policy Alternatives, Regina, SK.

Di Placido, C., Simon, T., Witte, T., Gu, D., & Wong, S. (2006). Treatment of gang members can reduce recidivism and institutional misconduct. *Law and Human Behavior, 30*, 93-114.

Edgar, K., & O'Donnell, I. (1998). *Mandatory drug testing in prisons: The relationship between MDT and the level and nature of drug misuse.* London, ON: Home Office Research Study 189.

Farrington, K. (1992). The modern prison as total institution? Public perception versus objective reality. *Crime and Delinquency, 38,* 6-26.

Fong, R. S., & Buentello, S. (1991). The detection of prison gang development: An empirical assessment. *Federal Probation, 55,* 66-69.

Fong, R., & Vogel, R. (1994-95). Comparative analysis of prison gang members, security threat group inmates and general population inmates. *Journal of Gang Research, 2,* 1-11.

Franklin, T., Franklin, C., & Pratt, T. (2006). Examining the empirical relationship between prison crowding and inmate misconduct: A meta-analysis of conflicting research results *Journal of Criminal Justice, 34,* 401-412.

Goffman, E. (1961). *Asylums: Essays on the social situation of mental patients and other inmates.* Toronto, ON: Anchor Books.

Grekul, J., & LaBoucane-Benson, P. (2008). Aboriginal gangs and their displacement. *Canadian Journal of Criminology and Criminal Justice, 50,* 60-82.

Griffin, M., & Hepfurn, J. (2006). The effect of gang affiliation on violent misconduct among inmates during the early years of confinement. *Criminal Justice and Behavior, 33,* 419-466.

Harris, M. (2003). *Con game: The truth about Canada's prisons.* Toronto, ON: McClelland & Stewart.

Harvey, J. (2007). *Young men in prison.* Cullompton, UK: Willan.

Hassine, V. (2006). In search of the convict code. In E. Latessa & A. Holsinger (Eds.), *Correctional contexts.* Los Angeles, CA: Roxbury.

Huey, M., & McNulty, T. (2005). Institutional conditions and prison suicide: Conditional effects of deprivation and overcrowding. *Prison Journal, 85,* 490-514.

Inciardi, J., & Lockwood, D. (1993). Drug use in prison: Patterns, processes and behavior. *Journal of Drug Issues, 23,* 119-130.

Irwin, J. (1962). Thieves, convicts and inmate culture. *Social Problems, 10,* 142-155.

Irwin, J. (2005). *The warehouse prison: Disposal of the new dangerous class.* London, UK: Oxford University Press.

Jackson, M. (2002). *Justice behind the walls; Human rights in Canadian prisons.* Vancouver, BC: Douglas & McIntyre.

Jackson, M. (Producer). (2004) Book review: Con game: The truth about Canadian prisons. Retrieved from http://justicebehindthewalls.net.

Jacobs, J. B. (1977). *Stateville: The penitentiary in mass society.* Chicago, IL: University of Chicago Press.

Kavanagh, S. (2016). Every Manitoba jail over capacity: Inmates 'will be living in tents,' warns advocate. Canadian Broadcasting Corporation, retrieved from: http://www.cbc.ca/news/canada/manitoba/jail-manitoba-capacity-inmates-1.3831682.

Keighley, K. (2017). Police-reported crime statistics in Canada. (2016). *Juristat: Canadian Centre for Justice Statistics, 3.*

Kelly, K., & Caputo, T. (2005). The linkages between street gangs and organized crime: The Canadian experience. *Journal of Gang Research, 13,* 17-31.

Kinlock, T., Gordon, M., Schwartz, R., O'Grady, K., Fitzgerald, T., & Wilson, M. (2007). A randomized clinical trial of methadone maintenance for prisoners: Results at one-month post- release. *Drug, Alcohol Dependence, 91,* 220-227.

Krughlanski, A., Gelfand, M., & Gunaratna, R. (2010). Detainee de-radicalization: A challenge for psychological science. *APS Observer, 23,* 1-3.

Lacombe, D. (2008). Consumed with sex: the treatment of sex offenders in risk society. *British Journal of Criminology, 48*, 55-74.

Lahm, K.F. (2008). Inmate-on-inmate assault: A multilevel examination of prison violence. *Criminal Justice and Behavior, 35,* 1120-137.

MacPherson, P. (2004). *Use of random urinalysis to deter drug use in prison: A review of the issues.* Ottawa, ON: Addictions Treatment Branch, Correctional Service of Canada.

Maier, K. & Ricciardelli, R. (2018). The "prisoners' dilemma:" how male prisoners experience and respond to penal threat while incarcerated. *Punishment & Society.* [pages forthcoming, online first]

Mann, W. E. (1967). *Society behind bars: A sociological scrutiny of Guelph reformatory.* Toronto, ON: Social Science Publishers.

Marron, K. (1996). *The slammer: The crisis in Canada's prison system.* Toronto, ON: Doubleday.

Martin, J. (2014). *Drugs on the dark net: How cryptomarkets are transforming the global trade in illicit drugs.* Springer.

McCorkle, R.C. (1992). Personal precautions to violence in prisons. *Criminal Justice and Behavior, 19*, 160-173. doi:10.1177/0093854892019002004.

McVie, F. (2001). Drugs in federal corrections. The issues and challenges. *Forum on Corrections Research, 13*, 7-9.

Melnitzer, J. (1995). *Maximum minimum medium: A journey through Canadian prisons.* Toronto, ON: Key Porter Books Ltd.

Motiuk, L., Boe, R., & Nafekh, M. (2003). *The safe return of offenders to the community.* Ottawa, ON: Correctional Services of Canada.

Neumann, P. (2014). *Prisons and terrorism: Radicalization and de-radicalization in 15 Countries.* London: International Centre for the Study of Radicalization and Political Violence.

Office of the Auditor General of British Columbia. (2015). An *audit of the adult custody division's correctional facilities and programs.* Retrieved at: http://www.bcauditor.com/files/publications/2015/special/report/AGBC%20Corrections%20report%20FINAL.pdf.

Office of the Correctional Investigator. (2017). *Annual report of the correctional investigator 2010-2011.* Retrieved from http://www.oci-bec.gc.ca.

Ontario Parole Board. (2010). Ontario parole board 2009-2010 annual report. Toronto, ON: Queen's Printer for Ontario.

Ottawa-Carlton Detention Centre Task Force. (2016). *Action plan.* Retrieved at: https://www.mcscs.jus.gov.on.ca/english/Corrections/OttawaCarletonDetentionCentreTaskForce/OCDCTaskForce-ActionPlan.html.

Ottawa Citizen. (2011, September 20). Smugglers use inventive ways to get drugs into prisons. Retrieved from http://www.ottawacitizen.com.

Paquin-Marseille, L., Grant, B.A., & Michel, S. (2012). *Review of the prison crowding and double-bunking literature.* Research Report, R-266. Ottawa, ON: Correctional Service Canada.

Pernanen, K., Cousineau, M., Brochu, S., & Sun, F. (2002). *Proportions of crimes associated with alcohol and other drugs in Canada.* Ottawa, ON: Canadian Centre for Substance Abuse.

Piché, J. (2014). A contradictory and finishing state: Explaining recent prison capacity expansion in Canada's provinces and territories. *Penal field,* 11, retrieved at: https://journals.openedition.org/champpenal/8797.

Plourde, C., & Brochu, S. (2002). Drugs in prison: A break in the pathway. *Substance Use and Misuse, 37*, 47-63.

Plourde, C., Brochu, S., Gendron, A., & Brunelle, N. (2012). Pathways of substance use among female and male inmates in Canadian federal settings. *The Prison Journal, 92*(4), 506-524.

Pelvin, H. (2017). *Doing Uncertain Time: Understanding the Experiences of Punishment in Pre-trial Custody* (Doctoral dissertation), University of Toronto.

Ricciardelli, R. (2019). *Also serving time: The prison officer experience in Canadian provincial and territorial correctional facilities.* Toronto: University of Toronto Press.

Ricciardelli, R. (2014a). *Surviving incarceration: Inside Canadian penitentiaries.* Waterloo: Wilfrid Laurier Press.

Ricciardelli, R. (2014b). Coping strategies: Investigating how male prisoners manage the threat of victimization in federal prisons. *The Prison Journal, 94*(4), 411-344.

Ricciardelli, R. (2014c). An examination of the inmate code in Canadian penitentiaries. *Journal of Crime and Justice, 37*(2), 234-255.

Ricciardelli, R. (2013). Establishing and asserting masculinities in Canadian penitentiaries. *The Journal of Gender Studies*, *24*(2), 170-191.

Ricciardelli, R., Maier, K. & Hannah-Moffat, K. (2015). Strategic masculinities: Vulnerabilities, risk, and the production of prison masculinities. *Theoretical Criminology, 19*(4), 491-513.

Ricciardelli, R. & Sit, V. (2016). Producing social (dis)order in prison: The effects of administrative controls on prisoner-on-prisoner violence. *The Prison Journal, 96*(2), 210-231.

Robinson, D., & Mirabelli, L. (1996). *Summary of findings of the 1995 CSC national inmate survey.* Correctional Service Canada, Correctional Research and Development.

Rothman, D.J. (1971). *The Discovery of the asylum: Social order and disorder in the new republic.* Toronto, ON: Little, Brown and Company.

Ruddell, R., Decker, S., & Egley, A. (2006). Gang intervention in jails: A national analysis. *Criminal Justice Review, 31,* 1-14.

Ruddell, R., & Gottschall, S. (2011). Are all gangs equal security risks? An investigation of gang types and prison misconduct. *American Journal of Criminal Justice, 36,* 265-279.

Schmid, T., & Jones, R. (1993). Ambivalent actions: Prison adaptation strategies of first-time, short-term inmates. *Journal of Contemporary Ethnography, 21,* 439-463.

Shewan, D., Gemmell, M., & Davies, J. B. (1994). Behavioural change amongst drug injectors in Scottish prisons. *Social Science and Medicine, 39*(11), 1585-1586.

Skillicorn, D.B. (2006) Social network analysis via matrix decompositions. In R.L. Popp & John Yen, (Eds.), *Emergent information technologies and enabling policies for counter-terrorism.* 367-392. New Jersey: Wiley- Press.

Skillicorn, D.B., Leuprecht, C., Stys, Y., & Gobeil, R. (2015). Structural differences of violent extremist offenders in correctional settings. *Global Crime, 16(3),* 238-258.

Sorensen, J., Wrinkle, R., & Gutierrez, A. (1998). Patterns of rule-violating behaviors and adjustment to incarceration among murderers. *The Prison Journal, 78,* 3222–231.

Sparks, R., Bottoms, A., & Hay, W. (1996). *Prisons and the problem of order.* Oxford: Clarendon.

Sprott, J., & Doob, A. (1998). Understanding provincial variation in incarceration rates. *Canadian Journal of Criminology, 40,* 305-322.

Statistics Canada. (2018). Table 35-10-0154-01. Retrieved from http://www5.statcan.gc.ca

Stys, Y., & Ruddell, R. (2013). Organized crime offenders in Canada: Risk, reform, and recidivism. *Journal of Offender Rehabilitation, 52(2),* 75-97.

Sykes, G.M. (1958). *The society of captives: A study of a maximum security prison.* Princeton University Press.

Sykes, G., & Messinger, S. (1960). The inmate social system. In R. Cloward et al. (Eds.), *Theoretical studies in the social organization of the prison* (pp. 6-9). New York, NY: Social Science Research Council.

Taillon, J. (2006). Offences against the administration of justice. *Juristat*, *26*(1).

Trammell, R. (2012). *Enforcing the convict code: Violence and prison culture.* Boulder, CO Lynne Rienner Publishers.

United Nations Congress on prevention of crime and treatment of offenders. (1958). Annex I(A), U.N. Doc. A/CONF.6/1.

Wallace, M., Turner, J., Matarazzo, A., & Babyk, C. (2009). *Measuring crime in Canada: Introducing the crime severity index and improvements to the uniform crime reporting survey.* Canadian Centre for Justice Statistics, Ottawa. Retrieved from http://www.statcan.gc.ca.

Walters, G. (1998). Time series and correctional analyses of inmate-initiated assaultive incidents in a large correctional system. *International Journal of Offender Therapy and Comparative Criminology, 42*, 124-132.

Weinrath, M. (2007). *An inquiry into inmate motivation for treatment or intervention at the remand stage of custody.* Winnipeg, MB: Report Prepared for Manitoba Corrections.

Weinrath, M. (2009a). Inmate perspectives on the remand crisis in Canada. *Canadian Journal of Criminology & Criminal Justice, 51*, 355-379.

Weinrath, M. (2009b). *A qualitative inquiry into inmate-staff relations, violence, drug use, prison gangs and programs, in Canadian federal and provincial correctional institutions.* Ottawa, ON: Correctional Service of Canada.

Weinrath, M., Murchison, M., & Markesteyn, T. (2012). Justice as method: the evaluation of the Mino-bimasdiziwin prison gang intervention program. In K. Gorkoff & R. Jochelson (Eds.), *Imagining Justice* (p.32-51). Blackwell, NS: Fernwood.

Weinrath, M. (2016). *Behind the walls: Inmates and correctional officers on the state of Canadian prisons.* Law and Society Series, Vancouver, BC: UBC Press.

Winterdyk, J., & Ruddell, R. (2010). Managing prison gangs: Results from a survey of US prison systems. *Journal of Criminal Justice, 38*, 730-736.

Wooldredge, J., & Steiner, B. (2009). Comparing methods for examining relationships between prison crowding and inmate violence. *Justice Quarterly, 26*, 795-826.

Zamble, E., & Porporino, F.J. (Eds.). (1988). *Coping, behavior, and adaptation in prison inmates.* New York, NY: Spinger-Verlag.

CASES CITED

R. v. Jordan, 2016 SCC 27, [2016] 1 S.C.R. 631

R. v. Summers, 2014 SCC 26, [2014] 1 S.C.R. 575

Women in Custody

6

Gillian Balfour

Learning Objectives

After reading this chapter, you should be able to:

- Understand the victimization – criminalization – incarceration continuum as it relates to women prisoners.

- Understand the global trends in the incarceration of women.

- Discuss with conditions of confinement in women's prisons with regards to mental illness, segregation, Indigenous women.

- Understand the challenges and controversies of prison reform.

INTRODUCTION

Women are the fastest growing prisoner population in the world. While men comprise more than 80% of prison populations, when we look more closely at these data, we see a troubling and steady increase in the rate of women's imprisonment, especially for Indigenous women, and women living with mental illness or cognitive disabilities. In Canada we have seen an overall increase of 50% in the rate of women confined to federal prisons over the past 20 years. For Indigenous women the rate is an even more staggering 70% increase. How can we make sense of these data other than to simply say "women are more dangerous or criminal than ever before"? To understand Canada's prisoner population today, and what happens to them in prison, we need to consider their complex pathways into prison: how they came to be incarcerated in the first place, as well as how laws and policies governing Canada's prisons have changed over time. In this chapter we will explore the lives of women in prison, some convicted of serious offences, most with histories of victimization, addiction, and mental illness. What offences are most women convicted of? What are their life experiences, and how are these experiences oftentimes a pathway to prison especially for Indigenous women? We will explore the controversial history of women's imprisonment in Canada, and how it was at one time internationally recognized as one of the most progressive correctional models. You will be introduced to what programs are designed for women prisoners, the controversies surrounding the treatment of women struggling with mental illness and Indigenous women, and how human rights litigation remains key to addressing the conditions of confinement in women's prisons in Canada.

Setting the Context

The imprisonment of women in Canada and elsewhere is difficult to trace in part because of the relatively few documented studies of women's prisons. Critical prison studies have produced a substantial body of literature of the men's prisons and the conditions of their confinement (see Crewe, 2009; Ignatieff, 1978; Jackson, 1983; Liebling et al., 2005; McCoy, 2015; Moran, 2015; Piché, Gaucher & Walby, 2014; Rusche & Kirschheimer, 2003). In Canada, the imprisonment of women has remained the subject of only a handful of critical studies (see Kilty, 2006; Pollack, 2009; Pollack & Eldridge, 2015), some of those historical (Sangster, 1999; Hannah-Moffat, 2001) or journalistic (Kershaw & Lasovich, 1991). Elizabeth Comack's examination of women's pathways to prison in Manitoba (1996; 2018), as well as Stephanie Hayman's (2005) account of the political claims-making surrounding the closure of the Prison for Women in Kingston Ontario in 2001, are examples of the rare studies of women doing time, the conditions of their confinement, and the challenges of prison reform. Women's own accounts of doing time have also been woven throughout prisoner writings (Fayter & Payne, 2017; Shook et al., 2017). However, in order to document systemic practices within Canadian prisons, researchers must increasingly rely upon Access to Information Requests or turn to the Office of the Correctional Investigator (OCI)[1] as oftentimes critical researchers are denied access to prisons and jails (Piché, 2011). Systematically collected data about provincial prisons (who is imprisoned and how they are treated) is even more scarce and difficult for critical prison scholars to access (Parkes et al., 2008). Yet, provincial prisons confine the largest group of prisoners in Canada. As a result annual government reports on women's federal and provincial prisons in Canada are increasingly difficult to access or do not exist. This shift in data collection and transparency with regards to Canada's prisons clearly signals a need for prisoner advocacy and an increase in critical prison scholarship to better understand who goes to prison and how they are treated once incarcerated. In the first section of this chapter, I describe some of the lives lived in Canada's women's prisons so as to capture the pains of imprisonment (Sykes, 1958) that have long existed.

Stories of Women in Custody

Dorothy Proctor was racialized and poor when she was first imprisoned in Kingston inside the Prison for Women at the age of 17, in the early 1960s for robbery. Decades later, in 1998 Dorothy Proctor launched a successful law suit against the Canadian federal government for damages resulting from the permanent harm of the LSD exposure. Through the legal proceedings, we learned that as a young prisoner, Dorothy was told by prison medical doctors that unless she participated in clinical experiments, she would be denied bedding and access to a toilet. When she was eventually released from the Prison for Women, she was severely addicted to drugs and suffered memory loss (Tyler, 1999). As her statement of claim for damages against Correctional Services Canada – what was then the Penitentiary Service – thirty years later asserts:

> This is a claim for general, special punitive and aggravated damages against the defendants arising from a period in the early 1960's when the plaintiff was a seventeen year old inmate at the prison for women in Kingston, Ontario. At that time, she had been the subject of LSD and electroshock experimentation. As a result of the said experimentation, the plaintiff claims to have suffered serious, irreparable physical and psychological damage which has rendered her incapable of experiencing any enjoyment in life or at obtaining or keeping any gainful employment. (*Proctor v. Queen*, 2000)

Marlene Moore was a young woman who entered the federal prison system in 1988 after being declared Canada's first female Dangerous Offender. Marlene never killed anyone – unlike most men designated as Dangerous Offenders – but she had a lengthy criminal record for assault and robbery. She was also a victim of childhood sexual abuse and neglect, and used self-harm to cope with her intense feelings of anger and fear of re-victimization. Correctional authorities responded to Marlene as a security risk because of her self-destructive behaviour by placing her in segregation for extended periods of time. Eventually, Marlene's physical and emotional health deteriorated; living in constant pain from infections and depression, she committed suicide. In a Coroner's Inquest into her death, which examined the policies and practices of the Correctional Services Canada (CSC), it was clear that prison officials at that time knew little about women's mental health needs, nor the relationship between victimization and how women responded to incarceration. As we will see later in this chapter, the inquiry into Marlene's death lead to significant transformations in research and policy with regards to federally sentenced women (Kershaw & Lasovich, 1991). Yet, with reforms in place several years later, the treatment of women with serious mental health needs continue to be met with isolation and punitive control.

Another death in custody – decades later in 2009 – strikes as eerily familiar to Marlene's tragic years of imprisonment and eventual death. Ashley Smith was 19 when she died inside one of Canada's newly designed federal correctional centres for women – Grand Valley Institution for Women in Kitchener, Waterloo. Considered to be progressive and inspired by a women-centered corrections model, GVI was soon revealed to the public through the video footage of Ashley's life behind bars in segregation, as a space of austere punitive practices for those women considered by correctional authorities to be too hard to handle (Bromwich, 2015). Following an announcement of an 11 million dollar settlement in a wrongful death suit against Correctional Services Canada, Julian Falconer, a lawyer for the family of Ashley Smith stated:

> This lawsuit was brought by the family to hold Correctional Services accountable for all of the inhumane and appalling conditions Ashley Smith was kept in. This lawsuit was very much about a conspiracy of senior correctional management to leave a young, mentally ill teen in

isolation without help and ultimately without the most basic of human needs. (*Globe & Mail,* May 4, 2011)

How did Ashley end up in segregation in a federal prison at such a young age? According to the New Brunswick provincial ombudsman's report, Ashley entered the provincial correctional system in New Brunswick at the age of 15 for throwing crab apples at a postal worker. Prior to this, Ashley's family had made repeated attempts to address her spiraling mental health needs in the community, and within a poorly funded youth correctional system ill equipped to meet Ashley's therapeutic requirements. Her complex needs resulted in increased aggression and alienation from her schools and community. Ashley was transferred into the federal women's correctional system at the age of 17, and within two years she was dead in a cell in the secure unit, where she had been held in long term segregation dressed only in a security gown under 24 hour surveillance. The cause of Ashley's death was officially recorded by CSC as self-asphyxiation. However, the Coroner's Inquest eventually ruled her death to be a homicide due to the conditions of her confinement: how she was treated by correctional authorities throughout her incarceration. Records released after her death show that Ashley had been transferred 17 times in 11 months across 4 different provinces, was forcibly injected with sedatives, duct taped to seats to prevent movement, was strip searched several times a day, exposed to chemical agents and tasers, as well as physical restraints.

Indigenous women make up a large proportion of women prisoners. Many of these women have long histories of significant trauma and victimization. Yvonne Johnson – a young Cree woman – entered the federal prison system in 1989 at the age of 26, after being convicted in the first degree murder of a man who had threatened to sexually assault children in the community. Documented in her biography, *Stolen Life: Journey of a Cree Woman* (Weibe, 1998), Johnson discloses a horrific life of physical and sexual violence at the hands of her father and brother. Yvonne was sentenced to 25 years in prison, and struggled with the loss of her three children to the foster care system and the haunting effects of her own victimization. Yvonne was eventually released in 2010 after serving 17 years, and will be on parole for the rest of her life.

The story of Renee Acoby – a Metis woman convicted of drug trafficking and sentenced to 30 months in prison – illustrates how the conditions of confinement, as well as the impact of the loss of a child can result in violence. Shortly before being incarcerated, Renee gave birth and her infant child remained with her in prison as part of a program for imprisoned mothers. Renee relapsed in her drug use while in prison, and her daughter was removed from her care and placed up for adoption.[2] Her life in prison quickly spiraled into one of resistance and defiance, as well as violence at times against prison authorities. She was charged for various institutional offences including hostage taking and attempting to escape prison. As a result of her institutional record for which she was criminally charged, she was declared a Dangerous Offender and cycled through maximum security and segregation for over 8 years (2003-2011) and under Management Protocol (see below for more discussion of this correctional practice). Renee befriended Ashley Smith while they were held in segregation together, and tried to help Ashley file a grievance about her mistreatment. To date, Renee is the only person ever to be designated a Dangerous Offender for conduct while incarcerated (Kerr, 2015). Why do more Indigenous women like Yvonne Johnson and Renee Acoby end up being incarcerated under the most punitive conditions, despite tragic personal histories of neglect and suffering? Can the Canadian prison system respond to the needs of incarcerated women, especially women convicted of serious violent offences who have also experienced significant trauma and loss? These are some of the questions we will think about throughout this chapter, but first we should put the incarceration of women in Canada in the global context.

Basic Facts and Trends

International prison data reveal that women are the fastest growing prisoner population globally. The World Prison Brief, produced by the Institute for Criminal Policy Research sets out that between 2000-2013, the number of incarcerated and detained girls and women has increased on each continent, and by as much as 53%. This increase cannot be explained by general population growth or overall prison population growth. The male prisoner population has increased by 20% during that same time (Walmsley, 2017). In Canada, earlier sentencing data indicated that women were being held in pretrial custody at a higher rate than men: "the growth in the number of women admitted to remand has been greater than the overall growth in remand. The number of adult females admitted to remand rose by 36% between 2001/2002 and 2006/2007 while the total number of adults admitted to remand was up 14%" (Babooram, 2008).

More recent data show that while there was an overall increase in the number of adult women remanded to pretrial custody (15,673 in 2012 to 22,054 in 2017), the largest increase occurred in one year (2016/17). With regards to the number of women sentenced to custody we see a similar pattern: the largest increase occurring in one year: 7,040 in 2016 to 10,806 in 2017. In sum, the number of women sentenced to custody and denied bail (remanded into pretrial custody), has increased from 25,610 in 2012 to 36,409 in 2017 (Statistics Canada, 2018). The sustained increase in the use of pre-trial custody or bail across Canada is particularly concerning when looking more closely at sentencing data. Myers (2017) reports that the number of persons in Canada held in pre-trial custody has tripled over the past 30 years and now eclipses the number of persons sentenced to incarceration. Provincial prison populations are comprised of sentenced and remanded persons, however, remanded prisoners represent over half of prisoners in Canada.

The Correctional Investigator stated in his 2018 annual report, that the over-incarceration of Indigenous prisoners represents "the most pressing social justice and human rights issue in Canada today" (Zinger, 2017, p.48). Over-incarceration is compounded by gender as the rate of Indigenous women's incarceration has outpaced that of men:

> In 2014/2015, Aboriginal women accounted for 39% of admissions of women to federal custody and 38% of admissions to provincial/territorial custody. In comparison, Aboriginal women comprised less than 5% of the total female population of Canada in 2015. Since 2001 there has been an increase in admissions for all three types of custody (remand, sentenced, and other) during the period for Indigenous women; the greatest change was observed in sentenced custody, whereas the proportion doubled, increasing from 18% in 2000/2001 to 37% in 2014/2015. (Mahony et al., 2017, p.39)

The persistent rise of incarceration rates for Indigenous women (and men) are striking as sentencing reforms were introduce in 1996 to address the problem of over-incarceration. In 1996, the federal government introduced amendments to the *Criminal Code* – section 718 – that sets out sentencing objectives and principles, including special consideration for Indigenous offenders so as to encourage the use of restorative justice and alternatives to incarceration whenever possible.[3] In a study of sentencing decisions in cases of Indigenous women convicted of serious personal injury offences, I found that sentencing judges oftentimes chose denunciation and deterrence as the priority of sentencing an Indigenous woman rather than restorative justice or rehabilitation (Balfour, 2013). Hannah-Moffat and Maurutto (2010) also found that in pre-sentencing reports in cases involving Indigenous women, conditions of poverty, homelessness, profound victimization, and lack of education were considered criminogenic risks for re-offending rather than mitigating factors. It would seem that paying special consideration to Indigenous women's lives under section 718 did not change how judges viewed the objectives of sentencing and the necessity of incarceration. In addition to sentencing reforms like section 718, the *Corrections and Conditional Release Act* sets out that CSC is also required to assess the unique programming needs of Indigenous prisoners.

When we read across these various data sources, a picture of who ends up in custody is troubling. First, we know that imprisonment is gendered as there has been a sustained growth globally in the number of women and girls in custody over the past two decades. Second, in Canada, over half of the provincial prison population is legally innocent (Myers, 2017). Third, the number of Indigenous women in provincial, territorial, and federal custody has grown steadily and outpaces that of Indigenous men. Finally, sentencing law reforms have not resulted in the intended decrease in rates of imprisonment for Indigenous women. These findings have significant implications for the management of prisons and the treatment of prisoners. As we will see, federal prisons in general have greater resources resulting in a sentencing trend towards a greater use of federal incarceration for women. This trend is concerning because prisons are security-focused institutions. They are not built or staffed in a manner that prioritizes mental health care or access to quality education, over control and discipline. Therefore, although women enter into federal prison oftentimes with significant addiction struggles, needs for trauma-centered care and opportunities for adult education and employment retraining, they experience prison as a space of control and discipline.

So why are more women going to prison, and what crimes are they convicted of? Are they becoming more criminal or violent, therefore prison rates are rising accordingly? Recent inmate population data tell us that by comparison, overall women are far less likely to be imprisoned for serious personal injury offences than are men. As reported by Mahony et al. (2017), women were more likely to be convicted of theft (35%), fraud (33%), possession of stolen property (27%), failure to appear in court (24%), or other offences relating to the administration of justice (breaching terms and conditions of a probation or parole order such as breaking curfew or failing to find employment). Within the small population of federally sentenced women prisoners, a majority of these women were convicted of drug related offences (24%) and violent offences (55%), as well as property related offences (30%). Within the federal prisons for women, the number of women over 50 has doubled since 2001, and half are serving their first federal sentence (Mahony et al., 2017).

The most recent data reported by Statistics Canada indicate that 75 percent of Indigenous women inmates are convicted of violent offences such as homicide, robbery, and assault whereas non-Indigenous women are more likely to be convicted of drug related offences (Kong & AuCoin, 2008). It is important to note, too, that Indigenous women are three times more likely than other women to be victims of violence, and five times more likely to be victims of femicide (murder of a women simply because they are women, see Statistics Canada 2006). As reported by Mahony et al. (2017) the rate of femicide amongst Indigenous women has tripled in the past 30 years whereas there has been little change in the rates of lethal violence against non-Indigenous women. These data together suggest a need to better understand the relationship between Indigenous women's histories of victimization, their risks for serious personal harm, and their longer custodial sentences due to the seriousness of their admitting offence. Trauma is connected to interpersonal violence in Indigenous women's lives, but it also influences how they experience imprisonment.

According to Statistics Canada (Kong & AuCoin, 2008) the proportion of federally sentenced women categorized as having high treatment needs doubled (from 26% to 50%). Women were significantly more likely than men to have treatment needs in the areas of employment/education (63% versus 57%) and marital/family violence (52% versus 43%), while males had more intervention needs in the areas of peers/social interaction (66% versus 61%), criminogenic attitudes (64% versus 35%), substance abuse problems (69% versus 62%), and difficulties with personal/emotional issues (87% versus 79%).

These data suggest women in prison are less educated, more likely to have experienced domestic violence, and have far more pro-social attitudes than men in prison. Another study compared provincial and federal women prisoner populations with regards to treatment needs, and produced similar findings, however, provincially sentenced women reported greater need for substance abuse programming and therapeutic supports for employment and community integration. These data illustrate how women sentenced to provincial prisons are likely to be street-involved or homeless with limited access to addiction treatment facilities (Statistics Canada, 2008).

The above data also illustrate the lack of employment in the lives of women prior to their incarceration. Lack of employment is recognized consistently as a key risk factor or pathway into prison for women prisoners, especially when compounded by factors of mental illness, addictions, and histories of victimization. Unemployment is also a risk factor for unsuccessful reintegration in the community once released from prison. For example, in a follow-up study of women prisoners with histories of substance abuse, Matheson, Doherty, and Grant (2008) found that women who were employed after their release were less likely to return to prison. "The overwhelming majority of women who returned to custody had not been employed during their release and the majority did not complete high school" (p. 35). Women are rendered more vulnerable to (re)-involvement in crimes such as prostitution, drug trafficking, and robbery poverty when they have limited education and lack job skills.

Another striking characteristic of women in custody is their responsibilities for single parenting prior to and during their incarceration. In 2004, approximately 25,000 children in Canada have a mother who is imprisoned.[4] CSC had initially agreed to implement a residential program for infants and their mothers, and a visitation program for older children to ensure parental contact was sustained. However, such initiatives were not been successfully implemented due in part to staunch opposition from the public (Hayman, 2005). In 2013 British Columbia's Supreme Court ruled that BC Corrections must reinstitute its Mother Child program in Alouette Correctional Centre for Women, after being cancelled in 2008. The court ruled that the cancelation of the program was a violation of the *Charter of Rights and Freedoms* on the grounds of gender discrimination as well as principles of procedural fairness: women are disproportionately more likely to be single parents and therefore punished more harshly as a result of not having access to their newborn children (*Inglis et al. v. The Ministry of Public Safety*).

Conditions of Confinement

The Prison for Women – or P4W as it became known as – was Canada's first and only federal prison for women built in 1935 and then closed in 2001 following the recommendations of the Task Force on Federally Sentenced Women (Correctional Services Canada, 1990). P4W was designed in the early 20th century in accordance with the principals of penitentiary design of the era that emphasized panopticon construction to maximize surveillance and prisoner isolation (Foucault, 1977). Discipline of women prisoners was both harsh and maternal. As Hannah-Moffat (2001) describes based on archival records of P4W matrons sought the redemption of "fallen women" through maternal discipline of domestic labour. However, for those women who were deemed unsalvageable due to their immorality (Minaker, 2006), or "Indianness" (Kline, 1994), conditions of confinement were more austere and punitive. Indigenous women, prostituted women, and those labelled as alcoholics were more likely to disciplined through harsh treatments of bread and water diets or time in solitary confinement (Sangster, 1999).

The Prison for Women was also a site of important progressive reforms in attempts to improve the conditions of confinement for some women, primarily white working class wayward girls. These efforts were informed by the humanitarian work of Elizabeth Fry – a Quaker who volunteered with women prisoners inside London's Newgate Prison and counseled prison governors on the importance of dignity in the treatment of prisoners. The first Elizabeth Fry Society in Canada was opened in Vancouver in 1939, then in Kingston Ontario in 1949 to provide support for women in conflict with the law. Volunteers worked tirelessly to provide women with social events such as sewing classes, and eventually escorted visits to the community. For example, in Kingston faculty from Queen's University went into the prison to offer educational programs to the women prisoners. In the 1970s, the Kingston Elizabeth Fry opened the first half way house for women.

By the 1980s, prisoner advocates embraced liberal feminist ideals of formal gender equality and launched a human rights complaint asserting that because there was only one federal prison for women and several federal prisons for men in various regions of the country, women were discriminated against as they could not serve their sentences close to family. As well, male prisoners had access to far more programming and educational opportunities. The remedy to this discriminatory treatment was to provide women access to programs inside men's prisons and to explore co-ed prisons that housed men and women together. Exchange of service agreements were also developed between federal and provincial governments, to allow women to serve federal sentences in provincial institutions so they could be closer to their families. These solutions proved unsuccessful as women's programming needs were significantly different from men's needs, and programming in provincial institutions very limited and ill-suited for federal inmates, who require more detailed correctional plans and have more significant needs for education, job training, and psychological services (Berzins & Hayes, 1987; Hayman, 2005).

Despite these attempts at prison reform, the conditions inside the Prison for Women continued to deteriorate. In 1989, nine women took their own lives inside the Prison for Women, including Marlene Moore. The Coroner's Inquest into her death, the Canadian Association of Elizabeth Fry Societies (CAEFS) and families of prisoners sought to have the institutional regulations regarding the treatment of high risk inmates, be critically examined to determine if the regulations – such as placing women who self-injure in isolation in segregation – contributed to Marlene's suicide. CSC was not found to be responsible for Marlene's death, but the federal government called for a Task Force on Federally Sentenced Women (TTFSW) to examine the needs of incarcerated women, and to propose recommendations to design a women-centered correctional model. Between 1989 and 1991 an unprecedented committee of Indigenous women, former inmates, feminist activists, academics, and senior officials from Corrections Canada, developed a research program that interviewed women in prison and on parole as to their life histories and prison experiences. The findings revealed the complex needs of incarcerated women, but also the context of women's offending: a high prevalence of sexual and physical victimization, profound poverty, lack of education and limited employment histories, chronic substance abuse, poor parenting, and for Indigenous women, the intergenerational effects of residential schools. The TTFSW report, *Creating Choices* was released calling for sweeping and unprecedented changes to the structure of women's imprisonment in Canada (see Shaw et al., 1991).

Creating Choices

The principles of *Creating Choices* were premised on a liberal feminist analysis of women's law breaking and institutional behaviour as resulting from the compounding effects of trauma, self-destructive coping strategies of self-injury or substance abuse, and social isolation. The recommendations for operational changes made by the TTFSW called for a woman-centered correctional model that aimed to empower women, provide meaningful and responsible choices, respect and dignity, supportive environments, and shared responsibility (Hannah-Moffat & Shaw 2000). Interviews with federally sentenced women revealed that for a majority of women, their experiences of sexual and physical violence was the context of their offending behavior, especially for Indigenous women prisoners; more than 60% of Indigenous women in prison have histories of sexual violence, and over 80% have experienced physical violence over their life course (Shaw, 1991; Shaw et al., 1991). This **victimization – criminalization continuum** (Faith, 1993) enables us to understand women's survival and coping with victimization when compounded by poverty and social isolation. Prior to their incarceration, criminalized women have often lived in **gendered conditions of endangerment**: those social and economic conditions that uniquely impact upon women in a manner that jeopardizes their safety and resilience, such as domestic violence, unstable housing, single parenting, welfare dependency, sexual exploitation, and untreated mental illness. These gendered conditions of endangerment compound the effects of victimization and are particularly evident in the lives of incarcerated women.

The most significant recommendation of the TTFSW was to close the infamous Prison for Women, and to design five new regional institutions for women, including a dedicated Healing Lodge for Indigenous women. The regional prisons were to be designed for more communal living with limited static security, such as no perimeter wall or segregation units; and corrections officers were not to wear uniforms. Key to the design of the new prisons was a mother-child program, sexual abuse trauma recovery, substance abuse treatment, and employment training. There was a call for greater community integration, with the facilities built closer to urban areas to promote access to community resources and more effective re-integration planning. The Healing Lodge was to be the centerpiece of this reform initiative – architecturally designed in accordance with Indigenous tradition with a strong connection to elders in the community. Eventually the Lodge was constructed on traditional lands of the Nankeet Band near Maple Creek in Saskatchewan. Opened in 1994, the Lodge was richly coloured and circular in design, included a Spiritual Lodge, communal cooking and eating areas for staff and prisoners, a ceramics workshop, as well as a childcare space for an envisioned mother-child program. Female correctional staff – or primary workers – were selected from local Indigenous communities as well as non-Indigenous women, and underwent unique training by participating as clients in various treatment programs, rather than as observers.

By 1998, however, conditions in the Lodge had become more carceral – searches of prisoners and visitors were now commonplace, primary workers no longer ate with the prisoners, and the focus on traditional Indigenous cultural practices with the prisoners was replaced by standard correctional programming and no maximum security women were permitted to be confined in the Lodge (Hayman, 2005). In efforts to understand the shift away from the spirit of the Healing Lodge as initially envisioned in *Creating Choices*, Hayman (2005, p.228) explains:

> prisons are places where …intimidation are common, and it is this reality that collides with the visionary nature of what aspired to at the Healing Lodge: to be a place where Aboriginal women may safely begin the healing journey back to their communities. However even this aspiration needs to be closely dissected as prisons are not places of healing, rather they are places of involuntary confinement where punishment is administered through the deprivation of liberty and autonomy.

It was clear that many of the recommendations would not be put into practice, and indeed, the spirit of *Creating Choices* was impacted upon by ideological shifts as CSC asserted greater authority. Between 1991 and 1994, inside the Prison for Women, conditions continued to deteriorate as staff were relocated to the new regional prisons. The inmates who remained at the Prison for Women were those deemed maximum security and were held under austere conditions and received little access to programming, health care, or mental health services. In April 1994, six women prisoners threatened security officers resulting in the warden ordering in the all-male tactical unit from Kingston Penitentiary for Men. Women had their clothes forcibly removed, were strip searched, physically restrained, and placed in segregation; eventually some were involuntarily transferred to the regional psychiatric centre. These events were captured on video and eventually revealed to the public on CBC television show, the Fifth Estate. A Commission was called to examine the policy and practices of CSC. The final report denounced the treatment of the women in segregation as "degrading, cruel and inhumane" and asserted there was an "absence of the rule of law" within CSC (Arbour, 1996). The system of correctional authority was deemed to be out control. The Commission recommended key institutional reforms to address prisoner rights, grievance processes, and to severely limit the use of administrative segregation. In response to the recommendations of the Arbour Inquiry Report, in 1996, CSC appointed the first Deputy Commissioner for women prisoners "to address the institutional environment that continues to present many challenges, and the principles of *Creating Choices* as the framework for effective policy and program development" (Correctional Services Canada, 2008). In the years that followed the release of Inquiry's report, however, a strained relationship between the CSC, the Canadian Human Rights Commission and the Correctional Investigator's office developed, resulting in numerous reports to the federal Minister in charge of Correctional Services of Canada, requesting more action be taken to meet the recommendations of the Inquiry, especially those with regards to the long term segregation of mentally ill inmates and Indigenous women.[5] CSC officials continued to assert that the principles of *Creating Choices* and the implementation plans for the new regional facilities did not address the matter of women who were classified as maximum security because of their use of instrumental violence (Correctional Services Canada 2003) nor did *Creating Choices* provide adequate direction or insight into the management of women with histories of interpersonal violence, self-injurious behaviour, and those women – many of whom are Indigenous and are living with serious mental illness.

After Creating Choices: Controversies and Challenges

Between 1996 and 2006, the implementation of the recommendations of *Creating Choices* was plagued with setbacks driven in part by missteps program development and staff training, as well as an influx of more federally sentenced women with significant mental health needs. In 2000, 8% of federally sentenced women were classified as maximum security whereas in 2002, the rate had jumped to 14% (Correctional Services Canada, 2003). This population of women is comprised of prisoners convicted of serious personal injury offences, 60% having received a sentence of greater than 6 years, is described by CSC as often having great difficulties living communally, in need of motivation to control their behaviour, and also having serious long standing mental health treatment needs. Their institutional behaviours are reported by correctional officers to be impulsive and volatile, engaging in self-harm, and assaultive towards others inmates and staff (ibid). CSC researchers turned their attention to the growing correctional program in women's prisons in the United States – gender responsive corrections.

Gender-responsive correctional programming was introduced into federal prisons for women in the mid-2000s, following its widespread implementation in the United States in response to the staggering rates of women's incarceration. As a correctional program, the gender-responsive model conceptualizes a woman's offending and institutional behaviour as driven by her primary need for relationships with others (spouses, children, friendships), also the impacts of abuse and trauma, such as mental health and addiction (Covington & Owen, 2003). A woman prisoner is in need of care to manage the effects of trauma and to build self-reliance and healthy relationship choices. "Relationships, children, past victimization, mental health, self-injury, self-esteem all become correctional targets" (Hannah-Moffat, 2010, p. 200). At the core of the correctional plan for high need and high risk women, is dialectical behavioural therapy (DBT) and psycho-education to challenge women's conduct. The premise of DBT was to challenge women's decisions to use violence that stem from high emotional distress that result in self-destructive or suicidal reactions to stressors (Laishes, 2002, p.28). In 2003, purpose-built secure units for maximum security women were introduced in all regional institutions. In short, between 1996 and 2003, conditions of confinement for federally sentenced women – especially for Indigenous and women with histories of serious mental illness – were increasingly defined by concerns for staff safety and institutional security. One of the most controversial institutional practices designed only for federally sentenced women, was the Management Protocol.

Management Protocol (2003-2010)

CSC introduced its Management Protocol (Sapers, 2008), apparently disregarding the principles of *Creating Choices*, as well as the recommendations of the Arbour Commission to restrict the use of segregation. This set of directives was aimed at prisoners who caused serious harm to themselves (self-harm or suicide attempts) or jeopardized the safety of others. Under the terms of the protocol, the treatment of prisoners was to be in accordance with the least restrictive measures that would allow for the protection of the public, staff, and inmates. Once classified under the Protocol, women were confined to a secure unit for a minimum of six months before being reintegrated back into the general prisoner population. This practice is exceptional in that no inmate can be legally held in segregation for more than 30 days without a review; thus through the implementation of the Protocol, CSC was able to extend the use of involuntary segregation to manage a segment of the prisoner population who were deemed a threat to institutional security. The Correctional Investigator cautioned in several of his annual reports to the Minister, that Management Protocol was being used by prison officials to manage mentally ill female inmates rather than those inmates whose criminal histories warranted maximum security detention (Sapers, 2008). Thus the increasing rates of mental illness amongst female prison populations was being met by an institutional response of greater isolation and control; and this particularly impacted upon women prisoners given their higher rates of mental illness, and Indigenous women (ibid). In the "Ten Year Status Report on Women's Corrections 1996-2006," CSC documented that although important changes had occurred in the treatment of maximum security women, CSC continued to be on the "prison side of the sentence" with limited improvements in reintegration planning and case management practices (Correctional Services Canada, 2006). As well, a staffing crisis was evident in women's institutions given the challenges of working with a small population with very complex needs.

In a review of documents produced by the Union of Canadian Correctional Officers (UCCO), I found that union executives strongly advocated for a super-maximum security prison design for female offenders. One of the first reports authored by the UCCO leadership committee targeted the failure of *Creating Choices* to address – in their view – the increasing level of violence and mental illness amongst women prisoners. While acknowledging the lack of services for mental health and addiction in the community, in their report *A New National Strategy for High Risk Women*, the UCCO leadership proposed a dedicated special handling unit within each regional prison for those women labelled extremely violent. The UCCO recommended a contained special handling unit within each prison, away from the secure units (maximum security). The UCCO describes the disruptive effect of the Protocol within the secure unit, the ineffectiveness of the Protocol in changing prisoners' behaviour, and the psychological and physical distress of frontline officers who have to work in these environments without adequate training and resources. On one hand, the UCCO provides a clear critique of the current practice of segregation as inhumane and unlikely to produce the reintegration of prisoners due to its psychological and social consequences of prolonged isolation. Yet, on the other hand, the UCCO advocates for a designated supermax unit for highly 'disturbed' female inmates to protect its members from violence in the workplace. In the following excerpt from their report, the UCCO does not recognize the harsh treatment by correctional officers and its impacts on women prisoners, such as the use of mace, cell extractions, and strip searches. Instead, they recast officers as the real victims of prisoner perpetrated violence:

> Given the increase in violent events in the institutions for women, action must be taken immediately to protect the personnel in these units. We believe that any delays in establishing such reinforced units could lead to other violent incidents initiated by these inmates whose history of violence could fill up several pages and which would thus again produce new victims amongst the CSC's personnel. (UCCO-SACC-CSN 2005, p.7)

The UCCO continued to call for an expanded use of segregation units in the women's regional prisons. In its submissions to the panel, the UCCO leadership referred to the violent confrontations at Prison for Women in 1994 and the untenable recommendation of the Arbour Commission to end the use of administrative segregation. The UCCO argued that, since the Arbour Commission, serious incidents such as the hostage taking of CSC personnel and inmates, severe assaults, injuries, and death threats continued in women's federal prisons. Indeed, the UCCO described the current conditions in women's prisons as "a wave of incidents that repeatedly involved a hard core of female inmates" (UCCO-CCAC-CSN 2007, p.39). Again, as in 2005, the UCCO recommended the following:

> a new Special Handling Unit designed to safely accommodate female inmates who pose a greater risk than the regular maximum security offenders. In order to foster a secure and humane approach to high-risk inmates, we propose the construction of a fortified secure area in one centrally located prison for women. This area would have to be independent and separate from the currently existing segregation sector and Secure Unit. (UCCO-CCAC-CSN 2007, p.4)

In short, the UCCO leadership continued to call for the (re)construction of a centralized super-max prison for "high risk" women. Four months after the submission of the UCCO's report to the panel, Ashley Smith died in a segregation cell at Grand Valley Institution. In the months that followed Smith's death, the UCCO continued to assert that her death could have been averted if their special handling unit proposal had been implemented, and that officers need to be protected from the psychological trauma of responding to the needs of mentally ill prisoners.

Prison protocols of routine strip searches and limited human contact compounds women's lived experiences of profound neglect and violence. The connection between women's use of instrumental violence and their histories of personal victimization, institutionalization, and mental illness has been reconstituted as a threat to public safety, prison staff and other inmates. Despite the findings of the Arbour Inquiry Report with regard to the arbitrary use of power and punitive use of segregation in the management of women prisoners, Dell, Filmore and Kilty (2009) found that prison staff continued to view segregation as a necessary response to women who "act badly" (p.296). Provincial jails and federal prisons across Canada are confronted by increasing rates of imprisonment, and populations with unprecedented needs for intense mental health support and services. As the following data indicates, the built capacity of federal women's prisons has increased dramatically over the past 25 years (see Table 6.1).

Throughout the decades since *Creating Choices* and the closure of the Prison for Women, rates of imprisonment have increased, and the punitiveness of the prisons has deepened. As expressed here by former Correctional Investigator Howard Sapers:

> My Office is increasingly concerned that we are moving farther and farther away from the progressive principles of women's corrections articulated 20 years ago in *Creating Choices*. The correctional model we aspired to create for federally sentenced women based on empowering women offenders through providing responsible and meaningful choices appears to be

Table 6.1 – Regional Facilities for Women			
Name	Location	Original Capacity (1995)	Current Capacity
Okimaw Ohci Healing Lodge	Saskatchewan	28	60
Nova Institution	Nova Scotia	24	99
Edmonton Institution for Women	Alberta	53	167
Grand Valley Institution	Ontario	72	215
Joliette Institution	Quebec	81	132
Source: CSC (2017) Women's Facilities http://www.csc-scc.gc.ca/women/002002-0002-eng.shtml			

giving way to a different reality. Indeed, conditions in the regional women's facilities, especially the maximum security units, are looking and feeling a lot like those that prevail within the male penitentiaries. (Sapers, 2010, p. 49)

In a study of searching protocols in women's federal prisons, I examined post-search reports from each of the five correctional institutions (Balfour, 2018). Data showed a highly discretionary use of searching as a form of prisoner discipline that varied across institutions. For example, Nova Institution – one of the smallest federal prisons – had the highest rate of cell searches and confiscation of personal items. Moreover, most of the items seized by correctional officers were not contraband in the form of drugs or potential weapons. Rather, confiscated items included make-up and personal hygiene products. Grand Valley Institution – one of the largest federal prisons for women – had a very low rate of confiscation of cell effects. I also considered the gender of correctional officers involved in the conduct and reporting of searches of women's cells. In almost all cases, women correctional officers were responsible for the cell searches and confiscation of personal items. One would expect to find a less punitive prison environment in a women's prison where female correctional officers are sensitized to the unique aspects of women's lives, such as victimization. However my data suggests that power dynamics between staff and prisoners in a women's prison continue to exist, but in a manner that reflects a **gendered organizational power** between women (Britton, 2003). Women correctional officers display their power over women prisoners by arbitrary confiscation of personal items that do not pose a threat to institutional security, such as drugs or weapons. These data suggest an intra-gendered hierarchy despite reforms intended to promote a women-centered correctional model.

With regards to more invasive searching practices such as strip searching, I found that strip searches are only reported when they occur outside of segregation and require coercion (use of force) by staff. Therefore, the rate of strip searching of prisoners within segregation is not reported systematically as part of the general search protocol. Furthermore, the reasons for strip searching of prisoners outside of segregation (in general population) was redacted (removed) by CSC so as not to be read by unauthorized personnel, in 95% of cases.

Prison Reform and Prisoner Rights

As the numbers of women sentenced to custody continue to rise and conditions of confinement are linked to institutional security priorities rather than programming and reintegration, some progressive work is being done on the outside to assist women on the inside. The use of segregation in women's provincial and federal prisons has become a flashpoint of human rights litigation in British Columbia and Ontario. The cases of Bobby Lee Worm and Christina Jahn reveal how harsh discipline and discrimination are intertwined in the lives of imprisoned women (see Box 6.1)

Box 6.1 – Human Rights Litigation and Conditions of Confinement

Worm v Attorney General of Canada

In 2006, 18 year old Cree woman, Bobby Lee Worm from Regina, was convicted of her first offence: robbery and assault. She was sentenced to 6 years of federal custody. Bobby Lee lived on the streets from a young age, and experienced severe physical and sexual abuse. Bobby Lee was addicted to drugs and suffered from severe PTSD due to her traumatic experiences. Once incarcerated, Bobby Lee continued to struggle with her addiction and periodic violence. She was confined on Management Protocol for nearly 4 years, confined to 10 by 7 foot cell with only a food slot in her cell door as her access to human contact. The B.C. Civil Liberties Association filed a claim against the Attorney General of Canada arguing that Management Protocol (indeterminant use of solitary confinement) constitutes torture, cruel, inhuman, and degrading treatment. Two days after the claim was filed, CSC released Worm from Management Protocol, and one month later the Protocol was cancelled. In 2013, Worm received an unspecified settlement from the CSC and Worm was released on day parole. This case shows the harsh treatment of women prisoners is also systemic: all women held under Management Protocol at the time of Worm's case were Indigenous. CSC's own internal policies with regards to maintaining order do not appear to be constrained by human rights laws, and litigation is increasingly necessary to ensure compliance with the CCRA, Charter of Rights and Freedoms, as well as international laws on torture (see Kerr, 2015). The continued need to challenge penal authority with regards to segregation and discrimination was made evident in another case of prisoner mistreatment at a provincial institution, the Ottawa Carleton Detention Centre.

Jahn v. Ministry of Community Safety and Correctional Services

Christina Jahn is a 42 year old woman living with severe mental health challenges of schizophrenia, depression, and borderline personality disorder, as well as late stage breast and bones cancers. After her arrest and conviction for theft and assault, she was sentenced to the Ottawa Carleton Detention Centre (OCDC). The police report recommended that she not be jailed but rather be sent to a treatment facility, however, no facility existed for women in Ontario at that time; only men had access to a dedicated mental health treatment facility. Once impris-

continued...

oned, she was placed in segregation due to mental health issues. Throughout her time in segregation, she documented the conditions of her confinement in letters to her family: lights left on in the cell 24 hours a day; water turned off in the cell toilet and sink; handcuffed while in a segregation cell; and missed chemotherapy appointments and cancer surgery. Each of these are violations of international and domestic laws with regards to access to medical care, degrading and humiliating treatment of prisoners, being physically restrained as coercive treatment, and sleep deprivation due to constant artificial light. Through her family's continual advocacy through filing complaints with the provincial Ombudsman to eventually have some of these conditions addressed, a formal human rights complaint was filed against the Ministry. In 2013, a settlement was reached wherein the Ministry was to comply with requirements to limit the use of segregation in cases of mental illness, to institute an immediate mental health screening and treatment protocol for prisoners, and to report annually on who is in segregation and the conditions of their confinement. However in 2017, the Canadian Human Rights Commission ruled that the Ministry had failed to comply with these requirements, and people with mental illnesses were still being placed in segregation or under "restrictive confinement" – a modified practice of segregation. In 2018, the Human Rights Tribunal of Ontario issued a landmark decision, filing a consent order against the Ministry setting out several requirements for compliance and reporting on the confinement of any prisoner to their cell in excess of 22 hours a day.

CONCLUSION

It would seem we are left a crossroads of prison abolition and reform. Despite well intended reforms introduced over twenty years ago that embraced the victimization – criminalization continuum as an analytical approach to understanding women's lives (Faith, 1993), it seems that correctional practices have retrenched a punitive response to women's high needs for safety and trauma recovery. This practice has particularly impacted upon Indigenous women and women living with mental illness. Although programming has become somewhat sensitized to the gendered forms of violence women experience and the impacts of victimization, correctional institutions remain paramilitary spaces responsible for a complex array of contradictory objectives: incapacitation and rehabilitation of prisoners. Incarcerated women's lives reflect those of the most marginalized women in our communities who lack access to housing, physical and sexual safety, employment, and mental health and addictions treatment. The discriminatory and degrading treatment of women prisoners who require treatment not punishment, has been successfully challenged by human rights advocates and lawyers. However, deaths in custody and ongoing human rights violations suggest a need for permanent judicial oversight of prisons and correctional authority; an unforeseen outcome of well-intended prison reforms initiated over twenty years ago.

KEY TERMS

Creating Choices
Gendered conditions of endangerment
Arbour Commission
Management protocol
Victimization-criminalization continuum
Dialectical Behavioural Therapy

Gendered organizational power
Christina Jahn
Yvonne Johnson
Marlene Moore
Dorothy Proctor
Ashley Smith

STUDY AND DISCUSSION QUESTIONS

1. What are some of the connections between women's victimization and their incarceration?
2. What are the key principles and recommendations of *Creating Choices*?
3. What were some of the controversies surrounding the implementation of *Creating Choices*?
4. Why would women who have served lengthy prison sentences have higher health care needs?
5. What are gendered conditions of endangerment?
6. Who is Christina Jahn and how did she change provincial prisons in Ontario?
7. Why was the implementation of Management Protocol a form of discrimination?
8. What are the claims of the UCCO with regards to federally sentenced women?
9. Why is prison reform so difficult to achieve?

HELPFUL WEBLINKS

*   **Canadian Association of Elizabeth Fry Societies**: http://www.caefs.ca
    This is the website for the national office of the Canadian Association of Elizabeth Fry Societies, and includes several helpful links to all aspects of prisoner advocacy for women and young girls.

*   **Fifth estate Beyond the Walls**: http://www.cbc.ca/fifth/episodes/2010-2011/behind-the-wall
    This is a link to a very powerful documentary about Ashley Smith while incarcerated at Grand Valley institution

*   **CSC**: http://www.csc-scc.gc.ca/text/pblcsbjct-eng.shtml#women
    This is an inventory of all publicly available research documents produced by CSC with regards to women prisoners.

*   **Canadian Families and Corrections Network:** https://www.cfcn-rcafd.org
    This organization focuses on families, children, and friends who have someone they care about in jail. Their mission is "to build stronger and safer communities by assisting families affected by criminal behavior, incarceration, and reintegration".

NOTES

[1] The Correctional Investigator is appointed by the Minister to act as an Ombudsman for federal prisoners, to conduct investigations with regard to prison conditions, and to respond to prisoner grievances. Each year the OCI reports to the Minister and makes recommendations as to operational improvements to ensure compliance with federal legislation.

[2] It is important to note that at the time of Renee's incarceration, a specialized program for incarcerated women with infant children called MotherCare, was in place in minimum and medium security prisons. This program was highly controversial with the public, and was soon cancelled despite being recognized as a best practice in prison programming. Mothering programs in prision are shown to reduce the negative effects of separation upon young children who are typically apprehended by protection services and placed in foster care almost immediately after their mother's detention. Residential mothering programs also show strong outcomes of successful reintegration for women (see Minaker, J. and Hogaveen, B. (eds.) (2016) *Criminalized Mothers, Criminalizing Motherhood*. Ontario, Demeter Press.

[3] The Criminal Code of Canada, section 718.2e sets out: "all available sanctions, other than imprisonment, that are reasonable in the circumstances and consistent with the harm done to victims or to the community should be considered for all offenders, with particular attention to the circumstances of Aboriginal offenders" (R.S.C., 1985, c. C-46).

4   Canadian Human Rights Commission. Protecting Their Rights: A Systematic Review of Human Rights in Correctional Services for Federally Sentenced Women. Ottawa: Canadian Human Rights Commission, 2003 at 6; and Voices for Children. Invisible Victims: The Children of Women in Prison. Voices for Children, 2004.On line: http://www.voicesforchildren.ca/report-Dec2004-1.htm

5   For complete discussion of the human rights complaints made against CSC by the Canadian Human Rights Commission, and the findings of the Correctional Investigator upon review of CSC's practices see Parkes, D. and Pate, K. (2006) "Time for Accountability: Effective Oversight of Women's Prisons." *Canadian Journal of Criminology and Criminal Justice,* 48(2): 251-285.

REFERENCES

Arbour, The Honorable Justice L. (Commissioner). (1996). *Commission of inquiry into certain events at the Prison for Women*. Ottawa: Solicitor General.

Babooram, A. (2008). The changing profile of adults in custody 2006-07. *Juristat, 28*, 10, Statistics Canada.

Balfour, G. (2006). Regulating women and girls. In G. Balfour & E. Comack (Eds.), *Criminalizing Women*. (pp. 153) Halifax: Fernwood Publishing.

Balfour, G. (2008). Falling between the cracks: The victimization, criminalization, and punishment of Aboriginal women in Canada. *Feminist Criminology, 3*(2),101-120.

Balfour, G. (2013). Do law reforms matter? Exploring the victimization– criminalization continuum in the sentencing of Aboriginal women in Canada. *International Review of Victimology, 19*(1), 85-102.

Balfour, G. (2018). Searching prison cells and prisoner bodies: Redacting carceral power and glimpsing gendered resistance in women's prisons. *Criminology & Criminal Justice, 18*(2), 139 155.

Berzins, L. & Hayes, C. (1987). The diaries of two change agents. In C. Adelburg & C. Currie. *Too few to count.* Vancouver: Press Gang.

Bloom, B., Owen, B.A., & Covington, S. (2003). *Gender-responsive strategies: Research, practice, and guiding principles for women offenders.* Washington, DC: National Institute of Corrections.

Boyce, J. (2014). Victimization of Aboriginal people in Canada. *Juristat.* Statistics Canada Catalogue no. 85-002-X.

Britton, D. (2003). *At work in the iron cage: The prison as a gendered organization.* New York: NYU Press.

Bromwich, R. (2015). *Looking for Ashley: Re-reading what the Smith case reveals about the governance of girls, mothers and families in Canada.* Demeter Press.

CAEFS (Canadian Association of Elizabeth Fry Societies). (2010). Criminalized and imprisoned Women. Retrieved from http://elizabethfry.ca

Calverley, D, (2010). Adult Correctional Services in Canada, 2008/2009. *Juristat, 30*, 3, Statistics Canada.

CHRC (Canadian Human Rights Commission). 2003. *Protecting their rights: A systemic review of human rights in correctional services for federally sentenced women*. Ottawa: Canadian Human Rights Commission.

Comack, E. (1996). *Women in trouble*. Halifax: Fernwood Publishing.

Comack, E. (2018). *Going back to jail*. Halifax: Fernwood Books.

Correctional Service Canada. (1990). *Creating Choices: The report of the task force on federally sentenced women*. Ottawa.

Correctional Services Canada. (2003). *Secure unit intensive supervision strategy*. Ottawa. Retrieved from http://www.csc-scc.gc.ca

Correctional Services Canada. (2006). *Ten year status report on women's corrections 1996-2006*. Ottawa: Minister of Public Safety and Emergency Preparedness.

Correctional Services Canada. (2008). *Transformation of federal corrections for women*. Retrieved from http://www.csc-scc.gc.ca

Correctional Services Canada. n.d. *Women offender programs and issues: Mother-Child program*. Retrieved from http://www.csc-scc.gc.ca

Covington, S., & Owen, B. (2005). *The gender-responsive strategies project: Approach and findings*. National Institute of Corrections Bulletin.

Crewe, B. (2009). *The prisoner society: Power, adaptation, and social life in an English prison*. Oxford: Oxford University Press.

Dell, C, Fillmore, C, & Kilty, J. (2009). Looking back ten years after the Arbour inquiry. *Prison Journal, 89*, 286-308.

Faith, K. (1993). *Unruly women: The politics of confinement and resistance*. Vancouver: Press Gang.

Fayter, R., & Payne, S. (2017). The impact of the conservative punishment agenda on federally sentenced women and priorities for social change. *Journal of Prisons and Prisoners, 26* (1&2), 10-30.

Foucault, M. (1977). *Discipline and punish* (A. Sheridan, trans.). New York: Pantheon.

Globe and Mail. (2011, May 4). *Ashley Smith's family settles wrongful death lawsuit*.

Hannah-Moffat, K. (2001). *Punishment in disguise: Penal governance and federal imprisonment of women in Canada*. Toronto: University of Toronto Press.

Hannah-Moffat, K. (2010). Sacrosanct or flawed: risk, accountability and gender responsive penal politics. *Current Issues in Criminal Justice, 22*(2), 193-215.

Hannah-Moffat, K, & Maurutto, P. (2010). Re-contextualizing pre-sentence reports: Risk and race. *Punishment and Society, 12*(3), 262-286.

Hannah-Moffat, K., & Shaw, M. (2000). *An ideal prison? Critical essays on women's imprisonment in Canada*. Halifax: Fernwood Publishing.

Heney, J. (1990). *Report on self-injurious behaviour inside Kingston's Prison for Women*. Ottawa: Correctional Service of Canada. Retrieved from http://www.csc-scc.gc.ca

Hayman, S. (2005). *Imprisoning our sisters: The new federal women's prisons in Canada*. Montreal: McGill Queen's University Press.

Ignatieff, M. (1978). *A just measure of pain: The penitentiary in the industrial revolution*. London: Macmillan.

Inglis et al. v. The Ministry of Public Safety. Retrieved from https://bccla.org/our_work/inglis-et-al-v-the-minister-of-public-safety/

Jackson, M. (1983). *Prisoners of isolation: Solitary confinement in Canada*. Toronto: University of Toronto Press.

Kerr, L. (2015). The origins of unlawful prison policies. *Canadian Journal of Human Rights, 4*(1), 89-119.

Kershaw, A., & Lasovich, M. (1991). *Rock-a-Bye baby: A death behind bars*. Toronto: Oxford University Press.

Kilty, J. (2006). Under the barred umbrella: is there room for a women-centered self-injury policy in Canadian corrections? *Criminology & Public Policy*, 5(1), 161-182.

Kline, M. (1994). The colour of law: The ideological representations of First Nations in legal discourse. *Social & Legal Studies, 3*(4), 451-476.

Kong, R., & AuCoin, K. (2008). Female prisoners in Canada. *Juristat, 28.* Statistics Canada. Retrieved from http://www.statcan.gc.ca

Laishes, J. (2002). *The 2002 mental health strategy for women prisoners.* Ottawa: Correctional Services Canada.

Liebling, A., & Arnold, H. (2005). *Prisons and their moral performance: A study of values, quality, and prison life.* London: Oxford University Press.

Mahony, T., Jacob, J., & Hobson, H. (2017). *Women in Canada: A gender based statistical report: Women in the criminal justice system.* Ottawa: Statistics Canada.

Matheson, F., Doherty, S., & Grant, B. (2008). Women offender substance abuse programming and community reintegration. Ottawa: Addictions Research Centre, Correctional Service of Canada.

McCoy, E. (2015). *Hard time: Reforming the penitentiary in nineteenth-century Canada.* Athabasca Press.

Minaker, J. (2006). Sluts and slags: The censuring of the erring female. In G. Balfour & E. Comack (Eds.), *Criminalizing women: Gender and injustice in neo-liberal times.* Halifax, NS: Fernwood Publishers.

Morin, D. (2015). Carceral geography: Spaces of incarceration, Surrey (UK): Ashgate.

Myers, N. (2017). Eroding the presumption of innocence: Pre-trial detention and the use of conditional release on bail. *British Journal of Criminology, 57,* 664-683.

Ontario Human Rights Commission. *Segregation and mental health in Ontario's prisons.* Toronto, Ontario: Ministry of Community Safety and Correctional Services.

Parkes, D., Bent, K., Peter, T., & Booth, T. (2008). Listening to their voices: Women prisoners and access to justice in Manitoba. *University of Windsor Year Book, Access to Justice, 26*(1), 85-119.

Piché, J. (2011). Going Public: Accessing Data, Contesting Information Blockades. *Canadian Journal of Law and Society, 26*(3), 635-643.

Piché, J; Gaucher, B., & Walby, K. (2014). Facilitating prisoner ethnography: An alternative approach to 'doing prison research differently.' *Qualitative Inquiry, 20*(4), 392-403.

Pollack, S., & Eldridge, T. (2015). Complicity and redemption: Beyond the insider/outsider research dichotomy. *Social Justice, 42(*2), 132-145.

Pollack, S. (2009). You can't have it both ways: Punishment and treatment of imprisoned women. *Journal of Progressive Human Services, 2,* 112-128.

Rusche, G., & Kirchheimer, O. (2003). *Punishment and social structure.* Transaction Publishers.

Sangster, J. (1999). Criminalized and the colonized: Ontario women confront the Ontario criminal justice system 1920-1960. *Canadian Historical Review, 80, 1.*

Sapers, H. (2008). *A Preventable Death. Report to Correctional Services of Canada.* Ottawa: Office of the Correctional Investigator.

Sapers, H. (2010). *Annual Report of the Office of Correctional Investigator 2009/2010.* Ottawa: Office of Correctional Investigator.

Shaw, M. (1991). *The federal female offender: Report on a preliminary study.* Ottawa: Solicitor General.

Shaw, M., Rodgers, K., Blanchette, J., Hattem, T., Seto, L., & Tamarack, L. (1991). *Paying the price: Federally sentenced women in context.* Ottawa: Solicitor General of Canada.

Shook, J., McInnis, B., Piché, J., & Walby, K. (2017). Special Issue–A dialogue on the Canadian federal penitentiary system and the need for penal reform. *Journal of Prisoners on Prisons, 26*(1&2), 1-314.

Statistics Canada. *Adult Custody Admissions to Correctional Service by Sex* (Table 35-10-0015-01). Retrieved from https://www150.statcan.gc.ca

Statistics Canada, Canadian Centre for Justice Statistics, Integrated Correctional Services Survey. Retrieved from http://www.statcan.gc.ca

Sykes, G. (1958). The pains of imprisonment. *The society of captives: A study of a maximum security prison*, 63-78.

Tyler, T. (December 18, 1999). *Prisoners used for 'frightening tests' new papers show. Toronto Star*.

UCCO-SACC-CSN. (2005). *A National Strategy for High Risk Women*. Dumont, Pierre and Preville, Marie-Josee.

UCCO-SACC-CSN National Executive Committee. (2007). *Rewards and consequences: A correctional service for the 21st century: A brief to the independent review panel studying the future of Correctional Service of Canada*. Retrieved from http://ucco-sacc-csn.ca

Walmsley, R. (2017). *World female imprisonment list*. International Centre for Prison Studies. Kings College. London.

Weibe, R. (1998). *A stolen life: The journey of a Cree woman*. Toronto: Alfred Knopf Canada.

Zinger, I. (2017). *The annual report of the office of Correctional Investigator 2016-2017*. Ottawa: Her Majesty the Queen in Right of Canada (1-90).

CASES CITED

Proctor v. Canada, [2000] O.T.C. 152

The Mass Imprisonment of Indigenous Peoples: Canada's Continued Colonial Agenda

7

Lisa Monchalin and Olga Marques

Learning Objectives

After reading this chapter, you should be able to:

- Understand colonialism and how it relates to Indigenous mass incarceration.

- Describe the impacts of residential schools and imposed laws.

- Compare Indigenous peoples' experiences with police, courts, and corrections.

- Explain how Indigenous peoples are criminalized by continuing colonialism.

- Describe how structural racism relates to Indigenous mass incarceration.

- Discuss the roles of Indigenous Elders, ceremonies, and healing in prisons.

- Understand what it means to decolonize.

While European explorers often said, "Indians have no law" Why? They couldn't see police; they didn't find courts; they didn't see uniforms, jails and all the trappings of power. But they also couldn't see the clan mothers, who are so important to our Native legal institutions.
– Robert Yazzie (Chief Justice Emeritus of the Navajo Nation), 1995 (quoted in Monchalin, 2016, p. 52).

INTRODUCTION

Indigenous peoples are the most overrepresented in the Canadian prison system compared to any other segment of the population. This overrepresentation has seen a continual growth, particularly among Indigenous women, whose prisoner population increased by 109% between 2001-2002 and 2011-2012 (The Office of the Correctional Investigator, 2016). According to the Office of the Correctional Investigator (2017), between 2007 and 2016, the federal Indigenous prison population increased by 39%, while the overall federal prison population only increased by less than 5%. For the last three decades in a row, the incarceration of Indigenous persons in federal prisons have continued to rise. While Indigenous peoples comprise about 5% of the total population in Canada, they represent 26.4% of federal prisoners, and with Indigenous women representing 37.6% of the total female federal prisoner population (p. 48).

To put it another way, Indigenous people are ten times more likely than non-Indigenous people to be put in prison. This rate of incarceration is even higher than at the height of apartheid in South Africa. For Indigenous people in Saskatchewan, this rate jumps to being 33 times more likely to be incarcerated (Macdonald, 2016). In 2016, the Correctional Investigator referred to some federal correctional institutions in the Prairie provinces as essentially "Indigenous prisons," given that 47% of those incarcerated in the Prairies are Indigenous. For instance, 59% of the persons incarcerated at Saskatchewan Penitentiary are Indigenous, 58% at Stony Mountain Institution in Manitoba, and in the Regional Psychiatric Centre in Saskatoon 61% of prisoners are Indigenous (The Office of the Correctional Investigator, 2016, p. 43). These realities help to clarify why "correctional officer" in the Prairie's is the fastest growing public sector occupation in Canada (Macdonald, 2016).

The mass incarceration of Indigenous peoples in Canadian prisons cannot be separated from the colonial context. As Monture-Angus (1998) states: "recognizing colonialism as a central explanation – if not *the* central explanation – for Aboriginal overrepresentation in the justice system is essential" (p. 363). Thus, in this chapter we ground understandings of the overrepresentation of Indigenous peoples within the context of both past and ongoing colonialism. To begin, we start by explaining Indigenous peoples advanced forms of laws and justice. We then outline what colonialism is, discuss imposed racist laws, as well as how Indigenous children were forced into residential schools. We then consider how, like residential schools, prisons are a continuation of colonial violence perpetrated against Indigenous peoples. This includes looking to the role of the current child welfare system, and education systems and their relation to over-incarceration as well. Discussion then turns to how structural racism is embedded within the entire criminal justice process from police, to courts, to corrections. We then shift to exploring healing, culture, and spirituality in prisons. Finally, we conclude by discussing Indigenous people's survival and resilience despite continued colonial oppression.

UNDERSTANDING INDIGENOUS MASS INCARCERATION WITHIN THE CONTEXT OF COLONIALISM

There have been many false narratives propagated in Canada regarding Indigenous peoples. One of these false narratives purports that Indigenous peoples did not have systems of justice before the arrival of the Europeans. Nothing can be further from the truth. Colonists tried very hard to destroy records of Indigenous people's societal structures and systems of governance, in an effort to abolish memory of them (Gunn Allen, 1992, p. 3; Means & Johnson, 2013, pp. 86-87). Indigenous peoples had, and still have, sophisticated systems of justice and techniques to deal with crime that were in place long before the arrival of the settlers. These systems and structures played a role in maintaining balance in communities across generations. Depending on the nation, there would be many different systems and approaches to dealing with crime. Just as there are many different nations across Canada, all with differing languages, cultures, and traditions – so too are there differing approaches to justice (Monchalin, 2016a, p. 53). For instance, in a study of six different Indigenous legal traditions: those from Coast Salish, Tsilhqot'in, Northern Secwepemc, Cree, Anishinabek, and Mi'kmaq, a key theme identified was diversity. As stated in their final report, "The first theme is diversity – there is wide range of principled legal responses and resolutions to harm and conflict in each Indigenous legal tradition" (Friedland, 2014, p. 8). For instance, one of the "biggest concepts" in Mi'kmaq society is *abeksikdawaebegik* (reconciliation), and there were two ways in which an offender was to take responsibility. First, restitution had to be given to their victims, and second, they had to advance empathy for their victims (Friedland, 2014, p. 8). In Coast Salish communities, responses to conflict or harms included "teaching responsibilities, conflict avoidance, providing guidance to wrongdoers, restitution, restoration, providing ongoing support and monitoring, retribution, and punishment for deterrence as a last resort when nothing else works to rectify the harmful behaviour." At the same time, Elders explained how punishment was only used if the other approaches all failed, and if the crime was severe (Friedland, 2014, pp. 10-11). Thus, there are a wide variety and reaching range of approaches to dealing with crime – none of which include the archaic prisons with bars, guards, weapons, and segregation cells that we see within the Canadian system today.

Furthermore, crime and disorder was rare among Indigenous populations at the time of contact and for some years after (Monture-Angus, 1998, p. 363). This is not to say that crime never happened, however, if it did, it was dealt with through various legal responses and approaches to justice that effectively maintained the well-being in communities since time immemorial (Monchalin, 2016a, pp. 52-53). As explained by Nishnawbe spiritual teacher Arthur Solomon, "We were not perfect but we had no jails and we had no judges or lawyers and no policemen," but rather, we did have "self-discipline and a code of moral conduct," including a philosophy of life based on the Creator and harmony with all of Creation (Solomon, 1990, p. 70). However, there has been an array of **colonial falsehoods** continually propagated within Canada having people believe otherwise, such as that Indigenous peoples had no forms of governance or laws – which is false. These untruths are spread throughout Canadian literature, histories, film, media, and popular culture to prioritize Euro-Canadian interests and goals over Indigenous peoples, communities, and lands. These colonial falsehoods play a role in keeping the population unaware of, or blind to, truths regarding Indigenous peoples and Indigenous histories. When people are blind to truths, assumptions and stereotypes are made regarding Indigenous peoples – notably when it comes to over-incarceration.

This is happening because of **colonialism**. According to Corntassel (2012) colonialism "is all about distorting Indigenous histories" as well as extinguishing Indigenous peoples collective and individual confidence (p. 86). Settler colonialism involves foreign peoples who come to lands not their own to exploit, steal, disconnect, and dislocate the original peoples of those lands, strictly for their own personal benefit. It comprises an attempt to control or eliminate people to steal Indigenous territories. Resources are stripped, while colonial falsehoods are spread rapidly about Indigenous peoples to not only convince the settlers, but Indigenous peoples too, that Indigenous peoples are a so-called "inferior" race and are a "problem" to be dealt with. Efforts are also made to control and oppress Indigenous peoples through legislation, and *their* foreign imported state institutions – such as through using their prisons, police, and court systems. In fact, as explained by McCaskill (1983), it is the justice system which is the central institution used by colonizers to unilaterally impose their way of life (p. 289).

"Indian" legislation was imposed on First Nations peoples in the 1850s and 1860s. In 1867, the totality of this legislation was consolidated to form **The Indian Act**. This is a federal law in Canada that is oppressive, discriminatory, and paternalistic. For instance, this Act made it illegal for First Nations people to practice cultures, dancing, or engage in ceremonies. If people were found engaging in these, they would be imprisoned and have their regalia confiscated. First Nations peoples were not allowed to enter a pool hall. Restrictions were placed on "Indians" ability to sell agricultural products. It was made illegal for First Nations people to hire a lawyer to advance land claims, and if found out, could face imprisonment (Monchalin, 2016a). Although some of the Act's worst provisions were removed in 1951, as well as 1985, it remains an archaic and racist piece of legislation that continues to regulate First Nations people's identities and lands today. For instance, it keeps an Indian registry, defining who is legally an "Indian" according to the governments system of registration. It also includes enforcing and regulating governance in the form of government-imposed band councils, to assimilate First Nations peoples. Sir John A Macdonald, Canada's first Prime Minister, made this aim of the Indian Act clear in 1887: "The great aim of our legislation has been to do away with the tribal system and assimilate the Indian people in all respects with the other inhabitants of the Dominion as speedily as they are fit to change" (Canada Parliament, 1887, p. 37). This aim does not seem to have changed.

Another assimilationist measure put in place by the government was the **Indian Residential Schools**. These schools were funded by the government, and administered by predominantly Catholic and Anglican religious dominations (Stonechild, 2006, p. 20). Although named "schools" these institutions were modelled off prisons and set up to indoctrinate children into Euro-Canadian Christian society. For instance, children were taken from their families, and placed into these institutions which were purposely far away from their homes. They were forbidden to speak their language. In addition, there were many extreme punishments in place if rules were not followed, including: having their mouths scrubbed out with *Ajax,* food and sleep deprivation, being put in isolation rooms, or into solitary confinement (Chansonneuve 2005, pp. 36-37). Children were taught that their parents were no good, and were savage, dirty, and pagans. They were conditioned to be ashamed of themselves, and told to forget everything their families taught them; and were further told that their cultures and ceremonies were works of the devil, and if practiced, they would burn in hell (Partridge, 2010, p. 51).

The implementation of these institutions was led by Sir John A. Macdonald. In operation from 1831 to 1996, an estimated 150,000 First Nation, Métis, and Inuit children attended (The Truth and Reconciliation Commission (TRC) of Canada, 2015, p. 3). Providing good quality education was not a priority. A 1948 survey identified that 40% of the teachers in these institutions did not have any professional training, but rather, many teachers were simply hired due to their "missionary zeal" (Stonechild, 2006, p. 20). The horrible abuses that went on against Indigenous children in these institutions has been well documented, and includes emotional, physical, and sexual abuses, resulting in one of the biggest genocides in Canada. At the sentencing of one of the child abusers, Arthur Henry Plint, B.C. Supreme Court Justice Douglas Hogarth explained that the residential school system was "nothing more than institutionalized pedophilia" (A. Smith, 2009, p. 9). In the telling of her story, Residential school survivor Nîno Mîkana Ikē Ka-Pimosēt (Helen Cote) who is Anisinābē, explained:

> For ten years the federal government of Canada and the Catholic Church imprisoned me. I was terrorized, raped and beaten. My child's body was not made for violent sexual and physical assaults. I became mentally ill at ten years old. I tried to escape my abuse and torture. Once

dogs were used to apprehend me. None of us were a threat to anyone. In that residential school we lived in fear. When we left that residential school, some of us promptly killed ourselves, or drowned our sorrows in drugs and alcohol. We went away to hide from our people, being too ashamed to look at them. Some of us died with our shame, therefore leaving our shame to be lived on in our children and grandchildren. (Cote & Schissel, 2008, p. 223)

Even though these institutions are now closed, intergenerational trauma still permeates generations of Indigenous peoples today. This means that trauma is transmitted generationally, whereby impacts are felt by families, including children and grandchildren of those who went to residential schools (Dion Stout & Kipling, 2003). Research has shown that this intergenerational trauma resulting from residential schools has cumulative negative impacts on well-being, and increased negative stressors in life – across several generations (Bombay, Matheson, & Anisman, 2014).

CANADIAN PRISONS AND THE CONTINUATION OF COLONIAL VIOLENCE

When Cree woman BobbyLee Worm received a six-year prison sentence for offences which included robbery, she ended up being put into a segregation cell for most of her prison term. Not only was BobbyLee a first-time offender, but she also suffered from post-traumatic stress, due to the trauma and abuse she had been subjected to in her life. In addition, many of her family members went to residential schools. While imprisoned in solitary confinement at the Fraser Valley Institution for Women in Abbotsford, British Columbia, she was placed in a three metre by three metre cell, known as "the hole." She was confined to her cell for up to 23 hours a day, with no human contact for months on end (*Supreme Court of British Columbia v. BobbyLee Worm and The Attorney General of Canada*, 2011, pp. 2-3). In 2013, she settled a lawsuit against the Correctional Service of Canada for what she endured, and in speaking about her experience, she stated:

> Solitary confinement does one thing. It breaks a person's will to live. Being locked up like that you feel like you're losing your mind. The only contact with another human is through a food slot. Days turn into nights and into days and you don't know if you'll ever get out. (*CBC News*, 2013)

The Office of the Correctional Investigator (2017) elucidates on how mental health problems are frequently intensified and worsened by segregation. When put into segregation, women report experiencing paranoia, extreme anxiety, with some feeling suicidal. They continue that the cells are isolated, dirty, and cold, and in one region, women are issued ear plugs in order to cope with screaming from those imprisoned in the same wings (p. 63). In Canada, Indigenous women are greatly overrepresented in segregation, including being more likely to be involuntary segregated, and have longer segregations as compared to non-Indigenous women (The Office of the Correctional Investigator, 2016, p. 62; Thompson & Rubenfeld, 2013, p. iii).

It is well documented in the literature that putting someone into solitary confinement can result in serious adverse effects, yet for Indigenous persons, segregation seems to be a regular, reoccurring practice. The United Nations Special Rapporteur, an independent expert appointed by the Human Rights Council, noted that there is extensive evidence that shows that the use of solitary confinement has serious health effects, ranging from hallucinations and mental illness, to insomnia and confusion. A significant adverse effect is that social and psychological contact is diminished completely down to the very least, to a degree that is inadequate for most prisoners to stay functioning mentally (The United Nations General Assembly, 2008). The use of solitary confinement for a prolonged period, whereby someone is held in a cell for "22 to 24 hours per day, and in some jurisdictions being allowed outside for up to one hour… may amount to cruel, inhuman or degrading treatment or punishment and, in certain instances, may amount to torture" (The United Nations General Assembly, 2008, p. 18).

These archaic practices – that Indigenous peoples are subjected to more often than non-Indigenous peoples – reinforce cycles of oppression and violence affecting Indigenous persons. They replicate and extend the trauma Indigenous peoples have underwent throughout history into today. It has been stated by some that "Canada's prisons are the 'new residential schools'" (Macdonald, 2016), and given the treatment that many Indigenous peoples are experiencing, this statement seems to have much credibility to it. Prisons are a continued extension of settler colonialism. They continue the institutionalization of Indigenous peoples with the intent to spiritually, mentally, and emotionally break-down Indigenous peoples. Prisons are evidence of the fact that we are still living in an era of **contemporary colonialism**. As Alfred and Corntassel (2005) outline, contemporary colonialism is:

> a form of post-modern imperialism in which domination is still the Settler imperative but where colonizers have designed and practise more subtle means (in contrast to the earlier forms of missionary and militaristic colonial enterprises) of accomplishing their objectives. (pp. 597-598)

Prisons have historically, and continue to be, the epitome of the colonial apparatus. Just like residential schools, prisons were not set-up to keep Indigenous families together. It is important to remember that correctional institutions operating in Canada are imports (primarily from England). In fact, the current criminal justice system, including police, courts, and corrections, are not only all imports – but they were brought to these lands to eliminate Indigenous presence to obtain Indigenous lands. As Arthur Solomon (1990) explained, colonizers created laws to "make sure the original people never got their source of power, the land, back again"(p. 90). With the arrival of the colonizers, these foreign systems of criminal justice were put in place. This began with the police, who were initially organized to manage and eliminate Indigenous presence. As Hildebrant (2008) explained, the original goals of the federal police in Canada were to gain the trust of Indigenous peoples "and then wean them from their customs and beliefs by enforcing laws intended to diminish the Native culture" (p. 36). And this "legacy of police administration has been so influential that even one-hundred years later their history is still written from a single perspective – one that only presents the view of the colonizer" (Hildebrandt, 2008, p. 35). Thus, these systems which are declared to achieve "justice" were not set-up in any way to achieve justice for Indigenous peoples, but rather, the opposite. These were set up to manage and eliminate, for the colonizers to reach their colonial goals of attainment of Indigenous territory. These systems and structures are still operating by these same goals. Agents of the state replicate the original goals of their forefathers. Prisons were not set up to eliminate crime, as that was never their intention; rather they are the central cog in the bureaucratic machine that keeps the criminal justice cycle continuing. All the while, Indigenous peoples continue to be syphoned in and out – continually trying to break their spirits.

Continuing colonialism is one of the primary drivers of Indigenous people's mass incarceration today. Rather than calling what is occurring against incarcerated Indigenous peoples, torture and continued oppression, neutral labels of "corrections" or "administrative segregation" due to "bad behaviour," are used. This is one of the manners through which settlers today ensue the same colonial goals of their forefathers. These goals have been handed down through various means, such as through popular discourse and cultures, as well as passed down and embedded within their societal institutions. As such, measures of assimilation and forced conformity that were pressed throughout history, continue. One of these methods is using the prison system. Prisons are a continuation of colonial violence against Indigenous peoples.

CRIMINALIZED BY CONTINUING COLONIALISM

Indigenous peoples have been targets throughout the entire criminal justice process. However, it doesn't just begin and end with the criminal justice process. There is an entire cycle embedded into the structures and institutions of society that fuel Indigenous peoples mass incarceration. For instance, another extension of both colonialism and prisons is the current child welfare system. Indigenous children are disproportionately taken away from families and placed into the child welfare system. According to the 2011 National Household Survey, of the roughly 30,000 children under the age of 14 in foster care, almost half (48.1%) were Indigenous children. Thus, in 2011, almost 4% of Indigenous children were in foster care as compared to 0.3% of non-Indigenous children (Statistics Canada, 2013, p. 5). This disproportionate overrepresentation is not driven by factors due to abuse. This is not to mean that abuse does not happen in Indigenous communities, however, when looking at the rationales behind the disproportionate dislocation of Indigenous children from their families, the overarching reason is neglect. Neglect, however, must be understood as a structural issue which is fuelled by poor housing, poverty, and substance misuse which are all interconnected to colonialism (Blackstock, 2011; Blackstock & Trocmé, 2005; Woods & Kirkey, 2013). It is not that Indigenous families do not *want* to care for their children, it is that, given the socio-economic and structural conditions that upend their lives and their living environments, some are unable to. Furthermore, the federal government discriminates against First Nations children in the child welfare system by providing inequitable child welfare services as compared to non-First Nations children. A ruling by the Canadian Human Rights Tribunal in January of 2016 found this to be true, after The First Nations Child and Family Caring Society of Canada along with the Assembly of First Nations filed a human rights complaint against the federal government in 2007 due to this discriminatory treatment – and won their case. This case showed that Canada discriminates on the basis of race, revealing that the federal government provides inequitable child welfare services for 163,000 First Nations children (Blackstock, 2016). For instance, the current funding formula leaves children in First Nations communities with 22% to 34% less child welfare funding as compared to what all other children in care in Canada receive (Jago, 2017).

The education system in Canada can also been yet another extension of both colonialism and prisons. Like the underfunded welfare system, schools in First Nations communities are also chronically underfunded. In 2011, First Nations children who went to school in their First Nation community received $3500 less, per student, per year as compared to provincial or private schools in Canada (Assembly of First Nations, 2011, p. 1; Campbell, Zeichner, Lieberman, & Osmond-Johnson, 2017, p. 11; Monchalin, 2016a, p. 18). In addition to less funding, schools located in First Nations communities also lack culturally-relevant curriculum, and in some cases, lack schools completely. For some youth, attending high schools means that they will have to leave their communities and stay with a host family, sometimes over 700 kilometers away, just to be able to attend high school.

In 2017, community gatherings in combination with an online survey collected opinions from Elders, parents, youth, First Nation leaders, and others who wanted to share their viewpoints on First Nations education. Participants in this study highlighted the need for culturally relevant education. For instance, many respondents felt that First Nation cultures must be an essential part of the school curriculum. This was a major issue of concern expressed by youth across the country, whereby they felt that Indigenous cultures should be offered in all grades. Youth also wanted to have the same quality of education offered on-reserve as off, as well as more schools on reserve so they would not have to leave their families and communities to be able to attend. Youth also expressed the need for proper infrastructure, including having access to safe drinking water in their schools (Hill+Knowlton Strategies Canada, 2017).

The experience of Indigenous student's off-reserve also seems to be one of disadvantage. For instance, in a 2002 study gathering the voices of Indigenous students, Indigenous students who left school, Indigenous adult community members, and teachers – on the circumstances of Winnipeg inner city schools – it was found that schools are racist, colonial, and Euro-centric. Schools were largely run by middle-class non-Indigenous people whose purpose is to advance dominant cultural values. As such, Indigenous students felt marginalized by such a system, feeling that their daily realities and cultural values were not reflected in the educational system. It was also found that there were few Indigenous teachers, and very little Indigenous content in the curriculum. On top of this, racism, including name calling and stereotyping was identified as being high (Silver, Mallett, Greene, & Simard, 2002, p. 3).

A research study gathering perspectives and experiences of both elementary and secondary First Nations and Métis students in Saskatchewan schools in 1997 and 1998 through talking circles and interviews, found that students generally have positive assessments of their education, and overall, students were serious about their education and have aspirations for their future (Schissel & Wotherspoon, 2003, p. 99). At the same time, students also expressed the need for teachers with experience, and who are Indigenous (p. 90). They value teachers and programming that are culturally relevant, and when this is present and integrated into their learning, they have enhanced success and a positive commitment to their education (p. 99). Yet like the study in Winnipeg, racism was also identified as prevalent, with more than 35% of high school students indicating that racism was their biggest barrier to learning. For instance, a First Nations student explained that his and other Indigenous students biggest barrier to learning was "prejudice, people calling us dumb First Nations and it sticks with us mentally" (pp. 82-83).

Given these realities, some Indigenous students in Canada have been pushed out of the school system which is overtly colonial and racist. Given the current educational structure, some argue that students are being pushed out of school and into prison, in what has been termed by many educators, students, lawyers, and civil rights advocates as the "**school-to-prison pipeline**" (C. D. Smith, 2009, p. 1012). In fact, according to the Assembly of First Nations (2012), "A First Nation youth is more likely to end up in jail than to graduate high school" (p. 3). As Smith (2009) explains, the "school-to-prison pipeline" is a phrase which "conceptually categorizes an ambiguous, yet seemingly systematic, process through which a wide range of education and criminal justice policies and practices collectively result in students of color being disparately pushed out of school and into prison" (p. 1012). A phrase used largely to reference Blacks, and Latinos in the United States, this concept can be clearly applied to the Canadian context in relation to Indigenous peoples.

Some of these criminal justice policies and practices that collectively result in Indigenous persons being pushed into prison are seemingly race-neutral policies. Such policies result in the disparate treatment of Indigenous peoples over time (Monchalin, 2016a, p. 144; Research Working Group of the Task Force on Race and the Criminal Justice System, 2012, p. 6). Consider the following examples outlined in Monchalin (2016a), such as the offence for driving with a suspended licence. This is not a policy that seems directly racist towards Indigenous peoples on the surface. Yet, because Indigenous peoples' have higher rates of poverty, means that they are also at a disadvantage to be able to pay a fine. Thus, Indigenous peoples experience the disparate impact of this. Poverty and unemployment also impacts people throughout various stages of the criminal justice process. For instance, if one is unemployed they have a lesser likelihood of attaining a good attorney, resulting in being less likely to get sentences reduced (p. 144). This results in Indigenous peoples being criminalized and put in prison for actions that are directly associated to factors such as poverty or lack of employment opportunities – both of which are directly tied to colonialism. Furthermore, it goes beyond these examples, as colonialism has fueled other factors correlated to Indigenous peoples being criminalized. As mentioned earlier in this chapter, Indigenous peoples went through immense trauma in residential schools. This trauma has been passed down generationally, resulting in losses to "mental, emotional, physical and spiritual well-being" (Partridge, 2010, p. 54). Today, and influenced by the "just get over it" rhetoric, Indigenous peoples are being criminalized for this residential school trauma, as well as the continuing trauma of colonialism. As explained by Arthur Solomon, the Sioux people referred to the colonizers as "*Wasichus*," which means, "those who take everything," and it is these *Wasichus* who "… make laws; and put fences around where no one can go; they put people in jail because they try to feed their hungry children" (Solomon, 1990, pp. 71-72).

STRUCTURAL RACISM: EMBEDDED IN THE ENTIRE CRIMINAL JUSTICE PROCESS

Overrepresentation is not due to Indigenous peoples committing more crimes. The data on mass incarceration demonstrates the numbers of Indigenous persons who are in prison, and this is in no way the same as the number of those who commit crimes. Indigenous peoples do not commit more crimes than non-Indigenous peoples. Rather, the criminal justice system is structurally racist, meaning that the social system and its structures establishes, replicates, and reinforces inequity among racialized groups. Understanding the criminal justice system through the lens of **structural racism**, or institutional racism highlights the racism that has been built into societal structures and its social institutions. For instance, within these structures and institutions, stereotypes about race pervade state agents attitudes, beliefs, and values, thus, resulting in these individuals acting in ways which uphold and reinforce stereotypes (Research Working Group of the Task Force on Race and the Criminal Justice System, 2012, p. 9).

These racist actions are seen at all levels of the criminal justice process, from arrest, to the court process, to corrections. As stated by Macdonald (2016),

> At every step, discriminatory practices, and a biased system work against an Indigenous accused, from the moment a person is first identified by police, to their appearance before a judge, to their hearing before a parole board. The evidence is unambiguous: If you happen to be Indigenous, justice in Canada is not blind.

Or put another way, as Chartrand (2018) states:

> The Canadian justice system works against Indigenous people at every level, from police checks and arrests to bail denial and detention, sentencing miscarriages and disparities and high incarceration rates.

At every level of the criminal justice system – from police, courts, and corrections – systemic and structural racism upends the experiences of Indigenous peoples. Siegel (2000) calls the police the "gatekeepers of the criminal justice process" (p. 498), as it is here where individuals are first marked, targeted, surveilled, and arrested, marking their entry into the criminal justice system. There is ample evidence showing how police have continued to treat Indigenous peoples brutally – and in many cases face no consequences for doing so. One horrific police practice has developed its own name because of its severity and reoccurrences: the **starlight tours**, also referred to as the freezing deaths. These deaths are a result of police seeking out Indigenous peoples on the street, usually late night, or early mornings, then driving them to the city limits, leaving them for dead in extreme weather conditions. This has resulted in many deaths of Indigenous peoples, due to hypothermia, and sometimes includes assaults as well (Monchalin, 2016a). This practice has been reported in various places throughout Canada, including Halifax, Toronto, Vancouver, and Winnipeg, yet Starlight Tours in Saskatoon is where attention started to be drawn to this issue in the 1990s and 2000s notably with the case of Cree teen Neil Stonechild, who was found dead and beaten by police officers beyond the northern outskirts of Saskatoon in 1990. A commission of inquiry into his death proved he was in police custody of officers Larry Hartwig and Brad Senger, who originally lied and said they did not have him in custody (Wright, 2004). Following the inquiry, the Saskatoon Police dismissed them from the force, however, neither of these police officers ever faced criminal charges (Monchalin, 2016a).

In 2000, also in Saskatoon, Darrel Night was picked up in the evening after walking back from a party. He too was driven to the outskirts of town and told by the police officers he was a "drunken fucking Indian," and when they left him for dead they yelled to him to "get the fuck out of here, you fucking Indian." The difference with Darrel's story is that he survived to tell it, by making it to a power plant that was about two kilometers away and getting the attention of their plant supervisor (Comack, 2012). This practice continues today, for instance, on a cold Saskatoon night in April of 2018, Ken Thomas also survived a starlight tour. After attending a concert, Ken went to a bar, stepped outside to have a cigarette, where he was then picked up by two police officers. He was told by the officers that he fit a description of someone who had been digging in vehicles. They then drove him to the outskirts of town and laughed at him as they left him there on a cold night. Ken being a marathon runner and a triathlon athlete, he was able to run back to town to keep warm (Irinici, 2018; *The Canadian Press*, 2018). A 1999 study examining First Nations Peoples experiences with police in the metro-Toronto area revealed that First Nations peoples often undergo very harsh treatment by the police. First Nations participants in the study revealed that the police mistreated them with persistent disrespect, they were offensive, and would engage them through cruel spoken interactions, intimidating and aggressive acts, and an excessively hostile demeanor (Neugebauer, 1999).

The court system is also laden with racism. Indigenous peoples are significantly underrepresented among all those who work in the administration of justice, including court officials, prosecutors, defence counsel, and as judges. What's more is that Indigenous peoples are also less likely to be represented on juries (Iacobucci, 2013, p. 2). This is problematic, as one defence lawyer noted that in some Prairie courtrooms, Indigenous defendants represent 85% of criminal caseloads (Macdonald, 2016). Without a balance of Indigenous peoples on the other side of the bench, and with colonial falsehoods running rampant, it becomes a recipe for racially charged outcomes. For instance, when 22-year-old Cree man Colten Boushie was shot point blank behind his head by a 56-year-old white farmer Gerald Stanley in Saskatchewan in August 2016 – an all-white jury, presided over by white judge – found Stanley not guilty. At the trial in February 2018 Stanley's defence was that the gun fired accidently, that it was a "freak accident" due to the guns mechanical failure known as a "hang fire" (NoiseCat, 2018). When the police went to notify Colten's mother, Debbie Baptiste, of his passing that evening, officers came into her home, some with their guns drawn, searched her home without permission, and proceeded to ask Debbie if she has been drinking. As the family explained, they were treated as if they were criminals (Giese, 2018). Then later in the same month of February 2018, another white man, 56-year-old Raymond Cormier, accused of murdering 15-year-old Tina Fontaine from Sagkeeng First Nation, whose body was found in Winnipeg's Red River, wrapped in a duvet cover and weighed down with rocks – was found not guilty. The recorded conversations whereby he spoke about killing her, and throwing her body in the water, was deemed circumstantial and not enough evidence for conviction. In this recording, Cormier stated: "You ever been haunted by something? What happened there really f—king it's not right. F—k. It's right on the shore. So, what do I do? Threw her in" (MacLean, 2018). Thus, for both Indigenous victims of crime, and for those who are accused, injustice is met at every juncture of the court process (See Box 7.1).

If Indigenous peoples find themselves reaching the point of corrections, they will have likely been subject to discriminatory treatment by the criminal justice system at every junction, and corrections

Box 7.1 – R v. Gladue 1999

In 1996, Parliament legislated a new principle, section 718.2(e) in the *Criminal Code*, with the intention of reducing the overrepresentation of Indigenous persons being admitted into prison. This provision directs judges to consider:

> all available sanctions other than imprisonment that are reasonable in the circumstances should be considered for all offenders, with particular attention to the circumstances of Aboriginal offenders

Then in 1999, the Supreme Court interpreted this section in *R v. Gladue*, a case which involved 19-year-old Cree and Métis woman Jamie Tanis Gladue. Gladue was accused of second-degree murder of her common-law husband. She pleaded guilty to manslaughter and was sentenced to three years in prison – a ruling that was upheld by the British Columbia Court of Appeal, as well as at the Supreme Court. In this Supreme Court Case, section 718.2(e) was interpreted, which argued that Indigenous persons must be sentenced in a way which gives greater weight to restorative justice and takes their background into consideration, such as historical injustices experienced by Indigenous peoples in Canada (Supreme Court of Canada, 1999). Furthermore, in 2012, the Supreme Court confirmed the Gladue ruling in *R. v. Ipeelee*, whereby Inuk man Manasie Ipeelee and Frank Ralph Ladue, from the Kaska Nation in the Yukon, had not complied with their long-term supervision orders (LTSO) by breaching the no substance use provision. In this case, the Supreme Court stated that judges have a statutory duty to consider Indigenous persons unique circumstances, and *Gladue* must be applied in any case involving Indigenous persons (The Supreme Court of Canada, 2012).

Yet since the provision of section 718.2(e) and the *Gladue* decision, there has not been any decrease in Indigenous people's disproportionate incarceration. As Martel et al. (2011) points out, since this ruling, there has been no decrease in the overrepresentation of Indigenous peoples being put into prisons (p. 251). Likewise, in an examination of whether 718.2(e) was successful in meeting its goal of reducing over-incarceration of Indigenous peoples in prison, Helana Fennig (2002) argues that it has not led to any decrease due to the fact that law reform does nothing to get to the root cause of Indigenous peoples overrepresentation in prison; further contending that Indigenous over-incarceration is a symptom of a much larger issue related to political, social, and economic disadvantage (as cited in Monchalin, 2016b, p. 360). Thus, mere tinkering with the colonial criminal justice system, rather than making structural changes to the colonial political, social, and economic systems of injustice, does not reduce overrepresentation of Indigenous peoples in prisons.

is many times no different. Incarceration practices are also racialized. Indigenous peoples are more likely to be placed in segregation, are less likely to receive parole, and more likely to have parole revoked for minor infractions (Chartrand, 2018). Incarcerated Indigenous peoples also serve disproportionately more of their sentence behind bars before first release, are under-represented in community supervision populations and over-represented in maximum security, are disproportionately involved in institutional security incidents, are subjected to more use of force interventions – as compared to non-Indigenous persons incarcerated (Sapers, 2012). Given Indigenous peoples discriminatory treatment within the correctional system, it might not be surprising that Indigenous peoples are also more likely to engage in self-injurious behaviour while incarcerated (ibid).

Indigenous people are at a disadvantage immediately upon intake, where Indigenous persons often become classified as higher risk on the Correctional Services Canada (CSC) **Custody Rating Scale**. This is a scale used to determine whether a person will be imprisoned in maximum, medium, or minimum security. Several studies have shown that such systems of classification are biased against minority and ethno-cultural and female populations (Hannah-Moffat & Shaw, 2001; Shaw & Hannah-Moffat, 2000; Webster & Doob, 2004). As Webster and Doob (2004) highlight, this Custody Rating Scale was created based on a homogenous group of white males in 1987. Many times, Indigenous women are unjustly over-classified in higher security classifications. Such misclassifications can be harmful and damaging to those incarcerated, especially when they are classified in a higher security risk level. For instance, as Webster and Doob (2004) state, "classification decisions determine many of the inmate's living conditions, including supervision levels, type of accommodation, geographical location of incarceration, use of restraints, and inmate privileges" (p. 397).

On the other hand, CSC has also funded a handful of research studies maintaining that the Custody Rating Scale instrument is not discriminatory nor does it have bias, arguing that it is appropriate for all populations (Barnum & Gobeil, 2012; Gobeil, 2008). As outlined in a report which examines its applicability with Indigenous women, they state: "There was no evidence that either the security classification as a whole or the CRS recommendation was over-classifying Aboriginal women … the over-representation of Aboriginal women at higher security levels is due to their higher level of risk and poorer institutional adjustment rather than a bias in initial security classification" (Barnum & Gobeil, 2012). In response to similar assertions by CSC, Webster and Doob (2004) argue that "CSC's claim of the scale's validity for women in general, and Aboriginal offenders in particular, is a dramatic oversimplification of their own findings and is profoundly misleading" (p. 411).

HEALING, CULTURE, AND SPIRITUALITY IN PRISONS

Indigenous peoples have survived, and continue to survive this advent of oppression, racism, and violence fueled in part by the criminal justice system. A key to this survival for many lies in the power of ceremonies, traditions, and cultures – that have kept peoples well-being and spirit balanced since time immemorial. Even with the disruptions caused by colonialism, the power of Indigenous cultures, spirituality, or in the remembrance of who one is and where they are from – has been central to survival today. Cultures and spirituality have also been brought inside prison walls, and have in many ways have provided a way to "cope with incarceration" (Waldram, 1993, p. 359). Initially Indigenous cultural ceremonies, and traditional medicines such as sweet grass, were banned inside of prisons in Canada (Solomon, 1990, p. 105). Staff persons and guards were known to make fun of and mock Indigenous spirituality (Morin, 1989). Having these practices allowed into prison was not an easy feat. Several Indigenous community organizations, peoples, and groups worked very hard to make this a reality. For instance, as Morin notes, this includes: "…the Native Clan in Manitoba, Native Counselling Services in Alberta, Allied Indian and Metis Society in B.C., and a number of other Native organizations from the community" (ibid).

In the 1960s and 1970s, Native Brotherhoods and Sisterhoods were forming inside prisons, and at this time, they were faced with much resistance.[1] For instance, when Indigenous prisoners tried to meet together as a group at an institution in Guelph, Ontario, they were only allowed to under the sponsorship of a Catholic chaplain (Solomon, 1990). Morin explains how important the Native Brotherhood groups have been inside prisons. He described them as being self-help groups for incarcerated Indigenous people, while at the same time they also promote a mutual understanding between Indigenous and non-Indigenous prisoners. At the Edmonton Maximum Security Institution in the 1980s for example, this group was instrumental in coordinating several programs for Indigenous prisoners, such as various ceremonies, life skills programs, peer group counselling, and as well as Powwows (Morin 1989) (see Box 7.2 and 7.3).

Indigenous cultures and traditions are essential and beneficial for Indigenous prisoners healing – since they were first instituted and continuing today. In 2001 a study examining First Nations peoples release from prisons, Indigenous cultures and traditions were found to be an essential part of prisoner's

Box 7.2 - An Insider's Perspective

First Nation Teachings and punitive prison sentences are polar opposites and yet when it comes to the rehabilitation of offenders, the Correctional Service of Canada has attempted to merge the two in the interest of alleviating the over representation of First Nation Offenders in the federal correctional system.

Since the Correctional Service of Canada (CSC) has acknowledged the need for an Aboriginal Spiritual aspect in the pursuit of healing First Nation members in 1992, there has been no evaluative assessment on the overall gains of the general population of Aboriginal offenders.

The Office of Public Safety in Ottawa states that assessments were completed in the areas of Healing lodges, and not for the pathways units as stated in the Roadmap to Strengthening Public Safety. This false statement supports the expansion of Pathways Units and gives a congratulatory pat on the back to CSC for the work supposedly completed in these areas.

Debra Hanuse, acting director of the law and legislation unit of the Assembly of First Nations, expressed the organizations support for this program based on statements from the Roadmap document:

Given the success of the Pathways Aboriginal Population Movement In lowering rates of recidivism among First Nations Inmates, we strongly support CSC plans to expand pathways Healing Units to all regions in both men 's and women's institutions. (Correctional Service of Canada Review Panel, 2007, p. 87)

The success alluded to here indicates that Pathways Units in medium security institutions are the answer to Aboriginal Healing through spirituality, when this is nothing more than a band aid solution that does not address the fundamental problem.

The majority of Aboriginal Offenders are the product of the fallout of colonialism, more specifically, the lack of traditional teachings that are the life lessons necessary for reintegration into society. These teachings cannot be packaged and delivered so that

offenders must seize these opportunities, pick up the tools of rehabilitation and use them. (Correctional Service of Canada Review Panel, 2007, p. 15)

If the offender was capable of, or had any faith in the "tools," these would have been put to use before incarceration. The problem is that the faith in the power of the traditional teachings has been lost and with the continual belittling of this walk there is small chance of an individual reacquiring the belief base necessary for faith in the traditional teachings.

The answer is the complete immersion in the teachings on a daily basis where they are incorporated into every aspect of life.

–KauKaught Anishnabe Nini

reintegration and healing. Of the seven interviews conducted with Indigenous peoples released from prison, "First Nations culture and traditional way of life" was identified as being a "priority" (Saulis, Fiddler, & Howse, 2001, p. 18). Several needs for Indigenous peoples released from prison were identified. This included, "Elder Counselling, traditional cultural guidance and healing circles, and structural transition programs for the individuals and community" (Saulis et al., 2001, p. 4). Similarly, in a study of 68 Indigenous ex-prisoners in Alberta, the importance of spirituality and cultures were identified as important in their successful exit from the system and in returning to the community (Heckbert & Turkington, 2001). Cultural identity was also identified as being "an important factor in the healing process" (p. 51). At the same time however, the study also found that Indigenous cultural activities and spirituality are not always respected or taken seriously inside prison. This included open displays of disrespect and discourtesy for Indigenous peoples, including disrespect of sacred items and Indigenous spaces (p. 51). Likewise, in a report by the Office of the Correctional Investigator in 2012, it was also found that there is inadequate awareness and knowledge of Indigenous peoples "cultures, spirituality and approaches to healing" within Canadian federal prisons among prison staff (Sapers, 2012, p. 6). **Elders** were noted as being especially essential in prisoners healing journeys in prisons, stating that they are "at the centre of any healing process" (p. 31). Yet, due to budgetary constraints, there is a limited availability of Elders in prison (pp. 27, 32). Elders are those who are respected in their community and seen as the wise ones who typically have traditional knowledge and teachings. Inside prisons, Elders bring a variety of assistance and healing to those incarcerated. For instance, this includes, providing counselling, or cultural or spiritual knowledge, or sometimes facilitating ceremonies. They first started going into prisons in the late 1960s and early 1970s on a volunteer basis. Then by the mid-1970s, and into the late 1980s their work started to become more formalized, and then by the late 1980s into the early 1990s their services in prison came to be written into policy, and eventually into law (Adema, 2014).

In an examination of case files and interviews with incarcerated Indigenous persons, some expressed concern that they did not have access to Elders who were of the same culture as them. This was concerning for some, as it meant that the teachings they were receiving were from a different Indigenous culture than their own (Johnston, 1997). It is important to realize that Indigenous peoples across Canada are from many different nations and cultures, all of which are diverse. This includes a wide variety of teachings, cultures, languages and traditions (Monchalin, 2016a, p. 3). A study which interviewed 30 incarcerated Indigenous men in the early 1990s, found that there was a **pan-Indian** approach to spirituality and culture being provided inside prisons (Waldram, 1993). A pan-Indian approach means that Indigenous cultures and peoples are lumped together, or that teachings from just one culture are applied to everyone – which can be problematic. At the same time, Waldram also found that while pan-Indianism exists, not all people rejected teachings from cultures different from their own and were okay with this. However, this was different for Inuit people who viewed such practices as foreign (Waldram, 1993). Waldram also noted how Indigenous persons who had the least knowledge of their cultural traditions tended to be less concerned about the nation-specific culture and traditions Elders were sharing in prisons, as they were searching for their roots and identity, and open to having the Elders help them trace their path (p. 356).

For many incarcerated Indigenous persons, their first deliberate exposure to Indigenous spirituality was inside prison walls. For instance, for some people, their first exposure to the **sweat lodge** was inside prison (Waldram, 1993). It is important to note, however, that the sweat lodge is not a ceremony that is part of all Indigenous people's traditions. This ceremony has a very long historical tradition, and the Plains Cree and the Lakota are among those whose traditions it is part. The ceremony involves cleansing and re-balancing ones spirit (Monchalin, 2016a). It involves a purification of both the individual and the collective, and as Arthur Solomon further explains, people pray for each other in a sweat, including "for the water, and for all of creation" (Solomon, 1994, p. 34). The sweat lodge structure is dome-like and circular. It will have hot rocks (referred to as "grandfathers") brought into the centre during several rounds. The heat increases as more grandfathers are brought in with each round. Inside, various medicines are used. However, which medicines are used, and how sweats are conducted will depend on the person who is facilitating it, and the traditions and teachings that they follow (Monchalin, 2016a).

Martel, Brassard, and Jaccoud contend that Indigenous cultures and spirituality might have become "oversimplified" or an "over-generalized version of aboriginal identity" because of formalization by CSC (Martel, Brassard, & Jaccoud, 2011, p. 242). This means that in some ways, Indigenous peoples have lost power over the delivery of their true cultures and traditions inside prisons, which extends to prison administration defining "what Aboriginal culture is (or is not)" (Martel et al., 2011, p. 243). In some instances, non-Indigenous peoples are those delivering Indigenous programming – in an attempt to teach Indigenous peoples how to be Indigenous (ibid). In other instances, CSC hires Indigenous people to deliver CSC programming, which they argue, co-opts Indigenous peoples to be an "agency Indian" when delivering CSC's colonial goals under the guise of being what CSC allows to be "Indigenous" (ibid., p. 250). Similarly, Adema contends that CSC has taken control of Indigenous cultural practices inside prisons, something that Indigenous persons, organizations, Elders, and community groups worked so hard to once bring in. This includes having Elders pulled under CSC structures and administration. As he further explained, this even included "CSC appropriating the role of the 'Elder' and defining it based on the Eurocentric expectations of spirituality" (Adema, 2014, p. 245). Yet at the same time, Adema reminds us that having Elders in prisons, as well as ceremonies, such as the sweat lodge, are a major inroad – one which has set the foundation for continued changes inside the colonial walls and structure of the prison. This is not to say that this is the complete solution to reducing Indigenous mass incarceration in Canadian prisons, but rather, Indigenous Elders, spirituality, cultures, and ceremony are certainly helping Indigenous persons survive while being locked up in these colonial institutions. As Adema explains, the Elders who went into prisons did so with "the goal to help prisoners survive a colonial institution, because the only way to fully decolonize the prison was penal abolition" (Adema, 2014, pp. 258-259). **Penal abolition** means to eliminate prisons altogether and replace them with more lasting and humane approaches to justice. To decolonize means the reversing and unravelling of colonialism, including its structures and institutions. It involves the return of Indigenous peoples lives and their land (Tuck & Yang, 2012, p. 1). According to Waziyatawin and Yellow Bird (2012), questioning the legitimacy of colonization, and recognizing the truth of its injustice, is the first step towards **decolonization.** They define decolonization as:

> the meaningful and active resistance to the forces of colonialism that perpetuate the subjugation and/or exploitation of our minds, bodies, and lands. Decolonization is for the ultimate purpose of overturning the colonial structure and realizing Indigenous liberation. (Waziyatawin & Yellow Bird, 2012, p. 3)

CONCLUSION: SURVIVAL, RESILIENCE, AND IDENTITY

> The criminal justice system, especially jail, does not work for us, or for anyone for that matter. As we heal, only then can we begin to implement alternatives to punishment that will heal both the Aboriginal and non-Aboriginal people. In the final analysis, dominant society must be part of the solution; it needs to be decolonized, too.
>
> — Nîno Mîkana Ikē Ka-Pimosēt (Helen Cote), Anisinābē, Cote First Nation (Cote & Schissel, 2008, p. 235).

Box 7.3 – A First Hand Perspective

My father is First Nations, of the Carrier Nation. My mother is Russian, descendant of the Dukhobors. Both sides of my family endured generations of conflict with state authority, which sought to oppress, assimilate, and destroy their cultures. My parents refused to teach me their languages, customs, or spirituality, due to fears of discrimination but they did hand down historic trauma. And being unable to cope with that trauma, I landed in prison.

I was always curious to learn of my roots and culture. When I discovered I could learn about First Nations teachings, culture, Spirituality, and customs while in prison, I was ecstatic and couldn't believe it. In the beginning, I was filled with wonder and awe regarding the Ceremonies of the Sweat Lodge, prayer and the Pipe and they helped me grow as a person. However, it didn't take long to become disillusioned. As I gained fuller understanding, I came to see the "Red Road" (what White institutions call their version of First Nations culture) was not a path to healing but merely a tapestry, covering a mirrored window that disguises the bars that confine us in their colonial matrix...

It all started to unravel when I found out I couldn't learn or practice my own heritage, the ways of the Coastal First Nations. Corrections recognizes only a very narrow, very shallow, paternalistically prescribed Spirituality that they have bastardized from Plains traditions and interwoven with European psychology. Although there are many First Nations cultures, most are not recognized by corrections and they insist their one size fits all. Any deviance from their prescribed cultural model is labelled manipulation, worthy of blame and punishment. Would they dare with others, for example to tell a Jehovah's Witness or a Muslim that Catholicism is the only recognized religion?

Corrections Elders, as well meaning as some of them might be, often would not qualify for Elder status in traditional First Nations communities. Many are not old enough, they don't have the traditional teachings, and they're not authorized to pass on the traditional teachings. Those that do meet traditional Elder standards never last long in corrections, as they believe in and adhere to their traditional teachings and customs. They would never pervert the teachings to conform to the correctional agenda. So, they choose to leave or are ejected by corrections. First Nations Spiritual teachers, unlike other faiths whose leaders are allotted staff positions, are contracted annually by CSC and thus can be quickly disposed if they do not conform. I've seen many good Elders suddenly disappear and many corrupt Elders stay in place, even when the prisoner population boycotts them for being more loyal to corrections than First Nations people and teachings. This is not to say all institutional Elders are corrupt but even those with the best intentions are constrained by institutional policies and operations.

Programming and security needs for First Nations prisoners are also prescribed, based on scores derived from actuarial risk-assessment measures that are constructed and normed in White culture. These assessment tools have been criticized for twenty years because their cultural bias elevates risk and need, which leads to incarceration at higher levels of security, which results in more time in segregation and longer waits for parole, which leads to higher rates of institutionalization and recidivism. These instruments are not accurate measures of risk but a self-fulfilling prophecy: these prisoners are not high risk when scored but due to the treatment they receive from corrections, their risk does elevate. Finally, the Supreme Court of Canada has Declared that CSC may no longer use these instruments on First Nations prisoners as corrections has not proven

continued...

the absence of cultural bias. Cultural bias is clear in the disproportionate rates of incarcerated First Nations prisoners, which continues to grow under auspices of these instruments.

When it comes to programs, the worst seemed designed to increase dysfunction while others disguise their North European, social and psychological concepts with First Nations terminology. In one of what I perceived to be the worst programs, the Aboriginal Family Violence Program, I was told to heal my childhood trauma by repressing my sad, painful memories ("cover them with your Magical Shaman Healing Blanket") and deluding myself with fantasies that everyone loved and nurtured me instead.

The Pathways units, which are touted as 24/7 traditional living and healing, are nothing more than large-scale, coerced segregation; institutional reservations. They are coerced because if a prisoner wants his case management team to believe his commitment to his "Healing Journey" (corrections terminology for "correctional plan") and earn a transfer to lower security or conditional release, enrolling in the Pathways unit is the preferred method for doing so. Enrolment requires waiving residual rights and freedoms to allow more frequent and invasive searching, less freedom of association and conscience, and less fairness in disciplinary procedures than the law allows. Just waiving your rights doesn't get you in right away. Each institution maintains a waitlist that amounts to 50% of the unit's capacity and admittance is through attrition when someone is expelled from the unit or transferred to lower security. The good news is, you don't forfeit your rights until you're in the unit.

First Nations prisoners have also lost their political voice. The Native Brotherhood (and Sisterhood, in women's prisons) was a representative body that was duly elected by the local First Nations population in each institution to represent their collective interests. During Harper's "tough on crime" regime (dumb on crime is more accurate, as his policies contradict research-based best practices), the Brotherhood was prohibited and replaced with Aboriginal Wellness Committee, whose members must be approved by the institutional administration and are expressly prohibited from political activity.

It's not only in the institutions that we have problems, either. While on parole, I was assigned a new parole officer who apparently became upset that I was thriving without corrections interventions. I was receiving funding for education and was gainfully employed in a First Nations community building much-needed new homes, recreation centres, and band offices. My PO was upset that the band didn't know my entire criminal and corrections history. I was informed I had to sign away my rights to privacy, so my PO could tell the Chief and Council all about my history and CSC's opinion of me, or else I was prohibited from entering any First Nations community. I complained to my PO's supervisors, who maintained the policy and threatened me with return to prison if I set foot in any First Nations community without first waiving my rights. Oddly, this requirement applied only if I was working in a First Nations community. I could go to school and work any non-Native community and it was not an issue. I filed a discrimination complaint with the Canadian Human Rights Tribunal and CSC settled in my favour, but it took three years and by then I had lost my funding for school due to deadlines and lost my employment.

In my view, Corrections is the new residential school. It continues to segregate us, oppress us, corrupts our Spirituality, and requires us to sign away rights and freedoms that everyone else enjoys to move forward through our sentences and regain our freedom.

— *One survivor*

Despite attempts at cultural and physical eradication, isolation, and containment, Indigenous peoples are still here, and have survived. This demonstrates how resilient Indigenous peoples are in the face of genocide. So while Indigenous peoples may have inherited trauma, **resilience** has been inherited as well (Pember, 2017). Resilience, or to be resilient, means that despite adversity, Indigenous peoples have survived due to such strength. There is much to be learned from how Indigenous peoples have survived. As mentioned earlier in this chapter, a key to this survival for many includes the importance or knowing who you are and where you are from. It includes the power of cultures, traditions, and ceremonies that reinforce identities and enhances well-being.

The colonial falsehoods which try to argue that Indigenous peoples' ceremonies, traditions, or methods of justice were primitive – must be dispelled. We learned from Waziyatawin and Yellow Bird (2012) that one of the first steps towards decolonization is recognizing the injustice of colonization – to wake up to the truth. Education is key. Unfortunately, colonialism has conditioned the population to believe that Eurocentric systems of education are somehow more legitimate than Indigenous methods, or that Indigenous methods of justice do not exist (Victor, 2007). Again, these are colonial falsehoods propagated to achieve the goals of the colonial project, and thus, continue the cycle of Indigenous mass incarceration.

Indigenous communities and peoples know what is best for themselves. There must be a move away from the hierarchical model that tells Indigenous peoples what to do, and how they should adapt to fit these colonial structures. This has not worked in the past and will not work in the future. There must be a **consciousness raising**. This means that society must wake up to truths and realities and develop a better awareness of injustices and why they are happening. In this case, it means becoming aware of the injustices perpetrated by colonialism. It means recognizing the injustices due to the distortion from the colonial project, and reconsider what is considered to be "the norm." As Alfred has explained:

> In order for indigenous peoples and the earth to survive, we must think outside of the concepts that form the present basis of our political, social and environmental relations, and focus on traditional notions of justice and power that are rooted in more natural and just premises. (Alfred, 1992, p. 11)

In conclusion, in this chapter we argued that Indigenous people's mass incarceration in Canadian prisons must not be separated from the context of colonialism. In this respect, we started this chapter explaining how Indigenous peoples have had systems of justice before the arrival of settlers, but then were put under imposed oppressive laws, and forced into residential schools. We also considered, how despite the closure of residential schools, their legacy of trauma is still felt today, and in many ways, prisons, the child welfare system, and education systems are all an extension of continued oppression and colonialism. We then turned to the related discussion of structural racism, and how it is deeply entrenched within the entire criminal justice process. Focus was then shifted to the importance of Elders, ceremonies, healing and spirituality in prisons, and how they help prisoners survive and cope with incarceration. Finally, we concluded by discussing Indigenous people's survival and resilience despite continued colonial oppression; emphasizing that in the face of genocide, Indigenous peoples are very resilient, and if change is to happen, Indigenous peoples must be listened too, and all peoples must contribute to a consciousness raising.

KEY TERMS AND CONCEPTS

Colonial falsehoods   Custody Rating Scale
Colonialism   Elders

Indian Residential Schools
Contemporary colonialism
School-to-prison pipeline
Structural racism
Starlight tours
The Indian ActPan-Indian

Sweat lodge
Penal abolition
Decolonization
Resilience
Consciousness raising

STUDY AND DISCUSSION QUESTIONS

1. What is meant by colonialism and how does it relate to Indigenous mass incarceration?
2. Why is it so important to understand Indigenous over-representation in prison within the context of colonialism?
3. What are the impacts of residential schools and imposed laws, and how do they contribute to the overrepresentation of Indigenous peoples in prisons today?
4. How does structural racism relate to Indigenous mass incarceration?
5. What are the roles of Indigenous Elders inside prisons, and how have their roles in prisons changed over time?
6. How and in what ways might a pan-Indian approach to spirituality and culture provided inside prisons be problematic?
7. What problems might arise from Indigenous cultures and spirituality being formalized by CSC?

HELFUL WEBLINKS

- **APTN Investigates: Indigenous People in Canada Behind Bars**
  http://aptnnews.ca/2017/11/03/aptn-investigates-indigenous-people-in-canada-behind-bars/
  A link to a video that examines the growing overrepresentation of Indigenous peoples in Canadian prisons.
- **Correctional Services Canada: Bringing the Grandchildren Home: Elders in Federal Correctional Facilities** http://www.csc-scc.gc.ca/media-room/009-1009-eng.shtml
  A link to a video that provides a closer look at Elders and the work they do inside of prisons with incarcerated Indigenous persons.

NOTES

[1] The Native Brotherhoods and Sisterhood movement began in 1964 from a group of mostly Cree-speaking Métis men in the Prince Albert Penitentiary (Adema, 2014, p. 247).

REFERENCES

Adema, S. (2014). Tradition and transitions: Elders working Canadian prisons, 1967-1992. *Journal of the Canadian Historical Association*, *25*(1), 243-275.

Alfred, T. (1992). The People. In Haudenosaunee Environmental Task Force (Ed.), *Words that come before all else: Environmental philosophies of the Haudenosaunee* (pp. 8-14). Native North American Travelling College.

Alfred, T., & Corntassel, J. (2005). Being Indigenous: Resurgences against contemporay colonialism. *Government and Opposition*, *40*(4), 597-614.

Assembly of First Nations. (2011). *Federal funding for First Nations Schools*. Retrieved from https://www.afn.ca/uploads/files/2_-_fact_sheet_-_funding_first_nations_schools.pdf

Assembly of First Nations. (2012). *A portrait of First Nations education. Chiefs assembly on education.* Gatineau. Retrieved from http://www.afn.ca/uploads/files/events/fact_sheet-ccoe-3.pdf

Barnum, G., & Gobeil, R. (2012). Revalidation of the custody rating scale for Aboriginal and non-Aboriginal women offenders. *Research Report R-273*. Ottawa.

Blackstock, C. (2011). The Canadian human rights tribunal on First Nations child welfare: Why if Canada wins, equality and justice lose. *Children and Youth Services Review, 33*(1), 187-194. Retrieved from http://dx.doi.org/10.1016/j.childyouth.2010.09.002

Blackstock, C. (2016). The complainant: The Canadian human rights case on First Nations child welfare. *McGill Law Journal, 62*(2), 285-328.

Blackstock, C., & Trocmé, N. (2005). Community based child welfare for Aboriginal children: Supporting resilience through structural change. In M. Ungar (Ed.), *Handbook for working with children and youth: Pathways to resilience across cultures and contexts* (pp. 105-120). Thousand Oaks: Sage Publications.

Bombay, A., Matheson, K., & Anisman, H. (2014). The intergenerational effects of Indian residential schools: Implications for the concept of historical trauma. *Transcultural Psychiatry, 51*(3), 320-338.

Campbell, C., Zeichner, K., Lieberman, A., & Osmond-Johnson, P. (2017). *Empowered educators in Canada: How high-performing systems shape teaching quailty.* San Francisco: Jossey-Bass.

Canada Parliament. (1887). Sessional papers: First session of the sixth parliament, *XX.*

CBC News. (2013, May 22). End solitary confinement, says former female inmate. Retrieved from http://www.cbc.ca/news

Chansonneuve, D. (2005). *Reclaiming connections: Understanding residential school trauma among Aboriginal people: A resource manual.* Ottawa: Aboriginal Healing Foundation. Retrieved from http://www.ahf.ca/downloads/healing-trauma-web-eng.pdf

Chartrand, V. (2018, February 18). Broken system: Why is a quarter of Canada's prison population Indigenous? *The Conversation.* Retrieved from https://theconversation.com/broken-system-why-is-a-quarter-of-canadas-prison-population-indigenous-91562

Comack, E. (2012). *Racialized policing: Aboriginal people's encounters with the police.* Black Point: Fernwood Publishing.

Corntassel, J. (2012). Living in a longer now: Moving beyond the state-centric system. In Waziyatawin & M. Yellow Bird (Eds.), *For Indigenous Minds Only: A Decolonization Handbook* (pp. 85-98). Santa Fe: School for Advanced Research Press.

Correctional Service of Canada Review Panel. (2007). *Roadmap to strengthening public safety.* Ottawa: Minister of Public Works and Government Services Canada. Retrieved from https://public-safety.gc.ca/cnt/cntrng-crm/csc-scc-rvw-pnl/report-rapport/cscrprprt-eng.pdf

Cote, H., & Schissel, W. (2008). Damaged children and broken spirits: A residential school survivor story. In C. Brooks & B. Schissel (Eds.), *Marginality & condemnation: An introduction to critical criminology (*2nd ed.) (pp. 220-237). Black Point: Fernwood Publishing.

Dion Stout, M., & Kipling, G. (2003). *Aboriginal people, resilience and the residential school legacy.* Ottawa: The Aboriginal Healing Foundation.

Friedland, H. (2014). *IBA accessing justice and reconciliation project: Final report.* Retrieved from http://indigenousbar.ca/indigenouslaw/wp-content/uploads/2013/04/iba_ajr_final_report.pdf

Giese, R. (2018, February 16). Why has Colten Boushie's mother had to work so hard just to prove her son's humanity? *Chatelaine.* Retrieved from http://www.macleans.ca/news

Gobeil, R. (2008). Assessing security reclassification with male Aboriginal and Non-Aboriginal offenders. *Research Report R-203*. Ottawa: Correctional Service of Canada.

Gunn Allen, P. (1992). *The sacred hoop: Recovering the feminine in American Indian traditions.* Boston: Beacon Press.

Hannah-Moffat, K., & Shaw, M. (2001). *Taking risks: Incorporating gender and culture into the classification and assessment of federally sentenced women in Canada.* Ottawa: Status of Women Canada.

Heckbert, D., & Turkington, D. (2001). *Turning points: A study of the factors related to the successful reintegration of Aboriginal offenders.* Ottawa: Research Branch: Correctional Services of Canada. Retrieved from http://publications.gc.ca/collections/collection_2010/scc-csc/PS83-3-112-eng.pdf

Helana Fennig, T. (2002). *Sentencing Aboriginal offenders: Section 718.2(e) of the Criminal Code of Canada and Aboriginal over-representation in Canadian prisons.* Simon Fraser University.

Hildebrandt, W. (2008). *Views from Fort Battleford: Constructed visions of an Anglo-Canadian west.* Regina: Canadian Plains Research Centre, University of Regina.

Hill+Knowlton Strategies Canada. (2017). *Let's talk on-reserve education: Survey report.* Retrieved from https://www.aadnc-aandc.gc.ca/eng/1509019844067/1509019955553

Iacobucci, T.H.F. (2013). *First Nations representation on Ontario juries: Report of the independent review conducted by The Honourable Frank Iacobucci.*

Irinici, A. (2018, April 24). Complaint filed against Saskatoon police accuses officers of conducting a 'starlight tour.' *CTV News Saskatoon.* Retrieved from https://saskatoon.ctvnews.ca

Jago, R. (2017, March 29). Budget 2017 Sets the stage for a nation-to-nation partnership with Indigenous people, but fails to mention the role of individual bands. *Policy options.* Retrieved from http://policyoptions.irpp.org

Johnston, J.C. (1997). *Aboriginal offender survey: Case files and interview sample.* Ottawa: Research Branch: Correctional Service Canada. Retrieved from http://www.csc-scc.gc.ca/research/092/r061-er61-eng.pdf

Macdonald, N. (2016, February). Canada's prisons are the 'new residential schools.' *Macleans.* Retrieved from http://www.macleans.ca

MacLean, C. (2018, February 22). Jury finds Raymond Cormier not guilty in death of Tina Fontaine. *CBC News.* Retrieved from http://www.cbc.ca

Martel, J., Brassard, R., & Jaccoud, M. (2011). When two worlds collide: Aboriginal risk management in Canadian corrections. *British Journal of Criminology, 51*(2), 235-255.

McCaskill, D. (1983). Native people and the justice system. In I.L. Getty & A.S. Lussier (Eds.), *As long as the sun shines and water flows: A reader in Canadian Native studies* (pp. 288-298). Vancouver: University of British Columbia Press.

Means, R., & Johnson, B. (2013). *If you've forgotten the names of the clouds, you've lost your way: An introduction to American Indian thought and philosophy.* Porcupine: Treaty Publications.

Monchalin, L. (2016a). *The colonial problem: An Indigenous perspective on crime and injustice in Canada.* Toronto: University of Toronto Press.

Monchalin, L. (2016b). The failed foreign system of criminal justice and the problem with Canada. In D. Long & O.P. Dickason (Eds.), *Visions of the heart: Issues invovling Aboriginal Peoples in Canada* (4th ed.) (pp. 351-373). Don Mills: Oxford University Press.

Monture-Angus, P. A. (1998). Lessons in decolonization: Aboriginal overrepresentation in Canadian criminal justice. In *visions of the heart: Canadian Aboriginal issues* (pp. 361-386). Scarborough: Thomson Nelson.

Morin, I. (1989). A Native perspective on corrections. *Saskatchewan Indian, October,* 15. Retrieved from http://www.sicc.sk.ca/archive/saskindian/a89oct15.htm

Neugebauer, R. (1999). First Nations People and law enforcement: Community perspectives on police response. In M. Corsianos & K.A. Train (Eds.), *From interrogating social justice: Politics, culture and identity* (pp. 247-269). Toronto: Canadian Scholars Press Inc.

NoiseCat, J.B. (2018, February 28). I am Colten Boushie. Canada is the all-white jury that acquitted his killer. *The Guardian*. Retrieved from https://www.theguardian.com

Partridge, C. (2010). Residential schools: The intergenerational impacts on Aboriginal Peoples. *Native Social Work Journal*, 7, 33-62.

Pember, M.A. (2017, October 3). Trauma may be woven into DNA of Native Americans intergenerational historic trauma is real. *Indian country today*. Retrieved from https://indiancountry medianetwork.com/news

Research Working Group of the Task Force on Race and the Criminal Justice System. (2012). Preliminary report on race and Washington's criminal justice system. *Washington Law Review*, *87*(1), 1-49.

Sapers, H. (2012). *Spirit matters: Aboriginal People and the corrections and conditional release act*. Ottawa: Office of the Correctional Investigator.

Saulis, M., Fiddler, S., & Howse, Y. (2001). *Release potential of federally-sentenced Aboriginal inmates to communities: A Community-based research project*. Ottawa: Research Branch: Correctional Service of Canada. Retrieved from http://publications.gc.ca/collections/collection_2010/scc-csc/PS83-3-110-eng.pdf

Schissel, B., & Wotherspoon, T. (2003). *The legacy of school for Aboriginal People: Education, oppression, and emancipation*. Don Mills: Oxford University Press.

Shaw, M., & Hannah-Moffat, K. (2000). Gender, diversity and risk assessment in Canadian corrections. *Probation Journal*, *47*(3), 163-172.

Siegel, L.J. (2000). Police and law enforcement. In L.J. Siegel (Ed.), *Criminology: The core* (7th ed.). Boston: Cenage.

Silver, J., Mallett, K., Greene, J., & Simard, F. (2002). *Aboriginal education in Winnipeg inner city high schools*. Winnipeg: Canadian Centre for Policy Alternatives. Retrieved from http://winnspace.uwinnipeg.ca/

Smith, A. (2009). Indigenous Peoples and Boarding Schools: A Comparative Study. *The Secretariat of the United Nations Permanent Forum on Indigenous Issues*, 1-58. https://doi.org/10.1017/CBO9781107415324.004

Smith, C.D. (2009). Deconstructing the pipeline : Evaluating school-to-prison pipeline equal protection cases through a structural racism framework. *Fordham Urban Law Journal*, *36*(5), 1009-1049.

Solomon, A. (1990). *Songs for the people: Teachings on the natural way*. (M. Posluns, Ed.). Toronto: NC Press Limited.

Solomon, A. (1994). *Eating bitterness: A vision beyond the prison walls*. Toronto: NC Press Limited.

Statistics Canada. (2013). *Aboriginal Peoples in Canada: First Nations People , Métis and Inuit*. https://doi.org/99-011-X2011001

Stonechild, B. (2006). *The new buffalo: The struggle for aboriginal post-secondary education in Canada*. Winnipeg: University of Manitoba Press.

Supreme Court of British Columbia v. BobbyLee Worm and The Attorney General of Canada. Notice of Civil Claim (2011). https://doi.org/S-111463

Supreme Court of Canada. R. v. Gladue (1999).

The Canadian Press. (2018, April 24). Man files complaint against Saskatoon police saying officers dropped him off outside city in the cold. *The Star*. Retrieved from https://www.thestar.com/news/canada

The Office of the Correctional Investigator. (2016). *Annual report of the office of the correctional investigator 2015-2016*. Ottawa: Her Majesty the Queen in Right of Canada. Retrieved from http://www.oci-bec.gc.ca/cnt/rpt/pdf/annrpt/annrpt20152016-eng.pdf

The Office of the Correctional Investigator. (2017). *Annual report office of the correctional investigator 2016-2017*. Ottawa: Her Majesty the Queen in Right of Canada. Retrieved from http://www.oci-bec.gc.ca/cnt/rpt/pdf/annrpt/annrpt20162017-eng.pdf

The Supreme Court of Canada. R. v. Ipeelee (2012).

The Truth and Reconciliation Commission (TRC) of Canada. (2015). *Honouring the truth, reconciling for the future: Summary of the final report of the truth and reconciliation commission of Canada*. Retrieved from http://www.myrobust.com/websites/trcinstitution/File/Reports/Executive_Summary_English_Web.pdf

The United Nations General Assembly. (2008). *Torture and other cruel, inhuman or degrading treatment or punishment.*

Thompson, J., & Rubenfeld, S. (2013). *A profile of women in segregation*. Retrieved from http://www.westcoastleaf.org/wp-content/uploads/2017/06/A-profile-of-women-in-segregation.pdf

Tuck, E., & Yang, K.W. (2012). Decolonization is not a metaphor. *Decolonization: Indigeneity, Education & Society, 1*(1), 1-40.

Victor, W. (2007). Indigenous justice: Clearing space and place for Indigenous epistemologies. *Prepared for the national centre for First Nation governance, December 2*, 1-28. Retrieved from http://fngovernance.org/ncfng_research/wenona_victor.pdf

Waldram, J. B. (1993). Aboriginal spirituality: Symbolic healing in Canadian prisons. *Culture, Medicine and Psychiatry, 17*, 345-362.

Waziyatawin, & Yellow Bird, M. (2012). Introduction: Decolonizing our minds and actions. In Waziyatawin & M. Yellow Bird (eds.). *For Indigenous minds only: A decolonization handbook* (pp. 1-14). Santa Fe: School for Advanced Research Press.

Webster, C., & Doob, A. (2004). Classification without validity or equity: An empirical examination of the custody rating scale for federally sentenced women offenders in Canada. *Canadian Journal of Criminology and Criminal Justice, 46*(4), 395-422.

Woods, M., & Kirkey, S. (2013, May 8). 'Tragic' number of Aboriginal children in foster care stuns even the experts. *Postmedia News*. Retrieved from http://www.canada.com

Wright, T.H.M.J.D.H. (2004). *Report of the commission of inquiry: Into matters relating to the death of Neil Stonechild*. Regina.

Yazzie, R. (1995). Healing as justice: The American experience. *Justice as Healing: A Newsletter on Aboriginal Concepts of Justice*. Saskatchewan: Un iversity of Saskatchewan. (Spring).

Limiting the State's Right to Punish

8

Debra Parkes, Kelly Hannah-Moffat and Amy Klassen

Learning Objectives

After reading this chapter, you should be able to:

- Understand the evolution of prisoners' rights in Canada.

- Understand the significance of these rights.

- Understand some of the primary methods of enforcing prisoners' rights.

- Consider the gap between law and correctional practice and reflect on the challenges of enforcing rights in a carceral context.

One must resist the temptation to trivialize the infringement of prisoners' rights as an insignificant infringement of the rights of people who do not deserve any better. When a right has been granted by law, it is no less critical that such rights be respected because the person entitled to it is a prisoner; indeed, it is always more important than the vigorous enforcement of rights be effected in the cases where the right is the most meaningful.
– Justice Louise Arbour

INTRODUCTION

What are the limits on the state's right to punish a person who violates the law? What constitutes too much punishment? When is punishment excessive? Why should prisoners have rights? Are they coddled and wasting court time with frivolous challenges? To answer such questions, we need to reflect on the meaning, context, purpose, and history of imprisonment, and on the significance of human rights in limiting the power of the state. The debate about prisoners' rights is filled with misconceptions and is often inappropriately juxtaposed with concerns about the rights of victims which are often seen to necessarily conflict with the rights of incarcerated people. We do not deny the insufficiency and importance of victim's rights, but by simply pitting the rights of victims against the rights of prisoners we cannot capture the significance and complexity of the issue, particularly since many people who are accused and convicted of a crime have experienced victimization. The breadth of the debate about prisoners' rights is expansive. It is not just about colour televisions or access to recreation facilities; it is about solitary confinement, over-crowded institutions, deaths in custody, and access to health care. These realities implicate our fundamental views of human rights and collective commitments to one another. Melnitzer (2000) argues that "civil rights of prisoners are the lowest common denominator of democracy" (p. 186). State power is ominous. Those subject to that power and those confined from the public view, like prisoners, need some assurances of accountability and protection from the arbitrary use and abuse of power by correctional officials who control virtually every aspect of a prisoner's life. Rights give prisoners some autonomy and control over their living conditions, while at the same time providing an essential check on the state's power to punish.

The debate about **rights**, which legally and morally ensure conformity with a particular norm is not to be confused with **privileges** which are often equated with an advantage or source of pleasure granted to a person. This discussion of rights is about the protection of fundamental legal, democratic, and human rights, such as freedom from discrimination, access to lawyers, privacy, limits on the use of solitary confinement and the use of force, the right to be informed about decisions, the right not to be subjected to cruel and unusual punishments, and the right to essential amenities such as showers, sanitary products, clothing, medical treatment, and exercise (UN, 2015).

Recognition and acknowledgement of these rights, along with the development of laws and administrative processes to secure those rights, are relatively new phenomena (see Box 8.1). This chapter will provide a brief history of prisoners' rights legislation, outline some of the official avenues of redress available to prisoners, and discuss some of the gaps between law and correctional practice and the significance of those gaps for a society committed to the rule of law.

THE SIGNIFICANCE OF PRISONERS' RIGHTS

The administration of a prison sentence is governed by the rule of law, a foundational principle which means that everyone from the most ordinary citizen to the head of state is subject to the law. The rule of law, in this context, means that the authority to punish comes from the law. In a society governed

Box 8.1 – Selected Legislation, Government Inquiries, and Legal Developments

1955 United Nations Standard Minimum Rules for the Treatment of Prisoners (SMRs) – As part of the international human rights movement developing in the aftermath of the Holocaust and the Second World War, this set of basic principles for the treatment of prisoners was articulated. The SMRs describe broad principles such as the need for treatment consistent with the dignity and value of human beings, while also setting specific standards for conditions of confinement including concerning accommodation, hygiene, food, exercise, health care, education, and rehabilitative programs.

1959 Parole Act – This Act created the National Parole Board (now called the Parole Board of Canada). For the first time in Canadian correctional history, parole decisions were determined and administered by an independent, national decision-making body.

1960 Canadian Bill of Rights – This law was enacted to affirm the dignity and worth of human beings and to declare certain fundamental freedoms. It was an essential step in the development of Canada's "rights culture," but it had a relatively little direct impact on imprisonment in Canada.

1969 Ouimet Committee – This Special Committee on Corrections reported to the Minister of Justice, taking the view that corrections should focus on rehabilitation rather than punishment. The Committee recommended a system of community corrections and called for the abolition of all forms of corporal punishment, which was still used in some prisons at the time.

1971 Swackhamer Inquiry – Following riots at some federal prisons, this Commission of Inquiry recommended a system of oversight of federal corrections, including a "visitors committee" to oversee penitentiary operations. This recommendation led to the creation of the Office of the Correctional Investigator (federal prison Ombudsperson) in 1973.

1972 Hugessen Task Force – This report made a series of recommendations to improve fairness and accountability in release (parole) decision-making. It recommended better access to information, a right to receive reasons for decisions, and the right to have assistance at parole hearings. It also called for the creation of five regional boards at the federal level.

1972 Abolition of Corporal Punishment – A law passed this year prohibited the use of corporal punishments, such as whipping and strapping, which were previously imposed as a sentence or as a disciplinary penalty for violation of prison rules.

1973 Office of the Correctional Investigator – The federal prison Ombudsperson was created through legislation in 1973. The Correctional Investigator primarily responds to prisoner complaints about treatment and conditions of confinement, conducting investigations and making recommendations. The Office issues an annual report and periodic reports on particular incidents (e.g., deaths in custody) or themes.

1975 Millhaven Inquiry – Responding to riots in federal prisons, this report articulated the vulnerability of prisoners in a climate that lacks awareness of rights, the rule of law, and due process.

continued...

1976 Abolition of the Death Penalty – The death penalty was abolished on July 26, 1976, but the last execution in Canada took place in December 1962. All remaining death sentences were commuted to life sentences in 1977.

1977 Canadian Human Rights Act – This law was enacted to prohibit discrimination by grounds such as gender, race, disability, and political or religious belief. Subsequent amendments have extended the grounds to include sexual orientation and gender identity. The Act applies to federally regulated activities and federal government entities including correctional services. Each province and territory has its own human rights act or code that applies to activities that are not federally regulated, including provincial correctional authorities. The Act also created the Canadian Human Rights Commission to investigate claims of discrimination as well as the Canadian Human Rights Tribunal to judge the cases.

1980 Martineau v. Matsqui Institutional Disciplinary Board – In this case, the Supreme Court of Canada, for the first time, affirmed that prison officials have to act "reasonably" in making decisions that involve prisoners' rights.

1982 Canadian Charter of Rights and Freedoms – The *Charter* is part of the *Constitution Act* 1982 which means that all laws and government actions must comply with its provisions. Some **Charter** rights such as the right to life, liberty and security of the person (section 7), the right to be free from cruel and unusual treatment or punishment (section 12), and the right to equality (section 15) have particular resonance in the prison context.

1990 Report of the Task Force on Federally Sentenced Women – Called "Creating Choices," this report articulated a different approach to women's corrections, one that would be women-centred and responsive to the unique needs and circumstances that bring women into conflict with the law. It was premised on an understanding of the evidence that women, as a group, are "high needs, low risk." A key recommendation of the Task Force was the closure of the Prison for Women and the creation of five new regional prisons for women, plus an Aboriginal Healing Lodge.

1992 Corrections and Conditional Release Act – This Act completely replaced the *Penitentiary Act* and the *Parole Act* that had previously governed federal imprisonment and conditional release.

1996 Report of the Commission of Inquiry into Certain Events at the Prison for Women in Kingston ("Arbour Commission") – Justice Louise Arbour was mandated by the Solicitor General to investigate and report on events that occurred at the Prison for Women in April 1993, namely the strip-searching of women prisoners by a male emergency response team in full riot gear and the subsequent illegal detention in segregation for many months. The report concluded that the rule of law and a culture of rights were not evident in correctional practice, despite the many laws and policies that purported to enforce them. The Report made many recommendations about women's corrections, but also about the need for judicial oversight and accountability over corrections generally.

continued...

1997 Task Force on Administrative Segregation – This task force was established in response to a recommendation from the Arbour Commission. It conducted a complete review of the use of administrative segregation by the Correctional Service of Canada. The goal was to ensure that all correctional staff and managers understood the legal and policy requirements and complied with the law in their decisions to place and maintain people in segregation. The task force report concluded that CSC staff did not fully appreciate their obligations under the law.

1999 R. v. Gladue – This decision of the Supreme Court of Canada interpreted s. 718.2(e) of the *Criminal Code*, which requires a sentencing judge to consider all available options other than imprisonment, with particular attention to the circumstances of Indigenous people. Subsequent decisions have declared that "Gladue analysis" – namely consideration of the ongoing impact of colonization and systemic racism and their contribution to the massive over-representation of Indigenous people in prison – is relevant to all decision-making in the criminal justice and correctional systems.

2002 Sauvé v. Canada – A majority of the Supreme Court of Canada declared that denying the vote to prisoners unjustifiably infringes the right to vote guaranteed to all citizens in section 3 of the *Charter*. The decision is rooted in a conception of prisoners as full rights holders under the *Charter*.

2004 May v. Ferndale institution – The Supreme Court of Canada affirmed the importance and flexibility of the ancient writ of *habeas corpus* which requires that prisoners have timely access to the courts to determine the legality of their detention.

2010 UN United Nations Rules for the Treatment of Women Prisoners and Non-custodial Measures for Women Offenders ("Bangkok Rules") – This United Nations document acknowledged the unique needs and circumstances of incarcerated women and was designed to complement the original UN Standard Minimum Rules for the Treatment of Prisoners which were primarily designed with men in mind. It specifically addressed rules related to women's health, pregnancy and parenting, hygiene concerns, suicide and self-harm prevention, and privacy, among other concerns.

2015 UN Standard Minimum Rules for the Treatment of Prisoners ("Mandela Rules") – The SMRs were substantially revised in 2015 to articulate and update the standards for conditions of confinement and set new limits on harmful correctional practices such as solitary confinement and the use of restraints. They also speak to such issues as the need for effective external oversight and monitoring of prisons.

2018 British Columbia Civil Liberties Association v. Canada – This decision of the British Columbia Supreme Court declared that the regime of administrative segregation (solitary confinement) in federal prisons violates the *Canadian Charter of Rights and Freedoms*, specifically section 7 (the right to life, liberty and security of the person) and section 15 (the right to equality). The decision has been appealed to the British Columbia Court of Appeal.

by the rule of law, the state (i.e., for our discussion, this means the Correctional Service of Canada or provincial and territorial correctional authorities, and their employees) must respect the fundamental rights of citizens. The premise is that either human rights belong to everyone or they are guaranteed to no one (Easton, 2010; Birgden & Perlin, 2008). The coercive authority of the state to punish individuals by confining them and depriving them of their liberty (precious and taken-for-granted freedom) is justified in law. The guarantee and enforcement of the rule of law are meant to ensure that punishment is fair and not arbitrary and that the experience of punishment is not inconsistent with the expectation of that punishment. For example, if a judge exercises legal authority to sentence a person to a period of incarceration, that judge expects that the person will be removed from society and denied liberty for a defined period. The judge may also expect the person to have access to programs and services that facilitate his or her reintegration into society, while at the same time ensuring the safety of the community. Judges who impose sanctions expect that their sentence will be administered by the law (Arbour, 1996). When the experience of incarceration is unduly harsh or unjust, it deviates from legal expectations and, thus, compromises the integrity of the sentence. The reality that punishment is not distributed evenly across society (for example, that Indigenous people are vastly over-represented in Canadian prisons and are more likely to be subjected to segregation and uses of force) represents a fundamental challenge to the legitimacy of our criminal justice system and assumptions about equality.

The central point is that prisoners are sentenced to a period of incarceration as punishment, not for punishment. This principle is enshrined in the United Nations Standard Minimum Rules for the Treatment of Prisoners, initially promulgated in 1955 and substantially updated in 2015. Those rules clearly state that:

- A prisoner's sense of dignity and worth as a human being must be respected and maintained through the entire course of imprisonment; and
- The suffering that results from the loss of liberty and freedom by the fact of incarceration is punishment enough.

Prisoners retain all the rights of non-incarcerated people, except those that are necessarily removed because of their imprisonment (e.g., their mobility and some aspects of their liberty). It is a premise of Canadian correctional law that prisons should not be punishing places; instead, they should help prisoners rehabilitate themselves (Correctional Service of Canada, 1998, p. 15).

There are a number of different legal sources of prisoners' rights, with differing levels of enforceability: international human rights law, Canadian constitutional law, legislation such as the *Correctional and Conditional Release Act* and the *Canadian Human Rights Act*, and the common law (judge-made laws like the doctrine of *habeas corpus*, which dates back nearly 1000 years). Many foundational prisoner rights are found in international human rights instruments such as the Universal Declaration of Human Rights (UN, 1946) which states that all individuals, including those who are imprisoned, are entitled to full and equal recognition and protection under the law. This means that prisoners have certain inalienable and fundamental rights and freedoms, such as the right to life, liberty, and security of person. Zinger (2006) maintains that:

> [c]ompliance with human rights obligations increases, though it does not guarantee, the odds of releasing a more responsible citizen. In essence, a prison environment respectful of human rights is conducive to positive change, whereas an environment of abuse, disrespect, and discrimination has the opposite effect: treating prisoners with humanity enhances public safety. Moreover, through respecting the human rights of prisoners, society conveys a strong message that everyone, regardless of their circumstance, race, social status, gender, religion, and so on, is to be treated with inherent respect and dignity. (p. 127)

At an elementary level, protecting prisoners' rights is an essential prerequisite for rehabilitation and successful reintegration.

These and other rights are of utmost importance to people who are incarcerated because of the vulnerability to abuse that comes with that status. In her examination of the Correctional Service of Canada's flagrant violations of federal women prisoners' rights, Justice Louise Arbour (1996) noted that "one must resist the temptation to trivialize the infringement of prisoners' rights as either an insignificant infringement of rights, or as an infringement of rights of people who do not deserve any better" (p. 182). She wrote:

> For example, the right not to be subject to body cavity searches is not particularly valuable to those who are unlikely ever to be subjected to such an invasive procedure. It is only valuable, and therefore should be enforced with the greatest vigour, in cases where such searches are likely to be undertaken. (pp. 182-183)

Arbour argued that even though law-abiding citizens may not identify with the position of prisoners, respecting and protecting prisoners' rights are critical because of the potential for abuse. Failure to protect the rights of prisoners jeopardizes the rights of all citizens (Easton, 2010).

THE EVOLUTION OF PRISONERS' RIGHTS

The premise that the correctional system should be bound by the rule of law and to the same due process standards as other parts of the criminal justice system is relatively new (see Box 8.1 for some key moments in the recognition and enforcement of prisoner's rights in Canada). Historically, prisoners were afforded few rights and subjected to hard labour and physical punishment. "Civil death," the concept that prisoners lost all civil and property rights, typified the legal approach to prisoners and was only abolished by English legislation in the late 19th century (Parkes, 2007). The last official vestige of civil death in Canada persisted until 2002 when the disenfranchisement of prisoners was found to be unconstitutional by the Supreme Court of Canada (*Sauvé v. Canada*, 2002).

The early to mid-20th century of corrections in Canada was primarily characterized by a legislative and judicial "hands-off" doctrine that entailed a broad delegation of power to administrative officials and a reluctance by courts to intervene in the affairs of prisons in response to prisoners' claims of inhumane conditions or treatment (Campbell, 1997; Landau, 1984; Jackson, 1983; Parkes 2007). Punishments were harsh, severe, and inhumane (see Chapter 2). Corporal punishments, such as hosing inmates with a powerful stream of water (used until 1913), dunking prisoners in troughs of ice (used until 1930), whipping and strapping (used until 1972), long periods of solitary confinement on a bread-and-water diet (used until 1976), and the death penalty (also legal until 1976), were commonplace (MacGuigan, 1977). This approach to corrections was influenced by a prevailing belief in the deterrent effect of imprisonment in austere conditions. Correctional officials believed that the harsher and more unpleasant the punishment, the higher the likelihood of conformity to the penal regime and the higher the chances of reform upon release from prison. While this belief may continue to be widely held among members of the public, academic research does not support the theory that harsh penalties or rare and unpleasant conditions of confinement deter or prevent crime. Some prisoner rights researchers have found quite the opposite (Easton, 2010).

Until the mid-1930s, there was little public or political interest in exposing these harsh conditions to external scrutiny. Prisoners had few substantive rights and procedural protections (Campbell, 1997). According to Landau (1984), the prison was an autonomous and secret system, with its own norms and no form of external scrutiny. Prisoners were proverbially "out of sight, out of mind," and matters of prison discipline were left to penitentiary wardens.

Unfortunately, one of the only ways that prisoners could bring public attention to their living conditions was by rioting. Riots were often sparked by inhumane conditions, a lack of meaningful programs, or the ineffective or non-existent complaint processes. In 1938, the Archambault Commission raised concerns about prison conditions and prison discipline, but government attention to prisoners' rights and significant developments in prisoners' rights litigation did not occur until the mid-1960s.

The overall correctional philosophy shifted in the postwar period from an ethos of deterrence and hard labour to one of rehabilitation. The rehabilitation model intended to turn the prison into a hospital to "treat" the "disease" of criminality. While the rehabilitative approach yielded many positive developments, including the introduction of programs such as individual counselling, it also led to further abuses of prisoners' rights. A wide variety of interventions and "treatments" were imposed on often involuntary "patients" (see Box 8.2). For example, the treatment techniques employed in British Columbia's Oakalla Prison (built in 1912 and then closed in 1991) included plastic surgery. These surgeries were first used in 1953 to correct "abnormalities" that were perceived to be linked to criminality, such as scars and unsightly or obscene tattoos (Richmond, 1975). Under the benevolent guise of treatment and rehabilitation, prisoners were subjected to cruel and dehumanizing treatments such as shock therapy, experimental drugs, forcible injections of mind-altering drugs, experimental surgeries, forced sterilization, prolonged segregation, sensory deprivation, indefinite periods of incarceration, and, in some instances, physical abuse (Ekstedt & Griffiths, 1988; Menzies, Chunn, & Boyd, 2001; Osborne, 2006; see Box 8.2). Some of these abuses continue today, and few prisoners have been compensated for these harms inflicted by the state. The introduction of a rehabilitative ethos raised various concerns about professional ethics, consent, and the right to be informed and refuse treatment.

The fact of incarceration does not negate an individual's fundamental right to refuse medical or psychological treatment. These rights extend to prisoners and "can only be limited in very narrow circumstances when mental incompetence prevents an individual from giving consent to treatment or when the person has a communicable disease covered by provincial legislation" (McKinnon, 1995, p. 47). However, we continue to see examples of these rights being violated, such as in the forced injection of a young woman, Ashley Smith, with psychotropic drugs while she was incarcerated (Beaudry, 2010). Smith died a year later in a prison segregation cell with a ligature around her neck while correctional officers watched.

By the mid-1970s, prison conditions worsened to the point that they could no longer be hidden. Society was becoming less tolerant of prison violence and abuse. Increasing public disillusionment with rehabilitative approaches and concerns about prisoner's rights led to another shift in correctional philosophy to more community-based interventions. This period saw a "humanizing of punishment," with the abolition of corporal punishment in 1972 and the death penalty in 1976. Several prison riots occurred throughout the 1960s and 1970s (for example, at Kingston Penitentiary in 1971 and in the US, the Attica uprising in 1971), which increasingly subjected the prison system to the scrutiny of public and parliamentary committees (Gosselin, 1982). The infamous riot at Kingston Penitentiary marked a turning point in Canadian corrections. The 1971 Swackhamer Inquiry, which criticized Kingston Penitentiary for the curtailment of programs and activities in the years before the riot, concluded that:

> Such things as access to hobby craft and sports, freedom to decorate cells and to dress in non-prison clothing on certain occasions, were not trivial privileges that could be limited or withdrawn without negative impact – but instead that these were significant factors in reducing the dehumanizing effects of incarceration. (Campbell, 1997, p. 297)

This finding, along with similar indictments of the prison's overall failure to rehabilitate or protect supported a shift away from punitive conditions of confinement toward normalizing the prison experience. Campbell (1997) has described how the recognition of these deplorable circumstances led to additional governmental inquiries, along with the establishment of new legal frameworks and support systems that allowed for external scrutiny and accountability through monitoring and prisoners' rights litigation.

Box 8.2 – The Dorothy Proctor Case

The treatment of Dorothy Proctor (1961 -), born on Cape Breton Island, while she was incarcerated at the Prison for Women, is an example of a profound violation of human rights in the name of correctional treatment. This case provides a glimpse into the involuntary treatment, specifically the experimental administration of lysergic acid diethylamide (LSD) and electro-convulsive therapy (ECT) on prisoners without their consent. In 1998, Dorothy Proctor filed a statement of claim against the Correctional Service of Canada concerning the psychiatric abuse she experienced while incarcerated at the Prison for Women in the early 1960s. Ms. Proctor was one of at least 23 prisoners who was given LSD as part of a 1962 study by Dr. Mark Eveson under the supervision of the Prison for Women's head of psychiatry, Dr. George Scott. Due to missing or destroyed records, only four of the other 23 women have been identified.

One purpose of these experiments was apparently to "alter the criminal disposition of offenders" and reduce recidivism. Ms. Proctor was 17 years of age, of African and Mi'kmaq descent, and serving a three-year sentence at P4W when she was selected as a participant for experimentation. According to court records, she was placed in segregation (solitary confinement) for lengthy periods of time as punishment for breaching various prison rules and subsequently compelled to undergo experiments with LSD and ECT under the direction of Dr. Eveson. These experiments were an unlawful use of the disciplinary power and flagrant violation of rights.

After repeatedly denying wrongdoing in the case, in March 1997, the Commissioner of the Correctional Service of Canada orders a Board of Investigation under section 20 of the *Corrections and Conditional Release Act* to investigate and report on Ms. Proctor's allegations. Although the board was not able to obtain individual records from the Correctional Service of Canada, its final report concluded that, among other things, Ms. Proctor was administered with LSD without her informed consent while she was in segregation and that she had sustained long-term adverse side effects as a result (including brain damage). It is debatable whether or not an incarcerated prisoner can ever provide informed consent to certain kinds of treatment. In this particular case, it is clear that Ms. Proctor was not informed of the potential long-term consequences of the use of this drug, and as a minor and a prisoner, she was not a position to decline treatment. The board recommended compensation and an apology for Ms. Proctor and the other unnamed prisoners involved in the experiments.

The case dragged on until April 2001 when the Attorney General and Dr. Eveson admitted to battery and negligence because there was no evidence of consent. The court accepted those declarations on May 8, 2001. There were further court proceedings, and the matter was eventually settled out of court. In the aftermath of the case, through various inquiries is was discovered that hundreds of inmates were found to have been subjected to scientific experimentation in Canadian prisons during the 1960s and 1970s.

Source: *Proctor v. Canada*, 2002 OTC 79 (Sup Ct).

Various inquiries recommended improvements in general living conditions and the development of formalized grievance and oversight processes. These recommendations contributed to the eventual creation of the Office of the Correctional Investigator (ombudsperson responsible for federal prisons) and the development of a formal institutionally based system for handling complaints and grievances in 1973. In addition to these procedural developments, essential changes in the Canadian legal landscape occurred from the late 1970s to early 1990s.

Legal decisions played a critical role in reshaping the correctional landscape by defining and refining law and policy concerning the rights of incarcerated people. For example, in *Martineau v. Matsqui Institutional Disciplinary Board* (1978), the Supreme Court of Canada signalled a move away from the judicial "hands-off" approach whereby courts were reluctant to interfere in correctional decision-making. For the first time, the court declared that correctional authorities have to act fairly when making decisions about the rights of prisoners. Other court rulings around this time affirmed that prisoners have a limited right to privileged communication with their lawyers (*Solosky v. R.*, 1980) and that prisoners had "residual liberty interests" as members of the general prison population (*R. v. Miller*, 1985). These interests were engaged when, for example, a prisoner was placed in segregation (solitary confinement), triggering the duty to act fairly and other principles of due process.

In 1977, Parliament passed the *Canadian Human Rights Act* which established the Canadian Human Rights Commission and a process for the adjudication of anti-discrimination claims, including in correctional services. The Commission investigated and reported on several matters relating to prisoners, including the treatment and conditions of confinement experienced by women prisoners, a group that makes up less than 10% of the prison population. Notably, in 1981, following a comprehensive year-long investigation into conditions at the Prison for Women, the Canadian Human Rights Commission found that a complaint of sex discrimination made by the advocacy group Women for Justice was substantiated. Federally sentenced women "were discriminated against on the basis of sex, and...in virtually all programs and facility areas, the treatment of federal women inmates was inferior to that of men" (Cooper, 1987, p. 139; Hannah-Moffat, 2000). The Commission concluded that the state had a legal and moral obligation to provide women with programs and facilities "substantially equivalent" to those provided to incarcerated men. It also noted that few women were involved in the development of policies and the senior management of the prison, and suggested that increased involvement of women in these areas could facilitate improvements (Hannah-Moffat, 2000). The federal government subsequently struck a Task Force on Federally Sentenced Women that reported in 1990, recommending sweeping changes to women's corrections.

Entrenchment of a constitutional *Bill of Rights*, the *Canadian Charter of Rights and Freedoms*, in 1982 signalled a new "rights revolution" of which prisoners would be a part (Parkes, 2007). The *Charter* is different from previous laws, even statutory bills of rights, in that it is entrenched in the constitution and cannot be changed through the normal legislative process. Judges have the power to declare invalid any laws or correctional decisions that violate the *Charter's* provisions. Although it brought about an unprecedented number of challenges to corrections and about conditional release issues, many prisoners' claims in the *Charter* era continued to be unsuccessful (Campbell, 1997, Parkes 2007). Judges often defer to the decisions of prison officials based on perceptions about correctional expertise, although there are good reasons to question that posture of deference (Kerr, 2015). Nevertheless, the *Charter* provides a vital means for challenging conditions of confinement and correctional decision-making.

Section 7 of the *Charter*, enshrining rights to life, liberty, and security of the person, is one of the most heavily litigated provisions. Issues raised under this section include concerns about prison disciplinary hearings, transfers to higher security prisons, random urinalysis, double-bunking (which incidentally also violates the UN Standard Minimum Standards for the Treatment of Prisoners), parole decision-making, and conditions in pre-trial detention, among others (Campbell, 1997; Parkes, 2007). Recently, the whole federal regime of administrative segregation – that is, placement in solitary confinement for a wide range of discretionary reasons – has been found to violate section 7 of the *Charter* (*British Columbia Civil Liberties Association v. Canada*, 2018; See Box 8.3). That decision has been appealed, but there is no question that the court ruling has caused the federal government to look for alternatives to the widespread use of solitary confinement.

Sauve v. Canada (2002) is another example of a successful prisoner *Charter* challenge. In this case, the Supreme Court of Canada invalidated a section of the *Canada Elections Act* that prohibited federal prisoners from voting. While section 3 of the *Charter* guarantees the right of all citizens to vote, prisoner voting bans remain common in many countries. The United States is an extreme example: more than 6.1 million Americans cannot vote due to felony disenfranchisement laws that sometimes involve a lifetime voting ban for a single felony conviction (Uggen, Larson & Shannon, 2016). The Court in *Sauvé* was divided, but a

Box 8.3 – Solitary Confinement and the Law

The widespread and prolonged use of solitary confinement, or segregation as it is called in Canadian prisons, is a pressing human rights issue. Since the founding of the first Canadian penitentiaries, prison administrators have used isolation cells to manage the prison population, but the damaging effects of solitary confinement are increasingly well known and many are calling for the abolition of this practice. The struggle to end solitary confinement illustrates many of the possibilities and challenges of enforcing prisoners' rights. In recent years, Canadians have become aware of the brutal practice of keeping people in solitary confinement through the tragic deaths of Ashley Smith (died in October 2007), Edward Snowshoe (died by suicide in August 2010), Terry Baker (died while in solitary confinement in July 2016), and others in prison segregation cells across the country.

However, reports, commissions of inquiry, and litigation decades earlier had highlighted the need to reign in the practice of segregating prisoners. In a case that went to the Federal Court in 1976, Jack McCann, a prisoner held in brutal conditions of isolation in the infamous "Penthouse" of the British Columbia Penitentiary successfully argued that his confinement amounted to cruel and unusual punishment contrary to the rights enshrined in the 1960 *Canadian Bill of Rights*. Calls to sharply limit the use of segregation and to require independent adjudication of decisions to place and maintain prisoners in segregation can be found in the 1996 Arbour Commission Report and the subsequent Task Force on Administrative Segregation, among others. The Correctional Service of Canada has persistently resisted calls for independent oversight and accountability over segregation decisions.

The rising Canadian awareness has coincided with international action to limit or abolish the use of solitary confinement. The 2015 Mandela Rules adopted by the United Nations General Assembly prohibit the imposition of indefinite or prolonged solitary confinement, and they prohibit it outright for women, children, and people with mental and physical disabilities whose conditions would be exacerbated by it. The Rules define solitary confinement as "the confinement of prisoners for 22 hours or more a day without meaningful human contact" and prolonged solitary confinement as "solitary confinement for a time period in excess of 15 consecutive days."

continued...

This mounting evidence of the harms of solitary confinement is the centrepiece of ongoing *Charter* litigation claiming that the whole regime of administrative segregation is unconstitutional. In 2018, Justice Leask issued his decision in *British Columbia Civil Liberties Association v. Canada*, finding that the rights of prisoners under sections 7 (life, liberty and security of the person) and 15 (equality) of the *Charter* were breached by administrative segregation regime. He found as the fact that administrative segregation (which has no hard time limits on its use and no independent adjudication) "places all Canadian federal inmates subject to it at significant risk of serious psychological harm, including mental pain and suffering, and increased incidence of self-harm and suicide. Some of the specific harms include anxiety, withdrawal, hypersensitivity, cognitive dysfunction, hallucinations, loss of control, irritability, aggression, rage, paranoia, hopelessness, a sense of impending emotional breakdown, self-mutilation, and suicidal ideation and behaviour. The risks of these harms are intensified in the case of mentally ill inmates. However, all inmates subject to segregation are subject to the risk of harm to some degree."

The BCCLA decision was a significant win for prisoners' rights. However, having declared the relevant sections of the CCRA invalid, Leask J. suspended that declaration for one year to allow the government to respond to the ruling. In October 2018, a month before the scheduled hearing of the government's appeal of the BCCLA decision, the Minister of Public Safety tabled Bill B-83 for First Reading in the House of Commons, a Bill that he says will bring an end to administrative segregation. The Bill describes "structured intervention units" that are akin to segregation units but where prisoners are meant to be provided with opportunities to be out of their cells for a minimum of four hours per day, rather than two hours per day under the current segregation regime. Many advocates are criticizing the proposed changes as mere "window dressing" or, worse, an expansion and normalization of conditions of isolation under a new name. Meanwhile, the BCCLA appeal was heard in November 2018, and a decision is pending.

Source: *British Columbia Civil Liberties Association v. Canada (Attorney General)*, 2018 BCSC 62.

majority held that the government's objectives for disenfranchising citizen prisoners, namely enhancing civic responsibility and providing additional punishment, were too vague and symbolic to justify limiting the right to vote.

The *Charter* and related litigation, as well as the findings of earlier inquiries, played a critical role in shaping the 1992 *Corrections and Conditional Release Act* (CCRA), the legislation currently governing federal corrections. The CCRA has three components: part one relates to conditions of confinement and the custodial portion of the prisoner's sentence; part two deals with the Parole Board of Canada and conditional release; and part three govern the Office of the Correctional Investigator, the ombudsperson for federal prisoners. The version of the CCRA passed in 1992 required that federal corrections be administered according to a set of principles, including that the Correctional Service of Canada (CSC) must "use the least restrictive measures consistent with the protection of the public, staff members and offenders" (s. 4(d)), that "offenders retain the rights and privileges of all members of society, except those rights and privileges that are necessarily removed or restricted as a consequence of sentence" (s. 4(e)), and that "correctional decisions must "be made forthrightly, with access by the offender to an effective grievance procedure" (s. 4(g)). Some of these principles have been modified by subsequent legislation, generally reflecting a watered down version of these rights. For example, following amendments in 2012, the foundational "least restrictive measures" principle now provides simply that measures be "limited to only what is necessary and proportionate to attain the purposes of this Act."

The CCRA also contains some specific rights such as an unqualified right to counsel in serious prison disciplinary matters (although no right to publicly-funded legal aid), a right to health care, and a right to notice or consultation concerning significant decisions other than those involving security. These rights are more specific than *Charter* rights and, therefore, may be more amenable to judicial review. Also, the Correctional Investigator, created in 1973, has played a role in seeking to bring more accountability and transparency to correctional decision-making, as well as performing the function of alerting government and the public to some severe abuses in the federal prison system. There has not been a similar overhaul and improvement of statutory rights of prisoners at the provincial level, where the majority of prisoners are incarcerated on any given day. In the current political climate, provincial politicians likely perceive that they have nothing to win and everything to lose by embarking on prisoner's rights reforms.

THE CHALLENGE OF OVERSIGHT AND ACCOUNTABILITY

Many concerns have been raised about the Correctional Service of Canada's unresponsiveness and indifference to infringements of prisoners' rights. Justice Louise Arbour was particularly critical of the Service's lack of accountability to the rule of law, as well as the inability of the Correctional Investigator and administrative processes such as the grievance and complaints process to make meaningful substantive and systemic changes. Justice Arbour articulated her concerns in the course of her investigations into troubling events that occurred at the Prison for Women in 1994, including the strip searching of women prisoners by a male emergency response team in full riot gear and the subsequent unlawful detention of the women in segregation for many months. In her Report, Justice Arbour argued that the Office of the Correctional Investigator, while playing a valuable role, is severely limited by its inability to compel compliance by the Correctional Service to its recommendations for change and improvements in correctional operations (Arbour, 1996). This lack of compliance is further complicated by what she called the Correctional Service's "disturbing lack of commitment to the ideals of justice" (1996, p. 198). For these reasons, Justice Arbour recommended increased judicial scrutiny and supervision of correctional practices. She also recommended the adoption of a meaningful judicial remedy in the form of a reduction of the sentence where a prisoner's rights are seriously violated:

> If illegalities, gross mismanagement of unfairness in the administration of a sentence renders the sentence harsher than that imposed by the court, a reduction of the period of imprisonment may be granted, such as to reflect the fact that the punishment administered was more punitive than the one intended. (Arbour, 1996, p. 183)

This kind of legal remedy would be akin to the rule contained in section 24(2) of the *Charter* which allows a judge to exclude from a criminal trial evidence that was obtained illegally (for example, where evidence was seized by the police in a search without a warrant or following an interrogation without the right to counsel). Arbour (1996) noted that this exclusionary rule has worked to promote compliance by state actors with the fundamental rights of people suspected or accused of a crime.

Similarly, reducing a sentence to account for unlawful conditions of confinement would not amount to a windfall for the prisoner. Our system is premised on the idea that people are sentenced to a term of lawful custody. Therefore, a "reduction in the term of imprisonment to reflect the illegality of unjustly imposed harsher conditions of imprisonment merely *restores the original sentence to its full intended effect*" [emphasis added] (1996, p. 184). While this recommendation has not been taken up by legislators or by most judges, we see a version of this principle in the few decisions where sentencing judges have reduced a sentence to account for particularly inhumane and unlawful conditions in pre-trial detention (Parkes, 2014, p. 609-611; e.g., *R v. Aqqiaruq,* 2009).

Justice Arbour's findings and recommendations centre on an awareness of the systemic nature of rights violations in prison. The infringement of a prisoner's rights is sometimes the result of a correctional officer's – or group of correctional officers' – malicious abuse of power. More often, however, it is a consequence of a systemic failure to endorse and respect the rule of law. Correctional systems tend to be impervious to outside criticism. Justice Arbour, like many observers, attributed the CSC's defensiveness and lack of accountability for and protection of rights to a "corporate culture, which fails to appreciate the need to obey both the spirit and the letter of the law" (Arbour, 1996, p. 181). While the CSC maintains that "humanizing the incarceration experiences through a rights-oriented correctional model promotes responsible behaviour that favours the safe and timely reintegration of offenders back into society" (Scott, 1998, p.3), the evidence suggests that Canada is still struggling with the concept of prisoners' rights. The legal framework of corrections includes legal rules, directives, and policies designed to protect prisoners from abuses and arbitrary decisions, but these rules are often ignored and compromised in practice.

In light of the Service's lack of accountability and protection of human rights, a working group was developed in 1997 to devise a strategic model for human rights. The report of the working group concluded that the CSC lacked a cohesive plan for ensuring that inmate and staff rights were protected (CSC, 1997). The working group noted that even though the CSC generated volumes upon volumes of internal policy documents, very little guidance was offered to frontline staff to fulfil these policy directives. The focus on procedural fine print gave the impression that the CSC was developing a culture that respected human rights, but the human rights working group found that the internal monitoring system used by the CSC failed to meet the requirements under the rule of law concerning human rights violations. The working group also reported that the CSC needed improved monitoring of prisoner and staff rights, particularly of incarcerated women and Indigenous people. The CSC's focus on policy development over implementation suggests that the CSC sees human rights as just another risk factor to manage. The CSC's 1997 report, "Human Rights and Corrections: A Strategic Model," cogently notes that:

> among the most challenging aspects of promoting a culture respectful of human rights in a correctional context is the conflict between widespread public perceptions about prisons and prisoners and the underlying premise, accepted by all correctional authorities, that offenders have both the right to be fairly and decently treated and the right to be helped towards a better life. This dilemma is further sharpened by the seeming contradiction between the need to apply measures that diminish personal rights while nevertheless insisting that such acts of intrusion or privation be carried out with proper respect for the very same rights.

This statement helps us understand why rights violations persist and are difficult to remedy.

The CSC has changed policies and procedures as a consequence of these investigations, but the changes that were undertaken have not remedied many of the structural difficulties consistently identified in these investigations and the annual and periodic reports of the Correctional Investigator or advocacy groups, such as Canadian Association of Elizabeth Fry Societies, John Howard Society or Amnesty International. The CSC has failed to act meaningfully on a large number of the recommendations made by many reports, commissions, and inquiries. Critics have marvelled at the continued ability of penal organizations to resist change (see, for example, Mann, 1998; Parkes & Pate, 2006). Mann (1998) argues that the creation and promotion of the prisoner complaint and grievance system appear to be a bureaucratically noble gesture, yet, in practice, its effectiveness, confidentiality, and objectivity are questionable. Many prisoners believe that the CSC's commitment to human rights represents a form of "bureaucratic window dressing" that fails in practice. The processes that enable such resistance are worthy of further interrogation.

Closed institutions, such as prisons, pose some accountability and research challenges. Todd Sloan's 2004 report for the Office of the Correctional Investigator, "Shifting the Orbit," insightfully argues that part of the reason correctional practices have not fundamentally changed, or been held accountable, is because they have been permitted to operate in a legislative and governmental vacuum. Although the CSC has submitted to some external scrutiny, it is not legally or organizationally required to follow the recommendation of overseers such as the Correctional Investigator; nor are they required to comply with the recommendation of numerous inquiries or investigations; nor are these recommendations externally audited. In short, there is little external and enforceable oversight of Canadian corrections. The CSC has steadfastly maintained institutional autonomy.

The Canadian experience suggests that introducing the rule of law with procedural and administrative guidelines has not eliminated abuses of power and violations of prisoners' rights. Prisoners' rights activists have spent many hours fighting to implement legal and administrative protection of prisoners' rights. Now that many of these mechanisms are available, critics are questioning and challenging the efficacy of these laws and policies. After all, what good is legal protection if prisoners are unaware of it or unwilling to use it, if correctional officials misinterpret or reinterpret the law because it is administratively inconvenient, or if the state fails to make necessary structural alterations?

IMPLICATIONS OF A PRISONERS' RIGHTS FOCUS IN CORRECTIONS

Recent decades have seen some developments in research about prisoners' rights. Easton (2010) argued that a rights-based approach is central to moving the construction of the prisoner from non-person to citizen (see Box 8.4 for an outline of the UN Standard Minimum Rules for the Treatment of Prisoners).

Despite the common public perception that prisoners forfeit their citizenship rights (e.g., the right to vote and the right not to be treated in cruel and unusual ways), prisoners remain citizens in the fullest sense of the word, other than relinquishing their liberty as a result of a custodial sentence. This conception of prisoners as rights holders were strongly endorsed by the Supreme Court in the 2002 prisoner voting rights case, *Sauvé v. Canada*. The five-member majority opinion found that the government's objectives for disenfranchising citizen prisoners, namely enhancing civic responsibility and providing additional punishment, were too vague and symbolic to justify limiting the right to vote, guaranteed to all citizens in section 3 of the *Charter*. The majority rejected the government's attempts to justify the voting ban in remarkably robust fashion, declaring that it was not open to the government to make prisoners "temporary outcasts from our system of rights and democracy" (para. 40).

Taking this idea further, Easton (2010) argued that more concerted efforts to protect the fundamental human rights and freedoms of prisoners would act as a precursor to protecting the freedoms and rights of non-incarcerated citizens. By improving human rights compliance, prison officials can improve the conditions of confinement so that additional punishments do not compound the already powerful consequence of incarceration. She argued that the essential aspect of human rights is that they are equally available to everyone, even those who appear not to deserve this consideration (Easton, 2010). Because human rights are universal by their very nature, protecting the rights of those who have violated the law, including committing serious crimes, helps protect the rights of everyone. Human rights compliance not only increases the perception of justice and procedural fairness for prisoners, but it also works to stabilize the prison order by eliminating arbitrary and discriminatory practices. Easton suggested that a human rights-based approach to penalty could challenge the effects of isolation and social exclusion on individuals confined in what Irving Goffman referred to as "total institutions" (Goffman, 1961). In total institutions, such as prisons, the

Box 8.4 – United Nations Standard Minimum Rules for the Treatment of Prisoners ("Mandela Rules")

In 2015, the United Nations General Assembly adopted significant revisions to the Standard Minimum Rules for the Treatment of Prisoners, which had initially been adopted in 1955. The new SMRs are named after the late President of South Africa, Nelson Mandela, who spent 27 years in prison in the course of his struggle against Apartheid and for human rights and equality. The Mandela Rules articulate a commitment to providing incarcerated people with humane, safe, and dignified conditions of custody.

Basic Principles

Rule 1

All prisoners shall be treated with the respect due to their inherent dignity and value as human beings. No prisoner shall be subjected to, and all prisoners shall be protected from, torture and other cruel, inhuman or degrading treatment or punishment, for which no circumstances whatsoever may be invoked as a justification. The safety and security of prisoners, staff, service providers and visitors shall be ensured at all times.

Rule 2

1. The present rules shall be applied impartially. There shall be no discrimination on the grounds of race, colour, sex, language, religion, political or other opinions, national or social origin, property, birth or any other status. The religious beliefs and moral precepts of prisoners shall be respected.

2. In order for the principle of non-discrimination to be put into practice, prison administrations shall take account of the individual needs of prisoners, in particular, the most vulnerable categories in prison settings. Measures to protect and promote the rights of prisoners with special needs are required and shall not be regarded as discriminatory.

Rule 3

Imprisonment and other measures that result in cutting off persons from the outside world are afflictive by the very fact of taking from these persons the right of self-determination by depriving them of their liberty. Therefore, the prison system shall not, except as incidental to justifiable separation or the maintenance of discipline, aggravate the suffering inherent in such a situation.

Rule 4

1. The purposes of a sentence of imprisonment or similar measures deprivation of a person's liberty are primarily to protect society against crime and to reduce recidivism. Those purposes can be achieved only if the period of imprisonment is used to ensure, so far

continued...

as possible, the reintegration of such persons into society upon release so that they can lead a law-abiding and self-supporting life.

2. To this end, prison administrations and other competent authorities should offer education, vocational training and work, as well as other forms of assistance that are appropriate and available, including those of a remedial, moral, spiritual, social and health- and sports-based nature. All such programmes, activities and services should be delivered in line with the individual treatment needs of prisoners.

Rule

1. The prison regime should seek to minimize any differences between prison life and life at liberty that tend to lessen the responsibility of the prisoners or the respect due to their dignity as human beings.

2. Prison administrations shall make all reasonable accommodation and adjustments to ensure that prisoners with physical, mental or other disabilities have full and active access to prison life on an equitable basis.

Source: United Nations. (2015). *Standard minimum rules for the treatment of prisoners*. Geneva: United Nations.

The Rules expand on these general principles, articulating limits on invasive practices such as searches of prisoners, use of restraints, and placement in solitary confinement. They also set standards for conditions of confinement (including hygiene, food, exercise, health care, education and rehabilitative programs, etc.) and speak to the need for monitoring and inspections of prisons, investigations into deaths in custody, and staff training.

The Rules form part of the international human rights framework that the Canadian state has committed itself to respect, although there are some ways in which the CSC and provincial correctional authorities do not adhere to the Rules (e.g., concerning double-bunking and the prolonged use of segregation). The Rules themselves are not justiciable, meaning that one cannot go to court and seek a remedy for the CSC violating one of the Rules. However, courts have treated these Rules and international human rights treaty provisions as interpretive tools in applying Canadian law.

potential for escalating hostility between staff and inmates can be alleviated through the use of an approach based on rights that could diffuse the possibility of informal and arbitrary punishments, such as arbitrary transfers and prolonged stays in solitary confinement.

Easton (2010) argued that understanding prisoners as rights holders and enforcing prisoners' rights will help focus public attention directly on the conditions of confinement. Researchers consistently document the important role played by the prison environment, not only in prisoner mental health but also regarding how prison staff members manage prisoners (Haney & Zimbardo, 1998). For example, concerning the use of solitary confinement, Haney (2003) examined the psychological impact that "supermax" solitary confinement has on inmates housed in these conditions over a long period. In the United States (and, in Canada, for that matter – see Box 8.3), prisoners now experience more extreme isolation and behavioural control than in the past, in part because of the massive increase in the prison population and the decreased focus on rehabilitation in prisons since the 1970s. Haney testified as an expert witness in the 2018 BCCLA *Charter* case on the legality of administrative segregation in Canada. Haney's research showed that more extended periods of isolation increased prisoner idleness, appetite, sleep problems, anxiety/panic, rage/loss of control, paranoia/hallucinations, and self-mutilation and that isolated housing was associated with increased rates of suicide and self-harm, deterioration in health (mental and physical), and increased levels of violence toward others (Haney, 2006). He found that prisoners often had to change their patterns of thinking, acting, and emotions to cope with the isolation caused by solitary confinement and that some inmates were not able to cope with prolonged isolation. As a result of their experience of isolation, some inmates lost their ability to control their behaviour and all sense of who they were and how they fit into the larger social world (Haney, 2003). Haney argued that because prisons have inadequate mental health services and are not equipped to deal with the influx of inmates with mental illnesses, many of the inmates housed in solitary confinement may have long-term disabilities. Similar to Easton (2010), he claimed that it is the lack of respect for human rights that allows additional punishments and arbitrary prison conditions to continue unabated.

In the context of universal rights, violations of prisoners' rights concerning arbitrary detention and decision-making have implications for human rights outside prisons. The 2010 interactions between the Toronto Police Service and G20 protestors illustrate how a lack of respect for prisoners' rights may be extended to the violation of non-prisoner rights, even in democratic states. It is crucial to recognize that the rationale for observing human rights is not merely that it is a requirement under domestic and international law or that it is more "humane," but rather "that rightful treatment is more likely to breed respect for the law and public welfare than the reverse" (CSC, 1997) and that compromising rights has a negative impact on *all* citizens.

SUMMARY

What are some limits on the state's right to punish? This chapter examines the importance of human rights as they relate to Canadian prisoners. It outlines the social, legal, and political significance of prisoners' rights by examining international and national laws, and discusses the rule of law, the history of prisoners' rights in Canada, and avenues of redress. It also presents the findings of the Arbour Commission and other oversight bodies. At a practical level, accountability for violations of prisoners' rights rests with individual administrators, prison officers, and the government that authorizes their powers. However, society at large is also responsible for feeding this "corporate culture" by turning a blind eye, being apathetic and advocating or silently endorsing punitive and austere penalties for a crime without consideration of the broader impact of such logic.

KEY TERMS AND CONCEPTS

Canadian Charter of Rights and Freedoms
Rights
Correctional Investigator
Rule of Law
Mandela Rules

Arbour Commission
Segregation
Corrections and Conditional Release Act
Duty to Act Fairly

STUDY AND DISCUSSION QUESTIONS

1. How does the rule of law influence the operation and organization of the Correctional Service of Canada? Is it enforced in correctional practice?
2. How should the state respond when a prisoner's rights are violated?
3. List and discuss the significance of five legislative or administrative developments in prisoners' rights.
4. Identify three gaps between legal norms and correctional practice. Show how they reflect a systemic problem rather than an individual problem.
5. Discuss Justice Arbour's proposal to reduce a prisoner's term of imprisonment to reflect the illegality of unjustly imposed harsh conditions of imprisonment.
6. What can we learn about the resistance of correctional systems to oversight and accountability by examining the history and ongoing use of solitary confinement in Canadian prisons?

HELPFUL WEBLINKS

- **Canadian Human Rights Commission** (www.chrc-ccdp.ca/default-eng.aspx) This web page outlines the various ways in which issues of human rights are addressed across Canada. It includes historical and current human rights cases and scholarly research.

- **Correctional Service of Canada** (http://www.csc-scc.gc.ca/index-en.shtml) This is the official website of the federal correctional system in Canada. It outlines the various aspects of criminal justice-mandated to the CSC by the federal government, and it highlights how the CSC handles human rights issues.

- **Office of the Correctional Investigator of Canada** (www.oci-bec.gc.ca/index-eng.aspx) This page outlines the various investigations undertaken by the correctional investigator (federal prison ombudsperson. It offers numerous reports and recommendations made to address human rights issues and conditions of confinement in federal prisons.

- **Canadian Association of Elizabeth Fry Societies** (www.elizabethfry.ca) This website highlights the various advocacy efforts undertaken on behalf of incarcerated women in Canada.

- **United Nations: Human Rights** (www.un.org/en/rights/index.shtml) This website is the home to the official UN human rights policies and the numerous projects currently sponsored by the United Nations to promote human rights issues across the world.

- **West Coast Prison Justice Society** (https://prisonjustice.org/) This non-profit organization located in British Columbia operates Prisoners' Legal Services, the only full-service clinic in Canada providing legal advocacy to federal and provincial prisoners. The WCPJS website has some plain language handbooks and resources on prisoners' rights in Canada.

REFERENCES

Arbour, L. (Commissioner). (1996). *Report of the commission of inquiry into certain events at the prison for women in Kingston.* Ottawa, ON: Public Works and Government Services of Canada.

Beaudry, P. (2010). *Ms. Ashley Smith: Psychiatric opinion based on record review.* Ottawa, ON: Office of the Correctional Investigator.

Birgden, A., & Perlin, M.L. (2008). Tolling for the luckless, the abandoned and forsaken: Therapeutic jurisprudence and international human rights law as applied to prisoners and detainees by forensic psychologists. *Legal and Criminological Psychology, 13,* 231-243.

British Columbia Civil Liberties Association v. Canada (Attorney General), 2018 BCSC 62.

Campbell, M. (1997). Revolution and counter-revolution in Canadian prisoners' rights. *Canadian Criminal Law Review, 2,* 285-329.

Cooper, S. (1987). The evolution of the federal women's prison. In E. Adelberg & C. Currie (Eds.), *Too few to count.* Vancouver, BC: Press Gang.

Correctional Service of Canada. (1997). *Human rights and corrections: A strategic model.* Ottawa, ON: Human Rights Division, Correctional Service of Canada.

Correctional Service of Canada. (1990). *Creating Choices: The report of the task force on federally sentenced women.* Ottawa, ON: Human Rights Division, Correctional Service of Canada.

Correctional Service of Canada. (1998). *Commemorating the 50th anniversary of the united nations universal declaration of human rights.* Ottawa, ON: Human Rights Division, Correctional Service of Canada.

Easton, S. (2010). *Prisoners' rights: Principles and practice.* New York, NY: Routledge.

Ekstedt, J., & Griffiths, C.T. (1988). *Corrections in Canada: Policy and practice.* Toronto, ON: Butterworths.

Goffman, E. (1961). *Asylums: Essays on the social situation of mental patients and other inmates.* New York, NY: Doubleday Anchor.

Gosselin, L. (1982). *Prisons in Canada.* Montreal, PQ: Black Rose Books.

Hannah-Moffat. K. (2000). *Punishment in disguise: Canadian federal women's penal reform.* Toronto, ON: University of Toronto Press.

Haney, C. (2003). Mental health issues in long-term solitary and "supermax" confinement. *Crime & Delinquency, 49,* 124-156.

Haney, C. (2006). *Reforming punishment: Psychological limits of the pains of imprisonment.* Washington, DC: American Psychological Association.

Haney, C., & Zimbardo, P. (1998). The past and future of U.S. prison policy: Twenty-five years after the Stanford prison experiment. *American Psychologist, 53,* 709-727.

Jacobs, J.B. (1980). The prisoner's rights movement and its impacts, 1960-1980. *Crime and Justice Annual Review, 2,* 429-448.

Jackson, M. (1983). *Prisoners of isolation: Solitary confinement in Canada.* Toronto, ON: University of Toronto Press.

Kerr, L. (2014). Contesting expertise in prison law. *McGill Law Journal, 60,* 43-94.

Landau, T. (1984). Due process, legalism, and inmates' rights: A cautionary note. *Canadian Criminology Reform, 2,* 151-163.

MacGuigan, M. (1977). *Report to parliament by the sub-committee on the penitentiary system in Canada.* Ottawa, ON: Supply and Services.

Mann, T. (1998). Human rights within CSC: One prisoner's perspective. *Let's Talk, 23*(4), 14-15.

Martineau v. Matsqui Institution, [1978] 1 S.C.R. 118.

McKinnon, C. (1995). The legal rights of offenders to refuse treatment. *Forum on Corrections Research, 7(3),* 45-47.

Melnitzer, J. (2000). Prisoners' rights: Inhuman rights. In J. Roberts (Ed.), *Criminal justice in Canada: A reader.* Toronto, ON: Harcourt Brace.

Menzies, R., Chunn, D.E., & Boyd, S.C. (2001). Introduction. In S. Boyd, R. Menzies, & D. Chunn (Eds.), *Abusing power: The Canadian experience.* Halifax, NS: Fernwood.

Ontario Court General Division. (1998). Statement of Claim. Dorothy Mills Proctor and Her Majesty the Queen in Right of Canada. Court File 98cv–6618.

Osborne, G.B. (2006). Scientific experiments on Canadian inmates, 1955 to 1975. *The Howard Journal, 45(3),* 284-306.

Parkes, D. & Pate, K. (2006). Time for accountability: effective oversight of women's prisons. *Canadian Journal of Criminology and Criminal Justice, 48(2),* 251-285.

Parkes, D. (2007). A prisoners' Charter? Reflections on prisoner litigation under the Canadian Charter of Rights and Freedoms. *U.B.C. Law Review, 40,* 629-676.

Parkes, D. (2014). The punishment agenda in the courts. *Supreme Court Law Review,* 67, 589-615.

Parkes, D. (2016). Women in prison: Liberty, equality and thinking outside the bars. *Journal of Law and Equality, 12,* 127-156.

Proctor v. Canada (AG), [2002] OTC 79 (SupCt).

R v Aqqiaruq, 2009 NUCJ 26.

R. v. Miller, [1985] 2 S.C.R. 613.

R. v. Gladue, [1999] 1 S.C.R. 688.

Richard, B. (2008). *The Ashley Smith report: A report of the New Brunswick ombudsman and child and youth advocate on the service provided to a youth involved in the youth criminal justice system.* Fredericton, NB: Office of the Ombudsman & Child and Youth Advocate.

Richmond, D.J. (1975). Prison doctor. In J. Ekstedt & C.T. Griffiths (Eds.), *Corrections in Canada: Policy and practice.* Toronto, ON: Butterworths.

Sapers, H. (2008). *A preventable death.* Ottawa, ON: Office of the Correctional Investigator.

Sauve v. Canada, [2002] 3 S.C.R. 519.

Solosky v. R, [1980] 1 S.C.R. 821.

Scott, A. (1998). Human rights and corrections. *Let's Talk, 23(4),* 2-3.

Solon, T. (2004). *Shifting the orbit: Human rights, independent review and accountability in Canadian corrections systems.* Ottawa, ON: Office of the Correctional Investigator.

Task Force on Administrative Segregation. (1997). *Commitment to legal compliance, fair decisions, and effective results: Reviewing administrative segregation.* Ottawa, ON: Correctional Service of Canada.

Uggen, C., Larson L., & Shannon, S. (2016). Six million lost voters: State-level estimates of felony disenfranchisement, 2016. Washington, DC: Sentencing Project.

United Nations. (1946). *Universal declaration of human rights.* Geneva: United Nations.

United Nations. (2010). *Rules for the treatment of women prisoners and non-custodial measures for women offenders.* Geneva: United Nations.

United Nations. (2015). *Standard minimum rules for the treatment of prisoners.* Geneva: United Nations.

Zinger. I. (2006). Human rights compliance and the role of external prison oversight. *Canadian Journal of Criminology and Criminal Justice, 48(2),* 127-140.

Offender Assessment, Classification, and Treatment in Canadian Corrections

Claire Goggin, Paul Gendreau, James Bonta, J. Stephen Wormith, Myles Ferguson, and Paula Smith

9

Learning Objectives

After reading this chapter, you should be able to:

- Describe the history and purpose of offender classification and case management.

- Describe the principles of risk, need, and responsivity and understand their role in offender classification, case management, and treatment.

- Explain the STICS model of offender supervision, its research base, and its implementation in Canadian corrections.

- Discuss the evolution of the rehabilitative ideal in corrections.

- Discuss the contribution of meta-analysis to the study of offender assessment, classification, and treatment.

- Compare and contrast the elements of effective and ineffective correctional programs.

INTRODUCTION

The purpose of this chapter is to review the evidence regarding the roles of offender assessment, classification, and correctional rehabilitation in evaluating criminal risk and preventing offenders from returning to a life of crime (i.e., recidivism). In the field of corrections, the concept of classification through the assessment of offender risk, criminogenic need, and responsivity (RNR) has been empirically-documented as an essential precursor to the delivery of effective correctional treatments. Moreover, although various definitions of correctional rehabilitation exist, there tends to be a general agreement about three aspects of effective treatments: 1) they are planned, 2) they target malleable features of an offender's personality and life circumstances that contribute to his/her crimi-

Box 9.1 – The PNR Principles

The principles of effective intervention that Andrews et al. (1990a) aimed to test were grounded in their narrative reviews, previous meta-analyses, as well as, the clinical wisdom and insight of many years of fieldwork and consultation with other experts in offender treatment. Mostly, the rationale underlying Andrews et al.'s (1990a) meta-analysis is captured in the following principles:

1. The need principle states that *effective treatments are those which target offender attributes that are robust predictors of recidivism*. There are two types of predictors: a) static (i.e., criminal history), and b) dynamic (i.e., anti-social values). The latter are typically referred to as criminogenic needs. The distinction between the two lies in the "changeable" nature of dynamic predictors.

2. The general responsivity principle holds that *effective treatments are behavioural*. Central to any behavioural program is the principle of operant conditioning; that is, when behaviour is contingently reinforced, it will be more readily "acquired" or learned. Positive reinforcers, usually pleasant or desirable conditions, tend to increase or strengthen the likelihood of a particular behavioural response. There are four basic types of reinforcers: a) material (i.e., money, goods); b) activities (i.e., recreation); c) social (i.e., attention, praise, approval); and d) covert (i.e., thoughts, self-evaluation).

3. The risk principle maintains that *higher-risk offenders are the optimal target group for behavioural intervention* as they tend to represent the highest risk to the public (see Bonta, 1996). In contrast, lower risk offenders require much less intervention. They have relatively few behaviour problems that require attention. Subjecting them to intensive services is not cost-effective; moreover, it may increase their rates of recidivism (Andrews & Bonta, 1998, p. 243).

4. Other factors also contribute to treatment effectiveness. These include: a) conducting programs in the community vs. institution, when feasible; b) ensuring that programs provide a structured relapse prevention (or "aftercare") component (Dowden, Antonowicz, & Andrews, 2003), where possible; and c) employing treatment staff who are interpersonally sensitive, well-trained, and clinically supervised. Among the most important of these factors is specific responsivity, that is, *matching treatment delivery styles and modalities to the learning styles of offenders* (Andrews & Bonta, 1998, p. 245; Gendreau, 1996a, pp. 122-123). Factors that should be considered in service delivery include offenders' lack of motivation to participate in the program, or their current emotional state (i.e., feelings of anxiety or depression).

nality, and 3) they employ techniques (i.e., various counselling and behaviour modification modalities) that use positive reinforcement strategies to shape pro-social attitudes, behaviours, and skills (Sechrest, White, & Brown, 1979, pp. 20-21). Of note, rehabilitation does not include specific deterrence types of interventions, such as incarceration, boot camp, and electronic monitoring, which are intended to suppress or punish future criminal behaviour by making the offender fearful of the consequences of committing crimes.

This chapter, then, presents a timely summary of the literature regarding the RNR principles which have been vital to establishing "what works" for whom in offender rehabilitation (Bonta & Andrews, 2017). Since these principles were first formulated (Andrews, Bonta, & Hoge, 1990a), dozens of quantitative reviews (i.e., meta-analyses) have been published examining critical aspects of correctional practice. These include comparisons of the utility of various risk assessment tools (Campbell, French, & Gendreau, 2009; Desmarais, Johnson, & Singh, 2016; Olver, Stockdale, & Wormith, 2014; Williams, Wormith, Bonta, & Sitarenios, 2017) and different types of treatment (Aos & Drake, 2013; Henwood, Chou, & Browne, 2015); evaluations of program effectiveness with various offender populations (Gutierrez, Chadwick, & Wanamaker, 2018; Hanson, Bourgon, Helmus, & Hodgson, 2009); assessments of the relationship between treatment delivery location (i.e., institution vs. community) and its effect on recidivism (Wodahl, Garland, Culhane, & McCarty, 2011); and analysis of the impact of program content and implementation (i.e., therapeutic integrity) on treatment effectiveness (Andrews & Dowden, 2005; Holdsworth, Bowen, Brown, & Howat, 2014). Results from these studies have produced a "road map" for evidence-based correctional assessment and programming that is accessible to all who share an interest in reducing criminal behaviour by maximizing offender classification and treatment effectiveness.

A BRIEF HISTORY OF OFFENDER CLASSIFICATION

The development of offender classification systems has been a critical step for advancement in criminology and corrections. The RNR principles (Andrews et al., 1990b) have emerged as critical dimensions of offender classification with the *Level of Service* (LS) family of instruments being among the most commonly used tools in this regard. Consequently, an essential theme of this chapter is the linkage between these principles and offender classification and treatment.

Although offenders can be dissimilar in many ways, a basic premise of correctional classification is that they also share certain features. Consequently, it is useful to subdivide them into practically meaningful categories according to joint symptoms, etiology, behavioural attributes, or other relevant characteristics. As such, offender classification serves four essential purposes for correctional administrators and practitioners: understanding, prediction, treatment, and case management (CM).

Early Offender Classification Models

Assessment of offender risk to re-offend is a crucial dimension on which offenders are classified and has led to an explosion in the development of offender risk assessment instruments which have best been described in "generational" terms (Andrews et al., 2006).

Clinical judgments characterized first generation assessments, typically using the current offence or criminal history, with little or no use of standardized assessment procedures. Given that anti-social behaviour involves a dynamic system of factors, predicting future criminal behaviour using mostly educated opinion proved elusive. Something more was needed to improve the predictive validity or value of clinical judgment.

Second generation statistical prediction models can be traced to the parole prediction instrument developed by Burgess (1928) in which offenders were scored as being either above or below the base rate of 21 items (e.g., type of offence, marital status, and psychiatric prognosis). The outcome was measured as success on parole (e.g., no violations, arrests). Such instruments dominated corrections until the early 1980s. In the early 1980s, the Correctional Service of Canada (CSC) adopted the *Statistical Information on Recidivism* (SIR) scale. The original instrument (Nuffield, 1982) was based on a sample of federal offenders released between 1970 and 1972. Although the SIR is still in use, there is some concern that it may no longer retain its predictive power given changes in the offender profile since it was first developed. Moreover, it is used only with non-Indigenous male offenders due to concerns about its applicability to Indigenous populations (Nafekh & Motiuk, 2002).

More Recent Offender Classification Models

The Level of Service family of risk instruments represent third-generation scales that have been successful both in Canada and other jurisdictions. The utility of the LS group of scales lies in their ability to classify offenders based on risk to re-offend, but also to identify factors which, through treatment, can remediate that risk. The scales do so by assessing offenders' level of functioning in the following domains: education and employment, family and marital, attitudes and orientation, substance use, companions, leisure and recreation, accommodations, financial, and emotional and personality, as well as criminal history. Their predictive validity and utility in the areas of offender classification and CM has been consistently demonstrated with different offender samples in Canada and beyond (see Bonta & Andrews, 2017).

Finally, fourth-generation assessments merge aspects of CM into the assessment process. The *Level of Service/Case Management Inventory* (LS/CMI; Andrews, Bonta, & Wormith, 2004), its predecessor, the *Level of Service Inventory-Ontario Revision* (LSI-OR; Andrews, Bonta, & Wormith, 1995), as well as the *Youth Level of Supervision/Case Management Inventory* (YLS/CMI; Hoge & Andrews, 2002) are three such examples. Two key elements separate these assessment tools from third generation predecessors. First, they expand the scope of inquiry beyond the traditional domains of offender risk and need to include non-criminogenic needs (i.e., factors that are not causally related to criminal behaviour but are relevant, nonetheless, to a comprehensive CM plan), and evaluate offender responsivity, the third principle in the RNR model. Secondly, these assessments include a CM component, which follows from assessment and classification and directs the case manager to develop a plan that is logically driven by the results of the assessment. In other words, fourth-generation assessment instruments serve a fully functioning CM role and provide all the tools needed to aid professionals in the planning, treatment, and management of correctional populations.

Offender Classification and Case Management

The concept of CM dates to the early 1990s when social workers began to care for the mentally disordered. With the deinstitutionalization of the mentally ill in the late 1960s, CM practices became strained, and agencies were forced to develop a more formal means of accessing services for large numbers of clients (Martin & Inciardi, 1993). Early CM was distinguished from traditional treatment in both style and service in that it was designed to be holistic and to have continuity over time, and its activities included the monitoring of services for the client.

Many of these clients were also offenders who required multiple services to manage their mental health needs and avoid further trouble with the law. Consequently, the concept of CM was imported into correctional work, first by those in the community, typically probation officers (POs), and then by institutional workers who saw the benefits of adopting such an approach in preparing inmates for release to the community.

Individual CM offers a means of planning, organizing, and supervising offenders thoroughly and comprehensively. In corrections, offenders are typically assigned to a specific worker. CM has a natural home in probation and parole because POs also work on an individual basis with a specific group of offenders, their "caseload" (see also Chapter 4). CM is increasingly provided by multidisciplinary teams in that representatives from diverse disciplines may be required to assist with offenders' rehabilitation needs.

Case Management Models

The most prevalent CM model used in Canadian corrections is one based on a restorative justice ideal which tends to reflect either a strength-based or positive approach. The former is premised on the belief that controlling offender behaviour requires more than just strict surveillance and supervision (Clark, 1997). The basis of the strength-based approach is that offenders are not merely "damaged goods" with a higher concentration of problems than others. Instead, like all of us, offenders have talents, capacities, past successes, and strengths that can be drawn upon to help them to pursue a better life. This perspective identifies offenders' strengths and resources to help them clearly understand their future goals and supports them in addressing any barriers to reaching those objectives. The expectation is that a strength-based focus can offer an effective alternative to coercive probation interventions (Kurtz & Linnemann, 2006).

In contrast, the assertive model is a highly integrated approach to service delivery that imposes a relatively high level of control over offenders. This may include CM, initial and ongoing assessments, psychiatric services, employment and housing assistance, family support and education, substance abuse services, as well as other services and supports critical to successfully maintaining offenders in the community.

A third variation of the restorative approach is that employed by CSC. Its Case Management Model is based on the supposition that, although multiple factors cause criminal behaviour, it is nevertheless learned and, therefore, can be mainly modified by addressing offenders' criminogenic needs. This perspective embodies the RNR principles which direct case managers to: a) provide direct services to higher risk/need offenders; b) target criminogenic needs in treatment; and c) use cognitive-behavioural interventions and tailor them to offenders' learning styles, motivations, abilities, and strengths (Bonta & Andrews, 2017).

In CSC, CM involves both institutional and community-based multidisciplinary teams who are in frequent contact with offenders. In addition to the Case Manager, who has primary responsibility for offenders, the team may also include correctional or vocational program instructors, mental health specialists, a Chaplain, and an Aboriginal liaison officer or Elder. The team works to develop and manage correctional offender plans that are based on an assessment of RNR factors. It also works to ensure that the goals of the offender's correctional plan remain the focus of targeted interventions. Once the offender is released into the community, the team may be expanded to include police officers, police liaison officers, mental health and social workers, volunteers, and caseworkers from aftercare agencies or community residential centres.

Case Management Challenges

Offender CM presents a few challenges, including ensuring continuity of service, the effective use of sanctions to maximize offender engagement in treatment, and best practice in determining program effectiveness (US Department of Justice, 1999). For example, discontinuity of service can have an impact on offender progress in two ways. Firstly, when inmates are transferred between institutions, it is critical that information regarding treatment history accompany them. When it does not, offender assessments must be re-administered resulting in additional strain on resources and delayed access to necessary programming. Secondly, there is a considerable advantage regarding treatment effectiveness in providing constancy of treatment programs within both the institutional and community contexts. Meeting both requirements facilitates a more seamless reintegration process for offenders.

A second challenge involves the use of sanctions as a CM tool. Offenders released from custody are typically required to comply with several conditions. A breach of conditions may result in a return to prison. The range of potential sanctions varies in intrusiveness and control, with the general-purpose being behaviour regulation. A system of graduated sanctions can be applied in response to offender misbehaviour. Conversely, more severe sanctions may require additional hours of community service or more significant restrictions on movement.

The third requirement of CM models is the need to include an evaluative component that can empirically document its effectiveness. Depending on the type of evaluation, effectiveness may vary by: a) staff training, personality, caseload, and/or experience; b) the program's targets; and c) the cost of attaining those targets. Thus, evaluation of a CM system can improve overall planning and effectiveness of the system.

Empirical research of CM in practice highlights a key concern; that is, the disconnect between classification and CM which occurs when workers doing the assessment and classification of offenders are not the persons responsible for the offender's subsequent CM or when there is little or no communication between assessors and case managers. Under such circumstances, the effect on offender outcomes has not been encouraging. For example, Harris, Gingerich, and Whittaker (2004) found in their study that Client Management Classification (CMC) case plans focussed on RNR principles saw recidivism decrease by 14%. However, only one-quarter of probationers were supervised in a manner that was entirely consistent with the results of risk assessment and consequently, CMC did not have a significant overall impact on offender outcome.

Enhancing Correctional Practice

Correctional practice is most effective when it is evidence-based and offered in a complete, theory-driven, and integrated manner. This means that it reduces the antisocial behaviour of offenders (i.e., recidivism), that it employs procedures that have been empirically evaluated as useful, and that the programs, services, and supervision are planned and delivered systematically following the RNR principles.

Andrews et al. (2004) introduced the LS/CMI, a combined assessment and CM protocol grounded in the RNR principles. It is also essential for classification and CM practices to be integrated at the agency level. To do so, however, there must be consistency within the organization's operational protocols, policies, and procedures.

A SURVEY OF CLASSIFICATION AND CASE MANAGEMENT PRACTICES IN CANADA

How do practices in Canadian correctional organizations stack up against the principles and ideals of offender classification and CM reviewed thus far? Some insight is provided into Canadian practices by way of a provincial and territorial correctional agency 2011 survey of assessment and classification instruments used with adult offenders in both community and institutional settings.

Assessment Practices

The survey revealed that provincial and territorial corrections use an impressive array of risk assessment instruments. The most consistently cited protocols were from the LS family of tools along with another third-generation risk/need assessment tools. Apart from Prince Edward Island, the practice of risk/needs assessment in institutional and community corrections is well established in Canada. It was also interesting to note that specialized risk assessment tools for sex offenders and domestic violence offenders were referenced in about half of the jurisdictions.

Only about half of respondents, however, reported using risk/needs assessments with inmates on remand or bail cases. Community-based assessments were most often used to determine reporting frequency or to identify programming needs and CM issues. In custody settings, they were typically used to establish initial security placement or changes in security classification, conditional release, programming, and CM. Assessments were usually administered within both settings at admission or within six months of admission. POs typically conducted assessments in the community while classification officers and correctional officers (COs) administered them in custody settings.

The agencies were also asked about staff training initiatives, their CM models, and the types of quality assurance mechanisms they had implemented. The utility of any assessment instrument is dependent on users' knowledge of the tool and the skill with which they administer it. Therefore, respondents' descriptions of training in the administration of the instruments and the implementation of quality assurance practices were of interest.

Results indicated considerable variation in the training practices across jurisdictions. This initially raised some concern, although, on closer inspection, it was apparent that some of the variability was attributed less to jurisdiction and more to the scale on which workers were being trained. For instance, second-generation risk scales such as the STATIC-99 (Hanson & Thornton, 2000), which is designed to assess risk among sexual offenders, requires less training than third-generation risk/need tools such as the LSI-R and much less training than a comprehensive fourth generation tool such as the LS/CMI. That said, there were meaningful differences among provinces and territories in training format and intensity (e.g., on-line vs. multi-day on-site training).

Most jurisdictions also reported some quality assurance mechanism, but the type and degree of quality assurance varied considerably. File audits (Nunavut) and reviews by supervisors (Alberta) were common procedures. Some organizations conducted annual peer reviews to assess inter-rater reliability (British Columbia), while others (Québec, New Brunswick) benefited from their use of an automated version of the instrument to design an ongoing monitoring process (see Figure 9.1). Some agencies included evaluations of assessment tools in a more substantial review of their offender CM process (Ontario). Another approach was to offer annual "booster sessions" as part of staff training (Prince Edward Island). With assessment practices such as these applied equally with institutional and community staff, the stage is set for the application of "meaningful," risk/need assessments and classification to offender CM.

Case Management Practices

The survey revealed that the approach to CM varied between institutional and community settings. For example, community case managers were typically POs who carried caseloads that ranged in size from 36 (Northwest Territories) to 76 (Ontario). In contrast, institutional CM employed three models: a) COs with limited (n = 4-15) caseloads (Manitoba, British Columbia); b) classification officers with moderate (n = 30-80) caseloads (Newfoundland and Labrador, Nova Scotia, New Brunswick); and c) staff with caseloads in the 30-40 range (Yukon, Nunavut). Regrettably, the survey was not sufficiently detailed to determine the implications of these different CM structures for active correctional practice.

Some jurisdictions did not articulate a clear CM model but rather described their offender supervision processes. Numerous jurisdictions had built CM models squarely on the principles of RNR

Figure 9.1 – Offender Assessment, Classification, Case Management Feedback Loop for Program Planning and Development

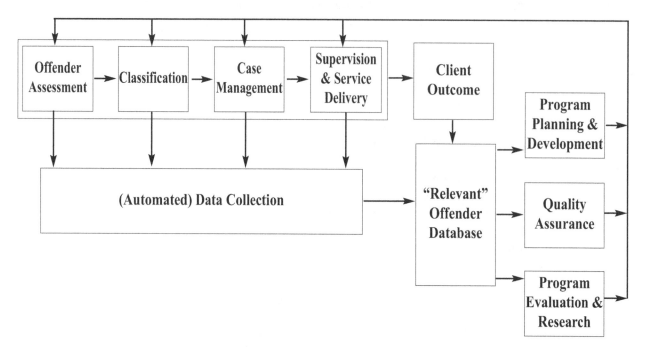

Source: Adapted from Wormith (1997, p. 28).

(Yukon) or the LS/CMI instrument (Manitoba, Québec). Others emphasized a multidisciplinary, "integrated" team approach to CM (Saskatchewan) or capitalized on CM's client centred focus and its capacity to respond to the continually evolving circumstances of the offender (British Columbia, Northwest Territories). A third approach included motivational interviewing during CM as a means of assisting offenders through the stages of change (New Brunswick). Although institutional CM was based on RNR and used the LS/CMI (Manitoba, Nova Scotia), some jurisdictions also noted that their CM models included institutional placement (Alberta) or mental health screening, particularly suicide prevention (Québec).

Quality assurance strategies were routine in most community-based agencies but varied as they did for assessment and classification. They included observation (British Columbia), case review and file review (Prince Edward Island), traditional auditing (Newfoundland and Labrador), in-house accreditation (Ontario), demonstrations of core competencies (New Brunswick), and the use of the *Correctional Program Assessment Inventory-2010* © (CPAI-2010 ©) in Ontario (Gendreau, Andrews, & Thériault, 2010). Quality assurance in institutions appeared to be less well established and tended to include occasional random reviews of files by managers (Manitoba) and ongoing monitoring of individual offender's progress by wardens (British Columbia) or classification committees (Nunavut). Several jurisdictions indicated that they were in the process of improving (Northwest Territories) and in some cases automating (British Columbia) their current provisions for quality.

Overall, the survey indicated that offender classification and CM in Canadian correctional practice is, on its face, evidence-based although the results should be interpreted with caution as they mostly relied on agency self-report. That is, the survey was descriptive and did not collect any systematic, empirical information regarding the effectiveness of CM with individual offenders. As such, it is useful to turn to an example of an effective correctional practice that it is both theories driven (i.e., RNR) and evidence-based.

THE STRATEGIC TRAINING INITIATIVE IN COMMUNITY SUPERVISION

The characteristics and skills required of an effective probation officer have been known for some time (Bonta & Andrews, 2017) and a training program developed from them can be gleaned from the literature (Andrews & Carvell, 1997). The only evaluation of a training program designed to enhance supervision in adherence with the RNR principles is that by Trotter (1996). The program emphasized prosocial modelling and problem-solving skills (i.e., cognitive-behavioural intervention) and empathy (i.e., establishing a positive rapport). Thirty POs attended five days of training, with 12 of them continuing to attend ongoing training sessions and apply the skills learned during client sessions, as evidenced by case notes. The 4-year recidivism rate for clients of POs who used the training was 53.8% as compared with 64% among clients of comparison POs (i.e., probation as usual).

The Strategic Training Initiative in Community Supervision (STICS) represents an essential evolution of classification and case management in Canada. The training model had two main components: a 3-day training workshop and ongoing clinical support. The training consisted of 10 modules ranging from a presentation of the evidence in support of RNR to the actual teaching of cognitive-behavioural skills. An important aspect of STICS training was the targeting of pro-criminal attitudes. POs were taught to recognize expressions of pro-criminal attitudes from their clients, teach their clients how attitudes shape behaviour, and how to adopt more prosocial attitudes. After training, the officers were provided ongoing clinical support through monthly meetings, refresher courses, and individualized feedback on their supervision, as a means of enhancing skills development.

The program involved random assignment of 80 POs to either training or routine supervision (Bonta, Bourgon, Rugge, Scott, Yessine, Gutierrez, & Li, 2011). Measurement of the POs' application of skills taught was based on audio recordings of a sample of supervision sessions over six months. The first hypothesis was that training would change the behaviour of the POs with their clients. Second, if officer behaviour did change, then a commensurate reduction in client recidivism was also predicted.

As anticipated, the trained officers did demonstrate more of the desired behaviours than the untrained POs. That is, they spent more time discussing the probationer's criminogenic needs, particularly pro-criminal attitudes. The experimental officers also spent less time on the conditions of probation and clients' non-criminogenic needs. Not only was the content of discussions between POs and clients in the expected direction but so too were the intervention techniques. There were significantly more STICS officers (75.8%) who had at least one discussion with clients regarding attitudes as compared with 10.5% of regular POs. Further, 69.7% of the STICS officers employed cognitive techniques as compared with 5.3% of comparison group POs. The impact of the program was evidenced in the recidivism rates for the two groups: 25% for clients of the STICS officers vs. 39.5% for the clients of regular POs.

How well, then, is what we know about effective assessment and classification being integrated with correctional treatment? The following section attempts to bridge our knowledge of these two critical areas with what we know about effective correctional rehabilitation.

THE RISE AND FALL AND RE-BIRTH OF THE REHABILITATIVE IDEAL

The over-riding objective of the criminal justice system is to enhance public safety by reducing criminal behaviour. Historically, attempts to reduce criminal behaviour have involved a combination of detention (i.e., incarceration), specific deterrence (i.e., inducing fear through sanctions), and rehabilitation (i.e., treatment).

The effectiveness of rehabilitation in reducing criminal behaviour has been vigorously debated over the last century. This is, in part, because the degree to which any correctional treatment gains acceptance among policy-makers depends not only on the amount and quality of the evidence of its effect but upon the social context of the times. Therefore, before presenting current evidence regarding the effectiveness of rehabilitation, we begin with a brief history of the ontogeny of the rehabilitative movement, and the social realities that have both encouraged and hindered its growth.

At a seminal conference in Cincinnati in 1870, the era's correctional experts agreed that the objectives for correctional treatment should be two-fold: a) to protect society and reform offenders, and b) to do so without being mean-spirited (Wines, 1871, p. 541). They spoke of instilling hope and emphasizing rewards over punishments (Wines), concepts that later resonated in 20th-century learning theory and behaviour modification strategies (Mowrer, 1960; Spiegler & Guevremont, 2010).

The Ascendency of the Rehabilitative Ideal

The treatment paradigm that evolved from the work of these late 19th century scholars, and one which was to remain unchallenged for many decades thereafter (Allen, 1981), had several important implications for latter-day rehabilitative practices. It was presumed that the genesis of offender criminality lay in a variety of psychological and social factors. As such, rehabilitation should, therefore, identify those factors that lead offenders into crime. Offenders could then be placed in treatment programs where their particular needs could be addressed. For example, offenders would be diagnosed, a treatment regime prescribed, and, crucially given the subsequent vilification of the rehabilitative ideal (Rothman, 1980), the treatment agency would have the discretion to determine the course of action necessary to effect change in the offender.

It was not until the mid-1950s that further reforms to the rehabilitative ideal were proposed. In 1954 the American Correctional Association was founded. Prisons became known as correctional institutions. For proponents of the rehabilitative ideal, the next two decades witnessed some exciting initiatives. Sophisticated classification systems were introduced (Warren, 1969). Prison-based treatment programs were implemented, ranging from individual and group counselling to therapeutic milieu, behaviour modification, and vocational and educational programming. With the emergence of community corrections in the 1960s, granting of parole was often made contingent upon the offender making satisfactory progress in institutional treatment programs. By 1975, when the American Probation and Parole Association was established, some parole/probation settings had developed innovative treatment programs reporting sizeable reductions in recidivism (see Ross & Gendreau, 1980). Further, it was felt that community re-integration strategies offered the most significant promise for optimizing the effect of rehabilitation.

Throughout this period, a few criminologists (e.g., Bailey, 1966; Cressey, 1958; Logan, 1972) argued that the evaluation literature provided little evidence of rehabilitation's effectiveness in reducing recidivism. At the time, these nay-sayers were largely ignored.

Times Change: Rehabilitation in Decline

The rehabilitation perspective was directly challenged by Martinson's (1974) publication *What works? Questions and answers about prison reform*, essentially a précis of a more comprehensive review by Lipton, Martinson, and Wilks (1975). Martinson's conclusions were based on an analysis of the outcome of 231 offender treatment studies published between 1945 and 1967. Consistent with the conclusions reached by the skeptics mentioned above, Martinson reasoned "that with few and isolated exceptions the rehabilitative efforts that have been reported so far have had no appreciable effect on recidivism" (p. 25). Furthermore, he sounded a note of despair when he stated, "we haven't the faintest clue about how to rehabilitate offenders and reduce recidivism" (p. 48). According to Walker (1985), Martinson's "nothing works" pronouncement "became an instant cliché and exerted an enormous influence on both popular and professional thinking" (p. 168). Many scholars and policymakers, Martinson included (Martinson, 1976) began to vigorously advocate for the punishment rather than treatment of offenders (Adams, 1976).

Why was Martinson's edict so eagerly received when others who had earlier expressed similar views were ignored? Neither end of the political continuum was satisfied with the *status quo* in criminal justice which each felt was the direct result of the rehabilitative ideal's destructive policies. For conservative policymakers, the apparent increase in prison disturbances and the availability of parole, which allowed offenders to serve only a fraction of their sentences in prison, were regarded as signs of weakness in the system. Also, there was evidence of increased crime rates during the latter 1970s. The conservative response was to "get tough" on criminals. They advocated for the abolition of parole, adoption of mandatory minimum sentences, and a fixed schedule of lengthier sentences, such as "three strikes and out" laws (i.e., life sentences upon third conviction regardless of offence type), as well as making prison living conditions much harsher (see Gendreau, Goggin, & Cullen, 1999). Only then could order be returned to the criminal justice system.

In contrast, liberal-minded advocates felt the system was out of control because the rehabilitative model gave carte blanche to correctional officials. This allowed them to exercise their discretion in an inequitable and coercive fashion. Prison officials were characterized as agents of social control who discriminated against the downtrodden. Moreover, treatment programs were scathingly described as degradation ceremonies that only widened the net and did more harm than good (see Binder & Geis, 1984; Fogel, 1979; Morris, 1974).

Unlike the conservative "get tough" agenda, liberals championed the "justice model" which minimized the goal of crime control and placed greater emphasis upon ensuring that justice was administered fairly. Regarding policy, undue discretion could be reined in by imposing fixed sentences, abolishing parole, and by making rehabilitation, where it was available at all, strictly voluntary. With appropriate protective legal mechanisms established, offenders could be protected from the vagaries of a capricious system (Conrad, 1981).

One can see, then, that Martinson's message arrived at the optimal moment to have maximum impact. Science had passed judgment: the rehabilitative model had no empirical support; its claims were exposed as fraudulent. Both the conservative and liberal schools were re-vitalized by the task of bringing order to the chaos that resulted from misguided rehabilitative policies.

We take pains to note that Martinson's (1974) and Lipton et al.'s (1975) conclusions were not entirely wrongheaded. On the heels of their publications, other reviewers (Greenberg, 1977; Wright & Dixon, 1977) confirmed the Lipton group's pessimistic findings as did a panel commissioned by the National Academy of Science (Sechrest et al., 1979) which thoroughly re-evaluated the results of Lipton et al.'s (1975) review. Indeed, challenges to the new "nothing works" orthodoxy were met with scorn. As a case in point, when Ted Palmer (1975) re-examined Martinson's sample, he noted that 48 percent of the programs showed reductions in recidivism. Furthermore, those programs that were conducted in the community, with juveniles or with moderate risk offenders, produced the best results.

Revivification of Rehabilitation: 1976 to the mid-1980s

Martinson's (1974) conclusions catalyzed to galvanize interest among rehabilitation's proponents to begin systematically documenting the effects of correctional programming. In truth, the rehabilitative ideal had been taken for granted (Palmer, 1992; Ross & McKay, 1978) and the process of its rejuvenation could only begin once its advocates acknowledged the naïveté and overconfidence which had prevailed in the 1950s and 1960s (Palmer, 1992) regarding correctional treatments.

Also, rehabilitation's prospects took a modest turn for the better when Martinson (1979) updated his previous review to include studies published since 1972. He now distanced himself from his "nothing works" stance and moved closer to Palmer's interactionist position by concluding:

> I have often said that treatment added to the networks of criminal justice is impotent...the conclusion is not correct...treatments will be found to be "impotent" under certain conditions, beneficial under others, and detrimental under still others. (Martinson 1979; p. 254)

Unfortunately, Martinson's recantation was generally ignored, demonstrating once again the potent effect that social context can have in influencing a message's receptivity.

Another source of optimism originated from outside the field of criminology. Criminologists were quite comfortable with the "nothing works" scenario in that the putative empirical reality was congruent with their ideological preferences (Binder & Geis, 1984; Cullen & Gendreau, 2000). Rather, the impetus for change came from psychology, a discipline with different intellectual and practice predispositions. Most of the proponents of change were from the so-called "Canadian School" of rehabilitation (Logan, Gaes, Harer, Innes, Karacki, & Saylor, 1991).

Members of the Canadian School adhered to the scientist-practitioner model within their discipline (clinical/community psychology) and most worked within Canadian correctional and governmental jurisdictions which were supportive of rehabilitation. They took for granted that the implementation, administration, and evaluation of offender assessment and treatment programs were key responsibilities. Being well-versed in learning theory and related behavioural treatments, they operated under the assumption that criminal behaviour, like most social behaviour, is learned and can, therefore, be modified through the application of a schedule of ethical and appropriate rewards and punishments. They rejected the implicit assumption of the "nothing works" doctrine that criminals, unlike non-criminals, were incapable of relearning or of acquiring new behavioural repertoires (Gendreau & Ross, 1979, p. 466). In response, this group undertook some literature reviews and demonstration projects (Andrews, 1980; Andrews & Kiessling, 1980) whose results they hoped would serve to validate the utility of the rehabilitative ideal and identify the specifics of useful, and ineffective, correctional practices.

They used these reviews to provide "bibliotherapy for cynics" (Gendreau & Ross, 1979). The authors uncovered scores of studies that reported reductions in recidivism, in some cases of considerable magnitude (i.e., 20% to 50%). Reviews of this type provided the foundation for developing some elementary principles of effective correctional treatments.

> For instance, it was found that a majority of the most effective programs were behavioural. Secondly, as psychologists, they were sensitive to individual differences, an idea towards which criminologists had long been inimical (Andrews & Wormith, 1989). Indeed, research into the effect of individual differences on recidivism (i.e., which offenders respond best to what types of treatments and therapies) underwent great advances in the late 1970s and early 1980s (for a detailed review see Gendreau & Ross, 1987, pp. 370-374). In addition to identifying what appeared to be useful program components, the Canadian group also shed light on aspects of

programs that resulted in increases in recidivism. Particularly crucial was the concept of therapeutic integrity.

As a testament to this unfortunate reality, the reader is directed to Quay's (1977) re-assessment of Kassebaum, Ward, and Wilner's (1971) popular prison counselling program. While the Kassebaum et al. (1971) research was cited as a prime example of a methodologically rigorous evaluation which demonstrated that treatment was ineffective, Quay discovered the reason for such a conclusion: the program had little therapeutic integrity. That is, it had a weak conceptual base, used counselling groups that were unstable, and employed unqualified, poorly-trained counsellors who did not believe in the efficacy of the program!

Other aspects of unsuccessful programs appeared to be related to individual difference factors and types of treatment. Some evidence indicated that even high-quality treatment services had little impact upon the recidivism of lower risk offenders, and Rogerian non-directive and psychodynamic oriented treatments were notably ineffective modalities (see Gendreau & Ross, 1983-84).

THE ROLE OF META-ANALYSIS: ESTABLISHING "WHAT WORKS" (AND "WHAT DOESN'T")

From the late 1980s to the present, the rehabilitative ideal has again been experiencing a "revival." This can be attributed both to the generation of new knowledge and, in our opinion, to recent developments in how that knowledge is cumulated. To this point, we have cited only the results of the narrative (or qualitative) reviews of offender treatment programs. Authors of such studies typically evaluate the truth of an issue (does treatment work?) by reading a few influential theoretical papers, examining some of the available evidence, and then selecting the results that tend to substantiate their "take" on the matter. Critics of the narrative review (Rosenthal, 1991) have pointed out that such reviews often omit crucial data and their conclusions can be subject to prejudice and ideology. Finally, most contemporary literature consists of, at a minimum, dozens of studies (Gendreau & Ross, 1987). There are limitations as to how much information one can systematically process when dealing with multiple outcomes, methodologies, and study characteristics. It is perhaps not surprising, then, that the conclusions of narrative reviews can be woefully imprecise, making them very difficult to replicate.

Quantitative research methodologies developed since the 1980s have proven useful in evaluating the effectiveness of treatment programs in medicine and psychology (Hunt, 1997). The techniques used to quantify the results of studies are subsumed under the term meta-analysis. In contrast to narrative reviews or box-score tabulations (i.e., how many studies produce a significant effect versus how many do not), a meta-analysis computes an "effect size" between treatment and outcome (i.e., recidivism) for each study.

In a meta-analysis, each primary study is also coded along some dimensions such as the type of subjects, offender risk level, type and dosage of treatment, therapist qualifications, study setting, and quality of research design. These factors can then be correlated with the overall treatment effect in order to assess their impact as moderators of effect size.

One should note, however, that meta-analysis is not foolproof (Smith, Gendreau, et al., 2009). The quality of the literature and the accuracy of the coding of study characteristics can affect the results. Nevertheless, the consensus is that to summarize large bodies of literature in order to generate rational policies; meta-analysis is a method far superior to narrative reviews (Gendreau & Smith, 2007).

We now turn to the results of meta-analyses conducted on offender treatment programs, with particular emphasis on recidivism prediction.

Early Results

The first meta-analyses of offender rehabilitation programs began to appear in the mid-1980s (Davidson, Gottschalk, Gensheimer, & Mayer, 1984). The pioneering reviews articulated familiar themes that would be validated in future meta-analyses. They were mostly limited to juvenile samples and the studies surveyed did not overlap to a large extent. On average, a modest majority ($n » 55\%$) of the effect sizes produced positive results vis-à-vis recidivism.

Lipsey (1992) later summarized the results of a vast database of juvenile interventions ($n = 443$ effect sizes). Sixty-four percent of these were positive (i.e., reduced recidivism) representing a noticeable improvement over the 50 percent baseline reported by Martinson and Palmer almost 20 years previously. The average reduction in recidivism within the Lipsey sample varied from 5% to 9% depending on the statistical adjustments made to the effect sizes. Subsequently, Lösel (1995) provided a comprehensive assessment of 13 meta-analyses of juvenile and adult treatment studies which were published between 1985 and 1995. He found that mean effect sizes ranged from .05 to .18 with an overall mean $r » .10$, translating into a reduction in recidivism of approximately 10%. Using Rosenthal's (1991) BESD statistic, this would mean that the recidivism rates for the treatment and control groups would be 45% and 55%, respectively. The results of further meta-analyses (Andrews, Dowden, & Gendreau, 1999; Bonta & Andrews, 2017; Redondo, Sanchez-Meca, & Garrido, 1999; see also Smith, Gendreau, et al., 2009) concurred with that of Lösel. It should also be noted that these positive results were not affected by methodological factors such as subject attrition, quality of research design, length of follow-up, or inclusion of published versus unpublished studies (Lipsey, 1992; 1999).

The Search for Principles of Effective Correctional Programming

The general trend in meta-analysis results was that behaviourally-oriented programs, or at least those with much structure (i.e., academic, vocational, family therapies), generally produced the most significant reductions in recidivism. Although the mean effect sizes were not significant in these instances (i.e., »10% reductions in recidivism) they were greater than those of non-behavioural or relatively unfocussed interventions (i.e., "group therapy," psychodynamic or milieu type therapies) which sometimes produced slight increases in recidivism. The Ross and Fabiano (1985) study, which was more of a box-score analysis, further suggested that the most significant impact of programming could be anticipated from cognitive-behavioural interventions. Davidson et al.'s (1984) attempt to analyze the influence of a large number of moderators on effect size estimates is particularly noteworthy given their findings that *professional training* (i.e., psychology, education), and *evaluator involvement* in the design, implementation, and control of an intervention were positively correlated with program success.

It is also worth noting that there is a cumulative effect on recidivism of adherence to the RNR framework when developing and delivering treatment programs. Bonta and Andrews (2017) categorized programs as to whether or not they followed these principles and reported a 23% reduction in recidivism rates for programs which did. It is also important to emphasize that these principles apply to diverse correctional populations, including females, minorities, youthful offenders, mentally disordered, violent, and sex offenders (Bonta & Andrews, 2017).

Finally, the results of recent research have underscored the importance of core correctional practices in maximizing the effectiveness of offender programming. These define the specific clinical skills and therapeutic practices that should be incorporated in service delivery (Bonta & Andrews, 2017). The data indicate that the inclusion of such practices in offender treatment is associated with reductions in recidivism in the range of 19% to 27% (Bonta & Andrews, 2017).

Before turning to prospects for rehabilitation, it is appropriate to point out one other significant contribution of meta-analysis; that is, its capacity to highlight what *doesn't work* in offender treatment.

Specific deterrence modalities, as noted previously, run counter to rehabilitation in that they aim to change behaviour through "get tough" strategies or by instilling fear through the use of punishment. Such tactics, favoured by politicians and the public alike, are not based on either a probative social science heuristic of criminal behaviour or any empirically-documented set of pre-requisite conditions for behaviour change, be that through persuasion or punishment (Gendreau, 1996a, p. 128-129; Gendreau et al., 1999). Instead, the deterrence rationale is rooted in vague "common-sense" notions which assume that one can effectively change behaviour by inducing psychological pain, increasing surveillance, or "breaking" offenders through humiliation (see Gendreau, Goggin, Cullen, & Paparozzi, 2002a).[1]

Future Prospects

In the concluding section, we look to the near future of correctional assessment, classification, and treatment research. Even given the cumulation of empirical evidence over the last 30 years in support of the effectiveness of well-designed and properly implemented assessment protocols and correctional programs, several compelling avenues of inquiry remain if we are to make "what works" work (Andrews, 2006, p. 595). These include refinements in the area of program eligibility and attrition, application of comprehensive risk assessment protocols to augment offender CM practices, monitoring of program integrity and program quality, and not least, being sensitive to the potential for retrenchment of the rehabilitative ideal.

Offender Treatment Attrition

Attrition rates in correctional treatment continue to dog programmers and facilitators alike and impede the accurate measurement of program impact. Further, an analysis of the predictors of attrition indicated that dropouts were among those assessed at highest risk and in greatest need for service. Specifically, they were more likely to be unemployed, have lower levels of education, exhibit anti-social personality tendencies, and have a prior incarceration history. Of note, these are consistent with known predictors of both recidivism and institutional misconducts (Gendreau, Goggin, & Law, 1997).

Germane to the present discussion, the most robust predictors of treatment attrition were aspects of offender responsivity; that is, negative attitudes toward treatment, disruptive behaviour during treatment, denial of the need for treatment, and lack of engagement in treatment. By designing primary studies to answer critical questions about the interplay of offender, clinician, and setting characteristics on offender behaviour (Andrews, Bonta, & Wormith, 2011; Smith, Gendreau, et al., 2009), future meta-analyses will be better positioned to tease out what needs to be done to reduce attrition rates and enhance program effectiveness.

Composite Risk-Need Assessment and Case Management

The principles of effective intervention described previously highlight the importance of assessing offender risk to re-offend, primarily as a means of identifying those most in need of treatment. Being able to evaluate offenders' risk to re-offend accurately, especially violently, is a practical concern shared by all front-line correctional workers.

As noted earlier, the LS/CMI (Andrews et al., 2004) is the latest in the LS family of risk scales and is an example of a 4th generation protocol. As such, it assesses the broad spectrum of empirically-documented risk factors for criminal behaviour plus includes sections that evaluate offender responsivity and allow for on-going documentation of case planning and program outcomes (Bonta & Andrews, 2017).

For subsequent "generations" of risk scales, the prediction of recidivism may be enhanced by an examination of the precursors to recidivism, especially violent recidivism, regarding both context and individual. As Campbell et al. (2009) have noted, the occurrence of violent behaviour, in particular, is time-sensitive and the ability to reliably predict its potential has direct practical utility for case managers.

At the same time, recent reviews of some of the commonly used risk assessment scales (Desmarais et al., 2016) have highlighted some areas of concern with the development and practice of offender risk assessment. These include inconsistencies in how risk factors/domains are defined, in methodological reporting standards (i.e., lack of validation studies, failure to report inter-rater reliabilities), and in the degree of predictive accuracy *per* scale (Taxman, 2018). To that end, next steps in assessment and classification include standardizing the operational definitions used in risk prediction as well as further refinements invalidating the results of such assessments with diverse correctional populations. Notably, the recent Supreme Court ruling in the Ewert case (*Ewert v. Canada,* 2018) underscores the urgency for researchers and correctional agencies alike to make a concerted effort to validate existing assessment protocols with populations (i.e., Indigenous peoples, females, mentally-disordered, seniors, etc.) whose characteristics and/or needs are necessarily distinct from the correctional samples upon whom such scales have traditionally been normed (i.e., Caucasian males).

CPAI-2010©

With the establishment of the principles of effective correctional programming, the ability to evaluate the degree to which programs observe such principles, as well as to measure the relationship between program "fidelity" (Bonta & Andrews, 2017, p. 244) and program effectiveness, has become both an empirical possibility and a professional obligation. In this regard, the CPAI-2010© is the instrument of choice (see Box 9.3). As noted previously, it is an empirically-based evaluation tool which provides a standardized measure of program quality (i.e., content) and integrity (i.e., the degree to which programs are implemented as designed). The tool is based on an extensive on-site review of offender, staff, and program characteristics, as well as risk/need assessment methods and outcome evaluation strategies. It has been used to evaluate treatment adherence across diverse programs and types of offenders within both institutional and community settings, with substantial validities being reported for programs which score well ($r \approx .40$) (Bonta & Andrews, 2017).

The importance of being able to adequately evaluate the potential for correctional programs to reduce recidivism in the context of the cash-strapped correctional jurisdictions cannot be overstated. Being able to gauge the impact of programs accurately allows agencies to make informed decisions about the programs they choose to implement, for whom, and under what conditions.

Nurturing the Rehabilitative Ideal

Notwithstanding the accumulation and dissemination of results from the "what works" literature, the process of reviving the rehabilitative ideal remains a challenge (Andrews & Bonta, 2010). As noted previously, there continue to be reported in the literature of program effects in the "real world" that are attenuated relative to those in "demonstration" programs (Lipsey & Cullen, 2007). Such results have sponsored additional interest in identifying the elements and aspects of program administration which may underlie these inconsistencies in reported efficacy (Wormith, Althouse, Simpson, Reitzel, Fagan, & Morgan, 2009). They have also, however, fueled a growing disenchantment with the role of rehabilitation in correctional policy, one that Cullen, Smith, Lowenkamp, and Latessa (2009) warn is permeating the "marketplace of ideas" (p. 112).

Box 9.2 – The Case of Mr. Jeffrey Ewert

Mr. Jeffrey Ewert is a federal offender who is presently serving two concurrent life sentences, having been convicted in 1984 of second-degree murder and attempted murder. He was born in 1962 to an Indigenous mother and non-Indigenous father and, at six months of age, was adopted into an urban non-Indigenous family in Western Canada. Mr. Ewert reports never having felt a sense of belonging in his adopted culture, in part due to a home environment characterized by parental substance use and mental illness and generalized bigotry towards his Indigenous heritage. His maladaptive behaviour began in childhood and continued through adolescence into adulthood. Despite being eligible for day parole in 1996 and full parole in 1998, Mr. Ewert never applied for either type of early release as he assumed it would not be granted given that, according to the risk instruments routinely used by CSC in making such determinations, he is assessed as high risk to re-offend (Hart, 2016).

This goes to the heart of Mr. Ewert's procedural grievances against CSC and his subsequent court challenges. That is, he has argued that the risk assessment tools used by CSC are culturally biased and invalid for use with Indigenous populations. Therefore, any decisions based on the results of such assessments are necessarily inaccurate and unreliable (Hart, 2016).

Between 2000 and 2005, Mr. Ewert filed some grievances against CSC regarding the agency's continued use of 5 actuarial risk assessment scale with Indigenous offenders. CSC uses the results of such assessments to determine institutional security classification as well as the need for treatment, parole eligibility, and risk to recidivate. CSC dismissed each of Mr. Ewert's grievances arguing, in part, that such tools were only one aspect of the broader assessment of offender risk and, further, that the service was currently researching to assess the validity of the tools with Indigenous populations (Hart, 2016).

In 2007, Mr. Ewert appealed CSC's rulings to the Federal Court in *Ewert v. Canada (Attorney General)* charging that the agency's continued use of the tools constituted a violation of his *Charter* rights under s. 7 and s. 15. Experts in the area testified that there was no substantive evidence of harm to or bias against Indigenous populations through the use of the specified tools. As a result, the Court dismissed Mr. Ewert's case but also indicated that CSC should elaborate on the progress of its on-going research agenda to empirically validate these tools with Indigenous populations. Despite assurances to the contrary, there was no evidence that CSC ever completed this research initiative (*Ewert v. Canada*, 2018).

Finally, in 2015 Mr. Ewert launched a new action against CSC in which he claimed that the agency's continued use of the tools was in breach of their responsibilities to him under s. 24(1) of the *Corrections and Conditional Release Act* (CCRA) which requires CSC to "take all reasonable steps to ensure that any information about an offender that it uses is as accurate, up to date and complete as possible" (*Ewert v. Canada*, 2015). The Court ruled in favour of the appellant and ordered CSC to cease using the specified risk assessment tools with Indigenous offenders until their empirical validity was established. This decision was later overturned on appeal (*Canada v. Ewert*, 2016) and, in March 2017, the case was appealed to the Supreme Court. In its June 2018, the Court concluded that CSC had breached its responsibilities under s. 24(1) of the CCRA, must henceforth cease using the tools in question and must begin an immediate program of research to evaluate the relative utility of these tools with Indigenous populations.

> ## Box 9.3 – The Correctional Program Assessment Inventory
>
> The Correctional Program Assessment Inventory (CPAI) was developed by Gendreau and Andrews (2000) as a means of measuring the relative quality of correctional treatment programs. Its genesis was due, in part, to the growing disillusionment that followed Martinson's (1974) pronouncement that "nothing works" in correctional treatment. The inventory was designed to evaluate the degree to which "real world" treatment programs were consistent with what the empirical record indicated were the keys to achieving meaningful behaviour change among offenders.
>
> The most recent version of the instrument, the CPAI-2010©, consists of eight dimensions that evaluate organizational culture, program implementation/maintenance, management/staff characteristics, client risk/need practices, program characteristics, dimensions of core correctional practice, and inter-agency communication and evaluation.
>
> Since its inception, the CPAI (Gendreau & Andrews, 2000), and later the CPAI-2010© (Gendreau et al., 2010) have been used to evaluate a variety of correctional programs including substance abuse treatment provided by CSC in both prison and community-based settings; large-scale offender treatment programs in several Canadian provinces; day treatment, boot camps, intensive supervision, and diversion programs in a number of U.S. states; and individual treatment programs in Canada, Australia, and New Zealand. Also, many of the core items of the CPAI-2010© (Gendreau et al., 2010) have been incorporated among the accreditation standards used by correctional services in Canada (i.e., CSC), the UK (i.e., prisons and probation), and several U.S. jurisdictions.

SUMMARY

In the absence of a sustained focus by all concerned – politicians, policy-makers, corrections personnel, and researchers – on evidence-based practices, the correctional treatment agenda is easily high-jacked by "quick-fix" aficionados. Witness, for example, the disquieting growth in the United States of what Latessa, Cullen, and Gendreau (2002) have labelled "correctional quackery." This is typified by programs which reflect an "ignorance" of the causes of crime and evidence-based behaviour change strategies. "Treatments" such as acupuncture, yoga, pet therapy, and ecumenical Christianity, among others (see Gendreau, Goggin, French, & Smith, 2006 for a complete list), command a share of the public purse which is unwarranted given their inability to reduce recidivism (Bonta & Andrews, 2003). They continue to be endorsed by policy-makers as well as the public.

At the same time, no authority deliberately sets out to spend finite resources on ineffective correctional treatments, but many unwittingly do when they attend more to "common sense" than evidence-based solutions. When viewed through the lens of the past half-century of progress in the development of evidence-based correctional practice, such policy initiatives are a potent reminder that knowledge transfer in the area of correctional programming is as critical a research priority as is knowledge cumulation.

On balance, however, we remain optimistic regarding the potential for empirically-based assessment protocols and offender treatments to continue to play a vital role in reducing criminal behaviour and enhancing public safety in Canada and elsewhere. The grounds for such optimism lie in the extensive knowledge that has been generated to date with regards to "what works" regarding risk assessment, CM, and correctional programming for whom and under what conditions. Moreover, this research represents knowledge cumulated through successive replications across multiple jurisdictions. Certainly, additional avenues of inquiry remain. These include: a) refinements in the science of program implementation; b) translating theory, research, and policy into front-line CM practice; c) the development of specific treatment "curricula"; d) adding to the knowledge base on assessment and correctional programming for diverse offender populations (e.g., females, Indigenous peoples, youth, mentally-disordered, seniors, etc.); and e) working to ensure government policy is based on sound research knowledge. Canada has been a leader in generating much of what we now know about effective correctional programming, including assessment, classification, CM, and treatment, and we look forward to continuing to contribute to that effort.

KEY TERMS AND CONCEPTS

Case Management
Correctional Rehabilitation
Criminogenic Needs
Effect Size
"Get Tough"
Graduated Sanctions
"Justice Model"
Level of Service/Case Management Inventory (LS/CMI)
Level of Service Inventory-Revised (LSI-R)
Martinson

Meta-Analysis
Moderators
Offender Classification
Offender Treatment Attrition
Operant Conditioning
Procriminal Behaviour
Prosocial Behaviour
Risk-Need-Responsivity (RNR)
Statistical Information on Recidivism (SIR)
Strategic Training Initiative in Community Supervision (STICS)

STUDY AND DISCUSSION QUESTIONS

1. Compare and contrast the four generations of risk prediction instruments.
2. Identify and discuss the eight stage CM model.
3. Discuss how the RNR model may be applied to offender assessment and rehabilitation.
4. Compare and contrast the conservative "get tough" view of rehabilitation *versus* the liberal "justice model" view.
5. Discuss the contributions of meta-analysis as a research technique in assessing the effectiveness of offender treatment programs.
6. "A 10% reduction in recidivism is of little practical value." To what extent do you agree or disagree with this statement and why?

HELPFUL WEBLINKS

* **Correctional Service of Canada** (CSC) at http://www.csc-scc.gc.ca
    This site provides research on relevant aspects of offender treatment in Canada, including risk assessment and classification, program development, and community corrections programs for diverse correctional populations.
* **Department of Justice Canada** at http://canada.justice.gc.ca/eng/dept-mandat.html
    The purpose of the Department is to ensure that the Canadian justice system is fair, accessible, and efficient. The Department also represents the Canadian government in legal matters.

- **Public Safety Canada** at http://www.publicsafety.gc.ca
    This site provides research on the Canadian correctional system, including offender treatment for specific populations, and aspects of treatment delivery in institutional and community settings.
- **National Institute of Corrections** (NIC) at http://www.nicic.gov/
    NIC is an agency within the US Department of Justice, Federal Bureau of Prisons. It was established to offer training assistance and consultation on matters pertinent to the operation of correctional agencies.

NOTES

[1]   Of note, deterrence-based policies have been in place in the United States since the early 1980s where they have translated into sizeable investments in new prison construction (Petersilia, 2011). This has had little effect on recidivism rates but has meant that the U.S. has the dubious distinction of being a leader in incarceration rates among Western democracies (i.e., 698/100,000) (Lipsey & Cullen, 2007; Walmsley, 2015). Moreover, states which most aggressively embraced the prison construction boom are now facing crippling budget deficits (Andrews & Bonta, 2010).

REFERENCES

Adams, S. (1976). Evaluation: A way out of rhetoric. In R. Martinson, T. Palmer, & S. Adams, (Eds.), *Rehabilitation, recidivism, and research* (pp. 75-91). Hackensack, NJ: National Council on Crime and Delinquency.

Allen, F. A. (1981). *The decline of the rehabilitative ideal: Penal policy and social purpose.* New Haven, CT: Yale University Press.

Andrews, D. A. (1980). Some experimental investigations of the principles of differential association through deliberate manipulations of the structure of service systems. *American Sociological Review, 45,* 448-462.

Andrews, D. A. (2006). Enhancing adherence to risk-need-responsivity: Making quality a matter of policy. *Criminology and Public Policy, 5,* 595-602.

Andrews, D. A., & Bonta, J. (1998). *The psychology of criminal conduct* (2nd ed.). Cincinnati, OH: Anderson Publishing Co.

Andrews, D. A., & Bonta, J. (2010). Rehabilitating criminal justice policy and practice. *Psychology, Public Policy, and the Law, 16,* 39-55.

Andrews, D. A., Bonta, J., & Hoge, R. D. (1990a). Classification for effective rehabilitation: Rediscovering psychology. *Criminal Justice and Behavior, 17,* 19-52.

Andrews, D.A., Bonta, J., & Wormith, J. S. (1995). *The Level of Service Inventory – Ontario Revision: Interview and scoring guide.* Toronto, Ontario, Canada: Ontario Ministry of the Solicitor General and Correctional Services.

Andrews, D. A., Bonta, J., & Wormith, J. S. (2004). *The Level of Service/Case Management Inventory (LS/CMI): User's Manual.* Toronto: Multi-Health Systems.

Andrews, D. A., Bonta, J., & Wormith, J. S. (2006). The recent past and near future of risk/need assessment. *Crime and Delinquency, 52,* 7-27.

Andrews, D. A., Bonta, J., & Wormith, J. S. (2011). The risk-need-responsivity (RNR) model: Does adding the Good Lives model contribute to effective crime prevention? *Criminal Justice and Behavior, 38,* 735-755.

Andrews, D. A., & Carvell, C. (1997). *Core correctional treatment – core correctional supervision and counselling: Theory, research, assessment and practice.* Ottawa, ON: Carleton University.

Andrews, D. A., & Dowden, C. (2005). Managing correctional treatment for reduced recidivism: A meta-analytic review of programme integrity. *Legal and Criminological Psychology, 10,* 173-187.

Andrews, D. A., Dowden, C., & Gendreau, P. (1999*). Clinically relevant and psychologically informed approaches to reduced re-offending: A meta-analytic study of human service, risk, need, responsivity, and other concerns in justice contexts.* Unpublished manuscript, Carleton University.

Andrews, D. A., & Kiessling, J. J. (1980). Program structure and effective correctional practices: A summary of the CaVIC research. In R. R. Ross & P. Gendreau (Eds.), *Effective Correctional Treatment.* Toronto, Ontario: Butterworth.

Andrews, D. A., & Wormith, J. S. (1989). Personality and crime: Knowledge destruction and construction in criminology. *Criminology, 28,* 369-404.

Andrews, D. A., Zinger, I., Hoge, R. D., Bonta, J., Gendreau, P., & Cullen, F. T. (1990b). Does correctional treatment work? A clinically relevant and psychologically informed meta-analysis. *Criminology, 28,* 369-404.

Aos, S., & Drake, E. (2013). *Prison, police, and programs: Evidence-based options that reduce crime and save money* (Doc. No. 13-11-1901). Olympia, WA: Washington State Institute for Public Safety.

Bailey, W. C. (1966). Correctional outcome: An evaluation of 100 reports. *Journal of Criminal Law, Criminology and Police Science, 57,* 153-160.

Binder, A., & Geis, G. (1984). Ad populum argumentation in criminology: Juvenile diversion as rhetoric. *Crime and Delinquency, 30,* 624-647.

Bonta, J. (1996). Risk-needs assessment and treatment. In A. T. Harland (Ed.), *Choosing correctional options that work,* (pp. 18-32). Thousand Oaks, CA: Sage.

Bonta, J., & Andrews, D. A. (2003). A commentary on Ward and Stewart's model of human needs. *Psychology, Crime and Law, 9,* 215-218.

Bonta, J., & Andrews, D. A. (2017). *The psychology of criminal conduct* (6th ed.). New York: Routledge.

Bonta, J., Bourgon, G., Rugge, T., Gress, C., & Gutierrez, L. (2013). Taking the leap: From pilot project to wide-scale implementation of the Strategic Training Initiative in Community Supervision (STICS). *Justice Research and Policy, 15,* 17-35.3

Bonta, J., Bourgon, G., Rugge, T., Scott, T.-L., Yessine, A. K., Gutierrez, L., & Li, J. (2011). An experimental demonstration of training probation officers in evidence-based community supervision. *Criminal Justice and Behavior, 38,* 1127-1148.

Burgess, E. W. (1928). Factors determining success or failure on parole. In A. A. Bruce, A. J. Harno, E. W. Burgess, & J. Landesco (Eds.), *The workings of the indeterminate sentence law and the parole system in Illinois.* Springfield, IL: State Board of Parole.

Campbell, M. A., French, S., & Gendreau, P. (2009). The prediction of violence in adult offenders: A meta-analytic comparison of instruments and methods of assessment. *Criminal Justice and Behaviour, 36,* 567-590.

Canada v. Ewert, 2016 FCA 203.

Clark, M.D. (1997). Strength-based practice: A new paradigm. *Corrections Today, 59,* 200-202.

Conrad, J. P. (1981). Where there's hope there's life. In D. Fogel, & J. Hudson (Eds.), *Justice as fairness: Perspectives of the justice model* (pp. 3-21). Cincinnati: OH: Anderson.

Cressey, D. R. (1958). The nature and effectiveness of correctional techniques. *Law and Contemporary Problems, 23,* 754-771.

Cullen, F. T., & Gendreau, P. (2000). Assessing correctional rehabilitation: Policy, practice, prospects. In J. Horney (Ed.) *National Institute of Justice criminal justice 2000: Changes in decision making and discretion in the criminal justice system.* (pp. 109-175). Washington, DC: Department of Justice, National Institute of Justice.

Cullen, F. T., & Gilbert, K. E. (1982). *Reaffirming rehabilitation.* Cincinnati, OH: Anderson.

Cullen, F. T., Smith, P., Lowenkamp, C. T., & Latessa, E. J. (2009). Nothing works revisited: Deconstructing Farabee's Rethinking Rehabilitation. *Victims and Offenders, 4,* 101-123.

Davidson, W., Gottschalk, R., Gensheimer, L., & Mayer, J. (1984). *Interventions with juvenile delinquents: A meta-analysis of treatment efficacy.* Washington, DC: National Institute of Juvenile Justice and Delinquency Prevention.

Desmarais, S. L., Johnson, K. L., & Singh, J. P. (2016). Performance of recidivism risk assessment instruments in the U.S. correctional settings. *Psychological Services, 13,* 206- 222.

Dowden, C., Antonowicz, D., & Andrews, D. A. (2003). The effectiveness of relapse prevention with offenders: A meta-analysis. *International Journal of Offender Therapy and Comparative Criminology, 47,* 516-528.

Ewert v. Canada (Attorney General), 2007 FC 13.

Ewert v. Canada, 2015 FC 1093.

Ewert v. Canada, 2018 SCC 30.

Fogel, D. (1979). *We are the living proof: The justice model for corrections* (2nd ed.). Cincinnati, OH: Anderson.

Gendreau, P. (1996a). The principles of effective intervention with offenders. In A. T. Harland (Ed.), *Choosing correctional interventions that work: Defining the demand and evaluating the supply* (pp. 117-130). Newbury Park, CA: Sage.

Gendreau, P. & Andrews, D. A. (2000). Correctional Program Assessment Inventory (CPAI) Saint John, NB: University of New Brunswick.

Gendreau, P., Andrews, D. A., & Thériault, Y. (2010). Correctional Program Assessment Inventory – 2010 © (CPAI-2010 ©) Beresford, NB.

Gendreau, P., Goggin, C., & Cullen, F. T. (1999). *The effects of prison sentences on recidivism.* Ottawa, Ontario: Solicitor General Canada.

Gendreau, P., Goggin, C., Cullen, F. T., & Paparozzi, M. (2002). The common-sense revolution and correctional policy. In J. McGuire (Ed.), *Offender rehabilitation and treatment: Effective programs and policies to reduce re-offending* (pp. 359-386. Chichester, UK: John Wiley & Sons.

Gendreau, P., Goggin, C., French, S., & Smith, P. (2006). Practicing psychology in correctional settings. In A. K. Hess, & I. B. Weiner, (Eds.), *The handbook of forensic psychology* (3rd ed.), (pp. 722-750.). Chichester: John Wiley & Sons.

Gendreau, P., Goggin, C., & Law, M. (1997). Predicting prison misconducts. *Criminal Justice and Behavior, 24,* 414-431.

Gendreau, P., & Ross, R. R. (1979). Effective correctional treatment: Bibliotherapy for cynics. *Crime and Delinquency, 25,* 463-489.

Gendreau, P., & Ross, R. R. (1983-84). Correctional treatment: Some recommendations for successful intervention. *Juvenile and Family Court, 34,* 31-40.

Gendreau, P., & Ross, R. R. (1987). Revivification of rehabilitation: Evidence from the 1980s. *Justice Quarterly, 4,* 349-407.

Gendreau, P., & Smith, P. (2007). Influencing the "people who count": Some perspectives on the reporting of meta-analytic results for prediction and treatment outcomes with offenders. *Criminal Justice and Behavior, 34,* 1536-1559.

Greenberg, D. F. (1977). The correctional effects of corrections: A survey of evaluations. In D. F. Greenberg (Ed.), *Corrections and punishment* (pp. 111-148). Beverly Hills: Sage.

Gutierrez, L., Chadwick, N., & Wanamaker, K. A. (2018). Culturally relevant programming versus the status quo: A meta-analytic review of the effectiveness of treatment of Indigenous offenders. *Canadian Journal of Criminology and Criminal Justice, 60,* 321- 353.

Hanson, R. K., Bourgon, G., Helmus, L, & Hodgson, S. (2009). The principles of effective correctional treatment also apply to sexual offenders: A meta-analysis. *Criminal Justice and Behaviour, 36,* 865-891.

Hart, S. D. (2016). Culture and violence risk assessment: The case of *Ewert vs. Canada. Journal of Threat Assessment and Management, 3,* 76-96.

Harris, P. M., Gingerich, R., & Whittaker, T. A. (2004). The "effectiveness" of differential supervision. *Crime & Delinquency, 50,* 235-271.

Henwood, K. S., Chou, S., & Browne, K. D. (2015). A systematic review and meta-analysis on the effectiveness of CBT informed anger management. *Aggression and Violent Behavior, 25*(Part B), 280-292.

Hoge, R. D., & Andrews, D. A. (2002). *Youth Level of Service/Case Management Inventory: User's manual.* Toronto, ON: Multi-Health Systems.

Holdsworth, E., Bowen, E., Brown, S., & Howat, D. (2014). Offender engagement in group programs and associations with offender characteristics and treatment factors: A review. *Aggression and Violent Behavior, 19,* 102-121.

Hunt, M. (1997). *How science takes stock: The story of meta-analysis.* New York: Russell Sage Foundation.

Kassebaum, G., Ward, D. A., & Wilner, D. M. (1971). *Prison treatment and parole survival: An empirical assessment.* New York: Wiley.

Kurtz, D., & Linnemann, T. (2006). Improving probation through client strengths: Evaluating strength-based treatments for at-risk youth. *Western Criminology Review, 7,* 9-19.

Latessa, E. J., Cullen, F. T., & Gendreau, P. (2002). Beyond correctional quackery: Professionalism and the possibility of effective treatment. *Federal Probation, 66,* 43-49.

Lipsey, M. W. (1992). Juvenile delinquency treatment: A meta-analytic inquiry into the variability of effects. In T. D. Cook, H. Cooper, D. S. Cordray, H. Hartmann, L. V. Hedges, R. J. Light, T. A. Lewis, & F. Mosteller (Eds.), *Meta-analysis for explanation: A casebook.* (pp. 83-127). New York: Russell Sage.

Lipsey, M. W. (1999). Can rehabilitative programs reduce the recidivism of juvenile offenders? An inquiry into the effectiveness of practical programs. *Virginia Journal of Social Policy and Law, 6,* 611- 641.

Lipsey, M. W., & Cullen, F. T. (2007). The effectiveness of correctional rehabilitation: A review of systematic reviews. *Annual Review of Law and Social Science, 3,* 297-320.

Lipton, D., Martinson, R., & Wilks, J. (1975). *The effectiveness of correctional treatment: A survey of treatment evaluation studies.* New York: Praeger.

Logan, C. H. (1972). Evaluation research in crime and delinquency: A reappraisal. *Journal of Criminal Law, Criminology and Police Science, 63,* 378-387.

Logan, C. H., Gaes, G. G., Harer, M., Innes, C. A., Karacki, L., & Saylor, W. G. (1991). *Can Meta-Analysis save correctional rehabilitation?* Washington, DC: Federal Bureau of Prisons, Department of Justice.

Lösel, F. (1995). The efficacy of correctional treatment: A review and synthesis of meta- evaluations. In J. McGuire (Ed.), *What Works: Reducing Reoffending* (pp. 79-111). West Sussex, UK: John Wiley.

Martin, S.S., & Inciardi, J.A. (1993). Case management approaches for the criminal justice client. In J.A. Inciardi (Ed.), *Drug treatment and criminal justice* (pp. 84-86). Thousand Oaks, CA: Sage.

Martinson, R. (1974). What works? Questions and answers about prison reform. *The Public Interest, 35,* 22-54.

Martinson, R. (1976). California and the crossroads. In R. Martinson, T. Palmer, & S. Adams (Eds.), *Rehabilitation, recidivism and research* (pp. 63-74). Hackensack, NJ: National Council on Crime and Delinquency.

Martinson, R. (1979). New findings, new views: A note of caution regarding sentencing reform. *Hofstra Law Review, 7,* 243-258.

Morris, N. (1974). *The future of imprisonment.* Chicago: University of Chicago Press.

Mowrer, O. H. (1960). *Learning theory and behavior.* New York: Wiley.

Nafekh, M., & Motiuk, L.L. (2002) *The Statistical Information on Recidivism – Revised 1 (SIR- R1) Scale: A psychometric examination.* Ottawa, ON: Correctional Service of Canada.

Nuffield, J. (1982). *Parole decision making in Canada.* Ottawa, ON: Ministry of the Solicitor General of Canada.

Olver, M. E., Stockdale, K. C., & Wormith, J. S. (2014). Thirty years of research on the Level of Service scales: A meta-analytic examination of predictive accuracy and sources of variability. *Psychological Assessment, 26,* 156-176.

Palmer, T. (1975). Martinson revisited. *Journal of Research in Crime and Delinquency, 12,* 133-152.

Palmer, T. (1992). *The re-emergence of correctional intervention.* Newbury Park, CA: Sage.

Petersilia, J. (2011). Beyond the prison bubble. *Federal Probation, 75,* 2-4.

Quay, H. C. (1977). The three faces of evaluation: What can be expected to work. *Criminal Justice and Behavior, 4,* 21-25.

Redondo, S., Sanchez-Meca, J., & Garrido, V. (1999). The influence of treatment programmes on the recidivism of juvenile and adult offenders: A European meta-analytic review. *Psychology, Crime and Law, 5,* 251-278.

Rosenthal, R. (1991). *Meta-analytic procedures for social research.* Beverly Hills, CA: Sage.

Ross, R. R., & Fabiano, E. A. (1985). *Time to think: A cognitive model of delinquency prevention and offender rehabilitation.* Johnson City, TN: Institute of Social Science and Arts.

Ross, R. R., & Gendreau, P. (1980). *Effective correctional treatment.* Toronto: Butterworths.

Ross, R. R., & McKay, B. (1978). Treatment in corrections: Requiem for a panacea. *Canadian Journal of Criminology, 20,* 279-295.

Rothman, D. J. (1980). *Conscience and convenience: The asylum and its alternatives in progressive America.* Boston: Little, Brown.

Sechrest, L., White, S. O., & Brown, E. D. (Eds.). (1979). *The rehabilitation of criminal offenders: Problems and prospects.* Washington, DC: National Academy of Sciences.

Smith, P., Gendreau, P., & Swartz, K. (2009). Validating the principles of effective intervention:A systematic review of the contributions of meta-analysis in the field of corrections. *Victims & Offenders, 4,* 148-169.

Spiegler, M. D., & Guevremont, D. C. (2010). *Contemporary behavior therapy* (5th ed.). Pacific Grove, CA: Brooks Cole.

Taxman, F. S. (2018). Risk assessment: Where do we go from here? In J. P. Singh, D. G. Kroner, J. S. Wormith, S. L. Desmarais, & Z. Hamilton (Eds.), *Handbook of recidivism risk/needs assessment tools* (pp. 271-284). Hoboken, NJ: John Wiley & Sons.

Trotter, C. (1996). The impact of different supervision practices in community corrections.

United States Department of Justice. (1999). *Case management in the criminal justice system.* Retrieved from http://www.nij.gov

Walker, S. (1985). *Sense and nonsense about crime: A policy guide.* Monterey, CA: Brooks/Cole.

Walmsley, R. (2015). *World prison population list* (11th ed.). London: International Centre for Prison Studies, King's College http://www.prisonstudies.org/sites/default/files/resources/downloads/world_prison_population_list_11th_edition_0.pdf

Warren, M. Q. (1969). The case for differential treatment of delinquents. *The Annals of the American Academy of Political and Social Science, 62,* 239-258.

Williams, K. M., Wormith, J. S., Bonta, J., & Sitarenios, G. (2017). The use of meta-analysis to compare and select offender risk instruments: A commentary on Singh, Grann, and Fazel (2011). *International Journal of Forensic Mental Health, 16,* 1-15.

Wines, E. C. (Ed.). (1871). Declaration of principles adopted and promulgated by the Congress. *Transactions of the National Congress on Penitentiary and Reformatory Discipline* (pp.541-567). Albany, NY: Weed-Parsons.

Wormith, J. S. (1997). Research to practice: Applying risk/needs assessment to offender classification. *Forum on Corrections Research, 9,* 26-31.

Wormith, J. S., Althouse, R., Simpson, M., Reitzel, L. R., Fagan, T. J., & Morgan, R. D. (2009). The rehabilitation and reintegration of offenders: The current landscape and some future directions for correctional psychology. *Criminal Justice and Behavior, 31,* 879-892.

Wright, W. F., & Dixon, M. C. (1977). Community prevention and treatment of juvenile delinquency. *Journal of Research in Crime and Delinquency, 14,* 35-67.

Conditional Release in Canada

10

Tracey Cyca & Tim Williams

Learning Objectives

After reading this chapter, you should be able to:

- Understand the history and purpose of conditional release and be able to compare it to how it is currently practiced.

- Describe the different types of conditional release and their success rates.

- Understand the division of responsibilities between the Parole Board of Canada and the Correctional Service of Canada.

- Understand the process and criteria used to grant conditional release.

- Describe the nature and purpose of risk assessment in the conditional release process.

- Explain the role of a parole officer in managing an offender's risk.

INTRODUCTION

The clear majority of offenders who receive a sentence of incarceration in Canada are released from prison before the end of their sentences with specific conditions to follow; this is known as **conditional release**. Parole is one type of conditional release, but there are several other types. The purpose of conditional release is to provide a transition period after incarceration during which offenders can be supervised and assisted to improve their chances of success, reduce the danger to the community, and minimize the negative effects of incarceration. If offenders fail to follow their conditions of release, they can be sent back to prison for the protection of society, without having committed a new offence. Conditional release also serves as an incentive to offenders to maintain good behaviour while incarcerated and to participate in correctional programs addressing the root causes of their criminal behaviour. An offender on conditional release is supervised by a parole officer until the **warrant expiry date** – that is, until the last day of their sentence as it was imposed by the courts.

This chapter will provide an overview of conditional release in Canada. It will *not* address the various temporary absence programs or systems of earned remission that are used within provincial and territorial jurisdictions throughout Canada to release offenders from provincial prisons.[1] Rather, this chapter will focus on federal conditional release, as it is implemented across Canada through a network of federal penitentiaries, parole offices, and parole board offices. The chapter will describe the origin and the evolution of federal conditional release, the different types of release, the dynamics of the decision-making process, and the detailed assessments that go into each case.

A HISTORY OF CONDITIONAL RELEASE

The origins of prisoner release programs date back to Victorian times. In French, the word *parol* means "word of honour" and was originally used to describe prisoners of war promising not to resume battle if released. In a similar way, parole allowed prisoners to be released (or paroled) if they gave their word that they would behave (USLegal, 2016).

In 1840, a British Naval Officer by the name of Alexander Maconochie, sailed to Van Dieman's Island (now Tasmania) to study their prison system. As a penal reformer, he found the treatment of the prisoners inhumane. A deeply religious man, he believed people could be reformed. He brought these beliefs to Norfolk Island Prison, off the coast of Australia, where he implemented the "marks system." Under this system, inmates could earn "marks" for hard work and good behaviour and use them in exchange for incentives such as food, cigarettes, and even early release (Morris, 2002). In 1854, Sir Walter Crofton built upon this philosophy of rehabilitation and successfully implemented a "marks" system at an Irish prison. His program was based on stages of progression and a belief that release should be earned through hard work and self-discipline (Barry, 1956; Carpenter & Crofton, 2010).

In the mid-nineteenth century United Kingdom, Ticket of Leave inmate release programs were being implemented. Canada's legal system was greatly influenced by that of the United Kingdom, and in 1899 the Canadian Parliament enacted the ***Ticket of Leave Act***. Prior to this, the only means of gaining an early release was to plead for a Royal Prerogative of Mercy (Daubney, 1988). These existed for centuries prior to the inception of parole and were petitions to the King or Queen for **clemency**. They were equivalent to pardons, served to shorten prison sentences, and were granted for humanitarian reasons or in order to mitigate unfair sentences. Royal Prerogatives of Mercy still exist today. The Parole Board of Canada considers them on behalf of the Governor General of Canada. They have always been and continue to be very rare.

Canada's *Ticket of Leave Act* (also known as *An Act to Provide for the Conditional Liberation of Convicts*) required parolees to inform police of their address, as well as any changes of address, to produce their certificate of release upon request, to abstain from further criminal activity, "to not habitually associate with notoriously bad characters" and finally "to not lead an idle and dissolute life without visible means of obtaining an honest livelihood" (Garson, 1956, p.143; Parole Board of Canada (PBC), 2018). The conditions placed on parolees today look remarkably similar but use an updated language (see Conditions on Release section). There was no mandatory supervision of offenders on tickets of leave; the legislation only required them to register with the police and to report regularly. The police were sceptical and suspicious about the early release of any offender and, at times, harassed parolees by placing unreasonable restrictions upon their movements or by advertising their status as prisoners (PBC, 2018).

Tickets of leave tended to be based on clemency or for pragmatic operational reasons, rather than as a transitional step used broadly to encourage rehabilitation. The legislation was intended for young and first-time offenders and was used to save money by releasing inmates rather than keeping them in prison (PBC, 2018). It was also used to alleviate some of the more extreme disparities in prison sentences, which created discontent among prison inmates, making prisons populations difficult to manage. In the first year of the Act, 71 people were granted tickets of leave (or licences). Fifty-nine were successful, 5 had their licence revoked for violating a condition, and another 7 committed a subsequent conviction (PBC, 2018). Even though it was initially considered an experiment, the Ticket of Leave program was viewed as a success, and it remained in place for 60 years.

The *Ticket of Leave Act* was subject to numerous inquiries and amendments. In 1913 the Remissions Branch was established within the Department of Justice and given responsibility for assessing all applications for clemency/parole. Decisions continued to have little to do with the idea of using parole to facilitate rehabilitation. Most releases continued to be granted for pragmatic purposes, humanitarian reasons, or as a reward for giving assistance to the Crown (PBC, 2018). Further, there was no across-the-board system of supervision by parole officers. Remissions officers only worked in Ottawa and sent representatives to visit prisons once a year to interview prospective parolees.

In 1936 the Archambault Commission studied the conditions of the prison system as well as parole. It criticized the Remission Service for being susceptible to political pressure and for failing to make parole a tool of reformation. The Commission also recommended the creation of an independent federal parole board. However, this report was shelved when WWII broke out, and all policy changes came to a halt. In 1956 the Fauteux Committee was appointed to examine the principles and procedures of the Remission Service. It reiterated many of the recommendations made in the Archambault report, noting that the ticket of leave system was still prone to political interference, and called for parole to be used as a tool to aid in rehabilitation. The committee suggested that parole is a "logical step in the reformation and rehabilitation of a person who is imprisoned" (PBC, 2018).

The government implemented many of the Fauteux Committee's recommendations. In 1959 Parliament enacted the *Parole Act* to replace the *Ticket of Leave Act*. As a result, the Remission Service was closed and the National Parole Board was created (now known as **Parole Board of Canada (PBC)**). The Parole Board was created in the form of a strong, separate entity known as an **administrative tribunal** and given full jurisdiction over conditional release decisions. In this way, the PBC operates at an arm's length from government, and its decisions are less susceptible to political pressure. Such independence allows the Board to look at the big picture and makes conditional release "more than just a way to get inmates to behave themselves in the institution" (PBC, 2018).

In 1969 the Ouimet Report came out with additional recommendations for change. Despite strong criticism of parole at the time, Ouimet upheld the notion of parole as a treatment-oriented correctional measure, and his report called for the increased use of community-based corrections and less reliance upon incarceration. Ouimet pointed out that the lowest-risk offenders were earning parole, but that the highest-risk offenders were forgoing parole applications and choosing, instead, to await their "earned remission dates" (which was awarded to inmates for merely complying with institutional rules). After spending more time in jail, these higher risk offenders were being released free and clear of any supervision. Ouimet therefore recommended community supervision, even for offenders who don't receive parole (i.e., "mandatory supervision"). The report also recommended a decentralization of Board members so that all parole candidates could have face-to-face hearings, and that federal/provincial jurisdiction would be clarified (Daubney, 1988). It further recommended an increase in the number of Board members and suggested that the department within the Parole Board responsible for case preparation and supervision (the National Parole Service) be merged with the Penitentiary Service, thereby making the National Parole Board more independent (PBC, 2018).

Both of Ouimet's key suggestions were implemented. In 1970, **Mandatory Supervision** (the precursor to today's **Statutory Release**) was introduced in Canada. Inmates with good behaviour no longer earned "time off" their sentences, only the right to serve their remission time in the community (Hamilton & Sinclair, 1991). In 1977, the National Parole Service and the Penitentiary Service combined to form the **Correctional Service of Canada (CSC)**, thereby uniting the community and the institutional sides of correctional operations within a single government agency and removing the Parole Board from correctional operations completely, making it a more fully independent decision-making body (PBC, 2018).

Additional changes were made to decision-making processes over the next three decades. In the 1970s, Board members were required to start providing written documentation outlining the rationale behind each of their decisions and offenders started being automatically scheduled for hearings at their parole eligibility dates (Speck, 2009). Capital punishment was abolished in 1976, and as a result, the Royal Prerogative of Mercy was transferred to the Parole Board of Canada. In 1982, the *Charter of Rights and Freedoms* was introduced which necessitated the development of more policies and procedural safeguards to ensure that the newly enshrined rights of offenders were being respected. Over time, victims' rights were expanded, and victims started being provided with more information, such as the parole eligibility dates of the person who had harmed them. Decision making policies were amended to become more transparent and to incorporate evidence-based information on risk and rehabilitation. In 1992, the *Corrections and Conditional Release Act (CCRA)* replaced both the *Parole Act* and the *Penitentiary Act* (PBC, 2018).

THE PURPOSE OF CONDITIONAL RELEASE

The *CCRA* contains three main themes: public safety and reintegration; openness and accountability; and procedural fairness. To protect public safety, the act emphasizes the use of risk assessment tools, especially for violent offenders. It also outlines the Board's role, the need for timely information, and the requirement that correctional staff take all necessary steps to obtain as much relevant information as possible to give to Board members. Release programs and eligibility dates are also outlined in the act (PBC, 2018). To address transparency, the *CCRA* formally recognizes the role of victims, allows the public to attend parole hearings, and allows for written copies of Board decisions to be obtained upon request (PBC, 2018). Finally, this Act "legislated statements of purpose and principles [which are] perceived as critical for fairness and equity" (PBC, 2018). The purpose of the *CCRA* is to "contribute to the maintenance of a just, peaceful and safe society by means of decisions on the timing and conditions of release that will best facilitate the rehabilitation of offenders and their reintegration into the community as law-abiding citizens" (*CCRA*, 1992, Sec. 100).

THE SPLIT IN JURISDICTION IN CANADIAN CORRECTIONS

In Canada, offenders who receive custodial sentences of two years or more, fall under the jurisdiction of the federal government (see Chapter 2). Offenders sentenced to a period of incarceration that is less than two years, fall under the jurisdiction of a provincial/territorial government and are incarcerated in institutions operated by provincial/territorial correctional authorities. This division of responsibility is known as the **two-year rule**. Despite the split, however, the Parole Board of Canada has the authority to release *both* federal and provincial/territorial inmates on federal conditional release, with two exceptions. Ontario and Quebec have their own provincial parole boards, that make conditional release decisions in relation to the provincial inmates within their provinces. These provincial boards are also authorized under the *CCRA* and therefore operate under the same parameters and guidelines as the Parole Board of Canada.

The split in jurisdiction is not absolute; the two levels occasionally overlap. For instance, some offenders who receive federal sentences (of two years or more) reside in parts of Canada without a nearby federal penitentiary. To accommodate such cases, the federal and provincial/territorial governments sometimes sign **Exchange of Services Agreements (ESA)**. These agreements allow federal offenders to serve all or part of their sentences in a provincial/territorial institution that is closer to their home communities. For instance, the North Slave Correctional Complex in Yellowknife, NWT, incarcerates federal offenders alongside its territorial inmates, under an ESA agreement. Another example of jurisdictional overlap occurs when provincial/territorial offenders receive federal conditional release. Overall, though, federal conditional release is not a popular option amongst provincial/territorial inmates. Of the 84,543 prisoners who served sentences in provincial jails in 2016/17, the Parole Board of Canada reviewed only 652 cases (see Malakieh, 2018, Table 4; Parole Board of Canada, 2016-2017, p. 21). This is because federal parole has the effect of lengthening provincial sentences. Inmates in provincial/territorial institutions continue to have the ability to earn remission based on their positive behaviour while incarcerated. These remission days are subtracted from the offender's sentence, meaning that offenders can gain an early release, free of any supervision. If they are granted parole, however, they are supervised by a federal parole officer until the original warrant expiry date, as imposed by the courts (see John Howard Society of Ontario, 2004).

TYPES OF CONDITIONAL RELEASE AND ELIGIBILITY DATES

There are four types of conditional release in Canada: temporary absences, day parole, full parole, and statutory release. Their purpose it to provide offenders with the opportunity to experience gradual release. This gives them a chance to slowly reintegrate into society as law-abiding citizens, while still having the supervision and support of corrections professionals. The four type of conditional release are graduated, each one providing progressively greater freedom and responsibilities and progressively greater contact with their outside supports in the community.

Temporary absences, day parole and full parole are *privileged* forms of conditional release. Each type of release is assigned an **eligibility date**, after which an offender becomes eligible for release. But none of these types of release are guaranteed. *If* a release is approved, the offender has an opportunity to take the next step in the reintegration process. The sentence is not shortened; the offender serves the full remainder of his or her sentence under supervision in the community. This allows for a gradual release process, helping offenders make the difficult transition from institutional confinement to living independently in the community. Statutory release, on the other hand, is not a privileged form of release.

As soon as a **warrant of committal** has been issued by the courts, an offender's sentence begins and the eligibility dates for the different types of conditional release are calculated (see Table 10.1).

Table 10.1 – Time Line of Federal Determinate Sentence and Conditional Release Eligibility Dates					
Warrant of Committal	**Unescorted Temporary Absences**	**Day Parole**	**Full Parole**	**Statutory Release**	**Warrant Expiry Date**
Sentence Begins	1/6 of sentence or 6 months (whichever is less)	6 months before 1/3 of sentence	1/3 of sentence or 7 years (whichever is less)	2/3 of sentence	Sentence Ends

These dates are calculated differently for offenders serving **determinate sentences** than for offenders serving **indeterminate sentences** (see Special Cases section).

Temporary Absences

During a temporary absence, the offender is temporarily released from the institution for a short period of time. Offenders are eligible for **Escorted Temporary Absences** (ETAs) as soon as they are admitted to an institution, and these can be granted at any time throughout the sentence. Most offenders are eligible for **Unescorted Temporary Absences** (UTAs) at one-sixth or 6 months of their sentence, whichever is later (Public Safety and Emergency Preparedness Canada, 2005). Offenders serving a life sentence or indeterminate sentence become eligible for UTAs 3 years prior to their full parole eligibility date. Inmates classified as maximum security are not eligible for UTAs.

ETAs require that the offender be supervised by a CSC staff member or an approved escort, and it is possible for more than one inmate at a time to be escorted. UTAs do not require any form of escort; however, the offender is sometimes required to report to a police station or parole office. The responsibility for granting UTAs is dependent on the type of sentence the offender is serving and the purpose of the release. Institutional heads (e.g., wardens) within CSC have the authority to grant UTAs for medical purposes and for sentences where death or serious harm did not occur. The PBC grants UTAs for life sentences, indeterminate sentences, Schedule I offences resulting in death or serious harm, and sentences for sexual offences involving a child (CSC, 2010)

ETAs and UTAs can be approved for medical, administrative, or compassionate reasons, as well as for family contact, personal development, community service, or parental responsibilities. The length of a TA is determined by its type and purpose (CSC, 2010). For example, an offender *may* be granted a UTA for compassionate reasons for up to 72 hours to attend a funeral. Another offender may be granted a UTA for personal development to attend a substance abuse clinic for up to 60 consecutive days. It is important to remember that not all releases are granted. They are dependent on an offender's security level, institutional performance, and the rationale for the temporary absence.

Work release is a special type of temporary absence. It allows inmates to leave the institution each day to work or volunteer in the community, under the supervision of an authorized person or organization. Work releases can be up to 60 days long, and inmates become eligible for them at the same time as they become eligible for UTAs. Any wages paid by employers during a work release are deposited directly into the offender's institutional savings account. There are strict restrictions upon how inmates can access and spend such monies; therefore, most of it usually remains unspent until the offender is granted conditional release. Given that offenders earn less than $10.00 per day working inside federal institutions, a paid 60-day, work release can be a huge asset for those who are hoping to establish their own residence in the community upon release.

Day Parole

Day parole is a form of conditional release where the inmate can leave the facility for the day, but must return each night to an institution or, more typically, some type of halfway house. Day parolees are subject to close supervision involving curfews, sign-in/sign-out procedures, head counts, and room searches. Day parolees also receive a great deal of support and assistance. Food is either provided or paid for, and rent, if charged at all, is typically based on an offender's ability to pay. Halfway houses that are operated by CSC directly are known as **Community Correctional Centres** (CCCs). Halfway houses that are operated under contract with CSC by **not-for-profit agencies** are known as: **Community-Based Residential Facilities** (CBRFs). And facilities operated under contract by First Nations communities are known as **Section 81 Healing Lodges**. The latter are unique in that they house serving inmates alongside conditionally released offenders, within the same facility.

An inmate serving a determinate sentence is eligible to apply for day parole 6 months prior to their full parole eligibility date. Offenders serving a life sentence or indeterminate sentence are eligible for day parole 3 years prior to their full parole eligibility date. The PBC has the discretion to grant day parole, and the offender is required to abide by specific conditions. Day parole can be used for an inmate to work, go to school, complete community service, or conduct familial responsibilities at home.

Full Parole

Full parole is like day parole in that the offender is required to follow conditions upon release. It is different in that offenders typically reside in their own private residence not a correctional facility. Offenders are normally eligible to apply for full parole after serving one third of their sentences. In certain cases, judges can set the period of parole eligibility. This is called **judicial determination**, and it is occassionally used for **Schedule I and II offences** (more serious). It allows a judge to set the full parole eligibility at one half of the sentence, or 10 years (whichever is later) (see Sec. 743.6 of the *Criminal* Code, 1985). The courts also set the full parole eligibility date at the time of sentencing for offenders serving indeterminate or life sentences.

Statutory Release

Statutory release (SR) is different from the above types of conditional release in that it is not dependent on the offender's involvement in rehabilitation programs or pre-release planning. That is, it is not a privileged release. The law states that the inmate *must* be released after serving two-thirds of their sentence. This is an alternate means of reintegrating the offender. When offenders do not receive day or full parole, they will still benefit from a period of supervision as they make the transition from the institution back into the community. Like the other types of release, the offender must still abide by specific conditions until their warrant expiry date. Offenders serving an indeterminate sentence, and those serving sentences for first and second-degree murder are not eligible for statutory release. These types of sentences do not have a warrant expiry date. Given that these offenders remain under sentence until the day they die, a statutory release date would be impossible to calculate.

The controversial aspect of statutory release is that offenders who reach their SR date often have performed marginally well in the institution, might have already been denied full parole or have had their granted conditional release revoked. The Parole Board of Canada often gets blamed if there are re-offences; however, these individuals were released by statute, not based on a Board decision, so the release is not attributable to a poor release decision. There have been some recommendations put forth calling for statutory release to be changed (Newark, 2011; Canadian Resource Centre for Victims of Crime, 2011). In *A Roadmap to Strengthening Public Safety*, Sampson et. al. (2007) suggest that statutory release be abolished in favour of *earned parole* – the premise being that release should be a privilege to be earned, not something dictated by a statutory schedule. But without statutory release, we would be faced with the prospect of the highest risk offenders being released at the very end of their sentences with virtually no supervision or support.

> Statutory release is like the mandatory requirement to wear seatbelts. We don't know who will be in an accident, but we do know that if everyone wears a seatbelt, lives will be saved, and injuries will be avoided. Similarly, we don't know who might reoffend, but we do know that we will have fewer crimes, and, most importantly, fewer victims. (Stewart, 2008)

Special Circumstances

Even though statutory release does not require a decision by the PBC, the Board does have the authority to impose certain restrictions. There are three special circumstances that provide alternatives to regular statutory release.

Statutory Release with Residency

In exceptional circumstances, the Board can impose a **residency condition** on the offender. That is, the offender will be released at his or her SR date, but will be required to live at a "community-based residential facility or in a psychiatric facility" (*CCRA*, 1992, p.79). This condition may remain until an offender's warrant expiry date. A residency condition is considered an "exceptional provision" and is only imposed when "in the absence of such a condition, the offender will present an undue risk to society by committing an offence listed in Schedule I before the sentence expiry" (NPB, 2011, p. 61). The CSC normally makes the referral to impose this condition; however, the Board can impose residency without a referral. The number of residency conditions imposed on statutory releases has steadily been increasing (PBC, 2010-11).

Detention

Another option available to the Board is to order the **detention** of the offender past their SR date (sometimes until the warrant expiry date). In other words, the offender is to remain in custody at an institution. This can only occur if the offender is serving a Schedule I or II offence of two years or more. Also, there must be reasonable grounds to believe the offender is "likely to commit an offence causing death or serious harm to another person, a sexual offence involving a child, or a serious drug offence" (*CCRA*, 1992, p.68) before the end of their sentence. This option requires that the offender's case be reviewed annually to determine if detention is still necessary.

One-Chance Statutory Release

For those offenders who have already been detained, the option of **one-chance statutory release** exists. Upon their annual review, the Board may grant SR. However, if the offender breaches any condi-

Box 10.1 – Interview with Day Parole Client

1. Describe the application process that you went through.

I had to request day and full parole myself. The intake parole officer at the institution I was in, said to waive parole for a later date, so I turned to other inmates for the help that I needed.

2. Describe your first day at the halfway house. What were some thoughts and feelings that you had?

The first I was at a different halfway house. I felt stressed and it was hard to get situated. It took some time before I was able to leave right away, so that it didn't feel like I was being trapped at the halfway house. So, for a short time, I wanted to go back to the institution. At the new halfway house, where I'm at now, I felt it was easier to get situated, and I also found the staff to be a little easier to work with.

3. Which is harder: being an inmate or a day parolee?

It depends on the halfway house I'm at and whether my Parole Officer and the staff that work at the house are willing to work with you. When they work with you, they either give you the freedom you want and need, or they'll find a way to work with you on whatever it is you need. When they work against you, it's just the opposite.

4. Tell me about the supports you receive at the halfway house.

At my new halfway house, they seem to want to be a good support and to work with me and to rehabilitate. At the previous house, I didn't seem to get much help. Mostly, I felt like I was on my own most of the time. At my current house, they provide those who need help with the things they need manage their time on the outside, like finding work and giving them bus tickets.

5. Describe your relationship with the staff of the halfway house.

My relations to the staff at this halfway house, for the most part, are pretty good. They want to work with and be supportive of you, rather than work against you.

6. Has living at the halfway house taught you some new life skills?

For the most part, no. I had life skills before, during, and will have them after I will leave this halfway house. But I do believe, for others, there can be life skills they can learn.

7. How does the day to day safety of the halfway house compare to the institution? Where did you feel more secure?

Yes, as of now, I feel more safe at the house than in the institution.

8. What would you change about the way halfway houses operate in Canada?

I don't really know, because it's my first and last time I will be going through all of this. But have come to notice that some places make you do more than you have to, which, in the long run can make it hard for you to rehabilitate or do the things you have to do to change, or stay out, or do well on the streets.

9. What's next for you?

What's next for me is to keep working in town until my warrant [expiry date], to go back to working the trade, and to be there for my loved ones, now and at/after warrant [expiry date] – to start my dreams with my girlfriend, soon-to-be wife, and to make a foundation – one where we can both be happy and make a future out of it. But, until then, I will just go step by step with her and myself and make the best of what we already have.

tion of their release and the Board subsequently revokes this release, the offender *must* serve the remainder of their sentence institutionally. As the name implies, the offender has one chance.

SPECIAL CASES AND THEIR CONDITIONAL RELEASE ELIGIBILITY DATES

Most offenders are serving determinate sentences (see Chapter 3). There are three types of cases that are exceptions to this rule: indeterminate sentences, life sentences and long-term offenders.

Indeterminate vs. Life Sentences

In 2016, offenders with a **life** or **indeterminate sentence** made up 23% of the inmate population (PSC, 2017). Indeterminate and life sentences are similar in that there is no statutory release date and no warrant expiry date, and either type may result in incarceration for life. However, they are different in how they are handed down. A life sentence is a sentence of life imprisonment given by a judge at the time of sentencing (e.g., for murder). An indeterminate sentence is a result of a designation that is given to an offender convicted of an offence that is ineligible for a life sentence. At the time of sentencing, the Crown can apply to the court to declare such an offender as a **Dangerous Offender** (DO). If the application is approved, the offender is given a sentence of imprisonment for an indeterminate length of time. A life sentence is a result of the type of offence committed, and an indeterminate sentence is a result of a special designation by the courts for offenders with a pattern of repeated and brutal violence.

Dangerous offenders are eligible for day parole at 4 years and full parole at 7 years; and the PBC must review the case every 2 years after that. Dangerous offenders who earn conditional release are subject to the same set of standard conditions as other offenders, as well as any special conditions that the PBC applies. As of Dec 31, 2016, there were 681 offenders with a special designation of DO (PSC, 2017). A life sentence in Canada is literally a life sentence. Many people believe that offenders serving life sentences are released after serving this court specified amount of time. In fact, they only become *eligible* for parole when they reach their eligibility dates; release is never guaranteed. If these offenders are in fact granted release, they will be supervised for the rest of their lives, and they can have their conditional release revoked even after they have been living in the community successfully for decades.

An interesting piece of legislation is the **judicial review** of parole eligibility. Section 745.6 of the *Criminal Code* was also known as the "faint hope clause." This piece of legislation was brought into effect in 1976 when the death penalty was abolished. It provided offenders serving a sentence with a parole eligibility of more than 15 years a sense of hope. Over the years, there were a total of 218 faint hope court decisions. Of these, 76% resulted in a reduction in the period of parole ineligibility (PSC, 2017). On Dec. 2, 2011, Canadian parliament passed Bill S-6, *An Act to amend the Criminal Code and another Act*. This legislation repealed the faint hope clause. Bill S-6 was very controversial, based, in part, upon media reports citing an internal study by Justice Canada that supported the Faint Hope Clause but was never released and therefore did not inform debate about the bill in parliament (Bebby, 2011).

Long-Term Offenders

In 1997, the *Criminal Code* was amended to include the long-term offender designation (CSC, 2013). A **Long-Term Supervision Order** (LTSO) is an option available to the courts to extend the period that an offender receives support and supervision from CSC. This designation is given to offenders who pose a significant risk to re-offend. These are typically sexual offences (64.5%), but other offences such as kidnapping, attempted murder and assault with a weapon are also eligible (PSC, 2017).

An LTSO is a period of community supervision that begins after the sentence is complete and cannot exceed 10 years. The majority (70.7%) of LTSOs are set for the maximum length of time, 10 years. This is intended to provide improved public safety, while avoiding the designation of DO and the accompanying indeterminate sentence.

Offenders being supervised under an LTSO designation are subject to the same standard conditions, as well as any special conditions assigned by the PBC. However, *unlike* other conditional releases, the PBC does not have the authority to revoke the order. They can recommend to the court that the offender be charged with a breach. If the offender is found guilty, in court, they can be handed a sentence of up to 10 years in prison (PBC, 2018).

THE ROLE AND DECISION-MAKING STRUCTURE OF THE PAROLE BOARD OF CANADA

Parole Officers working for Correctional Services of Canada write detailed reports containing specific recommendations about release, such as: whether conditional release should be granted, whether and what type of special conditions should be imposed to help manage an offender's level of risk in the community, and whether offenders should have their releases withdrawn. These are only recommendations, however, and the actual decision-making authority belongs to the PBC. This separation of responsibilities is an intentional feature of Canada's system of conditional release (see History of Conditional Release section). The creation of the Parole Board as a truly independent administrative tribunal made Canada's system of conditional release much more complex and administratively cumbersome, but it also embedded fundamental principles of justice into a decision making-process that has profound implications for offenders' freedom and liberty. Board members are required to make their decisions with the protection of the community as their paramount consideration, but also with compassion and fairness and with the recognition that offenders have the potential to achieve positive change (PBC, 2018).

The system has not been without its critics, however, and it has evolved a great deal since 1959. Parole Board positions are **Governor in Council (GIC) appointments**. This means that the Minister of Public Safety and Emergency Preparedness provides Cabinet with the names of specific individuals whom he/she recommends for appointment/reappointment to the PBC. Once approved by Cabinet, these individuals are formally appointed by the Governor General of Canada. It is an old-fashioned way of filling positions of power in society, and its critics have labelled it as a form of political patronage (Stilborn, 1989). Some critics suggest that Parole Board members should be hired based on merit alone and should be legally required to have expertise and competence in relation to the law, criminal justice, and risk assessment (Paparozzi & Guy, 2009). However, Canadian governments have made many changes over the years intended to transition GIC appointments away from patronage and towards a merit-based system (Scratch, 2006; Canada, 2016). Today's GIC appointments are made using a competitive process that specifies explicit competencies for candidates. Vacancies are advertised on a government website (http://www.appointments-nominations.gc.ca/) that stipulates the formal requirements of the position and provides a selection process that is open to any Canadian who might be interested and have the required qualifications.

The Review Process for Parole Decisions

Most offenders will require multiple decisions from the PBC over the course of their sentences. More serious categories of offenders (e.g., those on life sentences, or with extreme patterns of extreme violence) require a decision from the Parole Board to receive Temporary Absences from an institution. These same offenders may later apply to the Parole Board for day parole, then full parole, then perhaps for the removal or the revision of a special condition of release. If the Parole Board denies an offender parole, the offender can later reapply, or the Parole Board may decide to impose special conditions during statutory release or about detaining an offender until the end of the sentence. Even after an offender has been granted conditional release, the Parole Board will make the decision about whether to revoke that release any time the offender breaches a standard/special condition or is experiencing an increased level of risk to reoffend. Thus, the PBC functions as much more than a gatekeeper that decides who gets out of prison early. It is more like an absent yet omnipresent force hovering over an offender's case from as early as the 1/6-point in the sentence until as late as the last day of the sentence.

Any Parole Board decision made over the course of an offender's sentence is an extremely involved process, drawing upon the work of multiple individuals. Each time a member of an offender's **Case Management Team** (i.e., parole officer, program facilitator, correctional officer, psychologist/ psychiatrist, Aboriginal Liaison, etc.) writes/updates a plan, profile, or assessment, a copy of the document is shared with the PBC for its files. Added to these are official records such as: police reports, criminal records, victim impact statements, and court sentencing transcripts/presentence reports. So even before a decision has been requested, the PBC has already accumulated a substantial file in relation to an offender's case.

At the time of the decision, the Board receives a new raft of reports, which can include documents such as: Community Assessment(s); Correctional Plan Update(s); Assessment(s) for Decision; Psychological Risk Assessment(s); Psychiatric Assessment(s); letter(s) of support; security classification/ transfer document(s); and Correctional Program Report(s). For recidivists, the Parole Board will also review any archived file information prior to making its decision. Until recently, all reports were provided to the PBC in paper form. In 2014 the Board started transitioning from paper to electronic offender files, and they have now eliminated paper documents altogether. Rather than "share printing" new reports to remote PBC printers, the Correctional Service of Canada now E-shares information with the Board. This means that Board members are no longer required to spend hours in their offices pouring over paper files. They can review cases in the comfort of their own homes, if they so choose.

Before Parole Board members make their decision, a **case review officer** audits the offender file to ensure that all the required documents have been shared with both the Board and with the offender. This is necessary to ensure that offenders are aware of the information being used by the Board, so that they can speak to it in an informed manner. For recidivists with multiple volumes of archived files that predate formal sharing of information documentation procedures, the process of information-sharing can be time consuming and burdensome for both the Correctional Service of Canada and for the Parole Board. Once all this preparatory work has been completed and the file is ready, decisions are sometimes made based solely on a review of the written information that has been shared. In fact, when the Board initially commenced its work in 1959 these "paper decisions" were the only way the Board operated. Since 1969, however, the Parole Board has been conducting face-to-face parole hearings for major decisions.

The Parole Hearing Process

Hearings normally take place at the institution where the offender is incarcerated, or at parole offices, halfway houses, or healing lodges for offenders who have already earned release and are seeking additional freedoms. They are administered by a **hearing officer** who ensures that the offender is aware of his/her rights. The hearing officer also introduces everyone present, enters the decision into the Integrated Decision System (IDS), records the hearing, and escorts people in and out of the hearing room. Hearing officers also help Board members make their decisions by reviewing offender files prior to hearings and providing their insights regarding risk factors and any omissions or inconsistencies in the file.

There can be a surprisingly large number of people in the room at a parole hearing. In addition to the Hearing Officer, there are 1 to 3 Board members (depending on the category of the offence and the type of decision). Offenders are entitled to bring a community support (such as a husband, wife, pastor, or lawyer) to assist them. The offender's parole officer attends to answer questions and speak to the overall factors in the case. Victims are entitled to attend; they can simply observe or can choose to read their Victim's Statement. Victims are accompanied by a **regional communications officer** and sometimes by another support person of their own choosing. Police officers, the media, and members of the public can also attend hearings as observers but must apply to do so in advance. If the hearing is taking place in an institution, a Correctional Officer also attends to maintain security.

Commencing in 2008 the PBC started using video conferencing technology to conduct some of their hearings remotely. Much like the transition to electronic files, video conferencing has improved the working conditions for Board members and staff. They used to be on the road, up to 3 days per week, visiting far-flung institutions in their region, and frequently staying overnight in hotels. Traditional face-to-face hearings continue to occur for complex cases, but for more straightforward cases, Board members and staff can now conduct their hearings from the comfort of their offices. Observers also attend video conferenced hearings at the Parole Board offices. The downside of this type of hearing is the lack of face-to-face human contact and the possibility that many of the non-verbal cues in the room are missed.

Once all these preparations have been made, the case has been reviewed, and the offender has been given a chance to address the Board, it is time for the Board members to make their decision. If this decision is being made at a face-to-face hearing, everyone except for the hearing officer and the Board members leaves the hearing room, allowing the Board members to deliberate, to vote independently, and to reach their final decision. After the decision has been made, everyone reassembles to hear the Board's decision. Shortly after the final decision has been rendered (often within a matter of hours), the offender is provided with the reasons for the decision in writing (via the parole officer). These decisions are public documents and can be provided to members of the media or the public upon request.

Elder-Assisting Hearings

Parole board hearings have traditionally been laid out and organized in a way that resembles a judicial proceeding in court. Board members sit at one side of a board room table, and the offender, assistant, and parole officer sit on the opposite side of the table and speak when spoken to. The hearing assistant usually sits in between the two sides, at the end of the table. A correctional officer may stand, and everyone else sits at the back of the room and observes. Beginning in 1992, the PBC started conducting **Elder-assisted hearings** (Turnbull, 2014). These hearings are laid out much differently, with participants sitting in a circle, and draw upon the knowledge and presence of an Elder or cultural advisor. At the beginning and/or end of the hearing, the Elder will conduct a cultural ceremony such as a prayer or smudge if the offender has requested this. The Elder is also available to answer any questions the Board members might have about cultural or spiritual matters but has no decision-making authority (PBC, 2018B). Some hearings also include the passing of a sacred cultural object (such as an eagle feather) around the circle; this enables each participant to be heard and to speak openly. These hearings are not intended to be any less rigorous than a traditional parole hearing but, rather, are intended as a more culturally supportive hearing process for Indigenous offenders or offenders who have committed themselves to following an Indigenous way of life.

Decision Making Criteria for Conditional Release

Board members have a great deal of independence and broad discretion when reaching their decisions, but they are also bound by legislation. Section 100 of the *CCRA* states that conditional release must balance the protection of society with facilitating the rehabilitation and reintegration of offenders into the community. At times, however, these two purposes conflict. Board members face a dilemma when they encounter a case where a conditional release would clearly benefit an offender's rehabilitation and reintegration, but specific factors create concern about whether the release would pose an undue risk to the community. Section 100.1 resolves this dilemma by obligating the Board to prioritize protecting society over offender rehabilitation/reintegration. Conversely, Section 101c precludes Board members from playing it safe by arbitrarily denying release or imposing controls for reasons that are unrelated to community safety, rehabilitation, and reintegration. There are no sure bets or rigid criteria for Board members deciding whether to grant a conditional release. There is always a risk that a conditionally released offender may violate his/her conditions of release or even commit a new offence. At the end of the day, then, Board members must make a deeply discretionary decision about whether the potentially rehabilitative/reintegrative potential of a conditional release is outweighed by the offender's level of dangerousness to the community and risk to reoffend.

Managing Risk – The Role of a Parole Officer

Most parole officers in Canada are employed directly by the Correctional Service of Canada. CSC employs **institutional parole officers** who work inside federal institutions, initiating and leading the **case management process**, whereby offenders are assessed and classified (according to risk and need levels), provided with **Correctional Plans**, referred for **correctional interventions** (e.g., substance abuse treatment, cognitive behavioural group therapy), and ultimately either supported or denied support for conditional release. CSC also employs **community parole officers** to work in its parole offices and halfway houses, and sometimes in police stations, supervising, assessing, supporting, and managing offenders who have been granted conditional release. CSC also signs contracts with not-for-profit agencies such as the St. Leonard's Society, the Elizabeth Fry Society, the John Howard Society, and First Nations organizations to perform community parole supervision and/or to write community-related reports on its behalf. So, while most offenders on conditional release are supervised by a parole officer working for CSC, occasionally an offender is supervised by a contract parole supervisor, usually employed by a private, not-for-profit agency. In remote areas, though, contract parole supervisors are sometimes self-employed and sign a supervision or a report-writing contract with CSC directly.

The role of a parole officer (PO) is to "assess an offender's behaviour, accountability and potential risk to society" (CSC, 2013B). Parole officers supervise and manage their caseloads by maintaining regular contact with each offender. Much of this contact is made face to face. The frequency of contact on the community side is different for each offender and is dependent on the offender's risk factors. Meanwhile, a parole officer works with the offender to develop programming and treatment plans that address these risk factors. In addition to meeting with the offender, a PO manages the offender's risk by maintaining contact with the offender's family, employer, CSC program supervisors, police and anyone else who is in involved with the offender. These **collateral contacts** help to verify the offender's whereabouts, actions and behaviours, thus ensuring the risk level is manageable (CSC, 2008B).

If offenders in the community are not following their conditions this is considered a **breach of condition**. For example, if an offender has a condition to abstain from alcohol but comes to his parole meeting impaired, this would be a violation of his conditions and the parole officer would have to address this breach. It does not necessarily mean the release will be revoked. The parole officer must use his/her **discretion** to determine if the risk level is manageable. Before acting, the parole officer must take into consideration the unique characteristics of the offenders, their criminal history, as well as their recent behaviour while on release. In other words, responses to breaches are individualized to manage the offender's risk while protecting society.

Parole officers have several options available to them when an offender breaches a condition. If the PO assesses the risk as being low, he/she may decide to give the offender a warning, noting that there were exceptional circumstances and it is likely that the behaviour will not occur again. Any time a condition is violated, the PO must inform the Parole Board. If the PO assesses the risk level as being higher, he/she may choose to suspend the release. Again, this does not necessarily mean the release will be revoked. A **suspension** means the offender is placed in custody temporarily. During the period of suspension, the PO gathers information from the offender and collaterals to determine how serious the breach of conditions was. At this point, the PO has several options: a) cancel the suspension and release the offender from custody; b) refer the case to the PBC with a recommendation to change/add conditions; and c) refer the case to the PBC with a recommendation to revoke the release.

If the suspension is cancelled, the PO must still notify the PBC, indicate that the risk level is manageable, and identify what actions will be implemented to manage the risk level. Working with the offender, the parole officer will come up with new actions to manage and supervise the offender (see possible actions below). If the breach is in fact more serious and the risk is no longer manageable, the PO may recommend a change in conditions, or a **revocation** of the release. At this point, the final decision rests with the Parole Board. They may disagree with a revocation recommendation, reprimand the offender, and send him/her back on release in the community. Alternatively, they may agree with a revocation recommendation and choose to revoke the offender's release altogether. The PO must recommend the least restrictive measures. Incarceration is to be used as a last resort. The following are some possible actions that parole officers can take to manage a client's risk level (one or more of the above actions may be implemented at a time):

- Increase the frequency of contact with the offender
- Require the offender to submit regular urinalysis (this is only possible if the offender has a special condition to abstain from alcohol and drugs)
- Request the PBC to impose a special condition
- Impose an earlier curfew if the offender is residing in a community-based residential facility
- Refer the offender to an appropriate community correctional program (e.g. Substance abuse program)
- Refer the offender to psychological counselling
- Request the offender document high risk situations and develop a relapse prevention plan

If an offender's conditional release ends due to circumstances beyond their control (e.g., fatal illness), the PBC can also **terminate** the release. Essentially this means the offender returns to prison with no additional negative repercussions.

Risk Assessment

Institutional POs also complete actuarial risk assessments as part of the Offender Intake Assessment (OIA) process. These risk assessments are based on statistical probability, and they assist in categorizing the level of risk each offender poses, based on historical data gathered about offenders who have similar characteristics. Risk assessments are re-assessed by subsequent POs every 6 months or whenever a release decision is required, based on changes in the offender's behaviour and learning.

Assessments are conducted using computer-based tools that are part of CSC's online database called the Offender Management System (OMS). **Static risk factors** are based on historical or demographic characteristics of on offender's case that he/she *cannot* address through treatment or change, such as: age, criminal history, offence severity, and offence type. Based on these characteristics, the

Box 10.2 – Life as a Community Parole officer in the Correctional Service of Canada

Interview with Kelsey Uhl, on 2018-07-30. Ms. Uhl began her career with the Correctional Service of Canada (CSC) in 2007 as a summer student. From there, she earned a position as a parole supervisor at the Edmonton John Howard Society. In 2010, Ms. Uhl was hired as an institutional parole officer at the Edmonton Institution For Women, and 15 months later, she was redeployed to work at the Edmonton Area Parole Office in her current position.

1. What are the educational requirements to become a PO?

You need a bachelor's degree in the human sciences. I have a degree in criminology from Simon Fraser University. Throughout my university career, I also did some volunteering, at a halfway house, and then my last semester was a practicum.

2. What are the day to day duties of a PO?

Every day looks different. Some days I am out of the office, entirely, seeing offenders at their work sites, or their homes, or other locations, like a coffee shop or a halfway house. And some days, I plan as paperwork days, working on our required documentation and reports.

There are collateral contacts as well: keeping in touch with the offender's network, whatever that network looks like: their employer, their family, their friends, their spouses. The police are one of the best collaterals because they're one of the ones that aren't going to lie to me.

But the majority of my time is spent at the computer doing paperwork. We all get into this job for the face to face interactions with the offenders but that's really only 10-15% of my job.

There are also a lot of office meetings: meetings with your supervisor to keep them apprised of what is happening, meetings with the Mental Health Team, meetings with the Correctional Intervention Board. There are staff meetings regularly. We also attend parole board hearings by teleconference; for me, these are usually revocation hearings.

3. Describe what you like most about the job?

Hands down the thing I like most about the job is the flexibility. I can make my own schedule within the general guidelines of the office hours. Some of my colleagues work 7 to 3, some work 9 to 5, the office itself is open 8 to 4 – so whatever works for the individual, as long as we are getting our work done.

We also have the ability to work remotely on our laptops, so some days I love nothing more than working on reports or other paperwork from home in my sweatpants. I think having that option is a really positive thing for the wellbeing of staff. It's lovely, but it's also a double-edged sword because if you don't have good boundaries you can be firing up your laptop on evenings and weekends when you should be taking care of yourself.

4. Describe what you like least about the job?

I gave this one a lot of thought. Given the nature of the job there are any number of frustrations that you could potentially pick from – constant policy changes, difficult offenders, disturbing files, government "red tape." There are all kinds of things.

But the thing I have found most impactful in the past few years is the way this job sometimes changes your view of the world. When we're at work, we have to be constantly assessing the people around us, the area that we're in, all of the potential threats to our safety. And that's an important skill that we need in order to stay safe. But we get so good at doing this, that it becomes difficult to shut off. It becomes so automatic that you start to do

continued...

it in your non-work life. Over time, it can become less enjoyable to go out to the mall or a concert or a hockey game because you end up noticing that one person who is up to no good in a crowd of hundreds of perfectly lovely people, and your work brain starts assessing. I can't speak for all of my colleagues but for me there have been times when I've felt like I am just looking at the world as one big crime in progress. It's almost as though you end up having blinders on to the good stuff that happens in the world, and that can be exhausting and disheartening. It's a side effect of working in a high stress environment that is full of potential threats to yourself and others.

As a service, we have gotten much better at recognizing the impact of stress and vicarious trauma on our staff and encouraging self-care. I've done a lot of work on learning to separate my work and non-work lives and maintaining healthy boundaries in order to take care of myself. I have set some boundaries for myself that I find helpful, but may not work for everyone. So you have to make an active effort to look for the good in the world and to fill your non-work life with healthy things that fill your soul and with people who are uplifting to you.

5. Discuss the role of discretion in your position.

There are a lot of gray areas in this job. Even sometimes when you think there should be more black and white, every offender is different. The crimes themselves may have the same name, but the circumstances are entirely different or the motivations for a crime are entirely different. So you really have to treat each case as unique. Not all breaches need to be dealt with by a return to custody. If somebody incurs a new criminal charge, obviously, there's less discretion. But we have a great deal of discretion to deal with breaches, especially breaches of abstain conditions. Because we know that with addictions, people relapse, and that's part of the recovery process. There are a number of things we can implement before sending an offender back to jail – increase their reporting, increase urinalysis testing, add additional programs, we can ask the Parole Board to impose additional conditions, we can give them directions with regard to one of their conditions. It doesn't have to be a suspension. In all cases public safety is paramount. We need to be able to safely manage the risk to the public while balancing what might work best to address the breach.

6. Do you believe offenders on your caseload want to change?

Yes, I believe that the vast majority of them want to change. In my career, I can only think of a handful that I don't think wanted to change. They want to change and often times it's a matter of them not believing they can change, not having the support, not knowing how to change, not having the skills necessary to effect change – or learning the skills, trying them out, and giving up when the skills don't work perfectly the first time, so they get frustrated and give up.

7. Do you believe parole works?

I think it absolutely does. Statistically speaking all the research shows us that it does work. A gradual, structured, supervised release is much better for the longer-term success of offenders. We, in the community, say that that this is where the rubber meets the road. Offenders learn abstract or theoretical concepts through their programming in the institution, but the community is where they put their knowledge into practice. And we know that you have to practice something quite a bit in order to get good at it. Professional athletes have coaches who observe what they do and tell them what they can do differently, and how to improve. And I think it's the same with the parole officer and the Case Management Team; we expect mistakes along the way. We don't expect perfection. But then we need to talk about the mistakes and figure out, where did we go wrong? What can we do better next time? And I think that's a far better way to learn and a far better way to contribute to long term success.

offender's statistical probability of reoffending based on static factors is classified as high, medium, or low. **Dynamic risk factors** are individual characteristics or barriers that are statistically correlated with criminal behaviour. These risk factors *can* be addressed through intervention. Federal offenders' level of need is assessed in relation to seven dynamic factors: employment, marital/family, associates and social interaction, substance abuse, community functioning, personal and emotional orientation, and/or attitude. An overall rating of high, medium, or low is assigned based on the probability of reoffending based on these dynamic factors. A prioritized list of dynamic factors requiring specific intervention is also generated. These dynamic risk factors are assigned levels of "some need for improvement" or "considerable need for improvement." Dynamic risk factors *directly* related to the *current* offence are also assigned levels but are labelled as "contributing factors" and receive highest priority. In addition to these very general risk assessment tools, specialized assessments are conducted for specific categories of offenders, such as sex offenders, domestic violence perpetrators, or substance abusers.

Conditions on Release

Every offender on release is subject to a set of conditions. It doesn't matter what type of release he/she is given, the conditions must be followed. If the conditions are not followed, there are consequences. The parole officer has several options, including suspending the release and recommending to the Parole Board that they revoke the release. Regardless of the type of release, offenders are given a release certificate that they must always carry with them. This certificate outlines all the conditions they must follow. There are two types of conditions: standard conditions and special conditions.

Standard Conditions

These are the conditions that *every* offender on release must follow, regardless of type of release. They are very similar to the original ones in the *Ticket of Leave Act* of 1899, and they include:
- Report to your parole officer as directed
- Report any change in your family, domestic or financial situation
- Obey the law and keep the peace
- Carry and produce the release certificate if requested by a police officer or parole supervisor
- Report to the police if and as instructed by the parole supervisor
- Not to own or possess a weapon
- Always remain in Canada, and within the territorial boundaries fixed by the parole supervisor (CCRR, 2018, Sec. 161)

Special Conditions

Besides the above standard conditions, the PBC usually imposes additional conditions specific to each offender. Keeping in mind that the Board must consider the least restrictive measure, a **special condition** must be directly related to a contributing risk factor (see Chapter 9 for more on risk). Special conditions are used to aid in risk management, and each condition must be deemed "reasonable and necessary" to prevent the offender from returning to criminal activity (*CCRA*, 1992, p.79).

Depending on the offender and the individual circumstances surrounding the offence, there are a variety of special conditions that are possible. A special condition that is commonly added is to abstain from all drugs and alcohol. This is directly related to risk, as up to 80% of the federal offender population has substance abuse issues (Grant, Kunic, MacPherson, McKeown, & Hansen, 2003; Motiuk, Cousineau, & Gileno, 2005). Additional special conditions may include:

- Avoid children
- Avoid certain persons (specific names can be added)
- Follow a psychiatric treatment plan
- Take medication as prescribed
- Disclose all finances
- Submit to urinalysis testing as requested
- Reside at a specific location (e.g., Community-Based Residential Facility)
- Undergo psychological counselling
- Seek (or remain) employed (PBC, 2011).

The Board has the right to impose additional conditions or to remove conditions as it deems necessary and reasonable. If an offender violates a condition (standard or special) it is considered a sign that the level of risk to re-offend is increasing.

The Role of Victims in Conditional Release

Since the inception of the *CCRA* in 1992, victims have played a role in the conditional release process. More specifically, Section 2 of the *CCRA* outlines victims' rights and the integral role they play (*CCRA*, 1992). Once individuals register as victims, they are entitled to receive information from CSC. This includes the offender's name, the offence for which they were convicted, the start date and length of the sentence and all the conditional release eligibility and review dates (*CCRA*, 1992, p.14).

In 2012, Bill C-10, *The Safe Streets and Communities Act*, received royal assent. This piece of legislation gave victims the right to present a statement at PBC hearings. This **Victim Impact Statement** can be supplied in writing or via video, or it can be read out loud at a hearing. Victim impact statements give victims the opportunity to express how the crime has affected their lives, physically, emotionally, or financially. It also gives them an opportunity to express any concerns they have regarding their safety if the offender is released.

Bill C-10 also expanded the definition of victim. A victim is defined as someone "who has suffered physical or emotional harm, property damage, or economic loss as the result of the commission of the offence." (*CCRA*, 1992, p. 14). This definition now includes individuals who have custody of a victim's dependents. Finally, this piece of legislation broadened the amount of information that a victim is entitled to receive such as: the name of the institution where the offender resides, any disciplinary action taken against the offender while in custody, any programs the offender participated in, and reasons for transfers and temporary absences.

Most recently, the Canadian Victims' Bill of Rights (CVBR) was enacted (2015). This expanded the amount of information that victims are entitled to receive. Information regarding the offender's correctional plan, reviews, release dates and release destinations are now given to the victim, along with an updated photo of the offender. This Bill also legislats the process a victim can follow if they feel their rights have been violated (Minister of Justice, 2015).

Indigenous Canadians and Conditional Release

Research has demonstrated that there is an **over-representation** of Indigenous offenders in all areas of the Criminal Justice System (Calverley, 2010; LaPrairie, 2002). Conditional release is no exception. Since the landmark ruling of the Supreme Court in 1999 (*R.v. Gladue* – see Chapter 7) that stipulates an Indigenous offender's background must be taken into consideration (CC Sec. 718.2(e)), CSC has made several attempts to address the over-representation of offenders in the federal system, and the *CCRA* itself also been amended to address the issue. Along with the Aboriginal programming that has been introduced in the institutions, Sec. 81 of the *CCRA* outlines the process for building and running traditional healing lodges where offenders who are serving their sentence in the community can choose to reside. Further, Sec. 84 outlines the process for involving Aboriginal communities in release planning and supervision. The intent is to be able to provide the PBC with better information and planning specific to an Aboriginal offender so that they can make better release decisions. Finally, the PBC allows for Elder-assisted hearings that may include more Aboriginal practices.

Despite these changes, the statistics do not demonstrate any reduction in the over-representation (see Chapter 7 for further details). Over the ten-year period from 2006/7 – 2015/16, the grant rates for Indigenous offenders were lower than non-indigenous offenders for both day parole (66% vs. 70.1%) and full parole (17.3% vs. 26.4%) (PSC, 2017). Further, Indigenous offenders serve a higher proportion of their sentence before being released. On average, they serve 43.7% of their sentence before their first period of day parole supervision, compared to the 37.5% that non-indigenous offenders serve. This is true for full parole also (50.5% vs. 46%). Lastly, even though an Indigenous Cultural Advisor is available, only 40% of all federal hearings with Indigenous offenders were Elder assisted (PSC, 2017).

The Office of the Correctional Investigator conducted an assessment and produced the report, *Spirit Matters: Aboriginal People and the Corrections and Conditional Release Act* (2012). It outlined 10 recommendations that would improve the situation for Indigenous Canadians within Canada's correctional system. Recommendation #6 specifically addresses sec. 84. It indicates that "CSC should review the process for sec. 84 releases with the goal of significantly reducing the red tape and accelerating the process" (OCI, 2012).

In its recent Departmental Plan (2018-19), the Correctional Service of Canada and the Minister of Public Safety and Emergency Preparedness address the issue of correctional release plans. It indicates they will "support Indigenous offenders … [by] starting the release process as early in their sentences as possible using the newly launched Aboriginal Intervention Centres (located at 7 CSC institutions across the country)" (CSC, 2018).

Success and Failure Rates of Conditional Release in Canada

When Canadians are surveyed about their level of confidence in Canada's criminal justice system, they tend to express a great deal of confidence in the police, less confidence in the courts, low levels of confidence in the prison system, and the least confidence of all in the parole system (Roberts, 2005, p. 10-12). If Canadians were to examine the statistics, however, they might be surprised to learn that the clear majority of conditionally released offenders complete their releases without breaching their conditions or reoffending.

Temporary Absences

Between 2006 and 2016, 99% of escorted/unescorted temporary absences and 94% of work releases were completed successfully (Public Safety Canada, 2017, p. 101).

Day Parole, Full Parole, and Statutory Release

Between 2011 and 2016, the average successful completion rate was 89% for day parole, 85% for full parole, and 62% for statutory release. The percentage of successful releases also continues to improve over time. Whether we look at day parole, full parole, or statutory release, the percentage of offenders who have successfully finished their release has increased, almost every year, from 2011 to 2016. By the same token, the percentage of offenders whose parole has been revoked for breaches or new offences has dropped in all 3 categories, again, most years. Another clear and consistent trend is that, on average, day parole is more successful than full parole, and full parole is significantly more successful that statutory release (see Table 10.2).

One might be tempted to ask, "why not grant all offenders a period of day parole, given that it is more successful than other forms of release?" Such a suggestion, however, fails to consider the ques-

Table 10.2 – Successful Completion of Day Parole (DP), Full Parole (FP), and Statutory Release (SR)

Release Outcome	2011-12 (%)			2012-13 (%)			2013-14 (%)			2014-15 (%)			2015-16 (%)			Average (%)		
	DP	FP	SR	DP	FP	SR	DP	FP	SR	DP	FP	SR	DP	FP	SR	DP	FP	SR
Successful	87.7	78.6	61.3	88.6	85.0	60.0	89.3	85.0	61.5	90.5	87.0	63.2	91.1	87.6	63.1	89.4	84.6	61.8
Breached Conditions of Release	10.3	15.4	27.7	9.3	10.6	29.6	9.4	10.7	28.2	8.4	9.3	27.8	8.0	9.4	29.3	9.1	11.1	28.5
New Non-Violent Offence(s)	1.7	5.5	8.7	1.9	3.9	8.3	1.1	3.6	8.5	1.1	3.7	7.8	0.7	2.8	6.6	1.3	3.9	8.0
New Violent Offence(s)	0.3	0.5	2.3	0.2	0.6	2.1	0.2	0.7	1.8	0.0	0.0	1.2	0.2	0.2	0.9	0.2	0.4	1.7
Total	100	100	100	100	100	100	100	100	100	100	100	100	100	100	100	100	100	100

Source: Public Safety Canada, 2017, pp. 93-98

tion of causation. Are day parolees more successful because of their closely-supervised residential release, or do parolees who already have the best chances of success tend to apply for and receive day parole more often than higher risk offenders? Even though day parole has existed in Canada since 1969, we really don't know the answer to this question. One might similarly ask, "why not abolish statutory release, given that offenders who earn privileged forms of release, such as day or full parole, are so much more successful?" Once again, though, we can't assume that correlation equals causation. Yes, day/full parole release correlates positively with success, but is this correlation *caused* by the earlier, earned form of release? Or is the correlation caused by offenders who already have the best chances of success applying for and receiving parole, while those with poorer chances of success are choosing to "run down the clock" and wait for a statuary release? We really don't know, but we can't assume that all offenders would apply for parole if statutory release did not exist. Finally, it should be noted that the majority of statutory release cases succeed (60% - 63.2%), and even those who fail are mostly breaches or non-violent offences (6.6% - 8.7%).

ISSUES FOR THE FUTURE

Video Conferenced Parole Board Hearings – What are the implications of video conferenced hearings replacing at least some face-to-face parole hearings? Are offenders likely to receive a positive release decision when they are not in the same room as the decision maker? Do Board members have access to the same spectrum of information when observing hearing participants through a single camera lens? Is the technology being used of a sufficiently high calibre, given that individual freedom is at stake?

Section 84 has been in the *CCRA* since its inception. It is meant to encourage Aboriginal communities to be involved in the release process by proposing a plan for an inmate's release and integration into their community. However, Section 84 releases remain underutilized, poorly understood, and complex. Does Section 84 need to be rethought, revised, and retuned through legislative amendment, or are the problems more a matter of poor implementation and/or a lack of resources?

Aboriginal Intervention Centres – CSC is creating Aboriginal Intervention Centres (AIC), in each of its five regions. They are intended to speed up release planning and to increase the use of Section 84 releases. They will operate out of federal institutions. Is this the best means of engaging Indigenous communities in planning and participating in the release of Indigenous offenders? Or would a grass roots approach be more effective?

Earned vs. Automatic Release – As privileged forms of conditional release, day parole and full parole, tend to have stronger public support than statutory release which takes place automatically and places the onus on CSC and the PBC if it is to be denied via detention procedures. What are the characteristics of offenders who receive the latter type of release? What are the reasons they fail to earn parole?

CONCLUSION

Conditional release has a very long history in Canada but still evokes a great deal of public criticism. In its early days, conditional release was much less systematic, less graduated, and had much higher failure rates. Thanks to improvements such as better risk assessment tools, fairer decision-making processes, mandatory supervision of offenders, the detention of the highest risk cases, more release options, and targeted therapeutic intervention/supervision, today, the clear majority of conditionally released offenders successfully finish their sentences in the community. Nevertheless, releasing offenders prior to the end of their sentences always involves some element of risk to the community. It is an act of trust granted to someone who has publicly betrayed the trust of others in his or her past. Therefore, anytime a conditionally released offender commits a new crime, the release decision is easily criticized. As horrific and dramatic as these instances of reoffending might be, however, they don't change the big picture. On average, inmates who are given the opportunity to return to the community with support, structure, and supervision are more likely to achieve positive change and to succeed than those who are merely incarcerated and abruptly released. Conditional release can very successfully mitigate, but never eliminate, the inherent risk involved in returning offenders to the community.

KEY TERMS

Administrative Tribunal
Breach of Condition
Cabinet
Case Management Process
Case Management Team
Case Review Officer
Clemency
Collateral Contacts
Community Based Residential Facility
Community Correctional Centre
Community Parole Officer
Conditional Release
Correctional Interventions

Correctional Plan
Correctional Service of Canada
Corrections & Conditional Release Act
Dangerous Offender
Day Parole
Detention
Determinate Sentence
Discretion
Dynamic Risk Factors
Elder-assisted hearing
Eligibility Date
Escorted Temporary Absence
Exchange of Service Agreement

Elder-assisted hearing
Eligibility Date
Escorted Temporary Absence
Exchange of Service Agreement
Full Parole
Governor in Council Appointment
Hearing Officer
Indeterminate Sentence
Institutional Parole Officer
Judicial Determination
Judicial Review
Life Sentence
Long Term Supervision Order
Mandatory Supervision
Not for Profit Agency
One-Chance Statutory Release
Over-representation
Parole Board of Canada
Parole Hearing

Regional Communications Officer
Residency Condition
Revocation
Schedule I & II Offences
Section 81 Healing Lodge
Special Conditions
Standard Conditions
Static Risk Factors
Statutory Release
Suspension
Terminate
Ticket of Leave Act
Two-Year Rule
Unescorted Temporary Absence
Victim Impact Statement
Warrant Expiry Date
Warrant of Committal
Work Release

STUDY AND DISCUSSION QUESTIONS

1. Does conditional release contribute to public safety or diminish public safety?
2. Why do we need so many different types of conditional release? Are they equally relevant and necessary?
3. How does statutory release differ from other types of conditional release? Why does this type of release have the lowest success rate? Should it be abolished? Why?
4. Is statutory release with residency being used as an "exceptional provision" (as per the *CCRA*) given that the PBC is imposing residency more and more often? What might be some of the reasons be for this trend?
5. How can we effectively balance the rights and needs of offenders with the rights and needs of victims? Do you believe there is an imbalance? Provide an explanation for your answer.
6. What recommendations would you make to improve Canadians' understanding of conditional release?

HELPFUL WEBLINKS

- **Virtual Tour of a Hearing Room** at https://www.canada.ca/en/parole-board/services/parole/virtual-tour-of-a-hearing-room.html#a13
    This CSC webpage gives an outline of the view of a Parole Board Hearing. It shows all the different people involved and describes their role.
- **Spirit Matters: Aboriginal People and the Corrections and Conditional Release Act** at http://www.oci-bec.gc.ca/cnt/rpt/oth-aut/oth-aut20121022-eng.aspx
    This links directly to the report of the Office of the Correctional Investigator. It outlines his recommendations for dealing with the over-representation of Aboriginal People in the correctional system.

- **Department of Public Safety** report at https://www.publicsafety.gc.ca/cnt/rsrcs/pblctns/ccrso-2016/ccrso-2016-en.pdf
    This links directly to the report that contains a statistical overview of all corrections and conditional release statistics.
- **Correctional Service of Canada** website at http://www.csc-scc.gc.ca/victims/index-eng.shtml
    This link provides information relevant to victims of crime. It outlines the process for applying for information as well as what information is accessible.
- **Government of Canada** website that outlines the history of parole in Canada https://www.canada.ca/en/parole-board/corporate/history-of-parole-in-canada.html
- **Correctional Service of Canada** main webpage at http://www.csc-scc.gc.ca/index-en.shtml
    This has links to the different facilities, publications, and information related to corrections in Canada.

NOTES

[1]   Provincial/territorial systems of corrections in Canada operate independently of one another and vary significantly across jurisdictions; however, each of them offers some form of supervised temporary absence program in the community (see Calverley and Beattie (2004) for further details).

REFERENCES

Barry, J. (1956). Pioneers in criminology XII: Alexander Maconochie (1787-1860). *The Journal of Criminal Law, Criminology, and Police Science, 47*(2), 145-161.

Bebby, D. (2011, May 8). Ottawa study praising 'faint hope' clause for murderers never released. *The Globe and Mail*. Retrieved from https://www.theglobeandmail.com/news/politics/ottawa-study-praising-faint-hope-clause-for-murderers-never-released/article1322268/

Bill S-6. (2012). An Act to Amend the Criminal Code and another Act. 3rd Session, 40th Parliament, Elizabeth II, 2012. Retrieved from http://www.parl.gc.ca

Bill C-10. (2011). Safe streets and communities act. 1st Session, 41st Parliament, p. 60, Elizabeth II, 2011. Retrieved from http://www.parl.gc.ca

Calverley, D. (2010). Adult correctional services in Canada, 2008/2009. *Juristat, 30*(3).

Calverley, D., & Beattie, K. (2004). Community corrections in Canada. Retrieved from Statistics Canada, Canadian Centre for Justice Statistics, at: http://publications.gc.ca/Collection/Statcan/85-567-X/85-567-XIE2005001.pdf

Canada. Office of the Prime Minister. (2016, Feb 25). *Prime Minister announces new Governor in Council appointment process* [Press Release]. Retrieved from https://pm.gc.ca/eng/news/2016/02/25/prime-minister-announces-new-governor-council-appointment-process

Canadian Resource Centre for Victims of Crime. (2011). 2011/2012 priorities. Retrieved from http://crcvc.ca

Carpenter, M., & Crofton, W. (1872/2010). Reformatory prison discipline: As developed by the RT. Hon. Sir Walter Crofton, in the Irish convict prisons. Reprint. Charleston, NC: Nabu Press

Correctional Service of Canada. (2008). Commissioner's directives 715-2: Community super- vision and monitoring. Retrieved from http://www.csc-scc.gc.ca

Correctional Service of Canada. (2010). Commissioner's directives 710-3: Temporary absences and work releases. Retrieved from http://www.csc-scc.gc.ca

Correctional Service of Canada. (2013). CSC and Long Term Supervision Orders (LTSO). Retrieved from Government of Canada, Publications website at: http://publications.gc.ca/collections /collection_2014/scc-csc/PS84-15-2013-eng.pdf

Correctional Service of Canada. (2013B). Parole officer. Retrieved from http://www.csc-scc.gc.ca/publications/092/005007-2606-en.pdf

Correctional Service of Canada. (2018). Departmental Plan. Retrieved from http://www.csc-scc.gc.ca/careers/003001-1103-eng.shtml

Corrections and Conditional Release Act. (1992). Retrieved from Department of Justice Canada website at: http://laws-lois.justice.gc.ca

Corrections and Conditional Release Regulations. (2018). Retrieved from Department of Justice Canada website at: http://laws-lois.justice.gc.ca

Criminal Code. (1985). Retrieved from Department of Justice Canada website at: http://laws-lois.justice.gc.ca

Daubney, D. (1988). Taking responsibility: Report of the Standing Committee on Justice and Solicitor General on its review of sentencing, conditional release and related aspects of corrections. Retrieved from http://johnhoward.ca/wp-content/uploads/2016/12/1988-KE-9434-A22-S9-1988-Daubney-E.pdf

Garson, S. (1956). Report of a committee appointed to inquire to the principles and procedures followed in the remission service of the Department of Justice of Canada. John Howard Society. Retrieved from http://www.johnhoward.ca

Grant, B.A., Kunic, D., MacPherson, P., McKeown, C., & Hansen, E. (2003). The high intensity substance abuse program (HISAP): Results from the pilot programs. Research Report R-140. Ottawa, ON: Correctional Service Canada.

Hamilton, A.C. & Sinclair, C.M. (1991). Report of the Aboriginal Justice Inquiry. Retrieved from Government of Manitoba, Aboriginal Justice Implementation Commission website at: http://www.ajic.mb.ca/volumel/chapter12.html

John Howard Society of Ontario. (2014). Fact Sheet #20: Provincial parole in Ontario: The case for renewal. Retrieved from http://johnhoward.on.ca/wp-content/uploads/2014/09/facts-20-provincial-parole-in-ontario-the-case-for-renewal-may-2004.pdf

La Prairie, C. (2002). Aboriginal over-representation in the criminal justice system: A tale of nine cities. *Canadian Journal of Criminology, 44(2)*, 181-208.

Malakieh, J. (2018). Adult and youth correctional statistics in Canada, 2016/2017. Retrieved from Statistics Canada website at: https://www150.statcan.gc.ca/n1/pub/85-002-x/2018001/article /54972/tbl/tbl04-eng.htm

Minister of Justice. (2015). Canadian Victims Bill of Rights. Retrieved from Department of Justice Canada website at: http://laws-lois.justice.gc.ca

Motiuk, L., Cousineau, C., & Gileno, J. (2005). The safe return of offenders to the community: Statistical overview. Retrieved from Correctional Service of Canada, Research Branch, Correctional Operations and Programs at: http://www.csc-scc.gc.ca

Morris, N. (2002). Maconochie's gentlemen: The story of Norfolk Island and the roots of modern prison reform. New York, NY: Oxford University Press.

National Parole Board. (2011). *NPB policy manual*. Electronic version, *1*(21). Retrieved from http://www.pbc-clcc.gc.ca

Newark, S. (2011, September 13). Scott Newark: How to fix Canada's parole system. *National Post*. Retrieved from http://fullcomment.nationalpost.com

Office of the Correctional Investigator. (2012). Spirit matters: Aboriginal people and the corrections and conditional release act. Retrieved from http://www.oci-bec.gc.ca/cnt/rpt/pdf/oth-aut/oth-aut20121022-eng.pdf

Paparozzi, M., & Guy, R. (2009). The giant that never woke: Parole authorities as the lynchpin to evidence-based practices and prisoner re-entry. *Journal of Contemporary Criminal Justice, 25(4)*, 397-411.

Parole Board of Canada. (2016-2017). Performance monitoring report 2016-2017. Retrieved from Parole Board of Canada website at: https://www.canada.ca/content/dam/pbc-clcc/documents/publications/Performance-Monitoring-Report-2016-2017.pdf

Parole Board of Canada. (2010-2011). Performance monitoring report 2010-2011. National Parole Board: Performance Monitoring Division. Retrieved from http://pbcclcc.gc.ca

Parole Board of Canada. (2011). Special conditions. [Unpublished].

Parole Board of Canada. (2018). History of parole in Canada. Retrieved from https://www.canada.ca/en/parole-board/corporate/history-of-parole-in-canada.html

Parole Board of Canada. (2018B). Elder-assisted hearings. Retrieved from https://www.canada.ca/en/parole-board/corporate/publications-and-forms/fact-sheets/elder-assisted-hearings.html

Public Safety and Emergency Preparedness Canada. (2005). Sentence calculation: How does it work? (3rd ed.). Retrieved from http://www.publicsafety.gc.ca.

Public Safety Canada. (2017). Corrections and conditional release: Statistical overview annual report 2016. Public Works and Government Services Canada. Retrieved from http://www.publicsafety.gc.ca

Roberts, J. (2005). Public opinion and corrections: Recent findings in Canada. Retrieved from www.csc-scc.gc.ca/text/pa/ev-pblc-op/public_opinion_e.pdf

Sampson, R., Gascon, S., Glen, I., Louie, C., & Rosenfeldt, S. (2007). A roadmap to strengthening public safety: Report of the Correctional Service of Canada Review Panel. Minister of Public Works and Government Services Canada. Retrieved from http://www.publicsafety.gc.ca

Scratch, Lydia. (2006). *Governor in council appointments: Recent changes and suggestions for reform.* [Report No. PRB 06-21E]. Retrieved from the Parliamentary Information and Research Service, Library of Parliament website: https://lop.parl.ca/Content/LOP/ResearchPublications /prb0621-e.pdf

Speck, K.A. (2009). The evolution of conditional release in Canada. In risk assessment & risk management: A Canadian criminal justice perspective (pp. 76-80). International Centre for Criminal Law Reform and Criminal Justice Policy. Retrieved from http://www.icclr.law.ubc.ca

Stewart, G. (2008, May 15). Prison system's 'seatbelt' keeps crime in check. *The Kingston Whig Standard*.

Stilborn, J. (1989). *Political patronage: A newly troubled tradition.* [Report No. BP-199E]. Parliamentary Information and Research Service, Library of Parliament, Ottawa.

Turnbull, S. (2014). Aboriginalising the parole process: 'Culturally appropriate' adaptations and the Canadian federal parole system. *Punishment & Society, 16(4)*, 385-405

USlegal.com. (2016). History [Web Page]. Retrieved from https://criminallaw.uslegal.com/probation-and-parole/parole/history/

Adult Restorative Justice in Canada

11

Andrew Woolford and Amanda Nelund

Learning Objectives

After reading this chapter, you should be able to:

- Define restorative justice with respect to its processes and principles.

- Understand the origins of restorative justice and its development in Canada.

- Detail some of the ways that restorative justice can be used to work with adult offenders.

- Describe three adult-based restorative justice programs in Canada, as well as one example of the use of restorative justice in a correctional institution.

- Discuss some of the challenges faced and opportunities presented for restorative justice programs in Canada.

INTRODUCTION

Howard Zehr (1990), one of the early pioneers of **restorative justice** (RJ), describes the concept as follows: "crime is a violation of people and relationships. It creates obligations to make things right. Justice involves the victim, the offender, and the community in a search for solutions which promote repair, reconciliation, and reassurance" (p. 181). Of course, in practice, Zehr's ideal of justice is sometimes difficult to live up to, especially since some offenders may be unwilling to take responsibility for their actions (which is a precondition for involvement in most RJ programs), victims may have no interest in meeting with the person who harmed them, and community members may be indifferent to or too busy to involve themselves. But we will have more to say about the definition and implementation of RJ below.

For now, working with this very general definition, you can see how RJ is often viewed to be most appropriate for cases involving young offenders. Youth – a somewhat arbitrary designation that assumes a separate period of development between the stages of childhood and adulthood that runs from ages 12 to 17 – is a time of growth, transition, and formation. During this period, when young people are beset by the emotional highs and lows of puberty, it is possible that they might also "**drift**" (Matza, 1964) in and out of criminal engagements. For a variety of reasons, a young person may dabble in minor crimes such as drug usage, vandalism, or shoplifting, only to realize the error of his or her ways when it comes time to focus on responsibilities of adulthood. From the perspective of the **labelling theory**, however, this young person may not drift out of such **primary deviance** if the criminal justice system "labels" him or her a deviant. That is, if the criminal justice system stigmatizes the youth as a "bad" or "criminal" person by responding in a manner that seeks to degrade rather than reintegrate (Garfinkel, 1956; Braithwaite, 1989), the youth may move toward what is called **secondary deviance** and begin to accept the term "criminal" as her or his "**master status**" or primary identity (Becker, 1963).

Accepting, for the moment, the logic of this argument, it appears that RJ is well-suited to avoiding the dangers of labelling youth as criminals and, also, encouraging them to move away from secondary forms of deviance. Indeed, criminologist John Braithwaite (1989) has advanced the similar notion of "**reintegrative shaming**" to describe a justice process that works to prevent the stigmatization that is potentially experienced through formal criminal procedures. Braithwaite suggests that, when shaming wrongful behaviour through a reintegrative process, it is the act and not the person that is labeled. Community and family members, friends, and other actors, important to the offender, come together to clearly state that the offending act was wrong and unacceptable, but they also reinforce the positive qualities of the offender (e.g., "you've always been such a kind and caring person, how could you terrify the Smiths by breaking into their house?"). The end goal of such interactions is to shame the act committed by the youth in a fashion that reconnects him or her to family and community, rather than pushing the youth away and potentially toward further criminal activity.

We have belaboured this point about youth to highlight that our society often thinks differently about adults. Indeed, our correctional system assumes that adults, unlike youth, are largely formed in terms of their moral development. For this reason, once individuals reach the age of 18, they are presumed to be sufficiently self aware of, and, therefore, fully responsible for their actions (see Caulum, 2007). In this chapter, we do not accept this assumption. Although RJ does face challenges when used in adult criminal justice sentencing or within adult corrections, our main concern is that RJ approaches are also suited to adult offenders. We make this argument for several reasons. First, while youth may be in a more intensive stage of identity development, several studies of adult identity formation acknowledge that our identities are never finished projects (and we each have multiple identifications, some of which are more socially acceptable than others) (see, for example, Côté & Levine, 2002; Giddens, 1991; Levinson et al., 1976; Wrightsman, 1994). These identifications are an ongoing project – we negotiate and re-negotiate them throughout the course of our day-to-day lives. A police officer may be father to a seven-year-old daughter, a member of a faith community, and teammate to others on his local soccer team. But he must work at performing all of these identities in a competent fashion to have them resonate with him and others. However, in a moment of crisis, such as the loss of the daughter to an accidental death, he can throw all of these identities into jeopardy, making it difficult for this individual to maintain them in the wake of his ongoing trauma (Giddens, 1991). If the work of identity-building can be disrupted or weakened in such negative circumstances, RJ practitioners tend to believe that it can also be strengthened through positive and encouraging relationships with our significant others (Braithwaite, 1989).

Second, as you will see later in the chapter, RJ is not a single method or practice. Instead, RJ principles are the basis for a wide variety of justice interventions. Therefore, the RJ process that is used for a young offender will be very different from the one used for an adult offender. RJ is a flexible justice process that is designed to fit the type of offender or wrongdoer (Johnstone, 2002).

Finally, on occasion, members of the general public may engage in the fantasy that there are people in our society who lack any sense of right and wrong. For example, Comack and Bowness (2010) examine the prevalence of "us" versus "them" thinking in comments posted in response to news stories about an August 2008 police shooting of an Aboriginal man in Winnipeg. In several comments, discussion participants minimized the role played by race in the shooting, and instead argued that the death was the result of the victim's own irresponsibility and criminal character. However, rarely do we find people who are completely oblivious to normative notions of right and wrong and, therefore, irresponsible in every facet of life. Rather, most people are socialized to at least know, on some level, the core **norms** (i.e., standards of behaviour defined by shared social expectations) and **values** (i.e., standards of behaviour to which we attribute strong positive content) that are dominant in Canadian society. They can even perform these norms in many aspects of their lives. Indeed, it is difficult to imagine a person breaching norms constantly through the course of their day – they would have trouble navigating a variety of necessary interactions, such as riding a bus, collecting groceries, or meeting with their employer. Instead, according to Sykes and Matza (1957), norm violation tends to be selective. As well, when individuals do violate norms, they often feel compelled to rationalize their behaviour (e.g., "no one will notice, I'm not really harming anyone"), unless they are motivated by an impulse or desire that overrides this normative learning (e.g., addiction, although even in such cases rationalizations are not uncommon). RJ proponents (see, for example, Braithwaite, 1999; Johnstone, 2002) argue that these rationalizations and compulsions can and should be targeted through a well-designed RJ program that seeks to direct individuals toward following (rather than making excuses for violating) their normative orientation, and that this also is true for adult offenders.

In the remainder of this chapter, we will discuss the definition of restorative justice, including its origins and some of the various restorative justice processes that are intended to actualize restorative values. We, then, explore the relationship between RJ and correctional services, the position of RJ within the Canadian criminal justice system, and describe three RJ programs that work with adult offenders, as well as an example of a RJ program option available within the Canadian correctional system.

WHAT IS RESTORATIVE JUSTICE?

We begin this section by presenting a clear, thorough definition of restorative justice. Unfortunately, this is easier said than done. Early formulations of restorative justice often relied on opposing

Box 11.1 – The Old and New Paradigm (Zehr, 1995)

Retributive Justice	Restorative Justice
Crime defined by – violation of rules and relationships	Crime defined as – harm to people
Crime seen as categorically different from other harms and conflicts	Crime recognized as related to other harms and conflicts
State as victim	People and relationships as victims
State and offender are primary parties	Victim and offender are primary parties
Interpersonal dimensions irrelevant	Interpersonal dimensions central
Offence defined in technical, legal terms	Offence understood in full context: moral, social, economic, political
Wrongs create guilt	Wrongs create liability and obligations
Guilt is absolute, either/or	There are degrees of responsibility
Guilt is indelible	Guilt is removable through repentance and reparation
Debt is abstract	Debt is concrete
Debt paid by taking punishment	Debt paid by making right
Accountability = taking one's "medicine"	Accountability = taking responsibility
Blame fixing central	Problem solving central
Focus on past	Focus on future
Needs secondary	Needs primary
Batter, adversarial model normative	Dialogue normative
Imposition of pain normative	Restoration/reparation normative
One social injury added to another	Emphasis on repair of social injuries
Harm by offender balanced by harm to offender	Harm by offender balanced by making right
Victims' needs ignored	Victims' needs central
Restitution rare	Restitution normal
Sense of balance through retribution	Sense of balance through restitution

continued...

Box 11.1 – *continued*

State monopoly on response to wrongdoing	Victim, offender, community roles recognized
Offender has no responsibility for resolution	Offender has responsibility in resolution
Outcome encourages offender irresponsibility	Responsible behaviour encouraged
Offender denounced	Harmful act denounced
Offender stigmatized	Reintegration offered to offender
Justice tested by intent and process	Justice tested by its outcome
Process alienates	Process aims at reconciliation
Proxy professionals are the key actors	Victim and offender central – professional help available
Win-lose outcomes assumed	Win-win outcomes encouraged

RJ to criminal justice principles. Whereas criminal justice was said to focus on establishing blame and guilt, RJ was said to emphasize problem-solving, liabilities, and obligations. Whereas in criminal justice a wrongdoer's debt was owed to the state, in RJ the debt is owed to the people harmed (see Zehr, 1995 and Box 14.1). Such an oppositional strategy was criticized by subsequent theorists; however, because the vision of justice that is offered by RJ is developed in a manner that is parasitic on the criminal justice system, rather than seeking to truly imagine a justice that seeks to stand-alone on its own definitional terms rather than simply oppose criminal justice tendencies (Pavlich, 2005).

Though most of the contemporary literature on RJ begins with some sort of definition, theorists have been unable to agree on one definition. Indeed, several debates animate the restorative justice movement, making definitional agreement difficult. Theo Gavrielides (2007, pp. 34-43) identifies these "fault lines" as follows:

1. Is RJ a new paradigm or a complement to existing criminal justice options?
2. Does RJ rest within or outside the criminal justice system?
3. Should RJ be defined according to the processes it employs or the outcomes it aims to achieve?
4. How many stakeholders should be included in RJ processes?
5. Is RJ an alternative to punishment or an alternative form of punishment?
6. Is RJ a flexible approach or must it define a set of core practices?

These debates are unlikely to be resolved in their entirety in the near future, although efforts have been made to address and reconcile these tensions (Gavrielides, 2007).

Gavrielides third fault-line, perhaps, identifies the most frequent basis for definitional debate: should our definition be based on ideal processes, or the sort of outcomes we want to achieve, or the values to be reflected in those outcomes (see Braithwaite & Strang, 2001)?[1] An example of a process-based definition is offered by Tony Marshall (1996): "restorative justice is a process whereby all the parties with a stake in a particular offence come together to resolve collectively how to deal with the aftermath of the offence and its implications for the future" (p. 37). Here, RJ is defined as a process that adds the objective of restoration to the traditional justice objectives of reducing **recidivism** and rehabilitating offenders. If RJ can be used to achieve these criminal justice objectives, it follows that it can be used by the criminal justice system. Those working from this definition often see RJ as a program that can be run by criminal justice agencies such as the police, correctional services, or the courts (Marshall, 1996). For these theorists, RJ belongs squarely within the criminal justice field (see Gavrielides, 2005 for further discussion of the placement of RJ in relation to punishment, criminal justice, and ethics). And it is to be utilized only in response to criminal conflicts. Often this translates into the use of RJ in order to deal with lower level criminal cases, thereby keeping them out of the court system. Broadly speaking, those who understand RJ as a process view it as another tool in the criminal justice toolbox (see Duff, 2003).

Some definitions of RJ look quite different from those described above. These definitions conceptualize RJ as an alternative form of justice. Elizabeth Elliott (2011) holds RJ to be "a set of values for how to live peacefully together" (p. 70). Here, RJ, based on a set of key values, is a holistic approach to building conflict free relationships, and repairing relationships that have experienced conflict. Those values include respect, empathy, honesty, and inclusivity. Many authors and practitioners, working from this definition, see the criminal justice system as anathema to these values. Thus, this perspective does not see RJ as a way to achieve the justice system's goals. Instead, we are told, our objective should be the creation of peaceful, equal relationships, and communities. This set of goals necessarily broadens the contexts of RJ's usefulness. Those working from this perspective do not see RJ as a new tool for the criminal justice system. Rather, it is a new paradigm for our communities (Zehr, 1990). RJ, therefore, should be similar to the way that we deal with conflict in our families, our schools, our workplaces, and our communities.

This is a quick outline of a lively debate in the RJ literature. In order to keep the focus on corrections, we, herein, offer a somewhat narrower definition of RJ as a set of practices that aim to resolve conflict by including and responding to the needs and obligations of the offender, victim, and community. We say this with the caution since many people might find this definition overly restrictive (Elliott, 2011) and, furthermore, we will add the caveat that RJ can be thought of much more expansively.

A BRIEF HISTORY OF RESTORATIVE JUSTICE

Before elaborating on RJ principles and practices for solving conflict, we first offer a brief history of RJ. It is useful to look at the history of RJ in order to understand why it looks like it does today. Braithwaite argues (1996) that he "has yet to a find a culture which does not have some deep-seated restorative traditions" (p. 19). While this may be overstating the case, many RJ theorists have looked to different cultures for restorative ideals and practices. The Indigenous nations of both North America and Australia are often credited as cultures that primarily use RJ approaches (see, for example, Ross, 1996; Cuneen, 2002). One can see the influence of Indigenous ideas around connection, relationships, and healing throughout RJ literature. Similarly, there are also many religious influences on RJ, for example, Christian values, such as forgiveness and healing, and Mennonite communities were some of the first to practice RJ methods. Though we see these influences, and useful connections can be drawn between past and current notions of RJ (see Gavrielides & Winterdyk, 2011; Weitkamp, 2003), one must avoid historical oversimplifications. For example, caution is required when tracing a historical lineage from traditional Indigenous practices to current practices, such as circle sentencing. In particular, it should be remembered that not all Indigenous groups practiced justice similar to what we today call RJ, and current forms of Indigenous RJ are often state-led projects that are imposed under conditions where Indigenous peoples lack the powers of self-determination that once sustained their justice practices (Laroque, 1997; Nader, 1990; Woolford, 2009). As well, RJ proponents must be careful that their acknowledgment of Indigenous conflict resolution practices does not result in the co-optation or appropriation of such practices to achieve Euro-Canadian goals (e.g., the pacification of Indigenous communities and individuals), since this is hardly an appropriate response to a history of colonial land appropriation and forced assimilation (see Woolford, 2009).

The recent resurgence of restorative-type approaches to justice is difficult to pinpoint. Roughly speaking, in the 1970s criminal justice scholars committed to offender rehabilitation faced the argument that "**nothing works**" (Martinson, 1974; also see Chapter 11), which suggested that all our best efforts to reform offenders were too costly and likely to fail. In this intellectual atmosphere, Norwegian criminologist Nils Christie published an article that many RJ authors subsequently drew on. In "**Conflicts as Property**" (1977), Christie argues that we need to reconceptualize conflicts and their value. Conflicts, according to Christie, should be thought of as property, as something that communities owned. Conflicts, like other types of property, have value and use for their owners. Conflicts are valuable in that they create an opportunity for the people involved, and the broader community, to actively participate in social life. Conflicts and their resolution, through the active participation of the community, provide an occasion for discussing what is wrong and right. When a community has to resolve a conflict between two parties, it must discuss who did something wrong, why it was wrong, and what can be done to right it. This allows the community to set moral boundaries. This type of conflict resolution also allows community members to interact with the wrongdoer and this helps overcome the sense that this person is a "monster" or hardened "criminal." Christie argues that conflicts are valuable properties that are stolen from communities. Professionals, police, lawyers, and judges take conflicts away from the community and resolve them in formal, remote settings. This theft means that communities lose the valuable outcomes provided by conflict resolutions. Christie ends his article by calling for a victim-oriented, community court system run by the community with no professional involvement.

Ideas, like those advanced by Christie and others, advocating community as a source of effective normative regulation (see Barnett, 1977; Braitwaite, 1989; Kurki, 2000) soon began to influence the criminal justice practice. One of the first RJ programs is credited to justice practitioners in Canada. In 1974, a probation officer in Elmira, Ontario, saw an opportunity to react to a crime differently. Two young offenders were convicted of a string of vandalism offences. The probation officer thought it may be valuable for the youth, as part of their sentence, to actually meet the property owners they affected. The two young people personally apologized to all of their victims. The officer was so impressed by the impact this had on both the young people and the victims that, with the help of the Mennonite Central Committee, he started the first **victim-offender mediation** program (see Peachey, 2003).

KEY RESTORATIVE PRINCIPLES

Howard Zehr (2002, p.21) offers us three major questions as a good starting point for examining the key principles of RJ. He argues that the criminal justice system and RJ processes each ask three questions when they are dealing with harm.

Criminal Justice
- What laws are broken?
- Who did it?
- What do they deserve?

Restorative Justice

- Who is hurt?
- What are their needs?
- Whose obligations are these?

These questions highlight the main principles of each approach. The criminal justice system has, as its starting point, the violation of legal codes. If there is not a law in place prohibiting an act, the criminal justice system does not respond. The primary goals of the police and the judiciary in the trial stage are finding the responsible party and establishing their legal guilt. The focus is entirely on the offender with the victim relegated to the role of witness. The sentencing process determines and the corrections system administers whatever sentence the offender deserves. Punishing the offender is the outcome of the process. These principles are at the heart of the criminal justice response, and they vary considerably from restorative principles (Zehr, 1995).

The first question RJ asks illuminates two key principles. It shows, first, that the focus in RJ is not placed simply on legal crimes but more generally upon harm. This focus on harm remains even if RJ is used in a criminal justice context. RJ processes focus on all of the harm that occurred as a result of the conflict – and not solely on the legal harm. This means that many different types of harm may be taken into account. A mugging may involve monetary harm to the victim because their wallet was stolen; but there may be other types of harm involved as well, such as increased anxiety for the victim. RJ aims to address all types of harm (Zehr, 1995).

Another principle highlighted in the first question is RJ's commitment to empowering victims as equal stakeholders within restorative processes. RJ strives to include all stakeholders in a conflict; there is, however, a particular interest in assisting those who were harmed. RJ attempts to bring victims back from the periphery, where they are relegated by the criminal justice system, and give them a central role in a process of dealing with the harm they suffered.

The second and third questions that RJ asks highlight RJ's focus on needs and obligations. RJ works from the principle that when harm occurs, needs arise as a result. These needs must be met in order to satisfactorily resolve the conflict. A crime, or conflict, clearly harms the victims and creates the need for many things, including monetary restitution, information, and empowerment. RJ, though, does not just focus solely on victims' needs; the needs of all of the stakeholders are taken into account. The offender may need healing, rehabilitation, accountability, and/or reintegration. Communities may need healing, restoration, and strengthening. These three parties also have obligations to assist each other in meeting these needs. Offenders can give victims restitution and share their motivations for the act. Victims may be able to provide the offender with understanding or forgiveness. The community can assist in the reintegration of both the victim and the offender. RJ focuses on what needs to be done, and by whom, in order to restore all of those involved in a conflict.

A final, key principle of RJ is that of open and active engagement. Those who are involved in a conflict should be the ones involved in its resolution, and the process should be open to their involvement if they, in fact, want to participate. In the above principles, we see the assumption that the victim, offender, and community may all be present in the process. But they must not only be present – they should also be active in resolving the harm that occurred. RJ places much emphasis on discussion. In order to identify harm, needs, and obligations, the involved parties must articulate them. All stakeholders in a conflict should be involved in a restorative process.

RESTORATIVE JUSTICE PRACTICES

There are a variety of practices that adhere to these principles and, thus, fall under the label restorative justice. The most commonly identified are: **victim-offender mediation**, **family group conferencing**, **circles**, and **Restorative Boards**.

Victim-offender mediation (VOM) is a RJ practice that involves a victim and an offender coming together with a trained mediator. There is often extensive pre-meeting work that is done separately with both the victim and offender to determine why they want to participate and what they expect from the process. Most of these programs conduct the mediation in order to reach a final agreement where the offender commits to some form of restitution. This final agreement may serve as a guide to sentencing in the courts, or it may be established post-sentencing as an informal agreement between victim and offender. Various evaluations of VOM have found that it yields high levels of both victim satisfaction (Van Camp & Wemmers, 2013; Sherman & Strang, 2007; Rugge & Cormier, 2005) and offender satisfaction (Shapland, Robinson, & Sorsby, 2011; Rugge, Bonta, & Wallace-Capretta, 2005; Umbreit et al., 1995). These mediation sessions were conducted for a range of harms from petty crimes, such as vandalism and shoplifting, through to serious violent crimes, such as sexual abuse and homicide. This process involves the discussion of harm, needs, and obligations, and embodies the three RJ principles outlined above. It is somewhat limited, however, because of the absence of the community. Without a well-trained RJ mediator, there may be pressure for the parties to come to an agreement when they are not ready or do not want to cooperate.

Family conferencing, or just **conferencing,** is a second, common RJ process. Conferencing was first used in the New Zealand youth justice system with Maori families (see Consedine, 1995, 2003). Typically, a conference involves the offender and victim, their families and other support people, a facilitator, and possibly criminal justice and community representatives. The group discusses the crime, what exactly happened, why and how it affected the people gathered together. These sessions are conducted in order to achieve a final restitution agreement. The number of participants is clearly larger than those who participate in victim-offender mediation. This can allow for the participation of the community and the identification of its needs and obligations. Once again, it is important to have a trained mediator assist in the conference discussions. With a larger group, it becomes possible for more powerful members of the group to dominate the conversation and for less powerful members to be re-victimized in the process. And this need not be the case. Pennell and Burford (2002) have shown that conferencing can be used effectively even in cases with clear unequal power dynamics. Their pilot program in Newfoundland and Labrador used conferencing to cope with and resolve family violence. Other studies have also shown that victims who have participated in the conferencing process are more highly satisfied (McCold & Wachtel, 1998; Strang, 2001) than those who go through the formal criminal justice process (Latimer et al., 2001).

There are a variety of circle-based restorative justice processes, including peacemaking, healing, and sentencing circles (Stuart, 1996; Stuart & Pranis, 2006). Circles are generally traced back to the traditional justice practices of the North American Indigenous peoples. Like conferencing, circles are a practice that brings together the community to deal with harm. Although there may be variance between specific circles whey they are convened, most share a number of elements. Preparation is done with the offender, victim, and community prior to the circle. When the circle is eventually held, it will begin with a song or prayer, depending on the traditions held by the particular Indigenous group or groups involved. A symbolic object, such as an eagle feather, is passed around the circle to signify who has the right to speak and be heard. Circles involve the participants literally sitting in a circle. This signifies the equal rights and dignity of all of the members of the community. Everyone is given the chance to speak to how the crime impacted them and what they think the response should be. After all members of the circle have had their say, the community will move toward problem-solving and devising a sanction for the offender that must be agreed upon by all members of the circle. Finally, once the offender has fulfilled the terms of the sanction, a feast or other form of ceremony will be held to mark that person's accomplishment and full return to community life (see Ross, 1996).

A final restorative process is the restorative board (Gavrielides, 2007). Restorative boards are made up of community members. Offenders are either directed to these boards as part of their sentence (Galvrielides, 2007) or diverted to the board, in lieu of criminal sanctions (Woolford, 2009). The board members organize a meeting with the offender where the victim may or may not be present (Galvrielides, 2007; Woolford, 2009). The crime, its impact and possible resolutions are discussed. Restorative boards act as a way for citizens to be involved in the justice process and provide a chance for the offender to take responsibility for his or her crime. However, boards and other forms of justice panels have been criticized for not being sufficiently restorative (see Woolford, 2009). For example, Adam Crawford criticized the panels used in England and Wales for being overly managerial since they were primarily directed toward expediting minor cases through the justice system. They also tend to encourage reformalization as panel members often replicated legal styles of questioning to obtain information from offenders (see also Crawford & Newburn, 2002).

RESTORATIVE JUSTICE PRACTICES IN CORRECTIONS

The practices described above combine with correctional services in a number of ways. First, several of the practices can be used for the purposes of sentencing, and for deciding upon sanctions other than incarceration. But, in so doing, they rely upon agents of the correctional system, such as probation officers, to monitor restorative agreements. For example, a restorative conference might recommend that the offender attend anger management and alcoholics' anonymous programming, and abide by a curfew. These sanctions could, then, be made part of a probationary or conditional sentence by the judge who has oversight for the case. Once the judge has signed off on the restorative plan, the attached conditions are monitored by a probation officer or a representative from the restorative justice agency serving in a similar capacity. Second, restorative justice processes are also used post-sentencing as a means for reconciling the victim and offender, or, at least, providing the victim with a chance to ask questions of the offender as a means of assisting the victim in his or her healing process. A powerful example of such a process can be witnessed in the National Film Board of Canada documentary, "Glimmer of Hope." This film follows Don and Mary Struefert as they attend victim-offender reconciliation sessions with one of the men who raped and murdered their daughter, Carin, in 1991. The sessions, facilitated by Mark Umbreit, a well-known restorative justice author and practitioner, takes place within a correctional institution. The offender, Guy Sullivan, appears in his prison uniform. At the time of the meetings, Guy had already received multiple life sentences for his part in Carin's death, and the restorative sessions are focused primarily on assisting with the victim and offender process, and, also, dealing with this traumatic event. Third, restorative techniques can be incorporated into various forms of prison programming. For example, healing circles may be used among groups of prisoners who have similar behavioural tendencies or life experiences that strongly influence their offending. Along these lines, Healing Lodges run by Correctional Service of Canada, such as the Willow Cree Healing Centre in Saskatchewan or the Stan Daniels Healing Centre in Alberta, use Elder Healing Circles to help prepare inmates for release and reintegration into the community.

It should be noted, however, that some restorative justice advocates, who hold principle-driven visions of restorative justice, have expressed serious concerns about the use of restorative justice within the correctional system. Liz Elliott (2007), for example, examined prison education and correctional programming in Canada and found that total institutions like prisons, where the lives of inmates are regulated in their near entirety are, at best, contradictory spaces to implement restorative programming

For Elliott, correctional institutions are directed primarily toward "security" – a term she defines using its Latin root, meaning "without care." A contradiction arises when you seek to introduce practices of rehabilitation and care into this space, without care, where the focus is on punishment and regulating

Box 11.2 – Restorative Opportunities Program

Restorative Opportunities (RO) is a Correctional Service of Canada (CSC) program that offers people who have been harmed by a crime, either directly or indirectly, a chance to communicate with the offender who caused the harm.

RO is a post-sentence program in which participation is voluntary for everyone concerned. The program explores opportunities to use various victim-offender mediation models that best suit the needs of the participants, as defined by the participants, with the help of a professional mediator.

Victim-offender mediation is a process through which a trained community-based mediator prepares interested victims and offenders to communicate and provides them with the opportunity to meet in a safe, structured setting. During these meetings, participants can tell their story, explain to the offender the crime's physical, emotional and financial impact on their lives, explore unanswered questions about the crime and the offender, and participate directly in developing options to try to address the harms caused, where possible. Offenders are afforded opportunities to provide information and to gain insights that contribute to their accountability and personal growth.

This approach differs from conventional mediation in that the parties are not "disputants" in the usual sense; one is an admitted offender and the other is the victim or person(s) who experienced the harm. Furthermore, the process is not focused on reaching a settlement, but rather on open communication. This approach is in line with the values and principles of restorative justice that emphasize recognition of harm, choice, inclusion, facilitated dialogue, accountability, safety and truth.

Program models may vary, but they all have certain features in common: voluntary participation at all stages of the process, extensive preparatory work, confidentiality so as to avoid influencing National Parole Board decisions, and highly trained mediators who are perceived as neutral by both parties. Many encounters are face to face, but other options, such as exchanging letters or video messages, are also available. Alternatively, a mediator can act as a go-between, relaying messages between victims and offenders. The choice of model is guided by the participants' needs.

The goal of the RO program is to meet the needs of participants and to address the harms caused, while protecting against re-victimisation. Forgiveness is not a goal or expected result of a victim-offender mediation process and is not required in order to achieve a meaningful interaction. It may be a by-product in some cases; however, it is not explored unless it is raised as a need by the participants.

The reasons for which a person may choose to participate in victim-offender mediation are unique and individual. The decision to participate may stem from many months or years of thought and reflection. This process is not an easy one and is not for every victim; nor is it for every offender.

Source: http://www.csc-scc.gc.ca/restorative-justice/003005-1000-eng.shtml

freedom. In such circumstances, one can expect that it will be difficult to cultivate restorative values of relationship and mutual concern in a prison environment, although Elliott does not entirely rule out this possibility. The CSC is certainly seeking opportunities to further include RJ in its programming, so it remains to be seen whether attempts to foster care can flourish in a carceral setting (see Box 11.2).

RESTORATIVE JUSTICE IN CANADA

At the beginning of this chapter we spent some time articulating how, theoretically-speaking, RJ can be used just as effectively with adult offenders as it can with youth offenders. One of the reasons, we felt such justifications were necessary is that national efforts toward facilitating restorative approaches within the Canadian criminal justice system have been largely directed toward youth (Charbonneau, 2004; Hogeveen, 2006). A case in point is the *Youth Criminal Justice Act*, which emphasizes the use of extrajudicial measures (see Section 4 of the Act), and, in particular, conferencing, for first-time, nonviolent, youth offenders. This legal opening for the expansion of RJ does not, however, represent a national RJ strategy since each province is charged with determining how they will implement this portion of the *YCJA*.

A more general opening for RJ can be found in section 718 of the *Criminal Code* where, alongside the sentencing principles of denunciation, deterrence, and separation of offenders from the community (when necessary), there sits three principles that overlap with restorative values: rehabilitating offenders, providing reparations to victims and communities, and promoting a sense of responsibility within the offender, which includes having the offender acknowledge the harm that was done. As evidenced from the previous sections on the definition of RJ, these are the three principles that restorative justice advocates strive to incorporate into their programs.

Section 718.2 of the *Criminal Code* also makes room for restorative responses to crime. Specifically, part (e), which was the result of a 1996 amendment to the CC, instructs judges to consider alternative sentencing options whenever possible and, in particular, for Aboriginal offenders.

Section 718.2 was clarified by the decision in *R. v. Gladue* which was released by the Supreme Court of Canada on April 23, 1999 (see Box 11.3). In this decision, which referred to a second degree murder charge against an Aboriginal woman accused of the stabbing death of her boyfriend, section 718.2(e) was interpreted as a clear instruction to judges to change their sentencing practices and discontinue overreliance on incarceration, which was viewed, in part, as a cause of Aboriginal overrepresentation in Canadian correctional facilities.

The Gladue decision does not mean that Aboriginal offenders receive a lesser sentence simply because they are Aboriginal. Rather, the decision directs judges to consider two important factors when sentencing an Aboriginal person. First, Aboriginal peoples in Canada have a specific set of background and systemic experiences that impact upon potential criminal behaviour. These include extreme poverty, violence, the child welfare system, and the legacies of Indian Residential Schools, as well as other forms of forced assimilation. Second, these background factors have implications for the effectiveness of criminal sanctions and, therefore, require judges to consider sanctions that are more culturally and contextually appropriate (Parkes, 2011). Thus, judges may need to consider the Aboriginal offender's need for "healing" in relation to a history of addiction and abuse that has emanated from the violence of residential schools. Anything else would simply be an injustice and have little impact with respect to decreasing the likelihood of recidivism.

One sentencing model related to RJ that can gain wider usage in the post-Gladue era is the practice of circle sentencing, which is one of the circle types briefly touched upon above. Circle sentencing represents an adaptable and potentially culturally appropriate means for addressing the systemic and background factors that contribute to Aboriginal offending. We describe circle sentencing as "related

Box 11.3 – What is a Gladue Court?
By Claudia C. Belda, LECO 2006

Background to the Gladue Courts

On April 23, 1999, the Supreme Court released its decision regarding *R. v. Gladue*. The decision provided the Court's first interpretation of s. 718.2 (e) of the *Criminal Code*.

The Court stated that these amendments represented a change in the way judges should approach the sentencing process.

What is the Gladue Court?

The Gladue courts were a response to the Galdue decision. It was created by a group of Toronto Judges and the Aboriginal Legal Services of Toronto, and it began functioning in October 2001.

The court is available to all Aboriginal persons… However, it is up to the accused person to choose to have his or her matter heard by the Gladue Court.

The court accepts guilty pleas, conducts remands and trials, sentences offenders, and carries out bail hearings and variations.

How is the Gladue Court Different from a Regular Court?

The Gladue court is more beneficial to an Aboriginal offender simply because a judge must consider two things:

- The unique system or background factors which may have played a role in bringing the offender before the court; and
- The types of sentencing procedures and sanctions that may be appropriate in the circumstances of the offender, due to his or her Aboriginal heritage, including the examination of alternative justice processes such as Restorative Justice.

The above is done in order to address the finding of the Royal Commission's report on criminal law, "Bridging the Cultural Divide," which stated that the reason for the Euro-Canadian system of justice being unable to deal with Aboriginal offenders is due to the fact that there is:

> *fundamentally different world views of Aboriginal and non-Aboriginal people with respect to such elemental issues as the substantive content of justice and the process of achieving justice.*

It is a fact that Aboriginal offenders respond better to a Restorative Justice model that advocates sharing, reparation and a holistic approach, rather than the discriminatory, adversarial stance and incarceration that is often synonymous with the Criminal Justice system.

In order to make sure that those two considerations are properly explored, the Gladue courts have Gladue case workers, who are employed by Aboriginal Legal Services of Toronto. The job of the Gladue case worker is to prepare reports for the judges regarding the offender's background and alternative justice programs available to him or her after a finding of guilt.

All of these add up to a court that is more in tune with its user's background and environment, hence, the beginning of a better justice system.

For additional information please see the Aboriginal Legal Services of Toronto website at http://www.aboriginallegal.ca.

to RJ," since one must be careful to acknowledge that Aboriginal justice practices long preceded the current trend of RJ, and have, indeed, influenced the development of RJ. It would be another act of colonial appropriation to reduce the complex and culturally specific traditions of Aboriginal justice to simply another form or type of RJ. Unfortunately, the use of circles remains somewhat sporadic in Canada, and Aboriginal overrepresentation in the correctional system has increased rather than decreased in Canada's prisons since Gladue (Parkes, 2011; Roberts & Reid, 2017).

Circle sentencing, as it is currently practiced in Canada, does not represent a precise replication of Indigenous justice traditions. Instead, it is a hybrid of Canadian and Indigenous models (Anderson, 1999; Laroque, 1997). Circle sentencing can also take a variety of forms, depending on the regional and administrative context in which it is used. At a very general level, sentencing circles include most of the general elements of circles discussed above. However, what makes this a hybrid process is –

Box 11.4 – Resolutions and decisions adopted by the Economic and Social Council at its substantive session of 2002 (1-26 July 2002)/2002/INF/2/Add.2

2002/12 Basic principles on the use of restorative justice programmes in criminal matters

The Economic and Social Council,

Recalling its resolution 1999/26 of 28 July 1999, entitled "Development and implementation of mediation and restorative justice measures in criminal justice," in which the Council requested the Commission on Crime Prevention and Criminal Justice to consider the desirability of formulating United Nations standards in the field of mediation and restorative justice,

Recalling also its resolution 2000/14 of 27 July 2000, entitled: "Basic principles on the use of restorative justice programmes in criminal matters," in which it requested the Secretary-General to seek comments from Member States and relevant intergovernmental and non-governmental organizations, as well as institutes of the United Nations Crime Prevention and Criminal Justice Programme network, on the desirability and the means of establishing common principles on the use of restorative justice programmes in criminal matters, including the advisability of developing a new instrument for that purpose:

Taking into account the existing international commitments with respect to victims, in particular the Declaration of Basic Principles of Justice for Victims of Crime and Abuse of Power,

Noting the discussions on restorative justice during the Tenth United Nations Congress on the Prevention of Crime and the Treatment of Offenders, under the agenda item entitled "Offenders and victims: accountability and fairness in the justice process,"

Taking note of General Assembly resolution 56/261 of 31 January 2002, entitled "Plans of action for the implementation of the Vienna Declaration on Crime and Justice: Meeting the Challenges of the Twenty-first Century," in particular the action on restorative justice in order to follow up the commitments undertaken in paragraph 28 of the Vienna Declaration,

Noting with appreciation the work of the Group of Experts on Restorative Justice at their meeting held in Ottawa from 29 October to 1 November 2001,

continued...

Taking note of the report of the Secretary-General on restorative justice and the report of the Group of Experts on Restorative Justice,

1. *Takes note* of the basic principles on the use of restorative justice programmes in criminal matters annexed to the present resolution;

2. *Encourages* Member States to draw on the basic principles on the use of restorative justice programmes in criminal matters in the development and operation of restorative justice programmes;

3. *Requests* the Secretary-General to ensure the widest possible dissemination of the basic principles on the use of restorative justice programmes in criminal matters among Member States, the institutes of the United Nations Crime Prevention and Criminal Justice Programme network and other international, regional and non-governmental organizations;

4. *Calls upon* Member States that have adopted restorative justice practices to make information about those practices available to other States upon request;

5. *Also calls* upon Member States to assist one another in the development and implementation of research, training or other programmes, as well as activities to stimulate discussion and the exchange of experience on restorative justice; and

6. *Further calls upon* Member States to consider, through voluntary contributions, the provision of technical assistance to developing countries and countries with economies in transition, on request, to assist them in the development of restorative justice programmes.

37th plenary meeting 24 July 2002.

alongside the roles government agencies may play in referring cases to the circle by preparing community members for participation and providing some of the programming that may be recommended through the sanction – is that all the judicial actors will typically be part of the circle process. Although they are not elevated above or distinguished in any way in contrast to other members of the circle, they do bring their official knowledge to bear on the sentencing considerations undertaken by the circle. It should also be noted that the judge gives the final determination whether or not the sanction proposed, through the circle process, meets the standards of Canadian society. For example, Christopher Pauchay is an Aboriginal man who in 2008 left his two daughters to die in the cold, Saskatchewan night when he was severely intoxicated. The judge for the case, Provincial Court Judge Barry Morgan, was provided with a recommendation from a circle that Mr. Pauchay be permitted to remain in the community to serve his sentence and remain with his wife and son. This case, which was to be heard before a circle, caused some consternation among conservative political commentators like the *National Post*'s Jonathan Kay (2009). He argued that the severity of the crime meant that no consideration should be given to section 718.2(e). In the end, however, despite the worries of people like Kay, Judge Morgan rejected the circle's recommendations and sentenced Pauchay to three years in prison (*CBC News*, 2009).

While there are initiatives at the federal government level to advocate for restorative justice, such as the Criminal Code based opportunities for increased use of RJ for adults found in section 718, the inclusion of RJ in the new Victim's Bill of Rights as well as government reports recommending the expanded use of RJ (e.g., Standing Committee on Justice, 1988; Solicitor General of Canada, 1996), Canada leaves much of the implementation of RJ to local communities and the provinces/territories (FPT Working Group on Restorative Justice 2016). While a devolved framework like this one suits RJ, which is often described as a community-based process (Christie, 1977; Zehr, 1995), greater federal political support could open opportunities for increased resources for and knowledge of restorative justice programs. Indeed, many are still unaware that RJ options exist, despite the mainstream promotion of RJ in venues like the television show, Oprah, and the United Nations' endorsement of the principles of RJ (see Box 11.4).

However, there is also reason for caution when seeking a national RJ policy, since such a strategy is risky. Namely, the nature of government is such that they feel compelled to exercise a certain degree of control over programs that are run or funded through their official institutions. Governments tend to demand a great deal of accountability from the programs they support, and any government-funded or -run program, that underperforms or provokes public concern, could potentially reflect poorly on the sitting government (for examples from Manitoba, see Woolford & Curran, 2011). In terms of RJ, this means that the government will seek to hold RJ programs accountable by, for instance, requiring a number of "best practices" procedures be implemented. As well, the government might demand evaluation procedures that demonstrate clear value for their money by showing that the program does, indeed, meet government-defined goals (such as reduced recidivism). While specific RJ programs may not be opposed to implementing more efficient and effective practices, or lowering recidivism rates, such impositions may limit the flexibility and broader reach of RJ programs, requiring them to focus on running their agencies like any other government program, rather than striving for more ambitious RJ goals of community peace-building and transforming our societal approach to justice. In such circumstances, there is a concern that the formal institutionalization of RJ will lead to the dilution or erosion of RJ values (Elliott, 2007; Pavlich, 2018; Woolford & Ratner, 2003).

At present, Canada continues to have a locally differentiated approach to RJ for adult offenders (FPT Working Group on Restorative Justice 2016). To illustrate regional variations, we take a closer look at three Canadian programs.

FRASER REGION COMMUNITY JUSTICE INITIATIVE – LANGLEY BRITISH COLUMBIA

One of the longest-running RJ programs in Canada is the Fraser Region Community Justice Initiative Association (FRCJIA) in Langley, British Columbia. Founded in 1985, the FRCJIA has since expanded and diversified in numerous ways. Following its mission statement "to foster peacemaking and the resolution of conflict in the community through the development and application of RJ values, principles and processes" (FRCJIA, 2010), the FRCJIA has worked with both youth and adult offenders, victims, and community members to deal with the trauma caused by crime.

Some of the key challenges faced by any agency wishing to provide RJ services are funding and referrals. Reliance on a single source of funding is not an ideal option for agencies that wish to exercise a certain degree of autonomy, since funders often attach specific expectations or requirements to their funding. For example, many funders, whether government or private, often prefer to give program-specific funding that can only be put toward a specific program, such as a Victim Offender Reconciliation Program for family victims of homicide. This means that this funding cannot be directed toward the general costs of maintaining the agency, unless such administrative costs are built into the funding agreement. Thus, to cover general operating costs, and to allow greater flexibility in their programming, RJ agencies will often seek support from multiple funders. This is true for FRCJIA as it receives funding from a wide range of services and agencies such as: the Province of British Columbia, Correctional Service of Canada, Coast Capital Savings, Langley Mennonite Fellowship, the Hamber Foundation, Langley School District #35, TD Canada Trust, and through regular fundraising galas and other events.

Such a multitude of funding sources can, of course, present managerial challenges for the agency's directors. Many agencies in a similar position complain that their directors must now spend more and more of their time applying for new funds, meeting with funders, and evaluating programs to ensure that funding requirements are met (Woolford & Curran, 2013). Still, for the FRCJIA, this funding structure allows them to sustain a diversity of programming options, although, as can be expected, it is also difficult to sustain all these funding streams. For example, from 1981 to 2002, FRCJIA ran a Victim-Offender Reconciliation Program for adults and then ran one for youths from 1981 until 2004, but the program was terminated because of provincial funding cuts. The FRCJIA continues to run a Victim-Offender Mediation Program, which it cites as "one of the first programs in the world to utilize a combination of therapeutic and dispute resolution protocols in working with serious and violent crimes" (FRCJIA, 2010). This program focuses on assisting those who committed trauma-inducing crimes to ensure continuing accountability in their post-incarceration period. It was expanded in 2004 through a contract with Correctional Service of Canada that enabled FRCJIA staff to offer training and mentoring to clients across the country. The program is available to anyone "impacted by a criminal incident committed by someone serving time in a Canadian federal prison" (FRCJIA, 2010).

Another program offered through FRCJIA is Restorative Action Program (formerly Educating for Peacebuilding), which was established in 2000 in partnership with the Langley School District. Here, as with their Restorative Youth Services program, the FRCJIA has branched out to provide youth justice and youth peace building skills to change the culture of conflict in British Columbia.

The first challenge for any Agency developing RJ programs is, as mentioned, to secure funding to run the program. But once funding is in place, the next challenge, in addition to hiring and training competent staff members, is to obtain referrals from the criminal justice system's gatekeepers. Few conflicts are brought directly to the offices of RJ programs. In most cases, a professional working in the criminal justice system will refer a case to a program, like those offered by FRCJIA, because they feel that the case is well suited to a restorative intervention. For example, a defence lawyer may recognize that his or her client is truly remorseful for a wrongful act and has little interest in entering the adversarial arena of the courts. Or, a victim may approach crown counsel and request an opportunity to meet with the accused. Or, an offender housed in a federal penitentiary may request a meeting with the victim of his or her crime through a victim-offender reconciliation program. The reasons why a case may be referred to RJ are several, but it is highly likely that the referral is made or facilitated by a lawyer, judge, police officer, court clerk, nonprofit sector employee or volunteer, or some other actor with more intimate knowledge of the alternative programs. In the case of the FRCJIA's victim offender reconciliation program, this list expands to include victim/survivor referrals from victims, victims' therapists, victim serving agencies, and victim liaisons in prisons, and offender referrals are received on behalf of prisons from institutional staff who work closely with them (Gustafson, 2005).

Circles of Support and Accountability – Winnipeg Manitoba

Circles of Support and Accountability (COSA) is a national program that began in Hamilton, Ontario. This project is sponsored by the Initiatives for Just Communities organization, which operates under the auspices of the Mennonite Central Committee. In Winnipeg, as with other Canadian sites, COSA's focus is on high-risk offenders released from incarceration, or on parole or probation, who represent a potential threat to themselves and others. It relies on a small staff and team of volunteers to create networks of support to help such individuals assume non-harmful lives within their communities. While this is an offender-centred program, it embraces a restorative justice philosophy to work on healing the relationships, and potential relationships, damaged by criminal behaviour. It further seeks to holistically address the contextual, interpersonal, and individual factors that resulted in the offence or offence cycle. Throughout the entire process, offender accountability is emphasized, as is the need to establish strong and safe communities.

Dealing with serious offences in a post-carceral setting, means that COSA is not subject to criticism of restorative justice programs as a source of "**net-widening**," at least not in the usual way (Woolford & Ratner, 2003). COSA clearly does not simply serve as a means for dealing with wrongdoers who would otherwise be ignored by the criminal justice system, allowing the system to expand its "net" of social control. The latter occurs when RJ programs are assigned mostly minor cases, such as shoplifting and vandalism, that would not normally merit the cost and complexity of a formal trial. In these situations, RJ programs are viewed as a valuable means for providing consequences for those who commit minor crimes. However, COSA does allow the CJS to extend its reach by providing greater oversight over a group of offenders who are deemed a "high risk" to reoffend. To this extent, it is an appendage rather than alternative to the criminal justice system. But how it extends the net of control takes a gentler and more participatory form than most post-incarceration approaches to corrections. The individual with an offence history, who appears to have great risk to recidivate, is included in the decision-making processes regarding their safe and healthy reintegration into the community. They work alongside a COSA staff member and a team of COSA volunteers to honestly assess their own risk of re-offending, as well as to addresses the factors that typically spark their offence cycles. Overall, this time and volunteer-intensive practice is said to reduce recidivism rates by 72-83% (COSA, n.d.).

Nova Scotia Restorative Justice Program

The Nova Scotia Restorative Justice Program (NSRJP) is one of the most comprehensive, institutionalized restorative justice programs in the country. NSRJP began in 1999 and, reflecting the tendency we outlined earlier, was initially only available to youth. It was not until 2010 that the province ran a pilot project expanding the program to adults. The pilot was successful and today the program is available to youth and adults. We label this program "institutionalized" to highlight that it is not an informal or grass roots program. The NSRJP is fully funded and mandated by the province of Nova Scotia under the Public Safety and Security Division in the Department of Justice.

There are four referrals points where a case could move into restorative justice: police can refer before a charge is laid (pre-charge), Crown attorneys can refer a case to RJ after a charge is laid, judges can refer after a conviction and before a sentence is imposed (post-conviction/pre-sentence), and finally staff of either Correctional Services or Victim Services can refer after a sentence has been imposed (post-sentence). Each referral point admits different types of cases, with lower level offences being the only available ones for pre-charge. Each of these moments throughout the criminal justice process poses different benefits and weaknesses for restorative justice. For example, while the pre-charge point may reduce the number of cases that are processed by the justice system it may also contribute to net-widening. The post-sentence option allows even the most serious violent cases to be dealt with in restorative justice, but the concern noted earlier about the ability to practice RJ in carceral institutions can become an issue. An important note here is that although there are these options in terms of when a case goes to RJ all of them keep the control of the process in the hands of criminal justice system officials.

The goals of the program, as outlined on its website, are multiple:

The Restorative Justice Program is designed to:

1.1.1 reduce recidivism – it has been shown that face-to-face meetings with victims can have a profound effect on the future behaviour of offenders. The nature of the restorative process provides an opportunity to focus on the underlying causes of the criminal behaviour and the constructive reintegration of the offender into the community;

1.1.2 increase victim satisfaction – by having a forum in which victims can discuss the impact of the offence and identify the reparative measures to be taken, they will derive greater satisfaction;

1.1.3 strengthen communities – by promoting a restorative approach which invites community participation in achieving reconciliation between offenders and those harmed through the commission of an offence; and

1.1.4 increase public confidence in the justice system – greater participation by communities and victims in community-based restorative justice processes as an alternative or supplement to the formal criminal justice system will enhance public confidence.

There is tension throughout this list between the values of RJ and the goals of the criminal justice system. Is recidivism the primary goal of RJ? Should RJ be used to increase public confidence in the criminal justice system or to provide a radical alternative to that system? Archibald and Llewellyn (2007) also point to the ways in which government control means that the language of "service delivery," budgeting, and criminal justice evaluation all frame and impact the work of the restorative programming.

While the government retains key roles in the program, the actual restorative services are run by eight different community agencies and the Mi'kmaq Legal Support Network. The community agencies offer a variety of restorative programming that is delivered by both staff and volunteers. Each agency varies slightly in the type of programming they offer, often tailoring their programs to their community. For example, the Community Justice Society, the agency that serves the Halifax region, primarily uses talking circles. In 2015-16 the Society received 325 referrals that had a combined 921 criminal charges. This agency also offers a youth night, an Options to Anger group, and other community programming. There is some evidence that the incorporation of criminal justice values is being mitigated by having the programming run by these community agencies. A 2011 survey of staff and volunteers at Nova Scotia agencies found that participants rated punishment and denunciation the least important values for restorative justice and a majority felt that RJ in the province should be run by community agencies, governed by community boards (Crocker & Craig, 2011). Crocker (2016) goes as far as suggesting that rather than see the criminal justice co-opt RJ the reverse may happen; that practitioners may be able to bring RJ values into the criminal justice system.

RESTORATIVE JUSTICE IN CORRECTIONAL INSTITUTIONS

The Correctional Service of Canada generally acts from a distance when it comes to restorative justice. The Restorative Justice and Dispute Resolution division of the CSC funds community projects and works to provide information on and exposure for restorative justice (see the website http://www.csc-scc.gc.ca/text/rj/index-eng.shtml). One program, however, that the correctional service ran directly was the Restorative Justice Living Unit at the Grande Cache facility (Petrellis, 2007). This pilot project operated for nearly five years, and was designed with the goal of integrating restorative justice principles into the everyday lives of prisoners. The objective of the unit was to "provide a supportive and respectful environment that fosters and promotes accountability, healing, and restoration" (Petrellis, 2007, p. 2). Conflicts that arose on the unit were dealt with through peer mediation. Prisoners were mandated to attend weekly meetings on topics such as "Making Amends," "Hope and Beliefs," and "What is Restorative Justice?" (Petrellis, 2007). In 2005, there was an evaluation on the program. Eighty-nine percent of the participants reported an increased understanding of their crime

Box 11.5 – Principles and Goals from the Mandate for the Truth and Reconciliation Commission

There is an emerging and compelling desire to put the events of the past behind us so that we can work towards a stronger and healthier future. The truth telling and reconciliation process, as part of an overall holistic and comprehensive response to the Indian Residential School legacy, is a sincere indication and acknowledgement of the injustices and harms experienced by Aboriginal people and the need for continued healing. This is a profound commitment to establishing new relationships, embedded in mutual recognition and respect that will forge a brighter future. The truth of our common experiences will help set our spirits free and pave the way to reconciliation.

Principles

Through the Agreement, the Parties have agreed that an historic Truth and Reconciliation Commission will be established to contribute to truth, healing and reconciliation.

The Truth and Reconciliation Commission will build upon the "Statement of Reconciliation" dated January 7, 1998 and the principles developed by the Working Group on Truth and Reconciliation and of the Exploratory Dialogues (1998-1999). These principles are as follows: accessible; victim-centered; confidentiality (if required by the former student); do no harm; health and safety of participants; representative; public/transparent; accountable; open and honourable process; comprehensive; inclusive, educational, holistic, just and fair; respectful; voluntary; flexible; and forward looking in terms of rebuilding and renewing Aboriginal relationships and the relationship between Aboriginal and non-Aboriginal Canadians.

Terms of Reference 1.

Goals

The goals of the Commission shall be to:

  (a) Acknowledge Residential School experiences, impacts and consequences;
  (b) Provide a holistic, culturally appropriate and safe setting for former students, their families and communities as they come forward to the Commission;
  (c) Witness, support, promote and facilitate truth and reconciliation events at both the national and community levels;
  (d) Promote awareness and public education of Canadians about the IRS system and its impacts;
  (e) Identify sources and create as complete an historical record as possible of the IRS system and legacy. The record shall be preserved and made accessible to the public for future study and use;
  (f) Produce and submit to the Parties of the Agreement2 a report including recommendations3 to the Government of Canada concerning the IRS system and experience including: the history, purpose, operation and supervision of the IRS system, the effect and consequences of IRS (including systemic harms, intergenerational consequences and the impact on human dignity) and the ongoing legacy of the residential schools; and
  (g) Support commemoration of former Indian Residential School students and their families in accordance with the Commemoration Policy Directive (Schedule "X" of the Agreement).

and 44% reported an increased ability to empathize. The focus on problem solving and conflict resolution meant that offenders were able to safely, and respectfully, resolve most interpersonal conflicts without involving staff (Petrellis, 2007). The report did caution that it will implement another similar pilot that: will be more thoroughly integrated into the correctional system; will provide a need for greater communication among staff working on and off the restorative unit; and will seek more community support to transition the prisoners into the community after their release (Petrellis, 2007). This stands as an interesting and unique example of the ways that restorative practices are implemented in correctional settings.

CONCLUSION

Our overview of the three well-recognized and respected adult RJ programs in Canada, as well as one prison-based program, demonstrates that RJ is not solely a process suited to young offenders. Throughout the country, these, and other RJ programs, have successfully intervened in serious crimes by adult offenders. Other RJ programs were also established to deal with some of the most troubling harms known to our society, such as family violence (Pennell & Burrford, 2002) and child physical and sexual abuse (Ross, 1996). Indeed, even the Truth and Reconciliation Commission of Canada, which was created through the *Indian Residential School Settlement Act* (2006) as a means to teach Canadians the truth about the harmful nature of residential school and sought to begin the process of healing residential school abuses, draws upon the values, principles, and practices of RJ (Petoukhov, 2011) (see Box 11.5).

Each of these programs also operates in a specific political and funding context that has repercussions for its practice. Since few of these programs can operate without funding and resource support from the government and the criminal justice system, they are required to work in partnership with the CJS, making it very difficult for RJ to transform or revolutionize practices of justice (see Pavlich, 2005; Woolford, 2009). With the dependence of RJ on the state for funding and client referrals, comes greater potential for RJ to be co-opted and RJ values being displaced in favour of criminal justice system values. That is, RJ can more readily be turned toward criminal justice values as funding requirements and governmental goals are imposed as the priorities of RJ practice, making secondary those less quantifiable objectives such as healing, peace-building, and relationship-building – that are so often espoused in the RJ literature. With the introduction of RJ into correctional programming comes a new set of concerns: Is it possible to heal harm and build security in a punitive environment (Elliott, 2011)? Does the use of RJ in the Canadian prison system continue the process of "stealing crime" from communities by placing its resolution in distant correctional institutions (Christie, 1977)? Does practicing RJ in a manner that helps sustain the prison system truly initiate a "paradigm shift" toward a non-retributive response to criminal harms (Zehr, 1990)? These and other questions must be addressed as RJ is increasingly deployed to help put a more humane face on corrections.

KEY TERMS AND CONCEPTS

Conferencing Circles
Conflicts as Property
Drift
Labelling
Master Status
Net-widening
Norms
Nothing Works

Primary Deviance
Recidivism
Reintegrative Shaming
Restorative Board
Restorative Justice
Secondary Deviance
Values
Victim-Offender Mediation

STUDY AND DISCUSSION QUESTIONS

1. How is restorative justice currently used in Canada? Should it be used more broadly?
2. Is restorative justice well suited for use with adult offenders? Or is it better suited for young offenders?
3. In what ways does restorative justice provide victims with a more central role in the resolving the harms caused by crime? How does this compare and contrast with victim involvement in the formal criminal justice system?
4. In what ways might restorative justice values be threatened when restorative justice practices are funded or administered by the government?
5. Should restorative practices be utilized more frequently in prisons? What are some of the concerns about using RJ in prisons?

HELPFUL WEBLINKS

- **Corrections Service of Canada's restorative justice** page at http://www.csc-scc.gc.ca /text/rj/index-eng.shtml
  This link directs you to the Corrections Service of Canada's restorative justice page, where you will find information about restorative justice week, restorative opportunities, and the Ron Wiebe Award.

NOTE

[1] The terms "outcome-based" and "value-based" are both used in the literature to describe the substantive rather than procedural ideals that define RJ.

REFERENCES

Anderson, C. (1999). Governing Aboriginal justice in Canada: Constructing responsible individuals and communities through tradition. *Crime, Law & Social Change, 31*, 303-326.

Archibald, B., & Llewellyn, J. (2006). The challenges of institutionalizing comprehensive restorative justice: theory and practice in Nova Scotia. *Dalhousie Law Journal, 29*, 297-343.

Barnett, R. (1977). Restitution: A new paradigm of criminal justice. *Ethics, 87*, 279-301.

Becker, H. (1963). *Outsiders: Studies in the sociology of deviance*. New York, NY: Free Press.

Braithwaite, J. (1989). *Crime, shame and reintegration.* Cambridge, UK: Cambridge University Press.

Braithwaite, J. (1999). Restorative justice: Assessing optimistic and pessimistic accounts. *Crime and Justice: A Review of Research, 25,* 1-127.

Braithwaite, J. (1996). Restorative justice and a better future. *The Dalhousie Review, 76,* 9-32.

Caulum, M. (2007). Post adolescent brain development: A disconnect between neuroscience, emerging adults, and the corrections system. *Wisconsin Law Review, 3,* 729–758. CBC News. (2009, March 6). Father of girls who froze to death gets 3 years in prison. Retrieved from http://www.cbc.ca

Charbonneau, S. (2004). The Canadian youth criminal justice act 2003: A step forward for advocates of restorative justice? In E. Elliott & R. Gordon. (Eds.), *New directions in restorative justice: Issues, practice, evaluation.* Cullompton, UK: Willan Publishing.

Christie, N. (1977). Conflicts as property. *British Journal of Criminology, 17,* 1-15.

Circles of Support and Accountability. (n.d.). *Circles of support and accountability pamphlet.* Winnipeg: Initiatives for Just Communities.

Comack, E., & Bowness, E. (2010). Dealing the race card: Public discourse on the policing of Winnipeg's inner-city communities. *Canadian Journal of Urban Research, 19,* 34-50.

Consedine, J. (2003). The Maori restorative tradition. In G. Johnstone (Ed.), *A restorative justice reader: Texts, sources, context.* Cullompton, UK: Willan Publishing.

Consedine, J. (1995). *Restorative justice: Healing the effects of crime.* Lyttleton, NZ: Ploughshares.

Côté, J., & Levine, C. (2002). *Identity formation, agency, and culture: A social psychological synthesis.* Mahwah, NJ: Lawrence Erlbaum Associates.

Crawford, A. (2003). The prospects for restorative youth justice in England and Wales: A tale of two acts. In K. McEvoy & T. Newburn (Eds.), *Criminology, conflict resolution and restorative justice.* New York, NY: Palgrave Macmillan.

Crawford, A., & Newburn, T. (2002). Recent developments in restorative justice for young people in England and Wales: Community participation and representation. *British Journal of Criminology, 42,* 476-485.

Crocker, D. (2016). Balancing justice goals: restorative justice practitioners' views. *Contemporary Justice Review, 19,* 462-478.

Crocker, D. & Craig, R. (2011). *Results from a Survey of Staff, Board and Volunteers of the Nova Scotia Restorative Justice Program.* Unpublished report produced for the Nova Scotia Restorative Justice-Community University Research Alliance (NSRJ-CURA), Halifax, NS. Available at www.nsrjcura.ca

Cuneen, C. (2002). Restorative Justice and the politics of decolonization. In E. Weitkamp & H.J. Kerner (Eds.), *Restorative justice: Theoretical foundations.* Cullompton, UK: Willan Publishing.

Duff, A. (2003). Restorative punishment and punitive restoration. In G. Johnstone (Ed.), *A restorative justice reader: Texts, sources, context.* Cullompton, UK: Willan Publishing.

Elliott, E. (2011). *Security with care: Restorative justice and healthy societies.* Halifax, NS: Fernwood Publishing.

Elliott, E. (2007). Security, without care: Challenges for restorative values in prison. *Contemporary Justice Review, 10,* 193-208.

Federal-Provincial-Territorial Working Group on Restorative Justice. 2016. Restorative Justice in the Canadian Criminal Justice Sector. Retieved from http://www.csc-scc.gc.ca/restorative-justice/003005-4012-eng.shtml

Fraser Region Community Justice Initiative. (2010). *Annual report.* Retrieved from http://www.cjibc.org

Garfinkel, H. (1956). Conditions of successful degradation ceremonies. *American Journal of Sociology*, *61*, 420-424.

Gavrielides T. (2005). Some meta-theoretical questions for restorative justice. *Ratio Juris Journal, 18*, 84-106.

Gavrielides, T. (2007). Restorative justice theory and practice: Addressing the discrepancy. Helsinki: European Institute for Crime Prevention and Control.

Gavrielides, T., & Winterdyk, J. (2011). The fall and rise of restorative justice: An historical account of its notion, practices, and lessons learned. *Pakistan Journal of Criminology 3*(2), 107-124.

Giddens, A. (1991). *Modernity and self-identity: Self and society in the late modern age.* Stanford, CA: Stanford University Press.

Gustafson, D. (2005). Exploring treatment and trauma recovery implications of facilitating victim-offender encounters in crimes of severe violence: Lessons from the Canadian experience. In E. Elliott & R. Gordon (Eds.), *New directions in restorative justice: Issues, practice, evaluation.* Cullompton, UK: Willan Publishing.

Hogeveen, B. (2006). Unsettling youth justice and cultural norms: The youth restorative action project. *Journal of Youth Studies, 9*, 47-66.

Johnstone, G. (2002). *Restorative justice: Ideas, values, debates.* Devon, UK: Willan Publishing.

Kay, J. (2009, January 20). The folly of native sentencing circles, *The National Post*.

Kurki, L. (2000). Restorative justice and community justice in the United States. *Crime and Justice, 27*, 235-303.

Laroque, E. (1997). Re-examining culturally appropriate models in criminal justice applications. In M. Asch (Ed.), *Aboriginal and treaty rights in Canada: Essays on laws, equality, and respect for difference.* Vancouver, BC: UBC Press.

Latimer, J., Dowden, C., & Muise, D. (2001). *The effectiveness of restorative justice practices: A meta-analysis.* Ottawa, ON: Department of Justice.

Levinson, D., Darrow, C., Klein, E., Levinson, M., & McKee, B. (1976). Periods in the adult development of men: Ages 18-45. *The Counseling Psychologist, 6*, 21-25.

McCold, P., & Wachtel, B. (1998). *Restorative policing experiment: The Bethlehem Pennsylvania police family group conferencing project.* Piperville, PA: Community Service Foundation.

Marshall, T. (1996). The evolution of restorative justice in Great Britain. *European Journal on Criminal Policy and Research, 4*, 21-43.

Martinson, R. (1974). What works? Questions and answers about prison reform. *The Public Interest, 35*, 22-54.

Matza, D. (1964). *Delinquency and drift.* New Brunswick, NJ: Transaction Publishers.

Nader, L. (1990). *Harmony ideology: Justice and control in a mountain Zapotec village.* Stanford, CA: Stanford University Press.

Parkes, D. (2011). *Aboriginal peoples and the criminal justice system: The Gladue decision and its impacts.* Unpublished backgrounder prepared for Why Aren't Special Sentencing Provisions for Aboriginal Offenders Working? Seminar, Faculty of Law, University of Manitoba, March 16, 2011.

Pavlich, G. (2018). Transforming powers and restorative justice. In T. Gavrielides (Ed.), *The Routledge international handbook of restorative justice*. London: Routledge

Pavlich, G. (2005). *Governing paradoxes of restorative justice.* London, UK: GlassHouse Press.

Peachey, D.E. (2003). The Kitchener experiment. In G. Johnstone (Ed.), *A restorative justice reader: Texts, sources, context.* Cullompton, UK: Willan Publishing.

Pennell, J., & Burford, G. (2002). Feminist praxis: Making family group conferencing work. In H. Strang & J. Braithwaite (Eds.), *Restorative justice and family violence*. Cambridge, UK: Cambridge University Press.

Petoukhov, K. (2011). *An evaluation of the truth and reconciliation commission of Canada (TRC) through the lens of restorative justice and the theory of recognition*. Unpublished MA thesis, Department of Sociology, University of Manitoba.

Petrellis, T. (2007). *The restorative justice living unit at Grande Cache institution: Exploring the application of restorative justice in a correctional environment*. Ottawa, ON: Correctional Service Canada.

Roberts, J. V., & Reid, A. A. (2017). Aboriginal incarceration in Canada since 1978: Every picture tells the same story. *Canadian Journal of Criminology and Criminal Justice, 59*(3), 313-345.

Ross, R. (1996). *Returning to the teachings: Exploring Aboriginal justice*. Toronto, ON: Penguin Books.

Rugge, T., Bonta, J., & Wallace-Capretta, S. (2005). *Evaluation of the collaborative justice project: A restorative justice program for serious crime*. Ottawa, ON: Public Safety and Emergency Preparedness Canada.

Rugge, T., & Cormier, R. (2005). Restorative justice in cases of serious crime: An evaluation. In E. Elliott & E. Gordon (Eds.), *New directions in restorative justice: Issues, practice and evaluation*. Cullompton, UK: Willan.

Sherman, L. & Strang, H. (2007). *Restorative Justice: The Evidence*. London: The Smith Institute.

Shapland, J., Robinson, G., Sorsby, A. (2011). *Restorative justice in practice: Evaluating what works for victims and offenders*. New York: Routledge.

Solicitor General of Canada. (1996). *Corrections population growth: Report of the Federal/ Provincial/Territorial Ministers responsible for Justice*. Ottawa, ON: Solicitor General.

Standing Committee on Justice. (1988). *Taking responsibility: Report on the standing committee on justice and Solicitor General on its review of sentencing, conditional release and related aspects of corrections*. Ottawa, ON: Supply and Services Canada.

Strang, H. (2001). *Victim participation in a restorative justice process*. Oxford, UK: Oxford University Press.

Stuart, B. (1996). Circle Sentencing: Turning swords into ploughshares. In B. Galaway & J. Hudson (Eds.), *Restorative justice: International perspectives*. Monsey, NY: Criminal Justice Press.

Stuart, B., & Pranis, K. (2006). Peacemaking circles: Reflections on principal features and primary outcomes. In D. Sullivan & L. Tifft (Eds.), *Handbook of restorative justice: A global perspective*. London and New York: Routledge.

Sykes, G., & Matza, D. (1957). Techniques of neutralization: A theory of delinquency. *American Sociological Review, 22*, 664-670.

Tuari, J. M. (2009). An Indigenous perspective on the standardisation of restorative justice in New Zealand and Canada. *Indigenous Policy Journal*, xx, Fall, 1-24.

The Church Council on Justice and Corrections. (2011). *Restorative justice*. Retrieved from http://ccjc.ca

Umbreit, M., Coates, M., Kalanj, B., Lipkin, R., & Petros, G. (1995). *Mediation of criminal conflict: An assessment of programs in four Canadian provinces*. St. Paul, MN: Centre for Restorative Justice and Mediation, University of Minnesota.

Van Camp, T., & Wemmers J. (2013). Victim satisfaction with restorative justice: More than simply procedural justice. *International Review of Victimology, 19*(2), 117-143.

Van Ness, D. (2007). Regional reviews: E North America. In G. Johnstone & D. Van Ness (Eds.), *Handbook of restorative justice*. Cullompton, UK: Willan Publishing.

Weitekamp, E. (2003). The history of restorative justice. In G. Johnstone (Ed.), *A restorative justice reader*. Cullompton, UK: Willan.

Woolford, A., & Ratner, R. (2003). Nomadic justice: Restorative justice on the margins of law. *Social Justice, 30,* 177-194.

Woolford, A., & Curran, A. (2013). Community positions, neoliberal dispositions: Neoliberalism, welfare, and reflexivity within the social service field. *Critical Sociology, 39,* 45-63.

Woolford, A., & Curran, A. (2011). Limited autonomy, neoliberal domination, and ethical distancing in the social services. *Critical Social Policy, 31,* 583-606.

Woolford, A. (2009). *The politics of restorative justice: A critical introduction.* Halifax, NS: Fernwood Publishing.

Wrightsman, L.S. (1994). P*ersonality development in adulthood: volume 1: Theories and concepts.* Newbury Park, CA: Sage.

Zehr, H. (2002). *The little book of restorative justice.* Intercourse, PA: Good Books.

Zehr, H. (1995). Justice paradigm shift? Vales and visions in the reform process. *Mediation Quarterly, 12,* 207-216.

Zehr, H. (1990). *Changing lenses: A new focus for crime and justice.* Scottsdale, PA: Herald Press.

12

An Introduction to Prison and Penal Abolitionism in Canada

Justin Piché, Kevin Walby and
Nicolas Carrier

Learning Objectives

After reading this chapter, you should be able to:

- Describe the history of prison and penal abolition in Canada.

- Explain foundational abolitionist concepts.

- Outline an abolitionist critique of imprisonment and the penal system.

- Understand abolitionism and how it differs from liberal and conservative approaches to penal reform.

INTRODUCTION

Reflecting on the establishment of the modern prison in western democracies, Foucault (1977, p. 234) observed that penal reform, the pursuit of altering the form and the content of punishment, has remained a constant within prison, "as it were, its programme." Similar observations have been made about the entire penal system, including the police (Vitale, 2017). Approaches to social change within the penal field are shaped by political philosophies. Conservative reformers emphasize "law and order" programmes to re-legitimate "criminal justice" interventions (Walby, 2011), for instance through changes to penality informed by the principle of less eligibility, which aim to make sure that the criminalized are subject to living conditions below the standards afforded to the working poor and other vulnerable populations pushed to the margins (De Giorgi, 2006). Conservative penal reform efforts tend to gain salience in the wake of high-profile, rare events that become sensationalized in the media. For instance, the option for judges to consider consecutive sentences for first-degree murder was added to the *Criminal Code of Canada* in the wake of events such as the killings of Jessica Lloyd and Marie-France Comeau by then Canadian Forces Colonel Russell Williams (Spencer, forthcoming). On the other hand, liberal reformers seek to humanize and modernize practices of incarceration (Walby, 2011), by emphasizing the need to have evidence-based "correctional" practices or by building new, more sanitary jails, prisons and penitentiaries (Piché, 2014). Liberal penal reform tends to gain traction following tragedies relating to systemic problems within the penal system (Bromwich & Kilty, 2017). An example of liberal reforms includes attempts to place limits on the use of solitary confinement in Ontario (Sapers, 2017) following revelations that Indigenous prisoner Adam Capay had spent hundreds of days in segregation while awaiting trial (Patriquin, 2016).

In contrast to reformers of different political persuasions, abolitionists have concluded that meaningful reform is simply impossible (see Box 12.1). While they often advocate for changes in the ways in which we incarcerate, punish or otherwise confine individuals in the short-term, they fight for the abolition of the prison (e.g., Mathiesen, 1974), of the entire criminal legal system (e.g., Hulsman, 1986), or even the abolition of all forms of carceral control (e.g., Piché & Larsen, 2010).

In this chapter, we provide a history of prison and penal abolitionist thought and praxis in Canada, and how it has shaped and been shaped by developments elsewhere in the world. We first provide a history of prison and penal abolitionism in Canada by means of an oral history. We then summarize key ideas that orient abolitionist critiques of penality inside and outside the Canadian context, as well as visions for dismantling life-taking and building life-sustaining social relations. We also highlight how Canadian abolitionists remain active today in a context recently marked by penal intensification (Piché, 2014; Webster & Doob, 2015), engaging in concrete advocacy and activism to contest and scale-back the infliction of pain in the name of "justice." We conclude by reflecting on the contributions of Canadian abolitionists and the need to bolster solidarity efforts across different social movements as a means of extending the boundaries of abolitionist thought and praxis.

EMERGENCE OF PRISON AND PENAL ABOLITIONISM IN CANADA: A CONVERSATION WITH BOB GAUCHER

Beyond the recognition that Canadians founded the International Conference on Prison Abolition (now the International Conference on Penal Abolition / ICOPA), the breadth and depth of their contributions to abolitionist thought and praxis over time have often been overlooked (e.g., Brown & Schept, 2017). To demonstrate how abolitionist organizers situated in Canada have contributed to the development of abolitionism, the lead author conducted an interview with Bob Gaucher, a retired professor from the Department of Criminology at the University of Ottawa, who has been central to advancing prison

Box 12.1 – Proposed Reforms to Solitary Confinement Following the Death of Ashley Smith

In the span of just under a year under the supervision and control of Correctional Service Canada (CSC), Ashley Smith "was involved in approximately 150 security incidents," including several instances of self-harm and resistance that were met with use of force by staff (Sapers, 2008, p. 5). During that time, she was transferred 17 times and either placed in administrative segregation or otherwise isolated from other prisoners in mental health settings (ibid). Enduring prolonged solitary confinement, her behaviour deteriorated. Despite being placed on "24-hour suicide watch under direct staff supervision" a day prior at Grand Valley Institution – a federal penitentiary for women located in Kitchener, Ontario – on 19 October 2007 Ashley "wrapped a ligature around her neck, cutting off her air flow" (ibid, p. 6). With CSC staff and management failing to respond, she "died of asphyxiation" (ibid). Several years later, a *Coroner's Inquest Touching the Death of Ashley Smith* determined the cause of death to be a "Ligature strangulation and positional asphyxia" by means of "Homicide" due to the inaction on the part of CSC that contributed to the end of her life (Carlyle, 2013). The inquest made 104 recommendations to prevent future deaths in custody arising from the use of solitary confinement. The case of Ashley Smith's preventable death became a lightning rod for debates about the future of the practice in Canada (Bromwich & Kilty, 2017). Below, we provide a few quotes that illustrate how conservatives sought to essentially preserve the status quo with respect to solitary confinement, while liberals aimed to attenuate its damage and abolitionists sought to eradicate its use altogether, in the wake of this incident.

Conservative Stance

The Jury recommendations on this issue urged CSC to reduce its use of segregation, improve administration and oversight of the segregation process, and minimize the use of restraints to control self-injurious behaviour in favor of better therapeutic practices.

The Coroner's Jury also recommended that "indefinite solitary confinement" be abolished and that long-term segregation not exceed 15 days. They also wanted to see restrictions placed on the number of periods that offenders can spend segregated, including a requirement of no more than a cumulative total of 60 days in a calendar year.

To be clear, the term solitary confinement is not accurate or applicable within the Canadian federal correctional system. Canadian law and correctional policy allow for the use of administrative segregation for the shortest period of time necessary, in limited circumstances, and only when there are no reasonable, safe alternatives.

Administrative Segregation in the federal corrections system is not intended to be a form of punishment. It is an interim population management measure resulting from a carefully considered decision made by the Institutional Head to facilitate an investigation or to protect the safety and security of individuals and/or the institution.

> – *CSC (2014) under the leadership of then Public Safety Minister and Conservative MP Steven Blaney*

continued...

Liberal Stance

Today, the Government of Canada introduced legislation to restrict the use of administrative segregation and strengthen Canada's federal correctional system. The new legislation and regulations that will follow will increase accountability, transparency and oversight around the use of administrative segregation. This is an important step in ensuring that Canada's federal correctional system is effective, accountable and transparent, and that it helps inmates as they work towards rehabilitation and reintegration into society as law-abiding citizens.

For the first time, there will be a legislative framework that establishes a presumptive time limit for inmates confined in administrative segregation.

Under the current CCRA the Correctional Service of Canada must always release the inmate at the earliest appropriate time. Eighteen months after the legislation comes into force, there will be a presumption that an inmate must not remain in administrative segregation longer than 15 days, subject to security and safety concerns and there being no reasonable alternative. For the eighteen months prior, the presumptive limit will be 21 days.

Also for the first time, the legislation would provide independent external review of cases of inmates kept in administrative segregation beyond the presumptive release date, and for those who have, in the last calendar year, been in administrative segregation at least three times or for 90 cumulative days.

– PSC (2017) under the leadership of current Public Safety Minister and Liberal MP Ralph Goodale

Abolitionist Stance

Segregation is an inherently dangerous and inhumane practice. There is no evidence that it is possible to moderate or contain the damage it causes. Segregation is not necessary; there are examples in Canada where, when segregation was not an option, entire institutions have operated for extended periods of time without segregation units. When segregation is available, it is too often used as a default. If we truly wish to fix the problem, we must condemn and end the use of segregation outright.

– Senator Kim Pate (2018)

and penal abolition through his teaching, research, and activism. The conversation examines his contributions, alongside the work of three prominent abolitionists – Art Solomon, Claire Culhane and Ruth Morris. These actors were at the forefront of early organizing against prisons and punishment before abolitionism became an integral part of many social justice movements (Mayrl, 2013).

The "Beast" Meets Kesheyyanakwan, the "Fast Moving Cloud": Art Solomon's Struggle Against Colonial Government and Prisons

A leading Indigenous spiritual advisor and early proponent of prison abolition, Art Solomon (1914-1997) understood that many Canadian state institutions were explicitly designed to destroy Indigenous peoples by assimilating them into white settler society (Solomon, 1994). This was conducted through "strategies of annihilation" (Martel et al., 2011, p. 235), including the reserve system that dispossessed Indigenous peoples of their lands and confined them to small territories. Beyond this, children – including Art Solomon himself – were removed from their communities and confined in Residential Schools, where they were forcibly disconnected from their lands, cultures, languages, and spirituality (TRC, 2015). This pattern of cultural genocide persisted through practices such as the "60's scoop," where Indigenous children were removed from their homes and communities *en masse*, and adopted by white families (Sinclair, 2007). The mass removal and white-stream adoption of Indigenous children continues (Cardinal, 2018).

It is in this context that much of Art Solomon's work focused on what he called the "just us system," that is a 'criminal justice' system that arrests Indigenous peoples, processes them through courtrooms, and mass imprisons them (Sapers, 2013: paragraph 18) as an integral part of the on-going colonial rule of Canadian society. Bob Gaucher notes:

> Art brought this uniquely Indigenous perspective on the issues that appear within the abolitionist agenda…In his life, he observed how community control had been attacked in a genocidal attempt to destroy Aboriginal culture…that if you take away the ability of the community to manage itself then what you do is you completely disorganize that community. It becomes a state of anomie where there are no longer any kinds of traditional lines of understanding, family or community that are able to ameliorate situations that develop.

Art Solomon saw "criminal justice" as a means for the Canadian state to assert dominion over conflicts by criminalizing Indigenous people and subjecting many of those deemed responsible for "crime" – especially Indigenous peoples – to imprisonment. As Bob Gaucher remarks:

> Art sought to dismantle prisons and a very racist justice system. You have to understand, over-representation of Aboriginal people in our prison system…is a major characteristic of it since even before the Second World War. Even in the 1960s, when I was in PA [i.e. Saskatchewan Penitentiary in Prince Albert] I remember 40 percent of the institution was Aboriginal and Métis. They used to call the C-block "the reservation." That's long been a problem for Indigenous communities. Their criminalization was and remains an extension of Residential Schools. Art made that argument, that prisons were the university and at the educational root were the Residential Schools. Art brought a holistic view to make sense of the racial domination of Indigenous people and he saw prisons as the ultimate big brother.

For Art Solomon, abolition was more than fighting for an end to Indigenous incarceration. It was also a struggle to reassert Indigenous autonomy over their lives, including in the face of violence perpetrated under the guise of "criminal justice." As Bob Gaucher recounts:

> Art argued that community has to be the place where problems are resolved and so he introduced things like circles, which later became absorbed to some minor extent by the penal system itself in a bent way [i.e., sentencing circles]. Art was arguing that communities themselves have to be strengthened and have the ability to deal with their own problems. So, much as Indigenous lawyer, legal scholar and activist Trish Monture[1] also argued over the years, he saw the need to extract First Nations people from the clutches of the penal system so that their own communities can deal with the problems that we define as criminal justice problems. He didn't argue that there wasn't conflict, that there weren't problems within Indigenous communities, but he did argue that those communities didn't have any control, nor the power to deal with their own problems. What he really saw as an alternative was that Indigenous communities would use traditional means of reproducing harmony, that is the restoration of community harmony. He

saw criminalization and punishment as bullshit control that didn't resolve the issues that they were supposed to be addressing…Restoration of harmony, that was his focus. Intervention shouldn't be about punishment. It shouldn't be about guilt. It should be about restoration of harmony, of community. The problems of community break people apart. So, the solution was to bring them back together.

In his push to resist and dismantle colonial state structures, while reasserting Indigenous ways of being, Art was involved in many activities. Bob Gaucher notes that central to this was Art Solomon's work with prisoners through the Canadian Alliance in Solidarity with Native People (CASNP), as well as Native Brotherhood and Native Sisterhood groups:

His model starts with the idea of resistance and CASNP was very much an organization directed towards this. He pushed in his prison work with Indigenous peoples – many who have been the products of Residential Schools that didn't know their cultures – reintroducing and restoring their sense of spirituality. Art saw this reintroduction of spirituality and sense of community also as a means of dealing with a lot of problems within Indigenous communities, in contrast to the kind of instrumentality that they have in the criminal justice system. But he really did talk well about resistance. He used to say, "I've stared the monster in the face and I've laughed. I'm not scared of you." For Art, that resistance for Indigenous peoples starts by affirming their spirituality, the highest form of consciousness, in the face of colonial violence, including while imprisoned. As an elder and spiritual advisor, this is what he taught.

Art Solomon (1994, pp. 103-105) clearly noted that the current approach to imprisonment and punishment reproduces poverty and racism in Canada, and therein benefits wealthy, non-Indigenous communities. He viewed incarceration as the most repressive Canadian state edifice of colonial empire building, requiring that prison walls be torn down. Part of decolonizing was not just about abolishing institutions such as the prison, but also rebuilding Indigenous communities whose members would become reconnected to their cultures and lands with the autonomy to control their destinies. Art worked toward this anti-colonial and anti-racist vision by working with Indigenous prisoners as a spiritual advisor, as well as through local, national, and international consciousness raising efforts aimed at asserting Indigenous sovereignty.

A "One Woman Army":
Claire Culhane, Capitalism and Prisons as "The Best Fight in Town"

A prominent peace activist and feminist, Claire Culhane (1918-1996) spent her life fighting for social justice. As a young person, she engaged in numerous campaigns such as raising funds for Dr. Norman Bethune when he was providing care to supporters of the elected communist government during the Spanish Civil War. She also participated in relief work to help offset the ravages of poverty during the Great Depression of the 1930s and was a leading figure in the movement against the Vietnam War after she returned from work as a hospital administrator in the war-torn country. This hospital had become a conduit for intelligence to the United States, informing their aggression, which Claire Culhane (1972) was deeply concerned by. This activism merited Claire Culhane the title of "one woman army" in RCMP intelligence reports tracking her movements and interventions. This moniker would later become the title of a book by Mic Lowe (1992) documenting her life.

As the Vietnam War was coming to an end, Claire Culhane began to devote much of her time to other struggles, notably those behind bars. Among the many roles she took on in the 1970s was to become a member of the newly founded Citizens Advisory Board at British Columbia Penitentiary

(BC Pen) as the institution continued to be the site of numerous conflicts between prisoners, staff members and the administration, which culminated into the September 1976 riot. Bob Gaucher describes Claire Culhane's involvement in the incident:

> When Mary Steinhauser [a social worker in the prison] was shot to death by a guard during a hostage taking, Claire was on the Citizen's Advisory Board and refused to leave the institution. She stayed there through it all, and when it was over and she finally left, the Canadian Penitentiary Service barred her. They claimed she sent a prisoner's letter out during the incident and this gave them reason to bar her from the institution, but it was really because she scrutinized and monitored what in fact was going down.

Claire Culhane's commitment to prison abolition was related to broader struggles against inequality. As Bob Gaucher notes:

> Claire was an ardent opponent of capitalism and capitalist control – control of the bosses. She said prisons were "the best fight in town." It was all so obvious, how fucked up they were. This was repression at its most visible. She saw prisons as a fountain that allowed you to discuss it all…all the inequalities, the racism, all the problems that are part of this broader society, were evident in the prison. How they ran, what went down there. And so, prisons became "the best fight in town," that it was so obvious as an entry point to the discussion of these broader issues. She took prison and imprisonment itself very seriously.

With prison serving as the point of entry into struggles against capitalism, Claire Culhane promoted socialism, that is the redistribution of wealth to ensure that basic standards of living and the necessities of life were accessible to all, which she thought would translate into many benefits including less violence in Canadian society. As Bob Gaucher recalls:

> Claire was a structuralist. She thought it was the way society was organized that generated conflicts and harms. To address harm, you had to deal with the way society was organized. She certainly opposed harming others. But in her own understanding, she saw individual acts of violence as representative of broader structural issues. For her, that's where the solutions lay.

Claire Culhane's prison abolition and social justice work was animated by a deep commitment to public education and political persuasion. As Bob Gaucher notes, she privileged certain tactics in her struggles against the capitalist and punitive state:

> Claire was a political activist that believed in civil disobedience. On one occasion, she chained herself to the gates of Parliament. I was up there with her, distributing handouts that she made about conditions in Canadian prisons…She believed in exposé, that you had to expose what was going on. And that was central to her arguments and to her approach. Claire had prisoners across the system writing to her and she wrote to them. She made two cross-country tours every year, visiting every federal prison. She knew all the information about what was going down in Canadian prisons. Prisoners called her "*St. Claire*." She believed that if you saw injustices occurring you had to expose the problems and push people to do something about them…she was into creating demos, she traveled the country informing people. I brought her to the University of Ottawa in 1985 and it was one of the biggest talks I ever organized. I was surprised. I had a relatively small room that maybe held 90 people. But we had people standing in the aisles and anywhere there was space. There were people in the hall and colleagues of mine that were contributing to the work of the Correctional Service of Canada even showed up. She had quite the reputation and following. To reiterate, she was into exposé and she believed that you had to

show people what the fuck was actually going down in prisons, and if you did that, she had some hope at least, this would lead to some level of change, both structurally and for individual prisoners.

For Bob Gaucher, she "was a model of what an activist should be":

I've never met anybody in this country that comes even close to the contribution, and the absolute dedication and resistance of Claire Culhane. There has been nobody ever – and I say ever – that had the level of involvement and understanding of what was going on in Canadian prisons as she did. Her level of commitment, her level of understanding and her level of resist-ance…she supported civil disobedience. She thought you had to make noise, get their attention. I think those were all lessons for those of us on the left. Those of us who are against and resisting the social structures and the society we live in. We want something better. For me, Claire was an elder – she was inspiring. She would come out of meetings or talks that she did and would come out and say, "what are you going to do? What are you up to? What's your next move? Don't applaud me. Don't. I'm just doing what I should do. Go out there and do something." And people moved when she spoke. For instance, when she told my students about how she got arrested because the Post Office accused her of reusing stamps, when she was in fact only reusing the envelopes, saving money by crossing out the previous recipient and putting a label on it to send a letter to somebody else, they initiated a fundraising campaign to help fund her correspondence work with prisoners. She got things done…She also brought to bear tactics to organize resistance. For instance, she used to take on the Commissioner of penitentiaries all the time. She'd go and sit at national headquarters in Ottawa on Laurier. She'd get there at 7am and requested to see the Commissioner. She'd sit there all day waiting and if she didn't see him, she'd be back the next day at 7am. She brought this strength of character and absolute refusal to give into anything. She was the strongest person that I probably ever met. She worked 16 hours a day at it.

While Claire Culhane left a big mark, bringing at the forefront of public discussions how impris-onment primarily served the interests of capital as an instrument to control the poor and otherwise marginalized, her many activities with prisoners to make visible the harms of incarceration stood out. Chief among them was her commitment to building Prison Justice Day, which began on 10 August 1975 as a non-violent day of action inside Millhaven Institution. Prisoners refused to work and eat to commemorate the death of Eddie Nalon exactly a year earlier while in solitary confinement (Gaucher, 1989). Prison Justice Day now takes place inside and outside prison walls. As Bob Gaucher observes:

Claire is probably the principal person outside of prison walls that helped to establish and extend Prison Justice Day. She did early actions in Oakalla provincial prison in Vancouver, where there was no federal penitentiary for women at the time. She was also a major supporter of the penal press. If you look at early *Tightwire*[2] you'll find that Claire plays a prominent role in that as well. She saw Prison Justice Day as a main means of organizing resistance, both inside and outside. She supported prisoners' resistance by being a conduit of information as she traveled from institution to institution, informing people in Springhill what was going on at Stony Moun-tain and the like. Conduit is the best word that I can think of. She became a conduit to prison resistance across the country.

In the face of state efforts to thwart her work, including the institution of a lengthy ban prevent-ing her from physically accessing federal penitentiaries following the 1976 riot at BC Pen, Claire Culhane never wavered as documented in her books focusing on incarceration, including *Barred from prison: A personal account* (Culhane, 1979), *Still barred from prison: Social injustice in Canada* (Culhane, 1985) and *No longer barred from prison: Social injustice in Canada* (Culhane, 1991). Throughout it all she maintained contact with prisoners through correspondence and visited them in person as well once her access to these sites of confinement was restored, making visible their pain and the broader social injustices they represented. Claire Culhane was instrumental in placing prisoners at the centre of social change and positioning prison abolition as an anti-capitalist struggle.

Away From "An Expensive, Unjust, Immoral Failure": Ruth Morris and the Path toward Transformative Justice

Whereas Art Solomon and Claire Culhane initially came to abolitionism as part of broader struggles against domination and the Canadian state, Ruth Morris (1933-2001) saw her work against imprisonment and punishment as necessary for the progressive humanization of conflict resolution. Bob Gaucher describes how Ruth Morris first became familiar with abolitionism:

> It has to be understood and recognized that Quakers were central to Ruth's journey towards abolitionism. Fay Honey Knoop[3] was a Quaker, as was Ruth Morris. Quakers played an instrumental role in the emergence of the modern prison in North America and they felt a responsibility to build alternatives to it in lieu of its many harms and failures. Ruth was also influenced by Art Solomon, who may have come together with her through the World Council of Churches. So that coming together of spirituality was critical for some abolitionists and you have to give the Quakers a certain amount of credit despite critical mistakes that they made. I mean, their initial creation of the Pennsylvania system was a means of ameliorating what they saw as major problems with incarceration as it stood at that point in time. I think you can say that she was in that progressive tradition. Religious groups have to be considered when exploring the nexus of prison resistance and of alternatives to prison. You got to understand the context up to that point. Up until the mid-1970s there was real resistance going on to penal control, period. It was not spiritual groups and anti-penal resistors questioning imprisonment alone. It was part in parcel of a much broader political conversation where prisons were seen as instruments of, and the police where seen as an instrument of, state control. Just look at the Black Panther Party's ten-point program in the United States as an example.[4] I think Ruth in many ways represents the best of giving and caring religious traditions. The refusal to cast people aside. The belief that redemption, forgiveness and the restoration of harmony within communities is possible. It is the last point where I saw the real influence of Art Solomon on her… Ruth had this religiously-based commitment to social justice.

Ruth Morris' abolitionist stance evolved over time. As noted in *Stories of transformative justice* (Morris, 2000), she moved beyond the idea of "misery justice," that is moving from trying to humanize and change the existing system to prison abolition and developing community-based punishments. Having witnessed that the introduction of alternatives to imprisonment often failed to diminish the use of incarceration, while extending prison-like controls into the community (also see Cohen, 1985), Ruth Morris shifted her focus to penal abolition and building alternatives to punitive justice. This led to her promotion of restorative justice (see Chapter 14) as a way to dealing with conflict, but then realizing that such processes individualize accountability, which allows the structures that give rise to conflict to continue on. Considering that "the idea of restorative justice implied we had had justice, and lost it," she then advocated for transformative justice that focuses not just at the level of individuals impacted by "crimes," but seeks to alter the structures that are at the root of social conflicts and harms (Morris, 2000, p. 19; also see Box 12.2). As part of this shift in thought and practice, she also became outspoken about corporate and state harm, along with the need for fundamental structural changes to be made in our world as a means of achieving equality.

Box 12.2 – Questions Raised During the Pursuit of Justice in the Wake of "Crime"

Criminal Justice	Restorative Justice	Transformative Justice
• What laws have been broken? • Who did it? • What do they deserve? – Zehr (2002, p. 21)	• Who has been hurt? • What are their needs? • Whose obligations are these? – Zehr (2002, p. 21)	• How can we address the human needs arising from conflict (i.e., "answers, recognition of wrong, safety, restitution, and significance"), while doing something about "the social roots from which the crime arose"? – Morris (2000, p. 20)

Along the way, Ruth Morris engaged new communities in abolitionist discussions about what needs to be dismantled and built through various means such as creating the International Conference on Prison Abolition (ICOPA) in 1983, which continues to hold meetings in different parts of the world as the International Conference on Penal Abolition to reflect the idea that abolishing incarceration as an institution and practice requires the elimination of one of its core underlying logics – punishment (Delisle et al., 2015). This involves questioning the moral grounds upon which punishment could be justifiable. In regards to Ruth Morris' and ICOPA's journey, Bob Gaucher observes:

> It's the path that she took and it's important to understand that the community that she represented within ICOPA from fairly early on, and how it informed but also clashed with other strands of thought and praxis within ICOPA. One of the things that I find inspiring about Ruth – and to what extent this was the influence of people like Claire Culhane and Art Solomon – was her own sense of commitment, that she really gave wholeheartedly. She spent her own money. She raised money. She organized church groups. She spoke across this country and internationally. And she saw it as an international problem. She sought taking ICOPA to other venues, to other countries, that would both encourage people internationally to engage in abolitionist conversation, but also to inform them about what the alternatives were. And there were arguments about alternatives, and you see this in the transition of Ruth's own thinking and the development of understanding that occurred within ICOPA itself.

Throughout her life, Ruth Morris' pursuit of alternatives to state repression involved direct engagement with the penal system. Bob Gaucher recalls the value of such interventions, despite the risks involved with reform efforts being met by state cooptation of alternatives to meet punitive ends and the expansion of penal power, which has been a central preoccupation for abolitionists historically (e.g., Mathiesen, 1974) and remains so today (e.g., Ben-Moshe, 2013):

She started this bail reform group, a halfway house and many other initiatives in Toronto when she was engaged in prison abolition work…she did stuff inside the system. While others, like Art Solomon and Claire tried to ensure separation, keeping themselves clearly on the outside, Ruth served as a bridge between abolitionists and non-abolitionists…One of the things Ruth's approach really accomplished was by working within, it not only identified problems that she tried to address within the system, but she exposed the inability of working with the system to solve those problems. In that way, she made a real contribution. Yes, we want alternatives and we need to experiment to see what they look like in practice and whether they get absorbed into the existing system or really work towards building something new. Many of the alternatives put forward by Ruth prior to her shift towards penal abolition and transformative justice did get co-opted by the state, but the bail reform program in Toronto was important and did have some really positive spinoffs for some people who avoided the pains of jail. At the same time, it exposed to us, and also to her, to the reality that engaging with the state is dangerous work. Like Art Solomon used to say if you engage with and within the system, it will transform you into the system. That's capitalism, it has this ability to take whatever you throw at it and turn alternatives into its' own stuff.

A central theme throughout her work, captured at different moments in time in books such as *Crumbling walls: Why prisons fail* (Morris, 1989), *Penal abolition: The practical choice* (Morris, 1995), *The case for penal abolition* (West & Morris, 2000), *Stories of transformative justice* (Morris, 2000), and *Transcending trauma* (Morris, 2004) is that incarceration and later "criminal justice" as a whole, is an "expensive, unjust, immoral failure" (Morris, 2000, p. 5). Reflecting on her legacy, Bob Gaucher notes:

Just like Claire Culhane did her exposé to show what kind of bullshit was happening, Ruth Morris engaged people outside of the abolitionist movement into the abolitionist movement. In doing so, she educated them, expanding the number of people willing to entertain these ideas. Criminal justice is so entrenched…getting people to actually say, "well just a minute that doesn't work," is a mountain of a task. You see this with the police and all this adulation they get on cop shows and the news. It's hard at times to argue about police corruption and police transgressions as being systemic issues, rather than one-offs because they've created this image of the police as the great protector. Claire Culhane use to call it "a protection racket," you know? I think what Ruth Morris teaches us is to not close the door, to widen the scope of who you reach out to and include as many people as you can. If it means on the edges that your message is somewhat watered down when compared to the more radical stances of the likes of Art Solomon and Claire Culture, so what? Ruth herself exemplifies the way such thinking pulled her down the path. It's an important journey to be aware of.

Similar to Claire Culhane who privileged social change "from below" by working with prisoners, Ruth Morris' central contribution was to favour conflict resolution by involving those affected by criminalized acts in the justice process, while challenging the injustices "from above," including those that stem from Canada's adversarial, retributive penal process.

"Meet One, Teach One": Bob Gaucher and the Institutionalization of Abolitionism at the University of Ottawa

While some arrive to prison and penal abolitionist work through broader social justice organizing or working to humanize justice in the wake of conflicts and harms, others have adopted abolitionism after having experienced state repression first-hand. This was the case for Bob Gaucher (1945-), although he never put at the forefront that he had been a prisoner during his academic career, whether in his teaching or research activities. He reflected on his time behind bars, its impact and how he escaped the clutches of the state through education:

> When I was sixteen I received a 1-year sentence, which I served in an adult provincial prison – Fort Saskatchewan Gaol – outside of Edmonton. This clearly led me in the wrong direction and six months after the end of that sentence I was convicted of a B & E (Break and Enter) and sentenced to 2 years, which I served in the maximum-security Saskatchewan Penitentiary known as "PA" in Prince Albert, Saskatchewan. I was seventeen years old when I entered, and I served essentially the full two years (23 months and 22 days). During the last six months there I was in deep segregation / "the hole," from where I was released at the completion of my sentence. There were many other youths from my neighborhood and I made good friends amongst the more seasoned convicts from whom I learnt much about solidarity and resistance. I learnt what it meant to take a side – what resistance and solidarity were about under adverse conditions. I thought at that time that I was targeted by guards because of my age and as a possible weak link amongst my older more experienced friends or just because it pissed everyone off that I was constantly under the gun. A work stoppage in the Mason's Shop I was assigned to led to my appearance in Warden's Court where I was given the option of returning to work (i.e., doing what I was told) or going to "the hole." After I left Warden's Court I went to "the hole"! I wouldn't give in… they wouldn't give in, and so I spent the last six months of my sentence, which included all the goodtime I lost, in solitary confinement, for long periods, sleeping on a board and living on a "restricted diet" of one meal per day. Solitary can be hard to deal with, and though we could talk from cell to cell at night, the conditions were far from humane. I concluded that they were trying to destroy me, to kill my spirit, as a means of getting to my friends.

> I was in rough shape when I was released, angry and with little hope of a positive way forward. Though I tried, my lack of success in getting any type of toe hold in the Edmonton community led to a more serious approach and a year later, at age 20, I was arrested for Bank Robbery and eventually sentenced to 10 years. When I re-entered PA, older prisoners advised me that "you can do a deuce like that, but not a dime." Though I was still an angry kid, I heard them! A number of experiences helped turn me around. A good friend who completed a 12-year sentence for Bank Robbery shortly after I re-entered was back inside 4 months later doing another 12 years for a similar crime. I recall sitting in my cell thinking, "this isn't going to be me." Saskatchewan Penitentiary was a violent prison and it was difficult to avoid situations that demanded violent responses. There was one night I remember where I was trying to figure how to deal with the violence without getting "caught," which led me to reconsider what the future held. It's then that I resolved to "quit the game." Not so easy to do when you had rapidly built a reputation as a bad guy, and are now looking a years of imprisonment before release. But I was growing up, and I started to look outside the walls with a more conscious sense of self and society. And outside things were happening!

> I discovered that I could take university extension courses from Queen's University (Kingston) and was the first person in PA that did so, though other prisoners soon followed my lead. Over the next 2 years, I successfully completed 5 undergraduate courses and became eligible to enter second year as a full-time student in the Arts & Science undergraduate program. My reading and engagements went beyond these courses, as I tuned in to the rumblings from outside our cages. I became involved with the Native Brotherhood Group, discovered the American Indian Movement, and tried to learn Cree.

An older friend turned me on to Albert Camus' "The Rebel," and I engaged Sartre and the existentialist critique. I discovered Black Power, through the biography of Malcolm X, and the uprisings on the streets of Amerika. Even inside the walls we knew of the growing resistance to racism, class discrimination, and imperialism that was blossoming across the world. While I didn't buy into the emerging institutional conversation on rehabilitation, because I maintained my sense of indignation at what had occurred in my life (what were they doing sending a 17-year-old to a maximum-security pen for a minor property crime?), I didn't go looking for trouble and kept focused on a positive possible future. In the late 1960s, Pierre Trudeau's call for "a just society" included major changes to federal parole practices that increased granting rates, which I benefitted from in 1969. I left prison for Queen's University with a sense of solidarity with the people inside and having developed an understanding of the inequalities and discriminations that underlay criminalization and carceral practices in Canada and throughout the world.

The politicization and consequent resistance of youth to state control at home and imperialism abroad provide me with a sense of place in society that I previously lacked. There was a rational community that I felt part of that allowed me to channel my own sense of injustice and focus my resistance. I was finally able to make sense of the contradictions between the bullshit I had been told in the name of "society" and what I had actually experienced and witnessed in our criminal courts and prisons. I knew that the prison population of Saskatchewan Penitentiary was largely composed of the disenfranchised – Indigenous Peoples, Métis and the poor. The way prisoners were treated was symptomatic of the imperialism with which these groups were treated by Canadian society generally. I became involved in the anti-war movement, which included helping organize Queen's students' participation in the demonstration against Canadian complicity in Vietnam on Parliament Hill in Ottawa where I first heard Claire Culhane address an audience. I became the outside contact for a prisoners' group at Collins Bay Institution. These experiences have always informed me. All my subsequent involvements and activism with the penal abolition movement have been driven by my sense of solidarity with prisoners.

After completing his undergraduate at Queen's University in Kingston and his master's at Carleton University, Bob Gaucher began working for Statistics Canada where he got involved in a study that helped shape debates on capital punishment at a critical juncture in Canada's history (see Reed et al., 1976; Reed et al., 1977).

I got a job at Stats Can...The debate on capital punishment was starting to percolate and they gave me a homicide study to do. I spent two years working 10-hour days and weekends getting it done. What they asked us to do was provide all the information that addressed the nature of homicide in Canada. Initially, they had a bullshit scale. They had "domestic homicide," "kinship group," "during the commission of another offense," and "other" – and "other" was the biggest category. I broke it all out into a 10-point scale and that's what went to Parliament. It was well taken...the team at Stats Can presented the homicide study and we figured the study managed to switch at least 10 MPs to come onside with the abolition of capital punishment vote in 1976, which was a free vote that wasn't whipped by any of the parties in the House of Commons. Getting those votes was more than enough to win the day. I remember knocking heads with Solicitor General Warren Allmand at a John Howard Society dinner. I'd been asked to come on their board in Ottawa because they'd been my parole agency. Allmand was talking about replacing capital punishment with a life sentence with such a parole eligibility starting at 25 years. I got really upset with Allmand and asked him, "where did you get this number?" Back then, those getting sentenced to die were those convicted of first degree murder for killing a police officer or prison guard. I argued with him that people were doing an average 9½ years behind bars for second degree murder and 12 years for first degree murders, so why introduce life sentences with parole eligibility? Where did that come from? Yes, people were no longer going to be murdered by the state, but the trade-off would end-up being far more punitive for those who, at that time, weren't being sentenced to die...Allmand defended himself by talking about the 15-year clause, also known as "Faint Hope," which Harper got rid of. Despite the fact that Lifers are serving more of their sentences behind bars today, I remain proud of the fact that I contributed to a movement where people would have otherwise been subject to full blooded state murder.

During his time in university, which included the completion of a doctoral dissertation at Sheffield University supervised by Ian Taylor[5] on the early history of policing and penitentiaries in Canada prior to Confederation, Bob Gaucher followed debates about prisons and its alternatives. *The politics of abolition* (Mathiesen, 1974) and *Instead of prisons: A handbook for abolitionists* (Knopp et al., 1976) were among the works that cemented his abolitionist stance.

There was a liberal sensibility in the 1970s and a lot of us thought we we're going to get rid of a lot of this shit. Arguments about alternatives were there, which we didn't fully embrace but entertained. They were going to start diverting people from the penal system. As someone who was a 16-year-old kid who did really good in school, had no past record, and ended-up in jail, diversion made sense to me. I watched prison transform people into prisoners, transform them into outsiders. I don't think there's an appreciation of the extent to what it does to your psyche, to be trashed in that way – stripped, treated like a piece of meat...It's humiliating. You really have a sense that, no, you're not part of this anymore. They've thrown you aside, you're disen-franchised. I watched all of these young guys who were my friends, some who were teenagers when they came in. I watched them have their lives taken away from them or never being able to recover from state brutality.

However, while the prison and punishment were the focus, like Art Solomon and Claire Culhane, Bob Gaucher's work was informed by a commitment to dismantling broader structures of domination and building a world premised on the pursuit of equality. He notes:

Here lies the problem. There is the taken for granted context of capitalism, consumer capitalism and the problems it causes that is largely unquestioned...It's all about consumption the way we live. I personally see the solution in this country, in the world, is that we need to take seriously Indigenous understandings of how we live with Mother Nature, how we live with the environ-ment. To me, criminal justice is just a way of managing the capitalist economy, securing its place. It's got nothing to do with crime and justice. That's bullshit. Of course, we can't have people running around killing each other. No kidding. However, if you've got high murder rates there's something wrong with the organization of your society. That's the problem. You're not solving violence with piecemeal bullshit. Okay, we're going to legalize marijuana. It shouldn't have been illegal in the first place. This isn't going to change the nature of how we live and where we are. We need to go back to reflect upon the meaning of abolition. I've always thought as Claire Culhane and Art Solomon understood it. To have justice, we must deal with the struc-tural issues. Those in power don't give a shit how many prisoners there are. In the United States, do you think they give a shit if there's like two million prisoners or one million? You think the Koch brothers give one fucking hoot about that or Trump cares about that? They're about making money and pushing their self-serving vision where "I decide, I'm the one who makes the choices, nobody tells me what to do." That's the arrogance of being a billionaire, no sense of the collective and it's the arrogance that our society reproduces. I figured this out in the 1980s, while I watched everything we hoped for in the 1960s and the 1970s go south as Reagan, Thatcher and Mulroney took power. If we don't make structural change, we're not getting anywhere.

Given this take on the world, one may arrive at the conclusion that there is nothing to be done. However, as Bob Gaucher notes, when working in a context where social justice appears to be a distant possibility, there remains a lot to do and many possibilities for social change.

What I did is I started a Lifers group. I started rescuing individual prisoners because I guess it made me feel a little better and eased my conscience. It was also something that I could actually do that was real, when movement on bigger issues was not immediately feasible. When things are all going the other way, what do you do in the interim? While it doesn't mean that you don't keep arguing you have to be realistic too, right? If you want to be an abolitionist, okay, but take on what you can take on, even little things. I thought Thomas Mathiesen got it down pretty good in his arguments of negative reforms and you do what you can in the space that you get and try to make that space bigger…I tried to put prisoners on the agenda. What always drove me was my sense of solidarity with prisoners. Understanding who they are and what is going on behind the walls. So, I think of the *JPP* [*Journal of Prisoners on Prisons*] and getting the voices of prisoners in academic debates about imprisonment and punishment. As an academic I say this seriously, how can you make sense of prisons if you don't know what the perspective of prisoners are? I also made sure prisoners were involved in ICOPA. I always used to say, "could you have a women's liberation movement without women? How can you have a penal abolitionist movement without prisoners?" We need their input. They inform you about what's going down. That's what Claire Culhane understood. You can't understand what's going on unless someone there is in the action and tells you. Starting the *JPP* was a big contribution trying to give voice to prisoners. I saw it with the university students who were taken aback by the *JPP*. Jeez, prisoners can write a whole lot better than them. Their analysis was better than their own. It changed the nature of their perception of who's in prison and that's really important. It's humanizing. That's what I was trying to do with the John Howard Society – let's try to humanize. A prisoner is not just somebody that just keeps us afloat and makes us money, they're human beings. This is important for prisoners, who have an appreciation of what it means to be trashed, thrown aside, treated like shit…Teaching can also play an important role in the movement. As a professor at the University of Ottawa I liked the kids that I taught and I felt sorry for them, surrounded by all of this bullshit. If the reality is so encased around you then how do you see beyond it? It was a great struggle for me to be able to do that…One of the things I've been pleased about is that some students that I've taught have continued to carry the abolitionist torch in university and college settings like yourself, Vivanne Saleh-Hanna, Melissa Munn, Chris Bruckert, Claire Delisle and others. Many were members of the Infinity Lifers' Liaison Group going into penitentiaries for a long while. Other students of mine remain active in social justice causes. It means that I didn't waste my time. Teaching in criminology departments is a two-edged sword. You've got students who want to work for Canadian Security Intelligence Service and the like, who recruit on some campuses. You've got others who I found to be bright lights in my life and kept me going as the world got worse. Students really gave me a reason to continue.

Others have reflected on the relationship between abolition and teaching as well (e.g., Barraclough, 2010; Chartrand & Piché, forthcoming). While it is clear that abolitionists working in the Canadian context have not managed to eradicate imprisonment and the penal system, it is important to perhaps consider their contributions alongside forces of penal moderation (Doob & Webster, 2006) that have, at the very least, helped prevent the massive increase in imprisonment observed in some countries, notably the United States. On this point, Bob Gaucher observes the status and influence some Canadian abolitionists earned through their advocacy and organizing:

> Claire Culhane's MP [Member of Parliament] for many years was Svend Robinson, who was out front with all his support for prisoners and his support of abolitionist points of view. Senator Hastings was somebody I worked with from Calgary. He was concerned about Lifers. So, I think we always had influence in a minor way, influence on people on Parliament Hill. We're a more caring society. But, what you're doing is you're comparing it to a more than terrible situation. So, have we had any influence? I think we can have influence. And I think there is a possibility for reasoned debate. That was stopped for about 10 years under Harper's Conservatives, but I think by and large when you have Liberal governments they are more open. I think that it's rather astounding that with all this escalation of incarceration across the world, not just in the USA, but in parts of Europe and the UK that we've been able to maintain, not an acceptable level, but still prevent major spikes in incarceration. That should give everyone some hope. Claire Culhane and Ruth Morris were Order of Canada recipients. Art Solomon received honorary doctorates, including from McGill University. Kim Pate, who is now a Senator, has also been recognized in these ways. So, there is a level of recognition that social justice, prisons and punishment are issues, and that those that stand up for social justice should be recognized. If you make effort you can really actually achieve something.

A stalwart among Canadian abolitionists, Bob Gaucher clearly highlights how prison and penal abolitionism is anti-capitalist, anti-colonialist and anti-racist, while committed to knowledge generation, social action and conflict resolution "from below."

Rejoinders and Departures

While their tactics and their ways of arriving at prison and penal abolition differ, the figures noted above share a commitment to resisting state violence and fighting for a world that is more socially just. Their visions for a world without prisons and punishment overlapped in the sense that they all put working with the criminalized and imprisoned at the centre of their endeavours. Although Ruth Morris stood out with respect to her attempts to build capacity for alternatives to incarceration and punitive justice, Art Solomon, Claire Culhane and Bob Gaucher worked to broaden this aspect of abolitionism to consider more radical alternatives including decolonization and socialism, which have been core concerns for many Canadian abolitionists, both past (e.g., Monture-Angus, 1995) and present (e.g., Saleh-Hanna, 2015). From this history, one can get a sense of what leads some to take on an abolitionist stance (Mathiesen, 2008) as it relates to prisons and punishment, and what it implies in terms of what they seek to dismantle and build (Golstein et al., 2008). We return to these commitments in the next section by connecting the insights above to broader, international discussions on what is to be critiqued, dismantled and built.

CRITIQUE, DISMANTLE, BUILD

As noted above, one of the most pivotal thinkers representing the prison abolitionist position is Thomas Mathiesen. Mathiesen's work was formed based on his activism and advocacy with the Norwegian anti-prison organization KROM. In general terms, Mathiesen's (1986) position has three basic tenets. First, the abolition of prisons should be a goal of radical work in criminology and penal policy. Second, many so-called alternatives to prison are nearly as punitive and restrictive in nature, and should also be resisted. Third, short-term reforms are necessary, but such advocacy and organizing should not obscure the long-term goal of abolition. These ideas are articulated in Mathiesen's (1974) *The politics of abolition*. A key concept in that book is Mathiesen's notion of "the unfinished." The idea of the unfinished translates as permanent revolution or permanent change as a strategy for achieving abolitionist goals. Mathiesen also proposes the notions of positive and negative reforms. Positive reforms build-up or improve the efficiency of the penal system, and they re-legitimate existing organizations and power relations. Negative reforms decrease reliance on punitive justice by scaling-back or dismantling existing penal policies, practices, and institutions. Negative reforms are more consistent with abolitionist goals and the idea of the unfinished. Mathiesen cautions against the trap of short-term positive reforms, which in many cases further entrench penal power as illustrated by many of Ruth Morris' (2000) experiences with developing alternatives to incarceration and advancing restorative justice before she shifted to transformative justice advocacy and practice. Mathiesen's work and specifically *The politics of abolition* influenced abolitionist thinking and activism around the world (Ruggiero, 2010), notably in the United Kingdom (e.g., Ryan & Ward, 2014) and in Canada (e.g., Piché, 2014).

Mathiesen's work is just one position in a broader abolitionist field, which emerged out of organizing and activism. Like Bob Gaucher, some scholars and activists adopt an abolitionist approach after being criminalized (e.g., Bourque, 1988) or working in the penal system (e.g., Piché, 2009). There are core beliefs shared by prison abolitionists, which Scott (2013) summarizes.

First, imprisonment is a form of violence. As such, it is likely to fuel rather than to prevent future forms of harms (Scott, 2013, p. 94). Second, the prison is a social problem: it marginalizes and puts stress on the very communities that criminalization constructs as harmful (Clear, 2009). Prison is a form of punishment for the families of the incarcerated as well, leading to forced separation, stigmatization, as well as financial and emotional hardship (Comfort, 2008). Third, prison abolitionists adopt the position that while there is no overwhelming evidence that incarceration keep communities safe, there is plenty of evidence to show that this is not the case (Mathiesen, 1990). The faith placed in the ability of the prison to produce security is thus seen as dangerous. Fourth, the social uses of the prison reinforce existing power imbalances cutting through societies, notably those experienced by the poor and racialized, as well as those who do not adhere to gendered and sexual norms (Sim, 2009). Fifth, prisons are poor economic policy. They are extremely expensive and provide little to no value in return (Salib, forthcoming).

Imprisonment is seen as a social, economic, and policy failure (see Dilts, 2017). However, some abolitionists do not see the prison as a failure for its inability to achieve its own stated objectives (i.e. rehabilitation, deterrence, incapacitation, justice, etc.). Like Foucault (1977), they view the prison as "successful" and place the emphasis on the functions it serves, such as the control and containment of poor, colonized, racialized or otherwise marginalized persons (Davis, 2003; Sudbury, 2009; Ware et al., 2014). If we accept the thesis of *Discipline and punish* (Foucault, 1977), the prison is a success story in its ability to produce "criminals" and to normalize sanctions as a response to even the most minor forms of deviance.

American prison abolitionists have been central to this line of thinking, attributing mass incarceration in the United States to the emergence of a prison-industrial-complex (PIC) defined by Angela Davis (2003, p. 84) as "an array of relationships linking corporations, government, correctional communities, and media" that shape who ends up being criminalized and how they are punished. Yraida Guanipa (2011) reveals some of these relations by recounting her experience as a prison labourer while incarcerated in Florida that involved working for a corporation that managed scholarly publications accessed by college and university students and staff. In the United States and to a lesser degree elsewhere, prisons not only punish, but they also exploit the bodies of prisoners to derive profits for corporations and their shareholders. Nevertheless, the critique of the PIC in American prison abolitionism (Carrier & Piché, 2015a, 2015b) tends to be generalized too much. National criminal legal systems have different histories, and too often the PIC is used in a way that mask them, as if the interpretation of the American situation was valid for what is happening in other countries (Carrier et al., 2019). For instance, the analyses developed in the Canadian contexts by the likes of Art Solomon who linked patterns of social control to colonialism, as well as Claire Culhane who problematized the role of prisons in sustaining capitalist relations and vice-versa, show that the social uses of the penal system cannot be understood by simply transposing the American critique of the PIC or that of the weight of antebellum American violence on the penal present elsewhere.

Whether prison abolitionists conceptualize confinement as a failure or a perverse success, the main goal animating their work remains to dismantle and build alternatives to incarceration (Davis & Mendieta, 2005). However, for some abolitionists these critiques of penality targeting the prison do not go far enough. As Bob Gaucher notes above, the net-widening that occurred in many jurisdictions where community-based punishments were introduced, propelled some who seek to abolish imprisonment to pursue penal abolition. This entails a broader project of dismantling the criminal legal system as a whole, as it is theorized that without abolishing other punitive entities such as police and courts, jails and prisons will continue to be used if the retributive framework upon which they rely is not also eradicated (West & Morris, 2000; Hulsman, 1986). This is why so-called "alternatives" to prison such as those that fall under the label of "community corrections" (e.g., parole) are not viewed as permanent solutions for many abolitionists, as they stop short of challenging existing power structures and the penal system as it is. As Papendorf (2006) argues, Mathiesen's original inspiration was anti-prison struggles, not a full rejection of the penal system or state authority. However, dismantling the prison and penality also

Box 12.3 – Defining and Responding To the Use of Non-Medically Prescribed Opioids

Criminal Justice	Prison Abolitionism	Penal Abolitionism
The possession of non-medically prescribed opioids is a crime that ought to lead to the arrest, charging, conviction and punishment of drug users.	The possession of non-medically prescribed opioids is a crime that ought to lead to the use of an alternative to incarceration to address the needs of drug users.	Both meaning of the use of non-medically prescribed opioids and how to respond to ought to be decided upon by drug users themselves, which could open the door to other forms of regulation (e.g., commercial, health, etc.) or no regulations at all.

requires deconstructing the concept of "crime," a term which individualizes and masks structural determinants of problematic events, treating all harms as the same (i.e., a violation of state law).

Penal abolitionists believe that the identification and resolution of problematic situations need to be participatory, voluntary, and administered by communities for communities (Hulsman, 1986; Coyle, 2016; also see Box 12.3). One venue where this shift from prison to penal abolition took place can be traced to when the International Conference on Prison Abolition changed its name and focus to the International Conference on Penal Abolition (Delisle et al., 2015). In light of the continued normalization and proliferation of prison-like controls outside the penal system, including immigration detention, war camps and black sites where alleged terrorists are held with few legal protections there have also been calls for carceral abolition (e.g., Piché & Larsen, 2010). While not traditionally the nucleus of abolitionist organizing, calls to abolish carceral spaces other than prisons have grown with convergences with migrant justice work perhaps best epitomized by the popularization of the movement to Abolish ICE (Immigration and Customs Enforcement agency) in the United States when news of the forcible confinement of migrant children and their separation from their parents went mainstream in 2018 (e.g., Diaz, 2018). Among the challenges that merging penal and carceral abolitionism present are the following. A common strategy to question the legitimacy of the detention of illegalized migrants is to indicate that they are not "criminals" who have been charged, tried in open court and convicted. Doing so further naturalizes the idea that the prison is where criminalized individuals belong. Moreover, calls for "justice" regarding the fate of detained individuals will typically emphasize the absence of formal charges, thus mobilizing the very ideology of 'criminal justice' that penal abolitionists seek to undo (see Carrier, 2014).

Whether positioned as prison or penal abolitionists, the endeavour is not simply about dismantling oppressive structures, but also about building alternatives. Some abolitionists promote restorative justice processes such as victim-offender mediation and healing circles as a means of bringing parties in conflict, along with their communities of support, together on a voluntary basis to "conceptualize the problems with which we are confronted [with] and how we respond to them" (Elliott, 2011, p. 6). Such encounters are more likely to foster healing for those harmed (Roach, 2006; Morris, 2002), while promoting accountability among those who have harmed to work toward redress to the degree that is possible (Braithwaite, 1989). However, as noted above, restorative justice has been critiqued for individualizing accountability and extending the application of "criminal justice" categories (Pavlich, 2005). In this sense, abolitionists critique the embeddedness of restorative justice in the penal system and the cooption of these ideas by state punishing agencies like the police, courts, and prisons (Ruggiero, 2011). By mirroring punitive conceptions of accountability, restorative justice is vulnerable to cooptation and has been adopted by name at different stages of the "criminal" legal process, serving as a vehicle for punishment in some cases rather than a tool for healing (see, for example, Piché & Strimelle, 2007). The restorative approach has also been critiqued for failing to address broader structures of power that give rise to harm (Morris, 2000). For instance, in the case of domestic violence, one cannot separate the abuse of one partner by another from patriarchal ideas and practices that promote male domination (Ritchie, 2012). Thus, many prison and penal abolitionists promote transformative justice as a means of bringing those impacted by criminalized harms together not just to discuss who has been hurt, what needs they have, and who will work to address them, but also to identify and develop means to transform structures in our communities that promote violence (Morris, 2000; also see Box 12.4). For proponents of transformative justice like Ruth Morris, abolition necessitates non-state and non-punitive alternatives to conflict resolution, as well as socio-economic transformation to address inequalities and power structures that reproduce harm. State-run, top-down penal practices continue to create inequality, reproduce violence, and undertake morally unjustifiable actions against human lives (Sim, 2009).

Box 12.4 – Defining and Responding To Harm In the Case of Non-Consensual Physical Violence

Criminal Justice	Prison Abolitionism	Penal Abolitionism
Individuals in conflict have minimal input, if any, in defining the situation and appropriate responses. Assaults are criminal infractions. Infractions harm society. The formula for justice is the infliction of retaliatory harms. The absence of punishment is an injustice. Punishment might pursue different objectives (deterrence, rehabilitation, incapacitation, reparation, etc.). Punishment can include imprisonment.	Individuals in conflict have minimal input, if any, in defining the situation and appropriate responses. Assaults are criminal infractions. Infractions harm society. The formula for justice is the infliction of retaliatory harms. The absence of punishment is an injustice. Punishment might pursue different objectives (deterrence, rehabilitation, incapacitation, reparation, etc.). Punishment cannot include imprisonment.	Individuals in conflict define the situation and appropriate responses. Non-consenting instances of physical violence may be problematic situations. Situations are problematic from the perspective of the actors involved. The actors involved in a situation might not all agree that it is problematic. There is no pre-established formula for justice. Responses to problematic situations might pursue different objectives (reparation, healing, transformation, accountability, etc.), however, retaliatory harms are prohibited.

CONTEMPORARY ABOLITIONIST PRAXIS IN CANADA

Writing on the persistence of the modern prison, Angela Davis (2003, p. 15) remarks "it is hardly acceptable to engage in serious public discussions about prison life and radical alternatives to prison. It is as if prison were an inevitable fact of life…." Policing (Maynard, 2017) and courts (Lynch, 2016) also continue to be normalized, as are changing constellations of carceral controls meant to assert the state's power over territory in the face of mass human migration (Longazel et al., 2016), challenges to land sovereignty from Indigenous peoples (Pasternak, 2014), and other questions of "national security" (Moran, 2005; Welch, 2000).

In the face of many forms of injustice, it is easy to turn a blind eye, to focus one's attention elsewhere, or to settle for incremental reforms without demands for radical change along abolitionist lines. There are other challenges for abolitionist thought and action as well. As Davis and Rodríguez (2000) note, diversity and inclusion is an ongoing issue within the abolitionist movement, including in forums like ICOPA (also see Delisle et al., 2015).

Abolitionist proposals to eradicate prisons, "criminal justice" and other state institutions of control may appear to be impossible to achieve at present. However, Thomas Mathiesen (2008, p. 62) reminds us that "it is not impossible to nurture an abolitionist stance, a stance of saying 'no'," which "may contribute to what I would call *turning points*" where unforeseen possibilities for substantial social and political change arise. Showing that the movement is very much alive today, many groups and organizations are heading this call by advancing negative reforms (Mathiesen, 1974) to diminish the role and trauma of imprisonment and punishment in a march toward their abolition. To illustrate this, below we describe some of the kinds of abolitionist work occurring in the Canadian context, citing the online materials of groups (see *Recommended Websites*), to highlight how one can engage in such struggles.

Central to abolitionist organizing is public education as a means of sensitizing others to the idea that prisons at the very least or the criminal legal system in its entirety needs to be expunged from human societies. Groups based in Canada whose work is primarily focused on this objective include Joint Effort, which "is a women prison abolitionist group involved in solidarity work with women prisoners in the Lower Mainland" in British Columbia. Their efforts entail putting together activities behind bars such as discussion groups and workshops, as well as outside work that provides "public information about the situation of women in prison as well as lobbying government on various issues." Similarly, the Termite Collective based in Montreal, Quebec, features members inside and outside of prison. Together, the collective has documented ways in which the federal penitentiary system has become more austere through its campaign "Demand Prisons Change," as well as putting on plays highlighting current issues behind bars at community art festivals. Based in London, Ontario, the Prisoners Justice Film Festival also engages in public education through art by putting on a series of documentaries and films that highlight their belief "that policing, borders, prisons and institutionalization do not make our communities safer or more secure." They are also focused on "working to build safe, healthy communities based on sovereignty, social justice and self-determination."

There are also groups that engage in public education through publishing such as the *Journal of Prisoners on Prisons*, which features peer-reviewed papers written by current and past prisoners. The *JPP* fosters prisoner ethnographies that can reveal aspects of the penal system that otherwise remain unknown or often overlooked in mainstream criminology and criminal justice studies (Gaucher, 2002; Piché et al., 2014). By documenting the realities of incarceration and the shifting politics of punishment as lived by prisoners themselves, the journal seeks to challenge the legitimacy of the deprivation of liberty and the infliction of pain in the name of justice. Others seek to do this work through broadcasting programs that include interviews with prisoners and their allies, including prison radio programs based in Montreal, Quebec and Kingston, Ontario, as well as Star Raven based in Vancouver, British Columbia.

Challenging the penal status quo primarily through organizing campaigns is another approach some groups privilege in doing abolitionist work. For example, the Criminalization and Punishment Education Project (CPEP) has been campaigning to reduce crowding, while calling for improvements to the living conditions of prisoners who remain locked-up at the Ottawa-Carleton Detention Centre by putting on a series of public forums, writing op-eds, meeting with community groups and local politicians, and putting together videos. CPEP has been trying to build opposition to a newly announced jail in Ottawa through its #NOPE / No Ottawa Prison Expansion initiative. Other groups involved in opposing carceral expansion is Kingston, Ontario based EPIC / End the Prison Industrial Complex, which created a list of companies or profiteers who have made money by building cages for human beings as a means of shaming them for being involved in such work going forward.

Acknowledging that the struggle to dismantle penality and carcerality will not be won overnight, many abolitionists orient their work around improving the material conditions of the imprisoned, while fighting for their liberation. Halifax Prisoner Solidarity is one such group that does this through fundraising "dedicated to support political prisoners, with the understanding that all prisoners are political," with donations going "towards supporting political and anarchist prisoners and defendants." The West Coast Prison Justice Society takes this work further through its Prisoners' Legal Services initiative that seeks to defend prisoners in provincial and federal prisons in British Columbia against human rights abuses, while also fighting to abolish practices such as solitary confinement (WCPJS, 2016).

Another way that abolitionists are supporting prisoners is through letter writing that helps the incarcerated combat isolation by maintaining connections to the outside world. Montreal-based Prisoner Correspondence Project is one such group that "is a solidarity project for gay, lesbian, transsexual, transgender, gendervariant, two-spirit, intersex, bisexual and queer prisoners in Canada and the United States," linking them with people that are part of these same communities outside of prison. Also privileging correspondence work to build bridges inside and outside prison walls, members of the Centre for Justice Exchange at Bishop's University in Sherbrooke, Quebec file Access to Information requests and search for resources with prisoners to "1. Learn, co-create, and share ideas about justice and address challenges and barriers," "2. Raise awareness of resources available to individuals in and out of prison," and "3. Develop approaches to more inclusive understandings and practices of justice."

Combatting isolation also motivates several groups to organize books to prisoners drives. Among them are abolitionist collectives, including Books 2 Prisoners Ottawa based at Carleton University that engage in such work as a means of providing prisoners incarcerated for their involvement with social movements and politicized prisoners who are now active in social justice struggles with tools to deepen their political education. These groups are active throughout Canada (e.g., Nyki & Books to Bars Hamilton, 2013) and the United States (e.g., Law, 2013).

Some abolitionist groups also prioritize solidarity work with the loved ones of prisoners, ensuring that they are able to stay in contact with their family members, partners or friends who are behind bars. For instance, Winnipeg-based Bar None coordinates a rideshare to provincial and federal prisons in Manitoba, which "is one way to work against the damage incarceration does to the relationships that sustain communities." In Edmonton, Together Overcoming Darkness & Despair or the T.O.D.D. Support & Advocacy Foundation assists the loved ones of the criminalized and others in their journey through the penal system through "information and resource sharing, supported referrals, a weekly support group, court accompaniment and court support, visit transportation, confidential support and advocacy." In so doing, T.O.D.D. works toward "meaningful changes that create no more victims and hold people accountable," while combatting the damage of criminalization and punishment.

There are also abolitionist-oriented organizations based in Canada involved in public policy advocacy locally, provincially, federally, and internationally to improve the material conditions of criminalized populations in the short-term, while pursuing long-term abolitionist objectives. Notable among them is the Canadian Association of Elizabeth Fry Societies that advocates with and for criminalized women and girls "to ensure substantive equality in the delivery and development of services and programs," as well as their decarceration. Toronto-based PASAN has a narrower focus as "the only community-based organization in Canada exclusively providing HIV / AIDS and HCV prevention, education and support services to prisoners, ex-prisoners and their families." Such work includes advocating for harm reduction measures such as needle exchanges behind bars as a short-term negative reform, while problematizing the use of incarceration through initiatives like *Cell Count* magazine that highlights the brutalities of incarceration from the perspectives of those held captive in Canadian jails, prisons, and penitentiaries. Taking a wider view, the Canadian Friends Service Committee Quakers Fostering Justice is engaged in program advocacy, which includes research and advising governments on public policy in a manner "rooted in penal abolition...to eliminate the punitive mindset which pervades society and justice systems by transforming harmful approaches to ones that are healing."

While prison and penal abolitionists devote great attention and resources toward struggling against existing laws, institutions, policies, and practices geared toward the deprivation of liberty and the infliction of pain, a smaller number of groups have focused on building future justice infrastructure within the present. Among them is the Centre for Restorative Justice at Simon Fraser University in Burnaby, British Columbia. Co-founded by penal abolitionist Elizabeth Elliott (Elliott, 2011), the initiative teaches courses, conducts research, and engages in public education efforts geared toward promoting restorative justice as "non-retaliatory responses to violence." As restorative justice processes have been incorporated into the work of punitive justice organizations such as Correctional Service Canada over time (see, for example, Piché & Strimelle, 2007), Rittenhouse – which was founded by leading penal abolitionist Ruth Morris (Morris, 2000) – began to offer transformative justice training and encounters that push conflict resolution beyond meeting the individual needs generated by social harm to also include the identification and transformation of dominant structures that give rise to conflict.

While most of the formations described above tend to focus on imprisonment or conflict resolution as their entry points into abolitionist organizing, there are other groups doing work to dismantle and bring into being alternatives to "criminal justice." Notable among them are groups like Black Lives Matter in Toronto and elsewhere who have tabled an extensive political program to fight against anti-Black racism in various settings, which includes demands with respect to policing and incarceration. There are also groups like No One is Illegal and the End Immigration Detention Network that critique and demand alternatives to carceral controls operating in concert with and alongside the penal system such as immigration detention. Anarchist Black Cross (ABC) groups across the country have long been engaged in prisoner solidarity work as well, usually focusing on political prisoners, as well as prisoners of occupation and war. ABC groups follow anarchist principles, organizing in autonomous groups that are linked through a federation. Such on-going struggles push the boundaries of abolitionism as organizers forge ahead into the future, where we turn our attention to next.

CONCLUSION

Art Solomon, Claire Culhane, Ruth Morris and Bob Gaucher are among the key figures that have shaped a distinctly Canadian way of doing and thinking abolitionism, which in turn has been, and continues to be, influential on abolitionism as a transnational movement, notably through ICOPA. We have seen, via excerpts from an oral history co-constructed by Bob Gaucher and the lead author of this contribution, some issues that have stimulated forms of activism, which have led to the shift from prison to penal abolitionism. The work of Art Solomon has helped place the devastating impacts of colonial rule at the centre of Canadian abolitionism, something that is visible in the ways in which Bob Gaucher talks about the future abolitionists should strive for. It could be argued that many of the contemporary organized practices of prisoners' solidarity detailed above are the grandchildren of Claire Culhane's indomitable involvement which, as Bob Gaucher makes clear, touched the hearts and minds of many. Ruth Morris has been instrumental in making visible the narrowness and limits of both prison abolitionism and restorative justice, and her work speaks volumes about the possibility to engage in abolitionist struggles in pragmatic ways. Finally, Bob Gaucher's efforts have left an indelible mark on Canadian abolitionism, notably through helping to facilitate the work of the *Journal of Prisoners on Prisons* over the past three decades.

There are many forms of organizing currently happening on Canadian soil which are directly connected to the projects supporting criminalized and/or incarcerated individuals and their communities, working to dismantle jails, prisons and penitentiaries, creating alternatives to the penal system, and challenging forms of detention allowed outside the realm of "criminal justice." There certainly exists contradictions and tensions between different groups involved in abolitionist activism, which would take a whole other chapter to explain (see Carrier & Piché, forthcoming). What we can say by way of conclusion is that, moving forward, there is a need for more work to be done in Canada and elsewhere in the world on connecting abolitionism to broader visions for radical change such as social democracy (e.g., Davis & Mendieta, 2005) and anarchism (e.g., Dixon, 2014) to transform how human beings relate to each other, including how harms currently flowing from capitalism are conceived and responded to, as a means of ensuring our collective survival.

KEY TERMS

Prison Abolition
Penal Abolition
Positive Reforms
Negative Reforms
The Unfinished

STUDY AND DISCUSSION QUESTIONS

1. Who was Art Solomon and what were his core ideas about abolition?
2. Who was Claire Culhane and what were her core ideas about abolition?
3. Who was Ruth Morris and what were her core ideas about abolition?
4. Who is Bob Gaucher and what are his core ideas about abolition?
5. What core ideas about abolition are recurring in international contributions?
6. What is the difference between positive and negative reforms?
7. What is the difference between prison and penal abolition?
8. What are the main alternatives to confinement and punishment advanced by abolitionists?
9. What are the main tactics used by prison and penal abolitionists to achieve their objectives?
10. Can you think of ways you can challenge practices of imprisonment and punishment in your own community?

RECOMMENDED WEBSITES

- **Bar None** at https://barnoneblog.wordpress.com/
- **Black Lives Matter – Toronto** at https://blacklivesmatter.ca/
- **CAEFS / Canadian Association of Elizabeth Fry Societies** at http://www.caefs.ca/
- **Centre for Justice Exchange** at https://justiceexchange.ca/about/
- **Centre for Restorative Justice** at http://www.sfu.ca/crj.html
- **CPEP / Criminalization and Punishment Education Project** at http://www.cp-ep.org/
- **Demand Prisons Change** at https://demandprisonschange.wordpress.com/
- **End Immigration Detention Network** at https://endimmigrationdetention.com/
- **EPIC / End the Prison Industrial Complex** at https://epic.noblogs.org/
- **Halifax Prisoner Solidarity** at https://halifaxprisonersolidarity.noblogs.org/about/
- **Joint Effort** at http://prisonjustice.ca/joint-effort/
- **Journal of Prisoners on Prisons** at http://www.jpp.org/
- **No One Is Illegal** at http://www.nooneisillegal.org/
- **PASAN** at http://www.pasan.org/

- **Prisoner Correspondence Project** at https://prisonercorrespondenceproject.com/
- **Prisoners Justice Film Festival** at http://www.prisonersjusticefilmfestival.ca/about-2/
- **Prison Radio** at https://prisonradioshow.wordpress.com/about/
- **Quakers Fostering Justice** at http://quakerservice.ca/our-work/justice/
- **Rittenhouse** at http://www.rittenhouseanewvision.com/
- **Stark Raven** at http://prisonjustice.ca/stark-raven/
- **TODD / Together Overcoming Darkness & Despair Support & Advocacy Foundation** at https://toddcanada.org/about-us/
- **West Coast Prison Justice Society** at https://prisonjustice.org/

NOTES

[1] See Monture-Angus (1995).
[2] To access *Tightwire* and other penal press publications produced by Canadian prisoners consult http://penalpress.com.
[3] See Knopp et al. (1976).
[4] See Saleh-Hanna and Alston (2006-2007).
[5] Ian Taylor is best known for his contribution to "The New Criminology" (see Taylor et al., 1973).

REFERENCES

Barraclough, L. (2010). Reflections on teaching prison abolition. *The Radical Teacher*, *88*, 42-52.
Ben-Moshe, L. (2013). The tension between abolition and reform. In M. Nagel & A. J. Nocella III (Eds.), *The end of prisons: Reflections from the decarceration movement* (pp. 83-92). Rodopi Press.
Bourque, Y. (1988). Prison abolition. *Journal of Prisoners on Prisons, 1*(1), 1-7.
Braithwaite, J. (1989). *Crime, shame and reintegration*. New York: Cambridge University Press.
Bromwich, R., & Kilty, J. (Eds.) (2017). Law, vulnerability and segregation: What have we learned from Ashley Smith's carceral death? *Canadian Journal of Law & Society, 32*(2).
Brown, M. and Schept, J. (2017). New abolition, criminology and a critical carceral studies. *Punishment & Society, 19*(4), 440-462.
Cardinal, C. (2018). *Ohpikiihaakan-ohpihmeh (raised somewhere else): A 60s scoop adoptee's story of coming home*. Halifax: Fernwood Press.
Carlyle, J. (2013). *Coroner's inquest touching the death of Ashley Smith*. Toronto: Coroner's Court. Retrieved from http://www.csc-scc.gc.ca/publications/005007-9009-eng.shtml
Carrier, N. (2014). On some limits and paradoxes of academic orations on public criminology. *Radical Criminology*, *4*, 85-114.
Carrier, N., & Piché, J. (2015a). The state of abolitionism. *Champ pénal / Penal Field, XII*. Retrieved from http://journals.openedition.org/champpenal/9164
Carrier, N., & Piché, J. (2015b). Blind spots of abolitionist thought in academia: On longstanding and emerging challenges. *Champ pénal / Penal Field, XII*. Retrieved from http://journals.openedition.org/champpenal/9164
Carrier, N., & Piché, J. (forthcoming). On (In)justice: Undisciplined abolitionism in Canada. *Social Justice*.
Carrier, N., Piché, J., & Walby, K. (2019). Abolitionism and decarceration. In M. Deflem (Ed.), *The handbook of social control* (pp. 319-332). Hoboken: Wiley-Blackwell.

Chartrand, V., & Piché, J. (forthcoming). Abolition and pedagogy: Reflections on teaching a course on alternatives to punishment, state repression and social control. *Contemporary Justice Review.*

Clear, T. R. (2009). *Imprisoning communities: How mass incarceration makes disadvantaged neighborhoods worse.* Oxford: Oxford University Press.

Cohen, S. (1985). *Visions of social control.* Cambridge: Polity.

Comfort, M. (2008). *Doing time together: Love and family in the shadow of the prison.* Chicago: University of Chicago Press.

Correctional Service Canada [CSC]. (2014). *Response to the coroner's inquest touching the death of Ashley Smith.* Ottawa: Government of Canada. Retrieved from http://www.csc-scc.gc.ca/publications/005007-9011-eng.shtml

Coyle, M. (2016). Penal abolition as the end of criminal behavior. *Journal of Social Justice, 6,* 1-23.

Culhane, C. (1972). *Why is Canada in Vietnam? The truth about our foreign aid.* Madison: NC Press.

Culhane, C. (1979). *Barred from prison: A personal account.* Montreal: Arsenal Pulp.

Culhane, C. (1985). *Still barred from prison: Social injustice in Canada.* Montreal: Black Rose Books.

Culhane, C. (1991). *No longer barred from prison: Social injustice in Canada.* Montreal: Black Rose Books.

Davis, A. Y. (2003). *Are prisons obsolete?* New York: Seven Stories Press.

Davis, A.Y., & Mendieta E. (2005). *Abolition democracy: Beyond empire, prisons and torture.* New York: Seven Stories Press.

Davis, A. Y., & Rodríguez, D. (2000). The challenge of prison abolition: A conversation. *Social Justice, 27*(3), 202-223.

De Giorgi, A. (2006). *Re-thinking the political economy of punishment: Perspectives on post-Fordism and penal politics.* Aldershot: Ashgate.

Delisle, C., Basualdo, M., Ilea, A., & Hughes A. (2015). Organizing ICOPA 15 on Algonquin territory: Exploring social identity dynamics, collective decision-taking and controversies in the International Conference on Penal Abolition (ICOPA). *Champ pénal/Penal Field, XII.* Retrieved from http://journals.openedition.org/champpenal/9146

Diaz, D. (2018, July 3). These Democrats want to abolish ICE. *CNN.* Retrieved from https://www.cnn.com/2018/07/02/politics/abolish-ice-democrats-list/index.html

Dilts, A. (2017). Justice as failure. *Law, culture, and the humanities, 13*(2), 184-192.

Dixon, C. (2014). *Another politics: Talking across today's transformative movements.* Oakland: University of California Press.

Doob, A. N, & Webster, C. M. (2006). Countering punitiveness: Understanding stability in Canada's imprisonment rate. *Law & Society Review, 40*(2), 325-368.

Elliott, E. M. (2011). *Security with care: Restorative justice & healthy societies.* Winnipeg: Fernwood.

Foucault, M. (1977). *Discipline and punish: The birth of the prison.* New York: Vintage Books.

Gaucher, B. (1988). The prisoner as ethnographer. *Journal of Prisoners on Prisons, 1*(1), 1-6.

Gaucher, B. (Ed.) (2002). *Writing as resistance: The journal of prisoners on prisons anthology – 1988-2002.* Toronto: Canadian Scholars' Press.

Goldstein, B., Ritchie, B., Gilmore, C., Stein, D., Rodríguez, D., Ontiveros, I., Lawston, J., Sudbury, J., Welsing, M., Herzing, R., Solinger, R., & Omowale, Y. (Eds.) (2008). *Abolition now! Ten years of strategy and struggle against the prison industrial complex.* Oakland: AK Press.

Guanipa, Y. (2011). Commentary on imprisonment, prison labour and re-entry. *Journal of Prisoners on Prisons, 20*(1), 23-34.

Hulsman, L. (1986). Critical criminology and the concept of crime. *Contemporary Crises, 10*(1), 63-80.

Knopp, F. H., Boward, B., Brach, M. J., Christianson, S., Largen, M. A., Lewin, J., Lugo, J., Morris, M., & Newton, W. (Eds.) (1976). *Instead of prison: A handbook for prison abolitionists.* Syracuse: Prison Research Education Action Project.

Law, V. (2013). Defying dehumanization by sending books: A brief history of books through bars NYC. *Journal of Prisoners on Prisons, 22*(2), 149-152.

Longazel, J., Berman, J., & Fleury-Steiner, B. (2016). The pains of immigrant imprisonment. *Sociology Compass, 10*(11), 989-998.

Lowe, M. (1992). *One women army: The life of Claire Culhane.* Toronto: McMillan.

Lynch, M. (2016). *Hard bargains: The coercive power of drug laws in federal court.* New York: Russell Sage Foundation.

Martel, J., Brassard, R., & Jaccoud, M. (2011). When two worlds collide. Aboriginal risk management in Canadian corrections. *British Journal of Criminology, 51,* 235-255.

Mathiesen, T. (1974). *The politics of abolition: Essays in political action theory.* Oslo: Universitetsforlaget.

Mathiesen, T. (1986). The politics of abolition. *Contemporary Crisis, 10*(1), 81-94.

Mathiesen, T. (1990). *Prison on trial.* London: Sage.

Mathiesen, T. (2008). The abolitionist stance. *Journal of Prisoners on Prisons, 17*(2), 58-63.

Maynard, R. (2017). *Policing Black lives: State violence in Canada from slavery to the present.* Halifax: Fernwood.

Mayrl, D. (2013). Fields, logics, and social movements: Prison abolition and the social justice field. *Sociological Inquiry, 83*(2), 286-309.

Monture-Angus, P. (1995). *Thunder in my soul: A Mohawk woman speaks.* Winnipeg: Fernwood.

Moran, J. (2005). State power in the war on terror: A comparative analysis of the UK and the USA. *Crime, Law and Social Change, 44*(4/5), 335-359.

Morris, A. (2002). Critiquing the critics: A brief response to critics of restorative justice. *British Journal of Criminology, 42*(3), 596-615.

Morris, R. (1989). *Crumbling walls: Why prisons fail.* Oakville: Mosaic Press.

Morris, R. (1995). *Penal abolition: The practical choice.* Toronto: Canadian Scholars' Press.

Morris, R. (2000). *Stories of transformative justice.* Toronto: Canadian Scholars' Press.

Morris, R. (2004). *Transcending trauma.* Embrun: Winding Trail Press.

Nyki, & Books to Bars Hamilton (2013). The politics and practices of a books-to-prisoners organization. *Journal of Prisoners on Prisons, 22*(1), 122-125.

Papendorf, K. (2006). 'The unfinished': Reflections on the Norwegian prison movement. *Acta Sociologica, 49*(2), 127-137.

Pasternak, S. (2014). Jurisdiction and settler colonialism: Where do laws meet? *Canadian Journal of Law & Society, 29*(2), 145-161.

Pate, K. (2018, January 22). Segregation in prison must be banned. *Globe and Mail.* Retrieved from https://www.theglobeandmail.com/opinion/segregation-in-prison-must-be-banned/article37682823/

Patriquin, M. (2016, November 2). Why Adam Capay has spent 1,560 days in solitary. *Maclean's.* Retrieved from http://www.macleans.ca

Pavlich, G. (2005). *Governing paradoxes of restorative justice.* London: Glasshouse.

Piché, J. (2009). Penal abolitionism: A different kind of reform. *Criminal Justice Matters, 77,* 30-31.

Piché, J. (2014). A contradictory and finishing state: Explaining recent prison capacity expansion in Canada's provinces and territories. *Champ pénal / Penal Field, XI,* 26 pages.

Piché, J., Gaucher, B., & Walby, K. (2014). Facilitating prisoner ethnography: An alternative approach to "doing prison research differently." *Qualitative Inquiry, 20*(4), 392-403.

Piché, J., & Larsen, M. (2010). The moving targets of penal abolitionism: ICOPA, past, present and future. *Contemporary Justice Review, 13*(4), 391-410.

Piché, J., & Strimelle, V. (2007). Exploring the contours of restorative justice program evaluation frameworks: Pitfalls and opportunities. *International Journal of Restorative Justice, 3*(2), 40-56.

Public Safety Canada [PSC] (2017, June 19). *Government of Canada introduces legislative changes addressing issues in the federal corrections system*. Ottawa: Government of Canada. Retrieved from https://www.canada.ca

Reed, P., Bleszynski, T., & Gaucher, B. (1976). *Is justice really blind? A study of legal dispositions and sentences in homicide cases in Canada – 1961-73*. Ottawa: Statistics Canada.

Reed, P., Gaucher, B., & Bleszynski, T. (1977). *Repetitive violence among persons suspected or convicted of homicide in Canada – 1961-74*. Ottawa: Statistics Canada.

Ritchie, B. (2012). *Arrested justice: Black women, violence, and America's prison nation*. New York: New York University Press.

Roach, K. (2006). The institutionalisation of restorative justice in Canada: Effective reform or limited and limiting add-on? In I. Aertsen, T. Daems, & L. Roberts (Eds.), *Institutionalising restorative justice* (pp. 167-193). Portland: Willan Publishing.

Ruggiero, V. (2010). *Penal abolitionism*. Oxford: Oxford University Press.

Ruggiero, V. (2011). An abolitionist view of restorative justice. *International Journal of Law, Crime and Justice, 39*(2), 100-110.

Ryan, M., & Ward, T. (2014). Prison abolition in the UK: They dare not speak its name? *Social Justice, 41*(3), 107-119.

Saleh-Hanna, V. (2015). Black feminist hautology. *Champ pénal / Penal Field, XII*, 34 pages. Retrieved from https://journals.openedition.org/champpenal/9168

Saleh-Hanna, V., & Alston, A. O. (Eds.) (2006-2007). Special anniversary issue – Black panther party 1966-2006. *Journal of Prisoners on Prisons, 15*(2)/*16*(1), 250 pages.

Salib, P. (forthcoming). Why prison? An economic critique. *Berkeley Journal of Criminal Law*.

Sapers, H. (2008). *A preventable death*. Ottawa: Office of the Correctional Investigator of Canada. Retrieved from http://www.oci-bec.gc.ca/cnt/rpt/pdf/oth-aut/oth-aut20080620-eng.pdf

Sapers, H. (2013). *Spirit matters: Aboriginal people and the Corrections and Conditional Release Act*. Ottawa: Office of the Correctional Investigator of Canada. Retrieved from http://www.oci-bec.gc.ca/cnt/rpt/oth-aut/oth-aut20121022-eng.aspx

Sapers, H. (2017). *Segregation in Ontario: Independent review of Ontario corrections*. Toronto: Queen's Printer. Retrieved from https://www.mcscs.jus.gov.on.ca

Scott, D. (2013). Visualising an abolitionist real utopia: Principles, policy and praxis. In M. Malloch & B. Munro (Eds.), *Crime, critique and utopia* (pp. 90-113). London: Palgrave.

Sim J. (2009). *Punishment and prisons: Power and the carceral state*. London: Sage.

Sinclair, R. (2007). Identity lost and found: Lessons from the sixties scoop. *First Peoples Child & Family Review, 3*(1), 65-82.

Solomon, A. (1990). Songs for the people: Teachings of the natural way. Toronto: NC Press.

Solomon, A. (1994). *Eating bitterness: A vision beyond the prison walls – poems and essays of Arthur Solomon*. Madison: NC Press.

Spencer, D. (forthcoming). The hope principle? Exploring an unwritten principle of sentencing law. *Criminal Law Quarterly*.

Sudbury, J. (2009). Maroon abolitionists: Black gender-oppressed activists in the anti-prison movement in the U.S. and Canada. *Meridians, 9*(1), 1-29.

Taylor, I., Walton, P., & Young, J. (1973). *The new criminology: For a social theory of deviance*. London: Routledge.

Truth and Reconciliation Commission of Canada [TRC] (2015). *Calls to action*. Winnipeg. Retrieved from http://nctr.ca/assets/reports/Calls_to_Action_English2.pdf

Vitale, A. (2017). *The end of policing*. London: Verso.

Walby, K. (2011). Anarcho-abolitionism: A challenge to conservative and liberal criminology. In A. Doyle & D. Moore (Eds.), *Critical criminology in Canada* (pp. 288-307). Vancouver: University of British Columbia Press.

Ware, S., Ruzsa, J., & Dias, G. (2014). It can't be fixed because it's not broken: Racism and disability in the prison industrial complex. In L. Ben-Moshe, C. Chapman & A. C. Carey (Eds.), *Disability incarcerated: Imprisonment and disability in the United States and Canada* (pp. 163-184). New York: Palgrave Macmillan.

Webster, C. M., & Doob, A. N. (2015). US punitiveness 'Canadian style'? Cultural values and Canadian punishment policy. *Punishment & Society, 17*(3), 299-321.

Welch, M. (2000). The role of the immigration and naturalization service in the prison-industrial complex. *Social Justice, 27*(3), 73-88.

West Coast Prison Justice Society [WCPJS]. (2016). *Solitary: A case for abolition*. Vancouver: The Law Foundation of British Columbia.

West, W. G., & Morris, R. (Eds.) (2000). *The case for penal abolition*. Toronto: Canadian Scholars' Press.

Zehr, H. (2002). *The little handbook of restorative justice*. Intercourse (PA): Good Books.

13

The Future of Corrections in Canada

Rick Ruddell and Katharina Maier

Learning Objectives

After reading this chapter, you should be able to:

- Describe why correctional policymakers and administrators engage in forecasting.

- Identify the internal and external factors that can affect the future of Canadian correctional systems.

- Describe strategies used to predict future influences such as SWOT, PESTEL, and environmental scans.

- Explain the potential costs and benefits when correctional systems develop partnerships with external agencies.

INTRODUCTION

Contributors in the previous 12 chapters have highlighted the historical as well as the current issues and trends in Canadian adult corrections, including the management of special populations, relationships between community and institutional corrections, rehabilitative opportunities for inmates, the oversight of correctional systems, as well as the relationships between the police, courts and correctional agencies. All of these factors will play important roles in shaping the future of corrections. Trying to predict what occurs in the future is an important task in large correctional systems with billion-dollar budgets. Proactive correctional administrators, who are responsible for hundreds or thousands of staff, are constantly trying to determine the internal and external forces that will affect their organizations in order to reduce uncertainty and to meet the demands of the justice system. Leaders in smaller correctional centres and probation offices are also interested in predicting how their future operations will be impacted by various trends as these organizations may be more vulnerable to shifting conditions due to their small size.

There is a long history of scholars attempting to predict the future of corrections. A special issue of *The Prison Journal* published in 1987, for example, reported the predictions of 15 prominent scholars about the field of corrections 25 years into the future. While some of these predictions were accurate, such as Wolfgang's (1987, p. 88) warning of a loss of privacy due to the widespread use of computers, many of the contributing authors were optimistic that U.S. correctional populations would decrease and that "mediation, reconciliation, [and] restitution will become the major modes of correctional policies. Prisons will not vanish, but they will be emptied." Several contributors also predicted that community sanctions that were supported by halfway houses, group homes, and drug treatment programs would become commonplace. Others wrote about the need to use incapacitation selectively; reserving expensive correctional beds for the prisoners who posed the highest risks to public safety, and making a greater use of community-based alternatives (Seiter, 1987). Once incarcerated, the contributors argued that offenders should have access to rehabilitative programs that were relevant to the real-world. Few of these contributors predicted the introduction of get tough practices such as the expansion of mandatory minimum sentences, three-strikes, or truth in sentencing that lengthened sentences and required offenders to serve a greater proportion of their sentences prior to release.

Although many of the projections about the future of corrections made in the special issue of *The Prison Journal* were optimistic U.S. prison populations increased from the 1980s until they peaked in 2009 and have only decreased by about one percent a year since then (Carson, 2018). As noted in the previous chapters, by contrast, the use of incarceration has been more stable in Canada, and a review of Statistics Canada (2018a, 2018b) data shows the national incarceration rate, both federal and provincial, was 131 per 100,000 residents in 1979, and had only increased to 136 residents by 2016/2017. The rate of offenders on probation actually decreased somewhat during that timeframe, from 322 to 305 per 100,000 residents. Thus, while the U.S. forecasts were very imperfect, applying those predictions of stability and reliance upon community corrections to Canada would have been more accurate.

So if our predictions about correctional practices are not very accurate in the long term, why do we bother? Some correctional leaders are reluctant to engage in these exercises as they are so busy in their day-to-day activities they have little time to devote to considering future changes. Leaders concerned about the future, however, do not want their agencies to suffer because they failed to plan for different outcomes. One example of using information from a forecast to influence correctional centre operations is considering a city's possible growth and the demand for correctional centre beds in the future. Officials are able to use information about projected city populations to enable the planned expansion of a facility if more beds are later required. In addition to adding bed capacity, well-thought out expansion plans are flexible so they can accommodate changes in different populations, such as women or for persons with mental health problems (Jones, 2018). Thus, if these short term incarceration beds are required because the population increases, the facility can be expanded at less cost and disruption to the organization.

Predicting the future is much like forecasting the weather, and while it is a relatively easy to anticipate tomorrow's weather, it is more complicated to estimate next year's conditions. The **Police Futurists International** (2017) use six time frames in their forecasts of future trends, and they range from Immediate forecasts, which consider the next two years, to Distant forecasts, which try to predict changes 50 years and beyond. The following sections describe some potential changes in corrections until 2030, which is a mid-level orientation. Although many of these issues already influence what occurs in corrections they are likely to exert a greater impact on both community and institutional operations until 2030. In what follows, we briefly describe the internal and external factors influencing correctional operations, and then provide a more detailed list of specific issues that will shape the future of Canadian corrections.

PREDICTING THE FUTURE OF CORRECTIONS

Social scientists have used a number of different approaches to forecasting the future including examining **quantitative data** such as information about prison admissions dating back several decades. Researchers have also used **qualitative approaches** that solicit information from experts, or where correctional leaders working in small groups make forecasts based on scenarios (e.g., what are the potential impacts of a 25 percent funding cut to a community corrections budget?). Correctional administrators call their forecasting efforts by a number of different names including visioning the future (Russo, Drake, Schaffer, & Jackson, 2017) and **environmental scans** where the external forces that influence correctional practices, such as economic slowdowns that reduce prison budgets, are identified (National Institute of Corrections, 2017). Various federal agencies, including the Correctional Service of Canada (CSC), have also used SWOT and PESTEL analyses and they are briefly described below.

A **SWOT analysis** focuses on the internal and external attributes of an organization that can either help or hinder the agency's ability to meet their goals, including managing their futures by reducing uncertainty. Table 13.1 shows a sample SWOT table that was developed by Public Safety Canada (2010, p. 53). A SWOT analysis is often carried out using the observations and insight of an organization's staff members, who sometimes use a facilitator to help them condense the participant's feedback into clear, short, and specific factors that are easily understood by agency staff, stakeholders, and funders.

A **PESTEL analyses**, is a type of environmental scan that considers the political, economic, social, technological, legal and environmental factors that might influence an organization's future operations, and these forces are shown in Figure 13.1. A PESTEL analysis considers the following factors:

Political. Liberal and conservative politicians often have opposing positions on crime and punishment, and the crime control policies introduced by these parties influence all aspects of the justice system, including sentencing and corrections. The tough on crime policies of the Harper government, for instance, were softened by the Liberal government after the 2015 election.

Economic. Recessions or economic downturns can increase the amount of crime and the criminal justice system's ability to respond to crimes. Economic downturns can also negatively affect community and institutional corrections when these organizations are asked to "do more with less."

Table 13.1 – Sample SWOT Table		
Internal Factors	**Strengths** Attributes of the organization that are helpful to achieving the objective(s) **Corrections examples**: Veteran and professional staff members	**Weaknesses** Attributes of the organization that are harmful to achieving the objective(s) **Corrections examples**: Lack of funds for training staff members
External Factors	**Opportunities** External conditions that are helpful to achieving the objective(s) **Corrections examples**: Public support for correctional rehabilitation	**Threats** External conditions which could do damage to the objective(s) **Corrections examples**: Budget cutbacks

Source: Public Safety Canada (2010).

Social. Demographic changes, such as a large at-risk population (e.g., the percentage of 15 to 25 year-old males in a population) are associated with increased crime. Cultural changes can also influence correctional operations and public support for rehabilitating offenders, for example, may increase support for additional funding for community corrections.

Technological. Technology has led to new ways of carrying out crimes, such as internet-based fraud but correctional agencies have also benefitted from technology that has made it easier to supervise and monitor offenders (e.g. by using closed circuit television).

Environmental. Of all these factors, environmental conditions have had the least direct impact on correctional operations, although disasters such as fires and floods, have negatively influenced the operations of some rural correctional facilities. Climate change, however, may have a significant indirect effect on the economy if these changes influence agriculture, such as droughts, or rising sea water from melting over the long term floods coastal cities.

Legal. Supreme Court decisions, and legislative changes (such as the legalization of marijuana) play a significant role in the operations of justice systems and an appellate court's rulings can force policy changes in correctional facilities that can have a significant impact on their operations, such as the 2018 B.C. Supreme Court decision placing restrictions on the use of long-term segregation.

In addition to SWOT or PESTEL analyses, correctional leaders use a variety of forecasting methods that vary in their sophistication. Larger agencies, for example, tend to engage in state-of-the-art forecasting and the Correctional Service of Canada, for instance, has researchers who can produce predictions about the size of the correctional population based on analyzing decades of information about prison admissions and discharges, and they contrast those factors on other variables, such as

Figure 13.1 – PESTEL analysis

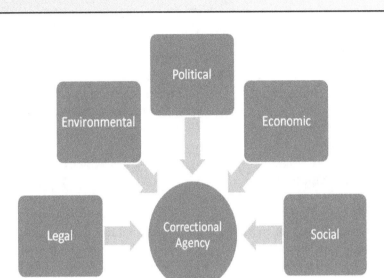

crimes reported to the police. Those analyses will focus on changes in the number of admissions and the average length of stay of these inmates (which determines the overall population), demographic trends (e.g., the number of young adult males in the population), and whether crime and arrest rates are increasing or decreasing. Other correctional administrators, by contrast, might write their predictions on the back of an envelope after holding informal discussions with other staff members.

Both internal and external forces have shaped the practice of contemporary corrections, and these factors include economic conditions, social and cultural changes, political and legal decisions, the shifting demographic characteristics of a population, and the responses of correctional systems to these changes. Some of these factors were briefly described above and while it is difficult enough to predict what the future will hold for any of one these issues, forecasting is more difficult when we examine all of these factors together. These external factors are shown in Box 13.1.

A review of the external factors shown in Box 13.1 reveals that all of these factors are largely out of the control of a correctional facility or system. For example, few predicted or anticipated the long-term consequences of the economic recession that started in 2008 and it has persisted much longer than most predicted. This downturn has had a significant impact on all criminal justice agencies, as well as the health, education, and social service agencies that can prevent crime and support the justice system (Ruddell & Jones, 2014). There are also unforeseen events, such as the 9/11 attacks that led to managing an increased number of offenders sentenced on terrorism-related offences, and the prospect of non-terrorist prisoners being socialized and recruited into these activities; what correctional administrators call **radicalization** (Correctional Service of Canada, 2014). These unforeseen acts or events are often called **black swan** events, and after these acts occur, most of us wonder why we had not anticipated the event.

All of the internal factors that will influence the future of Canadian corrections are related to activities initiated or carried out by the correctional personnel, partners, and stakeholders. For the most

Box 13.1 – External Factors Influencing the Future of Corrections

• Changes in economic prosperity or downturns • Changes in cultural values (e.g., attitudes towards punishing or rehabilitating offenders) • Public opinion about corrections • Legal decisions, such as the legalization of marijuana • New forms of crime (e.g., internet offences) • Changes in police enforcement, such as treating impaired driving as an infraction rather than a criminal offence • Technology, including drones that are used to smuggle contraband	• Political decisions (e.g., eliminating the "two-for-one" credit for remanded inmates) • Litigation/Lawsuits • Oversight carried out by provincial Ombudsmen or the federal Correctional Investigator • Changes in the composition of the general population (e.g., population of 15 to 25 year-old males) • Changes in the upper age limit for juvenile justice • Unforeseen events, such as the 9/11 attacks (also called black swan events)

part these activities are intended to make community and institutional corrections operate in a more efficient or effective manner, or make the conditions of community supervision or confinement more conducive to reducing a probationer's, parolee's, or inmate's recidivism. When both external and internal factors are compared, we contend that external factors have had a greater impact upon the operations of correctional systems.

TOP FIVE EXTERNAL FACTORS INFLUENCING THE FUTURE OF CORRECTIONS

Economic Prosperity and Corrections

One of the most significant influences affecting the police, courts, and corrections is the economic health of the nation. Prior research shows there are national economic downturns, or recessions, in Canada about every seven or eight years, although some provinces may also have significant downturns even when the national economic health is stable. One example is the economic downturn that started in Alberta in 2014 when oil prices dropped, and five years later that province still has not balanced its annual budgets. When economies constrict, there is typically less funding for correctional operations and rehabilitative programs and staffing are often cut (Scott-Hayward, 2011). A review of the literature shows that since the 1980s, there were economic cutbacks in every decade. Turner and colleagues (2015, p. 402) observe that governments in an economic downturn will often attempt to cut correctional costs by "closing prisons, reducing staff, and curtailing services and programming."

Canadians are experiencing record levels of personal and government debt (Blatchford, 2018a), there are high levels of unemployment in some provinces (Vomipero, 2018), investors are moving their funds to more business-friendly nations (Blatchford, 2018b), and inflation has been rising (Canadian Press, 2018). If these trends continue, a greater amount of government spending will be required to

Box 13.2 – Internal Factors Influencing the Future of Corrections

• Evidence-based practices • Violence reduction strategies • Correctional security • Technology (e.g., that increases security) • Environmentally friendly (sustainable) corrections initiatives • Correctional programming • Correctional health	• Staffing (recruiting, training and retaining correctional officers) • Stronger relationships between institutional and community corrections • Gang management interventions • Analysis of big data • Justice reinvestment

fund social programs and repay debt. The outcomes of these economic conditions, such as less social spending, might contribute to higher levels of crime, and this may place greater demands on the entire justice system, including community and institutional corrections. An increasing correctional population in tough economic times often results in overcrowding, and inmates are sometimes placed in crowded conditions, such as putting two inmates in cells designed for one person, or placing inmates in temporary housing arrangements, such as sleeping on cots in a gym. The use of these makeshift arrangements and other problems associated with overcrowding can sometimes result in increased violence, suicides, and deaths from other causes (Paperny, 2017), as well as reducing access to rehabilitative programming and a focus on only fulfilling the inmate's basic needs for shelter and food; what many call warehousing (Demers, 2014).

New Forms of Crime

New forms of crimes, or the changing characteristics of offenders have also influenced the operations of correctional systems. Few could have predicted, for instance, the impact of the mid-1980s crack cocaine epidemic in the U.S. that increased both violent crime and created a surge in correctional populations (Austin, Cuvelier, & McVey 1992). Since 2016 we have been confronting the increased abuse of opioids and this has created significant problems for first responders and medical services. Correctional institutions are also affected by those substance abuse problem and provincial correctional centres are confronting a spike in inmate deaths from opioids (Lowson, 2018). In response to the increased presence of these drugs and increased overdoses Alberta has introduced opioid addictions treatment programs in their correctional centres (Southwick, 2018). Efforts have also been made to introduce alternative criminal sentences for offenders with opioid addictions. For example, in 2015 the Nova Scotia Mental Health Court launched a drug treatment program designed specifically for individuals charged with crimes related to their opioid addiction.

While it is difficult to accurately predict the types of crimes that might emerge in the next decade, there are a growing number of internet-based offences reported to the police. Wexler (2018, pp. 4-7) reports that technology is changing the way that offenders victimize others and his observations are summarized as follows:

- New crimes, based on technology, are being carried out. One example is ransomware, where an individual's computer "freezes up" unless the user pays a ransom to an offender.

- Criminals are learning that internet-based crimes can provide greater rewards than street crime and offenders receive lesser penalties if caught and prosecuted.
- Offenders are adapting to crime-prevention technologies.
- Investigations of crimes are becoming more complex, and there are a greater number of sources of information (such as social media, information from security cameras, and a suspect's personal devices – from cell phones to Fitbits).
- The anonymity of offenders is increased by their use of the "dark web" to facilitate transactions for illegal goods or services.
- Local police services do not have the expertise or personnel to confront many of these technology-based offences.

Statistics Canada (2018c) reports that the total number of technology or internet violations increased by 58 percent between 2014 and 2016 (from 15,184 to 23,996 offences), and those numbers likely undercount the true number of victims of internet-based scams, as relatively few victims report these crimes to the police (see Wexler, 2018).

As a result, while the nature of crime in the future is changing, law enforcement seems to be lagging in their ability to respond to these crimes. Sentencing more technologically savvy offenders may influence correctional practices, including the need to supervise probationers convicted of internet-based crimes in the community; and whether their access to the internet is restricted because of a probation order, or managing the access to the internet for correctional centre and prison inmates.

Community corrections may also be impacted by a growing number of persons on electronic monitoring. Kilgore (2018) reports that in the United States, the number of persons supervised on electronic monitoring has doubled in the past ten years; and he calls this e-carceration. While electronic monitoring in Canada is less prevalent, cash-strapped provinces and territories might be interested in shifting the costs of incarceration from the institutions to the community. To produce financial benefits, however, electronic monitoring must reduce the size of the correctional population (Bonta, Wallace-Capretta, & Rooney, 1999). The Americans further shift the costs associated with electronic monitoring away from government as many probationers and parolees who are being electronically monitored must pay private corporations for their supervision.

The Changing Offender Profile: More Minority and Older Offenders

As highlighted in previous chapters correctional administrators have very little control over the persons admitted into their facilities. Police arrest suspects and some are remanded in custody until their court dates, and thereafter, the courts determine guilt and whether a community or custodial sentence is warranted, and if so, the length of that sentence. Thus, correctional facilities cannot always predict how many persons are admitted, the characteristics of these offenders, or how long these persons are held. The operations of a correctional facility, however, are affected by the characteristics of the persons who are admitted. From the 1990s to the 2000s there was a significant increase in the number of probationers and prisoners with many unmet needs such as persons with disabilities or mental illnesses, or gang members who posed significant risks to facility and public safety. To a large extent, the proportion of those offenders has stabilized since 2010, although the size of minority populations behind bars has been increasing and this group may pose challenges for community and institutional correctional systems in the future.

Statistics Canada (2017, p. 1) reports that in 2016, 4.9 percent of the Canadian population was of Indigenous ancestry, which was up 42.5 percent since 1996. The Indigenous population is over overrepresented in correctional populations. In the federal prison system, for example, Indigenous offenders account for over one-fifth (22.7 percent) of the population in 2015-16, and the number of these prisoners had grown by 16.6 percent in the previous four years (Public Safety Canada, 2017, p. 49). This over-representation is even more pronounced for Indigenous females who account for 31 percent of all female admissions to federal custody. In general, the number of women in federal institutions has risen significantly over the last decade, from 502 in 2007 to 688 in 2017 (Burke, 2017; see also Correctional Service of Canada, 2015).

Indigenous adults are also overrepresented in provincial and territorial corrections and account for about over one-quarter of all admissions in Canada, although the proportion is much higher in the Prairie Provinces and in Manitoba and Saskatchewan almost three-quarters of all admissions are Indigenous persons (Malakieh, 2018, p. 5). The growing number of Indigenous peoples in the general population suggests that their overrepresentation will continue, but that it will have a differential impact throughout the nation.

Another changing characteristic of the federal prison population is the increase in the number of offenders sentenced to terms of life imprisonment (also called indeterminate sentences). Public Safety Canada (2017, p. 57) reports that lifers represented almost one-quarter (23.4%) of all CSC offenders in 2015-16, and this total has been increasing as more offenders are sentenced to these sanctions and these offenders are living longer. As these individuals are under the supervision of the CSC for the rest of their lives, they will contribute to an aging custody population. Parallel with U.S. trends, there are a growing number of older inmates in federal and provincial corrections. Statistics Canada (2018d) reports that from 2000-01 to 2015-16, for example, the number of inmates aged 50 years and older admitted to provincial and territorial correctional facilities increased by 96 percent, and that trend is apt to continue as Canada's population ages. While older inmates tend to be more settled and engage in less misconduct than their younger counterparts, they often require a greater degree of health-care services, which places additional demands on institutional corrections.

Legislative Changes

Legislative changes can also have a significant long-term impact upon correctional practices, although it is sometimes difficult to predict the ultimate outcomes of new laws. The abolishment of accelerated parole review and the introduction of earned parole and adding more mandatory minimum sentences were predicted to increase the federal prison population. In response to those initiatives, the federal government increased the number of prison beds in anticipation of a greater number of offenders, but these prison population increases never occurred. Doob and Webster (2016) report that these legislative changes have not resulted in any discernible changes to Canada's incarceration rates. Similarly, Reitano (2017) observes that the national rate of persons supervised by the correctional system has been stable or decreasing although some provinces, such as Saskatchewan, are struggling with correctional centre overcrowding.

Sometimes legislation does not have the anticipated impact. The 2009 legislation that limited the "two-for-one" credit for remand – as discussed in Chapter 5 – was intended to decrease the provincial and territorial remand populations. Yet, the number of remanded individuals increased by 40 percent between 2005-06 and 2016-17 (Statistics Canada, 2018b). Some of these legislative changes are driven by political priorities of the ruling parties and while the Harper government in 2010 placed restrictions on the accelerated parole review process, the Liberal government in 2017 amended that legislation to streamline access to parole.

One change in the *Criminal Code of Canada* that may influence the operations of the justice system was the legalization of marijuana on October 17, 2018. Legalizing this drug is posited to reduce the number of drug-related arrests for possession and the number of persons supervised by community corrections personnel or admitted to a correctional centre. We cannot predict, however, the full impact of these new laws for individuals sentenced for the illegal distribution or sale of marijuana, or exceeding personal cultivation limits and these offences can result in 14-year prison sentences (Government of Canada, 2018).

Legal Decisions

The decisions of provincial Courts of Appeals and the Supreme Court of Canada can also influence correctional practices. In 2018, the British Columbia Supreme Court ruled that the long-term or indefinite use of solitary confinement (also called isolation or administrative segregation) was not constitutionally appropriate. The Court ruled that placing inmates in long-term solitary confinement "has significant adverse effects on the physical, psychological and social health of inmates" (Proctor, 2018, para. 9). Instead, the Justice who wrote the decision said that a 15-day placement in solitary confinement seemed to be defendable. The federal government has, however, appealed that decision, and it may be years before this matter is ultimately resolved if the Supreme Court of Canada decides to hear the case.

Other provincial Courts of Appeal are also hearing cases about the constitutionality of using risk assessments, which are developed using general offender populations, to assess the likelihood of prison misconduct and recidivism of Indigenous offenders. Furthermore, the Supreme Court may rule on criminal justice matters unrelated to corrections that may affect correctional populations. The *R. v. Jordan* decision in 2016, for example, placed strict limits on the length of time a case could be delayed in court. A year after that decision, the Canadian Broadcasting Corporation (CBC) reported that several hundred criminal cases were dismissed, including cases of "murders, sexual assaults, drug trafficking and child luring, all stayed by judges because the defendant's constitutional right to a timely trial was infringed" (Kane, 2017, para. 2).

Summary

Altogether, a number of external forces will shape the future of community and institutional corrections in Canada. While we identified the five factors we thought were the most important, the future of corrections may also be shaped by other external factors such as litigation, where inmates use the legal system to seek damages from a correctional system. In 2017 and 2018, for example, inmates launched a number of class action lawsuits – where lawyers represent inmates who have suffered a similar harm in a single case – on the overuse of solitary confinement (Bridges, 2018), the excessive cost of collect calls (*Global News*, 2017), and six prisoners are suing the province of Ontario because they were traumatized by witnessing a murder in their living unit (Richmond, 2017). Many of the issues raised in these lawsuits were previously addressed by external advocacy bodies, such as provincial ombudsmen or the federal prison system's correctional investigator. While these advocates have been around for decades, they seem to have little power to change systemic issues such as access to health care or conditions of confinement, which are most common complaints in the CSC (Public Safety Canada, 2017).

TOP FIVE INTERNAL FACTORS INFLUENCING THE FUTURE OF CORRECTIONS

Correctional Security

Correctional security includes a broad range of overlapping interventions, including violence reduction strategies, managing prison gangs, and providing meaningful correctional programming –

such as treatment and jobs that keeps inmates constructively occupied – also contributes to safer living conditions for the inmate. One of the most difficult tasks for correctional staff is ensuring a safe environment, especially given that Canadian federal prisons have a high proportion of violent offenders and 69 percent have been convicted of violent offences (Public Safety Canada, 2017), whereas the proportion of U.S. state prison inmates convicted of a violence offence is only 54 percent (Carson, 2018, p. 1). That difference may be one reason why murder rates in Canadian federal prisons are about four times their American counterparts. Public Safety Canada (2017, p. 70) reports there were 29 homicides in CSC institutions between 2004-05 and 2013-14 which translates into a rate of 1.7 homicides for every 1,000 federal inmates for those ten years. In the United States, by contrast, Noonan (2016, p. 4) reports the homicide rate in state and federal prisons was 0.4 murders for every 1,000 prisoners for the same years.

Being incarcerated in a provincial or territorial correctional center was safer, in terms of being killed, than living in a federal prison. While there were 29 murders in CSC facilities between 2004 and 2014, there were five homicides in correctional centres during the same time (Public Safety Canada, 2017, p. 70). So why should we care about what happens to these prisoners? We have to remember that almost all Canadian prisoners eventually return to the community and become our neighbours. When they return to the community more damaged because they were victimized or psychologically traumatized, they may be at a greater risk to commit further crimes. As a result, it is in our best interests that these ex-prisoners are healthy and well-adjusted when returned to the community.

There are a number of reasons why violence reduction strategies will become a greater priority in the future. There is, for instance, a growing recognition of the long-term destructive impacts of being victimized or witnessing violence. While one can see the physical injuries after an assault occurs, there is also acknowledgment of the psychological harm caused by these offences. Hochstetler, Murphy, and Simons (2004, p. 448) found that: "prison victimization contributes to the occurrence of depressive and post-traumatic stress symptoms" and that "prison victimization adds to the pains of pre-existing events." Victimization, coercion, and the possibility of being assaulted also contributes to an environment of fear. Hassine (2009, pp. 179-207) wrote extensively about the fear an inmate experiences in different correctional settings, and the short- and long-term consequences of this fright, such as anxiety, depression, sleep deprivation (which in turn leads to irritability) and paranoia. The ongoing exposure to fear and the stress it creates can lead to maladaptive behaviours – including joining a prison gang to reduce the likelihood of victimization – and fear and anxiety may also contribute to self-harm or suicide. These experiences may have a more destructive impact upon inmates who are already grappling with poor health, substance abuse and have poor coping skills.

Witnessing violence can also have a negative impact upon the individual (Blevins, Johnson Listwan, Cullen, & Lero Jonson, 2010; Boxer, Middlemass, & Delorenzo, 2009). Prolonged exposure to witnessing inmate assaults, their after-effects, or working with victims of violence can also result in **vicarious trauma**, heightened anxiety and irritability, and long-term disorders, such as **post-traumatic stress disorder** (PTSD). Daquin, Daigle, and Johnson Listwan (2017) found that parolees who had witnessed a greater amount of prison victimization had more arrests and parole violations than parolees with fewer experiences. Moreover, when levels of violence in a facility or housing unit are high, it is likely the environment is less favourable to rehabilitation due to the increased tension and stress associated with this misconduct.

Given these facts, there is apt to be an increased interest in violence reduction strategies over the next decade. Vanyur, Nink, Upchurch, Bodman, and Greenwald (2009) highlighted a number of steps that can be taken in reducing correctional violence. Their approach is preventative in nature and relies upon developing the staff members' expertise in managing offenders in a way that helps to reduce violence, as well as taking advantage of technology to aid in investigations. Levan (2016) also contends that older inmates can act as positive role models to newly admitted prisoners and they can use their informal power to reduce the tensions within a facility and counter gang recruitment.

Technology in Community and Institutional Corrections

Corrections is a labour-intensive industry as security personnel are required to supervise and control inmates, educators deliver programs, medical and mental health staff members work toward restoring the offenders' health, and administrative and support staff keep the institutions operating. Technology enables correctional systems to maximize the efforts of these personnel to increase security, efficiency, and manage administrative tasks. Since the early 1990s there has been an increased reliance on technological tools in correctional systems and these innovations have led to safer, more cost-effective, and efficiently run organizations.

Jackson and colleagues (2015, pp. 22-23) describe five different categories of correctional technology and they are summarized as follows:

- Facility operations and population services, which includes technologies and practices related to running correctional facilities, including their design, physical security, and process related to delivering products, education and health care to the inmates.
- Person-worn equipment and weapons/force, which covers uniforms, protective clothing (such as stab-resistant vests or riot gear), firearms, and less-than-lethal weapons, such as TASERS or pepper spray.
- Information and communications, which includes computerized information technology, sensors (such as drug or metal detectors), closed circuit television (CCTV), instruments devices that detect cellular phones (which are banned in all correctional facilities), and communications tools and systems such as the handheld radios carried by the staff members.
- Vehicles include ground, air – such as unmanned aerial drones – and water vehicles as well as their modifications.
- Doctrine, tactics, management, and behavioural knowledge development and training, and this category includes personnel education and training, innovation in policies and training technologies.

Corrections is a large industry in North America and many corporations will supply a range of technological tools to help a community-based agency or institution manage their probationers or inmates.

Over the next decade corporations will continue to produce tools and software that will be purchased by correctional systems to enhance security as well as operate more cost-efficiently by managing information about offenders and correctional operations. There has been more attention paid to collecting information from correctional agencies regarding offenders and their conduct in community and institutional settings, what some call **big data**. Because most information about community and facility operations is now computer-based, it is relatively easy to collect and analyze vast amounts of information about probationers and correctional centre or prison inmates. Researchers say that this information might be used to predict their behaviour, as well as helping to forecast risks to the public or facility safety (Corrections Technology Association, 2013).

Technology also poses risks to corrections. Inmates and their associates have access to the same types of technology, and may use these tools (such as contraband smart phones) to continue their criminal behaviors behind bars. Moreover, drones have been used to drop contraband to correctional centre or prison inmates and in January 2018, a drone dropped $26,500 of drugs and tobacco into the yard of a CSC facility in Abbotsford (Judd, 2018). While most contraband dropped by drones has been drugs or cellular phones, a handgun was dropped into the yard of a Quebec detention centre in 2015 (Cruz, 2015).

Correctional staff members sometimes resist the implementation of new technologies, and as a result, they will require training – not only in the use of these tools – but also to understand their advantages in promoting safety. Upchurch (2009) observed that the implementation phase of introducing new correctional technology tools must be carefully managed to increase staff acceptance. Thus, while we predict that technology will play a larger role in the future of corrections, there will be both positive and negative impacts of these changes.

Correctional Staffing

The orderly operation of correctional facilities relies upon the knowledge, skills, abilities, and dedication of the staff members, and the future of corrections will be shaped by these personnel. The number of institutional correctional officers in Canada is proportional to the size of the inmate population, and there is almost one corrections staff member for every federal prisoner. Most of those staff members are working in institutions. One of the challenges for correctional administrators in the future will be recruiting new officers and staff personnel from a shrinking pool of potential candidates.

There are several reasons for a shrinking labour pool, including that the Canadian population is aging and fewer young people are interested in correctional careers. In addition to a shrinking pool of potential job candidates, the standards for working in justice systems have increased. Correctional agencies want to hire officers with high levels of integrity, fitness, commitment to the organization, and clean drug-use histories. These expectations, however, are not consistent with the fact that many young adults today have experimented with drugs, are not physically fit, and have little interest in working with a single agency for their entire careers (Ruddell & Mays, 2009). Correctional agencies are also hamstrung by the fact that many facilities were constructed in rural and sparsely populated areas, and many potential job candidates are not interested in living in the countryside. Last, there is an increasing competition for the same type of candidates in justice systems and correctional agencies often pay less than other law enforcement organizations or the military.

The shrinking labour pool, however, might create career opportunities for members of minority groups, older workers, and women: groups that are currently under-represented as workers in some correctional systems. Historically, it was difficult for women to gain entry to some correctional careers, although now they are entering the field of corrections in increasing numbers, and in some U.S. jurisdictions they outnumber their male counterparts (Nink, 2008). Thus, correctional agencies in the future will likely have a more diverse workforce than existed in the past, and was overwhelmingly "pale and male."

The changing demographic characteristics of the population will also require that different models of staff supervision be developed, especially as aging baby boomers – many of whom are in managerial positions – are now supervising millennials (born between 1981 and 2000). Millennials have been criticized as having less organizational commitment, are often in a rush to get promoted, and feel that their knowledge, skills, and abilities are more relevant than their older coworkers. Ruddell and Mays (2009, p. 1) observed that while those traits "may be based on stereotypes, they do underscore the importance of acknowledging the intergenerational differences of today's law enforcement officers in day-to-day supervision as well as the development of retention strategies."

Not only will it be difficult to recruit new correctional officers, but it is difficult to retain them, and that will be a challenge for the future. One of the problems is that there is a growing number of correctional personnel suffering from psychological injuries. Over one-half of correctional workers in Carlton and colleagues' (2018) study of Canadian public safety personnel reported having symptoms associated with mental disorders, such as PTSD, or other mood and anxiety disorders (see also Henning,

2017). If untreated, these mental health disorders can lead to serious problems and in 2015, for example, 15 Canadian correctional officers committed suicide (TEMA, 2018). In addition to psychological injuries, there has been an increase in the number of provincial and federal corrections officers being assaulted on the job. Cottrill (2017) reports that in British Columbia the number of officers assaulted increased by 39 percent between 2014 and 2015.

As a result, during the next decade we predict that there will be increasing attention paid to correctional and probation officer wellness (Ferdik & Smith, 2017). Most wellness advocates now emphasize an "academy to retirement" approach to caring for the psychological and physical health of correctional staff members, and wellness will become a more important factor in the future as retaining employees is a more cost-effective approach compared to recruiting, training, and orientating new correctional officers.

Reducing Recidivism

Lowering the likelihood of an offender's return to custody typically depends on where they served their sentence, their sentence length, their access to rehabilitative programming, their strengths and weaknesses as well as the support they receive from their families and the correctional staff. An offender sentenced to a relatively short term of incarceration in a provincial correctional centre, for instance, may receive a job within the institution – which might help them to develop their vocational skills – but very little in the way of rehabilitative programming addressing their unmet needs in respect to alcohol and drug dependency, literacy, or criminal thinking. An offender in a federal institution, by contrast, may be sentenced to a longer sentence, but if convicted of a non-violent offence, their parole eligibility may occur before they can complete any correctional program. Consequently, many offenders do not participate in, nor complete, meaningful correctional interventions. Despite these limitations, Canada is at the forefront of correctional rehabilitation and the contributions of Donald Andrews and Jim Bonta in the development of correctional interventions based on the risk, needs, and responsivity (RNR) model have been adopted throughout the world. Much of this work was made possible through the federal correctional system that utilizes relatively small institutions, offers support for offender assessment, is committed to providing meaningful programming to offenders, and the parole system has a low officer to parolee ratio, which contributes to a safer transition of offenders into the community. It is worth noting that a majority of federal offenders on conditional release successfully complete day and full parole, at a rate of 91% and 88% respectively (Public Safety Canada, 2016).

Contributors in the preceding chapters have described the importance of reducing recidivism, and the need for positive and proactive relationships between community and institutional corrections. This communication and cooperation is important for a number of reasons, including enhancing opportunities for offenders and increasing public safety. Many offenders returning to the community from a correctional centre or penitentiary often feel optimistic about their likelihood of success (Berinbaum, 2009). The challenge for these ex-offenders, however, is that most will return to the same neighbourhoods where they were arrested, with the same dysfunctional friends and family members, a lack of legitimate employment opportunities, housing insecurity, and they will have to face the temptations of alcohol and drugs, as well as the influences of negative peers. All of these factors reduce the likelihood of a successful community reentry (Petersilia, 2009). Thus, while correctional systems may help offenders increase their skills and change their attitudes, they have little control over the conditions in the community that can push an ex-prisoner toward reoffending. Therefore, it is important that offenders develop as many meaningful social, vocational and interpersonal skills as possible to overcome barriers to a successful reentry. Non-governmental organizations can play a particularly important role in providing rehabilitative programming and direct support to former inmates living in the community.

Historically, many correctional programs were developed using commonly-held stereotypes about offenders or the "gut feelings" of administrators or politicians that were later proven to be wrong. Latessa, Cullen and Gendreau (2002) argued that rehabilitative programs should be based on interventions that had demonstrated their effectiveness through research, what we call **evidence-based practices**. These programs are often evaluated using cost-benefit analyses, which compare the costs of an intervention with the societal benefits of reduced crime: see, for example, the work carried out by the Washington State Institute for Public Policy (2018). Criminological research consistently shows that "conditional release is more effective in promoting a prisoner's successful reintegration into society as a law-abiding citizen than would be his/her sudden freedom – at sentence expiry – without any assistance or supervision" (Doob, Webster, & Manson, 2014, p. 305).

Public Safety Canada (2017) reports that inmates released on parole have lower recidivism rates compared to those released on their statutory release date. The timed, controlled, and gradual release from prison, in conjunction with the provision of rehabilitative programming, appear to positively impact recidivism rates while creating other social benefits. Although parole grant rates were on a decline for some years, they have steadily increased since 2010-11. One reason is that costs are significantly less for supervising offenders in the community (see below). Given the potential cost savings of implementing research-based interventions in corrections, policymakers will be motivated to continue their support for rehabilitative programming and community corrections in the future, and there will be an increased use of evidence-based practices and cost-benefit analyses.

Correctional Partnerships

Historically, correctional institutions were considered to be **closed systems**, meaning that they had limited interactions with their external environments. For most of the 20th century, many prisons and correctional centres were located in rural areas and were almost self-sufficient: inmates raised their own food, generated electricity, and cleaned and maintained (and sometimes constructed) these institutions. There were, however, limitations associated with this closed systems approach and as discussed in Chapter 8, a lack of public oversight sometimes resulted in abuses of authority. Moreover, by isolating themselves, correctional administrators could not take advantage of partnerships that allowed them to maximize their efforts to reduce recidivism.

The closed nature of correctional operations extended to relationships between the three elements of the criminal justice system – the police, courts, and corrections – and these relationships were often under-developed. As a result, one element of the system was not always aware what other agencies were doing, and this has been called operating in **silos** (which are the tall cylindrical structures used for storing grains on farms). This lack of communication and coordination also occurred within these systems. In institutional corrections, for instance, policies and practices are not always consistent between different facilities in correctional systems, or even within a single facility; resulting in the differential treatment of staff and offenders. This lack of coordination also occurred between institutional and community corrections, and in some cases, there is a lack of shared vision about goals within the same organization. Lacking a clear mission or shared values can lead to miscommunication, inefficient operations, a lack of coordination and conflict (Lin, 2000).

A lack of communication and inability to form effective working relationships can be understood within the geographical context of Canada (e.g., small populations within large provinces or the entire nation). Consequently, all of the elements of the justice system tended to act more independently than they do today. Problems arising from that approach included services that were sometimes duplicated and this results in waste, and some offenders "fell through the cracks" of the system, which increased recidivism. Moreover, victims were also overlooked and systems failed to provide notices to them (e.g., when an offender was being released), placed additional stressors on them.

In the future community and institutional agencies will increase their willingness to collaborate, analyze the effectiveness of their programs, learn about the efforts of other agencies, work toward solutions and integrate activities between these different agencies (Borakove et al., 2015, p. 7). Although there are costs and challenges associated with partnering with other government and non-government agencies, it is likely that working toward an **open systems** approach will continue into the future. Brosens, De Donder, Dury and Verte (2015) observe that closer ties are forming between correctional officials and university researchers. Historically, there was tension between these two groups, and some academics were very critical of the operations of correctional centres and prisons. Since 2000, however, there has been an increasing involvement of academics evaluating correctional services, developing assessment tools and correctional interventions, and supporting correctional administrators with different organizational challenges, such as delivering staff training. Some partnerships, such as the one between the Saskatchewan Ministry of Justice and the University of Saskatchewan have benefitted both organizations. As a result, it is likely that these relationships will continue in the future.

Last, while not a formal partnership *per se*, there has been an increased involvement of community stakeholders in both community and institutional corrections. In the past, these relationships were strained as some of these community organizations were hyper-critical of the operations of the police, courts, and corrections. Today, however, there is growing acknowledgement that these stakeholders can play an important role in advocating for inmates in a constructive manner that leads to positive change. Administrators in correctional systems, by contrast, also realize that many of these stakeholders have legitimate concerns, and if successfully resolved, the changes they advocate can also benefit the correctional system.

Summary

Some of the five internal changes we identified are a result of the changing culture in correctional facilities, where correctional leaders invest more time and resources in making their institutions more conducive to rehabilitation and returning inmates to the community with better skills and supports. It is possible that inmates will play a greater role in making correctional centres and prisons saner and safer places. Rowe (2018) observes how the California Department of Corrections and Rehabilitation has introduced a prison where inmates have adopted a culture that rejects gangs and promotes rehabilitation.

CONCLUSIONS

Despite the difficulty in making long-term forecasts, it is important that correctional practitioners and academics engage in these efforts, as incarceration is an expensive social policy that must be carefully managed. Malakieh (2018) reports that it cost an average of $288 per day to imprison a federal offender in 2016-17 and about three-quarters that amount ($213) to hold a provincial prisoner. One of the issues seldom considered in calculating the ultimate cost of incarceration are the indirect costs; including those borne by an offender's family and community (e.g., when we consider the high costs of phone calls or the expenses for a family to visit a loved one in a correctional centre or prison). These additional expenses include lost opportunities (e.g., when an individual loses their job because of a lengthy remand), the psychological effects of being abused while incarcerated or the impact of incarceration on an individual's future employment prospects. Some advocacy organizations have also suggested that incarcerating an individual can be **criminogenic**, which means that associating with more sophisticated offenders may push these individuals further into crime. McLaughlin and colleagues (2016, p. 2) estimate that for every dollar spent on corrections, there are another ten dollars in social costs.

Costs of supervising an offender in the community, by comparison, are a fraction of the institutional costs. According to Reitano (2017, p. 16), we spent about one seventh as much on community supervision compared to institutional corrections. Research suggests that community supervision (i.e., probation and parole) is not only more cost-effective (especially in the long-run), but may also positive influence recidivism rates (see Drake, 2018). When community supervision is coupled with the provision of treatment and rehabilitative services for offenders, these positive effects are enhanced.

There is also increased interest in developing or extending existing evidence-based correctional programs that promise lower recidivism rates. As highlighted in earlier chapters, and in the comments above, Canadian officials have implemented the risk, needs, and responsivity model, and that has proven to reduce recidivism (Bonta & Andrews, 2017). Developing this approach may lay the foundation for interventions oriented toward offenders who have not been reached by other approaches, such as gang members. Di Placidio and colleagues (2006), for example, have reported successful outcomes after working with these offenders in Canadian penitentiaries. When it comes to gang offenders, timing seems to be important. Interviews of current and former Alberta gang members conducted by Chalas and Grekul (2017, p. 376) revealed that one-third left their gangs after having children or a family, after they acknowledged the bleak future prospects of gang involvement (e.g., prison or death), or simply because they were too old for gang activities.

Many of the factors we identified as impacting the future of corrections are associated with lowering correctional costs, making confinement safer, and enhancing community safety. Innovations in technology, for instance, will enable officials to do their jobs in a more efficient manner, and the use of big data may ultimately enable us to make more accurate predictions about an offender's future behaviours. Activities related to violence reduction, by contrast, are intended to make correctional facilities safer, but will also reduce stress and recidivism, which in turn enhances public safety when offenders return home.

Forecasting future trends is always a precarious task as unforeseen or black swan events or new forms of offending (and offenders) can lead to dramatic changes in justice systems, as evidenced by the opioid epidemic or the 9/11 attacks. One inescapable fact, however, is that almost all Canadian offenders ultimately return to their communities. With the exception of offenders sentenced to life imprisonment or those designated as dangerous offenders, most prisoners will become our neighbors within a few years of being sentenced, and even "lifers" can earn their way back to the community. If they have received effective correctional programming and we have removed barriers to their reentry we have made good investments in our future safety. One important consideration is that we must work toward returning inmates to the community less damaged than when they were admitted to a correctional centre or prison.

A review of the literature shows that there has been, on average, at least one major economic crisis per decade in recent memory. During times of economic stress, there may be less public and political support for costly interventions intended to reform offenders. These short-term costs, however, should be balanced against the long-term financial consequences of failing to save an offender from a life of crime (Cohen & Piquero, 2009). Cost benefit analyses have demonstrated that effective correctional programming is a cost-effective investment in public safety (Washington State Institute for Public Policy, 2018). Thus, legislators, correctional policymakers, and administrators should adopt a long-term orientation toward corrections management.

One way of developing a futures orientation is to duplicate the efforts of the Police Futurists International (PFI) with a focus on corrections. In addition to sponsoring a website and publishing a newsletter, books and technical reports, the PFI also hosts meetings that enable persons interested in the future to collaborate and debate issues and trends. Given the costs as well as the consequences of failing to accurately forecast the future, it is important that forward looking correctional practitioners and academics establish their own organization.

KEY TERMS AND CONCEPTS

Big data

Black swan events

Closed systems

Criminogenic

Environmental scans

Evidence-based practices

Open systems

PESTEL analysis

Police Futurists International

Post-traumatic stress disorder (PTSD)

Quantitative data

Qualitative approaches

Radicalization

Silos

SWOT analysis

Vicarious trauma

Wellness programs

STUDY AND DISCUSSION QUESTIONS

1. What factor external to corrections will have the most impact upon the future of Canadian corrections in the next ten years?
2. What internal factor will have the most influence on the future of federal and provincial corrections in the next ten years?
3. Should budget limits be a factor in determining how much incarceration should be used? Why or why not?
4. Describe some of the potential advantages and disadvantages when correctional systems engage in partnerships with community organizations.
5. Describe some of the ways in which correctional administrators try to manage the futures of their organizations by forecasting.
6. After reading this book do you foresee a positive outcome for the practice of corrections in the next decade?

REFERENCES

Austin, J., Cuvelier, S., & McVey, A. (1992). Projecting the future of corrections: The state of the art. *Crime & Delinquency, 38*(3), 285-308.

Berinbaum, R. N. (2009). *Bridging the gap between prison and the community: An exploration of resettlement and desistance among female offenders in England and Canada.* Retrieved from http://www.internetjournalofcriminology.com

Blatchford, A. (2018a). Is Canadians' soaring debt too high? Our government hasn't a clue. *Financial Post.* Retrieved from http://business.financialpost.com/personal-finance/debt/no-way-to-know-if-debt-to-income-ratio-has-climbed-too-high-federal-officials

Blatchford, A. (2018b). Investment is flowing out of Canada and into U.S. after tax changes, RBC president says. *CBC News.* Retrieved from http://www.cbc.ca/news/business/royal-bank-investment-ceo-1.4602161

Blevins, K. R., Johnson Listwan, S., Cullen, F. T., and Lero Jonson, C. (2010). A general strain theory of prison violence and misconduct: An integrated model of inmate behavior. *Journal of Contemporary Criminal Justice, 26*(2), 148-166.

Bonta, J., & Andrews, D. A. (2017). *The psychology of criminal conduct.* New York: Taylor & Francis.

Bonta, J., Wallace-Capretta, S., & Rooney, J. (1999). Electronic monitoring in Canada. *Public Safety Canada.* Retrieved from https://www.publicsafety.gc.ca/cnt/rsrcs/pblctns/lctrnc-mntrng-cnd/index-en.aspx#_Toc449518646

Borakove, M. E., Wosje, R. Cruz, F., Wickman, A., Dibble, T., & Harbus, C. (2015). *From silo to system: What makes a criminal justice system operate like a system?* Arlington, VA: The Justice Management Institute.

Boxer, P., Middlemass, K., and Delorenzo, T. (2009). Exposure to violent crime during incarceration: Effects on psychological adjustment following release. *Criminal Justice and Behavior, 36*(8), 793-807.

Bridges, A. (2018). Province, feds breaching inmates' charter rights with 'administrative segregation': class action lawsuits. *CBC News.* Retrieved from http://nationalpost.com/news/ canada/inmates-at-ontario-jail-sue-province-for-15m-after-seeing-hearing-fellow-prisoner-killed

Brosens, D., De Donder, E., Dury, S., & Verte, D. (2015). Building a research partnership in a prison context: From collaboration to co-construction. *Sociological Research Online, 20*(3), 1-15.

Burke, D. (2017). Number of women in federal prisons is up, and advocates think they know why. *CBC News.* Retrieved from http://www.cbc.ca/news/canada/nova-scotia/women-prisons-crime-nova-institution-overcrowding-1.4347197

Canadian Press. (2018). Canadian inflation shoots above target, sparking prospect of interest rate Hikes. *Canadian Press.* Retrieved from https://www.huffingtonpost.ca/2018/03/23/inflation-canada-interest-rates_a_23393569/

Carleton, R. N., Afifi, T. O., Turner, S., Taillieu, T., Duranceau, S., et al. (2018). Mental disorder symptoms among public safety personnel in Canada. *The Canadian Journal of Psychiatry, 63*(1), 54-64.

Carson, E. A. (2018). *Prisoners in 2016.* Washington, DC: Bureau of Justice Statistics.

Chalas, D. M., & Grekul, J. (2017). I've had enough: Exploring gang life from the perspective of (Ex) members in Alberta. *The Prison Journal, 97*(3), 364-386.

Charron, M., Nemr, R., & Vaillancourt, R. (2009). *Aging of justice personnel.* Ottawa, ON: Statistics Canada.

Cohen, M. A., & Piquero, A. R. (2009). New evidence on the monetary value of saving a high risk youth. *Journal of Quantitative Criminology, 25*(1), 25-49.

Correctional Service of Canada. (2014). *Best practices in the assessment, intervention and management of radicalized offenders.* Ottawa, ON: Author.

Correctional Service of Canada. (2015). *Research results – Women offenders.* Retrieved from http://www.csc-scc.gc.ca/publications/005007-3014-eng.shtml

Corrections Technology Association. (2013). *Big data and corrections: What's the big issue?* Retrieved from http://www.correctionstech.org/meeting/2013/Presentations/RR7.pdf

Cottrill, J. (2017). Trouble in the big house. *OHS Canada.* Retrieved from https://www.ohscanada.com/features/trouble-big-house/

Cruz, J. (2015). Gun dropped via drone into Canada's most violent prison. *La Press.* Retrieved from http://www.guns.com/2015/12/21/gun-dropped-via-drone-into-canadas-most-violent-prison/

Daquin, J. C., Daigle, L. E., & Johnson Listwan, S. (2017). Vicarious victimization in prison: Examining the effects of witnessing victimization while incarcerated on offender reentry. *Criminal Justice and Behavior, 43*(8), 1018-1033.

Demers, J. (2014). *Warehousing prisoners in Saskatchewan*. Regina, SK: Canadian Centre for Policy Alternatives.

Di Placido, C., Simon, T. L., Witte, T. D., Gu, D., & Wong, S. C. P. (2006). Treatment of gang members can reduce recidivism and institutional misconduct. *Law and Human Behavior, 30*(1), 93-114.

Doob, T., & Webster, C. (2016). Weathering the storm? Testing long-standing Canadian sentencing policy in the twenty-first century. *Crime and Justice, 45*(1), 359-418.

Doob, A., Webster, C., & Manson, A. (2014). Zombie parole: The withering conditional release in Canada. *Criminal Law Quarterly, 61*(3), 301-328.

Drake, E. (2018). The monetary benefits and costs of community supervision. *Journal of Contemporary Criminal Justice, 34*(1), 47-68.

Ferdik, F. V., & Smith, H. P. (2017). *Correctional officer safety and wellness literature synthesis*. Washington, DC: National Institute of Justice.

Global News. (2017). Class action lawsuit launched over collect calls from prison. Retrieved from https://globalnews.ca/video/3778561/class-action-lawsuit-launched-over-collect-calls-from-prison

Government of Canada. (2018). *Legalizing and strictly regulating cannabis: the facts*. Retrieved from https://www.canada.ca/en/services/health/campaigns/legalizing-strictly-regulating-cannabis-facts.html

Hassine, V. (2009). *Life without parole: Living in prison today* (5th ed.). New York: Oxford University Press.

Henning, C. (2017). Behind prison walls: Correctional officers speak out about PTSD in new documentary. *CBC News*. Retrieved from http://www.cbc.ca/amp/1.4308785

Hochstetler, A., Murphy, D.S., & Simmons, R. L. (2004). Damaged goods: Exploring predictors of stress in prison inmates. *Crime & Delinquency, 50*(3), 436-457.

Jackson, B. A., Russo, J., Hollywood, J. S., Woods, D., Silberglitt, R., Drake, G. B., et al. (2015). Fostering innovation in community and institutional corrections. Santa Monica, CA: RAND.

Jones, E. (2018). Building jail expansion in phases would take 16 years, $6M to $8M a year, county says. *Lawrence Journal-World*. Retrieved from http://www2.ljworld.com/news/2018/feb/20/cost-16-year-phased-jail-expansion-pegged-65-8-mil/

Judd, A. (2018). Someone used a drone to drop $26,500 of drugs, tobacco over a B.C. prison wall. *Global News*. Retrieved from https://globalnews.ca/news/3961889/drone-drugs-b-c-prison-wall/

Kane, L. (2017). Failing everyone: 204 cases tossed over delays since Supreme Court's Jordan decision. *CBC News*. Retrieved from http://www.cbc.ca/news/politics/jordan-cases-stayed-1.4192823

Kilgore, J. (2018). Electronic monitors: how companies dream of locking us in our homes. *In these times*. Retrieved from http://inthesetimes.com/article/21084/electronic-monitors-GEO-Group_CoreCivic-mass-incarceration-prisons-jails

Latessa, E. J., Cullen, F., & Gendreau, P. (2002). Beyond correctional quackery: Professionalism and the possibility of effective treatment. *Federal Probation*, 66(1), 43-49.

Levan, K. (2016). *Prison violence: Causes, consequences and solutions*. New York: Routledge.

Lin, A. (2000). Reform in the making: The implementation of social policy in prison. Princeton, NJ: Princeton University Press.

Lowson, G. (2018). Spike in inmate deaths raises questions around opioid crisis in Ontario's prisons. *The Globe and Mail*. Retrieved from https://www.theglobeandmail.com/news/national/serious-questions-remain-five-months-after-mans-suspected-overdose-in-ontario-jail/article38274018/

Malakieh, J. (2018). *Adult and youth correctional statistics in Canada, 2016/2017*. Ottawa, ON: Canadian Centre for Justice Statistics.

McLaughlin, M., Pettus-Davis, C., Brown, D., Veeh, C., & Renn, T. (2016). *The economic burden of incarceration in the U.S.* St. Louis: George Warren Brown School of Social Work.

National Institute of Corrections. (2017). *Environmental scan, 2016.* Washington, DC: Author.

Nink, C. (2008). *Women professionals in corrections: A growing asset.* Centerville, UT: MTC Institute.

Noonan, M. E. (2016). *Mortality in state prison deaths, 2001-2014 – Statistical tables.* Washington, DC: Bureau of Justice Statistics.

Paperny, A. M. (2017). Canada's jailhouse secret: Legally innocent prisoners are dying. *Reuters.* Retrieved from https://ca.reuters.com/article/topNews/idCAKBN1AJ19V-OCATP

Petersilia, J. (2009). *When prisoners come home: Parole and prisoner re-entry.* New York: Oxford University Press.

Police Executive Research Forum. (2018). *The changing nature of crime and criminal investigations.* Washington, DC: Author.

Police Futurists International. (2017). *Futures research.* Retrieved from http://www.policefuturists.org/futures-research-2

Proctor, J. (2018). Indefinite solitary confinement in Canadian prisons ruled unconstitutional by B.C. Court. *CBC News.* Retrieved from http://www.cbc.ca/news/canada/british-columbia/charter-solitary-confinement-bc-ruling-1.4491526

Public Safety Canada. (2010). *Emergency management planning guide 2010-2011.* Ottawa, ON: Author.

Public Safety Canada. (2016). *Corrections and conditional release act: Statistical Overview.* Ottawa, ON: Author.

Public Safety Canada. (2017). *Corrections and conditional release act: Statistical overview.* Ottawa, ON: Author.

Reitano, J. (2017). *Adult correctional statistics in Canada, 2015/2016.* Ottawa, ON: Canadian Centre for Justice Statistics.

Richmond, R. (2017). Inmates at Ontario jail sue province for $15M after seeing, hearing fellow prisoner killed. *National Post.* Retrieved from http://nationalpost.com/news/canada/inmates-at-ontario-jail-sue-province-for-15m-after-seeing-hearing-fellow-prisoner-killed

Rowe, P. (2018). Echo yard, where normal prison rules no longer apply. *The San Diego Tribune.* Retrieved from http://www.sandiegouniontribune.com/news/public-safety/sd-me-echo-yard-20180408-story.html

Ruddell, R., & Jones, N. A. (2014). *The economics of Canadian policing five years into the great recession.* Regina, SK: Collaborative Centre for Justice & Safety.

Ruddell, R., & Mays, G. L. (2009). Shades of grey: Aging criminal justice personnel. *The Crime Report*, December 14, 2009, 1.

Russo, J., Drake, G. B., Shaffer, J. S., & Jackson, B. A. (2017). Envisioning an alternative future for the corrections sector within the U.S. criminal justice system. Santa Monica, CA: RAND.

Scott-Hayward, C. S. (2011). *The fiscal crisis in corrections: Rethinking policies and practices* (Updated). Retrieved from http://www.pewcenteronthestates.org/uploadedFiles/Vera_state_budgets.pdf?n=5515

Seiter, R. P. (1987). The future of corrections: A view from a state correctional administrator. *The Prison Journal, 67*(1), 71-75.

Southwick, R. (2018). Alberta to offer opioid addictions treatment at jails after successful Calgary pilot. *CBC News.* Retrieved from http://www.cbc.ca/news/canada/calgary/opioid-jails-alberta-health-addictions-treatment-1.4603966

Statistics Canada. (2017). Aboriginal peoples in Canada: Key results from the 2016 census. *The Daily.* Retrieved from http://www.statcan.gc.ca/daily-quotidien/171025/dq171025a-eng.pdf

Statistics Canada. (2018a). *Adult correctional services, average counts of offenders in federal programs*. Retrieved from http://www.statcan.gc.ca/

Statistics Canada. (2018b). *Adult correctional services, average counts of adults in provincial and territorial programs*. Retrieved from http://www.statcan.gc.ca/

Statistics Canada. (2018c). *Police-reported cybercrime, by cyber-related violation.* Retrieved from http://www.statcan.gc.ca/

Statistics Canada. (2018d). *Adult correctional services, custodial admissions to provincial and territorial programs by age group*. Retrieved from http://www.statcan.gc.ca/

Tarantino, R. (2009). Heated debate over two-for-one. Retrieved fromhttp://www.canadianlawyermag.com/article/heated-debate-over-two-for-one-474/

TEMA. (2018). *Reported Canadian public safety suicides*. Retrieved from tulson https://infogram.com/reported_canadian_first_responder_suicides

Turner, S. F., Davis, L. M., Fain, T., Braithwaite, H., Lavery, T., Choinski, W., & Camp, G. (2015). A national picture of prison downsizing strategies. *Victims & Offenders*, *10*(4), 401-419.

Upchurch, J. R. (2009). Approach with caution: How to successfully implement new correctional technology. *Corrections Today*, April, 28-30.

Vanyur, J. M., Nink, C., Upchurch, J. R., Bodman, J., & Greenwald, D. (2009). Investigating violence in prison. In N. E. Fearn & R. Ruddell (Eds.), *Understanding correctional violence* (pp. 143-176). Richmond, KY: Newgate Press.

Vomiero, J. (2018) Here's a province-by-province breakdown of Canada's record-low unemployment rates. *Global News*. Retrieved from https://globalnews.ca/news/3949024/canada-unemployment-rates-breakdown-by-province/

Washington State Institute for Public Policy. (2018). *Benefit-cost results: Adult criminal justice.* Retrieved from http://www.wsipp.wa.gov/BenefitCost

Wexler, C. (2018). Crime has been changing, and police agencies need to catch up, in the Police Executive Research Forum (ed.), *The changing nature of crime and criminal investigations* (pp. 4-9). Washington, DC: Police Executive Research Forum.

Wolfgang, M. E. (1987). The future of corrections. *The Prison Journal*, *67*(1), 88-89.

Subject Index

Author Index

CPSIA information can be obtained
at www.ICGtesting.com
Printed in the USA
LVHW100907080420
652570LV00001B/2

9 781897 1609